T0292419

Knowledge in Action

Knowledge in Action: Logical Foundations for Specifying and Implementing Dynamical Systems

Raymond Reiter

The MIT Press
Cambridge, Massachusetts
London, England

This book was set in Times Roman by the author using the LaTeX document preparation system.

Library of Congress Cataloging-in-Publication Data

Reiter, Raymond.
  Knowledge in Action: Logical Foundations for Specifying and Implementing
  Dynamical Systems / Raymond Reiter
     p.   cm.
  Includes bibliographical references and index.
  ISBN 978-0-262-18218-8 (hc.: alk. paper)—978-0-262-52700-2 (pb.)
  1. Knowledge representation (Information theory) 2. Expert systems
  (Computer science). 3. Logic, symbolic and mathematical.
  I. Title.
  Q387 .R48   2001
  006.3'32—dc21   2001030522
                                                   CIP

The MIT Press is pleased to keep this title available in print by manufacturing single copies, on demand, via digital printing technology.

For F.

Contents

Preface

The situation calculus has been with us since 1963, when John McCarthy first introduced it as a way of logically specifying dynamical systems in artificial intelligence, but for most of that time, it was not taken very seriously as a realistic formalism. True, it was the language of choice for investigating technical issues, like the frame problem, that arise in axiomatizing dynamics, but most AI researchers viewed it as just that—a theoretical tool without much practical importance. About nine years ago, Hector Levesque and I came to realize that the situation calculus had a lot more potential than was commonly believed, and we and our collaborators set out to demonstrate this, mainly by extending the language to incorporate features like time, concurrency, procedures, probability, etc., while taking care to do so in ways that provide for efficient implementations. This book is largely the result of that activity.

Insofar as its subject matter concerns the modeling of dynamical systems, this book crosses traditional academic boundaries. Its intended audience consists of graduate students and researchers in AI, databases, robotics, software agents, simulation, decision and control theory, computer animation, and, indeed, in any discipline whose central concern is with specifying and implementing systems that evolve over time. The academic world doesn't lack for books about dynamical systems, so what distinguishes this one? The simple answer is that its theoretical and implementation foundations rest on mathematical logic. In a nutshell, the central idea of the book is this: When faced with a dynamical system that you want to simulate, control, analyze, or otherwise investigate, first axiomatize it in a suitable logic. Through logical entailment, all else will follow, including system control, simulation, and analysis. Such a claim is by no means obvious, and to a large extent, this book is an exploration of this idea—in our case, using the situation calculus as the underlying logic.

This book is as much about implementing dynamical systems as it is about their theoretical and representational foundations. Therefore, it provides a large number of examples and, perhaps unusually for books of its kind, it includes all the code for these examples. This turned out to be feasible because the implementation language, Prolog, is so elegant and close to logic that once one gets the logical specification right, compilation into extremely compact Prolog code is in most cases absolutely trivial. How to perform this compilation—and the justification for it—is the subject of Chapter 5, and I believe that learning how to do this is one of the most important lessons of the book. This methodological theme pervades the book and can be captured by the slogan:

> No implementation without a sitcalc specification

To keep faith with this slogan I have been careful, throughout the book, to accompany all code with its logical specification in the situation calculus, even if, on occasion, this may seem a bit on the pedantic side. The payoffs are many: A logical specification states clearly and unambiguously what the modeling assumptions are, it helps enormously in coding and debugging an implementation, and it allows you to prove properties of the system model.

I have used this material on several occasions as the basis of a graduate course at the University of Toronto. Students were drawn from virtually all branches of computer science, but also included control theorists, electrical and computer engineers, and the occasional mathematician. The course ran for 13 weeks, two hours per week, which was enough time to comfortably cover most, but not all of the book. I think that Chapters 1–8, 11, and 12 contain the essential ideas and should form the core of any such course. Time permitting, Chapter 10 on planning can be a lot of fun. Chapter 9 on progression is perhaps the least important to include in a course, even though it tells rather a nice story about how STRIPS and the situation calculus are related. I assigned exercises from each chapter covered, trying for a balance between theoretical and implementation-based questions. The final course component was a project that gave expression to the students' individual interests and backgrounds. Frequently, these projects were inventive and ambitious; often, they led to graduate theses. Project topics ranged all over the map, including databases, computer animation, simulation of physical systems, program verification, theoretical foundations, and high-level robotics. My experience in teaching this course has been that once they learn how to use the situation calculus, students quickly realize how pervasive dynamics is in their own areas of interest, and relevant project topics immediately present themselves.

Acknowledgments

This book began in 1992, while Hector Levesque and I were at a retreat sponsored by the Canadian Institute for Advanced Research. It was a lovely spring afternoon, and we went out for a walk. I had recently written a paper on solving the frame problem in the situation calculus, and Hector suggested that maybe this solution could serve as a foundation for some kind of programming language. From this suggestion came Golog and a long-term effort by us and our collaborators to enrich the expressivity of the situation calculus. Much of this book is the result of that research program, and Hector's intellectual contributions are present on every page.

I had the good luck to write large chunks of this book during several wonderful summers in Rome. Gigina Aiello and Fiora Pirri made this possible by providing me with a second academic home at the University of Rome, La Sapienza. Grazie Fiora. Grazie Gigina. I am also grateful to Dov Gabbay who, in his usual resourceful way, managed to find me a fellowship to King's College, London, in the spring of 1998, during which time I worked on some of the ideas for this book.

In developing Chapters 10 and 12, I was on very shaky ground since I had very little previous experience with planning, and virtually none in probability and decision theory. Fahiem Bacchus was a great help in guiding me through the treacherous literature on planning. Craig Boutilier patiently acted as my primary informant about what's going on these days in probability and decision theory; he also provided valuable feedback on a preliminary draft of Chapter 12. Fahiem also helped out here by advising me on some of the many subtleties in the foundations of probability theory. Many others provided feedback on earlier drafts of parts of this book, and I'd like here to thank them for their contributions: Gerd Brewka, Robert Demolombe, Hojjat Ghaderi, Arie Gurfinkel, Pat Hayes, Danny House, Eric Joanis, Hesham Khalil, Iluju Kiringa, Yves Lespérance, Mohammad Mahdian, Victor Marek, Maurice Pagnucco, Dimitrie Paun, Javier Pinto, Fiora Pirri, Angus Stewart, and Michael Thielscher.

Working with a physical robot focuses the mind in ways that no amount of armchair theorizing can do. In getting our group's robot off the ground, we were helped enormously by Dieter Fox and Sebastian Thrun, who provided us with their worry-free RWI B21 navigation software, and who visited us on several occasions to help with its installation.

A number of the ideas in this book have been influenced by, and in many cases developed by, past and present members of the University of Toronto Cognitive Robotics Group. My thanks for your many contributions to: Alfredo Gabaldon, Sam Kaufman, Todd Kelley, Iluju Kiringa, Yves Lespérance, Hector Levesque, Fangzhen Lin, Yongmei Liu, Daniel Marcu, Sheila McIlraith, Javier Pinto, Richard Scherl, Sebastian Sardiña, Steven Shapiro, Misha Soutchanski, and Eugenia Ternovskaia. Apart from members of the group, discussions with a wide variety of people have influenced my thinking on dynamical systems. The list reads like a who's who of researchers in knowledge representation and the theory of actions: Fahiem Bacchus, Chitta Baral, Alex Borgida, Craig Boutilier, Gerd Brewka, Tom Costello, Giuseppe De Giacomo, Robert Demolombe, Marc Denecker, Pat Doherty, Charles Elkan, Alberto Finzi, Michael Fisher, Dov Gabbay, Michael Gelfond, Neelakantan Kartha, Bob Kowalski, Gerhard Lakemeyer, Vladimir Lifschitz, Jorg Lobo, Alan Mackworth, Victor Marek, John McCarthy, John-Jules Meyer, Rob Miller, John Mylopoulos, Maurice Pagnucco, Edwin Pednault, Fiora Pirri, David Poole, Stuart Russell, Fariba Sadri, Erik Sandewall, Len Schubert, Marek Sergot, Murray Shanahan, and Michael Thielscher. Thanks to you all.

One of the joys of doing science in Canada is that, by and large, its funding agencies make little attempt to steer researchers towards whatever are the currently fashionable application areas. I have benefited over the years from this no-strings-attached funding policy from the Canadian Institute for Advanced Research, the National Science and Engineering Research Council of Canada, the Institute for Robotics and Intelligent Systems, and the Centre for Information Technology of Ontario, and I want here to acknowledge their wisdom in sponsoring curiosity-driven research.

Finally, I'd like to thank Bob Prior, Katherine Innis, and the other staff at MIT Press for their help in getting this book out, Eugenia Ternovskaia for patiently preparing all the figures, Antonina Kolokolova for help with Latex fonts, and Gerhard Lakemeyer for providing me with his fine tuning of MIT's macros.

Ray Reiter
Toronto
January, 2001

1 Introduction

Heraclitus reminds us that we cannot step into the same river twice. As goes the river, so goes virtually every modeling task in artificial intelligence, computer animation, robotics, software agents, decision and control theory, simulation, databases, programming languages, etc. The world simply won't sit still, and all attempts to model any but its simplest features must take change seriously. It is not trivial to address this problem in its full generality, as suggested by the following partial list of phenomena that a comprehensive theory of dynamical systems and autonomous agents must accommodate:

- The causal laws relating actions to their effects.
- The conditions under which an action can be performed.
- Exogenous and natural events.
- Probabilistic action occurrences and action effects.
- Decision theory: Determining what to do and when to do it.
- Complex actions and procedures.
- Discrete and continuous time.
- Concurrency.
- Continuous processes.
- Hypothetical and counterfactual reasoning about action occurrences and time.
- Perceptual actions and their effects on an agent's mental state.
- Deciding when to look and what to look for.
- Unreliable sensors and effectors.
- Agent beliefs, desires and intentions and how these influence behaviour.
- Real time (resource bounded) behaviour.
- Non deliberative (reactive) behaviour.
- Revising an agent's beliefs in the presence of conflicting observations.
- Planning a course of actions.
- Execution monitoring of a course of actions; recognizing and recovering from failures.

Despite the many existing disciplines that focus on modeling dynamical systems of one kind or another, a story as general as this has yet to be told. This is not to say that your average system modeler lacks for tools of the trade; there are plenty of formalisms to choose from, including Petri nets, process algebras, dynamic and temporal logics, finite automata, Markov decision processes, differential equations, STRIPS operators, influence diagrams, etc. But as this list suggests, what's available is more like a Tower of Babel than a unifying representational and computational formalism. To be fair, this state of affairs is the natural outcome of disciplines organized by their applications; discrete event control theory is concerned with different problems than, say, programming language design, and neither appear to have anything in common with semantics for tense in natural language. We all solve problems that arise in our own, sometimes narrowly circumscribed fields of specialization, and in this sense, we are like the proverbial blind men, each acting in isolation, and each trying to figure out the elephant. Nevertheless, one can't help thinking that there really is an elephant out there, that at a suitable level of abstraction, there must be a unifying "theory of dynamics", one that subsumes the many special purpose mechanisms that have been developed in these different disciplines, and that moreover accommodates all the features of autonomous dynamical systems listed above.

During the past 15 years or so, a number of researchers in artificial intelligence have been developing mathematical and computational foundations for dynamical systems that promise to deliver the elephant.[1] The methodological foundations of all these approaches —indeed, of much of the theory and practice of artificial intelligence—are based on what Brian Smith [202] has called the *Knowledge Representation Hypothesis*:

> *Any mechanically embodied intelligent process will be comprised of structural ingredients that a) we as external observers naturally take to represent a propositional account of the knowledge that the overall process exhibits, and b) independent of such external semantical attribution, play a formal but causal and essential role in engendering the behaviour that manifests that knowledge.*

Adopting this hypothesis has a number of important consequences:

1. We are naturally led to employ mathematical logic as a foundation for the "propositional account of the knowledge that the overall process exhibits" called for in part a) of the hypothesis.

2. This "propositional account" differs substantially from the state-based approaches central, for example, to decision and control theory. Instead of explicitly enumerating states and their transition function, the Knowledge Representation Hypothesis favours sentences—descriptions of what is true of the system and its environment, and of the causal laws in effect for that domain.

3. Part b) of the Knowledge Representation Hypothesis calls for a causal connection between these sentences and the system's *behaviours*. How can sentences lead to behaviour? In logic, sentences beget sentences through logical entailment, so it is natural to view system behaviours as appropriate *logical consequences* of the propositional account of the domain. On this perspective, the *computational* component of a logical representation for a dynamical system consists of deduction. Determining how a sys-

---

1 Needless to say, this is still just a promise.

tem behaves amounts to *deducing how it must behave*, given the system's description.

4. Providing a propositional account for some domain amounts to giving an abstract *specification* for that problem. Even by itself, having a non-procedural specification for a problem domain is a good thing; at least it's clear what modeling assumptions are being made. But in addition to this, because these are logical specifications, one can hope to prove, entirely within the logic, various properties of the specification. In other words, there is a direct mechanism, namely logical deduction, for establishing correctness properties for the system.

5. In those cases where deduction can be performed efficiently, these system specifications are also *executable*. This means that, as a side effect of providing a logical specification, we often obtain a simulator for the system.

This book deals with a logical approach to modeling dynamical systems based on a dialect of first order logic called the *situation calculus*, a language first proposed by John McCarthy in 1963 [136]. The material presented here has evolved over a number of years in response to the needs of the University of Toronto Cognitive Robotics Project, and therefore, has been heavily influenced by the problems that arise there. Broadly speaking, the newly emerging field of cognitive robotics has, as its long term objectives, the provision of a uniform theoretical and implementation framework for autonomous robotic or software agents that reason, act and perceive in changing, incompletely known, unpredictable environments. It differs from "traditional" robotics research in emphasizing "higher level" cognition as a determiner for agent behaviours. Therefore, one focus of cognitive robotics is on modeling an agent's beliefs and their consequences. These include beliefs about what is true of the world it inhabits, about the actions that it and other agents (nature included) can perform and the effects of those actions on the agent and its environment, about the conditions under which such actions can be performed, about the mental states and physical abilities of its fellow agents in the world, and about the outcomes of its perceptions. In keeping with the Knowledge Representation Hypothesis, these beliefs are represented as logical sentences, in our case, using the situation calculus. Such beliefs condition behaviour in a variety of ways, and one goal of cognitive robotics is to provide a theoretical and computational account of exactly how it is that deliberation can lead to action. None of this is meant to suggest that these objectives are peculiar to cognitive robotics; many control theorists and roboticists are concerned with modeling similar phenomena. What distinguishes cognitive robotics from these other disciplines is its emphasis on beliefs and how they condition behaviour, and by its commitment to the Knowledge Representation Hypothesis, and therefore, to logical sentences as the fundamental mathematical representation for dynamical systems and agent belief states. Nevertheless, despite these differences in emphasis and methodology, the representational and computational problems that must be solved are generic to all dynamical system modeling. Basically, we are all trying to do the same thing.

This book is about modeling and implementing autonomous agents and dynamical systems in the situation calculus. It addresses many, but certainly not all, of the issues enumerated at the beginning of this chapter; to get an idea of its coverage, glance through the Table of Contents. In addition to its focus on theoretical foundations, the book also emphasizes implementations. Because these are in the logic programming language Prolog, the programs are quite compact and therefore, are given in their entirety. All these programs are freely available and—Need I say it?—without guarantees of any kind; Appendix C tells you how to download them.

2 Logical Preliminaries

Here, we briefly review some standard concepts in mathematical logic, and introduce the notation to be used throughout this book. The material on second-order logic and inductive definitions may be unfamiliar to some, but anyone unable to skim the section on first-order logic with perfect understanding is probably reading the wrong book.

2.1 First-Order Logic

2.1.1 Syntax

A *first-order language with equality* is specified by two disjoint sets of symbols, called the *vocabulary* of the language:

1. **Logical symbols**: The interpretation of these is fixed by the rules of first-order logic.

   (a) Parentheses of all shapes and sizes.

   (b) *Logical connectives*: $\supset, \neg$.

   (c) *Variables* (infinitely many): $x, y, z, x_1, y_1, z_1, \ldots$

   (d) *Equality*: $=$.

2. **Parameters**: These vary with the interpretation.

   (a) *Quantifier symbol*: $\forall$.

   (b) *Predicate symbols*: For each $n \geq 0$, a set (possibly empty) of symbols, called *n-place* or *n-ary* predicate symbols.

   (c) *Function symbols*: For each $n \geq 0$, a set (possibly empty) of symbols, called *n-place* or *n-ary* function symbols. 0-ary function symbols are called *constant* symbols.

Terms, atomic formulas (often simply called *atoms*), *literals, well-formed formulas* (often simply called *formulas*) are defined as usual, as are the concepts of *free* and *bound* occurrences of a variable in a formula. A *sentence* is a formula with no free variables. The symbols $\wedge, \vee, \equiv, \exists$ are defined to be suitable abbreviations in the standard way. The *language* defined over the above vocabulary is defined to be the set of all well-formed formulas constructible using this vocabulary.

Notational Conventions:

- A character string starting with a lowercase Roman letter occurring in a quantifier, or in an argument position of a predicate or function symbol in a formula will be a variable.

Uppercase Roman will be a constant.

- We will often omit leading universal quantifiers in writing sentences. The convention will be that any free variables in such formulas are implicitly universally quantified. So,

$$P(x, y) \supset (\exists z)[Q(y, z) \wedge R(x, w, z)]$$

abbreviates

$$(\forall x, y, w)[P(x, y) \supset (\exists z)[Q(y, z) \wedge R(x, w, z)]].$$

- The "dot" notation: In logical languages, a quantifier's scope must be indicated explicitly with parentheses. An alternative notation, which often obviates the need for explicit parentheses, is the "dot" notation, used to indicate that the quantifier preceding the dot has maximum scope. Thus, $(\forall x).P(x) \supset Q(x)$ stands for $(\forall x)[P(x) \supset Q(x)]$.

$$[(\forall x)(\exists y).A(x, y) \wedge B(x, y) \supset C(x, y)] \wedge R(x, y)$$

stands for

$$[(\forall x)(\exists y)[A(x, y) \wedge B(x, y) \supset C(x, y)]] \wedge R(x, y).$$

- Parenthesis reduction. We shall assume that $\wedge$ takes precedence over $\vee$, so that $P \wedge Q \vee R \wedge S$ stands for $(P \wedge Q) \vee (R \wedge S)$. Also, $\supset$ and $\equiv$ bind with lowest precedence, so $P \wedge Q \supset R \vee S$ stands for $(P \wedge Q) \supset (R \vee S)$, and $P \wedge Q \equiv R \vee S$ stands for $(P \wedge Q) \equiv (R \vee S)$.

2.1.2 Semantics

We begin, as usual, with the definition of a *structure* (sometimes called an *interpretation*) for a first-order language. This will tell us

1. What collection of things the universal quantifier symbol ($\forall$) ranges over—the *domain or universe of quantification*.

2. What the other parameters—the predicate and function symbols—denote with respect to the domain of the structure.

Formally, a structure $\mathcal{S}$ for a given first-order language is a function whose domain is the set of parameters of the language, and is defined by:

1. $\forall^{\mathcal{S}}$ is a nonempty set, called the *universe* or the *domain* of the structure $\mathcal{S}$. The universe is usually written $|\mathcal{S}|$.

2. For each n-ary predicate symbol P of the first-order language, $P^{\mathcal{S}} \subseteq |\mathcal{S}|^n$. These n-tuples of the universe are understood to be all, and only, those tuples on which P is true in the structure. This is called the *extension* of P in the structure $\mathcal{S}$.

3. For each n-ary function symbol f of the first-order language, $f^{\mathcal{S}}$ is an n-ary function

on $|\mathcal{S}|$, i.e. $f^{\mathcal{S}} : |\mathcal{S}|^n \to |\mathcal{S}|$. In particular, when $n = 0$, so that f is a constant symbol, $f^{\mathcal{S}}$ is simply some element of the universe.

SEMANTICS: TRUTH IN A STRUCTURE

We want to define when a sentence σ is *true* in a structure $\mathcal{S}$, denoted by $\models_{\mathcal{S}} \sigma$. To do so, we need a more general notion of truth for a formula (not necessarily a sentence). Suppose

1. ϕ is a formula of the given first-order language.

2. $\mathcal{S}$ is a structure for the language,

3. $s : V \to |\mathcal{S}|$ is a function, called a *variable assignment*, from the set V of variables of the language into the universe of $\mathcal{S}$.

We can now define $\models_{\mathcal{S}} \phi[s]$, meaning that the formula ϕ is true in the structure $\mathcal{S}$ when its free variables are given the values specified by s in the universe.

1. **Terms:** Define an extension $\bar{s} : T \to |\mathcal{S}|$ of the function s from the set T of all terms of the language into the universe.

   (a) For each variable v, $\bar{s}(v) = s(v)$.

   (b) If $t_1, \ldots, t_n$ are terms and f is an n-ary function symbol, then
   $$\bar{s}(f(t_1, \ldots, t_n)) = f^{\mathcal{S}}(\bar{s}(t_1), \ldots, \bar{s}(t_n)).$$

2. **Atomic Formulas:**

   (a) For terms t_1 and t_2,
   $$\models_{\mathcal{S}} t_1 = t_2[s] \text{ iff } \bar{s}(t_1) = \bar{s}(t_2).^1$$

   (b) For an n-ary predicate symbol P,
   $$\models_{\mathcal{S}} P(t_1, \ldots, t_n)[s] \text{ iff } <\bar{s}(t_1), \ldots, \bar{s}(t_n)> \in P^{\mathcal{S}}.$$

3. **Well-Formed Formulas:**

   (a) $\models_{\mathcal{S}} \neg\phi[s]$ iff not $\models_{\mathcal{S}} \phi[s]$.

   (b) $\models_{\mathcal{S}} (\phi \supset \psi)[s]$ iff $\models_{\mathcal{S}} \neg\phi[s]$ or $\models_{\mathcal{S}} \psi[s]$.

   (c) $\models_{\mathcal{S}} (\forall x)\phi[s]$ iff for every $d \in |\mathcal{S}|$, $\models_{\mathcal{S}} \phi[s(x|d)]$.
   Here, $s(x|d)$ is the function that is exactly like s except that for the variable x it assigns the value d.

---

1 Notice that we are slightly abusing notation here by using the same symbol $=$ for two different purposes. We could have avoided this ambiguity by denoting the equality predicate symbol in the language of first-order logic by something different than $=$, for example $\approx$, reserving $=$ for its standard usage in the metalanguage. But that seemed a bit pedantic.

Our interest will always be in the truth of sentences, not of arbitrary formulas. We needed the above notions for well-formed formulas in order to give a recursive definition of truth in a structure, even when our only interest is in sentences. With this definition in hand, we can now consider only sentences.

1. **Satisfiability:** A structure $\mathcal{S}$ *satisfies* a sentence σ, or σ *is true* in $\mathcal{S}$, iff $\models_\mathcal{S} \sigma[s]$ for every variable assignment s. A sentence is *satisfiable* iff there is a structure that satisfies it.

2. **Models:** A structure $\mathcal{S}$ is a model of a sentence σ iff $\mathcal{S}$ satisfies σ. $\mathcal{S}$ is a model of a set of sentences, possibly infinite, iff it is a model of each sentence in the set.

3. **Validity:** The sentence σ is valid, written $\models \sigma$, iff every structure of the first-order language is a model of the sentence σ.

4. **Unsatisfiability:** A sentence is unsatisfiable iff it has no models.

5. **Logical entailment:** Suppose Γ is a set of sentences, possibly infinite, and σ is a sentence. $\Gamma \models \sigma$ (Γ *entails* σ) iff every model of Γ is a model of σ. It is a standard result of first-order logic that $\Gamma \models \sigma$ iff there is a finite subset Γ' of Γ such that $\models \bigwedge \Gamma' \supset \sigma$, where $\bigwedge \Gamma'$ denotes the conjunction of the sentences in Γ'. This is often called the *Compactness Theorem for first-order logic*.

2.1.3 Soundness and Completeness

First-order logic can be axiomatized using a suitable set of sentences called *axioms* (usually a finite set of sentence *schemas*), together with *rules of inference* that permit the derivation of new formulas from old. These systems are used to construct *proofs* of sentences from sets of sentences called *premises*. $A \vdash \sigma$ means that, with respect to some given axiomatization of first-order logic, there is a proof of σ from the premises A. An axiomatization of first-order logic is *complete* iff $A \models \sigma$ implies $A \vdash \sigma$. An axiomatization of first-order logic is *sound* iff $A \vdash \sigma$ implies $A \models \sigma$.

First-order logic has many sound and complete axiomatizations, all of them equivalent. Examples include Gentzen and Hilbert style systems, etc. In this book, we won't be much concerned with particular axiomatizations of first-order logic, although the need for theorem-proving will arise frequently. So the symbol "$\vdash$" will not be used very often. Virtually all our claims and arguments will be semantic.

First-order logic is *not* decidable; the non-valid sentences are not recursively enumerable, although the valid sentences are.

2.1.4 Many-Sorted First-Order Languages

In the situation calculus, we shall find it convenient to distinguish three kinds of objects—situations, actions and other things. To do this, we will appeal to a *sorted* first-order language. In general, a sorted first-order language has variables and terms of different sorts. Semantically, the universe is partitioned into disjoint sub-universes, one such sub-universe for each sort. A variable will range over its own sub-universe, and a term will denote an element in its corresponding sub-universe. A predicate will be syntactically restricted to take arguments of certain prespecified sorts, as will functions. Moreover, functions will be required to deliver values of a prespecified sort. Many-sorted logical languages are strongly analogous to typed programming languages.

Syntax of a Many-Sorted First-Order Language. Assume given a nonempty set I, whose members are called *sorts*.

1. **Logical symbols:** As before, except that for each sort i, there are infinitely many variables $x_1^i, x_2^i, \ldots$, of sort i.

2. **Parameters**:

   (a) *Quantifier symbols:* For each sort i there is a universal quantifier symbol $\forall_i$.

   (b) *Predicate symbols:* For each $n \geq 0$ and each n-tuple $< i_1, \ldots, i_n >$ of sorts, there is a set (possibly empty) of n-ary predicate symbols, each of which is said to be of sort $< i_1, \ldots, i_n >$.

   (c) *Function symbols:* For each $n \geq 0$ and each $(n + 1)$-tuple $< i_1, \ldots, i_n, i_{n+1} >$ of sorts, there is a set (possibly empty) of n-ary function symbols, each of which is said to be of sort $< i_1, \ldots, i_n, i_{n+1} >$.

   Each term is assigned a unique sort, as follows:

1. Any variable of sort i is a term of sort i.

2. If $t_1, \ldots, t_n$ are terms of sort $i_1, \ldots, i_n$ respectively, and f is a function symbol of sort $< i_1, \ldots, i_n, i_{n+1} >$, then $f(t_1, \ldots, t_n)$ is a term of sort i_{n+1}.

Atomic formulas are defined as follows:

1. When t and t' are terms of the same sort, $t = t'$ is an atomic formula.

2. When P is an n-ary predicate symbol of sort $< i_1, \ldots, i_n >$ and $t_1, \ldots, t_n$ are terms of sort $i_1, \ldots, i_n$ respectively, then $P(t_1, \ldots, t_n)$ is an atomic formula.

Well-formed formulas are defined as usual, except that quantifiers must be applied to variables of the same sort. So $(\forall_i x^i)$ is permitted, but not $(\forall_i x^j)$ when i and j are different. Semantically, sorted formulas are interpreted by *many-sorted structures* as follows: As before, $\mathcal{S}$ is a function on the set of parameters, except this time it must assign to each parameter the correct sort of object.

1. $\mathcal{S}$ assigns to $\forall_i$ a nonempty set $|\mathcal{S}|_i$, called the *universe* of $\mathcal{S}$ of sort i. The universes of different sorts are required to be disjoint.

2. To each predicate symbol P of sort $< i_1, \ldots, i_n >$, $\mathcal{S}$ assigns a relation

$$P^{\mathcal{S}} \subseteq |\mathcal{S}|_{i_1} \times \cdots \times |\mathcal{S}|_{i_n}.$$

3. To each function symbol f of sort $< i_1, \ldots, i_n, i_{n+1} >$, $\mathcal{S}$ assigns a function

$$f^{\mathcal{S}} : |\mathcal{S}|_{i_1} \times \cdots \times |\mathcal{S}|_{i_n} \to |\mathcal{S}|_{i_{n+1}}.$$

The definitions of truth and satisfaction are as expected, under the intuition that $\forall_i$ means "for all members of the universe $|\mathcal{S}|_i$."

2.1.5 Reducing Many-Sorted Logic to Standard Logic

It turns out that many-sorted logics are no more powerful than ordinary unsorted first-order logic. To see why, consider an ordinary first-order language with all the predicate and function symbols of a given many-sorted language. In addition, it will have a new unary predicate symbol Q_i for each sort i. The intended meaning of $Q_i(t)$ is that term t is of sort i. Then we can transform every sentence σ of the many-sorted language into an ordinary first-order sentence σ^* in the following way:

Replace every subexpression $(\forall_i x^i) E(x^i)$ of σ by $(\forall x)[Q_i(x) \supset E(x)]$ where x is a variable chosen not to conflict with the others. Next define the following set Φ of ordinary first-order sentences:

1. $(\exists x) Q_i(x)$ for each sort i.

2. $(\forall x_1, \ldots, x_n).Q_{i_1}(x_1) \wedge \cdots \wedge Q_{i_n}(x_n) \supset Q_{i_{n+1}}(f(x_1, \ldots, x_n))$ for each function symbol f of sort $< i_1, \ldots, i_n, i_{n+1} >$.

Theorem In a many-sorted language, $\Sigma \models \sigma$ iff in its corresponding ordinary first-order language, $\Sigma^* \cup \Phi \models \sigma^*$.

Finally, a convention: When writing formulas in a sorted language, we will not use sorted quantifiers; their sorts will always be obvious from context.

2.1.6 Some Useful First-Order Inference Rules

For finding proofs by hand of the complex logical theorems required throughout this book, it is essential to use a collection of theorem-proving rules that reflect the natural thought processes that a mathematician invokes in proving theorems. Appendix A describes one such set of rules. They are not complete, but seem to work well surprisingly often. Of course, they are sound. If you have your own favorite theorem-proving methods, suitable for proving complicated theorems by hand, you can safely skip over this material.

2.1.7 A Limitation of First-Order Logic

Certain kinds of relations are not definable in first-order logic, for example, the *transitive closure* of a binary relation. We can think of a binary relation G as a directed graph (possibly infinite), where (v, v') is an edge in the graph from vertex v to vertex v' iff the relation G is true of (v, v'), i.e. iff $G(v, v')$ is true. By definition, the *transitive closure* T of this relation G is true of (v, v') iff there is a finite sequence of edges leading from v to v' in the graph G. Now, consider the problem of giving an explicit definition of the relation T in first-order logic, i.e., we want to write:

$$T(x, y) \equiv \tau(x, y),$$

where $\tau(x, y)$ denotes a first-order formula with free variables x and y that may mention the predicate G, and possibly other predicates as well, even T itself. Alas, one can prove—see Exercise 3 below for a precise statement of the problem, and for a proof—that no such first-order formula $\tau(x, y)$ is possible.

Fortunately, as we shall see later, there is a *second* order formula $\tau(x, y)$ that does explicitly define the transitive closure of G. Typically, a relation R will be second-order (but not first-order) definable whenever, in informal mathematics, it is defined inductively using the pattern:

"*R is the smallest set such that ...*" or

"*R is the intersection of all sets such that ...*"

This is the case for transitive graph closure. The transitive closure, $closure(G)$, of G is the smallest set such that:

1. $(v, v') \in closure(G)$ whenever $(v, v') \in G$.
2. If $(v, v') \in G$ and $(v', v'') \in closure(G)$, then $(v, v'') \in closure(G)$.

There is another way of saying this in informal mathematics. $closure(G)$ is the intersection of all sets $\mathcal{T}$ such that:

1. $(v, v') \in \mathcal{T}$ whenever $(v, v') \in G$.
2. If $(v, v') \in G$ and $(v', v'') \in \mathcal{T}$, then $(v, v'') \in \mathcal{T}$.

So don't fall into the common trap of trying to define transitive graph closure in the following naive way:

$$T(x, y) \equiv G(x, y) \vee (\exists z).G(x, z) \wedge T(z, y).$$

Here is a counterexample to this attempt:

Example 2.1.1: Consider the directed graph with two vertices a and b, and with a single directed edge $G(b, b)$. Consider a structure with universe $\{a, b\}$ that interprets G as $\{(b, b)\}$ and T as $\{(a, b), (b, b)\}$. In other words, the structure represents the graph G (by declaring that there is an edge from b to b, and no other edges), and it assigns *true* to $T(a, b)$ and $T(b, b)$. It is easy to check that this structure is a model of the above naive definition for transitive closure. In other words, there is a model of the graph together with the naive definition, and this model declares that (a, b) is in the graph's transitive closure, which it is not. This means that the naive definition does not correctly characterize the concept of transitive closure.

Notice what the naive definition does not capture: that T is the *smallest* binary relation with the property ...

Because our treatment of actions in the situation calculus will encounter limitations of first-order logic like those described above, we now consider second-order logic.

2.2   Second-Order Logic

2.2.1   Syntax

First-order logic permits quantification over individuals. Second-order logic provides quantification over predicates and functions.

- For all predicates P ...
- For all functions F ...

To enrich first-order logic with this ability, add to the definition of a first-order language the following new logical symbols:

1. *Predicate variables*: For each $n \geq 0$, infinitely many n-place predicate variables $X_1^n, X_2^n, \ldots$
2. *Function variables*:   For each $n \geq 0$, infinitely many n-place function variables $F_1^n, F_2^n, \ldots$

What we have been calling "variables" in first-order logic we will now call "individual variables". *Terms* are now expressions constructed from constant symbols and individual variables by applying function symbols (both function parameters and function variables). *Atomic formulas* are now of the form $P(t_1, \ldots, t_n)$ where the t_i are terms, and P is an n-ary predicate parameter or predicate variable. *Well-formed formulas* are as before, but with two new formula building operations, $(\forall X_i^n)\phi$ and $(\forall F_i^n)\phi$ when ϕ is a well-formed formula. A *sentence* is a well-formed formula with no free variables (individual, predicate or function).

2.2.2   Semantics

A *structure* for a second-order language will continue to be a function $\mathcal{S}$ on the set of parameters as in the first-order case, but the definition of satisfaction must now be extended. Let V now be the set of all variables (individual, predicate and function). Let s be a function on V that assigns to each variable the right kind of object in the structure.

1. $s(x)$ is a member of the universe.

2. $s(X^n)$ is an n-ary relation on the universe, i.e. a set of n-tuples of elements of the universe.

3. $s(F^n)$ is an n-ary function, i.e. a function from n-tuples of elements of the universe into the universe.

Now extend s to $\bar{s}$ as follows: $\bar{s}(F(t_1, \ldots, t_n)) = s(F)(\bar{s}(t_1), \ldots, \bar{s}(t_n))$. Here, F is an n-ary function variable. Next, extend the definition of satisfaction of a formula by a structure $\mathcal{S}$:

- Satisfaction of atomic formulas must be extended: For an n-ary predicate variable X, $\models_\mathcal{S} X(t_1, \ldots, t_n)[s]$ iff $< \bar{s}(t_1), \ldots, \bar{s}(t_n) > \in s(X)$.

- Satisfaction must be extended to include the new quantifiers:

  1. $\models_\mathcal{S} (\forall X^n)\phi[s]$ iff for every n-ary relation $R \subseteq |\mathcal{S}|^n$, $\models_\mathcal{S} \phi[s(X^n|R)]$. Here, $s(X^n|R)$ is the function that is exactly like s except that for the predicate variable X^n it takes the value R.

     This is the formal way of capturing the intuition that $(\forall X^n)\phi$ means that no matter what extension the n-ary predicate variable X^n has in a structure, ϕ will be true in that structure.

  2. $\models_\mathcal{S} (\forall F^n)\phi[s]$ iff for every n-ary function $f : |\mathcal{S}|^n \to |\mathcal{S}|$, $\models_\mathcal{S} \phi[s(F^n|f)]$. Here, $s(F^n|f)$ is the function that is exactly like s except that for the function variable F^n it takes the value f.

The notions of model, validity, unsatisfiability and logical entailment for first-order sentences, as defined in Section 2.1.2, have their natural generalization to second-order languages.

2.2.3   Inductive Definitions and Second-Order Logic

In this book, we shall be appealing to second-order logic to characterize the situation calculus. We will not need to quantify over function variables to do this. The major use we will make of second-order logic will be to describe *smallest* sets with certain properties. This is the sort of thing one does in logic and computer science all the time. For example, the concept of an arithmetic expression over the natural numbers can be defined to be the intersection of all sets P such that:

1. Every natural number is in P.

2. If e_1 and e_2 are in A, then so also are $-(e_1)$, $+(e_1, e_2)$ and $*(e_1, e_2)$.

The following second-order sentence is a way to specify the set of all such arithmetic expressions:

$$(\forall w).ae(w) \equiv$$
$$(\forall P).\{(\forall x)[natnum(x) \supset P(x)] \wedge$$
$$(\forall e)[P(e) \supset P(-(e))] \wedge$$
$$(\forall e_1, e_2)[P(e_1) \wedge P(e_2) \supset P(+(e_1, e_2))] \wedge$$
$$(\forall e_1, e_2)[P(e_1) \wedge P(e_2) \supset P(*(e_1, e_2))]\}$$
$$\supset P(w).$$

The informal concept of the intersection of all sets P with the above two properties is captured by universal second-order quantification over P.

Here is transitive graph closure again, which informally is defined as follows: The transitive closure, $closure(G)$, of G is the smallest set such that:

1. $(v, v') \in closure(G)$ whenever $(v, v') \in G$.

2. If $(v, v') \in G$ and $(v', v'') \in closure(G)$, then $(v, v'') \in closure(G)$.

Its second-order definition is:

$$(\forall x, y).T(x, y) \equiv$$
$$(\forall P).\{(\forall v, v')[G(v, v') \supset P(v, v')] \wedge$$
$$(\forall v, v', v'')[G(v, v') \wedge P(v', v'') \supset P(v, v'')]\}$$
$$\supset P(x, y).$$

The definitions of the above two concepts—the arithmetic expressions, and the transitive closure of a graph—are examples of so-called *inductive definitions*. They normally consist of one or more *base cases*, together with one or more *inductive cases*. For the arithmetic expressions, the base case treats natural numbers, and there are three inductive cases, one for characterizing the negative expressions, one for addition, and one for multiplication.

One cannot freely formulate inductive definitions and expect always to obtain something meaningful. There are rules to this game; for an example, and one of the rules, see Exercise 5 below.

The second-order versions of such inductive definitions naturally lead to second-order *induction principles* for proving properties of the members of these sets. Induction will play a major role in our theory of actions. To see how induction principles emerge from such second-order inductive definitions, consider the above definition of the arithmetic expressions. The following sentence is a trivial consequence of the definition:

$$(\forall P).\{(\forall x)[natnum(x) \supset P(x)] \wedge$$
$$(\forall e)[P(e) \supset P(-(e))] \wedge$$
$$(\forall e_1, e_2)[P(e_1) \wedge P(e_2) \supset P(+(e_1, e_2))] \wedge$$
$$(\forall e_1, e_2)[P(e_1) \wedge P(e_2) \supset P(*(e_1, e_2))]\}$$
$$\supset (\forall e).ae(e) \supset P(e).$$

This informs us that in order to prove that every arithmetic expression has a certain property P, say for the purposes of proving the correctness of an algorithm for parsing such expressions, it is sufficient to show that:

1. All natural numbers have property P.
2. Whenever e has property P, so does $-(e)$.
3. Whenever e_1 and e_2 have property P, so do $+(e_1, e_2)$ and $*(e_1, e_2)$.

This is simply the principle of induction on the syntactic structure of arithmetic expressions.

In the same way, we can obtain the following induction principle for transitive closure:

$$(\forall P).\{(\forall v, v')[G(v, v') \supset P(v, v')] \wedge$$
$$(\forall v, v', v'')[G(v, v') \wedge P(v', v'') \supset P(v, v'')]\}$$
$$\supset (\forall x, y).T(x, y) \supset P(x, y).$$

2.2.4 The Incompleteness of Second-Order Logic

Second-order logic is incomplete, meaning that there is no recursive axiomatization and rules of inference that can recursively enumerate all and only the valid second-order sentences. This is a consequence of the Gödel incompleteness theorem for arithmetic. So why, in this book, do we appeal at all to second-order logic? The main reason is that we shall be interested in *semantically characterizing* actions and their properties. This will mean, however, that our theory of actions will be incomplete in the same way as number theory is incomplete. We shall therefore also be interested in finding important special cases of our theory of actions, and special kinds of computations, that have first-order axiomatizations.

2.3 Exercises

1. Give second-order definitions for the following sets. In each case, obtain a second-order induction principle from the definition.

   (a) The set of natural numbers is the smallest set containing 0 and that is closed under the successor function. In other words, the smallest set N such that:

      i. $0 \in N$.
      ii. If $x \in N$ then $s(x) \in N$.

   (b) The set of LISP S-expressions is the smallest set containing all atoms, and that is closed under the binary function *cons*. Assume that the unary predicate *atom* has already been defined.

   (c) The set of all of Adam and Eve's descendents, defined as the smallest set D such that:

    i. $Adam \in D$ and $Eve \in D$.

    ii. If $x \in D$ and y is an offspring of x, then $y \in D$.

(d) The set of all propositional well-formed formulas, defined to be the smallest set P such that:

    i. Every propositional atom is in P.

    ii. If w_1 and $w_2 \in P$, then so also are $not(w_1)$ and $implies(w_1, w_2)$.

Assume that the unary predicate $atom$ has already been defined.

2. Give second-order definitions for the following relations on LISP lists. Use the constant symbol Nil to denote the empty list, and the binary function symbol $cons$, where $cons(a, l)$ denotes the result of adding the element a to the front of list l.

(a) $evenLength(l)$, meaning that list l has an even number of elements.

(b) $sublist(l_1, l_2)$, meaning that list l_1 is the result of deleting 0 or more elements from list l_2.

(c) $append(l_1, l_2, l)$, meaning that list l is the result of appending list l_1 to l_2.

3. This exercise will lead you to a proof that transitive closure is not first-order definable. It relies on the Compactness Theorem, which informs us that any unsatisfiable set of first-order sentences has a finite unsatisfiable subset. The proof is by contradiction, so assume that $\tau(x, y)$ is a first-order formula with two free variables, defining the transitive closure of a binary relation G. By this, we mean that for any structure S assigning an extension to the binary predicate symbol G, and for any variable assignment s, $\models_S \tau(x, y)[s]$ iff s assigns to the variables x and y a pair of domain elements of S that is in the transitive closure of G in that structure. All of which is a fancy way of saying that the set of pairs of domain elements of S that are in the transitive closure of G is precisely the set of domain element pairs that make τ true in the structure. Notice that the same formula τ must work for every graph G and every structure assigning an extension to G. Notice, finally, that $\tau(x, y)$, by hypothesis, says that, for some n, there is a sequence of n edges in the graph of G leading from x to y. Consider the following, infinitely many first-order formulas, each with two free variables x and y:

$\alpha_1(x, y) \quad G(x, y),$

$\alpha_2(x, y) \quad (\exists z_1).G(x, z_1) \wedge G(z_1, y),$

$\cdots$

$\alpha_n(x, y) \quad (\exists z_1, \ldots z_{n-1}).G(x, z_1) \wedge G(z_1, z_2) \wedge \cdots \wedge G(z_{n-1}, y),$

$\cdots$

$\alpha_n(x, y)$ says that there is a sequence of n edges in the graph of G leading from vertex

x to vertex y. Now, assume that the underlying first-order language has at least two constant symbols A and B. (Later, we shall see that this assumption is not necessary; it does, however, considerably simplify the proof.) For $n \geq 1$, let β_n be the sentence:

$$\tau(A, B) \wedge \neg\alpha_1(A, B) \wedge \cdots \wedge \neg\alpha_n(A, B).$$

β_n says that (A, B) is in the transitive closure of G, and A and B are not connected by any sequence of edges of length n or less.

Consider the infinite set of sentences $\{\beta_1, \ldots, \beta_n, \ldots\}$. Notice what this set claims: that (A, B) is in the transitive closure of G, but no finite sequence of edges in the graph G leads from A to B. So this set is obviously unsatisfiable. Now, use the compactness theorem to obtain a contradiction.

The above proof assumed that the underlying first-order language had at least two constant symbols A and B. But this assumption is unimportant; it is easy to see that if $\tau(x, y)$ defines the transitive closure of G in a first order language, it continues to do so for the enlarged language obtained by adding two new constant symbols A and B to the original language. We then use exactly the same proof as before.

4. Statements about the size of the domain of discourse are often not first-order definable.

   (a) Using the compactness theorem—see the previous exercise—prove that there is no first-order sentence that is true in a structure iff that structure has a finite domain. As before, the proof is by contradiction. Suppose that ϕ is such a first-order sentence. For $n \geq 2$, let $\sigma_{\geq n}$ be the sentence

   $$(\exists x_1, \ldots, x_n).x_1 \neq x_2 \wedge x_1 \neq x_3 \wedge \cdots \wedge x_{n-1} \neq x_n.$$

   Here, there are $n(n-1)/2$ conjuncts, expressing that the x's are pairwise unequal. $\sigma_{\geq n}$ says that there are at least n distinct individuals in the domain of discourse. Next, consider the infinite set of sentences $\{\phi, \sigma_{\geq 2}, \sigma_{\geq 3}, \ldots, \}$. This is unsatisfiable. Now use compactness to obtain a contradiction.

   (b) Prove the stronger result that there is no set (finite or infinite) of first-order sentences all of which are true on a structure iff that structure has a finite domain.

5. **Weird Inductive Definitions.** The very idea of an inductive definition can be problematic. Consider the following "inductive definition" of a smallest set W of natural numbers such that:

   (a) $0 \in W$.

   (b) If $x \notin W$, then $x + 1 \in W$.

   Give some examples of sets W that can reasonably be said to be characterized by this definition. What set(s) do we get by replacing the words "a smallest set W" by the words "the intersection of all sets W"?

This example reveals that not all "inductive definitions" make sense, or uniquely determine a set, which leads to the natural question: When are such definitions meaningful? There is no completely general answer to this question, but it is known that whenever negation is not mentioned in any of the defining conditions for the inductive definition, then a unique set is determined. The above weird definition does have a negative condition—$x \notin W$—in one of its conditions, so it is not guaranteed to uniquely define a set, and that is the case. Notice that all of the other examples of this chapter (transitive closure, Exercise 1 above, etc.) do fulfill this condition.

2.4 Bibliographic Remarks

All definitions and notation of this chapter are drawn from the excellent book on logic by Enderton [42]. The first-order inference rules of Appendix A are adapted from those used in the University of Texas theorem-proving system of Bledsoe [20]. These rules are very like those for natural deduction proof systems—see, for example, Barwise and Etchemendy [15]—but they differ by introducing many derived rules, e.g. for equality and equivalence substitution, and by using dynamic Skolemization and unification. Those of you unaccustomed to inventing axioms might find it useful to read Ernie Davis's Guide to Axiomatizing Domains in First-Order Logic. These are a useful set of principles for students of artificial intelligence; Appendix C contains a pointer. Except for the last four—the coloured blocks example is due to Robert Moore—the first-order theorem-proving exercises of Appendix A are all taken from Pelletier [157].

Considering how important they are in mathematics and computer science, it is not surprising that the theory of inductive definitions is a well-developed branch of mathematical logic. Moschovakis [150] is the classical book of the field. Leivant [104] discusses inductive definitions from the perspective of second-order logic.

3 Introduction to the Situation Calculus

In this chapter, we provide an intuitive introduction to the situation calculus, and show how one can represent actions and their effects in this language. We then use the situation calculus as a vehicle for illustrating two difficulties that arise in any attempt to formalize dynamic worlds, namely the qualification and frame problems. Our focus will be on the frame problem, and we show how, under suitable conditions, there is a simple solution with a number of desirable properties. Finally, we look at two settings—planning and database transactions—as examples that are well suited to formalization in the situation calculus.

3.1 The Situation Calculus

3.1.1 Intuitive Ontology for the Situation Calculus

The situation calculus is a second-order language specifically designed for representing dynamically changing worlds. All changes to the world are the result of named *actions*. A possible world history, which is simply a sequence of actions, is represented by a first-order term called a *situation*. The constant S_0 is used to denote the *initial situation*, namely, the empty sequence of actions. There is a distinguished binary function symbol do; $do(\alpha, s)$ denotes the successor situation to s resulting from performing the action α. Actions may be parameterized. For example, $put(x, y)$ might stand for the action of putting object x on object y, in which case $do(put(A, B), s)$ denotes that situation resulting from placing A on B when the current situation is s. Notice that in the situation calculus, actions are denoted by function symbols, and situations (world histories) are first-order terms. For example, $do(putDown(A), do(walk(L), do(pickup(A), S_0)))$ is a situation term denoting the sequence of actions $[pickup(A), walk(L), putDown(A)]$. Notice that the sequence of actions in such a history, in the order in which they occur, is obtained from a situation term by reading off the actions from right to left.

Generally, the values of relations and functions in a dynamic world will vary from one situation to the next. Relations whose truth values vary from situation to situation are called *relational fluents*. They are denoted by predicate symbols taking a situation term as their last argument. Similarly, functions whose values vary from situation to situation are called *functional fluents*, and are denoted by function symbols taking a situation term as their last argument. For example, in a world in which it is possible to paint objects, we might have a functional fluent $colour(x, s)$, denoting the colour of object x in that state of the world resulting from performing the action sequence s. In a mobile robot environment, there might be a relational fluent $closeTo(r, x, s)$, meaning that in that state of the world reached by performing the action sequence s, the robot r will be close to the object x.

3.1.2   Axiomatizing Actions in the Situation Calculus

The first observation one can make about actions is that they have *preconditions*: requirements that must be satisfied whenever they can be executed in the current situation. We introduce a predicate symbol $Poss$; $Poss(a, s)$ means that it is possible to perform the action a in that state of the world resulting from performing the sequence of actions s. Here are some examples:

- If it is possible for a robot r to pick up an object x in situation s, then the robot is not holding any object, it is next to x, and x is not heavy:

$$Poss(pickup(r, x), s) \supset [(\forall z)\neg holding(r, z, s)] \wedge \neg heavy(x) \wedge nextTo(r, x, s).$$

- Whenever it is possible for a robot to repair an object, then the object must be broken, and there must be glue available:

$$Poss(repair(r, x), s) \supset hasGlue(r, s) \wedge broken(x, s).$$

The next feature of dynamic worlds that must be described are the causal laws—how actions affect the values of fluents. These are specified by so-called *effect axioms*. The following are some examples:

- The effect on the relational fluent $broken$ of a robot dropping a fragile object:

$$fragile(x, s) \supset broken(x, do(drop(r, x), s)).$$

This is the situation calculus way of saying that dropping a fragile object causes it to become broken; in the current situation s, if x is fragile, then in that successor situation $do(drop(r, x), s)$ resulting from performing the action $drop(r, x)$ in s, x will be broken.

- A robot repairing an object causes it not to be broken:

$$\neg broken(x, do(repair(r, x), s)).$$

- Painting an object with colour c:

$$colour(x, do(paint(x, c), s)) = c.$$

3.1.3   The Qualification Problem for Actions

With only the above axioms, nothing interesting can be proved about when an action is possible. For example, here are some preconditions for the action $pickup$:

$$Poss(pickup(r, x), s) \supset [(\forall z)\neg holding(r, z, s)] \wedge \neg heavy(x) \wedge nextTo(r, x, s).$$

The reason nothing interesting follows from this is clear; we can never infer when a $pickup$ is possible. We can try reversing the implication:

$$[(\forall z)\neg holding(r, z, s)] \wedge \neg heavy(x) \wedge nextTo(r, x, s) \supset Poss(pickup(r, x), s).$$

Now we can indeed infer when a pickup is possible, but unfortunately, this sentence is *false*! We also need, in the antecedent of the implication:

$$\neg gluedToFloor(x, s) \wedge \neg armsTied(r, s) \wedge \neg hitByTenTonTruck(r, s) \wedge \cdots$$

i.e, we need to specify all the *qualifications* that must be true in order for a *pickup* to be possible! For the sake of argument, imagine succeeding in enumerating all the qualifications for *pickup*. Would that help? Suppose the only facts known to us about a particular robot R, object A, and situation S are:

$$[(\forall z)\neg holding(R, z, S)] \wedge \neg heavy(A) \wedge nextTo(R, A, S).$$

We still cannot infer $Poss(pickup(R, A), S)$ because we are not given that the above qualifications are true! Intuitively, here is what we want: When given only that the "important" qualifications are true:

$$[(\forall z)\neg holding(R, z, S)] \wedge \neg heavy(A) \wedge nextTo(R, A, S),$$

and if we *don't know* that any of the "minor" qualifications—$\neg gluedToFloor(A, S)$, $\neg hitByTenTonTruck(R, S)$—are true, infer $Poss(pickup(R, A), S)$. But if we happen to know that any one of the "minor" qualifications is false, this will block the inference of $Poss(pickup(R, A), S)$. Historically, this has been seen to be a problem peculiar to reasoning about actions, but this is not really the case. Consider the following fact about birds, which has nothing to do with reasoning about actions:

$$bird(x) \wedge \neg penguin(x) \wedge \neg ostrich(x) \wedge \neg pekingDuck(x) \wedge \cdots \supset flies(x).$$

But given only the fact $bird(Tweety)$, we want intuitively to infer $flies(Tweety)$. Formally, this is the same problem as action qualifications:

- The "important" qualification is $bird(x)$.
- The "minor" qualifications are: $\neg penguin(x)$, $\neg ostrich(x)$, $\cdots$

This is the classical example of the need for *nonmonotonic reasoning* in artificial intelligence. For the moment, it is sufficient to recognize that the qualification problem for actions is an instance of a much more general problem, and that there is no obvious way to address it. We shall adopt the following (admittedly idealized) approach: Assume that for each action $A(\vec{x})$, there is an axiom of the form

$$Poss(A(\vec{x}), s) \equiv \Pi_A(\vec{x}, s),$$

where $\Pi_A(\vec{x}, s)$ is a first-order formula with free variables $\vec{x}, s$ that does not mention the function symbol do. We shall call these *action precondition axioms*. For example:

$$Poss(pickup(r, x), s) \equiv [(\forall z)\neg holding(r, z, s)] \wedge \neg heavy(x) \wedge nextTo(r, x, s).$$

In other words, we choose to ignore all the "minor" qualifications, in favour of necessary and sufficient conditions defining when an action can be performed. Appendix B further discusses the qualification problem along with its close relative, the ramification problem.

3.1.4   The Frame Problem

As if the qualification problem were not bad enough, there is another well known problem associated with axiomatizing dynamic worlds; axioms other than effect axioms are required. These are called *frame axioms*, and they specify the action *invariants* of the domain, i.e, those fluents unaffected by the performance of an action. For example, the following is a positive frame axiom, declaring that the action of robot r' painting object x' with colour c has no effect on robot r holding object x:

$$holding(r, x, s) \supset holding(r, x, do(paint(r', x', c), s)).$$

Here is a negative frame axiom for not breaking things:

$$\neg broken(x, s) \wedge [x \neq y \vee \neg fragile(x, s)] \supset \neg broken(x, do(drop(r, y), s)).$$

Notice that these frame axioms are truths about the world, and therefore must be included in any formal description of the dynamics of the world. The problem is that there will be a vast number of such axioms because only relatively few actions will affect the value of a given fluent. All other actions leave the fluent invariant, for example: An object's colour remains unchanged after picking something up, opening a door, turning on a light, electing a new prime minister of Canada, etc. Since, empirically in the real world, most actions have no effect on a given fluent, we can expect of the order of $2 \times \mathcal{A} \times \mathcal{F}$ frame axioms, where $\mathcal{A}$ is the number of actions, and $\mathcal{F}$ the number of fluents.

These observations lead to what is called the *frame problem*:

1. The axiomatizer must think of, and write down, all these quadratically many frame axioms. In a setting with 100 actions and 100 fluents, this involves roughly 20,000 frame axioms.

2. The implementation must somehow reason efficiently in the presence of so many axioms.

WHAT COUNTS AS A SOLUTION TO THE FRAME PROBLEM?

Suppose the person responsible for axiomatizing an application domain has specified all the causal laws for that domain. More precisely, she has succeeded in writing down *all* the effect axioms, i.e. for each relational fluent F and each action A that causes F's truth value to change, axioms of the form:

$$R(\vec{x}, s) \supset (\neg)F(\vec{x}, do(A, s)), \,^{1}$$

and for each functional fluent f and each action A that can cause f's value to change, axioms of the form:

$$R(\vec{x}, y, s) \supset f(\vec{x}, do(A, s)) = y.$$

Here, R is a first-order formula specifying the contextual conditions under which the action A will have its specified effect on F and f. There are no restrictions on R, except that it must refer only to the current situation s. Later, we shall be more precise about the syntactic form of these effect axioms.

A solution to the frame problem is a systematic procedure for generating, from these effect axioms, all the frame axioms. If possible, we also want a *parsimonious* representation for these frame axioms (because in their simplest form, there are too many of them).

Why Seek a Solution to the Frame Problem?

Frame axioms are necessary to reason about the domain being formalized; they cannot be ignored. Nevertheless, one could argue that there is no need to have a solution to the frame problem; instead, the onus should be on the axiomatizer to provide the frame axioms. Still, a solution to the frame problem would be very convenient by providing:

- *Modularity.* As new actions and/or fluents are added to the application domain, the axiomatizer need only add new effect axioms for these. The frame axioms will be automatically compiled from these (and the old frame axioms suitably modified to reflect these new effect axioms).

- *Accuracy.* There can be no accidental omission of frame axioms.

We shall also find that a systematic solution to the frame problem, in particular the one we shall describe shortly, will make possible a very rich theory of actions, accompanied by a natural implementation.

3.2 A Simple Solution to the Frame Problem (Sometimes)

This section describes a straightforward solution to the frame problem, one that can be very efficiently computed and that yields extremely compact axioms. It is not, however, completely general; hence the caveat "Sometimes" in the section title. In fact, the solution applies only to deterministic actions *without* ramifications (state constraints). Readers unfamiliar with the concept of state constraints can safely ignore this comment for the time being; we shall return to this topic in Section 4.3.2 and Appendix B.

---

1 The notation ($\neg$) means that the formula following it may, or may not, be negated.

The solution that we shall describe is a synthesis of two proposals, one by Edwin Pednault, the other by Andrew Haas, as elaborated by Len Schubert, and proposed independently by Ernie Davis. To begin, we shall only consider relational fluents, i.e. relations whose truth values depend on the situation. Later, we shall consider functional fluents.

3.2.1   Frame Axioms: Pednault's Proposal

We illustrate this proposal with an example.

Example 3.2.1: Consider a simple electrical circuit consisting of various lightbulbs, each having its own on-off switch. When lightbulb x is on, flipping its switch, $flip(x)$, causes it to go off, and symmetrically when x is off. The fluent on has the following positive and negative effect axioms:

$$\neg on(x, s) \supset on(x, do(flip(x), s)),$$

$$on(x, s) \supset \neg on(x, do(flip(x), s)).$$

Now, rewrite these in the logically equivalent forms:

$$\neg on(x, s) \wedge y = x \supset on(x, do(flip(y), s)),$$

$$on(x, s) \wedge y = x \supset \neg on(x, do(flip(y), s)).$$

Next, suppose that these are *all* the causal laws relating the action $flip$ and the fluent on; we have described all the ways that flipping a switch can affect a light. Now, suppose that both $on(x, s)$ and $\neg on(x, do(flip(y), s))$ are true. In other words, light x was on in situation s, and in the situation resulting from flipping switch y, light x was off. Therefore, flipping the switch for y must have *caused* x to become off. Because we have axiomatized all the ways action $flip$ can affect on, the only way $\neg on(x, do(flip(y), s))$ could have become true is if the antecedent of its causal law, namely $on(x, s) \wedge y = x$ was true. Therefore, we conclude:

$$on(x, s) \wedge \neg on(x, do(flip(y), s)) \supset on(x, s) \wedge y = x.$$

This is logically equivalent to:

$$on(x, s) \wedge y \neq x \supset on(x, do(flip(y), s)).$$

This is exactly a positive frame axiom. It says that the action $flip(y)$ has no effect on the fluent $on(x, s)$ whenever y is different than x. We have obtained a frame axiom through purely syntactic manipulation of the effect axioms, by appealing to the assumption that these effect axioms capture all the causal laws relating the action $flip$ and the fluent on.

A symmetric argument yields the following negative frame axiom:

$$\neg on(x, s) \wedge y \neq x \supset \neg on(x, do(flip(y), s)).$$

The example illustrates a general pattern. Assume given a set of positive and negative effect axioms (one for each action $A(\vec{y})$ and fluent $F(\vec{x}, s)$):

$$\varepsilon_F^+(\vec{x}, \vec{y}, s) \supset F(\vec{x}, do(A(\vec{y}), s)), \tag{3.1}$$

$$\varepsilon_F^-(\vec{x}, \vec{y}, s) \supset \neg F(\vec{x}, do(A(\vec{y}), s)). \tag{3.2}$$

Here, $\varepsilon_F^+(\vec{x}, \vec{y}, s)$ and $\varepsilon_F^-(\vec{x}, \vec{y}, s)$ are first-order formulas whose free variables are among $\vec{x}, \vec{y}, s$. Notice that in these effect axioms the variable sequences $\vec{x}$ and $\vec{y}$ consist of distinct variables.

Pednault makes the following *Causal Completeness Assumption*:

Axioms (3.1) and (3.2) specify all the causal laws relating the action A and the fluent F.

With this completeness assumption, we can reason as follows: Suppose that both $F(\vec{x}, s)$ and $\neg F(\vec{x}, do(A(\vec{y}), s))$ hold. Then because F was true in situation s, action A must have caused it to become false. By the completeness assumption, the only way A could cause F to become false is if $\varepsilon_F^-(\vec{x}, \vec{y}, s)$ were true. This can be expressed axiomatically by:

$$F(\vec{x}, s) \wedge \neg F(\vec{x}, do(A(\vec{y}), s)) \supset \varepsilon_F^-(\vec{x}, \vec{y}, s).$$

This is logically equivalent to:

$$F(\vec{x}, s) \wedge \neg \varepsilon_F^-(\vec{x}, \vec{y}, s) \supset F(\vec{x}, do(A(\vec{y}), s)).$$

A symmetric argument yields the axiom:

$$\neg F(\vec{x}, s) \wedge \neg \varepsilon_F^+(\vec{x}, \vec{y}, s) \supset \neg F(\vec{x}, do(A(\vec{y}), s)).$$

These have precisely the syntactic forms of positive and negative frame axioms. Under the Causal Completeness Assumption, there is a systematic way to obtain these frame axioms from the effect axioms.

Example 3.2.2: Recall the earlier example effect axiom:

$$fragile(x, s) \supset broken(x, do(drop(r, x), s)).$$

Rewrite this in a logically equivalent form to conform to the pattern (3.1):

$$x = y \wedge fragile(x, s) \supset broken(x, do(drop(r, y), s)).$$

The causal completeness assumption yields a negative frame axiom for the fluent *broken* with respect to the action *drop*:

$$\neg broken(x, s) \wedge \neg[x = y \wedge fragile(x, s)] \supset \neg broken(x, do(drop(r, y), s)).$$

What happens when there is no causal relationship between an action and a fluent? For example, painting an object does not cause it to become broken or unbroken. In this case, there are two vacuous effect axioms:

$$false \supset broken(x, do(paint(y, c), s)),$$

$$false \supset \neg broken(x, do(paint(y, c), s)).$$

From these, using the same reasoning as before, we obtain the positive and negative frame axioms for *broken* with respect to *paint*:

$$\neg broken(x, s) \supset \neg broken(x, do(paint(y, c), s)),$$

$$broken(x, s) \supset broken(x, do(paint(y, c), s)).$$

This illustrates two problems with Pednault's proposal:

1. To systematically determine the frame axioms for all fluent-action pairs from their effect axioms, we must enumerate (or at least consciously consider) all these effect axioms, including the "vacuous" ones. In effect, we must enumerate all fluent-action pairs for which the action has no effect on the fluent's truth value, which really amounts to enumerating most of the frame axioms directly.

2. The number of frame axioms so obtained is of the order of $2 \times \mathcal{A} \times \mathcal{F}$, where $\mathcal{A}$ is the number of actions, and $\mathcal{F}$ the number of fluents, so we are faced with the usual difficulty associated with the frame problem—too many frame axioms.

Summary: Pednault's proposal

- For deterministic actions, it provides a systematic (and easily and efficiently implementable) mechanism for generating frame axioms from effect axioms.

- But it does not provide a parsimonious representation of the frame axioms.

3.2.2   Frame Axioms: The Davis/Haas/Schubert Proposal

Schubert, elaborating on a proposal of Haas, argues in favor of what he calls *explanation closure axioms* for representing the usual frame axioms. Independently, Davis proposed a very similar idea.

Example 3.2.3:   Consider a robot r that is holding an object x in situation s, but is not holding it in the next situation: Both $holding(r, x, s)$ and $\neg holding(r, x, do(a, s))$ are true. How can we explain the fact that *holding* ceases to be true? If we assume that the only way this can happen is if the robot r put down or dropped x, we can express this with the *explanation closure axiom*:

$$holding(r, x, s) \wedge \neg holding(r, x, do(a, s)) \supset a = putDown(r, x) \vee a = drop(r, x).$$

Notice that this sentence quantifies universally over a (actions). To see how this functions as a frame axiom, rewrite it in the logically equivalent form:

$$holding(r, x, s) \wedge a \neq putDown(r, x) \wedge a \neq drop(r, x)$$
$$\supset holding(r, x, do(a, s)). \tag{3.3}$$

This says that all actions other than $putDown(r, x)$ and $drop(r, x)$ leave $holding$ invariant,[2] which is the standard form of a frame axiom (actually, a set of frame axioms, one for each action distinct from $putDown$ and $drop$).

In general, an *explanation closure axiom* has one of the two forms:

$$F(\vec{x}, s) \wedge \neg F(\vec{x}, do(a, s)) \supset \alpha_F(\vec{x}, a, s),$$

$$\neg F(\vec{x}, s) \wedge F(\vec{x}, do(a, s)) \supset \beta_F(\vec{x}, a, s).$$

In these, the action variable a is universally quantified. These say that if ever the fluent F changes truth value, then α_F or β_F provides an exhaustive explanation for that change.

As before, to see how explanation closure axioms function like frame axioms, rewrite them in the logically equivalent form:

$$F(\vec{x}, s) \wedge \neg \alpha_F(\vec{x}, a, s) \supset F(\vec{x}, do(a, s)),$$

and

$$\neg F(\vec{x}, s) \wedge \neg \beta_F(\vec{x}, a, s) \supset \neg F(\vec{x}, do(a, s)).$$

These have the same syntactic form as frame axioms with the important difference that action a is universally quantified. Whereas, in the worst case, we expect $2 \times \mathcal{A} \times \mathcal{F}$ frame axioms, there are just $2 \times \mathcal{F}$ explanation closure axioms. This parsimonious representation is achieved by quantifying over actions in the explanation closure axioms.

Schubert argues that explanation closure axioms are independent of the effect axioms, and it is the axiomatizer's responsibility to provide them. Like the effect axioms, these are domain-dependent. In particular, Schubert argues that they cannot be obtained from the effect axioms by any kind of systematic transformation. Thus, Schubert and Pednault entertain conflicting intuitions about the origins of frame axioms.

Like Pednault, Schubert's appeal to explanation closure as a substitute for frame axioms involves an assumption.

The Explanation Closure Assumption

α_F *completely characterizes all those actions a that can cause the fluent F's truth value to change from true to false; similarly for* β_F.

---

2 To accomplish this, we require unique names axioms like $pickup(r, x) \neq drop(r', x')$. We shall explicitly introduce these later.

We can see clearly the need for something like this assumption from the example explanation closure axiom (3.3). If, in the intended application, there were an action (say, $eat(r, x)$) that could lead to r no longer holding x, axiom (3.3) would be false.

Summary: The Davis/Haas/Schubert Proposal

- Explanation closure axioms provide a compact representation of frame axioms: $2 \times \mathcal{F}$ of them. (This assumes the explanation closure axioms do not become too long. Later we shall provide an argument why they are likely to be short.)
- But Schubert provides no systematic way of automatically generating them from the effect axioms. In fact, he argues this is impossible in general.

Can we combine the best of the Pednault and Davis/Haas/Schubert ideas? The next section shows how to do this.

3.2.3 A Simple Solution (Sometimes)

We illustrate the method with an example.

Example 3.2.4: Suppose there are two positive effect axioms for the fluent $broken$:

$$fragile(x, s) \supset broken(x, do(drop(r, x), s)),$$

$$nextTo(b, x, s) \supset broken(x, do(explode(b), s)),$$

i.e, exploding a bomb next to an object will break the object. These can be rewritten in the logically equivalent form:

$$[(\exists r)a = drop(r, x) \land fragile(x, s)$$
$$\lor (\exists b)\{a = explode(b) \land nextTo(b, x, s)\}] \quad (3.4)$$
$$\supset broken(x, do(a, s)).$$

Similarly, consider the negative effect axiom for $broken$:

$$\neg broken(x, do(repair(r, x), s)).$$

In exactly the same way, this can be rewritten as:

$$(\exists r)a = repair(r, x) \supset \neg broken(x, do(a, s)). \quad (3.5)$$

Now appeal to the following causal completeness assumption:

Axiom (3.4) characterizes all the circumstances that can cause x to become broken.

Next, suppose $\neg broken(x, s)$ and $broken(x, do(a, s))$ are both true. Then action a must have caused x to become $broken$, and by the completeness assumption, this can happen only because

$$(\exists r)a = drop(r, x) \land fragile(x, s) \lor (\exists b)\{a = explode(b) \land nextTo(b, x, s)\}$$

was true. This intuition can be formalized by the following explanation closure axiom:

$$\neg broken(x, s) \wedge broken(x, do(a, s)) \supset (\exists r)a = drop(r, x) \wedge fragile(x, s) \vee$$
$$(\exists b)\{a = explode(b) \wedge nextTo(b, x, s)\}.$$

Similarly, (3.5) yields the following explanation closure axiom:

$$broken(x, s) \wedge \neg broken(x, do(a, s)) \supset (\exists r)a = repair(r, x).$$

3.2.4   Aside: Normal Forms for Effect Axioms

In the previous example, we rewrote one or more positive effect axioms as a single, logically equivalent positive effect axiom with the following syntactic normal form:

$$\gamma_F^+(\vec{x}, a, s) \supset F(\vec{x}, do(a, s)),$$

Similarly, we rewrote one or more negative effect axioms in the normal form:

$$\gamma_F^-(\vec{x}, a, s) \supset \neg F(\vec{x}, do(a, s)).$$

Here, $\gamma_F^+(\vec{x}, a, s)$ and $\gamma_F^-(\vec{x}, a, s)$ are first-order formulas with free variables among $\vec{x}, a, s$. The automatic generation of frame axioms appealed to these normal forms for the effect axioms. In this section, we precisely describe this transformation to normal form sentences. Readers who already understand this mechanism can skip to the next section.

Transformation of Effect Axioms to Normal Form: Each of the given positive effect axioms has the form:

$$\phi_F^+ \supset F(\vec{t}, do(\alpha, s)).$$

Here α is an action term (e.g. pickup(x), put(A,y)) and the $\vec{t}$ are terms. We write these effect axioms without leading quantifiers, so the free variables (if any) in these axioms are implicitly universally quantified.
Write this in the following, logically equivalent form:

$$a = \alpha \wedge \vec{x} = \vec{t} \wedge \phi_F^+ \supset F(\vec{x}, do(a, s)). \tag{3.6}$$

Here, $\vec{x} = \vec{t}$ abbreviates $x_1 = t_1 \wedge \cdots \wedge x_n = t_n$, and $\vec{x}$ are new variables, distinct from one another and distinct from any occurring in the original effect axiom. Now, suppose $y_1, \ldots, y_m$ are all the free variables, except for the *situation* variable s, occurring in the original effect axiom, i.e. all the variables (if any) that are implicitly universally quantified in this axiom. Then (3.6) is itself logically equivalent to:

$$(\exists y_1, \ldots, y_m)[a = \alpha \wedge \vec{x} = \vec{t} \wedge \phi_F^+] \supset F(\vec{x}, do(a, s)).$$

So, each positive effect axiom for fluent F can be written in the logically equivalent form:

$$\Psi_F \supset F(\vec{x}, do(a, s)),$$

where Ψ_F is a formula whose free variables are among $\vec{x}, a, s$. Do this for each of the k positive effect axioms for F, to get:

$$\Psi_F^{(1)} \supset F(\vec{x}, do(a, s)),$$
$$\vdots$$
$$\Psi_F^{(k)} \supset F(\vec{x}, do(a, s)).$$

Next, write these k sentences as the single, logically equivalent

$$[\Psi_F^{(1)} \vee \cdots \vee \Psi_F^{(k)}] \supset F(\vec{x}, do(a, s)).$$

This is the normal form for the positive effect axioms for fluent F.

Similarly, compute the normal form for the negative effect axioms for fluent F.

Readers familiar with the Clark completion semantics for logic programs will recognize the above transformation to normal form as very similar (but not identical) to the preliminary transformation of logic program clauses, in preparation for computing a program's *completion*.

Example 3.2.5: Suppose the following are all the positive effect axioms for fluent *tired*:

$$tired(Jack, do(walk(A, B), s)),$$

$$\neg marathonRunner(y) \wedge distance(u, v) > 2km \supset tired(y, do(run(u, v), s)).$$

Their normal form is:

$$\{[a = walk(A, B) \wedge x = Jack] \vee [(\exists u, v, y).a = run(u, v) \wedge$$
$$\neg marathonRunner(y) \wedge distance(u, v) > 2km \wedge x = y]\}$$
$$\supset tired(x, do(a, s)).$$

By properties of equality and existential quantification, this simplifies to:

$$\{[a = walk(A, B) \wedge x = Jack] \vee [(\exists u, v).a = run(u, v) \wedge$$
$$\neg marathonRunner(x) \wedge distance(u, v) > 2km]\}$$
$$\supset tired(x, do(a, s)).$$

3.2.5   A Simple Solution: The General Case

The example of Section 3.2.3 obviously generalizes. Suppose given, for each fluent F, the following two normal form effect axioms:

Positive Normal Form Effect Axiom for Fluent F

$$\gamma_F^+(\vec{x}, a, s) \supset F(\vec{x}, do(a, s)). \tag{3.7}$$

Negative Normal Form Effect Axiom for Fluent F

$$\gamma_F^-(\vec{x}, a, s) \supset \neg F(\vec{x}, do(a, s)). \tag{3.8}$$

Here, $\gamma_F^+(\vec{x}, a, s)$ and $\gamma_F^-(\vec{x}, a, s)$ are first-order formulas with free variables among $\vec{x}, a, s$. We make the following:

Causal Completeness Assumption:

Axioms (3.7) and (3.8), respectively, characterize all the conditions under which action a causes F to become true (respectively, false) in the successor situation.

In other words, these two sentences completely describe the causal laws for fluent F.

Hence, if F's truth value changes from *false* in the current situation s to *true* in the next situation $do(a, s)$ resulting from doing a, then $\gamma_F^+(\vec{x}, a, s)$ must have been *true*; similarly, if F's truth value changes from *true* to *false*. This informally stated assumption can be captured axiomatically by the following:

Explanation Closure Axioms

$$F(\vec{x}, s) \wedge \neg F(\vec{x}, do(a, s)) \supset \gamma_F^-(\vec{x}, a, s), \tag{3.9}$$

$$\neg F(\vec{x}, s) \wedge F(\vec{x}, do(a, s)) \supset \gamma_F^+(\vec{x}, a, s). \tag{3.10}$$

To make this work, we need:

Unique Names Axioms for Actions.

For distinct action names A and B,

$$A(\vec{x}) \neq B(\vec{y}).$$

Identical actions have identical arguments:

$$A(x_1, ..., x_n) = A(y_1, ..., y_n) \supset x_1 = y_1 \wedge \cdots \wedge x_n = y_n.$$

Proposition 3.2.6: *Suppose that T is a first-order theory that entails*

$$\neg(\exists \vec{x}, a, s).\gamma_F^+(\vec{x}, a, s) \wedge \gamma_F^-(\vec{x}, a, s). \tag{3.11}$$

Then T entails that the general effect axioms (3.7) and (3.8), together with the explanation closure axioms (3.9) and (3.10), are logically equivalent to:

$$F(\vec{x}, do(a, s)) \equiv \gamma_F^+(\vec{x}, a, s) \vee F(\vec{x}, s) \wedge \neg\gamma_F^-(\vec{x}, a, s). \tag{3.12}$$

Proof: Straightforward, but tedious. ∎

The requirement that $\neg(\exists \vec{x}, a, s).\gamma_F^+(\vec{x}, a, s) \wedge \gamma_F^-(\vec{x}, a, s)$ be entailed by the background theory T simply guarantees the consistency of the effect axioms (3.7) and (3.8). To see why, suppose this requirement were violated, so that for some $\vec{X}, A, S$ we have $\gamma_F^+(\vec{X}, A, S)$, and $\gamma_F^-(\vec{X}, A, S)$. Then we could simultaneously derive $F(\vec{X}, do(A, S))$

and $\neg F(\vec{X}, do(A, S))$ from the above two effect axioms. Notice that by the unique names axioms for actions, this consistency condition is satisfied by the example treating the fluent *broken* above.

We call formula (3.12) the *successor state axiom for fluent F*. For Example 3.2.4, the successor state axiom for *broken* is:

$$broken(x, do(a, s)) \equiv (\exists r)a = drop(r, x) \wedge fragile(x, s)\vee$$
$$(\exists b)\{a = explode(b) \wedge nextTo(b, x, s)\}\vee$$
$$broken(x, s) \wedge \neg(\exists r)a = repair(r, x).$$

3.2.6 A Simple Solution: Functional Fluents

We now treat the case of functional fluents, i.e. functions whose values vary from situation to situation. The analysis here turns out to be somewhat simpler than for relational fluents.

We begin with an example. Consider a simple blocks world in which an agent can create towers of blocks. The action $move(b, b')$ moves the block b, carrying all the blocks above it as a single tower, onto the block b'. The relational fluent $above(b, b', s)$ means that block b is above block b' in the tower in which b' occurs. The functional fluent $height(b, s)$ is the height above the table of the block b. Here are the effect axioms:

$$height(b, do(move(b, b'), s)) = height(b', s) + 1,$$

$$above(b, b', s) \supset$$
$$height(b, do(move(b', b''), s)) =$$
$$height(b'', s) + height(b, s) - height(b', s) + 1,$$

$$height(b, do(moveToTable(b), s)) = 1,$$

$$above(b, b', s) \supset$$
$$height(b, do(moveToTable(b'), s)) = height(b, s) - height(b', s) + 1.$$

These can be rewritten in the following, logically equivalent form, according to the transformations into normal form of Section 3.2.4:

$$\left\{ \begin{array}{l} (\exists b')[a = move(b, b') \wedge y = height(b', s) + 1] \vee \\ (\exists b', b'')[a = move(b', b'') \wedge above(b, b', s) \wedge \\ \qquad y = height(b'', s) + height(b, s) - height(b', s) + 1] \vee \\ a = moveToTable(b) \wedge y = 1 \vee \\ (\exists b', b'')[a = moveToTable(b') \wedge above(b, b', s) \wedge \\ \qquad y = height(b, s) - height(b', s) + 1] \\ \supset height(b, do(a, s)) = y. \end{array} \right\}$$

More generally, assume given a single effect axiom for a functional fluent f, with the following syntactic form:

$$\gamma_f(\vec{x}, y, a, s) \supset f(\vec{x}, do(a, s)) = y. \tag{3.13}$$

Here, $\gamma_f(\vec{x}, y, a, s)$ is a first-order formula whose free variables are among $\vec{x}, y, a, s$. For the above blocks world example, $\gamma_{height}(b, y, a, s)$ is the bracketed formula.

As in the case of relational fluents, there is a consistency property that such an effect axiom for f must respect, namely that the following sentence be entailed by the background theory:

$$\neg(\exists \vec{x}, y, y', a, s).\gamma_f(\vec{x}, y, a, s) \wedge \gamma_f(\vec{x}, y', a, s) \wedge y \neq y'. \tag{3.14}$$

This requirement simply guarantees the consistency of the effect axiom (3.13). To see why, suppose this requirement were violated, so that for some $\vec{X}, Y, Y', A, S$ we have $\gamma_F(\vec{X}, Y, A, S)$, $\gamma_f(\vec{X}, Y', A, S)$ and $Y \neq Y'$. Then we could simultaneously derive $f(\vec{X}, do(A, S)) = Y$ and $f(\vec{X}, do(A, S)) = Y'$ from the above effect axiom, and this is an inconsistency if $Y \neq Y'$. Notice that by the unique names axioms for actions, this consistency condition is satisfied by the above example treating the functional fluent *height*.

As before, to solve the frame problem for functional fluents, we make the following:

Causal Completeness Assumption:

Axiom (3.13) characterizes all the conditions under which action a can cause f to take on value y in the successor situation.

In other words, this sentence completely describes the causal laws for functional fluent f.

Hence, if action a is possible in the current situation s, and f's value changes from what it was in the current situation to something else in the next situation resulting from doing a, then $\gamma_f(\vec{x}, y, a, s)$ must have been *true*. This informally stated assumption can be captured axiomatically by the following:

Explanation Closure Axiom for Functional Fluents

$$f(\vec{x}, do(a, s)) \neq f(\vec{x}, s) \supset (\exists y)\gamma_f(\vec{x}, y, a, s). \tag{3.15}$$

To see that this is a frame axiom, rewrite it in the logically equivalent form:

$$\neg(\exists y)\gamma_f(\vec{x}, y, a, s) \supset f(\vec{x}, do(a, s)) = f(\vec{x}, s).$$

This says that f's function value does not change in passing from situation s to situation $do(a, s)$ provided $\neg(\exists y)\gamma_f(\vec{x}, y, a, s)$ is true.

It is a simple, but tedious, exercise to show that (3.13) and (3.15) are logically equivalent to the following:

Successor state axiom for functional fluent f:

$$f(\vec{x}, do(a, s)) = y \equiv \gamma_f(\vec{x}, y, a, s) \vee y = f(\vec{x}, s) \wedge \neg(\exists y')\gamma_f(\vec{x}, y', a, s).$$

Continuing with the above blocks world example, and assuming that the above effect axioms describe all the ways an action can affect the height of a block (the causal completeness assumption for this example), we obtain the following successor state axiom for *height*:

$$height(b, do(a, s)) = y \equiv$$
$$\gamma_{height}(b, y, a, s) \vee y = height(b, s) \wedge \neg(\exists y')\gamma_{height}(b, y', a, s),$$

where $\gamma_{height}(b, y, a, s)$ is the above bracketed formula.

3.2.7 A Simple Solution: Summary

Our proposed solution to the frame problem appeals to the following axioms:

1. Successor state axioms:

   (a) For each relational fluent F:

   $$F(\vec{x}, do(a, s)) \equiv \gamma_F^+(\vec{x}, a, s) \vee F(\vec{x}, s) \wedge \neg\gamma_F^-(\vec{x}, a, s).$$

   (b) For each functional fluent f:

   $$f(\vec{x}, do(a, s)) = y \equiv \gamma_f(\vec{x}, y, a, s) \vee f(\vec{x}, s) = y \wedge \neg(\exists y')\gamma_f(\vec{x}, y', a, s).$$

2. For each action A, a single action precondition axiom of the form:

   $$Poss(A(\vec{x}), s) \equiv \Pi_A(\vec{x}, s),$$

   where $\Pi_A(\vec{x}, s)$ is a first-order formula with free variables among $\vec{x}, s$.

3. Unique names axioms for actions.

Ignoring the unique names axioms (whose effects can be compiled), this axiomatization requires $\mathcal{F}+\mathcal{A}$ axioms in total, compared with the roughly $2 \times \mathcal{A} \times \mathcal{F}$ explicit frame axioms that would otherwise be required. Here, $\mathcal{F}$ is the number of fluents and $\mathcal{A}$ the number of actions. There still remains the possibility that fewer axioms come at the expense of prohibitively long successor state axioms, but fortunately, this is unlikely.

- A successor state axiom's length is roughly proportional to the number of actions that affect the value of the fluent.

- The intuition leading to the frame problem is that most actions do not affect the fluent. So few actions affect it. So its successor state axiom is short.

The conciseness and perspicuity of this axiomatization relies on two things:

1. Quantification over actions.

2. The assumption that relatively few actions affect a given fluent.

3.2.8   Some Limitations of These Action Descriptions

Recall that the solution to the frame problem applies only when the effect axioms have the special syntactic form:

$$R(\vec{x}, s) \supset (\neg)F(\vec{x}, do(A, s)).$$

Such axioms describe *deterministic* actions, and preclude *indeterminate* actions with uncertain effects, for example:

$$heads(do(flip, s)) \vee tails(do(flip, s)),$$

$$(\exists x)holding(x, do(pickupAblock, s)).$$

Effect axioms, and therefore the solution to the frame problem, are for primitive actions only; as yet, there are no constructs for complex actions, like the following:

- Conditional actions:

   if $carInDriveway$ **then** $drive$ **else** $walk$ **endif**.

- Iterative actions:

   while $[(\exists \, block)ontable(block)]$ **do** $removeAblock$ **endwhile**.

- Nondeterministic actions:

   $removeAblock = (\pi \, block)[pickup(block); putOnFloor(block)].$

   Here, ; means sequence and $(\pi \, block)$ means nondeterministically pick a block, and for that choice of a block, do the complex action following this operator.

- Recursive actions: If $down$ means move an elevator down one floor, define $d(n)$, meaning move the elevator down n floors.

   proc $d(n)$
      if $n = 0$ **then** no_op
      else $down$; $d(n - 1)$ **endif**
   endproc

In Chapter 6, we shall see how to define such complex actions within the situation calculus. Moreover, having done this, we will have a situation calculus-based programming language for tasks like discrete event simulation and high level robotic control. Probabilistic actions, like flipping a coin, will be treated in Chapter 12.

3.3   Deductive Planning with the Situation Calculus

Historically, the situation calculus has been most strongly identified with planning applications in artificial intelligence. This has basically been a textbook identification, since (rightly or wrongly) very few people actually use the situation calculus to do real world planning. Despite this, there is considerable value in giving a logical account of the planning problem; at the very least, this provides a *specification* of the planning task, one that planning systems—logic-based or not—ought to respect. This section gives such a formal account of planning within the situation calculus.

The planning problem is this: Given an axiomatized initial situation, and a goal statement, find an action sequence that will lead to a state in which the goal will be true.

Example 3.3.1: We treat the simple setting of a one-handed robot that can hold at most one object in its hand, pick up and drop things, and walk about.

Action precondition axioms:

$$Poss(pickup(r, x), s) \equiv robot(r) \wedge [(\forall z)\neg holding(r, z, s)] \wedge nextTo(r, x, s),$$

$$Poss(walk(r, y), s) \equiv robot(r),$$

$$Poss(drop(r, x), s) \equiv robot(r) \wedge holding(r, x, s).$$

Effect axioms:

$$holding(r, x, do(pickup(r, x), s)),$$

$$\neg holding(r, x, do(drop(r, x), s)),$$

$$nextTo(r, y, do(walk(r, y), s)),$$

$$nextTo(r, y, s) \supset nextTo(x, y, do(drop(r, x), s)),$$

$$y \neq x \supset \neg nextTo(r, x, do(walk(r, y), s)),$$

$$onfloor(x, do(drop(r, x), s)),$$

$$\neg onfloor(x, do(pickup(r, x), s)).$$

The solution to the frame problem of the previous section yields the following:

Successor state axioms:

$$holding(r, x, do(a, s)) \equiv \\ a = pickup(r, x) \vee holding(r, x, s) \wedge a \neq drop(r, x), \tag{3.16}$$

$$nextTo(x, y, do(a, s)) \equiv \\ a = walk(x, y) \vee (\exists r)[nextTo(r, y, s) \wedge a = drop(r, x)] \vee \\ nextTo(x, y, s) \wedge \neg(\exists z)[a = walk(x, z) \wedge z \neq y], \tag{3.17}$$

$$onfloor(x, do(a, s)) \equiv \\ (\exists r)a = drop(r, x) \vee onfloor(x, s) \wedge \neg(\exists r)a = pickup(r, x). \tag{3.18}$$

Initial situation:

$$chair(C), \quad robot(R), \quad nextTo(R, A, S_0), \quad (\forall z)\neg holding(R, z, S_0). \qquad (3.19)$$

The distinguished constant S_0 always denotes the initial situation in the situation calculus. So initially, a robot R is next to the object A; moreover, R is not holding anything.

As specified in our approach to the frame problem, we also need:

Unique names axioms for actions:

$$pickup(r, x) \neq drop(r', y),$$

$$pickup(r, x) \neq walk(r', y),$$

$$walk(r, y) = walk(r', y') \supset r = r' \wedge y = y',$$

$$etc.$$

Here are some facts derivable from these axioms:

From (3.16),

$$holding(R, A, do(pickup(R, A), S_0)). \qquad (3.20)$$

From (3.20), (3.16) and unique names for actions,

$$holding(R, A, do(walk(R, y), do(pickup(R, A), S_0))). \qquad (3.21)$$

From (3.17),

$$nextTo(R, y, do(walk(R, y), do(pickup(R, A), S_0))). \qquad (3.22)$$

From (3.22) and (3.17),

$$nextTo(A, y, do(drop(R, A), do(walk(R, y), do(pickup(R, A), S_0)))). \qquad (3.23)$$

From (3.18),

$$onfloor(A, do(drop(R, A), do(walk(R, y), do(pickup(R, A), S_0)))). \qquad (3.24)$$

Suppose we want to derive:

$$(\exists s).nextTo(A, B, s) \wedge onfloor(A, s).$$

i.e., that there is an action sequence leading to a state of the world in which the object A is next to B and A is on the floor. The above is a constructive proof of this sentence, with

$$s = do(drop(R, A), do(walk(R, B), do(pickup(R, A), S_0))).$$

We can interpret this situation term as a *plan* to get A onto the floor next to B: First, R picks up A, then it walks to B, then it drops A. *The key idea here is that plans can be synthesized as a side-effect of theorem-proving.*

So the general picture of planning in the situation calculus, with respect to some background axioms, is to prove that some situation satisfies the goal statement G:

$$Axioms \vdash (\exists s)G(s).$$

Any variable-free binding for s obtained as a side-effect of a proof is a plan guaranteed to yield a situation satisfying the goal G. This is exactly the idea behind Prolog, in which programs are executed by a theorem-prover for the side-effect of obtaining bindings for the existentially quantified variables in the goal theorem.

There is one slight problem with this pretty picture of deductive planning that needs fixing. Notice that the proof of (3.23) and (3.24), from which the above plan was obtained, did not use any of the action precondition axioms. Therefore, the following two sentences could just as easily have been derived:

$$nextTo(A, y, do(drop(C, A), do(walk(C, y), do(pickup(C, A), S_0)))),$$

$$onfloor(A, do(drop(C, A), do(walk(C, y), do(pickup(C, A), S_0)))).$$

These also give a constructive proof of the sentence

$$(\exists s).nextTo(A, B, s) \wedge onfloor(A, s),$$

with

$$s = do(drop(C, A), do(walk(C, B), do(pickup(C, A), S_0))).$$

In other words, the chair C picks up A, then it walks to B, then it drops A. The obvious problem here is that the first plan, in which the robot R does the work, conforms to the action precondition axioms, while the second plan does not; according to these axioms, robots can pick things up, and go for walks, but chairs cannot. More precisely, the robot's plan is *executable* according to the action precondition axioms, meaning that one can prove, from the axioms, that:

$$Poss(pickup(R, A), S_0) \wedge Poss(walk(R, B), do(pickup(R, A), S_0)) \wedge$$
$$Poss(drop(R, A), do(walk(R, B), do(pickup(R, A), S_0))).$$

In other words, the action $pickup(R, A)$ is possible initially; $walk(R, B)$ is possible in the next situation resulting from doing the first action; finally, $drop(R, A)$ is possible in the situation resulting from doing the first two actions. On the other hand, there is no proof that this sequence of actions, as performed by the chair, is executable, and so the chair's actions should not be viewed as a plan. These considerations lead to the following,

Definition 3.3.2: Official Definition of a Plan for the Situation Calculus

Let $\mathcal{D}$ be a set of situation calculus axioms characterizing some application domain, σ a variable-free situation term, and $G(s)$ a situation calculus formula whose only free variable is the situation variable s. Then σ is a plan for G (relative to $\mathcal{D}$) iff

$$\mathcal{D} \models executable(\sigma) \wedge G(\sigma).$$

One way to determine such a σ is to prove the sentence $(\exists s).executable(s) \wedge G(s)$. Any binding for s obtained as a side-effect of a proof is a plan guaranteed to be executable and to yield a situation satisfying the goal G.

There still remains the problem of logically specifying the relation $executable(s)$; that will be done in Section 4.2.4 below.

We shall revisit the planning problem in Chapter 10, which develops systematic techniques for computing plans in the situation calculus.

3.4 Formalizing Database Transactions in the Situation Calculus

3.4.1 Motivation and Background

One way that databases evolve over time is as a result of *transactions*, whose purpose is to update the database with new information. For example, an educational database might have a transaction specifically designed to change a student's grade. This would normally be a procedure that, when invoked on a specific student and grade, first checks that the database satisfies certain preconditions (e.g., that there is a record for the student, and that the new grade differs from the old), and if so, records the new grade. This is obviously a *procedural* notion; transactions also *physically modify* the database.

Ideally, we would prefer a *specification* of the entire evolution of a database to serve as a formal foundation for an implementation of an evolving database. This section proposes such a specification of database transactions by appealing to the situation calculus. We shall discover that databases also suffer from the frame problem, and that our solution applies equally to the database setting.

3.4.2 Database Updates: A Proposal

We represent databases in the situation calculus, and treat updatable relations as fluents, i.e. they will take a situation argument. Moreover, we view update transactions as situation calculus actions. Of course, for this proposal to work, we need a solution to the frame problem for database relations. To see that databases do suffer from the frame problem, notice that a grade-changing transaction does not affect a student's grade in a different course, or his student number, or the courses in which he is enrolled, etc.

3.4.3 The Basic Approach: An Example

We describe an example of an education database with the following characteristics:

Database Relations

1. $enrolled(st, course, s)$: st is enrolled in $course$ in situation s.

2. $grade(st, course, grade, s)$: The grade of st in $course$ is $grade$ in situation s.[3]

3. $prerequ(pre, course)$: pre is a prerequisite course for $course$. Notice that course prerequisites are assumed not to change from one situation to another.

Database transactions:

1. $register(st, c)$: register st in course c.

2. $change(st, c, g)$: change the grade of st in course c to g.

3. $drop(st, c)$: drop st from course c.

Initial Database

These will be arbitrary first-order sentences, the only restriction being that fluents mention only the initial situation S_0. Some typical examples of sentences true in the initial database are:

$enrolled(Sue, C100, S_0) \lor enrolled(Sue, C200, S_0)$,

$(\exists c)enrolled(Bill, c, S_0)$,

$(\forall p).prerequ(p, P300) \equiv p = P100 \lor p = M100$,

$(\forall p)\neg prerequ(p, C100)$,

$(\forall c).enrolled(Bill, c, S_0) \equiv c = M100 \lor c = C100 \lor c = P200$,

$enrolled(Mary, C100, S_0)$, $\neg enrolled(John, M200, S_0)$,
$grade(Sue, P300, 75, S_0)$.

Now we axiomatize the transaction preconditions, and the effects on the database relations of the transactions.

Transaction Precondition Axioms:

- A student can register in a course iff she has obtained a grade of at least 50 in all prerequisites for the course:

$$Poss(register(st, c), s) \equiv \{(\forall p).prerequ(p, c)$$
$$\supset (\exists g).grade(st, p, g, s) \land g \geq 50\}.$$

- It is possible to change a student's grade iff he has a grade that is different than the new grade:

$$Poss(change(st, c, g), s) \equiv (\exists g').grade(st, c, g', s) \land g' \neq g.$$

---

3 Notice that it would be more natural to represent $grade$ as a functional fluent: $grade(st, course, s) = g$ iff the grade of st in $course$ is g when the database is in situation s. However, conventional databases, especially relational databases, only provide mechanisms for representing relations, not functions. Accordingly, when formalizing databases in the situation calculus, we shall treat functions, like $grade$, as relations.

- A student may drop a course iff the student is currently enrolled in that course:

$$Poss(drop(st, c), s) \equiv enrolled(st, c, s).$$

Transaction Effect Axioms:

$$\neg enrolled(st, c, do(drop(st, c), s)),$$

$$enrolled(st, c, do(register(st, c), s)),$$

$$grade(st, c, g, do(change(st, c, g), s)),$$

$$g' \neq g \supset \neg grade(st, c, g', do(change(st, c, g), s)).$$

By solving the frame problem with respect to these effect axioms, we obtain the following successor state axioms for the database relations:

$$enrolled(st, c, do(a, s)) \equiv a = register(st, c) \vee$$
$$enrolled(st, c, s) \wedge a \neq drop(st, c),$$

$$grade(st, c, g, do(a, s)) \equiv a = change(st, c, g) \vee$$
$$grade(st, c, g, s) \wedge (\forall g')a \neq change(st, c, g').$$

3.4.4 Querying a Situation Calculus Database

Notice that on the above situation calculus perspective on databases, all updates are *virtual*; the database, consisting as it does of a set of logical sentences, is never physically changed. Axioms are forever. How then do we query a database after some sequence of transactions has been "executed"? For example, suppose we want to know whether John is enrolled in any courses after the transaction sequence $drop(John, C100), register(Mary, C100)$ has been "executed". The trick is to formulate this as a query with respect to the hypothetical future resulting from the performance of this transaction sequence:

$$Database \models (\exists c)enrolled(John, c, do(register(Mary, C100),$$
$$do(drop(John, C100), S_0))).$$

This is an example of what is called the *projection problem* in AI planning. Such a sequence of update transactions is called a database *log* in database theory. In this setting, the AI projection problem becomes formally identical to the database problem of evaluating a query with respect to a database log. We shall have much more to say later about the projection problem, database logs and queries, and related issues.

3.5 Exercises

1. Suppose that the following are all of the effect axioms about an electrical system:

$$fuseOk(s) \wedge \neg lightOn(s) \supset lightOn(do(flipSwitch, s)),$$

$$lightOn(s) \supset \neg lightOn(do(flipSwitch, s)),$$

$$\neg fuseOk(do(shortCircuit, s)),$$

$$lightOn(s) \supset \neg lightOn(do(shortCircuit, s)).$$

(a) Give the normal form positive and negative effects axioms (Section 3.2.5) for the fluent $lightOn$.

(b) Obtain Pednault's solution to the frame problem for fluent $lightOn$.

(c) Give the explanation closure axioms (positive and negative) for the $lightOn$ fluent.

(d) Obtain the successor state axioms for the fluents $lightOn$ and $fuseOk$.

(e) Prove that the resulting action theory entails that

$$fuseOk(S_0) \supset (\exists s)lightOn(s).$$

2. The AI literature on change frequently appeals to one or more "classical" examples. Usually, despite their seeming simplicity, there is some historical reason for the example; it illustrates some desirable general property, or some special difficulty for existing (at the time) approaches. For each of the following examples, axiomatize it appropriately with action precondition and effect axioms, obtain successor state axioms, then solve the problem.

(a) **The monkey and bananas problem:** (The very first planning problem!)

A monkey is in a room containing a bunch of bananas hanging from the ceiling, and a chair. The monkey can't reach the bananas from the floor, but can if standing on the chair, provided the chair is underneath the bananas, which initially it is not. Neither, initially, is the monkey near the chair. In this scenario, four actions are possible:

- $walk(x)$ - The monkey walks to object x.
- $pushUnder(x, y)$ - The monkey pushes object x to a location under y.
- $climb(x)$ - The monkey climbs onto object x.
- $grab(x)$ - The monkey grabs object x.

Fluents:

- $onCeiling(x, s)$ - Object x is on the ceiling in situation s.
- $holding(x, s)$ - The monkey is holding x in situation s.
- $nextTo(x, s)$ - The monkey is next to x in situation s.
- $on(x, s)$, - The monkey is on x in situation s.
- $below(x, y, s)$ - Object x is below object y in situation s.

Deductively obtain a plan whereby the monkey gets the bananas. Make sure that the plan you obtain is executable.

(b) **The Yale shooting problem:**

Fluents:

- $alive(s)$ - Joe is alive in situation s.
- $loaded(s)$ - The gun is loaded in situation s.

Actions:

- $load$ - Load the gun. This can always be done, whether or not the gun is currently loaded.
- $shoot$ - Shoot the gun. This requires that the gun be loaded, and has the effect that Joe will not be alive.
- $wait$ - A no-op; it has no effect on any fluent, and can always be performed.

Show that, regardless of the initial situation, Joe will not be alive after the sequence $load, wait, shoot$ takes place.

3. Axiomatize the game of tic-tac-toe on a 3×3 board, with two players, X and O who move alternately. When X moves, she chooses a blank square and marks an "X" in it. Player O marks unmarked squares with an "O". Use the following relational fluents:

- $xsquare(squ, s)$: The square squ contains an "X" in situation s. Similarly, $osquare(squ, s)$ means squ contains an "O", and $bsquare(squ, s)$ means squ is blank. Assume the squares are numbered $1, \ldots, 9$.
- $xturn(s)$: In situation s it is X's turn to make a move.
- $oturn(s)$: In situation s it is O's turn to make a move.

Use the following actions:

- $xmove(squ)$: X places an X in square squ.
- $omove(squ)$: O places an O in square squ.

You will find it useful to introduce an abbreviation $wins(p, s)$, meaning that player p wins the game in situation s. $wins$ can be easily expressed in terms of the fluents $xsquare$ and $osquare$.

4. Let $favoriteBook(p, s)$ be a functional fluent, denoting person p's favorite book in situation s. Give effect axioms for the following facts about this fluent:

After John reads what is, in the current situation, Mary's favorite book, that book will become his favorite book in the next situation.

After Mary reads Moby Dick, her favorite book will be Moby Dick.

Using these, determine the successor state axiom for $favoriteBook$. Then prove that in the situation resulting from Mary reading Moby Dick, followed by Mary reading Middlemarch, followed by John reading what is, in the current situation, Mary's favorite book, John's favorite book will be Moby Dick.

5. Formalize the following toy airline reservation system along the lines of the example database system of this chapter. This will involve formulating suitable intuitively plausible effect and action precondition axioms, and deriving the corresponding successor state axioms.

Fluents:

- $seatsAvailable(flight\#, date, n, s)$ - There are n seats available in the situation s for $flight\#$ on $date$.

- $hasReservation(person, flight\#, date, s)$ - $person$ has a reservation in the situation s for $flight\#$ on $date$.

- $seatReserved(person, seat\#, flight\#, date, s)$ - Obvious meaning.

Transactions:

- $reserve(person, flight\#, date)$ - Reserve space for $person$ on $flight\#$ for $date$.

- $assignSeat(person, seat\#, flight\#, date)$ - Obvious meaning.

- $cancelReservation(person, flight\#, date)$ - Cancel the booking.

3.6 Bibliographic Remarks

The situation calculus has been a part of the artificial intelligence zeitgeist almost from the very beginning of the field. It is included in the standard material of every introductory course on AI, and it is the language of choice for investigations of various technical problems that arise in theorizing about actions and their effects. Nevertheless, historically the AI community has not taken the situation calculus seriously as a foundation for practical work in planning, control, simulation or robotics. There were good representational and computational reasons for this. Representationally, there were no suitably rich accounts for the most basic ingredients of a theory of actions, like time, concurrency, continuous processes, or procedures. Neither was there a good story for the frame and qualification problems. Computationally, it was seen as a first-order language requiring necessarily inefficient theorem-proving methods. One purpose of this book is to show that these historical limitations of the situation calculus have been largely overcome by recent research, and that the resulting enriched language has many representational and computational advantages for modeling dynamical systems.

The basic conceptual and formal ingredients of the situation calculus are due to John

McCarthy [136] in 1963. The frame problem was first observed by John McCarthy and Pat Hayes [141]; since then, it has been the subject of a large body of technical research (e.g. Brown [28]), as well as philosophical speculation (e.g. Pylyshyn [170]). Two excellent recent books on theories of actions, with specific focus on solutions to the frame and related problems are by Sandewall [187] and by Shanahan [195]. See also the book by Shoham [199] for an earlier treatment of causality and the frame problem. The companion to the frame problem—the qualification problem—was also first observed by McCarthy [137], although he had in mind a somewhat more general notion of the scope of this problem than that prevailing today, which concerns only the qualifications relevant to action preconditions.

The first uses of the situation calculus were in planning, following the influential proposal of Green [71]. Indeed, Shakey, the very first autonomous robot project, was based on Green's account of planning, using resolution theorem-proving with a situation calculus axiomatization of the robot's actions and environment. This was in the late 1960's and early 1970's, before very much was known about the frame problem or theorem-proving, and this first attempt at a situation calculus-based approach to high level robotics was abandoned in the face of the extreme computational inefficiencies that were encountered (Fikes and Nilsson [50]).

The solution to the frame problem of Section 3.2 was described in Reiter [173]; it combines elements of earlier proposals by Pednault [154], Davis [36], and by Haas [76], as elaborated by Schubert [192]. Independently, Elkan [41] proposed a similar solution. The significance of the consistency condition (3.11) in deriving successor state axioms (Proposition 3.2.6) was first noted by Pednault [154], and generalized slightly by Reiter [173] to fit his solution to the frame problem.

The situation calculus-based approach to formalizing databases evolving under update transactions was described by Reiter in [175]. This approach to database updates is extended by Bertossi, Arenas and Ferretti [18], who also provide an implementation that interfaces to a relational database system, and to automated theorem-provers for proving properties of the situation calculus database description. For more information on relational databases, see Maier [131], and for a relational database perspective on update transactions, see Abiteboul [1]. Our perspective on databases, in which the initial database is any first-order theory, not necessarily relational, is closest to that held by the deductive database community; see, for example, Minker [147].

The monkey-bananas problem—the very first planning problem—was proposed by John McCarthy in 1963 and reprinted in [136]; in that paper, McCarthy also gave an axiomatization from which he showed that the monkey can indeed get the bananas.

The Yale Shooting Problem was proposed by Hanks and McDermott in 1986 [80], not because it is very difficult—it is trivial under our approach to the frame problem—but because they wanted to point out that all the formal approaches to solving the frame problem at that time got it wrong. All these approaches were based on nonmonotonic reasoning techniques; in fact, solving the frame problem was one of the principal motivations for the development of these logics (Reiter [172]). Accordingly, the Hanks-McDermott paper presented a serious challenge to these formalisms. The final outcome of this challenge was a flurry of activity on the part of the nonmonotonic research community to correct their story on the frame problem, a job that by now has largely been completed successfully.

While the situation calculus was perhaps the first logical proposal within artificial intelligence for representing system dynamics, it has not remained the only such approach. Others include the event calculus, first formulated by Kowalski and Sergot [98] (see also Miller and Shanahan [146]), Sandewall's features and fluents [187, 189] and its related temporal action logics developed by Doherty , Gustafsson , Karlsson and Kvarnström [40], the family of $\mathcal{A}$ languages of Gelfond and Lifschitz [60], the fluent calculus of Hölldobler and Schneeberger [89] (see also Thielscher [212], and for the most recent version of the language, Thielscher [214]), and temporal logics by Allen [2] and McDermott [142]. This is an embarrassing richness of proposals; a few attempts have been made to compare some of them with the situation calculus (Kowalski and Sadri [97]; Van Belleghem, Denecker, and De Schreye [16]; Thielscher [213]).

4 Foundations of the Situation Calculus

In the previous chapter, we provided an intuitive introduction to the situation calculus, and an indication of some of the things it is good for. We now consider formally specifying a language and an axiomatization for the situation calculus, as well as the precise forms that theories of actions should have. Having done this, we shall be able to prove various useful theoretical and computational results about actions, and establish the foundations on which the remainder of this book rests.

4.1 The Language of the Situation Calculus

The language $\mathcal{L}_{sitcalc}$ adopted here is a second-order language with equality. It has three disjoint sorts: *action* for actions, *situation* for situations, and a catch-all sort *object* for everything else depending on the domain of application. Apart from the standard alphabet of logical symbols—we use $\wedge$, $\neg$ and $\exists$, with the usual definitions of a full set of connectives and quantifiers—$\mathcal{L}_{sitcalc}$ has the following alphabet:

- Countably infinitely many individual variable symbols of each sort. We shall use s and a, with subscripts and superscripts, for variables of sort *situation* and *action*, respectively. We normally use lower case roman letters other than a, s, with subscripts and superscripts for variables of sort *object*. In addition, because $\mathcal{L}_{sitcalc}$ is second-order, its alphabet includes countably infinitely many predicate variables of all arities.

- Two function symbols of sort *situation*:
  1. A constant symbol S_0, denoting the initial situation.
  2. A binary function symbol $do : action \times situation \rightarrow situation$. The intended interpretation is that situations are finite sequences of actions, and $do(a, s)$ denotes that sequence formed by adding action a to the sequence s.

- A binary predicate symbol $\sqsubset : situation \times situation$, defining an ordering relation on situations. The intended interpretation of situations is as finite action sequences, in which case $s \sqsubset s'$ means that s is a proper subsequence of s'.

- A binary predicate symbol $Poss : action \times situation$. The intended interpretation of $Poss(a, s)$ is that it is possible to perform the action a in situation s.

- For each $n \geq 0$, countably infinitely many predicate symbols with arity n, and sorts $(action \cup object)^n$. These are used to denote situation independent relations like

$$human(Joe), \quad oddNumber(n), \quad movingAction(run(agent, loc1, loc2)).$$

- For each $n \geq 0$, countably infinitely many function symbols of sort

$$(action \cup object)^n \rightarrow object.$$

These are used to denote situation-independent functions like

$$sqrt(x), \quad height(MtEverest), \quad agent(pickup(person, object)).$$

- For each $n \geq 0$, a finite or countably infinite number of function symbols of sort

  $$(action \cup object)^n \rightarrow action.$$

  These are called *action functions*, and are used to denote actions like $pickup(x)$, $move(A, B)$, etc. In most applications, there will be just finitely many action functions, but we allow the possibility of an infinite number of them.

  Notice that we distinguish between function symbols taking values of sort *object* and those—the action functions—taking values of sort *action*. In what follows, the latter will be distinguished by the requirement that they be axiomatized in a particular way by what we shall call *action precondition axioms*.

- For each $n \geq 0$, a finite or countably infinite number of predicate symbols with arity $n+1$, and sorts $(action \cup object)^n \times situation$. These predicate symbols are called *relational fluents*. In most applications, there will be just finitely many relational fluents, but we do not preclude the possibility of an infinite number of them. These are used to denote situation dependent relations like $ontable(x, s)$, $husband(Mary, John, s)$, etc. Notice that relational fluents take just one argument of sort *situation*, and this is always its last argument.

- For each $n \geq 0$, a finite or countably infinite number of function symbols of sort

  $$(action \cup object)^n \times situation \rightarrow action \cup object.$$

  These function symbols are called *functional fluents*. In most applications, there will be just finitely many functional fluents, but we do not preclude the possibility of an infinite number of them. These are used to denote situation dependent functions like $age(Mary, s)$, $primeMinister(Italy, s)$, etc. Notice that functional fluents take just one argument of sort *situation*, and this is always its last argument.

Notice that only two function symbols of $\mathcal{L}_{sitcalc}$—S_0 and do—are permitted to take values in sort *situation*.

4.2   Axioms for the Situation Calculus

There is a strong analogy between the situation calculus and a part of number theory. Accordingly, we begin with a diversion into the world of natural numbers.

4.2.1   Number Theory

In 1889, Giuseppe Peano provided the first axiomatization of the natural numbers. Here, we focus on a fragment of full number theory that characterizes the successor function, and the less-than relation. Full number theory would also have axioms characterizing addition and multiplication, but these turn out not to be relevant here. Accordingly, we introduce the following vocabulary for a second-order language (with equality):

- A single constant symbol 0.
- A unary function symbol σ (successor function).
- A binary relation symbol $<$ (the less than relation).

The axioms for this part of number theory are:

$$\sigma(x) = \sigma(y) \supset x = y,$$

$$(\forall P).P(0) \wedge (\forall x)[P(x) \supset P(\sigma(x))] \supset (\forall x)P(x),$$

$$\neg x < 0,$$

$$x < \sigma(y) \equiv x \leq y.$$

Here, $x \leq y$ is an abbreviation for $x < y \vee x = y$.

The second sentence is a second-order induction axiom; it is a way of characterizing the domain of discourse to be the *smallest* set such that

1. 0 is in the set.
2. Whenever x is in the set, so is $\sigma(x)$.

This second-order fragment of arithmetic is *categorical* (it has a unique model). Normally, textbooks on the subject describe first-order number theory, which you obtain by replacing the second-order axiom by an induction *schema* representing countably infinitely many first-order sentences, one for each instance of P obtained by replacing P by a first-order formula with one free variable. The resulting first-order fragment of arithmetic is *not* categorical; it has (infinitely) many distinct models.

This leads to the natural question: Why not use the second-order axiom instead of the axiom schema? The answer is, because second-order logic is incomplete; there is no "decent" axiomatization of second-order logic that will yield all the valid second-order sentences; the valid sentences of second-order logic are not recursively enumerable, or equivalently, there is no recursive axiomatization for second-order logic (Section 2.2.4). That being the case, why appeal to second-order logic at all? The main reason is that *semantically*, but not syntactically, it characterizes the natural numbers. We shall encounter the same phenomenon in semantically characterizing the situation calculus.

4.2.2   Foundational Axioms for Situations

We now focus on the domain of situations. The primary intuition about situations that we wish to capture axiomatically is that they are finite sequences of actions. We want also to be able to say that a certain sequence of actions precedes another. The four axioms we are about to present capture these two properties of situations:

$$do(a_1, s_1) = do(a_2, s_2) \supset a_1 = a_2 \wedge s_1 = s_2, \tag{4.1}$$

$$(\forall P).P(S_0) \wedge (\forall a, s)[P(s) \supset P(do(a, s))] \supset (\forall s)P(s). \tag{4.2}$$

Compare these to the first two axioms for the natural numbers.

Axiom (4.2) is a second-order induction axiom, and has the effect of limiting the sort *situation* to the smallest set containing S_0, and closed under the application of the function *do* to an action and a situation. Any model of these axioms will have as its domain of situations the smallest set S satisfying:

1. $\sigma_0 \in S$, where σ_0 is the interpretation of S_0 in the model.

2. If $\sigma \in S$, and $A \in \mathcal{A}$, then $do(A, \sigma) \in S$, where $\mathcal{A}$ is the domain of actions in the model.

Notice that axiom (4.1) is a unique names axiom for situations. This, together with the induction axiom, imply that two situations will be the same iff they result from the same sequence of actions applied to the initial situation. Two situations S_1 and S_2 may be different, yet assign the same truth values to all fluents. So a situation in the situation calculus must not be identified with the set of fluents that hold in that situation, i.e with a *state*. The proper way to understand a situation is as a *history*, namely, a finite sequence of actions; two situations are equal iff they denote identical histories. This is the major reason for using the terminology "situation" instead of "state"; the latter carries with it the connotation of a "snapshot" of the world. In our formulation of the situation calculus, *situations are not snapshots, they are finite sequences of actions*. While states can repeat themselves—the same snapshot of the world can happen twice—situations cannot.

There are two more axioms, designed to capture the concept of a subhistory:

$$\neg s \sqsubset S_0, \tag{4.3}$$

$$s \sqsubset do(a, s') \equiv s \sqsubseteq s', \tag{4.4}$$

where $s \sqsubseteq s'$ is an abbreviation for $s \sqsubset s' \vee s = s'$.[1] Here, the relation $\sqsubset$ provides an ordering on situations; $s \sqsubset s'$ means that the action sequence s' can be obtained from the sequence s by adding one or more actions to the front of s.[2] These axioms also have their

---

1 Unlike $\sqsubset$, $\sqsubseteq$ is *not* a predicate symbol of $\mathcal{L}_{sitcalc}$; it is an *external* notation—a convenient shorthand—standing for the situation calculus formula that it abbreviates. So whenever you encounter an external expression of the form $s \sqsubseteq s'$, you are to mentally replace it with the legitimate situation calculus formula $s \sqsubset s' \vee s = s'$ for which it is an abbreviation. A good way to view abbreviations in logic is as macros that expand, wherever they are used, into their definitions. Logicians often appeal to such macros as a way of keeping a language, and an axiomatization, to a bare minimum. That is what we are doing here by treating $\sqsubseteq$ as an abbreviation. First, it need not be included in $\mathcal{L}_{sitcalc}$; secondly, an axiom $s \sqsubseteq s' \equiv s \sqsubset s' \vee s = s'$ need not be included among the foundational axioms of the situation calculus.

2 Readers familiar with the programming language LISP will have noticed that in the situation calculus, the constant S_0 is just like NIL, and *do* acts like *cons*. Situations are simply *lists* of primitive actions. For example, the situation term $do(C, do(B, do(A, S_0)))$ is simply an alternative syntax for the LISP list $(C\ B\ A)$ $(=$

analogues in the last two axioms of the preceding fragment of number theory.

The above four axioms are *domain independent*. They will provide the basic properties of situations in any domain specific axiomatization of particular fluents and actions. Henceforth, call them Σ. It takes a little bit of proving, but one can show that the situations in any model of Σ can be represented by a tree. Figure 4.1 shows one such tree, for a model M of Σ with n individuals $\alpha_1, \ldots, \alpha_n$ in M's domain of actions.

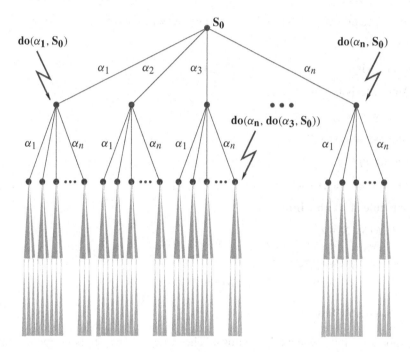

Figure 4.1: The tree of situations for a model with n actions.

We have abused notation slightly in this figure; strictly speaking, do should be do^M, and S_0 should be S_0^M. Nothing in this figure should suggest to the reader that there can be only finitely many actions in a model of Σ. There are models of Σ with action domain of any

---

$cons(C, cons(B, cons(A, NIL))))$. Notice that to obtain the action *history* corresponding to this term, namely the performance of action A, followed by B, followed by C, we read this list from right to left. Therefore, when situation terms are read from right to left, the relation $s \sqsubset s'$ means that situation s is a proper subhistory of the situation s'. The situation calculus induction axiom (4.2) is simply the induction principle for lists: If the empty list has property P and if, whenever list s has property P so does $cons(a, s)$, then all lists have property P.

cardinality.

4.2.3   Some Consequences of the Foundational Axioms

The following are some logical consequences of the foundational axioms Σ:

$S_0 \neq do(a, s)$,

$do(a, s) \neq s$,

Existence of a predecessor: $s = S_0 \lor (\exists a, s')s = do(a, s')$,

$S_0 \sqsubseteq s$,

Transitivity: $s_1 \sqsubset s_2 \land s_2 \sqsubset s_3 \supset s_1 \sqsubset s_3$,

Anti-reflexivity: $\neg s \sqsubset s$,

Unique names: $s_1 \sqsubset s_2 \supset s_1 \neq s_2$,

Anti-symmetry: $s \sqsubset s' \supset \neg s' \sqsubset s$,

$\neg do(a, s) \sqsubseteq s$,

$s \sqsubseteq s' \land s' \sqsubseteq s \supset s = s'$.

The Principle of Double Induction

$(\forall R).R(S_0, S_0) \land$
$\quad\quad [(\forall a, s).R(s, s) \supset R(do(a, s), do(a, s))] \land$
$\quad\quad [(\forall a, s, s').s \sqsubseteq s' \land R(s, s') \supset R(s, do(a, s'))]$
$\quad\quad\quad\quad \supset (\forall s, s').s \sqsubseteq s' \supset R(s, s')$.

4.2.4   Executable Situations

A situation is a finite sequence of actions. There are no constraints on the actions entering into such a sequence, so that it may not be possible to actually execute these actions one after the other. For example, suppose the precondition for performing the action $putdown(x)$ in situation s is that the agent is holding x: $holding(x, s)$. Suppose also that in situation S_0, the agent is not holding A: $\neg holding(A, S_0)$. Then $do(putdown(A), S_0)$ is a perfectly good situation, but it is not executable; the precondition for performing $putdown(A)$ is violated in S_0. Moreover, $do(pickup(B), do(putdown(A), S_0))$ is not an executable situation either. In fact, no situation whose first action is $putdown(A)$ is executable. Similarly, an action A_1 may be executable in S_0, but the action A_2 may not be possible in $do(A_1, S_0)$, in which case no sequence of actions beginning with these two would be executable. We emphasize that action sequences in which an action violates its precondition are perfectly good situations. They simply are not physically realizable; they are "ghost" situations.

Normally, we shall be interested only in *executable* situations, namely, those action histories in which it is actually possible to perform the actions one after the other. To characterize such situations, introduce an abbreviation:

$$executable(s) \overset{def}{=} (\forall a, s^*).do(a, s^*) \sqsubseteq s \supset Poss(a, s^*). \tag{4.5}$$

So *executable(s)* means that all the actions occurring in the action sequence s can be executed one after the other.

4.2.5 Further Consequences of the Foundational Axioms

There are a number of consequences of these abbreviations and the foundational axioms Σ:

$$executable(do(a, s)) \equiv executable(s) \wedge Poss(a, s),^3$$

$$executable(s) \equiv s = S_0 \vee (\exists a, s').s = do(a, s') \wedge Poss(a, s') \wedge executable(s'),$$

$$executable(s') \wedge s \sqsubseteq s' \supset executable(s).$$

The Principle of Induction for Executable Situations

$$(\forall P).P(S_0) \wedge (\forall a, s)[P(s) \wedge executable(s) \wedge Poss(a, s) \supset P(do(a, s))] \supset$$
$$(\forall s).executable(s) \supset P(s).$$

The Principle of Double Induction for Executable Situations

$$(\forall R).R(S_0, S_0) \wedge$$
$$[(\forall a, s).Poss(a, s) \wedge executable(s) \wedge R(s, s) \supset R(do(a, s), do(a, s))] \wedge$$
$$[(\forall a, s, s').Poss(a, s') \wedge executable(s') \wedge s \sqsubseteq s' \wedge R(s, s') \supset R(s, do(a, s'))]$$
$$\supset (\forall s, s').executable(s') \wedge s \sqsubseteq s' \supset R(s, s').$$

The principle of induction for executable situations is a very useful consequence of the foundational axioms. It is specifically designed for proving sentences of the form $(\forall s).executable(s) \supset \phi(s)$, i.e. that $\phi(s)$ is true for all executable situations s, and it says that to do so it is sufficient first to prove $\phi(S_0)$, then to prove:

$$(\forall a, s).\phi(s) \wedge executable(s) \wedge Poss(a, s) \supset \phi(do(a, s)).$$

Notice how this induction principle differs from the induction axiom (4.2) of the foundational axioms. (4.2) is used to prove properties of *all* situations, executable or not, while

---

3 Keep in mind that *executable(do(a, s))* and *executable(s)* are both abbreviations, so an expression like *executable(do(a, s))* $\equiv$ *executable(s)* $\wedge$ *Poss(a, s)* really stands for that situation calculus formula obtained from this expression by expanding these abbreviations. Similarly in the next two expressions, and elsewhere throughout the book.

the above principle is devoted to proving properties only of executable situations.

The principle of *double induction* for executable situations is used to prove sentences of the form

$$(\forall s, s').executable(s') \wedge s \sqsubseteq s' \supset R(s, s').$$

4.3   Reasoning about Situations Using Induction

There are many settings in which mathematical induction on situations is necessary to prove useful properties in the situation calculus. Typically, these are statements of the form "For all (executable) situations, property ϕ will be true". More precisely, these are theorems to be proved, having the syntactic form: $(\forall s)\phi(s)$, or $(\forall s).executable(s) \supset \phi(s)$, for some situation calculus formula $\phi(s)$ with one free variable s. Here are some examples:

Reasoning about the physical world. The dynamics of electrical and mechanical artifacts can be axiomatized in the situation calculus. Having done so, one will be well positioned to prove various properties of the system, and such proofs often require induction. In Section 4.3.1 below, we shall describe a simple electrical circuit consisting of two switches Sw_1 and Sw_2 connected to a light, and we shall prove that the light will be on iff both switches are in the same state (open or closed):

$$(\forall s).light(s) \equiv [open(Sw_1, s) \equiv open(Sw_2, s)].$$

This has the typical syntactic form for a proof by the simple induction axiom of the foundational axioms.

Planning. The standard logical account of planning views this as a theorem proving task (Section 3.3). To obtain a plan whose execution will lead to a world situation s in which the goal $G(s)$ will be true, establish that

$$Axioms \models (\exists s).executable(s) \wedge G(s).$$

Sometimes we would like to establish that no plan could possibly satisfy a goal. This is the problem of establishing that

$$Axioms \models (\forall s).executable(s) \supset \neg G(s),$$

i.e. that in all executable future world situations, G will be false. This sentence has the typical pattern calling for a proof by induction using the induction principle for executable situations.

Integrity constraints in database theory.   In database theory, an *integrity constraint* specifies what counts as a legal database state; it is a property that every situation must satisfy. For example,

- Grades are functional: No matter how the database evolves, no one may have two different grades for the same course in the same database situation.
- No one's salary may decrease during the evolution of the database.

The concept of an integrity constraint is intimately connected with that of database *evolution*. No matter how the database evolves, the constraint must be true in all database futures. Therefore, in order to make formal sense of integrity constraints, we need a prior theory of database evolution. How do databases change? One way (not the only way) is via predefined update *transactions*, as formally specified using the situation calculus in the last chapter. We shall assume that transactions provide the only mechanism for such database changes. Therefore, we can appeal to our earlier situation calculus theory of database transactions (Section 3.4) in defining integrity constraints and their role in maintaining database integrity. We shall identify a possible future of a database with a situation, and represent integrity constraints as first-order sentences, universally quantified over situations.

- No one ever has two different grades for the same course in any database situation:
$$(\forall s, st, c, g, g').grade(st, c, g, s) \land grade(st, c, g', s) \supset g = g'. \tag{4.6}$$
- Salaries never decrease in any executable situation:
$$(\forall s, s', p, \$, \$').executable(s') \land s \sqsubseteq s' \land sal(p, \$, s) \land sal(p, \$', s')$$
$$\supset \$ \leq \$'. \tag{4.7}$$

We can now define what we mean by a database satisfying its constraints.

Definition 4.3.1: Constraint Satisfaction
A database *satisfies* an integrity constraint IC iff

$$Database \models IC.$$

So, for example, to establish that a database satisfies the integrity constraint (4.6), we must prove that the database entails it. This sentence has the typical syntactic form calling for an inductive proof, using the induction axiom (4.2), with induction hypothesis $P(s)$ as:

$$(\forall st, c, g, g').grade(st, c, g, s) \land grade(st, c, g', s) \supset g = g'.$$

4.3.1 Some Examples of Inductive Proofs

Example 4.3.2: Consider an electric circuit with two switches, Sw_1 and Sw_2, and an action $toggle(sw)$ that opens the switch sw if it is closed, and closes it if it is open. The circuit is connected to a light that changes its state from on to off and off to on whenever one of the switches is toggled.

$$open(sw, do(a, s)) \equiv \neg open(sw, s) \land a = toggle(sw) \lor$$

$$open(sw, s) \land a \neq toggle(sw).$$

$$light(do(a, s)) \equiv \neg light(s) \land [a = toggle(Sw_1) \lor a = toggle(Sw_2)] \lor$$
$$light(s) \land a \neq toggle(Sw_1) \land a \neq toggle(Sw_2).$$

The property we wish to prove of this setting is:

$$(\forall s).light(s) \equiv [open(Sw_1, s) \equiv open(Sw_2, s)]. \tag{4.8}$$

In other words, it will always be the case that the light will be on iff both switches are open or closed (= not open) together. This sentence has the right syntactic form for an application of the induction principle (4.2) for arbitrary situations. So, take $P(s)$ to be:

$$light(s) \equiv [open(Sw_1, s) \equiv open(Sw_2, s)].$$

Assume further that (4.8) is true of the initial situation:

$$light(S_0) \equiv [open(Sw_1, S_0) \equiv open(Sw_2, S_0)].$$

The proof is long and tedious, but is otherwise straightforward. It requires the fact that $Sw_1 \neq Sw_2$, as well as a unique names axioms for the action $toggle(sw)$.

Example 4.3.3: We want to prove that no person can carry himself in any executable situation:

$$(\forall s).executable(s) \supset (\forall x)\neg carrying(x, x, s). \tag{4.9}$$

Assume the following action precondition axiom for $pickup$, and successor state axiom for $carrying$:

$$Poss(pickup(x, y), s) \equiv x \neq y \land \neg carrying(x, y, s).$$

$$carrying(x, y, do(a, s)) \equiv a = pickup(x, y) \lor$$
$$carrying(x, y, s) \land a \neq putdown(x, y).$$

Assume further that initially, no one is carrying himself:

$$\neg carrying(x, x, S_0).$$

The sentence (4.9) has the right syntactic form for a proof by induction on executable situations (Section 4.2.5), with $P(s)$ as $\neg carrying(x, x, s)$. The proof is straightforward. Notice that there are *non-executable* situations in which someone *is* carrying himself. For example, it is trivial to derive $carrying(Sam, Sam, do(pickup(Sam, Sam), S_0))$. The situation $do(pickup(Sam, Sam), S_0)$ is simply not physically realizable; it is a ghost situation. So the restriction in (4.9) to executable situations is essential. This was not the case for the previous example.

Example 4.3.4: We want to prove that salaries never decrease over any executable situation:

$$(\forall s, s', p, \$, \$').executable(s') \wedge s \sqsubseteq s' \wedge sal(p, \$, s) \wedge sal(p, \$', s') \supset \$ \le \$'.$$

Assume the following background axioms:

- To change a person's salary, the new salary must be greater than the old:

$$Poss(changeSal(p, \$), s) \equiv (\exists \$').sal(p, \$', s) \wedge \$' < \$.$$

- Successor state axiom for *sal*:

$$sal(p, \$, do(a, s)) \equiv a = changeSal(p, \$) \vee$$
$$sal(p, \$, s) \wedge (\forall \$')a \ne changeSal(p, \$').$$

- Initially, the relation *sal* is functional in its second argument:

$$sal(p, \$, S_0) \wedge sal(p, \$', S_0) \supset \$ = \$'.$$

- *Unique names axiom* for *changeSal*:

$$changeSal(p, \$) = changeSal(p', \$') \supset p = p' \wedge \$ = \$'.$$

The sentence to be proved is logically equivalent to:

$$(\forall s, s').executable(s') \wedge s \sqsubseteq s' \supset$$
$$(\forall p, \$, \$').sal(p, \$, s) \wedge sal(p, \$', s') \supset \$ \le \$'.$$

This has the right syntactic form for an application of the double induction principle for executable situations of Section 4.2.5, with $R(s, s')$:

$$(\forall p, \$, \$').sal(p, \$, s) \wedge sal(p, \$', s') \supset \$ \le \$'.$$

The rest of the proof is straightforward. As was the case in the previous example, the restriction to executable situations in the current example is essential; it is trivial to derive $sal(Mary, 100, do(changeSal(Mary, 100, S_0))$, even when initially, $Mary$'s salary is 200: $sal(Mary, 200, S_0)$.

4.3.2 State Constraints

The previous discussion of inductive proofs in the situation calculus dealt with two qualitatively different classes of sentences whose proofs required induction: Sentences universally quantified over *all* situations, executable or not, and sentences universally quantified over executable situations only. Sentences (4.6) and (4.8) are examples of the first kind, while (4.7) and (4.9) are of the second. Sentences of the first kind use the simple induction axiom (4.2) of the foundational axioms for the situation calculus, or the principle of double induction over all situations derived in Section 4.2.3, and *do not make use of action precondition axioms*. The second class of sentences require induction (simple or double) over executable situations, as derived in Section 4.2.5, and typically do require the information in action precondition axioms to make the proofs by induction go through. Both classes of sentences describe *global* properties of the background theory of actions, global because these are properties that must be true of *all* (executable) situations. Our perspective on such sentences is that they are *inductive invariants* of the background axioms, i.e. they must be provable, normally using induction, from these axioms.

Both kinds of sentences are examples of what are called *state constraints* in the literature on theories of actions; database researchers generally call them *integrity constraints*. By whatever name, they are a source of deep theoretical and practical difficulties in modeling dynamical systems, and we do not treat this topic in any depth in this book. Appendix B contains a brief discussion that clarifies how sentences of the first and second kinds are intimately connected to the frame and qualification problems (Section 3.1.3), respectively.

4.4   Basic Theories of Action

Recall that Σ denotes the four foundational axioms for situations. We now consider some metamathematical properties of these axioms when combined with a specification of the initial situation, successor state and action precondition axioms, and unique names axioms for actions. Such a collection of axioms will be called a *basic theory of actions*. First we must be more precise about what counts as successor state and action precondition axioms.

Definition 4.4.1: The Uniform Formulas
Let σ be a term of sort *situation*. Inductively define the concept of a term of $\mathcal{L}_{sitcalc}$ that is *uniform in* σ as follows:

1. Any term that does not mention a term of sort *situation* is uniform in σ.
2. If g is an n-ary non-fluent function symbol, and $t_1, \ldots, t_n$ are terms that are uniform in σ and whose sorts are appropriate for g, then $g(t_1, \ldots, t_n)$ is uniform in σ.
3. If f is an $(n+1)$-ary functional fluent symbol, and $t_1, \ldots, t_n$ are terms that are uniform in σ and whose sorts are appropriate for f, then $f(t_1, \ldots, t_n, \sigma)$ is uniform in σ.

The formulas of $\mathcal{L}_{sitcalc}$ that are *uniform in* σ are inductively defined by:

1. Any formula that does not mention a term of sort *situation* is uniform in σ.
2. When F is an $(n+1)$-ary relational fluent and $t_1, \ldots, t_n$ are terms uniform in σ whose sorts are appropriate for F, then $F(t_1, \ldots, t_n, \sigma)$ is a formula uniform in σ.
3. If U_1 and U_2 are formulas uniform in σ, so are $\neg U_1$, $U_1 \wedge U_2$ and $(\exists v)U_1$ provided v is a variable not of sort *situation*.

Thus, a formula of $\mathcal{L}_{sitcalc}$ is uniform in σ iff it does not mention the predicates $Poss$ or $\sqsubset$, it does not quantify over variables of sort *situation*, it does not mention equality on situations, and whenever it mentions a term of sort *situation* in the situation argument position of a fluent, then that term is σ.

Example 4.4.2: When f, g are functional fluents, F is a relational fluent, and P is a non-fluent predicate, the following is uniform in σ:

$$(\forall x).x = f(g(x,\sigma),\sigma) \wedge (\exists y)F(g(A,\sigma), y, \sigma) \supset$$
$$\neg P(x, B) \vee P(f(f(x,\sigma),\sigma), g(x,\sigma)).$$

No formula that mentions $Poss$ or $\sqsubset$ is uniform in any situation term σ. The following are not uniform in σ:

$$holding(x, do(pickup(x), \sigma)), \quad do(a, \sigma) \neq \sigma, \quad (\exists s)holding(x, s),$$
$$resigned(primeMinister(Canada, do(elect(p, \sigma)), \sigma)).$$

Definition 4.4.3: Action Precondition Axiom

An action precondition axiom of $\mathcal{L}_{sitcalc}$ is a sentence of the form:

$$Poss(A(x_1, \cdots, x_n), s) \equiv \Pi_A(x_1, \cdots, x_n, s),$$

where A is an n-ary action function symbol, and $\Pi_A(x_1, \cdots, x_n, s)$ is a formula that is uniform in s and whose free variables are among $x_1, \cdots, x_n, s$.

The uniformity requirement on Π_A ensures that the preconditions for the executability of the action A are determined by the current situation s.

Definition 4.4.4: Successor State Axiom

1. A successor state axiom for an $(n + 1)$-ary relational fluent F is a sentence of $\mathcal{L}_{sitcalc}$ of the form:

$$F(x_1, \ldots, x_n, do(a, s)) \equiv \Phi_F(x_1, \ldots, x_n, a, s), \tag{4.10}$$

where $\Phi_F(x_1, \ldots, x_n, a, s)$ is a formula uniform in s, all of whose free variables are among $a, s, x_1, \ldots, x_n$. Notice that we do not assume that successor state axioms have the exact syntactic form as those obtained earlier by combining the ideas of Davis/Haas/Schubert and Pednault. The discussion there was meant to motivate one way that successor state axioms of the form (4.10) might arise, but nothing in the development that follows depends on that earlier approach.

   As for action precondition axioms, the uniformity of Φ_F guarantees that the truth value of F in the successor situation $do(a, s)$ is determined entirely by the current situation s. In systems and control theory, this is called the *Markov property*.

2. A successor state axiom for an $(n + 1)$-ary functional fluent f is a sentence of $\mathcal{L}_{sitcalc}$

of the form:

$$f(x_1, \ldots, x_n, do(a, s)) = y \equiv \phi_f(x_1, \ldots, x_n, y, a, s),$$

where $\phi_f(x_1, \ldots, x_n, y, a, s)$ is a formula uniform in s, all of whose free variables are among $x_1, \ldots, x_n, y, a, s$. As for relational fluents, the uniformity of ϕ_f in the successor state axioms for functional fluents guarantees the Markov property: The value of a functional fluent in a successor situation is determined entirely by properties of the current situation, and not by any other situation. Just as for relational fluents, we do not assume that successor state axioms have the exact syntactic form as those obtained earlier by combining the ideas of Davis/Haas/Schubert and Pednault.

Basic Action Theories. Henceforth, we shall consider theories $\mathcal{D}$ of the following forms:

$$\mathcal{D} = \Sigma \cup \mathcal{D}_{ss} \cup \mathcal{D}_{ap} \cup \mathcal{D}_{una} \cup \mathcal{D}_{S_0}$$

where,

- Σ are the foundational axioms for situations.
- $\mathcal{D}_{ss}$ is a set of successor state axioms for functional and relational fluents.
- $\mathcal{D}_{ap}$ is a set of action precondition axioms.
- $\mathcal{D}_{una}$ is the set of unique names axioms for actions.
- $\mathcal{D}_{S_0}$ is a set of first-order sentences that are uniform in S_0, so that S_0 is the only term of sort *situation* mentioned by the sentences of $\mathcal{D}_{S_0}$. Thus, no sentence of $\mathcal{D}_{S_0}$ quantifies over situations, or mentions $Poss$, $\sqsubset$ or the function symbol do. $\mathcal{D}_{S_0}$ will function as the initial theory of the world (i.e. the one we start off with, before any actions have been "executed"). Often, we shall call $\mathcal{D}_{S_0}$ the *initial database*. Notice that the initial database may (and often will) contain sentences mentioning no situation term at all, for example, unique names axioms for individuals, like $John \neq Mary$, or "timeless" facts like $isMountain(MtEverest)$, or $dog(x) \supset mammal(x)$.

Definition 4.4.5: Basic Action Theory

A *basic action theory* is any collection of axioms $\mathcal{D}$ of the above form, with the following additional *functional fluent consistency property*:
Suppose f is a functional fluent whose successor state axiom in $\mathcal{D}_{ss}$ is:

$$f(\vec{x}, do(a, s)) = y \equiv \phi_f(\vec{x}, y, a, s).$$

Then

$$\mathcal{D}_{una} \cup \mathcal{D}_{S_0} \models (\forall \vec{x}).(\exists y)\phi_f(\vec{x}, y, a, s) \land$$
$$[(\forall y, y').\phi_f(\vec{x}, y, a, s) \land \phi_f(\vec{x}, y', a, s) \supset y = y'].$$

Why require this consistency property? The reason is that it provides a sufficient condition for preventing a source of inconsistency in f's successor state axiom. Notice what it says: that the conditions defining f's value in the next situation, namely ϕ_f, actually define a value for f, and that this value is unique. The solution to the frame problem for functional fluents of Section 3.2.6 does satisfy this functional fluent consistency property (Exercise 14b below). The consistency condition for functional fluents leads to the following result:

Theorem 4.4.6: (Relative Satisfiability)
A basic action theory $\mathcal{D}$ is satisfiable iff $\mathcal{D}_{una} \cup \mathcal{D}_{S_0}$ is.

This result assures us that provided the initial database together with the unique names axioms for actions are satisfiable, then unsatisfiability cannot be introduced by augmenting these with the foundational axioms for the situation calculus, together with action precondition and successor state axioms. In the absence of the above functional fluent consistency property, it is easy to construct examples of basic action theories for which this theorem is false (Exercise 14a below).

4.5   Regression

There is a central computational mechanism that arises again and again in the development of the situation calculus. This is called *regression*, and it forms the basis for many planning procedures and for automated reasoning in the situation calculus. The intuition underlying regression is this: Suppose we want to prove that a sentence W is entailed by some basic action theory. Suppose further that W mentions a relational fluent atom $F(\vec{t}, do(\alpha, \sigma))$, where F's successor state axiom is $F(\vec{x}, do(a, s)) \equiv \Phi_F(\vec{x}, a, s)$. Then we can easily determine a logically equivalent sentence W' by substituting $\Phi_F(\vec{t}, \alpha, \sigma)$ for $F(\vec{t}, do(\alpha, \sigma))$ in W. After doing so, the fluent atom $F(\vec{t}, do(\alpha, \sigma))$, involving the complex situation term $do(\alpha, \sigma)$, has been eliminated from W in favour of $\Phi_F(\vec{t}, \alpha, \sigma)$, and this involves the simpler situation term σ. In this sense, W' is "closer" to the initial situation S_0 than was W. Moreover, this operation can be repeated until the resulting goal formula mentions only the situation term S_0, after which, intuitively, it should be sufficient to establish this resulting goal using only the sentences of the initial database. Regression is a mechanism that repeatedly performs the above reduction starting with a goal W, ultimately obtaining a logically equivalent goal W_0 whose only situation term is S_0. We have only indicated how regression works by reducing relational fluent atoms in W; there is an analogous way of reducing functional fluent terms. This section makes this idea precise, and establishes that a proof of the resulting regressed sentence need only appeal to the initial database together with unique names axioms for actions.

In preparation for describing the regression operator, we introduce a very convenient abbreviation for certain situation terms.

Abbreviation: $do([a_1, \ldots, a_n], s)$.

$$do([\,], s) \stackrel{def}{=} s,$$

$$do([a_1, \ldots, a_n], s) \stackrel{def}{=} do(a_n, do(a_{n-1}, \ldots do(a_1, s) \ldots)) \quad n = 1, 2, \ldots$$

$do([a_1, \ldots, a_n], s)$ is a compact and suggestive notation for the situation term

$$do(a_n, do(a_{n-1}, \ldots do(a_1, s) \ldots)),$$

denoting that situation resulting from performing the action a_1, followed by $a_2, \ldots$, followed by a_n, beginning in situation s.

Definition 4.5.1: The Regressable Formulas

A formula W of $\mathcal{L}_{sitcalc}$ is *regressable* iff

1. Each term of sort *situation* mentioned by W has syntactic form $do([\alpha_1, \ldots, \alpha_n], S_0)$ for some $n \geq 0$, where $\alpha_1, \ldots, \alpha_n$ are terms of sort *action*.

2. For each atom of the form $Poss(\alpha, \sigma)$ mentioned by W, α has the form $A(t_1, \ldots, t_n)$ for some n-ary action function symbol A of $\mathcal{L}_{sitcalc}$.

3. W does not quantify over situations.[4]

4. W does not mention the predicate symbol $\sqsubset$, nor does it mention any equality atom $\sigma = \sigma'$ for terms σ, σ' of sort *situation*.

The essence of a regressable formula is that each of its *situation* terms is rooted at S_0, and therefore, one can tell, by inspection of such a term, exactly how many actions it involves. It is not necessary to be able to tell what those actions are, just how many they are. In addition, when a regressable formula mentions a *Poss* atom, we can tell, by inspection of that atom, exactly what is the action function symbol occurring in its first argument position, for example, that it is a *move* action.

Example 4.5.2: The following are all regressable formulas:

- Can the actions in the sequence

$$walk(A, B), enter(office(Sue)), giveCoffee(Sue)$$

---

4 Strictly speaking, this condition is of no real consequence. Because of condition 1, the variable s of quantification in $(\forall s)W$ cannot be mentioned in W, so the quantifier is doing no real work. But this no-quantification condition will slightly simplify the analysis to follow.

be executed one after the other beginning in S_0?

$$Poss(walk(A, B), S_0) \land$$
$$Poss(enter(office(Sue)), do(walk(A, B), S_0)) \land$$
$$Poss(giveCoffee(Sue)), do([walk(A, B), enter(office(Sue))], S_0)).$$

- In a blocks world, are there two different blocks such that, after one is moved to the table and the other then moved onto A, all blocks other than A will be clear?

$$(\exists x, y).x \neq y \land (\forall z).z \neq A \supset$$
$$clear(z, do([moveToTable(x), move(y, A)], S_0)).$$

- In a blocks world, are there two actions such that after doing the first, block A will be on the table, and after doing the second, no other blocks will be on the table?

$$(\exists a, a').onTable(A, do(a, S_0)) \land$$
$$(\forall x).x \neq A \supset \neg onTable(x, do([a, a'], S_0)).$$

- The above examples remain regressable if one or more of their quantifiers are deleted. In other words, we treat *formulas* as well as sentences.

- Regressable formulas can mention functional fluents:

$$velocity(x, do(drop(x), S_0)) \leq velocity(y, do([pickup(y), throw(y)], S_0)).$$

- The availability of functional fluents allows quite complex (sometimes strange) situations and regressable formulas to be represented. For example,

$$happy(Mary,$$
$$do(pickup(Mary,$$
$$favoriteBook(John,$$
$$do(read(John, MobyDick), S_0))),$$
$$do(walkTo(John,$$
$$houseOf(Mary, do(divorce(Mary, John), S_0))),$$
$$do(marry(Mary, John), S_0))))$$

claims that Mary would be happy in result of the following sequence of actions: First, Mary marries John, then John walks to the house that Mary would have owned had she initially divorced John, then Mary picks up what John's favorite book would be had he initially read Moby Dick.

The following are not regressable:

$$Poss(a, S_0), \quad holding(x, do(pickup(A), s)).$$

We begin by defining a simple version of regression, restricted to the case that there are no functional fluents. Later, we generalize it for functional fluents.

Definition 4.5.3:   The Regression Operator: Simple Version

Suppose that W is a regressable formula of $\mathcal{L}_{sitcalc}$, and that W mentions no functional fluents. The *regression operator* $\mathcal{R}$ when applied to W is determined relative to a basic theory of actions of $\mathcal{L}_{sitcalc}$ that serves as a background axiomatization. In what follows, $\vec{t}$ is a tuple of terms, α is a term of sort *action*, σ is a term of sort *situation*, and W is a regressable formula of $\mathcal{L}_{sitcalc}$ that mentions no functional fluents. We emphasize here that *the regression operator is defined only for regressable formulas that do not mention any functional fluents.*

1. Suppose W is an atom. Since W is regressable, there are four possibilities:

   (a) W is a situation-independent atom (i.e. W is an equality atom between terms of the same sort *object* or *action*, or W is an atom whose predicate symbol is not a fluent). Then
   $$\mathcal{R}[W] = W.$$

   (b) W is a relational fluent atom of the form $F(\vec{t}, S_0)$. Then
   $$\mathcal{R}[W] = W.$$

   (c) W is a regressable $Poss$ atom, so it has the form $Poss(A(\vec{t}), \sigma)$ for terms $A(\vec{t})$ and σ of sort *action* and *situation* respectively. Here, A is an action function symbol of $\mathcal{L}_{sitcalc}$. Then there must be an action precondition axiom for A of the form
   $$Poss(A(\vec{x}), s) \equiv \Pi_A(\vec{x}, s).$$

   Without loss of generality, assume that all quantifiers (if any) of $\Pi_A(\vec{x}, s)$ have had their quantified variables renamed to be distinct from the free variables (if any) of $Poss(A(\vec{t}), \sigma)$. Then
   $$\mathcal{R}[W] = \mathcal{R}[\Pi_A(\vec{t}, \sigma)].$$

   In other words, replace the atom $Poss(A(\vec{t}), \sigma)$ by a suitable instance of the right-hand side of the equivalence in A's action precondition axiom, and regress that expression. The above renaming of quantified variables of $\Pi_A(\vec{x}, s)$ prevents any of these quantifiers from capturing variables in the instance $Poss(A(\vec{t}), \sigma)$.

   (d) W is a relational fluent atom of the form $F(\vec{t}, do(\alpha, \sigma))$. Let F's successor state axiom in $\mathcal{D}_{ss}$ be
   $$F(\vec{x}, do(a, s)) \equiv \Phi_F(\vec{x}, a, s).$$

   Without loss of generality, assume that all quantifiers (if any) of $\Phi_F(\vec{x}, a, s)$ have had their quantified variables renamed to be distinct from the free variables (if any) of $F(\vec{t}, do(\alpha, \sigma))$. Then

$\mathcal{R}[W] = \mathcal{R}[\Phi_F(\vec{t}, \alpha, \sigma)]$.

In other words, replace the atom $F(\vec{t}, do(\alpha, \sigma))$ by a suitable instance of the right-hand side of the equivalence in F's successor state axiom, and regress this formula. The above renaming of quantified variables of $\Phi_F(\vec{x}, a, s)$ prevents any of these quantifiers from capturing variables in the instance $F(\vec{t}, do(\alpha, \sigma))$.

2. For non-atomic formulas, regression is defined inductively.

$\mathcal{R}[\neg W] = \neg \mathcal{R}[W]$,

$\mathcal{R}[W_1 \wedge W_2] = \mathcal{R}[W_1] \wedge \mathcal{R}[W_2]$,

$\mathcal{R}[(\exists v)W] = (\exists v)\mathcal{R}[W]$.

As described above, regression is defined only for regressable formulas of $\mathcal{L}_{sitcalc}$. For example, $\mathcal{R}[Poss(a, S_0)]$ and $\mathcal{R}[holding(x, do(pickup(A), s))]$ are undefined, because in both cases, the regression operator is being applied to non-regressable formulas.

Intuitively, the regression operator eliminates $Poss$ atoms in favour of their definitions as given by action precondition axioms, and replaces fluent atoms about $do(\alpha, \sigma)$ by logically equivalent expressions about σ as given by successor state axioms. Moreover, it repeatedly does this until it cannot make such replacements any further, after which it delivers the resulting formula. Because the regression operator applies only to regressable formulas, this resulting formula will only mention the situation term S_0. Because regression repeatedly substitutes logically equivalent formulas for atoms, what the operator delivers will be logically equivalent to what it started with. This is the content of the following:

Theorem 4.5.4: *Suppose W is a regressable sentence of $\mathcal{L}_{sitcalc}$ that mentions no functional fluents, and $\mathcal{D}$ is a basic theory of actions. Then $\mathcal{R}[W]$ is a sentence uniform in S_0. Moreover,*

$$\mathcal{D} \models W \equiv \mathcal{R}[W],$$

Because W and $\mathcal{R}[W]$ are logically equivalent, then for the purpose of proving W with background axioms $\mathcal{D}$, it is sufficient to prove $\mathcal{R}[W]$. Because $\mathcal{R}[W]$ mentions only the situation term S_0, one would expect that most of the axioms of $\mathcal{D}$ would be irrelevant to its proof. This is indeed the case.

Theorem 4.5.5: (The Regression Theorem)
Suppose W is a regressable sentence of $\mathcal{L}_{sitcalc}$ that mentions no functional fluents, and

$\mathcal{D}$ is a basic theory of actions. Then,

$$\mathcal{D} \models W \quad \text{iff} \quad \mathcal{D}_{S_0} \cup \mathcal{D}_{una} \models \mathcal{R}[W].$$

From a computational perspective, Theorem 4.5.5 is perhaps the most important result of this book. It reduces the evaluation of regressable sentences to a first-order theorem-proving task *in the initial theory* $\mathcal{D}_{S_0}$, together with unique names axioms for actions. No successor state axioms or action precondition axioms are required in this theorem proving task. (Of course, they are used to perform the regression steps, but after that, they are no longer necessary.) In particular, none of the foundational axioms of Σ are required, and this means especially that the second-order induction axiom is not required. As we shall see throughout this book, answering regressable queries is at the heart of almost every computation we shall want to perform. This means that we shall be repeatedly appealing to the regression operator to do these computations, and to the Regression Theorem to justify this decision.

Example 4.5.6: The following examples are with reference to the action precondition and successor state axioms of the education database of Section 3.4.3.

- $\mathcal{R}[Poss(drop(Bill, C100), S_0)] = enrolled(Bill, C100, S_0)$.
- $\mathcal{R}[(\exists p)Poss(register(p, C100), S_0)] =$
  $(\exists p)(\forall p').prerequ(p', C100) \supset (\exists g).grade(p, p', g, S_0) \wedge g \geq 50$.
- $\mathcal{R}[Poss(drop(Bill, C100), do(register(p, c), S_0))] =$
  $\mathcal{R}[enrolled(Bill, C100, do(register(p, c), S_0))] =$
  $\mathcal{R}[register(Bill, C100) = register(p, c) \vee$
  $\quad enrolled(Bill, C100, S_0) \wedge register(p, c) \neq drop(Bill, C100)] =$
  $register(Bill, C100) = register(p, c) \vee$
  $\quad enrolled(Bill, C100, S_0) \wedge register(p, c) \neq drop(Bill, C100)$

Notice that this last regressed expression can be considerably simplified using the unique names axioms for actions. Henceforth, we shall perform such simplifications without further comment. The justification will be that always, we shall be regressing for the purpose of using the Regression Theorem to prove the formula we started with, and therefore, $\mathcal{D}_{una}$ will be available for simplification purposes. The last example thus simplifies to:

$Bill = p \wedge C100 = c \vee enrolled(Bill, C100, S_0)$.

- $\mathcal{R}[enrolled(Sue, c, do(drop(Bill, c), do(register(p, c), S_0)))] =$
  $\mathcal{R}[drop(Bill, c) = register(Sue, c) \vee$
  $\quad enrolled(Sue, c, do(register(p, c), S_0)) \wedge drop(Bill, c) \neq drop(Sue, c)] =$

$\mathcal{R}[enrolled(Sue, c, do(register(p, c), S_0))] \wedge Bill \neq Sue] =$
$\mathcal{R}[\{register(p, c) = register(Sue, c) \vee$
$\quad enrolled(Sue, c, S_0) \wedge register(p, c) \neq drop(Sue, c)\} \wedge Bill \neq Sue] =$
$\{p = Sue \vee enrolled(Sue, c, S_0)\} \wedge Bill \neq Sue$

4.6 Using Regression

There are two standard settings in AI where regression is useful: Proving that a given action sequence is executable, and the so-called *projection problem*. We consider each of these in turn.

4.6.1 Executable Ground Action Sequences

In this section, we provide a regression-based method for computing whether a ground situation is executable.[5] It is easy to prove (Exercise 15 below) that for each $n \geq 0$,

$$\Sigma \models (\forall a_1, \ldots, a_n).executable(do([a_1, \ldots, a_n], S_0)) \equiv$$
$$\bigwedge_{i=1}^{n} Poss(a_i, do([a_1, \ldots, a_{i-1}], S_0)). \tag{4.11}$$

From this, and the regression theorem, we obtain:

Corollary 4.6.1: *Suppose that $\alpha_1, \ldots, \alpha_n$ is a sequence of ground action terms of $\mathcal{L}_{sitcalc}$. Then*

$$\mathcal{D} \models executable(do([\alpha_1, \ldots, \alpha_n], S_0))$$

iff

$$\mathcal{D}_{S_0} \cup \mathcal{D}_{una} \models \bigwedge_{i=1}^{n} \mathcal{R}[Poss(\alpha_i, do([\alpha_1, \ldots, \alpha_{i-1}], S_0))].$$

This corollary provides a systematic, regression-based method for determining whether a ground situation $do([\alpha_1, \ldots, \alpha_n], S_0)$ is executable. Moreover, it reduces this test to a theorem-proving task *in the initial database* $\mathcal{D}_{S_0}$, together with unique names axioms for actions.

Example 4.6.2: Executability Testing

We continue with the education database example of Section 3.4.3, and compute whether the following transaction sequence is executable:

---

5 Recall that a *ground* term is one that mentions no variables.

$register(Bill, C100), drop(Bill, C100), drop(Bill, C100).$

Intuitively, this should fail because the first $drop$ leaves $Bill$ unenrolled in $C100$, so that the precondition for the second $drop$ will be false.

First compute

$\mathcal{R}[Poss(register(Bill, C100), S_0)] \wedge$
$\mathcal{R}[Poss(drop(Bill, C100), do(register(Bill, C100), S_0))] \wedge$
$\mathcal{R}[Poss(drop(Bill, C100), do(drop(Bill, C100), do(register(Bill, C100), S_0)))],$

which is

$\mathcal{R}[(\forall p).prerequ(p, C100) \supset (\exists g).grade(Bill, p, g, S_0) \wedge g \geq 50] \wedge$
$\mathcal{R}[enrolled(Bill, C100, do(register(Bill, C100), S_0))] \wedge$
$\mathcal{R}[enrolled(Bill, C100, do(drop(Bill, C100), do(register(Bill, C100), S_0)))].$

Using unique names axioms for actions, this simplifies to:

$\{(\forall p).prerequ(p, C100) \supset (\exists g).grade(Bill, p, g, S_0) \wedge g \geq 50\} \wedge$
$true \wedge$
$false.$

So the transaction sequence is indeed not executable.

Example 4.6.3: Executability Testing: Another Example

Consider next the sequence

$change(Bill, C100, 60), register(Sue, C200), drop(Bill, C100).$

This requires computing

$\mathcal{R}[(\exists g')grade(Bill, C100, g', S_0) \wedge g' \neq 60] \wedge$
$\mathcal{R}[(\forall p)prerequ(p, C200) \supset$
$\qquad\qquad (\exists g).grade(Sue, p, g, do(change(Bill, C100, 60), S_0)) \wedge g \geq 50] \wedge$
$\mathcal{R}[enrolled(Bill, C100, do(register(Sue, C200),$
$\qquad\qquad\qquad do(change(Bill, C100, 60), S_0)))].$

Using unique names axioms for actions, this simplifies to

$\{(\exists g').grade(Bill, C100, g', S_0) \wedge g' \neq 60\} \wedge$
$\{(\forall p).prerequ(p, C200) \supset$
$\qquad\qquad Bill = Sue \wedge p = C100 \vee (\exists g).grade(Sue, p, g, S_0) \wedge g \geq 50\} \wedge$
$\{Sue = Bill \wedge C200 = C100 \vee enrolled(Bill, C100, S_0)\}.$

So the transaction sequence is executable iff this sentence is entailed by the initial database together with unique names axioms for actions.

4.6.2   The Projection Problem and Query Evaluation

As normally encountered in AI, the projection problem is this: Given a sequence of ground action terms, and a formula, G, determine whether G is true in the situation resulting from performing these actions. In other words, we are interested in answering queries of the form: Would G be true in the world resulting from the performance of the given sequence of actions? When formulated in the situation calculus, the problem is this:

Definition 4.6.4: The Projection Problem
Suppose $\mathcal{D}$ is a basic action theory, $\alpha_1, \ldots, \alpha_n$ is a sequence of ground action terms, and $G(s)$ is a formula with one free variable s, whose only situation term is s. Determine whether:

$$\mathcal{D} \models G(do([\alpha_1, \ldots, \alpha_n], S_0)).$$

For example, a projection query for the sequence of actions

$$walk(A, office(Sue)), enter(office(Sue)), giveCoffee(Sue)$$

might be: Will Sue have coffee after the performance of this sequence?

$$\mathcal{D} \models hasCoffee(Sue, do([walk(A, office(Sue)), enter(office(Sue)),$$
$$giveCoffee(Sue)], S_0)).$$

Our concern is with answering projection queries like this, and the Regression Theorem gives us an immediate mechanism when $G(do([\alpha_1, \ldots, \alpha_n], S_0))$ is a regressable sentence: To solve the projection problem, it is both necessary and sufficient to regress $G(do([\alpha_1, \ldots, \alpha_n], S_0))$, and ask whether the resulting sentence is entailed by the initial database together with unique names for actions.

Planning and database query evaluation are two settings, among many, where the projection problem arises naturally, and where this regression-based approach is useful.

- **Planning.** To verify that a proposed plan $do([\alpha_1, \ldots, \alpha_n], S_0)$ satisfies a goal G, show that the axioms entail the projection query $G(do([\alpha_1, \ldots, \alpha_n], S_0))$.
- **Database Query Evaluation.** To answer a query G against a transaction sequence, answer the projection query G in the resulting situation.

Example 4.6.5: Querying a Database

Consider again the education database example, and the transaction sequence:

$$\mathbf{T} = change(Bill, C100, 60), register(Sue, C200), drop(Bill, C100).$$

Suppose that the query is:

$$(\exists st).enrolled(st, C200, do(\mathbf{T}, S_0)) \wedge$$
$$\neg enrolled(st, C100, do(\mathbf{T}, S_0)) \wedge$$
$$(\exists g).grade(st, C200, g, do(\mathbf{T}, S_0)) \wedge g \geq 50.$$

We must compute $\mathcal{R}$ of this query. After some simplification, using the unique names axioms for actions, and assuming that $\mathcal{D}_{S_0} \models C100 \neq C200$, we obtain

$$(\exists st).[st = Sue \vee enrolled(st, C200, S_0)] \wedge$$
$$[st = Bill \vee \neg enrolled(st, C100, S_0)] \wedge$$
$$[(\exists g).grade(st, C200, g, S_0) \wedge g \geq 50].$$

Therefore, the answer to the query is obtained by evaluating this last formula in $\mathcal{D}_{S_0}$, together with unique names axioms for actions.

Unfortunately, it is not difficult to imagine successor state axioms for which such regressed queries are exponentially long in the length of the transaction sequence (Exercise 13 below), so this approach is not always feasible. In response to this, we shall revisit the database query problem in Section 4.8.3 to seek conditions under which it can be solved with reasonable computational complexity.

Notice that this approach to the projection problem is a very special case of the Regression Theorem, which justifies answering regressable queries by regression. The regressable queries are a much larger class than the projection queries, because the former can ask about any number of future situations, whereas projection queries are about a single situation. Also, regressable queries can involve non-ground situation terms (Example 4.5.2), while projection queries are about ground terms.

4.7 Regression with Functional Fluents

Definition 4.5.3 described the regression operator for regressable formulas without functional fluents. The possibility of functional fluents complicates the definition somewhat, although conceptually, the idea remains straightforward. Here, we generalize the earlier definition. First, we need:

Definition 4.7.1: Prime Functional Fluent Terms
A functional fluent term is *prime* iff it has the form $f(\vec{t}, do([\alpha_1, \ldots, \alpha_n], S_0))$ for $n \geq 1$ and each of the terms $\vec{t}, \alpha_1, \ldots, \alpha_n$ is uniform in S_0. Thus, for prime functional fluent terms, S_0 is the only term of sort *situation* (if any) mentioned by $\vec{t}, \alpha_1, \ldots, \alpha_n$.

Remark 4.7.2: Let $g(\vec{\tau}, do(\alpha, \sigma))$ have the property that every term of sort *situation* that it mentions has the form $do([\alpha_1, \ldots, \alpha_n], S_0)$ for some $n \geq 0$. Then $g(\vec{\tau}, do(\alpha, \sigma))$ mentions a prime functional fluent term.

Proof: For $n \geq 0$, define the *length* of the situation term $do([a_1, \ldots, a_n], S_0)$ to be n. The proof is by induction on the sum of the lengths of all terms of sort *situation* mentioned by $g(\vec{\tau}, do(\alpha, \sigma))$ (with base case 1). ∎

Example 4.7.3:   Suppose $f(\cdot, \cdot, \cdot), r(\cdot)$ and $h(\cdot)$ are functional fluent symbols, and $g(\cdot, \cdot)$ is an ordinary function symbol. Then the functional fluent term

$$f(g(h(do(A, S_0)), h(S_0)), f(B, r(S_0), do(A, do(B, S_0))), do(h(do(C, S_0)), S_0))$$

mentions three prime functional fluent terms:

$h(do(A, S_0))$,

$f(B, r(S_0), do(A, do(B, S_0)))$ and

$h(do(C, S_0))$.

Definition 4.7.4:   The Regression Operator

The *regression operator* $\mathcal{R}$ when applied to a regressable formula W of $\mathcal{L}_{sitcalc}$ is determined relative to a basic theory of actions of $\mathcal{L}_{sitcalc}$ that serves as a background axiomatization. In what follows, $\vec{t}, \vec{\tau}$ are tuples of terms, α and α' are terms of sort *action*, σ and σ' are terms of sort *situation*, and W is a regressable formula of $\mathcal{L}_{sitcalc}$. We emphasize here that *the regression operator is defined only for regressable formulas of $\mathcal{L}_{sitcalc}$.*

1. Suppose W is a regressable *Poss* atom, so it has the form $Poss(A(\vec{t}), \sigma)$ for terms $A(\vec{t})$ and σ of sort *action* and *situation* respectively. Here, A is an action function symbol of $\mathcal{L}_{sitcalc}$. The definition of regression in this case remains the same as in Definition 4.5.3.

2. Suppose W is a regressable atom, but not a *Poss* atom. There are three possibilities:

   (a) If S_0 is the only term of sort *situation* (if any) mentioned by W, then

   $$\mathcal{R}[W] = W.$$

   (b) Suppose that W mentions a term of the form $g(\vec{\tau}, do(\alpha', \sigma'))$ for some functional fluent g. Then because W is regressable, this term satisfies the conditions of Remark 4.7.2, and therefore, $g(\vec{\tau}, do(\alpha', \sigma'))$ mentions a prime functional fluent term. Let this prime term have the form $f(\vec{t}, do(\alpha, \sigma))$, and suppose f's successor state axiom in $\mathcal{D}_{ss}$ is

   $$f(\vec{x}, do(a, s)) = y \equiv \phi_f(\vec{x}, y, a, s).$$

Without loss of generality, assume that all quantifiers (if any) of $\phi_f(\vec{x}, y, a, s)$ have had their quantified variables renamed to be distinct from the free variables (if any) of $f(\vec{t}, do(\alpha, \sigma))$. Then

$$\mathcal{R}[W] = \mathcal{R}[(\exists y).\phi_f(\vec{t}, y, \alpha, \sigma) \wedge W|_y^{f(\vec{t}, do(\alpha, \sigma))}].^6$$

Here, y is a variable not occurring free in $W, \vec{t}, \alpha$ or σ. Notice that, relative to f's successor state axiom, we have simply replaced W by a logically equivalent formula $(\exists y).\phi_f(\vec{t}, y, \alpha, \sigma) \wedge W|_y^{f(\vec{t}, do(\alpha, \sigma))}$, and we next regress this formula. The above renaming of quantified variables of $\phi_f(\vec{x}, y, a, s)$ prevents any of these quantifiers from capturing variables in the instance $f(\vec{t}, do(\alpha, \sigma))$.

Although it is not immediately obvious, it is necessary to focus on prime functional fluent terms in the above regression step to guarantee that the regression operator actually terminates. Without some such requirement, regression can loop.

(c) The only remaining possibility is that W is a relational fluent atom of the form $F(\vec{t}, do(\alpha, \sigma))$, and moreover, W does not mention a functional fluent term of the form $g(\vec{t}, do(\alpha', \sigma'))$. The definition of regression in this case remains the same as in Definition 4.5.3.

3. For non-atomic formulas, regression is defined inductively, just as in Definition 4.5.3.

Example 4.7.5: Consider the following successor state axioms:

$$loc(x, do(a, s)) = y \equiv a = go(x, y) \vee loc(x, s) = y \wedge \neg(\exists y')a = go(x, y').$$

$$nicePlace(x, do(a, s)) \equiv x = Rome \vee x = Paris \vee$$
$$nicePlace(x, s) \wedge a \neq earthquake.$$

We perform the following regression calculation, where, for the purposes of simplifying the expressions, we assume that the initial database contains unique names axioms for the people mentioned. The calculation includes logical simplifications with unique names axioms for actions.

$$\mathcal{R}[nicePlace(loc(Hal, do(go(Sue, Rome), do(go(Sam, Toronto), S_0))),$$
$$do(a, S_0))] =$$

$$\mathcal{R}[(\exists y).\{go(Sue, Rome) = go(Hal, y) \vee$$
$$loc(Hal, do(go(Sam, Toronto), S_0)) = y \wedge$$
$$\neg(\exists y')go(Sue, Rome) = go(Hal, y')\} \wedge nicePlace(y, do(a, S_0))] =$$

$$(\exists y).\mathcal{R}[loc(Hal, do(go(Sam, Toronto), S_0)) = y] \wedge$$

---

6 In general, when ϕ is a formula, and t and t' are terms, then $\phi|_t^{t'}$ denotes that formula obtained from ϕ by replacing all occurrences of t' in ϕ by t.

$$\mathcal{R}[nicePlace(y, do(a, S_0))] =$$

$$(\exists y).(\exists y''')\{go(Sam, Toronto) = go(Hal, y''') \lor$$
$$loc(Hal, S_0) = y''' \land \neg(\exists y')go(Sam, Toronto) = go(Hal, y') \land y''' = y\} \land$$
$$\mathcal{R}[nicePlace(y, do(a, S_0))] =$$

$$(\exists y).loc(Hal, S_0) = y \land \mathcal{R}[nicePlace(y, do(a, S_0))] =$$

$$(\exists y).loc(Hal, S_0) = y \land$$
$$[y = Rome \lor y = Paris \lor nicePlace(y, S_0) \land a \neq earthquake].$$

The proof turns out to be rather delicate, but one can show that the Regression Theorem continues to hold with the above regression operator. This means that in a basic action theory, to prove a regressable sentence with functional fluents, it is both necessary and sufficient to regress it, and prove its regressed form using only the initial database, together with unique names axioms for actions. Therefore, the executability testing procedure of Section 4.6.1, and the query evaluation mechanism for the projection problem of Section 4.6.2, continue to apply.

4.8   Database Logs and Historical Queries[7]

In what follows, we shall restrict ourselves to a situation calculus language $\mathcal{L}_{sitcalc}$ with no functional fluents. Let $\mathbf{T}$ be a sequence of ground actions, so that $do(\mathbf{T}, S_0)$ denotes the situation resulting from "performing" the actions of $\mathbf{T}$ in turn, starting in S_0. In database theory, such a sequence $\mathbf{T}$ is often called a database *log*. Recall that for us, all database updates are *virtual*; the database is never physically modified. Intuitively, a database log contains all the information necessary to query the database resulting from "performing" the transactions in the log. Queries that make use of all, or parts, of such a log will be called *historical* queries. In this section, we investigate systematic ways of using a log for answering such queries. In addition to the projection problem, which is concerned with querying the final situation $do(\mathbf{T}, S_0)$ of a log $\mathbf{T}$, we shall also consider queries about the intermediate situations reached by the log, for example:

- Was Mary's salary ever less than it is now?

  $$(\exists s, \$, \$').s \sqsubseteq do(\mathbf{T}, S_0) \land$$
  $$sal(Mary, \$, s) \land sal(Mary, \$', do(\mathbf{T}, S_0)) \land \$ < \$'.$$

- Was John ever simultaneously enrolled in both $C100$ and $M100$?

  $$(\exists s).s \sqsubseteq do(\mathbf{T}, S_0) \land enrolled(John, C100, s) \land enrolled(John, M100, s).$$

- Has Sue always worked in department 13?

---

7 This section may be safely skipped on first reading.

$$(\forall s).s \sqsubseteq do(\mathbf{T}, S_0) \supset emp(Sue, 13, s).$$

We shall not be able to give a fully general solution for historical queries, but instead, will focus on restricted classes of queries, and restricted classes of basic action theories, that admit good theoretical and computational properties, and for which we can give a complexity analysis. One such restriction will be to *context-free* successor state axioms.

Definition 4.8.1: Context-Free Successor State Axiom

This has the form

$$F(\vec{x}, do(a, s)) \equiv \gamma_F^+(\vec{x}, a, s) \vee F(\vec{x}, s) \wedge \neg\gamma_F^-(\vec{x}, a, s), \tag{4.12}$$

where both $\gamma_F^+(\vec{x}, a, s)$ and $\gamma_F^-(\vec{x}, a, s)$ are independent of the situation s. To emphasize this independence from s, we write them as $\gamma_F^+(\vec{x}, a)$ and $\gamma_F^-(\vec{x}, a)$. Here are some examples:

$$holding(p, x, do(a, s)) \equiv a = pickup(p, x) \vee$$
$$holding(p, x, s) \wedge a \neq drop(p, x) \wedge \neg(\exists u)a = put(p, x, u).$$

$$onGround(x, do(a, s)) \equiv heavierThanAir(x) \wedge (\exists p)a = drop(p, x) \vee$$
$$onGround(x, s) \wedge \neg(\exists p)a = pickup(p, x).$$

In addition, all the successor state axioms of the education database of Section 3.4.3 are context-free. The following is not context-free:

$$broken(x, do(a, s)) \equiv (\exists r)a = drop(r, x) \wedge fragile(x, s) \vee$$
$$(\exists b)\{a = explode(b) \wedge nextTo(b, x, s)\} \vee$$
$$broken(x, s) \wedge \neg(\exists r)a = repair(r, x).$$

Intuitively, a successor state axiom for fluent F is context-free iff F's truth value in the next situation $do(a, s)$ depends on F's truth value in the current situation s, but is independent of the truth values of any other fluents in s.

We shall also require that one, or both of γ_F^+ and γ_F^- be *decidable with respect to* $\mathcal{D}_{S_0}$ and $\mathcal{D}_{una}$, in the sense that for any ground instances $\gamma_F^+(\vec{X}, A)$ and $\gamma_F^-(\vec{X}, A)$ of γ_F^+ and γ_F^-, either $\mathcal{D}_{S_0} \cup \mathcal{D}_{una} \models \gamma_F^+(\vec{X}, A)$ or $\mathcal{D}_{S_0} \cup \mathcal{D}_{una} \models \neg\gamma_F^+(\vec{X}, A)$, and either $\mathcal{D}_{S_0} \cup \mathcal{D}_{una} \models \gamma_F^-(\vec{X}, A)$ or $\mathcal{D}_{S_0} \cup \mathcal{D}_{una} \models \neg\gamma_F^-(\vec{X}, A)$.

4.8.1 Querying All Past Situations

In this section, we focus on queries of the form "Has relational fluent F always been true over the duration of the log $\mathbf{T}$?"

$$(\forall s).s \sqsubseteq do(\mathbf{T}, S_0) \supset F(\vec{X}, s), \tag{4.13}$$

where $\vec{X}$ is a tuple of ground terms. Our concern is with deriving systematic and relatively efficient methods for evaluating such queries when given a log $\mathbf{T}$. We shall assume that F's successor state axiom is context-free, with the form (4.12). The point of departure is the following sentence, obtained in Exercise 7 below, which, in the case that $\gamma_F^-(\vec{x}, a, s)$ is independent of s, is:

$$(\forall s'').[(\forall s)(s \sqsubseteq s'' \supset F(\vec{x}, s))] \equiv F(\vec{x}, S_0) \wedge \neg(\exists a, s').do(a, s') \sqsubseteq s'' \wedge \gamma_F^-(\vec{x}, a).$$

Using this, we obtain:

$$(\forall s)[s \sqsubseteq do(\mathbf{T}, S_0) \supset F(\vec{x}, s)] \equiv$$
$$F(\vec{x}, S_0) \wedge (\forall a, s').do(a, s') \sqsubseteq do(\mathbf{T}, S_0) \supset \neg\gamma_F^-(\vec{x}, a). \qquad (4.14)$$

Suppose $\mathbf{T} = [A_1, \ldots, A_n]$. Then it is easy to see that:

$$(\forall a, s')[do(a, s') \sqsubseteq do(\mathbf{T}, S_0) \supset \neg\gamma_F^-(\vec{x}, a)] \equiv (\forall a). \bigwedge_{i=1}^n a = A_i \supset \neg\gamma_F^-(\vec{x}, a),$$
$$\equiv \bigwedge_{i=1}^n \neg\gamma_F^-(\vec{x}, A_i).$$

Hence, (4.14) is equivalent to:

$$(\forall s)[s \sqsubseteq do(\mathbf{T}, S_0) \supset F(\vec{x}, s)] \equiv F(\vec{x}, S_0) \wedge \bigwedge_{i=1}^n \neg\gamma_F^-(\vec{x}, A_i).$$

This yields the following evaluation procedure for queries of the form (4.13):

1. If $\mathcal{D}_{S_0} \cup \mathcal{D}_{una} \models \bigwedge_{i=1}^n \neg\gamma_F^-(\vec{X}, A_i)$ then return the answer to the query $F(\vec{X}, S_0)$.
2. Else if $\mathcal{D}_{S_0} \cup \mathcal{D}_{una} \models \bigvee_{i=1}^n \gamma_F^-(\vec{X}, A_i)$ then answer "no".
3. Else, answer "I don't know".

From a complexity point of view, life becomes much simpler if we assume that ground instances of γ_F^- are decidable with respect to $\mathcal{D}_{S_0}$ and $\mathcal{D}_{una}$. In this case, the above procedure simplifies to:

1. If $\mathcal{D}_{S_0} \cup \mathcal{D}_{una} \models \bigwedge_{i=1}^n \neg\gamma_F^-(\vec{X}, A_i)$ then return the answer to the query $F(\vec{X}, S_0)$.
2. Else answer "no".

Example 4.8.2: Consider querying whether Sue has always worked in department 13:

$$(\forall s).s \sqsubseteq do(\mathbf{T}, S_0) \supset emp(Sue, 13, s).$$

Assume the successor state axiom for emp is:

$$emp(p, d, do(a, s)) \equiv a = hire(p, d) \vee$$
$$emp(p, d, s) \wedge a \neq fire(p) \wedge a \neq quit(p).$$

Suppose that $\mathcal{D}_{S_0}$ contains unique names axioms for terms of sort other than *action* and *situation*, for example, $Sue \neq Mary$. Then, ground instances of γ_{emp}^- are decidable with respect to $\mathcal{D}_{S_0}$ and $\mathcal{D}_{una}$, and we obtain the following evaluation procedure:

1. If neither $fire(Sue)$ nor $quit(Sue)$ are elements of $\mathbf{T}$, then return the answer to query

$emp(Sue, 13, S_0)$.

2. Else return "no".

Suppose that $\gamma_F^-(\vec{x}, a, s)$ is independent of s, that γ_F^- is decidable with respect to $\mathcal{D}_{S_0}$ and $\mathcal{D}_{una}$ and that this decision procedure has "reasonable" complexity.[8] Then the computational complexity of answering queries of the form (4.13) adds at most linear complexity (in the length of the log) to the complexity of evaluating a ground fluent atom in the initial situation.

Notice that this complexity result holds when the only atoms mentioned by the formula $\gamma_F^-(\vec{x}, a)$ are equality atoms between terms of sort *action* (a very common occurrence; see the many examples in this book), and when a unique names assumption is enforced for terms of sort other than *action* and *situation* (for example, $John \neq Mary$).

4.8.2 Querying Some Past Situation

This section focuses on queries of the form "Has relational fluent F ever been true over the duration of the log **T**?"

$$(\exists s).s \sqsubseteq do(\mathbf{T}, S_0) \wedge F(\vec{X}, s), \tag{4.15}$$

where $\vec{X}$ is a tuple of ground terms. We begin with the following sentence, obtained in Exercise 8 below, which, in the case that $\gamma_F^+(\vec{x}, a, s)$ is independent of s is:

$$(\forall s').[(\exists s)(s \sqsubseteq s' \wedge F(\vec{x}, s))] \equiv s' = S_0 \wedge F(\vec{x}, S_0) \vee$$
$$(\exists a, s'').s' = do(a, s'') \wedge [\gamma_F^+(\vec{x}, a) \vee (\exists s).s \sqsubseteq s'' \wedge F(\vec{x}, s)].$$

Using this, we obtain:

$$[(\exists s)(s \sqsubseteq do(\mathbf{T}, S_0) \wedge F(\vec{x}, s))] \equiv do(\mathbf{T}, S_0) = S_0 \wedge F(\vec{x}, S_0) \vee$$
$$(\exists a, s'').do(\mathbf{T}, S_0) = do(a, s'') \wedge [\gamma_F^+(\vec{x}, a) \vee (\exists s).s \sqsubseteq s'' \wedge F(\vec{x}, s)].$$

When $\mathbf{T} = [A_1, \ldots, A_n], n \geq 1$, define:

$$last(\mathbf{T}) = A_n, \text{ and } butlast(\mathbf{T}) = [A_1, \ldots, A_{n-1}].$$

Then it is easy to see that the above is logically equivalent to:

$$[(\exists s)(s \sqsubseteq do(\mathbf{T}, S_0) \wedge F(\vec{x}, s))] \equiv do(\mathbf{T}, S_0) = S_0 \wedge F(\vec{x}, S_0) \vee$$
$$\gamma_F^+(\vec{x}, last(\mathbf{T})) \vee (\exists s).s \sqsubseteq do(butlast(\mathbf{T}), S_0) \wedge F(\vec{x}, s).$$

This yields a recursive procedure for evaluating queries of the form (4.15), in the case that ground instances of γ_F^+ are decidable with respect to $\mathcal{D}_{S_0}$ and $\mathcal{D}_{una}$:

---

8 By "reasonable" here, we mean a complexity that is essentially constant relative to the length of the log, for example, one that is polynomial in the size of the formula γ_F^-.

proc $query(\mathbf{T})$
    If $\mathbf{T} = [\ ]$, then return the answer to the query $F(\vec{X}, S_0)$.
    Else if $\mathcal{D}_{S_0} \cup \mathcal{D}_{una} \models \gamma_F^+(\vec{X}, last(\mathbf{T}))$ then answer "yes".
    Else, return $query(butlast(\mathbf{T}))$.
endProc

COMPLEXITY ANALYSIS

Suppose that $\gamma_F^+(\vec{x}, a, s)$ is independent of s, that γ_F^+ is decidable with respect to $\mathcal{D}_{S_0}$ and $\mathcal{D}_{una}$ and that this decision procedure has "reasonable" complexity. Then the computational complexity of answering queries of the form (4.15) adds at most linear complexity (in the length of the log) to the complexity of evaluating a ground fluent atom in the initial situation.

4.8.3 The Projection Problem Revisited

Recall that by appealing to regression, Section 4.6.2 provided a very general mechanism for addressing the projection problem, which concerns answering queries of the form $Q(do(\mathbf{T}, S_0))$. The idea of that section was to regress the query $Q(do(\mathbf{T}, S_0))$, and to evaluate the regressed query in the initial database. Unfortunately, there are successor state axioms for which such regressed queries are exponentially long in the length of the log (Exercise 13 below). Accordingly, here we consider the special case where F's successor state axiom is context-free, and we consider queries of the form $F(\vec{X}, do(\mathbf{T}, S_0))$, where $\vec{X}$ is a tuple of ground terms.

We begin with the following sentence, derived in Exercises 4.9, question 6, which is, in the case that F's successor state axiom is context-free (so that both $\gamma_F^+(\vec{x}, a, s)$ and $\gamma_F^-(\vec{x}, a, s)$ are independent of s):

$$F(\vec{x}, s) \equiv s = S_0 \wedge F(\vec{x}, S_0) \vee$$
$$(\exists a, s').s = do(a, s') \wedge [\gamma_F^+(\vec{x}, a) \vee F(\vec{x}, s') \wedge \neg \gamma_F^-(\vec{x}, a)].$$

Using this, we obtain:

$$F(\vec{x}, do(\mathbf{T}, S_0))) \equiv do(\mathbf{T}, S_0)) = S_0 \wedge F(\vec{x}, S_0) \vee$$
$$(\exists a, s').do(\mathbf{T}, S_0)) = do(a, s') \wedge [\gamma_F^+(\vec{x}, a) \vee F(\vec{x}, s') \wedge \neg \gamma_F^-(\vec{x}, a)]$$

Using the functions *last* and *butlast* of the previous section, this can be written as:

$$F(\vec{x}, do(\mathbf{T}, S_0))) \equiv do(\mathbf{T}, S_0)) = S_0 \wedge F(\vec{x}, S_0) \vee$$
$$\gamma_F^+(\vec{x}, last(\mathbf{T})) \vee F(\vec{x}, butlast(\mathbf{T})) \wedge \neg \gamma_F^-(\vec{x}, last(\mathbf{T}))$$

This yields a recursive procedure for evaluating queries of the form $F(\vec{X}, do(\mathbf{T}, S_0))$, in the case that ground instances of γ_F^+ and γ_F^- are decidable with respect to $\mathcal{D}_{S_0}$ and $\mathcal{D}_{una}$:

proc $query(\mathbf{T})$

    If $\mathbf{T} = [\ ]$, then return the answer to the query $F(\vec{X}, S_0)$.

    Else if $\mathcal{D}_{S_0} \cup \mathcal{D}_{una} \models \gamma_F^+(\vec{X}, last(\mathbf{T}))$ then answer "yes".

    Else if $\mathcal{D}_{S_0} \cup \mathcal{D}_{una} \models \gamma_F^-(\vec{X}, last(\mathbf{T}))$ then answer "no".

    Else, return $query(butlast(\mathbf{T}))$.

endProc

COMPLEXITY ANALYSIS

Suppose that F's successor state axiom is context-free, that γ_F^+ and γ_F^- are both decidable with respect to $\mathcal{D}_{S_0}$ and $\mathcal{D}_{una}$ and that this decision procedure has "reasonable" complexity. Then the computational complexity of answering queries of the form $F(\vec{X}, do(\mathbf{T}, S_0))$ adds at most linear complexity (in the length of the log) to the complexity of evaluating a ground fluent atom in the initial situation.

4.9 Exercises

1. Prove the consequences of the foundational axioms of Sections 4.2.3 and 4.2.5. (The proofs of the principles of induction and double induction are not so straightforward.)

2. One of the consequences of the foundational axioms that you proved in the previous question is:

$$executable(do(a, s)) \equiv executable(s) \wedge Poss(a, s)$$

This suggests that, instead of introducing the abbreviation (4.5) for $executable(s)$, we could have proposed the following "abbreviation":

$$executable(do(a, s)) \stackrel{def}{=} executable(s) \wedge Poss(a, s)$$

Give two reasons why this proposal makes no sense.

3. Since situations are simply sequences (or lists, if you prefer) of primitive actions, it might be convenient to have available many of the standard list processing abilities provided by LISP. So, define each of the following as abbreviations:

    (a) $null(s)$, which is true iff s is the empty action sequence.

    (b) $a \in s$, which is true iff action a is one of the actions occurring in the action history s.

    (c) $first(s, a)$, which is true iff a is the first action to occur in the history s, if it has one.

    (d) $last(s, a)$, which is true iff a is the last action to occur in the history s, if it has one.

(e) $allButLast(s, s')$, which is true iff s' is the history obtained from s by removing its last action occurrence, if it has one.

(f) $maxCommonSubsequ(s_1, s_2, s)$, which is true iff s is the maximal initial subhistory common to both s_1 and s_2.

In the above, a_1 is the first action occurrence in the situation

$$s = do(a_n, do(a_{n-1}, \ldots, do(a_1, S_0) \cdots)),$$

and a_n is the last. For any $i \leq n$, $do(a_i, do(a_{i-1}, \ldots, do(a_1, S_0) \cdots))$ is an initial subhistory of s.

4. **Alternative Foundational Axioms for Situations.** Consider introducing the subhistory predicate $\sqsubset$ as a second order definition:

$$s \sqsubset s' \equiv (\forall P).(\forall a, s_1) P(s_1, do(a, s_1)) \land$$
$$(\forall s_1, s_2, s_3)[P(s_1, s_2) \land P(s_2, s_3) \supset P(s_1, s_3)] \qquad (4.16)$$
$$\supset P(s, s').$$

This says that $\sqsubset$ is the smallest transitive relation such that $s \sqsubset do(a, s)$ for all situations s and actions a. Next, introduce the two axioms:

$$S_0 \sqsubseteq s, \qquad (4.17)$$
$$S_0 \neq do(a, s). \qquad (4.18)$$

Prove that the four foundational axioms (4.1) - (4.4) of Section 4.2.2 are logically equivalent to (4.1), (4.16), (4.17) and (4.18). Hints:

- For proving that the alternative axioms entail the original:

  (a) To obtain induction from (4.16), use (4.17), and take $P(\sigma, \sigma')$ in (4.16) to be $Q(\sigma) \supset Q(\sigma')$, where Q is a unary predicate variable.

  (b) Prove that $\sqsubset$ is transitive. Then prove $\neg S_0 \sqsubseteq S_0$. Use these two results to help prove (4.3).

  (c) To prove the ($\Rightarrow$) direction of (4.4), first prove that $s \sqsubset do(a, s)$, then use (4.16), taking $P(\sigma, \sigma')$ to be $\sigma \sqsubset \sigma' \land (\exists a, s).\sigma' = do(a, s) \land \sigma \sqsubseteq s$.

- For proving that the original foundational axioms entail the alternatives:

  (a) Use the results of Section 4.2.3.

  (b) To prove the ($\Rightarrow$) half of (4.16), do induction on s' in:

$$(\forall s).s \sqsubset s' \supset (\forall P).(\forall a, s_1) P(s_1, do(a, s_1)) \land$$
$$(\forall s_1, s_2, s_3)[P(s_1, s_2) \land P(s_2, s_3) \supset P(s_1, s_3)]$$
$$\supset P(s, s').$$

5. Suppose that we have obtained the successor state axiom for relational fluent F from the effect axioms using our solution to the frame problem. Then this axiom has the

form:
$$F(\vec{x}, do(a, s)) \equiv \gamma_F^+(\vec{x}, a, s) \vee F(\vec{x}, s) \wedge \neg\gamma_F^-(\vec{x}, a, s). \tag{4.19}$$

Prove that this, together with the foundational axioms Σ, entails the following "closed form" solution for F:

$$F(\vec{x}, s) \equiv F(\vec{x}, S_0) \wedge \neg(\exists a, s')[do(a, s') \sqsubseteq s \wedge \gamma_F^-(\vec{x}, a, s')] \vee$$
$$(\exists a', s')[do(a', s') \sqsubseteq s \wedge \gamma_F^+(\vec{x}, a', s') \wedge$$
$$\neg(\exists a'', s'')[do(a', s') \sqsubset do(a'', s'') \sqsubseteq s \wedge \gamma_F^-(\vec{x}, a'', s'')]].$$

Notice that this *says* the intuitively correct thing: F is true in s iff

(a) F is true initially, and no subsequent action falsifies F, or,

(b) Some previous action a' caused F to become true, and no subsequent action a'' falsified F prior to s.

6. Prove that Σ together with the successor state axiom (4.19) entails the following "closed form" solution for F:

$$F(\vec{x}, s) \equiv s = S_0 \wedge F(\vec{x}, S_0) \vee$$
$$(\exists a, s').s = do(a, s') \wedge [\gamma_F^+(\vec{x}, a, s') \vee F(\vec{x}, s') \wedge \neg\gamma_F^-(\vec{x}, a, s')].$$

Notice what this *says*: F is true in s iff

(a) s is the initial situation, and F is true initially, or

(b) The very last action of s caused F to be true, or

(c) F was true in the situation previous to s, and the last action of s did not falsify F.

7. Prove that Σ together with the successor state axiom (4.19) entails the following:

$$(\forall s').[(\forall s)(s \sqsubseteq s' \supset F(\vec{x}, s))] \equiv$$
$$F(\vec{x}, S_0) \wedge \neg(\exists a, s'').do(a, s'') \sqsubseteq s' \wedge \gamma_F^-(\vec{x}, a, s'').$$

In other words, F is true in *every* situation up to and including s' iff

(a) F is true initially, and

(b) No action of s' falsifies F.

8. Prove that Σ together with the successor state axiom (4.19) entails the following:

$$(\forall s').[(\exists s)(s \sqsubseteq s' \wedge F(\vec{x}, s))] \equiv s' = S_0 \wedge F(\vec{x}, S_0) \vee$$
$$(\exists a, s'').s' = do(a, s'') \wedge [\gamma_F^+(\vec{x}, a, s'') \vee (\exists s).s \sqsubseteq s'' \wedge F(\vec{x}, s)].$$

In other words, F is true in *some* situation up to and including s' iff

(a) s' is the initial situation, and F is true initially, or

(b) The very last action of s' caused F to be true, or

(c) F is true in some situation up to and including the situation previous to s'.

9. (a) Prove that Σ together with the successor state axiom (4.19) entails the following *generalized explanation closure*:

$$(\forall s, s').s \sqsubseteq s' \wedge F(\vec{x}, s) \wedge \neg F(\vec{x}, s') \supset$$
$$(\exists a, s'').\gamma_F^-(\vec{x}, a, s'') \wedge s \sqsubseteq do(a, s'') \sqsubseteq s'.$$

Hint: Use the double induction principle of Section 4.2.3.

(b) *The stolen car problem:* Consider the following scenario:

Fluents:

 - $parked(s)$ - The car is parked in situation s.

Actions:

 - $park$ - Park the car, with identically $true$ preconditions.
 - $steal$ - Steal the car, with precondition that the car be parked.
 - tow - Tow the car, with precondition that the car be parked.

Initially, the car is parked.

Show that in all situations, if the car is not parked, then there must be an earlier situation in which the car was stolen or towed:

$$(\forall s).\neg parked(s) \supset (\exists s').do(tow, s') \sqsubseteq s \vee do(steal, s') \sqsubseteq s.$$

10. The sentences derived in the previous exercises have dual forms, obtainable by replacing F by $\neg F$, γ_F^+ by γ_F^-, and γ_F^- by γ_F^+. This then yields sentences suitable for proving properties of $\neg F$. Prove these dual forms.

11. Prove the following induction principle for base cases other than S_0:

$$(\forall P)(\forall s).P(s) \wedge (\forall a, s')[P(s') \wedge s \sqsubseteq s' \supset P(do(a, s'))]$$
$$\supset (\forall s').s \sqsubseteq s' \supset P(s'),$$

12. Axiomatize assignment statements for a simple programming language. Use the term $assign(var1, var2)$ to denote the action of assigning the value of program variable $var1$ to program variable $var2$. Use the functional fluent $value(var, s)$ to denote the value of program variable var in situation s. Formulate a plan for exchanging the values of two program variables X and Y, using an auxiliary variable Z, and prove the correctness of this plan using regression.

13. Give an example of successor state axioms and a query for which the regression approach to the projection problem leads to a regressed query whose length is exponential in the length of the log.

14. (a) Suppose one did not insist on the functional fluent consistency property of Section 4.4 in defining basic action theories. Show that Theorem 4.4.6 would then be false by giving an example of an unsatisfiable basic action theory for which $\mathcal{D}_{una} \cup \mathcal{D}_{S_0}$ is satisfiable.

  (b) Prove that the solution to the frame problem for functional fluents of Section
      3.2.6 satisfies the functional fluent consistency property, provided the consistency
      condition (3.14) holds.

15. Prove (4.11).

16. Why is the decidability of the γ_F necessary for the correctness of the query evaluation
    procedures of Section 4.8? (Hint: In first-order logic, provability of a disjunction does
    not necessarily imply the provability of one of its disjuncts.)

17. Analyse the projection problem for queries of the form $\neg F(\vec{X}, do(\mathbf{T}, S_0))$.

18. Let $\mathcal{D}$ be a basic action theory, and suppose that $\mathcal{D}_{S_0} \cup \mathcal{D}_{una}$ is decidable, meaning
    that for any sentence of $\mathcal{L}_{sitcalc}$ uniform in S_0, it is decidable whether it is entailed by
    $\mathcal{D}_{S_0} \cup \mathcal{D}_{una}$. Prove that $\mathcal{D}$ is decidable for the class of regressable sentences.

19. The task here is to axiomatize the operations of a Turing machine, with the objective
    of proving some undecidability results for the situation calculus. To simplify the rep-
    resentation, we appeal to the fact that the halting problem is undecidable for the class
    of deterministic binary Turing machines (just two tape symbols—call them A and B),
    starting on a one way infinite tape all of whose squares initially contain B's. Introduce
    the following predicates and fluents:

    • $transTable(q, c, q', c', m)$. This is a situation-independent predicate describing
      the Turing machine's transition table: When in state q scanning tape symbol c,
      the machine enters state q', overprints c with tape symbol c', and moves its tape
      head in the direction m, which is one of L (left) or R (right).

    • $blank(i, s)$. Tape square i contains the blank symbol (namely, B) in situation s.
      Initially, all tape squares are blank.

    • $state(q, s)$. In situation s, the machine's state is q. Assume there is a distin-
      guished *initial state* Q_0, and a distinguished *halt* state Q_H.

    • $scan(i, s)$. The machine's head is scanning tape square i in situation s. Initially,
      the head is scanning tape square 0.

The axiomatization has just one action constant: $trans$, meaning that the machine
makes a transition.

Numbering the tape squares: Use the constant symbol 0 for the first square, and a
unary function symbol $succ : Object \rightarrow Object$ for denoting the positive integers.
So the tape squares are numbered

   $0, succ(0), succ(succ(0)), \ldots$

Give an initial database, an action precondition axiom, and successor state axioms
representing the operation of such a Turing machine.

Hence, prove that the planning problem is undecidable for finite situation calculus action theories consisting of:

(a) Just one action constant with action precondition axiom stating that the preconditions for this action are always *true*.

(b) One unary function symbol: $Object \rightarrow Object$.

(c) Three binary predicate fluents, with successor state axioms for these fluents.

(d) A decidable initial database. (Why is this important?)

(e) Finitely many 0-ary predicate symbols.

The last item refers to an encoding of the non-fluent machine transition predicate $transTable(q, c, q', c', m)$. For a given Turing machine, all the arguments to this predicate are drawn from finite domains, so instead of it, we could have used the finitely many 0-ary predicates $transTable_{q,c,q',c',m}()$, with c, c' ranging over $\{A, B\}$, q, q' ranging over the finitely many states of the Turing machine, and m ranging over $\{L, R\}$.

4.10   Bibliographic Remarks

The material on induction and its importance in the situation calculus is taken from Reiter [174]. The foundational axioms for the situation calculus of Section 4.2.2 are taken from Pirri and Reiter [165]. Similar axioms were proposed in Pinto [159], Reiter [174] and Lin and Reiter [125].

Our view of situations as action sequences differs from earlier treatments of the situation calculus, in which, at least intuitively, situations were identified with *states*. The state-based perspective was already present in the early work of McCarthy and Hayes [141] who write: "A situation *s* is the complete state of the universe at an instant of time." This idea seems not to have been explored much in the literature, although ontologies different than ours have been occasionally proposed for the situation calculus (e.g. Costello and McCarthy [140]). The fluent calculus is an interesting action theory that combines states with situations (Thielscher [212, 214]).

The concept of *regression* is an old one in AI (Waldinger [216]), and forms the basis of a number of planning algorithms. Pednault uses it extensively in his paper on the frame problem [154], and also discusses it in [155]. The relative satisfiability of basic action theories and the soundness and completeness of regression for these theories (Theorems 4.4.6 and 4.5.5) are proved in (Pirri and Reiter [165]).

As presented here, basic action theories are *Markovian*, in the sense that the right-hand sides of action precondition and successor state axioms can only mention the current situation; they may not refer to the past. In many settings, it is extremely convenient to allow *non-Markovian* axioms. It is possible to formulate a non-Markovian situation calculus, but this requires a reexamination of some of the fundamental definitions and results given in this chapter. In particular, regression needs to be generalized, and proved sound and complete. Gabaldon [58] has provided such an account.

The alternative foundational axioms for situations of Exercises 4.9, question 4, are based on suggestions by Fiora Pirri, Eugenia Ternovskaia, and Hector Levesque and Gerhard Lakemeyer .

5 Implementing Basic Action Theories

This chapter presents a method for implementing basic action theories in the logic programming language Prolog, one that will be used throughout this book. The justification for the approach relies on a fundamental result due to Keith Clark about the relationship between a logical theory consisting of axioms, all of which are definitions, and a corresponding Prolog program. Roughly, this result states that whenever the Prolog program succeeds on a sentence, then that sentence is logically entailed by the theory, and whenever it fails on a sentence, then the negation of that sentence is entailed by the theory. A consequence of Clark's theorem is that Prolog provides a natural implementation for such theories. Moreover, important special cases of basic action theories fit this pattern, so that a correct implementation for these is immediately obtained.

The first task is to describe Clark's theorem. We assume that the reader has some experience with programming in Prolog; without this, much of the following will appear rather mysterious.

5.1 Logical Foundations of Prolog

Definition 5.1.1: Definitions and Definitional Theories

A first-order sentence is a *definition* iff it has the syntactic form

$$(\forall x_1, \ldots, x_n).P(x_1, \ldots, x_n) \equiv \phi,$$

where P is an n-ary predicate symbol other than equality, and ϕ is a first-order formula with free variables among $x_1, \ldots, x_n$. Sometimes we call this sentence a *definition of P*. A set of axioms is *definitional* iff its axioms consist of one definition for each predicate symbol, except for equality. A definitional axiom set may include arbitrary sentences mentioning only the equality predicate. The *if-half* of the above definition of P is the sentence $(\forall x_1, \ldots, x_n).\phi \supset P(x_1, \ldots, x_n)$.

It is permitted that ϕ be identically *true* or *false* in a definition, so

$$(\forall x_1, \ldots, x_n).P(x_1, \ldots, x_n) \equiv true$$

and

$$(\forall x_1, \ldots, x_n).P(x_1, \ldots, x_n) \equiv false$$

are perfectly acceptable definitions of P. They are logically equivalent to

$$(\forall x_1, \ldots, x_n)P(x_1, \ldots, x_n) \text{ and } (\forall x_1, \ldots, x_n)\neg P(x_1, \ldots, x_n)$$

respectively, and therefore stipulate that P is always true or false. Notice that in a definition of P, the arguments to P must be *distinct variables*, so the following is a good definition of P:

$$(\forall x, y).P(x, y) \equiv P(A, x) \vee \neg(\exists z)Q(x, y, z).$$

The following can never be a definition of Q, no matter what ϕ is:

$$(\forall x, y).Q(A, f(x), y) \equiv \phi.$$

Definition 5.1.2: Atoms, Literals, Clauses and Goals

As in logic, by an *atom* is meant a formula of the form $P(t_1, \ldots, t_n)$, where P is an n-ary predicate symbol, and $t_1, \ldots, t_n$ are terms. A *literal* is an atom or the negation of an atom. A *clause* is a sentence of the form $L_1 \wedge \cdots \wedge L_m \supset A$ where A is a non-equality atom, and $L_1, \ldots, L_m$ are literals. The case $m = 0$ is permitted, in which case the corresponding clause is simply A. A Prolog program is a finite sequence of clauses. Prolog uses a different syntax for clauses than does logic, representing the above clause by A :- $L_1, \ldots, L_m$. and when $m = 0$, by A. Moreover, instead of the logical negation sign $\neg$, Prolog uses the "negation-as-failure" symbol not. In what follows, we shall stick to the standard logical syntax for clauses. A *normal goal* is a conjunction of literals. These are the permitted goals for a Prolog program consisting of clauses of the above form. So we are treating the case where both clauses and goals may mention negative literals and the Prolog interpreter appeals to negation-as-failure in evaluating these.

Definition 5.1.3: Proper Prolog Interpreter

A *proper* Prolog interpreter is one that evaluates a negative literal not A, using negation-as-failure, and moreover, does so *only when (at the time of evaluation)* the atom A *is ground*. When A is not ground, the interpreter may suspend its evaluation, working on other literals until (with luck) A does become ground, or it may abort its computation. Either way, it never tries to fail on non-ground atoms.

Theorem 5.1.4: (Clark's Theorem)

Suppose T is a set of definitions for every predicate symbol except for equality in some first-order language with finitely many predicate symbols, together with the following equality sentences:

1. *For every pair of distinct function symbols f and g of the language (including constant symbols),*

    $$f(\vec{x}) \neq g(\vec{y}).$$

2. *For every n-ary function symbol of the language,*

$$f(x_1, \ldots, x_n) = f(y_1, \ldots, y_n) \supset x_1 = y_1 \wedge \cdots \wedge x_n = y_n.$$

3. *For every term $t[x]$ (other than x itself) that mentions the variable x,*

$$t[x] \neq x.$$

Notice that this is an axiom schema, standing for the (perhaps) infinitely many axioms obtained from the schema by replacing $t[x]$ by one of the terms of the language mentioning x.

Suppose that a Prolog program, $program(T)$, can be obtained from the definitions of T by writing the if-halves of all the definitions of T as Prolog clauses.[1] *Then,*

1. *Whenever a proper Prolog interpreter succeeds on a normal Prolog goal G with answer substitution θ, then $T \models (\forall)G\theta$. Here, $(\forall)G\theta$ denotes the result of universally quantifying all the free variables (if any) of $G\theta$.*

2. *Whenever a proper Prolog interpreter returns failure on a normal Prolog goal G, then $T \models (\forall)\neg G$ where the quantification is over all free variables mentioned by G.*

When the above theorem says that "a proper Prolog interpreter returns failure", it means that after a finite computation, the interpreter returns, having failed to obtain a derivation. It *does not* mean that the interpreter fails to return, for example by looping forever.

This is an extremely important theorem. It guarantees the soundness of a Prolog implementation of a definitional theory; Prolog's negation-as-failure mechanism on the if-half of the definitions does the right thing with respect to logical negation in the original theory. As we shall see shortly, Clark's theorem will guarantee the correctness of a natural Prolog implementation of basic theories of action for the purposes of evaluating regressable sentences.

5.1.1 Why Insist on a Proper Prolog Interpreter?

Without this requirement, it is easy to invent examples of definitional theories and normal goals for which the Prolog version of the if-halves does the wrong thing. For example, consider the definitional theory:

$$P(x) \equiv x = A,$$

$$Q(x) \equiv x = B.$$

Its if-halves have the trivial Prolog program:

```
p(a).  q(b).
```

---

1 Notice that in forming $program(T)$, we discard T's unique names equality axioms.

The normal goal not p(X), q(X). should succeed (with X = b). In other words, by Clark's theorem, the definitional theory with which we began, plus the equality theory, should entail $\neg P(B) \wedge Q(B)$, which it does. Unfortunately, almost every current Prolog system will fail on this goal because, in evaluating the goal from left to right the interpreter evaluates not p(X) by negation-as-failure, and the call to p(X) succeeds (with X = a), so the goal fails. The fault lies with the interpreter's willingness to try negation-as-failure on the non-ground atom p(X).

Given that most Prolog systems do the wrong thing on negative, non-ground atoms,[2] what guarantees can a programmer have about her implementation? The answer seems to be that she is on her own. It is her responsibility to ensure that her program clauses are written so that negative literals are evaluated last under Prolog's left-to-right evaluation of clause bodies; then their variables are more likely to become bound to ground terms when it is their turn to be evaluated. She must also ensure that the goals posed to her program are such that they will produce ground atoms whenever, during the execution of the program, negation-as-failure is used. At least she will have the assurances granted by Clark's theorem; if her program uses negation-as-failure only on ground atoms, then it is doing the right thing with respect to the definitional theory from which the program was obtained.[3]

5.1.2 More on the Equational Theory of Clark's Theorem

The first two conditions on the equality sentences in Clark's theorem are straightforward to understand. They are *unique names axioms* for the function symbols, and specify that two function terms are to be treated as equal iff their main function symbols are identical, and their arguments are equal. The third condition, namely that $t[x] \neq x$, seems more puzzling. It captures the effects of the "occurs check" of Prolog's unification algorithm; whenever term t mentions variable x, then t and x fail to unify.[4] The schema $t[x] \neq x$ can also be viewed as a strengthening of the first two unique names axioms, in the sense that, although it is not logically entailed by them, it is the case that whenever x is instantiated by a ground term $f(t_1, \ldots, t_n)$, then this instantiated version will be a consequence of these two unique names axioms (Exercise 3 below). The schema seems to be necessary for the proof of Clark's theorem so we shall have to live with it; this involves, in part,

---

2 There are exceptions; Eclipse Prolog provides two negation operators, one of which suspends itself on negative, non-ground atoms, hoping that their free variables will eventually become bound during the rest of the computation, at which point the operator resumes.

3 Unfortunately, negation-as-failure is not the only source of unsoundness in Prolog systems. The unification algorithm used by these omits the "occurs check", and therefore further compromises the logical purity of the language. But that's another story.

4 As already remarked, most Prolog implementations omit the occurs check, but Clark's Theorem presupposes a logically pure Prolog.

understanding that it provides a strengthening of the first two unique names axioms. Notice that when the function symbols of the language consist of constants only, then these three equality axioms reduce to simply the set of inequalities $C \neq C'$ for all pairs of distinct constant symbols of the language.

Example 5.1.5: Consider a first-order definitional theory about family relationships.

$$offspring(x, y) \equiv x = John \wedge y = Mary \vee x = John \wedge y = Bill \vee$$
$$x = Sam \wedge y = Sue \vee x = Sue \wedge y = Mike \vee x = Fiora \wedge y = Ben \vee$$
$$x = Fiora \wedge y = Gio \vee x = Pam \wedge y = Tom,$$

$$male(x) \equiv x = John \vee x = Bill \vee x = Sam \vee x = Mike \vee x = Ben \vee$$
$$x = Gio \vee x = Tom,$$

$$father(x, y) \equiv offspring(y, x) \wedge male(y),$$

$$mother(x, y) \equiv offspring(y, x) \wedge \neg male(y),$$

$$siblings(x, y) \equiv x \neq y \wedge (\exists z).offspring(z, x) \wedge offspring(z, y).$$

The if-halves of these definitions are, after some logical simplification:

$$offspring(John, Mary), \; offspring(John, Bill), \; offspring(Sam, Sue),$$
$$offspring(Sue, Mike), \; offspring(Fiora, Ben), \; offspring(Fiora, Gio),$$
$$offspring(Pam, Tom),$$

$$male(John), \; male(Bill), \; male(Sam), \; male(Mike), \; male(Ben),$$
$$male(Gio), \; male(Tom),$$

$$offspring(y, x) \wedge male(y) \supset father(x, y),$$

$$offspring(y, x) \wedge \neg male(y) \supset mother(x, y),$$

$$offspring(x, z) \wedge offspring(y, z) \wedge x \neq y \supset siblings(x, y).$$

These are all syntactically appropriate Prolog clauses, and therefore Clark's theorem assures us that provided the constants Sue, Tom, etc., satisfy unique names axioms—they denote different individuals—then the following Prolog program is *sound* with respect to the original definitions, in the sense that any answer returned by Prolog, using negation-as-failure in place of logical negation, is guaranteed to be entailed by the definitional theory we started with, provided negation-as-failure is invoked only on ground atoms.

```
offspring(john,mary). offspring(john,bill). offspring(sam,sue).
offspring(sue,mike). offspring(fiora,ben). offspring(fiora,gio).
offspring(pam,tom).
male(john). male(bill). male(sam). male(mike). male(ben).
male(gio). male(tom).
```

```
father(X,Y) :- offspring(Y,X), male(Y).
mother(X,Y) :- offspring(Y,X), not male(Y).
siblings(X,Y) :- offspring(X,Z), offspring(Y,Z), not X = Y.
```

5.2   Lloyd-Topor Normal Forms for Arbitrary Definitions and Goals

Clark's theorem justifies a simple Prolog implementation of definitional theories under suitable assumptions about equalities of terms, but as formulated, it severely restricts the kinds of definitions to which it applies to those whose if-halves have logically equivalent Prolog clauses. It works fine for the above definitions for family relationships. But it does not directly apply to a large class of definitions, of which the following is an example:

$$(\forall x, y).subset(x, y) \equiv (\forall z).member(z, x) \supset member(z, y).$$

The if-half of this is:

$$(\forall x, y).(\forall z)[member(z, x) \supset member(z, y)] \supset subset(x, y),$$

and this is not the right syntactic form for a Prolog clause.

Similarly, while Clark's theorem guarantees that Prolog treats normal goals properly, for example, $mother(Ben, x) \land \neg mother(Mary, x)$, it says nothing about more general goals, for example,

$$(\forall x).father(x, Bill) \supset (\exists y).father(y, Bill) \land y \neq x \land \neg male(y).$$

This last formula is not the right syntactic form for a normal Prolog goal, which must be a conjunction of literals.

In order to extend the range of definitions and goals for which Clark's theorem guarantees a correct Prolog implementation, we appeal to a series of transformations, due to John Lloyd and Rodney Topor. These are rules for systematically transforming if-halves of definitions of the syntactic form $W \supset A$ into a syntactic form suitable for implementation as Prolog clauses. Here, A must be an atomic formula, but W may be an arbitrary first-order formula, possibly involving quantifiers, in which case we require that the quantified variables of W be different from one another, and from any of the free variables mentioned in W. The following transformation rules are applied repeatedly until no rules can be performed. The resulting formulas are then guaranteed to be in Prolog clausal form. We represent the formula $W \supset A$ in the form $\Psi \land \Phi \land \Theta \supset A$, where one or both of Ψ and Θ may be missing.

1. Replace $\Psi \land \neg(W_1 \land W_2) \land \Theta \supset A$ by
    $\Psi \land (\neg W_1 \lor \neg W_2) \land \Theta \supset A$.

2. Replace $\Psi \land (W_1 \lor W_2) \land \Theta \supset A$ by

$\Psi \wedge W_1 \wedge \Theta \supset A$, and

$\Psi \wedge W_2 \wedge \Theta \supset A$.

3. Replace $\Psi \wedge \neg(W_1 \vee W_2) \wedge \Theta \supset A$ by
   $\Psi \wedge \neg W_1 \wedge \neg W_2 \wedge \Theta \supset A$.

4. Replace $\Psi \wedge (W_1 \supset W_2) \wedge \Theta \supset A$ by
   $\Psi \wedge (\neg W_1 \vee W_2) \wedge \Theta \supset A$.

5. Replace $\Psi \wedge \neg(W_1 \supset W_2) \wedge \Theta \supset A$ by
   $\Psi \wedge \neg[\neg W_1 \vee W_2] \wedge \Theta \supset A$.

6. Replace $\Psi \wedge (W_1 \equiv W_2) \wedge \Theta \supset A$ by
   $\Psi \wedge (W_1 \supset W_2) \wedge (W_2 \supset W_1) \wedge \Theta \supset A$.

7. Replace $\Psi \wedge \neg(W_1 \equiv W_2) \wedge \Theta \supset A$ by
   $\Psi \wedge \neg[(W_1 \supset W_2) \wedge (W_2 \supset W_1)] \wedge \Theta \supset A$.

8. Replace $\Psi \wedge \neg\neg W \wedge \Theta \supset A$ by
   $\Psi \wedge W \wedge \Theta \supset A$.

9. Replace $\Psi \wedge (\forall x_1, \ldots, x_n)W \wedge \Theta \supset A$ by
   $\Psi \wedge \neg(\exists x_1, \ldots, x_n)\neg W \wedge \Theta \supset A$.

10. Replace $\Psi \wedge \neg(\forall x_1, \ldots, x_n)W \wedge \Theta \supset A$ by
    $\Psi \wedge (\exists x_1, \ldots, x_n)\neg W \wedge \Theta \supset A$.

11. Replace $\Psi \wedge (\exists x_1, \ldots, x_n)W \wedge \Theta \supset A$ by
    $\Psi \wedge W \wedge \Theta \supset A$.

12. Replace $\Psi \wedge \neg(\exists x_1, \ldots, x_n)W \wedge \Theta \supset A$ by
    $\Psi \wedge \neg p(y_1, \ldots, y_k) \wedge \Theta \supset A$, and
    $(\exists x_1, \ldots, x_n)W \supset p(y_1, \ldots, y_k)$.
    Here, $y_1, \ldots, y_k$ are all the free variables in $(\exists x_1, \ldots, x_n)W$, and p is a new predicate symbol not already appearing in the formulas.

Example 5.2.1: The above definition of *subset* has as the Lloyd-Topor normal form for its if-half:

$\neg p(x, y) \supset subset(x, y)$,
$member(z, x) \wedge \neg member(z, y) \supset p(x, y)$.

5.2.1 What Are the Lloyd-Topor Auxiliary Predicates?

Except for the last, all of the Lloyd-Topor transformations replace a sentence by a logically equivalent sentence so there are no surprises in them. However, the last rule introduces an auxiliary predicate whose logical status may appear mysterious. This new predicate arises because a new definition is being introduced into the definitional theory whose if-halves are being transformed by the Lloyd-Topor rules. To see why this is so, consider again the subset example, whose definition was:

$$subset(x, y) \equiv (\forall z).member(z, x) \supset member(z, y).$$

This is logically equivalent to:

$$subset(x, y) \equiv \neg(\exists z)\neg[member(z, x) \supset member(z, y)].$$

Now, introduce a new predicate symbol p, defined by:

$$p(x, y) \equiv (\exists z)\neg[member(z, x) \supset member(z, y)].$$

Then the original definition of subset can be equivalently written as:

$$subset(x, y) \equiv \neg p(x, y).$$

The if halves of these two definitions are:

$$(\exists z)\neg[member(z, x) \supset member(z, y)] \supset p(x, y),$$

$$\neg p(x, y) \supset subset(x, y).$$

After applying some of the first eleven Lloyd-Topor transformations to the first of these, we recover the Prolog program of Example 5.2.1.

5.2.2   Accommodating Arbitrary Goals

The Lloyd-Topor transformations can also be used to replace an arbitrary goal, which need not be a conjunctions of literals, by a normal goal—indeed, a single atom. The trick is to treat an arbitrary goal G as a definition by introducing a new predicate $answer$, as follows. Suppose $\vec{x}$ are all the free variables of G. Introduce the new definition $answer(\vec{x}) \equiv G$, and add it to the set of definitions under consideration. This new definition is also transformed, along with the other definitions, by the Lloyd-Topor rules. Now, treat $answer(\vec{x})$ as the goal, instead of G.

Example 5.2.2: The following goal, with free variable x, is not a normal goal:

$$(\forall y).father(y, x) \supset (\exists z).father(z, x) \wedge z \neq y \wedge \neg male(z).$$

Introduce the predicate $answer(x)$ and the definition

$$answer(x) \equiv [(\forall y).father(y, x) \supset (\exists z).father(z, x) \wedge z \neq y \wedge \neg male(z)].$$

Next, consider only the if-half of this definition of $answer(x)$ and use the Lloyd-Topor transformations to obtain:

$$\neg p(x) \supset answer(x),$$

$father(y, x) \land \neg q(x, y) \supset p(x),$

$father(z, x) \land z \neq y \land \neg male(z) \supset q(x, y).$

Here, p and q are new predicate symbols, as required by the transformation rules. Now, with these clauses introduced into the Prolog program, one can pose the normal goal $answer(x)$ instead of the original goal.

It is not hard to see that after applying the Lloyd-Topor transformations to a collection of formulas of the form $W \supset A$, one ends up with a set of Prolog clauses. What is the relationship between this Prolog program, the above treatment of arbitrary goals via the $answer$ predicate, and the definitions with which we began?

Theorem 5.2.3: Clark's Theorem Generalized

Suppose T is a set of definitions for all predicate symbols[5] in some first-order language with finitely many predicate symbols, together with the following equality sentences:

1. *For every pair of distinct function symbols f and g of the language (including constant symbols),*

   $$f(\vec{x}) \neq g(\vec{y}).$$

2. *For every n-ary function symbol of the language,*

   $$f(x_1, \ldots, x_n) = f(y_1, \ldots, y_n) \supset x_1 = y_1 \land \cdots \land x_n = y_n.$$

3. *For every term $t[x]$ (other than x itself) that mentions the variable x,*

   $$t[x] \neq x.$$

Suppose that $program(T)$ is a Prolog program obtained from the definitions of T by applying the Lloyd-Topor transformations to the if-halves of all the definitions of T.[6] Suppose further that G is a normal goal. (We include here the possibility that G is the special answer atom $answer(\vec{x})$, in which case the definition for $answer(\vec{x})$ has been transformed by the Lloyd-Topor rules, and these transformed clauses are also included in $program(T)$). Then,

1. *Whenever a proper Prolog interpreter succeeds on the goal G with answer substitution θ, then $T \models (\forall)G\theta$. Here, $(\forall)G\theta$ denotes the result of universally quantifying all the free variables (if any) of $G\theta$.*

2. *Whenever a proper Prolog interpreter returns failure on the goal G, then $T \models (\forall)\neg G$*

---

5 Recall that equality is *not* a predicate symbol of any first-order language. It is a built-in predicate of first-order logic, with a fixed interpretation that makes it mean "equals". See Section 2.1.1. Therefore, we do not require that there be a definition for equality in T.

6 Notice that in forming $program(T)$, we discard the unique names equality axioms of T.

where the quantification is over all free variables mentioned by G.

5.2.3   Definitional Theories: Soundness, Completeness, and Closed Worlds

Clark's Theorem, as generalized in Theorem 5.2.3, provides a foundation for Prolog programming. It guarantees the *soundness* of Prolog implementations for definitional theories.
By soundness here is meant that whenever the Prolog interpreter returns an answer, that
answer is correct in the sense that it is a logical consequence of the definitional theory
we started with. Clark's theorem does *not* guarantee the *completeness* of these implementations, which is to say, whenever the definitional theory entails an answer, there is no
guarantee that the corresponding Prolog program will compute that answer. Consider, as
an example, the following definitional theory:

$$p(x) \equiv true, \quad q(x) \equiv x = A.$$

Its Prolog program is:

    p(X). q(a).

The goal p(X), not q(X). will not succeed under a proper Prolog interpreter, despite the fact
that the definitional theory (with unique names axioms, of course) entails $p(B) \wedge \neg q(B)$.

    There are various conditions under which the program for a definitional theory will be
guaranteed complete, but these tend to be very restrictive. We will not pursue the completeness question further here, but will simply take comfort in the soundness guarantee
afforded by Clark's theorem.

    A more serious consideration is the restriction to definitional theories required by
Clark's theorem. Just how expressive are definitional theories? What features of an application domain are representable by such theories, and what features are not? In other
words, by virtue of Clark's theorem, what can be expressed with a Prolog implementation
of an application domain? There are two principal limitations of definitional theories:

1. For Clark's theorem to apply, these theories must contain suitable unique names axioms. This is a severe restriction on the denotations of terms; different terms denote different things. So one cannot say, for example, that $father(Sue) = Bill$,
   or $HighestMountainInTheWorld = Everest$.

2. All predicates must be definitions. Therefore, one cannot express incomplete information about an application domain, for example existential facts like $(\exists x)loves(Sue, x)$,
   or disjunctions like $loves(John, Mary) \vee loves(John, Sue)$. Such sentences simply
   cannot be shoe-horned into definitional form. Other examples include stating that the
   only thing known about whom John loves is that she is not Sally, but there may be
   someone other than Sally whom he does love: $\neg loves(John, Sally)$. Or that John

loves Mary, and possibly someone else as well: $loves(John, Mary)$.

These observations suggest that definitional theories, and therefore their Prolog implementations, provide very limited mechanisms for representing incomplete information, i.e. information reflecting some state of ignorance about what is true of an application domain. For this reason, such axiomatizations are said to be *closed world* representations. In contrast, full first-order logic provides a representational vehicle for *open worlds*; application domains involving arbitrary degrees of incomplete information are readily representable using existential quantification, disjunction and negation. Indeed, this ability to axiomatize incomplete information is a source of much of the expressive power and richness of first-order logic. So it is a great pity to give up much of this power by embracing closed world definitional theories. The advantage in doing so—and it is a significant advantage— is the extraordinary simplicity of Clark's translation to Prolog of these theories, and the resulting computational efficiency of these programs. Moreover, as we shall see later in this book, there are many applications for which such closed world definitional theories are appropriate. Nevertheless, there are also many applications requiring open world axiomatizations. The most obvious of these is robotics; in such settings, it is naive to expect that a robot will have complete information about the initial state of its world, for example, which doors are open and which closed. Indeed, in the presence of complete information about its world, it is not clear why a robot would ever need sensors!

5.3 Basic Action Theories, Definitions, and Regressable Queries

The primary objective of all this talk about definitions, Lloyd-Topor normal forms and Prolog is an implementation for a large class of basic action theories that will be provably correct for the purposes of proving regressable sentences. This may seem a lot of work for solving just one problem, but as we shall discover throughout this book, proving regressable sentences lies at the heart of virtually every computation we shall want to do in the situation calculus; the foundational work we are engaged in now will pay off handsomely later.

The basic idea of our approach is to use Clark's theorem and the Lloyd-Topor transformations to justify a Prolog implementation for basic action theories of the situation calculus. It is central to Clark's approach that the given logical theory be definitional; all its axioms except those for equality must be definitions. Now action precondition and successor state axioms are "almost" in definitional form, but not quite (why?). The purpose of this section is to formulate suitable conditions under which these theories can be recast in definitional form for the purpose of proving regressable sentences.

5.3.1 Definitional Form for Action Precondition Axioms

Recall that an action precondition axiom for action function A has the syntactic form $Poss(A(\vec{x}), s) \equiv \Pi_A(\vec{x}, s)$. This is not in definitional form since the arguments to $Poss$ do not consist of variables only (because of the first argument term $A(\vec{x})$). Our purpose here is to recast these action precondition axioms in definitional form.

Suppose the situation calculus language $\mathcal{L}_{sitcalc}$ has just finitely many action function symbols $A_1, \ldots, A_n$. Then there will be finitely many action precondition axioms of the form:

$$Poss(A_1(\vec{x}), s) \equiv \Pi_{A_1}(\vec{x}, s)$$
$$\vdots \tag{5.1}$$
$$Poss(A_n(\vec{z}), s) \equiv \Pi_{A_n}(\vec{z}, s).$$

Definition 5.3.1: Definition for $Poss$
Given finitely many action precondition axioms of the form (5.1), we call the following the *definition for $Poss$*:

$$Poss(a, s) \equiv$$
$$(\exists \vec{x})[a = A_1(\vec{x}) \wedge \Pi_{A_1}(\vec{x}, s)] \vee \cdots \vee (\exists \vec{z})[a = A_n(\vec{z}) \wedge \Pi_{A_n}(\vec{z}, s)]. \tag{5.2}$$

Notice that we make no claim about logical equivalence between the action precondition axioms (5.1) and the definition for $Poss$ (5.2). In fact, they are *not* logically equivalent in general (why?).

(5.2) provides exactly what is needed, namely a definition for $Poss$. Moreover, it is easy to see that the if-half of this definition is logically equivalent to:

$$\Pi_{A_1}(\vec{x}, s) \supset Poss(A_1(\vec{x}), s),$$
$$\vdots$$
$$\Pi_{A_n}(\vec{z}, s) \supset Poss(A_n(\vec{z}), s).$$

These can be transformed into Lloyd-Topor normal form. Provided, as we shall do, this definition for $Poss$ can be shown to be sufficient for proofs of regressable sentences, we shall be guaranteed a correct Prolog implementation.

5.3.2 Definitional Form for Successor State Axioms

For the purposes of proving regressable sentences, and under suitable conditions on the initial database, the successor state axiom for a relational fluent F can be replaced by a definition for F, as we now describe. As was the case for action preconditions, the motivation for doing this is to appeal to Clark's theorem to justify a Prolog implementation for basic action theories. Because Prolog does not provide for clauses defining functions, only predicates, we shall assume there are no functional fluents in the underlying situation calculus language.

Definition 5.3.2: Closed Initial Database

Suppose $\mathcal{L}_{sitcalc}$ has no functional fluents. An initial database $\mathcal{D}_{S_0}$ of $\mathcal{L}_{sitcalc}$ is in *closed form* iff:

1. For every relational fluent F of $\mathcal{L}_{sitcalc}$, $\mathcal{D}_{S_0}$ contains exactly one sentence of the form $F(\vec{x}, S_0) \equiv \Psi_F(\vec{x}, S_0)$, where $\Psi_F(\vec{x}, S_0)$ is a first-order formula that is uniform in the situation term S_0, and whose free variables are among $\vec{x}$.

2. For every non-fluent predicate symbol P of $\mathcal{L}_{sitcalc}$, $\mathcal{D}_{S_0}$ contains exactly one sentence of the form $P(\vec{x}) \equiv \Theta_P(\vec{x})$ where $\Theta_P(\vec{x})$ is a situation-independent first-order formula whose free variables are among $\vec{x}$.

3. The rest of $\mathcal{D}_{S_0}$ consist of the following equality sentences:

    (a) For each pair of distinct function symbols f and g of sort *object*, including constant symbols,
    $$f(\vec{x}) \neq g(\vec{y}).$$

    (b) For each function symbol f of sort *object*,
    $$f(x_1, \ldots, x_n) = f(y_1, \ldots, y_n) \supset x_1 = y_1 \wedge \cdots \wedge x_n = y_n.$$

    (c) For each term t of sort *object* other than the variable x of sort *object*,
    $$t[x] \neq x.$$

    (d) For each term τ of sort *action* other than the variable a of sort *action*,
    $$\tau[a] \neq a.$$

    In other words, the remaining sentences of $\mathcal{D}_{S_0}$ are precisely the unique names axioms for the sort *object* required by Clark's theorem, together with the schema $\tau[a] \neq a$ for sort *action*, also required by this theorem.

A closed initial database provides a very limited representational vehicle. The only thing such a database can say about a fluent F is that it is characterized by an equivalence. On this assumption, as described in Section 5.2.3, there are many things that cannot be said about F's initial truth values. For example, one cannot say that $(\exists x)F(x, S_0)$, or $F(A, S_0) \vee F(B, S_0)$, or even simply that $F(A, S_0)$ is all that is known to be true of F. Similarly for the non-fluent predicate symbols, which are also defined by equivalences. Moreover, we are restricted to unique names for terms of sort *object*, so we cannot say that syntactically different terms denote the same thing, as in $murderer(Caesar) = Brutus$.

Despite the representational limitations imposed by such initial databases, we are willing to make these assumptions because, first, as we are about to see, it will lead to a natural Prolog implementation, and secondly, despite the above restriction to equivalences and unique names, it does allow us to model many interesting dynamical systems. In fact, much of the remainder of this book will consist of examples of dynamical systems whose axiomatizations involve closed initial databases and that therefore have straightforward Prolog implementations.

Definition 5.3.3: Definitions for Fluents

Let F be a relational fluent whose successor state axiom is:

$$F(\vec{x}, do(a, s)) \equiv \Phi_F(\vec{x}, a, s).$$

Suppose further that $\mathcal{D}_{S_0}$ is a closed initial database, so it contains a single axiom for F of the form

$$F(\vec{x}, S_0) \equiv \Psi_F(\vec{x}, S_0).$$

Then the following sentence is said to be a *definition for F*:

$$F(\vec{x}, s) \equiv s = S_0 \wedge \Psi_F(\vec{x}, S_0) \vee (\exists a, s').s = do(a, s') \wedge \Phi_F(\vec{x}, a, s'). \tag{5.3}$$

Unlike the case for the definition for $Poss$, F's successor state axiom and initial situation axiom are together logically equivalent to the definition (5.3) (Exercise 4 below).

For our purposes, the fluent definition (5.3) has the nice property that its if-half is logically equivalent to the pair of sentences:

$$\Psi_F(\vec{x}, S_0) \supset F(\vec{x}, S_0),$$

$$\Phi_F(\vec{x}, a, s) \supset F(\vec{x}, do(a, s)).$$

The first is the if-half of F's equivalence in the closed initial database, while the second is the if-half of the equivalence in F's successor state axiom. Both if-halves are readily implemented as Prolog clauses after performing the Lloyd-Topor transformations to $\Psi_F(\vec{x}, S_0)$ and $\Phi_F(\vec{x}, a, s)$, respectively.

The following is our main result. It informs us that for the purpose of proving regressable sentences, the definitions for $Poss$ and for fluents (together with certain unique names axioms) are all that are needed.

Theorem 5.3.4: *Let $\mathcal{D}$ be a basic action theory in a situation calculus language $\mathcal{L}_{sitcalc}$ with the following properties:*

1. *$\mathcal{L}_{sitcalc}$ has no functional fluents, and it has just finitely many relational fluents and action function symbols.*

2. $\mathcal{D}_{S_0}$ *is in closed form. Let* $\mathcal{D}_{S_0}^{\Delta}$ *be* $\mathcal{D}_{S_0}$ *with all the equivalences for relational fluents removed. Therefore,* $\mathcal{D}_{S_0}^{\Delta}$ *consists of definitions for all non-fluent predicate symbols of* $\mathcal{L}_{sitcalc}$, *together with certain unique names axioms.*

- *Let* $\mathcal{D}_{ap}^{\Delta}$ *consist of the single definition (5.2) for Poss.*
- *Let* $\mathcal{D}_{ss}^{\Delta}$ *consist of definitions of the form (5.3), one for each relational fluent* F.
- *Let* $\mathcal{D}_{unsit}$ *consist of the two unique names axioms for situations in* Σ, *namely:*

   $S_0 \neq do(a, s),$

   $do(a_1, s_1) = do(a_2, s_2) \supset a_1 = a_2 \wedge s_1 = s_2,$

   together with all instances of the schema

   $t[s] \neq s,$

   for every term of sort situation *other than s itself that mentions the situation variable* s.

Then $\mathcal{D}$ *and* $\mathcal{D}_{S_0}^{\Delta} \cup \mathcal{D}_{ap}^{\Delta} \cup \mathcal{D}_{ss}^{\Delta} \cup \mathcal{D}_{una} \cup \mathcal{D}_{unsit}$ *are equivalent for regressable sentences in the following sense: Whenever* G *is a regressable sentence of* $\mathcal{L}_{sitcalc}$,

$$\mathcal{D} \models G \quad \textit{iff} \quad \mathcal{D}_{S_0}^{\Delta} \cup \mathcal{D}_{ap}^{\Delta} \cup \mathcal{D}_{ss}^{\Delta} \cup \mathcal{D}_{una} \cup \mathcal{D}_{unsit} \models G.$$

Proof: Exercise 5 below for the $\Rightarrow$ half. The $\Leftarrow$ half is non-trivial, and we omit it here.
∎

Remark 5.3.5:   The above theorem assumes the schema $t[s] \neq s$, for every term of sort *situation* other than s itself. In fact, all instances of this schema are already entailed by the foundational axioms Σ of $\mathcal{D}$, so by adopting this schema, we are making no new assumptions.

Proof: Exercise 3 below. ∎

Theorem 5.3.4 tells us that under suitable circumstances, one can prove regressable sentences by appealing to the axiomatization $\mathcal{D}_{S_0}^{\Delta} \cup \mathcal{D}_{ap}^{\Delta} \cup \mathcal{D}_{ss}^{\Delta} \cup \mathcal{D}_{una} \cup \mathcal{D}_{unsit}$. These axioms constitute a definitional theory, and therefore Clark's theorem applies, as follows.

Corollary 5.3.6: Implementation Theorem
Let $\mathcal{D}$ *be a basic action theory satisfying the conditions of Theorem 5.3.4, and let* $\mathcal{P}$ *be the Prolog program obtained from the following sentences, after transforming them by the Lloyd-Topor rules:*

1. For each definition of a non-fluent predicate of $\mathcal{D}_{S_0}$ of the form $P(\vec{x}) \equiv \Theta_P(\vec{x})$:

$\Theta_P(\vec{x}) \supset P(\vec{x}).$

2. For each equivalence in $\mathcal{D}_{S_0}$ of the form $F(\vec{x}, S_0) \equiv \Psi_F(\vec{x}, S_0)$:

$\Psi_F(\vec{x}, S_0) \supset F(\vec{x}, S_0).$

3. For each action precondition axiom of $\mathcal{D}_{ap}$ of the form $Poss(A(\vec{x}), s) \equiv \Pi_A(\vec{x}, s)$:

$\Pi_A(\vec{x}, s) \supset Poss(A(\vec{x}), s).$

4. For each successor state axiom $F(\vec{x}, do(a, s)) \equiv \Phi_F(\vec{x}, a, s)$ of $\mathcal{D}_{ss}$:

$\Phi_F(\vec{x}, a, s) \supset F(\vec{x}, do(a, s)).$

Then $\mathcal{P}$ provides a correct Prolog implementation of the basic action theory $\mathcal{D}$ for the purposes of proving regressable sentences.[7] To formulate a query G (which must be a regressable sentence) for execution by this program, first apply the Lloyd-Topor transformations to G according to Section 5.2.2, and issue the resulting query to the program.

For the purposes of implementing dynamical systems, the Implementation Theorem is perhaps the most important result of this book. It justifies a particularly simple Prolog implementation for posing regressable queries to basic action theories with closed initial databases. Of course, we have seen that this restriction to closed initial databases is quite strong. Nevertheless, there are many settings in which such closed theories are appropriate, and whenever that is the case, the Implementation Theorem tells us what to do.

Example 5.3.7: With reference to the education database of Section 3.4.3, we construct a Prolog program according to the Implementation Theorem.

Transaction Precondition Axioms. These contribute the following if-halves to the Prolog program:

$\{(\forall p).prerequ(p, c) \supset (\exists g).grade(st, p, g, s) \wedge g \geq 50\} \supset$
$$Poss(register(st, c), s),$$

$(\exists g').grade(st, c, g', s) \wedge g' \neq g \supset Poss(change(st, c, g), s),$

$enrolled(st, c, s) \supset Poss(drop(st, c), s).$

The Lloyd-Topor transformations applied to these yield the Prolog clauses:

$\neg p(st, c, s) \supset Poss(register(st, c), s),$

---

7 Here, by "correct Prolog implementation" we mean, as described more precisely in Theorem 5.2.3, that whenever a proper Prolog interpreter succeeds on a regressable sentence, that sentence is entailed by $\mathcal{D}$, and whenever it fails on such a sentence, the negation of this sentence is entailed by $\mathcal{D}$.

$prerequ(p, c) \wedge \neg q(st, p, s) \supset p(st, c, s),$

$grade(st, p, g, s) \wedge g \geq 50 \supset q(st, p, s),$

$grade(st, c, g', s) \wedge g' \neq g \supset Poss(change(st, c, g), s),$

$enrolled(st, c, s) \supset Poss(drop(st, c), s).$

Successor State Axioms. Next, consider the clauses obtained from the if-halves of the equivalences in the successor state axioms.

$a = register(st, c) \vee enrolled(st, c, s) \wedge a \neq drop(st, c) \supset$
$$enrolled(st, c, do(a, s)),$$

$a = change(st, c, g) \vee grade(st, c, g, s) \wedge (\forall g')a \neq change(st, c, g') \supset$
$$grade(st, c, g, do(a, s)).$$

The Lloyd-Topor transformations applied to these yield the Prolog clauses:

$a = register(st, c) \supset enrolled(st, c, do(a, s)),$

$enrolled(st, c, s) \wedge a \neq drop(st, c) \supset enrolled(st, c, do(a, s)),$

$a = change(st, c, g) \supset grade(st, c, g, do(a, s)),$

$grade(st, c, g, s) \wedge \neg r(a, st, c) \supset grade(st, c, g, do(a, s)),$

$a = change(st, c, g) \supset r(a, st, c).$

Initial Database. For the Implementation Theorem to apply, the initial database must be in closed form. We shall assume the following equivalences for the fluents $grade$ and $enrolled$, and the non-fluent $prerequ$:

$prerequ(p, c) \equiv p = C100 \wedge c = M100 \vee p = C200 \wedge c = M100,$

$grade(st, c, g, S_0) \equiv st = Mary \wedge c = C100 \wedge g = 40 \vee$
$$st = Mary \wedge c = C200 \wedge g = 60,$$

$enrolled(st, c, S_0) \equiv st = John \wedge c = C100 \vee st = John \wedge c = C200.$

The if-halves of these are, after some logical simplification involving properties of equality:

$prerequ(C100, M100), \quad prerequ(C200, M100),$

$grade(Mary, C100, 40, S_0), \quad grade(Mary, C200, 60, S_0),$

$enrolled(John, C100, S_0), \quad enrolled(John, C200, S_0).$

The Implementation Theorem guarantees that this program correctly implements the original basic action theory for the education database, whenever the queries are regressable.

5.3.3   Unfolding the Lloyd-Topor Auxiliary Predicates

The need to introduce auxiliary predicates is an annoying feature of the Lloyd-Topor transformations. Fortunately, they can be eliminated by a process called *unfolding*, as we now
describe. The basis for this is a simple observation: The evaluation of any Prolog program
with such a predicate will be exactly the same as if we replace it in the antecedent of the
clause in which it occurs by the antecedent of the clause defining it, then delete this clause
that defines it. Schematically, the claim is that an auxiliary predicate *Aux* introduced by
the Lloyd-Topor transformations produces a program of the form:

$$\cdots \wedge \neg Aux \wedge \cdots \supset A,$$

$$W \supset Aux,$$

and this has the same evaluation as the simpler program

$$\cdots \wedge \neg W \wedge \cdots \supset A.$$

That being the case, why is the concept of an auxiliary predicate needed at all in defining
the Lloyd-Topor transformations? The reason is that such predicates simplify the statement
and proof of Clark's theorem; they serve no other purpose. The principal way in which they
do this is through the concept of a proper Prolog interpreter. Recall that Clark's theorem
requires such an interpreter. Recall also that a proper interpreter never tries negation-as-
failure on non-ground *atoms*, including the atoms involving auxiliary predicates. If, instead
of introducing these auxiliary predicates the Lloyd-Topor transformations appealed only to
the unfolded version of the program, the definition of a proper Prolog interpreter could no
longer be restricted to negation-as-failure on atoms only. It would require rather complicated conditions on complex expressions—the W in the above schematic. To avoid such
complications in the proof of their theorem, Lloyd and Topor introduced the simplifying
device of auxiliary predicates. Nevertheless, when it comes to *implementing* definitional
theories, these predicates get in the way, especially when they arise as the *answer* predicates, introduced to deal with arbitrary goals that are not conjunctions of literals. Our
purpose here is to formulate equivalent, but simpler rules that remove the need for auxiliary predicates.

5.3.4   Revised Lloyd-Topor Transformations

As noted above, the Lloyd-Topor Transformations introduce auxiliary predicates. They
also (through the rules 2 and 12) sometimes create two clauses from one. The revised
transformations that we now give take a sentence of the form $W \supset A$, where A is an atom
and W is an arbitrary first-order formula, possibly involving quantifiers, in which case we
require that the quantified variables of W be different from one another, and from any of

the free variables mentioned in W. The output of these revised transformations is *a single Prolog executable* formula $lt(W) \supset A$, without introducing new predicates and clauses. Here, $lt(W)$ is a formula defined inductively on the syntactic structure of W, as follows:

1. When W is a literal,

$$lt(W) = W.$$

2. $\quad lt(W_1 \wedge W_2) = lt(W_1) \wedge lt(W_2).$

3. $\quad lt(W_1 \vee W_2) = lt(W_1) \vee lt(W_2).$

4. $\quad lt(W_1 \supset W_2) = lt(\neg W_1 \vee W_2).$

5. $\quad lt(W_1 \equiv W_2) = lt((W_1 \supset W_2) \wedge (W_2 \supset W_1)).$

6. $\quad lt((\forall x)W) = lt(\neg(\exists x)\neg W).$

7. $\quad lt((\exists x)W) = lt(W).$

8. $\quad lt(\neg\neg W) = lt(W).$

9. $\quad lt(\neg[W_1 \wedge W_2]) = lt(\neg W_1) \vee lt(\neg W_2).$

10. $\quad lt(\neg[W_1 \vee W_2]) = lt(\neg W_1) \wedge lt(\neg W_2).$

11. $\quad lt(\neg[W_1 \supset W_2]) = lt(\neg[\neg W_1 \vee W_2]).$

12. $\quad lt(\neg[W_1 \equiv W_2]) = lt(\neg[(W_1 \supset W_2) \wedge (W_2 \supset W_1)]).$

13. $\quad lt(\neg(\forall x)W) = lt((\exists x)\neg W).$

14. $\quad lt(\neg(\exists x)W) = \neg lt(W).$

Example 5.3.8: We continue with the education database of Example 5.3.7, and use the revised Lloyd-Topor transformations to create a correct Prolog implementation without auxiliary predicates.

Transaction Precondition Axioms. The revised transformations, applied to the if-halves of the transaction precondition axioms, yield:

$$\neg(prerequ(p, c) \wedge \neg(grade(st, p, g, s) \wedge g \geq 50)) \supset Poss(register(st, c), s),$$

$$grade(st, c, g', s) \wedge \neg g' = g \supset Poss(change(st, c, g), s),$$

$$enrolled(st, c, s) \supset Poss(drop(st, c), s).$$

Successor State Axioms. The revised transformations, applied to the if-halves of the successor state axiom equivalences, yield:

$$a = register(st, c) \vee enrolled(st, c, s) \wedge \neg a = drop(st, c) \supset$$
$$enrolled(st, c, do(a, s)),$$

$$a = change(st, c, g) \vee grade(st, c, g, s) \wedge \neg a = change(st, c, g) \supset$$
$$grade(st, c, g, do(a, s)).$$

Initial Database. This is the same as in Example 5.3.7.

These implications are precisely what one gets from those obtained in Example 5.3.7, but keeping disjunctions instead of splitting into two distinct clauses, and unfolding the auxiliary predicates. Finally, to obtain the corresponding Prolog program, replace all occurrences of ¬ by Prolog's not, and replace disjunction and conjunction by Prolog's disjunction and conjunction operators ; and , respectively.

The following is the resulting Prolog program for the above education database. It is in Eclipse Prolog, but this is largely compatible with other standard Prologs like CProlog or Quintus. It is the first example of how to implement the situation calculus that we shall use again and again in this book, so it is important to thoroughly understand it.

Prolog Implementation of an Education Database

```
:- dynamic(enrolled/3).    % Compiler
:- dynamic(grade/4).       % directives

%  Transaction Precondition Axioms

poss(change(St,C,G),S) :- grade(St,C,G1,S), not G = G1.
poss(drop(St,C),S) :- enrolled(St,C,S).
poss(register(St,C),S) :-
         not (prerequ(P,C), not (grade(St,P,G,S), G >= 50)).

%  Successor State Axioms.

enrolled(St,C,do(A,S)) :- A = register(St,C) ;
                          enrolled(St,C,S), not A = drop(St,C).
grade(St,C,G,do(A,S)) :- A = change(St,C,G) ;
                         grade(St,C,G,S), not A = change(St,C,G).

%  Initial Database

enrolled(john,c100,s0).    enrolled(john,c200,s0).
grade(mary,c100,40,s0).    grade(mary,c200,60,s0).
prerequ(c100,m100).        prerequ(c200,m100).
```

As determined in Corollary 5.3.6, this program is correct only for answering regressable queries. In Section 4.5, we used regression for this purpose, so it is of interest to inquire about the relationship between regression and the above Prolog program. A moment's thought will reveal that with respect to this program, *the Prolog backchaining inter-*

preter is performing the regression steps, as well as the theorem-proving of the regressed formula in the initial situation. Prolog implements the regression operator of Section 4.5 by applying the operator to a formula in a depth-first manner; the atoms in the antecedent of a clause are regressed back to the initial situation in the left-to-right order in which they occur in that clause. Moreover, whenever an atom mentions only the initial situation, Prolog tries to prove this atom using its initial database. The Prolog interpreter is functioning as a regression-based theorem-prover.

Example 5.3.9: Next, we treat an example query to this database that requires the revised Lloyd-Topor transformations. Consider the situation term

$$do(drop(John, C100), do(register(Mary, M100),$$
$$do(change(Mary, C100, 75), S_0))).$$

This represents the transaction log

$$[change(Mary, C100, 75), register(Mary, M100), drop(John, C100)],$$

and we denote it by S. The query is: In situation S, is it the case that $John$ and $Mary$ are all and only the students who are enrolled in some course?

$$(\forall st)[(\exists c)enrolled(st, c, S) \equiv st = John \lor st = Mary].$$

After applying the revised Lloyd-Topor transformations to this, we obtain:

$$\neg[enrolled(st, c, S) \land \neg st = John \land \neg st = Mary \lor$$
$$(st = John \lor st = Mary) \land \neg enrolled(st, c, S)].$$

See the sample program execution below for the evaluation of this query.

The perceptive reader will have noticed that in this query, negation-as-failure will be invoked on a non-ground atom, for example, in the evaluation of $\neg enrolled(st, c, S)$. During this evaluation, the variable st will be bound (to $John$ or $Mary$), but c will be unbound. Fortunately, this does not violate Clark's theorem. To see why, we must consider the Lloyd-Topor transformation of this query *with* auxiliary predicates, because the generalized form of Clark's theorem is formulated only for this setting. After performing these transformations, we obtain:

$$\neg p \supset answer,$$

$$enrolled(st, c, S) \land \neg st = John \land \neg st = Mary \supset p,$$

$$st = John \land \neg q(st) \supset p,$$

$$st = Mary \land \neg q(st) \supset p,$$

$$enrolled(st, c, S) \supset q(st).$$

Clearly, in evaluating the goal *answer*, negation-as-failure will not be invoked on a non-ground atom, so by Clark's theorem, this evaluation will return the correct answer. This example does illustrate a general problem with the revised Lloyd-Topor transformations; one cannot readily tell, by a simple inspection of the output of these transformations, whether a negation-as-failure violation occurs. It seems that one must inspect the clauses obtained by the transformations *with* auxiliary predicates to determine this. While it is possible to avoid having to go this route (Exercise 6 below), we shall not consider this issue any further here.

Next, we pose some regressable queries to the above program.

Querying the Education Database

```
/*  Is the following transaction sequence executable?
    [change(mary,c100,75), register(mary,m100), drop(john,c100)]  */

[eclipse 2]: poss(change(mary,c100,75),s0),
             poss(register(mary,m100),do(change(mary,c100,75),s0)),
             poss(drop(john,c100),do(register(mary,m100),
                                     do(change(mary,c100,75),s0))).
yes.


/*  Which students are enrolled in which courses after the
    above transaction sequence?  */

[eclipse 3]: enrolled(St,C,do(drop(john,c100),
                             do(register(mary,m100),
                                do(change(mary,c100,75),s0)))).
St = mary
C = m100      More? (;)

St = john
C = c200      More? (;)

no (more) solution.


/*  Is there an executable transaction sequence of the form:
    [change(mary,c100,75), register(mary,m100), drop(St,C)],
    (Note the variables!), and if so, in which courses is St
    enrolled after this action sequence?  */

[eclipse 4]: poss(change(mary,c100,75),s0),
             poss(register(mary,m100),do(change(mary,c100,75),s0)),
             poss(drop(St,C),do(register(mary,m100),
```

```
                              do(change(mary,c100,75),s0))),
              enrolled(St,C1,do(drop(St,C), do(register(mary,m100),
                              do(change(mary,c100,75),s0)))).
C1 = c200
St = john
C = c100      More? (;)

C1 = c100
St = john
C = c200      More? (;)

no (more) solution.

/*  With respect to the database log
    [change(mary,c100,75), register(mary,m100), drop(john,c100)]
    is it the case that john and mary are all, and only, the
    students enrolled in some course. This query was treated in
    Example 5.3.9, and its Lloyd-Topor form, which is what we
    pose now, was determined there.  */

[eclipse 5]: S = do(drop(john,c100),do(register(mary,m100),
                    do(change(mary,c100,75),s0))),
             not (enrolled(St,C,S), not St = john, not St = mary ;
                  (St = john ; St = mary), not enrolled(St,C,S)).
St = St
C = C
S = do(drop(john, c100), do(register(mary, m100),
       do(change(mary, c100, 75), s0)))
yes.

/*  The answer is "yes". Notice that Prolog creates no bindings for
    the variables St and C because they are in the scope of
    negation-as-failure, and this never binds variables.  */
```

5.4 Exercises

1. (a) Invent your own mini-database application, and axiomatize it in the style of the example of Section 3.4.3.

   (b) Give a Prolog implementation of your mini-database, and try it out on some queries. Be sure that at least some of these queries are complex enough to require the revised Lloyd-Topor transformations to Prolog executable form.

2. Implement your axiomatization for the monkey and bananas problem of Exercise 3.5, and verify that your plan is both executable and correct. Specify axiomatically the closed initial database that your program represents.

3. This question concerns the axiom schema $t[x] \neq x$ of Clark's theorem.

   (a) Prove, by induction on the syntactic form of $t[x]$ that each instance of this schema is independent of the first two unique names axioms: it is not entailed by these.

   (b) Prove that each *ground* instance of $t[x] \neq x$ in which x is replaced by a ground term is entailed by the first two unique names axioms.

   (c) Prove that basic theories of actions guarantee this schema for every term $t[s]$ of sort *situation*. Specifically, prove that $\Sigma \models (\forall s)t[s] \neq s$, whenever t (and hence s) are of sort *situation*.

4. Prove that in any basic action theory, F's successor state axiom and initial situation axiom are together logically equivalent to the definition (5.3). Hint: Use the sentence

   $$s = S_0 \vee (\exists a, s')s = do(a, s'),$$

   from Section 4.2.3.

5. Using the Regression Theorem 4.5.5, prove the $\Rightarrow$ half of Theorem 5.3.4.

6. Consider the revised Lloyd-Topor transformations of Section 5.3.4, and the problem of recognizing negation-as-failure violations as discussed in Example 5.3.9. In connection with these transformations, devise an algorithm for marking variables occurring in the scope of a negation operator with the property that whenever such a marked variable is ground during a negation-as-failure evaluation, the conditions for Clark's theorem will hold, in which case the Prolog evaluation will be guaranteed to be sound.

5.5 Bibliographic Remarks

Logic programmers might think that our presentation of the foundations of Prolog (Section 5.1) has got the story exactly backwards. The usual approach to describing the semantics of Prolog—see, for example, Lloyd [129]—begins with a Prolog program $\mathcal{P}$. Next, by applying some straightforward rules to the clauses of $\mathcal{P}$, one transforms $\mathcal{P}$ into what we have called a definitional theory, and what logic programmers call the *Clark completion* of the program. It is this resulting definitional theory that defines the semantics of the original program $\mathcal{P}$. One then argues that a proper Prolog interpreter does the right thing on $\mathcal{P}$ by invoking Clark's Theorem (Theorem 5.1.4). We have done the opposite. Our point of departure was to start with a definitional theory, show how to obtain a Prolog program from it, then use Clark's Theorem to justify the program as an implementation for the original theory. Chacun à son goût.

The Lloyd-Topor transformations are taken from Lloyd's book [129] where Clark's theorem in its original and generalized forms are proved. Clark's results were first reported in [35].

Eclipse Prolog is the logic programming language that will be used throughout this book. Very little of our code will be so fancy as to be incompatible with other commonly used Prolog systems like CProlog or Quintus. We chose Eclipse primarily because, as implied by its name—the ECRC Constraint Logic Parallel System—it provides built in constraint solving libraries that we shall use later for temporal reasoning. Eclipse is available free to academic institutions; for details on obtaining the language, and its documentation, see Appendix C.

6 Complex Actions, Procedures, and Golog

Chapter 4 outlined a situation calculus-based approach for representing, and reasoning about, simple actions, while Chapter 5 provided an implementation for these. These same issues have yet to be addressed for complex actions and procedures, for example:

- **if** *car In Driveway* **then** *drive* **else** *walk* **endIf**
- **while** ($\exists block$) *ontable(block)* **do** *remove A block* **endWhile**
- **proc** *remove A block* (πx)[*pickup(x)*; *putaway(x)*] **endProc**

Here, we have introduced a procedure declaration *remove A block*, and also the nondeterministic operator π; ($\pi\ x$)$\delta(x)$ means nondeterministically pick an individual x, and for that x, perform $\delta(x)$. We shall see later that this kind of nondeterminism is very useful for robotics and similar applications.

The objective of this chapter is to provide a situation calculus-based account of such complex actions and procedures. The end result will be Golog, a novel logic programming language for modeling complex behaviours.

6.1 Complex Actions and Procedures in the Situation Calculus

Our approach will be to define complex action expressions using some additional extralogical symbols (e.g., **while**, **if**, etc.) that act as *abbreviations* for logical expressions in the language of the situation calculus. These extralogical expressions should be thought of as *macros* that expand into genuine formulas of the situation calculus. So below, we define the abbreviation $Do(\delta, s, s')$, where δ is a complex action expression. *Intuitively, $Do(\delta, s, s')$ will macro-expand into a situation calculus formula that says that it is possible to reach situation s' from situation s by executing a sequence of actions specified by δ.* Note that complex actions may be nondeterministic, that is, may have several different executions terminating in different situations.

Do is defined inductively on the structure of its first argument as follows:

1. **Primitive actions:**

$$Do(a, s, s') \overset{def}{=} Poss(a[s], s) \wedge s' = do(a[s], s).$$

The notation $a[s]$ means the result of restoring the situation argument s to all functional fluents mentioned by the action term a (see the next item below). For example, if a is $goTo(location(Sam))$, and if *location* is a functional fluent, meaning that its value is situation dependent, then $a[s]$ is $goTo(location(Sam, s))$.

2. **Test actions:**

$$Do(\phi?, s, s') \overset{def}{=} \phi[s] \wedge s = s'.$$

Here, the test expression ϕ is a *situation-suppressed expression* (not a situation calculus formula) consisting of a formula in the language of the situation calculus, but with all situation arguments suppressed. $\phi[s]$ denotes the situation calculus formula obtained from ϕ by restoring situation variable s into all fluent names (relational and functional) mentioned in ϕ.

Example 6.1.1:

- If ϕ is $(\forall x).onTable(x) \wedge \neg on(x, A)$,

  then $\phi[s]$ stands for $(\forall x).onTable(x, s) \wedge \neg on(x, A, s)$.

- If ϕ is $(\exists x)nextTo(x, location(Mary))$,

  then $\phi[s]$ stands for $(\exists x)nextTo(x, location(Mary, s), s)$.

3. **Sequence:**

$$Do(\delta_1; \delta_2, s, s') \overset{def}{=} (\exists s'').Do(\delta_1, s, s'') \wedge Do(\delta_2, s'', s').$$

4. **Nondeterministic choice of two actions:**

$$Do(\delta_1 \mid \delta_2, s, s') \overset{def}{=} Do(\delta_1, s, s') \vee Do(\delta_2, s, s').$$

5. **Nondeterministic choice of action arguments:**

$$Do((\pi\ x)\ \delta(x), s, s') \overset{def}{=} (\exists x)\ Do(\delta(x), s, s').$$

6. **Nondeterministic iteration:** Execute δ zero or more times.

$$Do(\delta^*, s, s') \overset{def}{=}$$
$$(\forall P).\{(\forall s_1) P(s_1, s_1)\ \wedge$$
$$(\forall s_1, s_2, s_3)[Do(\delta, s_1, s_2) \wedge P(s_2, s_3) \supset P(s_1, s_3)]\}$$
$$\supset\ P(s, s').$$

In other words, doing action δ zero or more times takes you from s to s' iff (s, s') is in every set (and therefore, the smallest set) such that:

(a) (s_1, s_1) is in the set for all situations s_1.

(b) Whenever doing δ in situation s_1 takes you to situation s_2, and (s_2, s_3) is in the set, then (s_1, s_3) is in the set.

The above definition of nondeterministic iteration utilizes the standard second order way of expressing this set. Some appeal to second-order logic appears necessary here because transitive closure is not first-order definable, and nondeterministic iteration appeals to this closure.[1]

Conditionals and while-loops can be defined in terms of the previous constructs as follows:

if ϕ **then** δ_1 **else** δ_2 **endIf** $\overset{def}{=}$ $[\phi?\,;\,\delta_1]\,|\,[\neg\phi?\,;\,\delta_2]$,

while ϕ **do** δ **endWhile** $\overset{def}{=}$ $[\phi?\,;\,\delta]^*\,;\,\neg\phi?$.

Example 6.1.2:

- Walk to the car, get in, start it, then drive to Ottawa.

    $walkToCar\,;\,enterCar\,;\,startCar\,;\,driveTo(Ottawa)$.

- Move one of the blocks on the table onto the floor.

    $(\pi\,b).block(b)\wedge onTable(b)?\,;\,pickup(b)\,;\,putOnFloor(b)$.

- Move everything off the table onto the floor.

    while $(\exists x)onTable(x)$ **do**
    $\qquad (\pi\,x).onTable(x)?\,;\,pickup(x)\,;\,putOnFloor(x)$.
    endWhile

Example 6.1.3: We show the result of macro expanding $Do(\delta, S_0, s)$ when δ is the complex action

$(\pi\,x).A(x)\,;\,\phi?\,;\,[B(x)\,|\,C(x)\,;\,\psi?]$.

δ says: Nondeterministically choose a value for x, and for this choice, do the primitive action $A(x)$, then test whether ϕ is true in the resulting situation, and if so, do primitive action $B(x)$ or do primitive action $C(x)$ followed by the test of ψ. The situation calculus formula that expresses this is the following macro-expansion of $Do(\delta, S_0, s)$:

$(\exists x).(\exists s_1).Poss(A(x), S_0) \wedge s_1 = do(A(x), S_0) \wedge (\exists s_2).\phi[s_1] \wedge s_1 = s_2 \wedge$
$\qquad [Poss(B(x), s_2) \wedge s = do(B(x), s_2) \vee$
$\qquad\quad (\exists s_3).Poss(C(x), s_2) \wedge s_3 = do(C(x), s_2) \wedge \psi[s_3] \wedge s_3 = s].$

Using logical properties of equality, this simplifies to:

$(\exists x).Poss(A(x), S_0) \wedge \phi[do(A(x), S_0)] \wedge$
$\qquad [Poss(B(x), do(A(x), S_0)) \wedge s = do(B(x), do(A(x), S_0)) \vee$
$\qquad\quad Poss(C(x), do(A(x), S_0)) \wedge \psi[do(C(x), do(A(x), S_0))] \wedge$
$\qquad\qquad s = do(C(x), do(A(x), S_0))].$

---

1 See the discussion concerning the non-first-order definability of transitive closure in Section 2.1.7.

Notice what this *says*: The situation s reached by executing the program δ beginning with the initial situation is

1. $do(B(x), do(A(x), S_0))$ if, for some x, $A(x)$ is possible in S_0, ϕ is true after doing $A(x)$, and $B(x)$ is possible after doing $A(x)$, or

2. $do(C(x), do(A(x), S_0))$ if, for some x, $A(x)$ is possible in S_0, ϕ is true after doing $A(x)$, $C(x)$ is possible after doing $A(x)$, and ψ is true after doing $C(x)$.

These values for the situation s are the possible execution histories for the action δ; they represent all the possible symbolic execution traces of the action. To calculate one or more of these execution traces requires a background axiomatization of action precondition and successor state axioms and an initial database. (The latter are required because the formulas $\phi[do(A(x), S_0)]$ and $\psi[do(C(x), do(A(x), S_0))]$ will normally be composed of fluents, and therefore their truth values will be determined by successor state axioms and the initial database.) Therefore, evaluating δ relative to such background axioms is the following theorem-proving task:

$$Axioms \vdash (\exists s) Do(\delta, S_0, s).$$

In other words, find some final situation s for which the above macro-expansion is provable from the background axioms. Any instance of s obtained as a side-effect of a proof (e.g. 1 or 2 above for particular values of x) will be an execution trace of δ. As we shall see below, this idea will form the basis of an interpreter for Golog, a situation calculus-based programming language whose semantics is specified by the macro-expansion rules given earlier.

Of course, when a complex action involves nondeterministic iteration, its macro-expansion is more complicated because it is second-order. Nevertheless, the *content* of its macro-expansion is the same: It expands into a second-order situation calculus formula that says that it is possible to reach a final situation from the initial situation by executing a sequence of actions specified by the complex action. Moreover, determining a final situation is the same theorem-proving task as before, but this time in second-order logic.

6.1.1 Procedures

Next, we extend the above definitions for complex actions to include procedures. The difficulty with giving a situation calculus semantics for recursive procedure calls using macro expansion is that there is no straightforward way to macro expand a procedure body when that body includes a recursive call to itself.

1. We begin with an auxiliary macro definition: For any predicate variable P of arity $n + 2$, taking a pair of situation arguments:

$$Do(P(t_1, \ldots, t_n), s, s') \stackrel{def}{=} P(t_1[s], \ldots, t_n[s], s, s').$$

In what follows, expressions of the form $P(t_1, \ldots, t_n)$ occurring in programs will serve as procedure calls, and $Do(P(t_1, \ldots, t_n), s, s')$ will mean that executing the procedure P on actual parameters $t_1, \ldots, t_n$ causes a transition from situation s to s'. Notice that in the macro expansion, the actual parameters t_i are first evaluated with respect to the current situation s ($t_i[s]$) before passing them to the procedure P, so the procedure mechanism being defined is *call by value*. Because we now want to include procedure calls among our actions, we extend the definition of complex actions to consist of any expression that can be constructed from primitive actions and procedure calls using the complex action constructors of 1 - 6 above.

2. Next, we define a situation calculus semantics for *programs* involving (recursive) procedures. In the standard block-structured programming style, a program will consist of a sequence of declarations of procedures $P_1, \ldots, P_n$, with formal parameters $\vec{v}_1, \ldots, \vec{v}_n$ and procedure bodies $\delta_1, \ldots, \delta_n$ respectively, followed by a main program body δ_0. Here, $\delta_1, \ldots, \delta_n, \delta_0$ are complex actions, extended by actions for procedure calls, as described in 1 above. So a program will have the form:

   proc $P_1(\vec{v}_1)\ \delta_1$ **endProc** ; $\cdots$; **proc** $P_n(\vec{v}_n)\ \delta_n$ **endProc** ; δ_0

   We define the result of evaluating a program of this form as follows:

   $$Do(\{\textbf{proc}\ P_1(\vec{v}_1)\ \delta_1\ \textbf{endProc} ; \cdots ; \textbf{proc}\ P_n(\vec{v}_n)\ \delta_n\ \textbf{endProc} ; \delta_0\}, s, s')$$

   $$\stackrel{def}{=} (\forall P_1, \ldots, P_n).[\bigwedge_{i=1}^{n} (\forall s_1, s_2, \vec{v}_i).Do(\delta_i, s_1, s_2) \supset P_i(\vec{v}_i, s_1, s_2)]$$

   $$\supset Do(\delta_0, s, s').$$

   This is our candidate for the semantics of a program. Its situation calculus macro expansion says the following: When $P_1, \ldots, P_n$ are the smallest binary relations on situations that are closed under the evaluation of their procedure bodies $\delta_1, \ldots, \delta_n$, then any transition (s, s') obtained by evaluating the main program δ_0 is a transition for the evaluation of the program.

Example 6.1.4:

1. Given that *down* means move an elevator down one floor, define $d(n)$, meaning move an elevator down n floors.

   proc $d(n)\ (n = 0)?\ |\ d(n - 1)$; *down* **endProc**

2. Parking an elevator on the ground floor:

proc $park$ $(\pi\ m)[atfloor(m)?\ ;\ d(m)]$ **endProc**

3. $cleanUp$ means put away all the blocks into the box.

   proc $cleanUp$
     $(\forall x)[block(x) \supset in(x, Box)]?\ |$
     $(\pi\ x)[(\forall y)\neg on(y, x)?\ ;\ put(x, Box)]\ ;\ cleanUp$
   endProc

4. A blocks world program consisting of three procedure declarations devoted to creating towers of blocks, and a main program that makes a seven block tower, while ensuring that block A is clear in the final situation.

   proc $makeTower$ (n) % Make a tower of n blocks.
     $(\pi\ x, m)[tower(x, m)?\ ;$ % $tower(x, m)$ means that there is a
                           % tower of m blocks whose top block is x.
           if $m \leq n$ **then** $stack(x, n - m)$
           else $unstack(x, m - n)$
           endIf]
   endProc ;

   proc $stack$ (x, n) % Put n blocks on the tower with top block x.
     $n = 0?\ |\ (\pi\ y)[put(y, x)\ ;\ stack(y, n - 1)]$
   endProc ;

   proc $unstack$ (x, n) % Remove n blocks from the tower x.
     $n = 0?\ |\ (\pi\ y)[on(x, y)?\ ;\ moveToTable(x)\ ;\ unstack(y, n - 1)]$
   endProc ;

   % main: create a seven block tower, with A clear at the end.
   $makeTower(7)\ ;\ \neg(\exists x)on(x, A)?$

6.1.2   Programs and Executable Situations

An important property of the above definitions is that every successful program evaluation leads to an executable situation.

Theorem 6.1.5: *Suppose that δ is a program, and Σ are the foundational axioms for the situation calculus. Then*

$$\Sigma \models (\forall s).Do(\delta, S_0, s) \supset executable(s).$$

This should be intuitively clear because any situation s reached by evaluating δ must consist of a sequence of some of δ's primitive actions, and the macro-expansion for primitive actions requires that $Poss$ must hold for these. Therefore, whenever $Do(\delta, S_0, s)$ holds, $Poss$ must hold for all the primitive actions of s, and therefore, s must be executable. This somewhat informal argument can be tightened up, but we won't do so here.

The importance of this result is that when such a program is being used to specify the behaviour of an agent—say a robot—then any successful evaluation of the program is guaranteed to yield an executable action sequence *according to the agent's representation of what the world is like*. In other words, relative to the agent's "mental picture" of the world, as represented by its action precondition and successor state axioms, etc., the robot has every reason to believe that it can physically perform the action sequence computed by its program in the actual world. Of course, when it comes to physically perform these actions, it may well discover that the actual world does not conform to its mental picture, but that's another story, to which we shall return later. For the moment, it is sufficient to remark that such agents compute their programs off-line—in their heads, so to speak—in order to obtain an action sequence, and that Theorem 6.1.5 guarantees that any such sequence will be executable relative to the agent's mental image of the world.

6.1.3 Why Macros?

Programs and complex actions "macro expand" to (sometimes second-order) formulas of the situation calculus; *complex behaviours are described by situation calculus formulas.* But why treat these programs via macro expansion instead of as first class objects (terms) in the language of the situation calculus? To see why, consider the complex action

   while $[(\exists block)onTable(block)]$ **do** $removeAblock$ **endWhile**.

Now ask what kind of thing is $onTable(block)$. It is not a fluent, since these take situations as arguments. But it is meant to stand for a fluent since the expression $onTable(block)$ will be evaluated with respect to the current situation of the execution of the **while**-loop. To see what happens if we avoid the macro approach, suppose we treat complex actions as genuine first-order terms in the language of the situation calculus.

- We must augment this language with new distinguished function symbols ?, ;, |, π, and perhaps $while, ifThenElse$.
- Moreover, since a **while**-loop is now a first-order term, the p in $while(p, a)$ must be a first order term also. But p can be any "formula" standing for a situation calculus formula, e.g., $onTable(block), (\exists x, y).onTable(x) \wedge \neg red(x) \vee on(x, y)$.
- So we must introduce new function symbols into the language: $\widehat{on}, \widehat{onTable}, \widehat{and}, \widehat{or}, \widehat{exists}, \widehat{not}$ etc. ($\widehat{on}$ is needed to distinguish it from the fluent on.) Now these "formulas" look like genuine terms:

   $\widehat{onTable}(block),$

$$exists(X, exists(Y, or(and(\widehat{onTable}(X), not(\widehat{red}(X))), \widehat{on}(X, y)))).$$

Notice that X and Y here must be constants. In other words, we must *reify* situation-suppressed fluents and formulas about fluents. This makes the resulting first-order language much more complicated.

- Even worse, we must *axiomatize* the correspondence between these reified formulas and the actual situation calculus formulas they stand for. In the axioms for Do, such reified formulas get evaluated as

$$Do(p?, s, s') \equiv apply(p, s) \wedge s = s'.$$

Here, $apply(p, s)$ is true iff the reified situation-suppressed formula p, with its situation argument s restored (so that it becomes a genuine situation calculus formula), is true. So *apply* must be axiomatized. These axioms are schemas over fluents F and reified formulas p, p_1, p_2 and the quantified "variables" X of these expressions.

$$apply(\hat{F}(t_1, \ldots, t_n), s) \equiv F(apply_1(t_1, s), \ldots, apply_1(t_n, s), s),$$

where $apply_1$ restores situation arguments to functional fluents. Also needed are:

$$apply(and(p_1, p_2), s) \equiv apply(p_1, s) \wedge apply(p_2, s),$$

$$apply(or(p_1, p_2), s) \equiv apply(p_1, s) \vee apply(p_2, s),$$

etc.

All of this would result in a much more complex theory. To avoid this technical clutter, we have chosen to take the above macro route in defining complex actions, and to see just how far this idea can be pushed. As we shall see, it is possible to develop a very rich theory of actions this way.

6.1.4   Programs as Macros: What Price Must Be Paid?

By opting to define programs as macros, we obtain a much simpler theory than if we were to reify these actions. The price we pay for this is a less expressive formalism. For example, it is impossible to *quantify* over complex actions, since these are not objects in the language of the situation calculus. This means, for example, that programs cannot be synthesized using conventional theorem-proving techniques. In this approach to program synthesis, one obtains a program satisfying the goal formula $Goal$ as a side-effect of proving the following entailment:

$$Axioms \models (\exists \delta, s).Do(\delta, S_0, s) \wedge Goal(s).$$

Here, $Axioms$ are those for the foundations of the situation calculus, together with application specific successor state, action precondition and initial situation axioms. On this account, program synthesis is formally the same task as planning (Section 3.3). But the program to be synthesized is being existentially quantified in the theorem, so that this theorem cannot even be expressed in our language.

On the other hand, many other program properties are, in principle, provable within the formalism. Moreover, doing so is (conceptually) straightforward precisely because program executions are formulas of the situation calculus.

1. *Correctness*: To show that, for a given initial situation, whenever program δ terminates, it does so in a situation satisfying property P:

$$Axioms \models (\forall s).Do(\delta, S_0, s) \supset P(s).$$

Or, the stronger claim that for all initial situations satisfying property I, whenever program δ terminates, it does so in a situation satisfying property P:

$$Axioms \models (\forall s_0, s).I(s_0) \land Do(\delta, s_0, s) \supset P(s).$$

2. *Termination:* To show that program δ terminates for a given initial situation:

$$Axioms \models (\exists s)Do(\delta, S_0, s).$$

Or, the stronger claim that program δ terminates for all initial situations satisfying property I:

$$Axioms \models (\forall s_0).I(s_0) \supset (\exists s)Do(\delta, s_0, s).$$

In other words, the above macro account is well-suited to applications where a program δ is *given*, and the job is to prove it has some property. As we will see, the main property that will concern us is execution: given δ and an initial situation, find a terminating situation for δ, if one exists. To do so, we prove the termination of δ as above, and then extract from the proof a binding for the terminating situation.

6.1.5   Golog

The program and complex action expressions defined above can be viewed as a programming language whose semantics is defined via macro-expansion into sentences of the situation calculus. We call this language Golog, for "alGOl in LOGic". Golog appears to offer significant advantages over current tools for applications in dynamic domains like the high-level programming of robots and software agents, process control, discrete event simulation, complex database transactions, etc. The next section presents a simple example.

6.2   An Elevator Controller in Golog

Here we show how to axiomatize the primitive actions and fluents for a simple elevator, and we write a Golog program to control this elevator.

Primitive actions:

- $up(n)$. Move the elevator up to floor n.
- $down(n)$. Move the elevator down to floor n.
- $turnoff(n)$. Turn off call button n.
- $open$. Open the elevator door.
- $close$. Close the elevator door.

Fluents:

- $currentFloor(s) = n$. In situation s, the elevator is at floor n.
- $on(n, s)$. In situation s, call button n is on.

Primitive Action Preconditions:

$$Poss(up(n), s) \equiv currentFloor(s) < n.$$

$$Poss(down(n), s) \equiv currentFloor(s) > n.$$

$$Poss(open, s) \equiv true.$$

$$Poss(close, s) \equiv true.$$

$$Poss(turnoff(n), s) \equiv on(n, s).$$

Successor state axioms:

$$currentFloor(do(a, s)) = m \equiv a = up(m) \vee a = down(m) \vee$$
$$currentFloor(s) = m \wedge \neg(\exists n)a = up(n) \wedge \neg(\exists n)a = down(n).$$

$$on(m, do(a, s)) \equiv on(m, s) \wedge a \neq turnoff(m).$$

Notice that we no longer determine successor state axioms by first writing effect axioms, then transforming these according to the solution to the frame problem of Section 3.2; rather, we directly write the successor state axioms. After a little bit of experience, most people find it natural and straightforward to directly write such axioms, and in the remainder of this book, we shall do just that.

An abbreviation:

$$nextFloor(n, s) \stackrel{def}{=} on(n, s) \wedge$$
$$(\forall m).on(m, s) \supset |m - currentFloor(s)| \geq |n - currentFloor(s)|.$$

This defines the next floor to be served as a nearest floor to the one where the elevator happens to be.

The Golog procedures:

> **proc** $serve(n)$
> $goFloor(n)$; $turnoff(n)$; $open$; $close$ **endProc**.

> **proc** $goFloor(n)$
> $(currentFloor = n)?$ | $up(n)$ | $down(n)$ **endProc**.
>
> **proc** $serveAfloor$
> $(\pi\, n)[nextFloor(n)?\,;\; serve(n)]$ **endProc**.
>
> **proc** $control$
> [**while** $(\exists n)on(n)$ **do** $serveAfloor$ **endWhile**] ; $park$
> **endProc**.
>
> **proc** $park$
> **if** $currentFloor = 0$ **then** $open$ **else** $down(0)$; $open$ **endIf**
> **endProc**.

Initial situation:

> $currentFloor(S_0) = 4, \quad on(b, S_0) \equiv b = 3 \vee b = 5.$

Notice that this last axiom specifies that, initially, buttons 3 and 5 are on, and moreover no other buttons are on. In other words, we have a definition about which call buttons are initially on. It is this definitional character of the initial situation that will justify, in part, the Prolog implementation described below in Section 6.3.

Running the program:

This is the theorem-proving task of establishing the following entailment:

> $Axioms \models (\exists s)Do(control, S_0, s).$[2]

Here, $Axioms$ consists of the foundational axioms for the situation calculus, together with the successor state, action precondition and initial situation axioms for the elevator. Notice especially what this entailment says, and why it makes sense.

- Although the expression $Do(control, S_0, s)$ looks like an atomic formula, Do is a macro not a predicate, and the expression stands for a much longer second-order situation calculus formula. This will mention only the primitive actions $up, down, turnoff,$ $open, close$ and the fluents $currentFloor, on,$ as well as the distinguished situation calculus symbols $do, S_0, Poss.$

- Because the macro-expansion of $(\exists s)Do(control, S_0, s)$ is a situation calculus sentence, it makes sense to seek a proof of it using as premises the axioms that characterize the fluents and actions of this elevator world.

---

2 Strictly speaking, we must prove the sentence $(\exists s)Do(\Pi; control, S_0, s)$ where Π is the sequence of procedure declarations just given. The call to $control$ in this sentence serves as the main program. See the definition of Golog programs and their semantics in Section 6.1 above.

A successful "execution" of the program, i.e. a successful proof, might return the following binding for s:

$$s = do(open, do(down(0), do(close, do(open, do(turnoff(5),$$
$$do(up(5), do(close, do(open, do(turnoff(3), do(down(3), S_0))))))))))).$$

Such a binding represents an execution trace of the Golog program for the given description of the initial situation. This trace, namely, the action sequence

$down(3)$, $turnoff(3)$, $open$, $close$, $up(5)$, $turnoff(5)$, $open$, $close$, $down(0)$, $open$,

would next be passed to the elevator's execution module for controlling it in the physical world. Notice especially that, as described here, Golog programs are executed *off-line*. Nothing happens in the external world during this off-line computation. Only after the program terminates (assuming it does terminate) is its execution trace passed to a real world execution module that physically performs the actions—causing an elevator to serve suitable floors, or a robot to perform some action sequence.

As one can see from the example, Golog is a logic programming language in the following sense:

1. Its interpreter is a general-purpose theorem-prover. In its most general form, this must be a theorem-prover for second-order logic; in practice (see Section 6.3 below), first-order logic is sufficient for many purposes.

2. Like Prolog, Golog programs are executed for their side-effects, namely, to obtain bindings for the existentially quantified variables of the theorem.

6.3 Implementation

In this section, we discuss an implementation of the Golog language in Prolog. We begin by presenting a very simple version of this interpreter. Next, we discuss the correctness of this implementation, and show how it is related to proving regressable sentences. Finally, we show how the elevator example above would be written for this interpreter and some execution traces.

6.3.1 An Interpreter

Given that the execution of Golog involves finding a proof in second-order logic, it is perhaps somewhat surprising how easy it is to write a Golog interpreter. The following shows the entire program in Prolog. In order to exploit the Prolog language, this implementation does not allow functional fluents; all fluents are assumed to be relational. Moreover, because it relies on Prolog for all the necessary theorem-proving, the interpreter also makes

certain assumptions about the underlying basic theory of actions, specifically, that its initial
database is closed as described in Section 5.3.2. We shall return to this point later, when
we discuss the correctness of the Golog interpreter.

A Golog Interpreter in Prolog

```prolog
:- dynamic(proc/2).             % Compiler directives. Be sure
:- set_flag(all_dynamic, on).   % to load this file first!

:- op(800, xfy, [&]).     % Conjunction
:- op(850, xfy, [v]).     % Disjunction
:- op(870, xfy, [=>]).    % Implication
:- op(880,xfy, [<=>]).    % Equivalence
:- op(950, xfy, [:]).     % Action sequence
:- op(960, xfy, [#]).     % Nondeterministic action choice

do(E1 : E2,S,S1) :- do(E1,S,S2), do(E2,S2,S1).
do(?(P),S,S) :- holds(P,S).
do(E1 # E2,S,S1) :- do(E1,S,S1) ; do(E2,S,S1).
do(if(P,E1,E2),S,S1) :- do(?(P) : E1 # ?(-P) : E2,S,S1).
do(star(E),S,S1) :- S1 = S ; do(E : star(E),S,S1).
do(while(P,E),S,S1):- do(star(?(P) : E) : ?(-P),S,S1).
do(pi(V,E),S,S1) :- sub(V,_,E,E1), do(E1,S,S1).    /*  Generate a new
          Prolog variable, and substitute it into the action E.  */
do(E,S,S1) :- proc(E,E1), do(E1,S,S1).
do(E,S,do(E,S)) :- primitive_action(E), poss(E,S).

% sub(Name,New,Term1,Term2): Term2 is Term1 with Name replaced by New.

sub(X1,X2,T1,T2) :- var(T1), T2 = T1.
sub(X1,X2,T1,T2) :- not var(T1), T1 = X1, T2 = X2.
sub(X1,X2,T1,T2) :- not T1 = X1, T1 =..[F|L1], sub_list(X1,X2,L1,L2),
                    T2 =..[F|L2].
sub_list(X1,X2,[],[]).
sub_list(X1,X2,[T1|L1],[T2|L2]) :- sub(X1,X2,T1,T2),
                                   sub_list(X1,X2,L1,L2).

/* The holds predicate implements the revised Lloyd-Topor
   transformations on test conditions.  */

holds(P & Q,S) :- holds(P,S), holds(Q,S).
holds(P v Q,S) :- holds(P,S); holds(Q,S).
holds(P => Q,S) :- holds(-P v Q,S).
holds(P <=> Q,S) :- holds((P => Q) & (Q => P),S).
```

```
holds(-(-P),S) :- holds(P,S).
holds(-(P & Q),S) :- holds(-P v -Q,S).
holds(-(P v Q),S) :- holds(-P & -Q,S).
holds(-(P => Q),S) :- holds(-(-P v Q),S).
holds(-(P <=> Q),S) :- holds(-((P => Q) & (Q => P)),S).
holds(-all(V,P),S) :- holds(some(V,-P),S).
holds(-some(V,P),S) :- not holds(some(V,P),S).   % Negation
holds(-P,S) :- isAtom(P), not holds(P,S).        % by failure.
holds(all(V,P),S) :- holds(-some(V,-P),S).
holds(some(V,P),S) :- sub(V,_,P,P1), holds(P1,S).


/* The following clause treats the holds predicate for all atoms,
   including Prolog system predicates. For this to work properly,
   the Golog programmer must provide, for all atoms taking a
   situation argument, a clause giving the result of restoring
   its suppressed situation argument, for example:
         restoreSitArg(onTable(X),S,onTable(X,S)).              */


holds(A,S) :- restoreSitArg(A,S,F), F ;
              not restoreSitArg(A,S,F), isAtom(A), A.

isAtom(A) :- not (A = -W ; A = (W1 & W2) ; A = (W1 => W2) ;
     A = (W1 <=> W2) ; A = (W1 v W2) ; A = some(X,W) ; A = all(X,W)).

restoreSitArg(poss(A),S,poss(A,S)).
```

The do predicate here takes three arguments: a Golog action expression, and terms standing for the initial and final situations. Normally, a query has the form do(e,s0,S), so that an answer will be a binding for the final situation S. In this implementation, a legal Golog action expression e is one of the following:

- $e_1 : e_2$. Sequence.
- ?(p). Test action, where p is a condition (see below).
- $e_1 \# e_2$. Nondeterministic choice of e_1 or e_2.
- if(p,e_1,e_2). Conditional.
- star(e). Nondeterministic repetition.
- while(p,e). Iteration.
- pi(v,e). Nondeterministic assignment, where v is a Prolog constant (standing for a Golog variable) and e is a Golog action expression that uses v.
- a. The name of a user-declared primitive action or defined procedure (see below).

A condition p in the above is either an atomic formula or an expression of the form p_1 & p_2,

$p_1 \vee p_2$, $-p$, $p_1 \Rightarrow p_2$, $p_1 \Leftrightarrow p_2$, all(v,p), or some(v,p), where v is a Prolog constant and p is a condition using v. In evaluating these conditions, the interpreter applies the revised Lloyd-Topor transformations (Section 5.3.4), uses negation as failure to handle logical negation $(-)$, and consults the user-supplied successor state axioms and initial database to determine which fluents are true.

6.3.2 Assumptions Underlying the Implementation

The interpreter presupposes a background basic action theory implemented with suitable Prolog clauses. As we shall see, the Golog evaluation of programs amounts to proving regressable sentences. Therefore, we can appeal to the results of Chapter 5 on a correct Prolog implementation for regressable sentences for the purposes of specifying Prolog clauses for the background basic action theory. We recall here what were the underlying assumptions for such a Prolog implementation.

1. $\mathcal{L}_{sitcalc}$ has no functional fluents, and it has just finitely many relational fluents and action function symbols.

2. The basic action theory has a closed initial database $\mathcal{D}_{S_0}$. This means:

   (a) $\mathcal{D}_{S_0}$ contains suitable unique names axioms.

   (b) $\mathcal{D}_{S_0}$ contains a definition for each non-fluent predicate symbol.

   (c) For each relational fluent F, $\mathcal{D}_{S_0}$ contains an equivalence of the form:

   $$F(\vec{x}, S_0) \equiv \Psi_F(\vec{x}, S_0).$$

Under the above assumptions on a basic action theory, Corollary 5.3.6 guarantees us that the following clauses, after conversion by the revised Lloyd-Topor transformations, provide a correct Prolog implementation for proving regressable sentences.

1. For each definition of a non-fluent predicate of $\mathcal{D}_{S_0}$ of the form $P(\vec{x}) \equiv \Theta_P(\vec{x})$:

   $$\Theta_P(\vec{x}) \supset P(\vec{x}).$$

2. For each equivalence in $\mathcal{D}_{S_0}$ of the form $F(\vec{x}, S_0) \equiv \Psi_F(\vec{x}, S_0)$:

   $$\Psi_F(\vec{x}, S_0) \supset F(\vec{x}, S_0).$$

3. For each action precondition axiom $Poss(A(\vec{x}), s) \equiv \Pi_A(\vec{x}, s)$ of $\mathcal{D}_{ap}$:

   $$\Pi_A(\vec{x}, s) \supset Poss(A(\vec{x}), s).$$

4. For each successor state axiom $F(\vec{x}, do(a, s)) \equiv \Phi_F(\vec{x}, a, s)$ of $\mathcal{D}_{ss}$:

   $$\Phi_F(\vec{x}, a, s) \supset F(\vec{x}, do(a, s)).$$

Therefore, we assume that the underlying basic action theory for a Golog application satisfies the above properties 1 and 2, and that its Prolog implementation consists of clauses of the form 1 - 4.[3] In addition, the Golog implementation (like the elevator, below) expects the following parts:

1. a collection of clauses of the form primitive_action(act), declaring each primitive action.

2. a collection of clauses of the form proc(name,body) declaring each defined procedure (which can be recursive). The body here can be any legal Golog action expression.

3. a collection of clauses of the form

   restoreSitArg(fluentAtom,S,fluentAtom[S]),

one for each fluent. For example, in a blocks world, there should be an atomic clause restoreSitArg(on(X,Y),S,on(X,Y,S)), meaning that the result of restoring the situation argument S to the situation-suppressed fluent atom on(X,Y) is on(X,Y,S). This is used by the interpreter's holds predicate for evaluating Golog test expressions. The clauses for holds recursively decompose test expressions until they reach an atomic test expression A; this is evaluated by the last clause in the program for holds. There are two possibilities:

   (a) A is a fluent atom (like on(X,Y)). Then restoreSitArg(A,S,F) will succeed, and F will be the result of restoring the current situation argument to A. The interpreter then lets Prolog evaluate F (using the clauses for the successor state axioms and the initial database) to determine its truth value.

   (b) A is an atom, but not a fluent atom, so not restoreSitArg(A,S,F) succeeds. In this case, A must be an atom of a non-fluent predicate of the basic action theory, or a Prolog atom, involving a Prolog system predicate or a user-defined predicate. In either case, it is passed to Prolog for evaluation. This is how the Golog interpreter provides an escape to Prolog; if a predicate is not declared to be a fluent via restoreSitArg, it is treated as an ordinary Prolog atom to be evaluated by the Prolog interpreter.

6.3.3 Correctness of the Interpreter for Basic Action Theories with Closed Initial Database

While this interpreter might appear intuitively to be doing the right thing, at least in cases where the usual Prolog closed world assumption is made about the initial database, it turns out to be non-trivial to state precisely in what sense it is correct. On the one hand, we have the specification of *Do* as a formula in second-order logic, and on the other, we have the above do predicate, characterized by a set of Prolog clauses, together with a collection of Prolog clauses for the background basic action theory, as described in the previous section.

---

3 The Golog programmer is responsible for performing the revised Lloyd-Topor transformations on these clauses in order to obtain Prolog executable clauses. The implementation does not do these transformations for her.

The exact correspondence between the two depends on a number of factors. Here, we shall only indicate by an example one reason why this implementation is correct for basic action theories with closed initial database.

Recall the complex action δ from Example 6.1.3:

$$(\pi\, x).A(x)\,;\ \phi?\,;\ [B(x)\,|\,C(x)\,;\ \psi?].$$

We saw there that the macro-expansion of $Do(\delta, S_0, s)$ is logically equivalent to:

$$(\exists x).Poss(A(x),\, S_0) \wedge \phi[do(A(x),\, S_0)] \ \wedge$$
$$[Poss(B(x),\, do(A(x),\, S_0)) \wedge s = do(B(x),\, do(A(x),\, S_0)) \ \vee$$
$$Poss(C(x),\, do(A(x),\, S_0)) \wedge \psi[do(C(x),\, do(A(x),\, S_0))] \ \wedge$$
$$s = do(C(x),\, do(A(x),\, S_0))].$$

To evaluate this program relative to a basic action theory $\mathcal{D}$ requires determining whether

$$\mathcal{D} \models (\exists s)Do(\delta, S_0, s),$$

and if so, extracting from the proof a binding for the existentially quantified variable s. If it exists, this binding provides an execution trace of δ. Now by simple properties of equality, $(\exists s)Do(\delta, S_0, s)$ is logically equivalent to:

$$(\exists x).Poss(A(x),\, S_0) \wedge \phi[do(A(x),\, S_0)] \ \wedge$$
$$[Poss(B(x),\, do(A(x),\, S_0)) \vee Poss(C(x),\, do(A(x),\, S_0)) \ \wedge$$
$$\psi[do(C(x),\, do(A(x),\, S_0))]]].$$

Therefore, we must establish that:

$$\mathcal{D} \models (\exists x).Poss(A(x),\, S_0) \wedge \phi[do(A(x),\, S_0)] \wedge$$
$$[Poss(B(x),\, do(A(x),\, S_0)) \vee Poss(C(x),\, do(A(x),\, S_0)) \wedge \qquad (6.1)$$
$$\psi[do(C(x),\, do(A(x),\, S_0))]]].$$

By definition, the program test conditions ϕ and ψ mention no terms of sort *situation*, and $\phi[do(A(x), S_0)]$ is the situation calculus formula obtained from ϕ by restoring the situation argument $do(A(x), S_0)$ to all situation-suppressed fluents mentioned by ϕ. Thus, $\phi[do(A(x), S_0)]$ and $\psi[do(C(x), do(A(x), S_0))]$ are regressable formulas, and therefore the sentence of the entailment (6.1) is also regressable. Then the Implementation Theorem (Corollary 5.3.6) informs us that the Prolog clauses 1 - 4 of the previous section for the basic action theory $\mathcal{D}$ is a correct implementation for establishing the entailment (6.1). More precisely, if we perform the revised Lloyd-Topor transformations to the sentence of (6.1), and pose this as a query to the Prolog clauses 1 - 4 for $\mathcal{D}$, then if this Prolog query succeeds, the entailment (6.1) will be true, and if this query fails, then $\mathcal{D}$ entails the negation of the sentence of (6.1). This is exactly what the Golog interpreter of Section 6.3.1 does. To see this, imagine symbolically unwinding the Prolog call do(δ,s0,S). The result will be the Prolog query:

```
poss(a(X),s0), holds(φ,do(a(X),s0)),
  ( poss(b(X),do(a(X),s0)) ; poss(c(X),do(a(X),s0)),
                          holds(ψ,do(c(X),do(a(X),s0)))) ).
```

Here, X is a new variable, introduced by the interpreter's clause for nondeterministic choice of action arguments during its expansion of δ. Now the interpreter predicate holds(C,S) does two things: It implements the revised Lloyd-Topor transformation on the test condition C, and it restores the situation argument S to the situation-suppressed fluent atoms of C. Therefore, if we symbolically unwind the holds predicate in the above Prolog query, the result will be Prolog's version of the revised Lloyd-Topor transformation for the sentence of (6.1). Therefore, by the Implementation Theorem, the Prolog clauses for $\mathcal{D}$ are correct for answering this query.

Of course, the Golog interpreter does not first symbolically unwind the do and holds predicates before evaluating the result. Rather, it does so incrementally, in left-to-right order, evaluating the atomic pieces of the sentence as they are generated. But this is just an implementation detail, and an intelligent one at that, because failures are detected earlier under this incremental evaluation mechanism.

Although the above argument for the correctness of the Golog interpreter was made with respect to the given program δ, it should be clear that, at least for complex actions without nondeterministic iteration and procedures, which have second-order macro-expansions, the same argument will work. For a hint as to why this kind of an argument extends to nondeterministic iteration, and hence to **while** loops, see Exercise 11 below.

To summarize: When δ is a Golog complex action without nondeterministic iteration or procedures,

1. $(\exists s)Do(\delta, S_0, s)$ is logically equivalent to a regressable sentence.

2. The Golog interpreter incrementally generates and evaluates the revised Lloyd-Topor transformation of this regressable sentence.

3. The Implementation Theorem (Corollary 5.3.6) guarantees the correctness of this procedure.[4]

We emphasize again that correctness of the above interpreter relies on the Implementation Theorem, and hence on the standard Prolog closed world assumption that the initial database—the facts true in the initial situation S_0—is closed. This was the case for the

---

4 Perceptive readers will have noticed that we have here overstated the claim that $(\exists s)Do(\delta, S_0, s)$ must be logically equivalent to a regressable sentence. For example, when δ is $(\pi\, a)a$, or when δ is $(\exists a)Poss(a)$?, the macro expansion in both cases is $(\exists a)Poss(a, S_0)$, and this is not regressable. The problem stems from possible interactions between quantification over actions and the $Poss$ predicate. The proof that the Golog interpreter correctly handles these cases as well requires a picky argument that's not worth the effort to go into here.

logical specification of the elevator example of Section 6.2. For many applications, this is a reasonable assumption. For many others this is unrealistic, for example in a robotics setting in which the environment is not completely known to the robot. In such cases, a more general Golog interpreter is necessary. In Chapter 10 we shall show how one might use a Golog interpreter to evaluate test expressions by first regressing them back to the initial situation (as in Section 4.5), then using a theorem-prover to establish the resulting regressed expression.

6.3.4   The Elevator Example

The following clauses implement the above elevator example:

The Elevator Controller

```
% Primitive control actions

primitive_action(turnoff(N)).  % Turn off call button N.
primitive_action(open).        % Open elevator door.
primitive_action(close).       % Close elevator door.
primitive_action(up(N)).       % Move elevator up to floor N.
primitive_action(down(N)).     % Move elevator down to floor N.


% Definitions of Complex Control Actions

proc(goFloor(N), ?(currentFloor(N)) # up(N) # down(N)).
proc(serve(N), goFloor(N) : turnoff(N) : open : close).
proc(serveAfloor, pi(n, ?(nextFloor(n)) : serve(n))).
proc(park, if(currentFloor(0), open, down(0) : open)).

/* control is the main loop. So long as there is an active call
   button, it serves one floor. When all buttons are off, it
   parks the elevator.    */

proc(control, while(some(n, on(n)), serveAfloor) : park).


% Preconditions for Primitive Actions.

poss(up(N),S)  :- currentFloor(M,S), M < N.
poss(down(N),S) :- currentFloor(M,S), M > N.
poss(open,S).
poss(close,S).
poss(turnoff(N),S)  :- on(N,S).


% Successor State Axioms for Primitive Fluents.
```

```
currentFloor(M,do(A,S)) :- A = up(M) ; A = down(M) ;
              not A = up(N), not A = down(N), currentFloor(M,S).

on(M,do(A,S)) :- on(M,S), not A = turnoff(M).

% Initial Situation. Call buttons: 3 and 5. The elevator is at floor 4.

on(3,s0).    on(5,s0).    currentFloor(4,s0).

/* nextFloor(N,S) is an abbreviation that determines which of the
   active call buttons should be served next. Here, we simply
   choose an arbitrary active call button.    */

nextFloor(N,S) :- on(N,S).

% Restore suppressed situation arguments.

restoreSitArg(on(N),S,on(N,S)).
restoreSitArg(nextFloor(N),S,nextFloor(N,S)).
restoreSitArg(currentFloor(M),S,currentFloor(M,S)).
```

There are two things to notice especially about these clauses:

1. The restoreSitArg declarations for restoring suppressed situation arguments to all situation dependent atoms occurring in test conditions.

2. The clause for nextFloor(N,S). $nextFloor(n, s)$ was introduced as an abbreviation into the elevator axiomatization, so strictly speaking, it is not a fluent; it is not even a legal expression in the situation calculus language defining this elevator. The above Prolog implementation for the elevator has a clause for nextFloor(N,S) that describes this abbreviation. So we are using Prolog here to *to expand this abbreviation*; whenever nextFloor is mentioned in a test condition (as in the serveAfloor procedure), Golog evaluates this test first by restoring its suppressed situation argument, next by calling Prolog which, by backchaining into the clause for nextFloor, expands its abbreviation, finally by Prolog evaluating this expansion.

Next, we show some queries to the interpreter for this program.

Running the Elevator Program

```
[eclipse 2] do(pi(n,?(on(n)) : goFloor(n)),s0,S).

S = do(down(3), s0)    More? (;)
```

```
S = do(up(5), s0)      More? (;)

no (more) solution.
%-----------------------------------------------------
[eclipse 3] do(pi(n, turnoff(n) #
                      ?(nextFloor(n)) : goFloor(n)),s0,S).

S = do(turnoff(3),s0)     More? (;)

S = do(turnoff(5),s0)     More? (;)

S = do(down(3),s0)     More? (;)

S = do(up(5),s0)     More? (;)

no (more) solution.
%-----------------------------------------------------
[eclipse 4] do(control,s0,S).

S = do(open,do(down(0),do(close,do(open,do(turnoff(5),do(up(5),
do(close,do(open,do(turnoff(3),do(down(3),s0))))))))))   More? (;)

S = do(open,do(down(0),do(close,do(open,do(turnoff(3),do(down(3),
do(close,do(open,do(turnoff(5),do(up(5),s0))))))))))    More? (;)

S = do(open,do(down(0),do(close,do(open,do(turnoff(5),do(up(5),
do(close,do(open,do(turnoff(3),do(down(3),s0))))))))))    More? (;)

S = do(open,do(down(0),do(close,do(open,do(turnoff(3),do(down(3),
do(close,do(open,do(turnoff(5),do(up(5),s0))))))))))    More? (;)

no (more) solution.
```

The first query asks the interpreter to nondeterministically go to a floor whose call button is on. The answers show that there are only two ways to do this: either go down to floor 3 or up to 5.

The second query asks the interpreter to either turn off a call button or to go to a floor that satisfies the test nextFloor. Since this predicate has been defined to hold only of those floors whose button is on, this gives us four choices: turn off floor 3 or 5, or go to floor 3 or 5.

The final query calls the main elevator controller, control, to serve all floors and then park the elevator. There are only two ways of doing this: serve floor 3 then 5 then park, or serve floor 5 then 3 then park. Note that we have not attempted to prune the backtracking to avoid duplicate answers.

6.3.5   The University of Toronto Implementation of Golog

The actual implementation of Golog being used at the University of Toronto is in Eclipse
Prolog and incorporates a number of additional features for debugging and for efficiency
beyond those of the simple interpreter presented above.

For example, one serious limitation of the style of interpreter presented here is the
following: determining if some condition (like currentFloor(0)) holds in a situation involves
looking at what actions led to that situation, and unwinding these actions all the way back
to the initial situation. In other words, the interpreter is performing *regression*. Doing this
repeatedly with very long sequences of actions can take considerable time. Moreover, the
Prolog terms representing situations that are far removed from the initial situation end up
being gigantic.

However, it is possible in many cases to *progress* the initial database to handle this.
The idea is that the interpreter periodically "rolls the initial database forward" in response
to the actions generated thus far during the evaluation of the program. This progressed
database becomes the new initial database for the purposes of the continuing evaluation of
the program. In this way, the interpreter maintains a database of just the current value of all
fluents, and the distance from the initial situation is no longer a problem. The full Golog
implementation employs such a progression mechanism. Chapter 9 considers database
progression in more detail.

6.4   Discussion

Golog is designed as a logic programming language for dynamic domains. As its full
name (alGOl in LOGic) implies, Golog attempts to blend ALGOL programming style
into logic. It borrows from ALGOL many well-known, and well-studied programming
constructs such as sequence, conditionals, recursive procedures and loops.

However, unlike Algol and most other conventional programming languages, programs
in Golog decompose into primitives that in most cases refer to actions in the external world
(e.g., picking up an object or telling something to another agent), as opposed to commands
that merely change machine states (e.g., assignments to registers). Furthermore, these
primitives are defined by the programmer, by formulating suitable action precondition and
successor state axioms in first-order logic; which is to say, the programmer axiomatically
specifies the "execution machine" for her program. This feature of Golog supports the
specification of dynamical systems at the right level of abstraction. Moreover, because the
primitive actions have been axiomatized, their effects can be formally reasoned about, as

can the effects of Golog programs. This feature supports the possibility of proving various properties of Golog programs, such as correctness and termination.

Golog programs are evaluated with a theorem-prover. The user supplies precondition axioms, one per action, successor state axioms, one per fluent, a specification of the initial state of the world, and a Golog program specifying the behaviour of the agents in the system. Executing a program amounts to finding a ground situation term σ such that

$$Axioms \models Do(program, S_0, \sigma).$$

This is done by trying to prove

$$Axioms \models (\exists s)Do(program, S_0, s),$$

and if a (constructive) proof is obtained, such a ground term $do([a_1, a_2, \ldots, a_n], S_0)$ is obtained as a binding for the variable s. Then the sequence of actions $[a_1, a_2, \ldots, a_n]$ is sent to the primitive action execution module. This looks very like logic programming languages such as Prolog. However, unlike such general purpose logic programming languages, Golog is designed specifically for specifying agents' behaviours and for modeling dynamical systems. In particular, in Golog, actions play a fundamental role.

The version of Golog presented here omits many important considerations. The following is a partial list:

1. *Sensing and knowledge.* When modeling an autonomous agent, one must consider the agent's *perceptual actions*, e.g., acts of seeing, hearing, etc. Unlike ordinary actions that affect the environment, perceptual actions affect an agent's mental state, i.e., its state of *knowledge*. Chapter 11 provides a situation calculus account of knowledge, and within this setting, solves the frame problem for perceptual actions.

2. *Sensing actions.* In the presence of sensing actions, the purely off-line method described above for executing Golog program is no longer adequate. For example, suppose the sensing action $sense_P$ reads the truth value of P, and the primitives a and b are always possible. Then the following program $\mathcal{P}$ is perfectly reasonable:

   $sense_P$; **if** P **then** a **else** b **endIf**

   and should be executable with respect to any initial situation. However, it is not the case that

   $$Axioms \models Do(\mathcal{P}, S_0, \sigma)$$

   for any ground situation term σ. That is, at off-line execution time, the agent does not know the truth value of P and therefore does not know the exact sequence of primitive actions that corresponds to the execution of this program. This means that the program cannot be executed entirely off-line; some combination of off- and on-line execution must be provided for Golog programs *with* sensing actions, a topic we shall return to in Chapter 11.

3. *Exogenous actions.* We have assumed that all events of importance are under the agent's control. That is why, in the elevator example, we did not include a primitive action $turnon(n)$, meaning push call button n. Such an action can occur at any time, and is not under the elevator's control; rather, it is under the control of external agents. $turnon(n)$ is an example of an *exogenous* action. Other such examples are actions under nature's control—it starts to rain, a falling ball bounces on reaching the floor. In writing an elevator or robot controller, one would not include exogenous actions as part of the program, because the robot is in no position to cause such actions to happen. Chapter 8 describes *Reactive* Golog, which allows one to write Golog simulations that do allow for exogenous action occurrences.

4. *Concurrency and reactivity.* Once we allow for exogenous events, it becomes very useful to write programs that monitor certain conditions, and take appropriate actions when they become true. For example, in the middle of serving a floor, smoke might be detected by the elevator, in which case, normal operation should be suspended, and an alarm should be sounded until the alarm is reset. So what is needed is a concurrent version of Golog where a number of complex actions of this sort can be executed concurrently (at different priorities). This form of concurrency would allow a natural specification of controllers that need to quickly react to their environment while following predetermined plans. Chapter 8 describes *Reactive* Golog that provides for interrupt mechanisms of this kind.

5. *Continuous processes.* It might seem that, by virtue of its reliance on discrete action occurrences, the situation calculus cannot represent continuous processes and their evolution in time, like an object falling under the influence of gravity. However, one can view a process as a fluent—$falling(s)$—which becomes true at the time t that the instantaneous action $startFalling(t)$ occurs, and becomes false at the time t of occurrence of the instantaneous action $endFalling(t)$. One can then write axioms that describe the evolution in time of the falling object. We shall consider this approach to time and continuous processes in Chapter 7. This means that one can write Golog simulators of such dynamical systems. Moreover, with this extension to the situation calculus, the Golog programmer can now write controllers that allow a robot to react appropriately to such predictable (by the robot) exogenous events in its environment.

6.5   Proving Properties of Golog Programs

Anyone writing controllers for complex systems (chemical plants, airport traffic control systems, robots, etc.) should give some thought to providing formal evidence for the reliability of his implementation. Because of their foundations in the situation calculus, Golog programs are well-suited to logical proofs of program properties. Traditionally in computer science, there are two broad classes of properties that are addressed: *(partial) correctness*, and *termination*. As indicated in Section 6.1.4, the first refers to proving that if a program terminates, it does so in a situation satisfying some desirable property. The second requires a proof that the program indeed terminates. Not all interesting program properties fit into these two categories, mainly because not all programs are designed to terminate. Operating systems and robot control programs are two such examples, so the above notions of correctness and termination don't even make sense in such settings. (Moreover, the macro approach to defining Golog does not even permit nonterminating programs (why?); a different approach is needed.)

In this section, we provide a brief excursion into the topic of proving properties of Golog programs. Our purpose is not to develop a comprehensive theory; this topic is as yet largely unexplored, and in any case, would take us too far afield. Rather, we want only to indicate how one might go about developing a general story within the Golog framework, and how this might relate to the "traditional" computer science account. We shall focus only on proving correctness properties, and to keep the ideas simple, but not trivial, we consider programs with loops but not with procedures.

6.5.1 Induction Principle for While Loops

In "traditional" computer science proofs of program properties, the only interesting verification techniques involve induction, and this is typically invoked to prove properties of loops and recursion. It is in this setting that so-called *loop invariants* arise. In this section we explore how loop invariants and inductive proofs of program properties arise in the Golog setting.

Theorem 6.5.1: *The following is a valid second-order sentence:*

$$(\forall s, s').Do(\textbf{while } \phi \textbf{ do } \alpha \textbf{ endWhile}, s, s') \supset \neg\phi[s'].$$

Proof: Exercise 12 below. ∎

This informs us that *if* the **while** loop terminates, then the loop's test condition ϕ will be false in the terminating situation—no surprise here. Notice the important caveat "*if* the **while** loop terminates"; there is no guarantee that the loop will terminate. Therefore, proofs that appeal to results like this one are called *partial correctness* proofs, or simply *correctness* proofs. Proving termination is a separate problem.

Theorem 6.5.2: *The following induction principle for* **while** *loops is a valid second-order sentence:*

$$(\forall P, s).P(s) \wedge (\forall s', s'')[P(s') \wedge \phi[s'] \wedge Do(\alpha, s', s'') \supset P(s'')]$$
$$\supset (\forall s').Do(\textbf{while } \phi \textbf{ do } \alpha \textbf{ endWhile}, s, s') \supset P(s').$$

Proof: Exercise 13 below. ∎

This is the fundamental induction principle for loops. It says that if one ever wants to prove that some property P is true of a terminating situation s' for a **while** loop, it is sufficient to prove first that P holds in the loop's beginning situation s, and then prove that P is a *loop invariant*, namely, that P's truth value is preserved after every iteration of the loop. Notice again that this is a *correctness* property; it says that *if* the loop terminates, P will be true in a terminating situation. It does not help in establishing that the loop *will* terminate; that is a separate problem.

6.5.2   Example: A Blocks World

We illustrate a proof of a program property using the following blocks world:

Actions

- $move(x, y)$: Move block x onto block y, provided they are different, and both are clear.
- $moveToTable(x)$: Move block x onto the table, provided x is clear and is not on the table.

Fluents

- $clear(x, s)$: Block x has no other blocks on top of it, in situation s.
- $on(x, y, s)$: Block x is on (touching) block y, in situation s.
- $ontable(x, s)$: Block x is on the table, in situation s.

This setting can be axiomatized as follows:

Action Precondition Axioms

$$Poss(move(x, y), s) \equiv clear(x, s) \wedge clear(y, s) \wedge x \neq y,$$

$$Poss(moveToTable(x), s) \equiv clear(x, s) \wedge \neg ontable(x, s).$$

Successor State Axioms

$$clear(x, do(a, s)) \equiv$$
$$(\exists y)\{[(\exists z)a = move(y, z) \vee a = moveToTable(y)] \wedge on(y, x, s)\} \vee$$
$$clear(x, s) \wedge \neg(\exists y)a = move(y, x),$$

$$on(x, y, do(a, s)) \equiv a = move(x, y) \lor$$
$$on(x, y, s) \land a \neq moveToTable(x) \land \neg(\exists z)a = move(x, z),$$

$$ontable(x, do(a, s)) \equiv a = moveToTable(x) \lor$$
$$ontable(x, s) \land \neg(\exists y)a = move(x, y).$$

Unique Names Axioms for Actions

$$move(x, y) \neq moveToTable(z),$$

$$move(x, y) = move(x', y') \supset x = x' \land y = y',$$

$$moveToTable(x) = moveToTable(x') \supset x = x'.$$

Consider the following Golog program that nondeterministically moves blocks around, so long as there are at least two blocks on the table:

$$\gamma = \textbf{while } (\exists x, y)[ontable(x) \land ontable(y) \land x \neq y] \textbf{ do}$$
$$(\pi\, u)moveToTable(u) \mid (\pi\, u, v)move(u, v)$$
$$\textbf{endWhile}$$

We prove that whenever this program terminates, it does so with a unique block on the table, provided there was some block on the table to begin with:

$$(\forall s, s').Do(\gamma, s, s') \supset [(\exists x)ontable(x, s) \supset (\exists! y)ontable(y, s')].[5]$$

Proof:

To begin, $(\exists! y)ontable(y, s')$ abbreviates

$$(\exists y)ontable(y, s') \land (\forall u, v)[ontable(u, s') \land ontable(v, s') \supset u = v].$$

The second conjunct follows immediately from Theorem 6.5.1. It remains to establish

$$(\forall s, s').Do(\gamma, s, s') \supset [(\exists x)ontable(x, s) \supset (\exists y)ontable(y, s')].$$

We do this by induction, using Theorem 6.5.2, taking the induction hypothesis $P(s)$ to be $(\exists y)ontable(y, s)$. So, for this P, we must prove:

$$(\forall s, s').Do(\gamma, s, s') \supset [P(s) \supset P(s')].$$

By Theorem 6.5.2, we need only prove the induction step:

$$(\forall s', s'').\{P(s') \land (\exists x, y)[ontable(x, s') \land ontable(y, s') \land x \neq y]\land$$
$$Do((\pi\, u)moveToTable(u) \mid (\pi\, u, v)move(u, v), s', s'')\} \supset P(s''). \quad (6.2)$$

By the macro-expansion rules,

$$Do((\pi\, u)moveToTable(u) \mid (\pi\, u, v)move(u, v), s', s'')$$

---

[5] The notation $(\exists! y)\phi(y)$ means that there is a unique y such that $\phi(y)$. It is an abbreviation for the formula $(\exists y)\phi(y) \land (\forall u, v).\phi(u) \land \phi(v) \supset u = v$.

expands to:

$$(\exists u)Do(moveToTable(u), s', s'') \vee (\exists u, v)Do(move(u, v), s', s''),$$

which in turn expands to:

$$(\exists u)[Poss(moveToTable(u), s') \wedge s'' = do(moveToTable(u), s')] \vee$$
$$(\exists u, v)[Poss(move(u, v), s') \wedge s'' = do(move(u, v), s')].$$

This means that to establish (6.2), we must establish the following two sentences:

$$(\forall x, y, u, s', s'').[P(s') \wedge ontable(x, s') \wedge ontable(y, s') \wedge x \neq y \wedge$$
$$Poss(moveToTable(u), s') \wedge s'' = do(moveToTable(u), s')] \supset P(s''),$$

and

$$(\forall x, y, u, v, s', s'').[P(s') \wedge ontable(x, s') \wedge ontable(y, s') \wedge x \neq y \wedge$$
$$Poss(move(u, v), s') \wedge s'' = do(move(u, v), s')] \supset P(s'').$$

Replacing the second occurrences of P in these two sentences in accordance with the induction hypothesis that $P(s)$ is $(\exists z)ontable(z, s)$, and doing some simplification, yields:

$$(\forall x, y, u, s').[P(s') \wedge ontable(x, s') \wedge ontable(y, s') \wedge x \neq y \wedge$$
$$Poss(moveToTable(u), s')]$$
$$\supset (\exists z)ontable(z, do(moveToTable(u), s')),$$

and

$$(\forall x, y, u, v, s').[P(s') \wedge ontable(x, s') \wedge ontable(y, s') \wedge x \neq y \wedge$$
$$Poss(move(u, v), s')]$$
$$\supset (\exists z)ontable(z, do(move(u, v), s')).$$

The first sentence follows from *ontable*'s successor state axiom, and the second, by using the successor state axiom for *ontable* together with the unique names axioms for actions.

6.6 Summary

Golog is a logic programming language for implementing applications in dynamic domains like robotics, process control, intelligent software agents, database update transactions, discrete event simulation, etc. Its basis is a formal theory of actions specified in an extended version of the situation calculus.

Golog has a number of novel features, both as a programming language, and as an implementation tool for dynamic modeling.

1. Formally, a Golog program is a macro that expands during the evaluation of the program to a (usually second-order) sentence in the situation calculus. This sentence

mentions only the primitive, user-defined actions and fluents. The theorem-proving task in the evaluation of the program is to prove this sentence relative to a background axiomatization consisting of the foundational axioms of the situation calculus, the action precondition axioms for the primitive actions, the successor state axioms for the fluents, and the axioms describing the initial situation.

2. Golog programs are normally evaluated to obtain a binding for the existentially quantified situation variable in the top-level call

$$(\exists s) Do(program, S_0, s).$$

The binding so obtained by a successful proof is a symbolic trace of the program's execution, and denotes that sequence of actions that is to be performed in the external world. At this point, the entire Golog computation has been performed off-line. To effect an actual change in the world, this program trace must be passed to an execution module that knows how to physically perform the sequence of primitive actions in the trace.

3. Because a Golog program macro-expands to a situation calculus sentence, properties of this program (termination, correctness, etc.) can be proved directly within the situation calculus.

4. Unlike conventional programming languages, whose primitive instruction set is fixed in advance (assignments to variables, pointer-changing, etc.), and whose primitive function and predicate set is also predefined (values and types of program variables, etc.), Golog primitive actions and fluents are user-defined by action precondition and successor state axioms. In the simulation of dynamical systems, this facility allows the programmer to specify her primitives in accordance with the naturally occurring events in the world she is modeling. This, in turn, allows programs to be written at a very high level of abstraction, without concern for how the system's primitive architecture is actually implemented.

5. The Golog programmer can define complex action *schemas*—advice to a robot about how to achieve certain effects—*without specifying in detail how to perform these actions*. It becomes the theorem-prover's responsibility to figure out one or more detailed *executable* sequences of primitive actions that will achieve the desired effects.

   while $[(\exists \, block) ontable(block)]$ **do** $(\pi \, b) remove(b)$ **endWhile**

is such an action schema; it does not specify any particular sequence in which the blocks are to be removed. Similarly, the elevator program does not specify in which order the floors are to be served. On this view of describing complex behaviours, the Golog programmer specifies a skeleton plan; the evaluator uses deduction, in the context of a specific initial world situation, to fill in the details. Thus Golog allows

the programmer to strike a compromise between the often computationally unfeasible
classical planning task, in which a plan must be deduced entirely from scratch, and detailed programming, in which every little step must be specified. This is not to say that
Golog cannot represent classical planning problems. As an extreme case, the program

while ¬*Goal* **do** $(\pi\ a)[Appropriate(a)?\ ;\ a]$ **endWhile**

repeatedly selects an appropriate action and performs it until some goal is achieved.
Finding an executable sequence of actions in this case is simply a reformulation of the
planning problem. Chapter 10 treats the planning problem in more detail.

There are several limitations to the version of Golog that has been presented here. The
implementation only works correctly under the Prolog built-in closed world assumption
(Section 5.2.3). Adapting Golog to work with non-Prolog theories in the initial situation
requires using a general purpose theorem-prover for proving logical consequences of the
initial situation. Handling sensing actions requires the system's knowledge state to be
modeled explicitly (see Chapter 11) and complicates the representation and updating of
the world model. Exogenous events also affect the picture as the system may no longer
know what the actual history is. In many domains, it is also necessary to deal with sensor
noise and "control error".

6.7   Exercises

1. Implement some complex transactions for your earlier database example of Exercise
   5.4, question 1a (or a new one if you prefer), and try them out.

2. Axiomatize the following blocks world for a one-handed robot:

   Actions

   - $pickup(x)$: Pickup block x, provided it is clear, it is on the table and the robot's
     hand is empty.
   - $putDown(x)$: Put down x onto the table, provided the robot is holding x.
   - $stack(x, y)$: Put x onto y, provided the robot is holding x and y is clear.
   - $unstack(x, y)$: Pickup x from y, provided the robot's hand is empty, x is clear,
     and x is on y.

   Fluents

   - $clear(x, s)$: Block x has no other blocks on top of it, in situation s.
   - $on(x, y, s)$: Block x is on (touching) block y, in situation s.
   - $ontable(x, s)$: Block x is on the table, in situation s.

- *handempty(s)*: The robot's hand is empty, in situation s.

- *holding(x, s)*: The robot is holding block x, in situation s.

Next, implement, and test, the following Golog procedures:

(a) *flattenTower(b)*: Place all the blocks in the tower whose top block is b onto the table.

(b) *reverseTower(b)*: Create a tower consisting of the blocks of the tower whose top block is b, but with the blocks in reverse order.

(c) *appendTowers(b1, b2)*: Stack all the blocks in the tower whose top block is $b1$ onto the tower whose top block is $b2$. The resulting tower has as its top block the *bottom* block of the original tower with top block $b1$.

(d) Same as the previous procedure except that the resulting tower has $b1$ as its top block.

(e) *makeOneTower*: Create a single tower consisting of all the blocks.

3. **Shopping at the Supermarket.** Write a Golog program for a robot that shops at a supermarket for items on a shopping list (bread, oranges, beluga caviar, etc.). Initially, the robot is at home; then it drives to the supermarket, enters the store, picks up a shopping cart, and proceeds to shop. As it selects items from the list, it places them in its shopping cart, then it pushes the cart to the appropriate area of the supermarket to pick up the next item. Finally, it goes to the check-out counter to pay, carries the groceries to its car, and drives home. Be careful about axiomatizing the effects of pushing the shopping cart from one place to another; you must guarantee that everything in the cart moves with the cart. Similarly for carrying the groceries to the car, and for driving the car home. By running your program, verify that everything that was purchased actually ended up at the robot's home.

4. Use Golog to implement a simple agent program that helps a user manage her files. The primitive actions available to the agent include compressing a file and removing a file. The behaviours of the agent include:

- compressing files that haven't been accessed for a given period of time;

- removing unnecessary TeX/LaTeX files that haven't been accessed for a given period of time, i.e. files with the extensions .dvi, .log, .aux, .bbl, etc.

The agent maintains information about the user's files such as: what the files are, their names, content types, last access times, etc. Think of programming additional behaviours and the creative use of nondeterminism.

5. **The Towers of Hanoi Problem.** There are three pegs, A, B and C, and $n \geq 0$ discs of different sizes. Initially, all the discs are stacked on peg A, in order of decreasing size,

the largest disc on the bottom. The problem is to move the discs from peg A to peg B, one at a time, in such a way that no disc is ever placed on a smaller disc. Peg C may be used for temporary storage of discs. By suitably modifying the standard recursive solution found in virtually every programming textbook, write a Golog program to solve this problem. Use the action $move(p_1, p_2)$, meaning move the top disc on peg p_1 to peg p_2.

6. **The n-Queens Problem.** Given an $n \times n$ chess board, find a placement of n queens such that no two queens can attack each other. (In other words, no two queens are placed on the same row, column, or diagonal.) Write a nondeterministic Golog program to solve this problem. Use the single action $place(row, column)$, meaning place a queen on the square specified by $(row, column)$, and a fluent $occupied(row, column, s)$, meaning that $(row, column)$ is occupied by a queen in situation s. Implement your specification.

7. **Getting Out of a Maze.** Consider a rectangular array of cells, some of which are occupied by obstacles. In addition, there are two distinguished cells: *start* and *end*. The problem is to find a path through this maze from *start* to *end*, by successively visiting adjacent, non-diagonal cells, without revisiting any cells.

    (a) Axiomatize this setting in the situation calculus. Use the following actions, predicates and fluents:
    - $move(x, y)$: The only action of this domain, meaning move to the adjacent cell (x, y) immediately north, south, east or west of the one you are in (no diagonal moves), provided (x, y) lies within the maze, it is not occupied, and it hasn't been visited before.
    - $inRange(x, y)$: The cell (x, y) lies within the rectangular maze.
    - $occupied(x, y)$: The cell (x, y) is occupied by an obstacle.
    - $adjacent(x, y, x', y')$: Cell (x, y) is non-diagonally adjacent to cell (x', y').
    - $visited(x, y, s)$: In situation s, the cell (x, y) has already been visited.
    - $position(s)$: A functional fluent whose value in situation s is the cell occupied by the maze-traverser.

    (b) Write a nondeterministic Golog program to traverse a maze.

    (c) Implement the above axioms and program, and try it out.

    (d) Improve on this program by giving it the heuristic of always moving to a cell that is closest to the *end*, whenever that is possible.

8. (a) Use Golog to implement a procedure $max(array, top, index)$ that binds $index$ to an index in the linear $array$ containing the maximum element of the array in the range [1..top]. First do this recursively.

(b) Now do this nondeterministically, without recursion.

To clarify what is wanted in problems (a) and (b), here is an example of a run of a nondeterministic *max* program, when given the seven element array:

```
val(a,[1],3,s0).
val(a,[2],5,s0).
val(a,[3],2,s0).
val(a,[4],1,s0).
val(a,[5],7,s0).
val(a,[6],7,s0).
val(a,[7],6,s0).

[eclipse 2]: do(maxnondet(a,7,Index),s0,S).

Index = 5
S = s0    More? (;)

Index = 6
S = s0    More? (;)

no (more) solution.
```

9. Using both versions of *max* from the previous problem, implement two Golog programs for sorting a linear array. This requires the ability to do assignments. Of course, Golog does not actually *do* assignments, so you will have to fake it with a primitive action $assign(value, identifier)$. Actually, to fake assignments to arrays as well as scalars, you will probably want something like $assign(value, identifier, idx)$, so that $assign(3, X, [\ ])$ assigns 3 to the scalar identifier X, and $assign(3, A, [5, 6])$ assigns 3 to the [5,6]-th element of the (binary) array A. Moreover, in order to recover the values of identifiers and arrays, you will probably want a functional fluent $val(identifier, idx, s)$, or in the Prolog implementation, $val(identifier, idx, v, s)$.

To clarify what this problem seeks, here is an example of a run of a sort program, when given the above seven element array:

```
[eclipse 2]: do(sort(a,7),s0,S).

S = do(assign(2,a,[2]),do(assign(1,a,[1]),do(assign(3,a,[3]),
    do(assign(2,a,[1]),do(assign(5,a,[4]),do(assign(1,a,[2]),
    do(assign(6,a,[5]),do(assign(6,a,[5]),do(assign(7,a,[6]),
    do(assign(6,a,[5]),do(assign(7,a,[7]),do(assign(6,a,[6]),
    s0)))))))))))))

yes
```

10. (a) Using Do, define a macro for a new program constructor, called $constrain(a, p)$, meaning perform complex action a subject to condition p. Here p is a predicate taking a pair of situation arguments, and the idea is that p specifies some relationship that must hold between the situation in which a is performed, and the resulting situation after a is performed. Use the first part of the macro definition for procedures (Section 6.1), namely that part dealing with predicate symbols taking pairs of situation arguments.

Examples:

- Go to a room other than the one you are in with the same colour as the one you are in: $(\pi\, r)constrain(go(r), sameColour)$.

$$sameColour(s, s') \equiv (\exists r, r', c).inRoom(r, s) \wedge inRoom(r', s')$$
$$\wedge\, r \neq r' \wedge colour(r, c, s) \wedge colour(r', c, s').$$

- Go to the kitchen, making sure you pass through the dining room en route: $constrain(go(Kitchen), passThrough(DiningRoom))$.

$$passThrough(r, s, s') \equiv (\exists s'').s \sqsubseteq s'' \sqsubseteq s' \wedge inRoom(r, s'').$$

(b) Modify the Golog interpreter to include this new constructor.

(c) Write a small Golog program that uses this constructor in an interesting way, and test it out on your modified Golog interpreter.

11. Keeping in mind that Do is a macro that expands to a second-order situation calculus formula, prove that the following sentence is valid, where δ is any fixed Golog complex action:

$$Do(\delta^*, s, s') \equiv s = s' \vee Do(\delta\,;\,\delta^*, s, s'). \tag{6.3}$$

Hint: For the $\Leftarrow$ direction, first prove $(\forall s)Do(\delta^*, s, s)$. Then expand $Do(\delta\,;\,\delta^*, s, s')$ using the macros for ; and δ^*, where the latter expands into an expression universally quantified over P. Next expand $Do(\delta^*, s, s')$ of the left-hand side into an expression universally quantified over Q. Finally, take $P = Q$, and do a little more work. For the $\Rightarrow$ direction, expand the left-hand side into an expression universally quantified over P, take $P(s, s')$ to be $s = s' \vee Do(\delta\,;\,\delta^*, s, s')$, and make use of the $\Leftarrow$ direction, which you have already proved.

This means that a *sound* Golog interpreter can be designed for nondeterministic iteration (and hence for **while** loops) using this result, and *this interpreter will not require a theorem-prover for second-order logic.* Basically, this interpreter, in proving $Do(\delta^*, s, s')$ succeeds with $s = s'$, or it tries to prove $Do(\delta\,;\,\delta^*, s, s')$. This last attempted proof will succeed if the theorem-prover succeeds on $Do(\delta, s, s')$, or if it succeeds on $Do(\delta^2\,;\,\delta^*, s, s')$, etc. In other words, the proof of $Do(\delta^*, s, s')$ will succeed if it succeeds on $Do(\delta^n, s, s')$ for some n. This is exactly the theorem-proving mechanism for nondeterministic iteration used in the Prolog implementation of Golog, and in fact, the validity of (6.3) is the formal justification for the soundness of this clause of the interpreter. Notice that this interpreter clause is the if-half of (6.3).

12. Prove Theorem 6.5.1.

13. This exercise will lead you to a proof of Theorem 6.5.2.

   (a) First, prove that the definition of nondeterministic iteration entails the following induction principle:

$$(\forall P, s).P(s) \wedge (\forall s', s'')[P(s') \wedge Do(a, s', s'') \supset P(s'')]$$
$$\supset (\forall s').Do(a^*, s, s') \supset P(s').$$

   Hint: Replace the occurrence of $Do(a^*, s, s')$ by its definition:

$$(\forall Q).(\forall s)Q(s, s) \wedge (\forall s_1, s_2, s_3)[Q(s_1, s_2) \wedge Do(a, s_2, s_3) \supset Q(s_1, s_3)]$$
$$\supset Q(\sigma, \sigma').$$

   Next, choose a suitable instance for the predicate variable Q, namely,

$$Q(s, s') = P(s) \supset P(s').$$

   (b) Using the previous result, prove Theorem 6.5.2. Hint: Take a to be $\phi?; \alpha$.

14. For the blocks world of Section 6.5.2, invent a Golog while loop, and prove some correctness property of it.

6.8 Bibliographic Remarks

Much of the material for this chapter derives from the Golog overview paper by Levesque, Reiter, Lespérance, Lin, and Scherl [120].

As remarked above, the macro approach to defining Golog's semantics precludes classical deductive techniques for program synthesis in Golog. Manna and Waldinger [132] clearly describe the theorem-proving approach to program synthesis.

Except for procedures, the semantics of Golog via macro-expansion draws considerably from dynamic logic (Goldblatt [70]; Harel, Kozen, and Tiuryn [82]). In effect, it reifies as situations in the object language of the situation calculus, the possible worlds with which the semantics of dynamic logic is defined. The macro definition for Golog procedures corresponds to the more usual Scott-Strachey *least fixed-point* definition in standard programming language semantics (Stoy [207]).

The Golog interpreter and the entire Golog framework has been the subject of experimentation with various applications at the University of Toronto. The most advanced is a robotics application—mail delivery in an office environment (Lespérance, Levesque, Lin,

Marcu, Reiter, and Scherl [107]). The high-level controller of the robot programmed in Golog is interfaced to an existing robotics package that supports path planning and local navigation. The system is currently used to control two different autonomous robots: an RWI B21 and a Nomad200 ([93]). Another application involves tools for home banking (Ruman [183]; Lespérance, Levesque, and Ruman [110]). In this case, a number of software agents written in Golog handle various parts of the banking process (responding to buttons on an ATM terminal, managing the accounts at a bank, monitoring account levels for a user, etc.).

ConGolog (De Giacomo, Lespérance, and Levesque [64]), a version of the language supporting concurrency (including interrupts, priorities, and support for exogenous actions) has also being implemented, and experiments with various applications have been performed, e.g., multi-elevator co-ordination, meeting scheduling (Shapiro, Lespérance, and Levesque [197]).

In process control and robotics applications it is necessary to take seriously the possibility of control error and sensor noise. For a situation calculus approach to these issues, see (Bacchus, Halpern, and Levesque [8]).

Dixon's Amala [39] is a programming language in a conventional imperative style. It is designed after the observation that the semantics of embedded programs should reflect the assumptions about the environment as directly as possible. This is similar to our concern that language primitives should be user-defined, at a high level of abstraction. However, while Golog requires that these primitives be formally specified within the language, Amala does not. One consequence of this is that programs in Golog can be executed by a theorem-prover, but not those in Amala.

Like the classical AI planning work (Section 3.3) of Green [71] and Fikes and Nilsson [49], Golog requires primitives and their effects to be formally specified. The major difference is that Golog focuses on high-level programming rather than plan synthesis at run-time. But sketchy plans are allowed; nondeterminism can be used to infer the missing details. In our elevator example, it was left to the Golog interpreter to find an executable sequence of actions to serve all active call buttons.

Situated automata (Rosenschein and Kaelbling [182]) share with Golog the same objective of designing agents using a high level language, and then compiling these high-level programs into low-level ones that can be immediately executed. In the framework considered here, the low-level programs are simply sequences of primitive actions.

Shoham's *AGENT-0 programming language* [200] includes a model of commitments and capabilities, and has simple communication acts built-in; its agents all have a generic rule-based architecture; there is also a global clock and all beliefs are about time-stamped propositions. However, there is no automatic maintenance of the agents beliefs based on a specification of primitive actions as in Golog and only a few types of complex actions are handled; there also seems to be less emphasis on having a complete formal specification of the system. A number of other groups are also developing formalisms for the specification of artificial agents. See Wooldridge and Jennings [218] for a detailed survey of this research.

Transaction logic (Bonner and Kifer [22]) was designed to define complex database transactions, and like Golog, provides a rich repertoire of operators for defining new transactions in terms of old. These include sequence, nondeterministic choice, conditionals and iteration. The Bonner-Kifer approach focuses on the definition of complex transactions in terms of *elementary* updates. On the assumption that these elementary updates successfully address the frame problem, any complex update defined in terms of these elementary ones will inherit a correct solution to the frame problem. Bonner and Kifer do not address the frame problem for these elementary updates; this task is left to the database designer.

The *strategies* of McCarthy and Hayes [141] were a surprisingly early proposal for representing complex actions in the situation calculus. McCarthy and Hayes even appeal to an Algol-like language for representing their strategies, and they include a mechanism for returning symbolic execution traces, as sequences of actions, of these strategies. Moreover, they sketch a method for proving properties of strategies. While McCarthy and Hayes provide no formal development of their proposal, it nevertheless anticipates much of the spirit and technical content of the Golog project.

The literature on program verification in computer science is enormous. Our approach to this in Section 6.5 is actually quite close to Hoare-style proof systems (Hoare [87]; Apt and Olderog [5]), but we have sentences, like that for while loops in Theorem 6.5.1, instead of rules of inference. Liu [128] provides a thorough account of embedding Hoare proof systems into the Golog framework. Shapiro [196] studies proofs of ConGolog program properties. For a different logical foundation for programming language semantics and verification, see Hehner [83].

Given the idea of a logic-based programming language for robot control, it is interesting to ask about its expressivity; can every conceivable control task be expressed in the language? This is the question addressed by Lin and Levesque [123], where a much simpler situation calculus-based programming language than Golog is introduced, and proved to be universal in a suitably defined sense.

7 Time, Concurrency, and Processes

So far, we have ignored three fundamental properties of real actions—they occur in time, they normally have durations, and frequently they occur together, i.e., concurrently. The situation calculus, as presented to this point, provides no way of representing these features of actions. Indeed, insofar as actions are currently represented in the situation calculus, they occur sequentially, and atemporally. This chapter is devoted to expanding the situation calculus ontology and axiomatization to accommodate a more realistic picture of action occurrences.

7.1 Concurrency and Instantaneous Actions

Modeling the possibility of concurrent action execution leads to many difficult formal and conceptual problems. For example, what can one mean by a concurrent action like $\{walk(A, B), chewGum\}$? Intuitively, both actions have durations. By this concurrent action, is it meant that both actions have the same duration? That the time segment occupied by one is entirely contained in that occupied by the other? That their time segments merely overlap? What if there are three actions and the first overlaps the second, the second overlaps the third, but the first and third do not overlap; do they all occur concurrently? A representational device in the situation calculus for overcoming these problems is to conceive of such actions as *processes*, represented by relational fluents, and to introduce durationless (instantaneous) actions that initiate and terminate these processes. For example, instead of the monolithic action representation $walk(x, y)$, we might have instantaneous actions $startWalk(x, y)$ and $endWalk(x, y)$, and the process of walking from x to y, represented by the relational fluent $walking(x, y, s)$. $startWalk(x, y)$ causes the fluent $walking$ to become true, $endWalk(x, y)$ causes it to become false. Similarly, we might represent the $chewGum$ action by the pair of instantaneous actions $startChewGum$ and $endChewGum$, and the relational fluent $chewingGum(s)$. It is straightforward to represent these fluents and instantaneous actions in the situation calculus. For example, here are the action precondition and successor state axioms for the walking action:

$$Poss(startWalk(x, y), s) \equiv \neg(\exists u, v)walking(u, v, s) \wedge location(s) = x,$$

$$Poss(endWalk(x, y), s) \equiv walking(x, y, s),$$

$$walking(x, y, do(a, s)) \equiv a = startWalk(x, y) \vee$$
$$walking(x, y, s) \wedge a \neq endWalk(x, y),$$

$$location(do(a, s)) = y \equiv (\exists x)a = endWalk(x, y) \vee$$
$$location(s) = y \wedge \neg(\exists x, y')a = endWalk(x, y').$$

With this device of instantaneous *start* and *end* actions in hand, arbitrarily complex concurrency can be represented. For example,

$\{startWalk(A, B), startChewGum\}, \{endChewGum, startSing\},$
$\{endWalk(A, B)\}$

is the sequence of actions beginning with simultaneously starting to walk and starting to chew, followed by simultaneously ending to chew and starting to sing, followed by ending the walk (at which time the singing process is still going on).

7.2   Concurrency via Interleaving

Before focusing on true concurrency, in which two or more actions start and end at exactly the same times, we consider what other forms of concurrency can be realized in the situation calculus as developed thus far. As we shall see, a surprisingly rich theory of *interleaved concurrency* can be expressed within the sequential situation calculus, provided we appeal to instantaneous *start* and *end* actions, as in the previous section. In computer science, concurrency is most often modeled via *interleaving*. Conceptually, two actions are interleaved when one of them is the next action to occur after the other, and usually an interleaving account of such a concurrent occurrence is considered appropriate if the outcome is independent of the order in which the actions are interleaved.

We can provide interleaved concurrent representations for walking and chewing gum, such as

$do([startWalk(A, B), startChewGum, endChewGum, endWalk(A, B)], S_0),$

in which the gum-chewing process is initiated after the walking process, and terminated before the end of the walking process. Or, the gum-chewing can start before the walking, and terminate before the walking ends:

$do([startChewGum, startWalk(A, B), endChewGum, endWalk(A, B)], S_0).$

In other words, we can represent any overlapping occurrences of walking and chewing gum, *except for exact co-occurrences of any of the instantaneous initiating and terminating actions*. For many applications, this is sufficient. The great advantage is that interleaved concurrency can be represented in the sequential situation calculus, and no new extensions of the theory are necessary.

It is important to have a clear picture of exactly what, conceptually, is being modeled by interleaved concurrency with instantaneous actions like $startWalk(x, y)$ and *endChew-Gum*. Since as yet, we have no explicit representation for time, the situation calculus axioms capture a purely qualitative notion of time. Sequential action occurrence is the only temporal concept captured by the axioms; an action occurs *before* or *after* another. It may occur one millisecond or one year before its successor; the axioms are neutral on this question. So a situation $do([A_1, A_2, \ldots, A_n], S_0)$ must be understood as a world history in which, after a nondeterministic period of time, A_1 occurs, then, after a nondeterministic period of time, A_2 occurs, etc. If, for example, this action sequence was the result of a Golog robot program execution, then the robot's action execution system would make the decision about the exact times at which these actions would be performed sequentially in the physical world, but the axioms, being neutral on action occurrence times, contribute nothing to this decision. Later, we shall show how to incorporate time into the situation calculus, after which one can axiomatically specify the times at which actions are to occur.

7.2.1 Examples of Interleaved Concurrency

Imagine a door with a spring handle. The door can be unlocked by turning the handle, but the agent must hold the handle down, for if not, the spring loaded mechanism returns the handle to its locked position. To open the door, an agent must turn the handle, and hold it down while she pushes on the door. The concurrent handle turning and door pushing causes the door to open. Neither action by itself will open the door. This is easy to do in the situation calculus if we view the action of turning and holding the handle down, which intuitively has a duration, as a composite of two instantaneous actions, $turnHandle$ and $releaseHandle$, whose effects are to make the fluent $locked(s)$ false and true respectively. In the same spirit, we treat the action of pushing on a door, which also intuitively has a duration, as a composite of two instantaneous actions $startPush$ and $endPush$, whose effects are to make the fluent $pushing(s)$ true and false respectively. The appropriate successor state axiom for $open$ is:

$$open(do(a, s)) \equiv pushing(s) \wedge a = turnHandle \vee$$
$$\neg locked(s) \wedge a = startPush \vee open(s).$$

Those for $pushing$ and $locked$ are:

$$pushing(do(a, s)) \equiv a = startPush \vee pushing(s) \wedge a \neq endPush,$$

$$locked(do(a, s)) \equiv a = releaseHandle \vee locked(s) \wedge a \neq turnHandle.$$

Another interesting example is the following. Turning on the hot water faucet causes hot water to run (denoted by the fluent $hot(s)$); similarly for turning on the cold. Both the hot and cold water faucets share a common spout, so if only the hot water is running, you will burn your hand.

$$Poss(turnonHot, s) \equiv \neg hot(s),$$

$$Poss(turnonCold, s) \equiv \neg cold(s),$$

$$Poss(turnoffHot, s) \equiv hot(s),$$

$$Poss(turnoffCold, s) \equiv cold(s),$$

$$hot(do(a, s)) \equiv a = turnonHot \lor hot(s) \land a \neq turnoffHot,$$

$$cold(do(a, s)) \equiv a = turnonCold \lor cold(s) \land a \neq turnoffCold.$$

The following successor state axiom captures the conditions for burning oneself:

$$burn(do(a, s)) \equiv hot(s) \land a = turnoffCold \lor \neg cold(s) \land a = turnonHot \lor burn(s).$$

7.2.2 Limitations of Interleaved Concurrency

Despite the wide applicability of interleaved concurrency with instantaneous actions, there are examples for which true concurrency appears to be more appropriate and convenient. The standard example that seems not to be representable by an interleaving account—but see Exercise 4 below—is the scenario of a duel, in which an instantaneous shoot action by one duelist causes the death of the other. Being alive is a precondition for shooting. If both duelists shoot simultaneously, both die, whereas, in the absence of true concurrency, only one death can result from a duel. A more interesting setting where true concurrency seems appropriate is in the modeling of physical systems, such as a number of objects tracing out trajectories under Newtonian equations of motion. These equations may predict the simultaneous collisions of several objects, and an interleaving axiomatization for predicting and simulating these occurrences is clumsy and unnatural. Section 7.9 below shows how to axiomatize such physical systems using true concurrency.

7.3 The Sequential, Temporal Situation Calculus

In this section, we add an explicit representation for time to the sequential situation calculus. This will allow us to specify the exact times, or a range of times, at which actions in a world history must occur. For simplicity, and because we remain interested in interleaved concurrency, we continue to consider instantaneous actions. We want to represent the fact that a given such action occurs at a particular time. Recall that in the situation calculus, actions are denoted by first-order terms, like $startMeeting(Susan)$ or $bounce(ball, wall)$. Our proposal for adding a time dimension to the situation calculus is to add a new temporal argument to all instantaneous actions, denoting the actual time at which that action occurs. Thus, $startMeeting(Susan, t)$ might be the instantaneous action of $Susan$ starting a meeting at time t, and $bounce(ball, wall, 7.3)$ might be the instantaneous action of $ball$ bouncing against $wall$ at time 7.3.

We now investigate how to extend the foundational axioms for the sequential situation calculus (Section 4.2.2) to accommodate time. These four foundational axioms remain exactly the same as before; it will be necessary only to add one new axiom to them, and to introduce two new function symbols into $\mathcal{L}_{sitcalc}$.

First, introduce a new function symbol $time : action \rightarrow reals$. $time(a)$ denotes the time of occurrence of action a. This means that in any application involving a particular action $A(\vec{x}, t)$, we shall need an axiom specifying the occurrence time of the action A:

$$time(A(\vec{x}, t)) = t,$$

for example, $time(startMeeting(person, t)) = t$. Next, it will be convenient to have a new function symbol $start : situation \rightarrow reals$. $start(s)$ denotes the start time of situation s. This requires the new foundational axiom:

$$start(do(a, s)) = time(a). \tag{7.1}$$

Notice that we do not define the start time of S_0; this is arbitrary, and may (or may not) be specified to be any real number, depending on the application. Notice also that we are imagining temporal variables to range over the reals, although nothing prevents them from ranging over the integers, rationals, or anything else on which a binary relation $<$ is defined. In this connection, we are not providing axioms for the reals (or integers), but rely instead on the standard interpretation of the reals and their operations (addition, multiplication, etc.) and relations ($<$, $\leq$, etc.).

Next, we need to reconsider the relation $executable(s)$ on situations. Recall that this was defined to be an abbreviation for a formula that intuitively says that all the actions occurring in the action sequence s can be executed one after the other. Consider the situation

$$do(bounce(B, W, 4), do(startMeeting(Susan, 6), S_0)),$$

in which the time of the second action precedes that of the first. Intuitively, such an action sequence should not be considered possible, and we suitably amend the abbreviation $executable(s)$ of (4.5):

$$executable(s) \stackrel{def}{=} (\forall a, s^*).do(a, s^*) \sqsubseteq s \supset \\ Poss(a, s^*) \wedge start(s^*) \leq time(a). \tag{7.2}$$

Now, $executable(s)$ means that all the actions in s are possible, and moreover, the times of those action occurrences are nondecreasing.

Finally, notice that the constraint $start(s^*) \leq time(a)$ in abbreviation (7.2) permits action sequences in which the time of an action may be the same as the time of a preceding action. For example,

$$do(endLunch(Bill, 4), do(startMeeting(Susan, 4), S_0)),$$

might be a perfectly good executable situation. This situation is defined by a sequence of two actions, each of which has the same occurrence time. We allow for this possibility because often an action occurrence serves as an enabling condition for the simultaneous occurrence of another action. For example, cutting a weighted string at time t enables the action $startFalling(t)$. Both actions occur at the same time, but conceptually, the falling event happens "immediately after" the cutting. Accordingly, we want to allow the situation $do(startFalling(t), do(cutString(t), S_0))$.

The four axioms of Σ, namely the old foundational axioms for the situation calculus, together with (7.1) are the foundational axioms for the *sequential, temporal situation calculus*.

7.3.1   Concurrent Temporal Processes

With the capacity to explicitly represent time, we can now give an interleaving account for processes that overlap temporally in arbitrarily complex ways. Figure 7.1 illustrates a possible time line for instances of three overlapping processes, $walking(x, y, s)$, $singing(s)$, and $chewingGum(s)$.

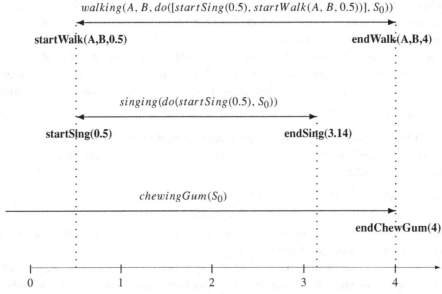

Figure 7.1: Temporal Processes in the Situation Calculus.

The indicated instances of the *singing* and *walking* processes begin together (but the first initiates "before" the second), and they terminate at different times. The instance of the *chewingGum* process was in progress initially (and therefore does not have an initiating action) and it terminates at the same time as the *walking* process.

7.4   Sequential, Temporal Golog

With the above axioms and abbreviations for the sequential, temporal situation calculus in hand, it is easy to modify the Golog semantics and interpreter to accommodate time. Semantically, we need only change the definition of the *Do* macro for primitive actions (Section 6.1) to:

$$Do(a, s, s') \stackrel{def}{=} Poss(a[s], s) \wedge start(s) \leq time(a[s]) \wedge s' = do(a[s], s). \qquad (7.3)$$

Everything else about the definition of *Do* remains the same. To suitably modify the Golog interpreter of Section 6.3.1, replace the clause

```
do(E,S,do(E,S)) :- primitive_action(E), poss(E,S).
```

by

```
do(E,S,do(E,S)) :- primitive_action(E), poss(E,S),
                   start(S,T1), time(E,T2), T1 =< T2.
```

Finally, because of the new predicate, *start*, taking a situation argument, the earlier Golog interpreter must be augmented by the clauses:

```
restoreSitArg(start(T),S,start(S,T)).
start(do(A,S),T) :- time(A,T).
```

We can now write sequential, temporal Golog programs. However, to execute such programs, the Golog interpreter must have a temporal reasoning component. It must, for example, be able to infer that $T_1 = T_2$ when given that $T_1 \leq T_2 \wedge T_2 \leq T_1$. While such a special purpose temporal theorem-prover could be written and included in the Golog interpreter, this would involve a great deal of effort. To illustrate the use of temporal Golog, we shall instead rely on a logic programming language with a built-in constraint solving capability.   Specifically, we shall appeal to the ECRC Common Logic Programming System ECLIPSE 3.5.2, which provides a built-in Simplex algorithm for solving linear equations and inequalities over the reals. So we shall assume that our Golog program makes use of linear temporal relations like $2 * T_1 + T_2 = 5$ and $3 * T_2 - 5 \leq 2 * T_3$, and rely on ECLIPSE to perform the reasoning for us in the temporal domain. ECLIPSE provides a special syntax for those relations over the reals recognized by its built-in theorem-prover. These relations are: $=, \neq, \geq, >, \leq, <$, which are represented in ECLIPSE by the infix

$=, \$ <>, \$ >=, \$ >, \$ <=, \$ <$, respectively. So, in ECLIPSE, the above modification
of the Golog interpreter to include time is:

```
do(E,S,do(E,S)) :- primitive_action(E), poss(E,S),
                   start(S,T1), time(E,T2), T1 $<= T2.
```

All other clauses of the earlier interpreter of Section 6.3.1 will work correctly under
ECLIPSE.

7.4.1 Example: A Coffee Delivery Robot

Here, we describe a robot whose task is to deliver coffee in an office environment. The
robot is given a schedule of the preferred coffee periods of every employee, as well as
information about the times it takes to travel between various locations in the office environment. The robot can carry just one cup of coffee at a time, and there is a central coffee
machine from which it gets coffee. The robot's task is to schedule coffee deliveries in such
a way that, if possible, everyone gets coffee during his/her preferred time periods.

Primitive actions:

- $pickupCoffee(t)$. The robot picks up a cup of coffee from the coffee machine at time
  t.
- $giveCoffee(person, t)$. The robot gives a cup of coffee to $person$ at time t.
- $startGo(loc_1, loc_2, t)$. The robot starts to go from location loc_1 to loc_2 at time t.
- $endGo(loc_1, loc_2, t)$. The robot ends its process of going from location loc_1 to loc_2 at
  time t.

Fluents:

- $robotLocation(s)$. A functional fluent denoting the robot's location in situation s.
- $hasCoffee(person, s)$. $person$ has a cup of coffee in situation s.
- $going(loc_1, loc_2, s)$. In situation s, the robot is going from loc_1 to loc_2.
- $holdingCoffee(s)$. In situation s, the robot is holding a cup of coffee.

Situation-Independent Predicates and Functions:

- $wantsCoffee(person, t_1, t_2)$. $person$ wants to receive coffee at some point in the
  time period $[t_1, t_2]$.
- $office(person)$. Denotes the office inhabited by $person$.
- $travelTime(loc_1, loc_2)$. Denotes the amount of time that the robot takes to travel
  between loc_1 and loc_2.
- CM. A constant denoting the location of the coffee machine.
- $Sue, Mary, Bill, Joe$. Constants denoting office people.

Primitive Action Preconditions:

$$Poss(pickupCoffee(t), s) \equiv \neg holdingCoffee(s) \land robotLocation(s) = CM,$$

$$Poss(giveCoffee(person, t), s) \equiv holdingCoffee(s) \land$$
$$robotLocation(s) = office(person),$$

$$Poss(startGo(loc_1, loc_2, t), s) \equiv \neg(\exists l, l')going(l, l', s) \land loc_1 \neq loc_2 \land$$
$$robotLocation(s) = loc_1,$$

$$Poss(endGo(loc_1, loc_2, t), s) \equiv going(loc_1, loc_2, s).$$

Successor State Axioms:

$$hasCoffee(person, do(a, s)) \equiv (\exists t)a = giveCoffee(person, t) \lor$$
$$hasCoffee(person, s),$$

$$robotLocation(do(a, s)) = loc \equiv (\exists t, loc')a = endGo(loc', loc, t) \lor$$
$$robotLocation(s) = loc \land \neg(\exists t, loc', loc'')a = endGo(loc', loc'', t),$$

$$going(l, l', do(a, s)) \equiv (\exists t)a = startGo(l, l', t) \lor$$
$$going(l, l', s) \land \neg(\exists t)a = endGo(l, l', t),$$

$$holdingCoffee(do(a, s)) \equiv (\exists t)a = pickupCoffee(t) \lor$$
$$holdingCoffee(s) \land \neg(\exists person, t)a = giveCoffee(person, t).$$

Initial Situation:

Unique names axioms stating that the following terms are pairwise unequal:

$$Sue, \ Mary, \ Bill, \ Joe, \ CM,$$
$$office(Sue), \ office(Mary), \ office(Bill), \ office(Joe).$$

Initial Fluent values:

$$robotLocation(S_0) = CM, \quad \neg(\exists l, l')going(l, l', S_0),$$
$$\neg holdingCoffee(S_0), \quad start(S_0) = 0, \quad \neg(\exists p)hasCoffee(p, S_0).$$

Coffee delivery preferences. The following expresses the fact that all, and only, the tuples satisfying the *wantsCoffee* relation are $(Sue, 140, 160), \ldots, (Joe, 90, 100)$. In other words, this relation is definitional.

$$wantsCoffee(p, t_1, t_2) \equiv$$
$$p = Sue \land t_1 = 140 \land t_2 = 160 \lor p = Mary \land t_1 = 130 \land t_2 = 170 \lor$$
$$p = Bill \land t_1 = 100 \land t_2 = 110 \lor p = Joe \land t_1 = 90 \land t_2 = 100.$$

Robot travel times:

$$travelTime(CM, office(Sue)) = 15, \quad travelTime(CM, office(Mary)) = 10,$$

$travelTime(CM, office(Bill)) = 8,$ $travelTime(CM, office(Joe)) = 10.$
$travelTime(l, l') = travelTime(l', l),$ $travelTime(l, l) = 0.$

Action Occurrence Times:

$time(pickupCoffee(t)) = t,$ $time(giveCoffee(person, t)) = t,$
$time(startGo(loc_1, loc_2, t)) = t,$ $time(endGo(loc_1, loc_2, t)) = t.$

Golog Procedures:

proc $deliverCoffee(t)$ % Beginning at time t the robot serves coffee to everyone,
                              % if possible. Else the program fails.

   $now \leq t?$;
   $\{[(\forall p, t', t'').wantsCoffee(p, t', t'') \supset hasCoffee(p)]?$
      |
      if $robotLocation = CM$ **then** $deliverOneCoffee(t)$
         else $goto(CM, t)$; $deliverOneCoffee(now)$
      endIf\} ;
   $deliverCoffee(now)$
endProc

The above procedure introduces a functional fluent $now(s)$, which is exactly the same as the fluent $start(s)$. We prefer it here to $start$ because it has a certain mnemonic value, but like $start$, it denotes the *current time*.

proc $deliverOneCoffee(t)$ % Assuming the robot is at the coffee machine,
                                 % it delivers one cup of coffee.
   $(\pi p, t_1, t_2, wait)[\{wantsCoffee(p, t_1, t_2) \wedge \neg hasCoffee(p) \wedge wait \geq 0 \wedge$
               $t_1 \leq t + wait + travelTime(CM, office(p)) \leq t_2\}?$;
            $pickupCoffee(t + wait)$;
            $goto(office(p), now)$;
            $giveCoffee(p, now)$
endProc

proc $goto(loc, t)$ % Beginning at time t the robot goes to loc.
   $goBetween(robotLocation, loc, travelTime(robotLocation, loc), t)$
endProc

proc $goBetween(loc_1, loc_2, \Delta, t)$ % Beginning at time t the robot goes from loc_1
                                  % to loc_2, taking Δ time units for the transition.
   $startGo(loc_1, loc_2, t)$; $endGo(loc_1, loc_2, t + \Delta)$
endProc

The following sequential, temporal Golog program implements the above specification.

Sequential, Temporal Golog Program for a Coffee Delivery Robot

```
% Golog Procedures.

proc(deliverCoffee(T),
  ?(some(t, now(t) & t $<= T)) :
  (?(all(p,all(t1,all(t2,wantsCoffee(p,t1,t2) => hasCoffee(p)))))
   #
   pi(rloc, ?(robotLocation(rloc)) :
            if(rloc = cm, /* THEN */ deliverOneCoffee(T),
            /* ELSE */ goto(cm,T) : pi(t, ?(now(t)) :
                                          deliverOneCoffee(t))) :
            pi(t, ?(now(t)) : deliverCoffee(t))))).

proc(deliverOneCoffee(T),
  pi(p, pi(t1, pi(t2, pi(wait, pi(travTime,
    ?(wantsCoffee(p,t1,t2) & -hasCoffee(p) & wait $>= 0 &
      travelTime(cm,office(p),travTime) &
      t1 $<= T + wait + travTime & T + wait + travTime $<= t2) :
    pi(t, ?(t $= T + wait) : pickupCoffee(t)) :
    pi(t, ?(now(t)) : goto(office(p),t)) :
    pi(t, ?(now(t)) : giveCoffee(p,t)))))))).

proc(goto(L,T),
  pi(rloc,?(robotLocation(rloc)) :
    pi(deltat,?(travelTime(rloc,L,deltat)) :
      goBetween(rloc,L,deltat,T)))).

proc(goBetween(Loc1,Loc2,Delta,T),
    startGo(Loc1,Loc2,T) :
  pi(t, ?(t $= T + Delta) : endGo(Loc1,Loc2,t))).

% Preconditions for Primitive Actions.

poss(pickupCoffee(T),S) :- not holdingCoffee(S), robotLocation(cm,S).
poss(giveCoffee(Person,T),S) :- holdingCoffee(S),
                                robotLocation(office(Person),S).
poss(startGo(Loc1,Loc2,T),S) :- not going(L,LL,S),
                                not Loc1 = Loc2, robotLocation(Loc1,S).
poss(endGo(Loc1,Loc2,T),S) :- going(Loc1,Loc2,S).

% Successor State Axioms.
```

```
hasCoffee(Person,do(A,S)) :- A = giveCoffee(Person,T) ;
                             hasCoffee(Person,S).
robotLocation(Loc,do(A,S)) :- A = endGo(Loc1,Loc,T) ;
                     robotLocation(Loc,S), not A = endGo(Loc2,Loc3,T).
going(Loc1,Loc2,do(A,S)) :- A = startGo(Loc1,Loc2,T) ;
                     going(Loc1,Loc2,S), not A = endGo(Loc1,Loc2,T).
holdingCoffee(do(A,S)) :- A = pickupCoffee(T) ;
                     holdingCoffee(S), not A = giveCoffee(Person,T).


% Initial Situation.

robotLocation(cm,s0).

start(s0,0).

wantsCoffee(sue,140,160).    wantsCoffee(bill,100,110).
wantsCoffee(joe,90,100).     wantsCoffee(mary,130,170).

travelTime0(cm,office(sue),15).   travelTime0(cm,office(mary),10).
travelTime0(cm,office(bill),8).   travelTime0(cm,office(joe),10).

travelTime(L,L,0).
travelTime(L1,L2,T) :- travelTime0(L1,L2,T) ; travelTime0(L2,L1,T).

% The time of an action occurrence is its last argument.

time(pickupCoffee(T),T).        time(giveCoffee(Person,T),T).
time(startGo(Loc1,Loc2,T),T).   time(endGo(Loc1,Loc2,T),T).

% Restore situation arguments to fluents.

restoreSitArg(robotLocation(Rloc),S,robotLocation(Rloc,S)).
restoreSitArg(hasCoffee(Person),S,hasCoffee(Person,S)).
restoreSitArg(going(Loc1,Loc2),S,going(Loc1,Loc2,S)).
restoreSitArg(holdingCoffee,S,holdingCoffee(S)).

% Primitive Action Declarations.

primitive_action(pickupCoffee(T)).
primitive_action(giveCoffee(Person,T)).
primitive_action(startGo(Loc1,Loc2,T)).
primitive_action(endGo(Loc1,Loc2,T)).

% Fix on a solution to the temporal constraints.
```

```
chooseTimes(s0).
chooseTimes(do(A,S)) :- chooseTimes(S), time(A,T), rmin(T).

% "now" is a synonym for "start".

now(S,T) :- start(S,T).
restoreSitArg(now(T),S,now(S,T)).

% Utilities.

prettyPrintSituation(S) :- makeActionList(S,Alist), nl,
                           write(Alist), nl.

makeActionList(s0,[]).
makeActionList(do(A,S),L) :- makeActionList(S,L1), append(L1,[A],L).

coffeeDelivery(T) :- do(deliverCoffee(T),s0,S), chooseTimes(S),
                     prettyPrintSituation(S), askForMore.

askForMore :- write('More? '), read(n).
```

One problem with this constraint logic programming approach to coffee delivery is that the execution of the Golog call do(deliverCoffee(1),s0,S) will not, in general, result in a fully instantiated sequence of actions S. The actions in that sequence will not have their occurrence times uniquely determined; rather, these occurrence times will consist of all feasible solutions to the system of constraints generated by the program execution. So, to get a fixed schedule of coffee delivery, we must determine one or more of these feasible solutions. The relation chooseTimes(S) in the above program does just that. It takes a situation term as its argument. Beginning with the first action in that situation history, chooseTimes determines the time of that action (which, in general, will be a Prolog variable since the ECLIPSE constraint solver will not have determined a unique value for that action's occurrence time). It then minimizes (via rmin(T)) that time, relative to the current set of temporal constraints generated by executing the coffee delivery program. Then, having fixed the occurrence time of the first action, it repeats with the second action, etc. In this way, chooseTimes selects a particular solution to the linear temporal constraints generated by the program, thereby producing one of many possible schedules for the robot.

The following is the output obtained by running this coffee delivery program under the temporal Golog interpreter of Section 7.4. Before loading and running these programs, the ECLIPSE rational constraint solver must be loaded from its library by entering lib(r). There are two, qualitatively different solutions to this scheduling problem.

Running the Coffee delivery Program

```
[eclipse 2]: coffeeDelivery(1).

[pickupCoffee(80), startGo(cm,office(joe),80),
 endGo(cm,office(joe),90), giveCoffee(joe,90),
 startGo(office(joe),cm,90), endGo(office(joe),cm,100),
 pickupCoffee(100), startGo(cm,office(bill),100),
 endGo(cm,office(bill),108), giveCoffee(bill, 108),
 startGo(office(bill),cm,108), endGo(office(bill),cm,116),
 pickupCoffee(125), startGo(cm,office(sue),125),
 endGo(cm,office(sue),140), giveCoffee(sue, 140),
 startGo(office(sue),cm,140), endGo(office(sue),cm,155),
 pickupCoffee(155), startGo(cm,office(mary),155),
 endGo(cm,office(mary),165), giveCoffee(mary,165)]
More?  y.

[pickupCoffee(80), startGo(cm,office(joe),80),
 endGo(cm,office(joe),90), giveCoffee(joe,90),
 startGo(office(joe),cm,90), endGo(office(joe),cm,100),
 pickupCoffee(100),startGo(cm,office(bill),100),
 endGo(cm,office(bill),108), giveCoffee(bill,108),
 startGo(office(bill),cm,108), endGo(office(bill),cm,116),
 pickupCoffee(120), startGo(cm,office(mary),120),
 endGo(cm,office(mary),130), giveCoffee(mary,130),
 startGo(office(mary),cm,130), endGo(office(mary),cm,140),
 pickupCoffee(140), startGo(cm,office(sue),140),
 endGo(cm,office(sue),155), giveCoffee(sue,155)]
More?  y.

no (more) solution.
```

7.4.2 A Singing Robot

To simplify the exposition, we did not endow the above program with any interleaving execution of processes, as described in Section 7.3.1. This would, however, be easy to do. Suppose we wanted the robot to sing a song, but only while it is in transit between locations. Introduce two instantaneous actions $startSing(t)$ and $endSing(t)$, and a process fluent $singing(s)$, with action precondition and successor state axioms:

$Poss(startSing(t), s) \equiv \neg singing(s).$

$Poss(endSing(t), s) \equiv singing(s),$

$singing(do(a, s)) \equiv (\exists t)a = startSing(t) \lor singing(s) \land \neg(\exists t)a = endSing(t).$

Then the following version of the Golog procedure *goBetween* turns the robot into a singing waiter:

proc *goBetween(loc*1, *loc*2, Δ, *t)*
   *startGo(loc*1, *loc*2, *t)* ;
   startSing(t) ; *endSing(t + Δ)* ;
   *endGo(loc*1, *loc*2, *t + Δ)*
endProc

This provides a temporal, interleaving account of the concurrent execution of two processes: singing and moving between locations.

7.4.3 Plan-Execution Monitoring

While we now know how to specify and compute robot schedules with temporal Golog, it would be a serious mistake to believe that the problem of controlling a robot over time has therefore been solved. It would be unrealistic to expect a robot to execute a schedule like that returned by the coffee delivery program. Frequently, it will be impossible to meet the exact times in such a schedule, for example, if the robot is unexpectedly delayed in traveling to the coffee machine. Moreover, travel times cannot be precisely predicted, and errors necessarily arise due to mechanical factors like the robot's wheels slipping on a smooth floor. So a coffee delivery schedule like that computed above must be viewed as an idealized artifact; its physical realization by a real robot is unlikely to succeed at the exact times called for by the schedule. How then can one make use of such a schedule in controlling an imperfect robot in an imperfect world? This is an instance of the general problem of specifying how a robot can monitor, and correct, its own execution when it is following a predetermined plan, like the coffee delivery schedule. Insofar as is possible, the robot should follow its plan, but it is permitted, at plan-execution time, to make suitable modifications to that plan in order to accommodate unexpected situations. How does the robot determine that its current plan has failed? How does it repair a failed plan? When does it give up completely on a plan, and what does it do instead?

   Plan execution monitoring is a difficult and largely unsolved problem, and we are not about to tackle it here. Nevertheless, it is instructive to look at the problem a bit more closely. To begin, the robot can detect plan failure only by sensing its environment. It sees that it is not in John's office; it reads its internal clock to determine that it is now too late to serve Mary her coffee. So it seems that if we are to take plan-execution monitoring seriously, *we need an account of sense actions.* Notice that such actions are fundamentally different from the "ordinary" actions (picking up a block, moving an elevator) we have considered thus far. Ordinary actions change the physical world; sense actions do not. Except in quantum mechanics, reading the time does not cause any physical changes to the world. What then are the effects of sense actions? Rather than changing the state of the world, *sense actions change the mental state of the sensing agent.* After performing such an action, the agent may come to know something he did not know before—it's now 3PM; John is in his office. In fact, sense actions are often called *knowledge-producing actions.* So it seems that, in order to model sense actions, we shall need a situation calculus account that distinguishes between the state of the physical world, and the mental state of an agent, and that, moreover, formalizes what it means for an agent to know something. With such a formal story in hand, we can then axiomatically express causal laws for sense actions, such as: sensing a clock causes the sensing agent to know what time it is. Furthermore, we can extend our approach to the frame problem for ordinary actions to include sense actions. All of which is an extended advertisement and motivation for Chapter 11, which gives just such a formal treatment of sense actions.

Returning to the original problem, we can imagine a coffee delivery robot that monitors its own execution, recomputing what remains of the schedule, after it has determined (by sensing its internal clock) the actual occurrence times of its actions. We do not instantiate a schedule's action occurrence times (as we did using chooseTimes(S)), but leave these free, subject to the constraints generated by the Golog program. Whenever the robot physically performs an action, it senses the action's actual occurrence time, adds this to the constraints, then computes a remaining schedule, or fails if no continuing schedule can be found.

7.5   The Concurrent, Non-Temporal Situation Calculus

In this section, we focus on true concurrency for primitive actions, ignoring time for the moment. So the picture will be the same as for the sequential situation calculus that has been developed so far, except that many actions may occur together. This means that there will be no explicit representation for the time of an action occurrence, and situations will be sequences of concurrent action occurrences instead of sequences of single action occurrences as in our earlier development. To represent concurrent actions, we shall use sets of simple actions. To avoid the conceptual problems described in Section 7.1, we shall restrict ourselves to actions all of which have equal, but unspecified durations. These durations could be zero, in which case concurrent actions will be represented by sets of instantaneous actions.

We now consider how to represent such concurrent actions in the situation calculus, which we do by treating concurrent actions as sets, possibly infinite, of simple actions. As we shall see later, the possibility of infinitely many actions occurring concurrently must be taken seriously, so that the obvious notation $a_1 \| a_2 \| \cdots \| a_n$ cannot accommodate this possibility. Because concurrent actions are sets of simple actions, we can use the notation $a \in c$ to mean that simple action a is one of the actions of the concurrent action c. We do not axiomatize sets, but instead rely on the standard interpretation of sets and their operations (union, intersection, etc.) and relations (membership, subset, etc.). This is in the same spirit as our treatment of time; we did not axiomatize the reals for this purpose, but instead relied on the standard interpretation of the reals and their operations (addition, multiplication etc.) and relations ($<$, $\leq$, etc.). To distinguish the sorts *action* of simple actions and *concurrent*, we use variables $a, a', \ldots$, and $c, c', \ldots$, respectively.

Next, we consider how to generalize the foundational axioms of the sequential situation calculus (Section 4.2.2) to provide for concurrency. As we do so, keep in mind that, conceptually, all simple actions have identical, but unspecified durations and the co-occurrence of two or more such actions means that they all begin and end together. To begin, we need to view situations as sequences of concurrent actions, so we extend the function symbol do to take concurrent actions as an argument. Then we have situation terms like $do(\{startMeeting(Sue), collide(A, B)\}, S_0)$.

After extending do in this way, the rest is easy; simply replace each *action* variable in the foundational axioms by a variable of sort *concurrent action*:

$$(\forall P).P(S_0) \wedge (\forall c, s)[P(s) \supset P(do(c, s))] \supset (\forall s)P(s), \tag{7.4}$$

$$do(c, s) = do(c', s') \supset c = c' \wedge s = s', \tag{7.5}$$

$$\neg s \sqsubset S_0, \tag{7.6}$$

$$s \sqsubset do(c, s') \equiv s \sqsubseteq s'. \tag{7.7}$$

The abbreviations for $executable(s)$ becomes:

$$executable(s) \overset{def}{=} (\forall c, s^*).do(c, s^*) \sqsubseteq s \supset Poss(c, s^*).$$

Notice that now the predicate $Poss$ is permitted to take a concurrent action as its first argument, so in axiomatizing a particular application, we shall need to specify the conditions under which certain concurrently occurring actions are possible. What can one say in general about the preconditions of concurrent actions? At the very least, we need:

$$Poss(a, s) \supset Poss(\{a\}, s), \tag{7.8}$$

$$Poss(c, s) \supset (\exists a)a \in c \wedge (\forall a)[a \in c \supset Poss(a, s)]. \tag{7.9}$$

This last axiom tells us that if a concurrent action is possible, then it contains at least one action, and all its simple actions are possible. As we shall see later, the converse need not hold.

The six axioms (7.4) - (7.9) are the foundational axioms for the *concurrent, non-temporal situation calculus*. Notice that, except for axioms (7.8) and (7.9), these are identical to those for the sequential situation calculus, with the exception that they refer to concurrent actions instead of simple actions.

7.6   Axiomatizing Concurrent Worlds

7.6.1   Successor State Axioms

In the sequential situation calculus, we provided a solution to the frame problem by appealing to a systematic way of obtaining successor state axioms from the effect axioms. For the concurrent setting, we have to generalize these successor state axioms slightly; this turns out to be quite straightforward, as the following example shows:

$$pickingUp(x, do(c, s)) \equiv startPickup(x) \in c \ \lor$$
$$pickingUp(x, s) \land endPickup(x) \notin c.$$

The next example axiomatizes the two duelists scenario that, intuitively, cannot be captured by an interleaving account of concurrency. Suppose that $shoot(x, y)$ is the instantaneous action of person x shooting person y.

$$dead(x, do(c, s)) \equiv (\exists y)shoot(y, x) \in c \lor dead(x, s).$$

Then it is easy to prove that

$$dead(Tom, do(\{shoot(Tom, Harry), shoot(Harry, Tom)\}, S_0))$$

and

$$dead(Harry, do(\{shoot(Tom, Harry), shoot(Harry, Tom)\}, S_0)),$$

but that

$$dead(Harry, do(\{shoot(Tom, Harry)\}, S_0))$$

and

$$\neg dead(Tom, do(\{shoot(Tom, Harry)\}, S_0)) \equiv \neg dead(Tom, S_0).$$

7.6.2   Action Precondition Axioms

The earlier approach to axiomatizing dynamic worlds in the situation calculus relied on a collection of *action precondition axioms*, one for each simple action, and we also rely on such axioms here. However, concurrency introduces certain complications, which we now describe.

THE PRECONDITION INTERACTION PROBLEM

In the case of action preconditions for concurrent actions, the converse of (7.9) need not hold. Two simple actions may each be possible, their action preconditions may be jointly consistent, yet intuitively they should not be concurrently possible. We call this the *pre-condition interaction problem*. Here is a simple example:

$$Poss(startMoveLeft, s) \equiv \neg movingLeft(s),$$
$$Poss(startMoveRight, s) \equiv \neg movingRight(s).$$

Intuitively, $Poss(\{startMoveLeft, startMoveRight\}, s)$ should be false. Such impossible combinations of actions are the reason that the foundational axiom (7.9) was not a biconditional; the converse of axiom (7.9) can be false.

Notice that the precondition interaction problem arises only when modeling true concurrency. This is one reason why, whenever possible, one should appeal to an interleaving account for concurrency.

INFINITELY MANY ACTIONS CAN CO-OCCUR

Nothing prevents one from writing:

$$Poss(A(x), s) \equiv true,$$

in which case $A(x)$ can co-occur, for all x. So if x ranges over the natural numbers (or the reals, or ...) we get lots of possible co-occurrences. This is the principal reason that we chose to represent concurrent actions by sets, rather than a function symbol $\|$, because one cannot always denote a concurrent collection of actions by $a_1 \| a_2 \| \cdots \| a_n$. Unfortunately, there does not seem to be a natural way, in the foundational axioms, to rule out the possibility of infinitely many co-occurring actions.

Notice that this problem cannot arise for interleaved concurrency, which is yet another reason for modeling concurrency with interleaving, whenever possible.

7.7 The Concurrent, Temporal Situation Calculus

Section 7.3 extended the sequential, non-temporal situation calculus to represent time by providing an explicit time argument to actions. We now investigate how to modify and extend the foundational axioms for the concurrent, non-temporal situation calculus (Section 7.5) to accommodate time. As before, actions will be viewed as instantaneous, and will have an explicit temporal argument denoting the time at which the action occurs. We remain committed to the induction axiom (7.4), and unique names axiom (7.5) for situations, as in Section 7.5, as well as the axioms for $\sqsubset$. Recall that for the sequential, temporal situation calculus, we introduced a function symbol $time$, where $time(a)$ denotes the time of occurrence of action a, and we shall also need this function here. As before, this means that in any application involving a particular action $A(\vec{x}, t)$, there must be an axiom telling us the time of the action A:

$$time(A(\vec{x}, t)) = t.$$

A concurrent action makes no intuitive sense if it is empty, or if it contains two or more simple actions whose occurrence times are different, for example

$$\{startMeeting(Sue, 3), bounce(B, W, 4)\}.$$

Accordingly, define the notion of a coherent concurrent action to be one for which there is at least one action in the collection, and for which all of the (instantaneous) actions in the collection occur at the same time. This can be done with an abbreviation:

$$coherent(c) \overset{def}{=} (\exists a)a \in c \land (\exists t)(\forall a')[a' \in c \supset time(a') = t].$$

Now, extend the function *time* from simple actions to concurrent ones:

$$coherent(c) \supset [time(c) = t \equiv (\exists a)(a \in c \land time(a) = t)]. \tag{7.10}$$

Next, it will be convenient to have a function *start*: $start(s)$ denotes the start time of situation s. This requires the axiom:

$$start(do(c, s)) = time(c). \tag{7.11}$$

Notice that we do not define the start time of S_0; this is arbitrary, and may (or may not) be specified to be any real number, depending on the application.

We also need to slightly revise the abbreviation (7.2) for $executable(s)$ to accommodate concurrent actions:

$$executable(s) \overset{def}{=} (\forall c, s^*).do(c, s^*) \sqsubseteq s \supset Poss(c, s^*) \land start(s^*) \leq time(c).$$

Now, $executable(s)$ means that all the concurrent actions in s are possible, and moreover, the times of those action occurrences are nondecreasing.

Finally, as for the non-temporal concurrent case,

$$Poss(a, s) \supset Poss(\{a\}, s), \tag{7.12}$$

and we need to generalize axiom (7.9) of the concurrent, non-temporal situation calculus to the following:

$$Poss(c, s) \supset coherent(c) \land (\forall a)[a \in c \supset Poss(a, s)]. \tag{7.13}$$

This tells us that if a concurrent action is possible, then it is coherent and all its simple actions are possible. Because of the precondition interaction problem, we do not adopt the converse of (7.13) as an axiom.

The sentences (7.10)–(7.13)—together with the axioms (7.4)–(7.7) of Section 7.5 for induction, unique names for situations, and $\sqsubseteq$—are the foundational axioms for the *concurrent, temporal situation calculus*.

7.8 Concurrent, Temporal Golog

With an axiomatization for the concurrent, temporal situation calculus, it is easy to modify the Golog semantics and interpreter to accommodate these features. Semantically, we need only change the definition (7.3) of the *Do* macro for sequential, temporal Golog to apply to concurrent actions instead of simple actions:

$$Do(c, s, s') \overset{def}{=} Poss(c[s], s) \wedge start(s) \leq time(c[s]) \wedge s' = do(c[s], s).$$

Everything else about the definition of *Do* remains the same. To suitably modify the sequential, temporal Golog interpreter of Section 7.4, replace the clause

```
do(E,S,do(E,S)) :- primitive_action(E), poss(E,S),
                   start(S,T1), time(E,T2), T1 =< T2.
```

by

```
do(C,S,do(C,S)) :- concurrent_action(C), poss(C,S),
                   start(S,T1), time(C,T2), T1 =< T2.
```

Suitable clauses must also be included for concurrent_action and time. The following is the resulting interpreter.

A Prolog Interpreter for Concurrent, Temporal Golog

```
do(E1 : E2,S,S1) :- do(E1,S,S2), do(E2,S2,S1).
do(?(P),S,S) :- holds(P,S).
do(E1 # E2,S,S1) :- do(E1,S,S1) ; do(E2,S,S1).
do(if(P,E1,E2),S,S1) :- do(?(P) : E1 # ?(-P) : E2,S,S1).
do(star(E),S,S1) :- S1 = S ; do(E : star(E),S,S1).
do(while(P,E),S,S1):- do(star(?(P) : E) : ?(-P),S,S1).
do(pi(V,E),S,S1) :- sub(V,_,E,E1), do(E1,S,S1).
do(E,S,S1) :- proc(E,E1), do(E1,S,S1).
do(C,S,do(C,S)) :- concurrent_action(C), poss(C,S), start(S,T1),
                   time(C,T2), T1 =< T2.

/* The time of a concurrent action is the time of its first simple
   action. This assumes that the concurrent action is coherent: it is
   non-empty, and all its simple actions occur at the same time. */

time([A | C],T) :- time(A,T).

% The start time of situation do(C,S) is the time of C.

start(do(C,S),T) :- concurrent_action(C), time(C,T).
```

```
%  Restore suppressed situation arguments.

restoreSitArg(start(T),S,start(S,T)).
restoreSitArg(poss(A),S,poss(A,S)).

%  Concurrent actions are Prolog lists.

concurrent_action([]).     concurrent_action([A | R ]).

%  coherent actions defined.

coherent([A | R]) :- time(A,T), sameTime(R,T).
sameTime([],T).
sameTime([A | R],T) :- time(A,T), sameTime(R,T).

/*  The operator declarations, and clauses for holds and sub are
    the same as for the earlier Golog interpreter.   */
```

The next section illustrates the use of this interpreter for simulating physical systems.

7.9   Natural Actions

A natural application of the concurrent, temporal situation calculus is in modeling dynamic physical systems, where the system evolution is due to *natural actions*, namely, actions like a falling ball bouncing when it reaches the floor. Such actions obey natural laws, for example the Newtonian equations of motion. The fundamental property of such natural actions, that needs to be formally captured, is that they must occur at their predicted times, provided no earlier actions (natural or agent initiated) prevent them from occurring. Because several such actions may occur simultaneously, a theory of concurrency is needed. Because such actions may be modeled by equations of motion, continuous time must be represented. Since the concurrent, temporal situation calculus has these properties, it will provide the foundations of our approach to natural actions. This section is devoted to spelling out the details of this approach.

7.9.1   Representing Physical Laws

Our focus will be on natural actions, namely those that occur in response to known laws of physics, like a ball bouncing at times determined by Newtonian equations of motion. These laws of physics will be embodied in the action's precondition axioms, for example:

$$Poss(bounce(t), s) \equiv isFalling(s) \wedge$$
$$\{height(s) + vel(s)[t - start(s)] - 1/2G[t - start(s)]^2 = 0\}.$$

Here, $height(s)$ and $vel(s)$ are the height and velocity, respectively, of the ball at the start of situation s.

Notice that the truth of $Poss(bounce(t), s)$ *does not* mean that the bounce action must occur in situation s, or even that the bounce action must eventually occur. It simply means that the bounce is physically possible at time t in situation s; a *catch* action occurring before t should prevent the bounce action.

7.9.2 Permissiveness of the Situation Calculus

Before continuing with our treatment of natural actions, it is important to think a little more carefully about the nature of agents and the actions that they can perform, as they have been modeled in the situation calculus developed thus far.

Recall that a situation is nothing but a history—a sequence of primitive actions. Among all such situations, we distinguished those that are executable, in the sense that the actions making up the sequence are all physically possible; their action preconditions are true in the situations in which they are to occur. These executable situations s were captured by the abbreviation $executable(s)$ (Section 4.6.1). But the truth of an action's preconditions does not mean that the action *must* be mentioned in every executable situation. For example, suppose A and B are two actions that are always possible: $Poss(A, s) \equiv true$, $Poss(B, s) \equiv true$. Then $do([A, \ldots, A], S_0)$ is an executable situation for any finite sequence of A's; B need not occur in every executable situation, despite the fact that its action preconditions are always possible. In this sense, the situation calculus, as presented so far, is *permissive* with respect to action occurrences; there are perfectly good executable world futures that do not include certain actions, even when it is possible to perform them. One useful way to think about this aspect of the situation calculus is that the executable situations describe all the possible ways that the world can evolve, assuming that the agent capable of performing the primitive actions has the "free will" to perform, or withhold, her actions. Thus, any particular situation represents one world history in which the agent has chosen to perform the actions in that sequence, and has chosen to withhold other actions not in the sequence.

In augmenting the situation calculus with natural actions, we can no longer allow such permissiveness in defining the executable situations. Nature does not have the free will to withhold her actions; if the time and circumstances are right for a falling ball to bounce against the floor, it must bounce. This means that in modeling physical laws in the situation calculus, we can no longer rely on our earlier concept of permissive executable situations. The executable situations must be extended so they remain permissive with respect to the free will agents in the world, but are *coercive* with respect to natural actions. The next section formally defines this new concept of an executable situation.

7.9.3   Natural Actions and Executable Situations

As discussed in the previous section, in the space of all situations, we want to single out the executable situations, i.e. those that respect the property of natural actions that they must occur at their predicted times, provided no earlier actions (natural or free-will-agent initiated) prevent them from occurring. First, introduce a predicate symbol *natural*, with which the axiomatizer can declare suitable actions to be natural, as, for example, *natural(bounce(t))*. Next, capture this new concept of an executable situation with the following abbreviation:

$$executable(s) \stackrel{def}{=}$$
$$(\forall c, s^*)[do(c, s^*) \sqsubseteq s \supset Poss(c, s^*) \land start(s^*) \leq time(c)] \land$$
$$(\forall a, c, s')[natural(a) \land Poss(a, s') \land do(c, s') \sqsubseteq s \supset$$
$$a \in c \lor time(c) < time(a)].$$

The first condition on the right-hand side is simply the old definition of an executable situation for the temporal, concurrent situation calculus (Section 7.7). It requires of the new definition for *executable(s)* that each of the concurrent actions in *s* must be possible, and the occurrence times of the actions *s* must be nondecreasing. The second condition on the right-hand side imposes an additional constraint on situations with respect to the occurrences of natural actions. This may initially be a bit difficult to understand; the following is provable from this abbreviation, and provides a more intuitive inductive characterization of the executable situations:

$$executable(S_0).$$

$$executable(do(c, s)) \equiv executable(s) \land Poss(c, s) \land start(s) \leq time(c) \land$$
$$(\forall a).natural(a) \land Poss(a, s) \land a \notin c \supset time(c) < time(a).$$

Here, *c* is a concurrent action that, in general, will include simple actions due to free-will-agents, as well as natural actions. In making sense of this definition, keep in mind that the "laws of motion" for natural actions are encoded in the actions' precondition axioms, as described above in Section 7.9.1. Intuitively, we get a next executable situation $do(c, s)$ from the current situation *s* iff:

1. *s* is executable, and,

2. *c* is possible and *c* doesn't occur before the start of *s*, and,

3. Whenever *a* is a natural action that can occur in situation *s* (and therefore, being natural, it must occur *next* unless something happens before it), but *a* is not in *c* (and hence doesn't occur next), then *c* must occur before (not after, not at the same time as) *a*'s predicted occurrence time.

Now, the executable situations characterize all possible world evolutions, where the non-natural actions are under the control of one or more agents with the free will to perform or withhold such action occurrences, and where the natural actions must occur if the time and circumstances predict their occurrences.

7.9.4 An Example: Enabling Actions

In the discussion following the presentation of axiom (7.2), we noted the possibility of situations containing two or more concurrent actions with the same occurrence times. We now provide an example where this is a desirable feature of our axiomatization. Consider a scenario in which an agent is holding an object. At some time, chosen under her own free will, she releases the object, enabling it to start falling. The $startFalling$ action is a natural action, which is to say, it must occur immediately after the release action. For simplicity, assume that once the object starts to fall, it continues falling forever.

$$start(S_0) = 0, \quad holding(S_0), \quad \neg falling(S_0),$$

$$natural(a) \equiv (\exists t)a = startFalling(t),$$

$$Poss(release(t), s) \equiv holding(s) \wedge start(s) \leq t,$$

$$Poss(startFalling(t), s) \equiv \neg holding(s) \wedge \neg falling(s) \wedge start(s) \leq t,$$

$$falling(do(c, s)) \equiv (\exists t)startFalling(t) \in c \vee falling(s),$$

$$holding(do(c, s)) \equiv (\exists t)catch(t) \in c \vee holding(s) \wedge \neg(\exists t)release(t) \in c.$$

Then the following is an executable situation:

$$do(\{startFalling(1)\}, do(\{release(1)\}, S_0)).$$

The following are *not* executable situations:

$$do(\{startFalling(2)\}, do(\{release(1)\}, S_0)),$$

$$do(\{release(1)\}, do(\{startFalling(1)\}, S_0)).$$

7.9.5 Zeno's Paradox

Executable situations admit infinitely many distinct action occurrences over a finite time interval. Consider the natural action A:

$$Poss(A(t), s) \equiv t = (1 + start(s))/2,$$

with $start(S_0) = 0$. Then for any $n \geq 1$, the situation $do([A(1/2), \ldots, A(1 - 1/2^n)], S_0)$ is executable. This means that if B is another action, natural or not, with $Poss(B(t), s) \equiv t = 1$, then $B(1)$ never gets to be part of any executable situation; it never happens! This is arguably the right intuition, given the idealization of physical reality involved in the axiomatization of A. There does not appear to be any simple way to prevent Zeno's paradox from arising in temporal axiomatizations like ours. Of course, this is not really a paradox, in the sense that such examples do not introduce any inconsistencies into the axiomatization.

7.9.6   The Natural-World Assumption

This is the sentence:

$$(\forall a)natural(a). \qquad\qquad\qquad\qquad (NWA)$$

The Natural-World Assumption restricts the domain of discourse of actions to natural actions only.

Lemma 7.9.1: *The following is a consequence of the foundational axioms and the definition of an executable situation:*

$$executable(do(c, s)) \wedge executable(do(c', s)) \wedge NWA \supset c = c'.$$

Intuitively, the above lemma tells us that natural worlds are *deterministic*: If there is an executable successor situation, it is unique. The following theorem extends Lemma 7.9.1 to *histories*: When there are only natural actions, the world evolves in a unique way, if it evolves at all.

Theorem 7.9.2: *The foundational axioms for the concurrent, temporal situation calculus together with the definition of an executable situation entail the following:*

$$executable(s) \wedge executable(s') \wedge NWA \supset s \sqsubseteq s' \vee s' \sqsubseteq s.$$

7.9.7   Least-Natural-Time Points

The following abbreviation plays a central role in theorizing about natural actions:

$$lntp(s, t) \stackrel{def}{=} (\exists a)[natural(a) \wedge Poss(a, s) \wedge time(a) = t] \wedge \qquad (7.14)$$
$$(\forall a)[natural(a) \wedge Poss(a, s) \supset time(a) \geq t].$$

Intuitively, the *least-natural-time point* is the earliest time during situation s at which a natural action can occur.

Remark 7.9.3: (7.14) entails the following:

$$lntp(s, t) \wedge lntp(s, t') \supset t = t'.$$

So, when it exists, the least-natural-time point is unique. Unfortunately, it need not exist, for example, when $(\forall a).natural(a) \equiv (\exists x, t)a = B(x, t)$, where x ranges over the nonzero natural numbers, and $Poss(B(x, t), s) \equiv t = start(s) + 1/x$. Another such example is when $(\forall a).natural(a) \equiv (\exists t)a = A(t)$, and $Poss(A(t), s) \equiv t > start(s)$.

The Least-Natural-Time Point Condition

In view of the possibility of "pathological" axiomatizations, for which the least-natural-time point may not exist (see comments following Remark 7.9.3), we introduce the following sentence:

$$(\forall s).(\exists a)[natural(a) \wedge Poss(a, s)] \supset (\exists t)lntp(s, t). \qquad (LNTPC)$$

Normally, it will be the responsibility of the axiomatizer to prove that his axioms entail $LNTPC$. Fortunately, under some very reasonable assumptions (Theorem 7.9.5 below), we can often prove that axiomatizations of natural worlds do entail $LNTPC$. The following theorem indicates why the $LNTPC$ is important for natural worlds.

Theorem 7.9.4: *The foundational axioms for the concurrent, temporal situation calculus together with the above definitions entail:*

$$LNTPC \wedge NWA \supset$$
$$executable(do(c, s)) \equiv \{executable(s) \wedge Poss(c, s) \wedge start(s) \leq time(c) \wedge$$
$$(\forall a)[a \in c \equiv Poss(a, s) \wedge lntp(s, time(a))]\}.$$

This theorem informs us that for natural worlds satisfying $LNTPC$, we obtain the next executable situation from the current one by assembling into c all the possible actions occurring at the least-natural-time point of the current situation, provided this collection of natural actions is possible, and the least-natural-time point is greater than or equal to the start time of the current situation. Intuitively, this is as it should be for natural worlds. So, when $LNTPC$ holds, this theorem provides a complete characterization of the executable situations. What are some useful conditions guaranteeing $LNTPC$?

The normal settings where we wish to model natural actions involve a domain closure assumption specifying that there are just finitely many natural action types $A_1, \ldots, A_n$ with arguments determined by conditions $\phi_i(\vec{x}_i, t)$, where the ϕ_i are first-order formulas with free variables among $\vec{x}_i, t$:

$$natural(a) \equiv (\exists \vec{x}_1, t)[\phi_1(\vec{x}_1, t) \wedge a = A_1(\vec{x}_1, t)] \vee \cdots \vee$$
$$(\exists \vec{x}_n, t)[\phi_n(\vec{x}_n, t) \wedge a = A_n(\vec{x}_n, t)]. \qquad (7.15)$$

For example, in the case of two balls B_1 and B_2 moving between two walls W_1 and W_2 that we shall treat below, the domain closure axiom is:

$natural(a) \equiv$

   $(\exists b, w, t)[(b = B_1 \vee b = B_2) \wedge (w = W_1 \vee w = W_2) \wedge a = bounce(b, w, t)] \vee$
   $(\exists b_1, b_2, t)[b_1 = B_1 \wedge b_2 = B_2 \wedge a = collide(b_1, b_2, t)].$

This says that

   $bounce(B_1, W_1, t), \quad bounce(B_2, W_1, t), \quad bounce(B_1, W_2, t),$
   $bounce(B_2, W_2, t), \quad collide(B_1, B_2, t)$

are all, and only, the natural actions.

The following is a very general sufficient condition for $LNTPC$ to hold when the natural actions satisfy a domain closure axiom. Its proof is a straightforward exercise in first-order theorem-proving.

Theorem 7.9.5: *The domain closure assumption (7.15) entails*

$$\bigwedge_{i=1}^{n} (\forall s) \left\{ \begin{array}{l} (\exists \vec{x}_i, t)[\phi_i(\vec{x}_i, t) \wedge Poss(A_i(\vec{x}_i, t), s)] \supset \\ \quad (\exists \vec{y}_i, t')[\phi_i(\vec{y}_i, t') \wedge Poss(A_i(\vec{y}_i, t'), s) \wedge \\ \quad [(\forall \vec{z}_i, t'')[\phi_i(\vec{z}_i, t'') \wedge Poss(A_i(\vec{z}_i, t''), s) \supset t' \leq t'']] \end{array} \right\}$$
$$\supset LNTPC.$$

This theorem tells us that whenever a domain closure axiom of the form (7.15) holds for the natural actions, then in order to verify that $LNTPC$ is true, it is sufficient to verify that for each action type A_i:

$$(\forall s).(\exists \vec{x}_i, t)[\phi_i(\vec{x}_i, t) \wedge Poss(A_i(\vec{x}_i, t), s)] \supset$$
$$(\exists \vec{y}_i, t')[\phi_i(\vec{y}_i, t') \wedge Poss(A_i(\vec{y}_i, t'), s) \wedge$$
$$[(\forall \vec{z}_i, t'')[\phi_i(\vec{z}_i, t'') \wedge Poss(A_i(\vec{z}_i, t''), s) \supset t' \leq t'']]$$

This, in turn, says that if the action type A_i is possible at all in situation s, then there is a least time t' for which it is possible.

Theorems 7.9.4 and 7.9.5 provide the theoretical foundations for a situation calculus-based simulator for physical systems that we now describe.

7.9.8 Simulating Natural Worlds

With the above account for natural actions in hand, we can write concurrent, temporal Golog programs that simulate natural worlds. We illustrate how to do this with an example. Two perfectly elastic point balls, B_1 and B_2, of equal mass, are rolling along the x-axis on a frictionless floor, between two walls, W_1 and W_2, that are parallel to the y-axis. We expect them to bounce indefinitely between the two walls, occasionally colliding with each other. Such bounces and collisions will cause the balls' velocities to change discontinuously. Let $wallLocation(w)$ denote the distance from the y-axis of wall w.

Primitive Actions and their Precondition Axioms:

- $collide(b_1, b_2, t)$. Balls b_1 and b_2 collide at time t.

- $bounce(b, w, t)$. Ball b bounces against wall w at time t.

$$Poss(collide(b_1, b_2, t), s) \equiv vel(b_1, s) \neq vel(b_2, s) \wedge t > start(s) \wedge$$
$$t = start(s) - \frac{pos(b_1, s) - pos(b_2, s)}{vel(b_1, s) - vel(b_2, s)}$$

$$Poss(bounce(b, w, t), s) \equiv vel(b, s) \neq 0 \wedge t > start(s) \wedge$$
$$t = start(s) + \frac{wallLocation(w) - pos(b, s)}{vel(b, s)}$$

Fluents and Their Successor State Axioms:

- $vel(b, s)$. A functional fluent denoting the velocity of ball b in situation s.

- $pos(b, s)$. A functional fluent denoting the position (x-coordinate) of ball b in situation s.

$$pos(b, do(c, s)) = pos(b, s) + vel(b, s) * (time(c) - start(s)).$$

On hitting a wall, a ball's new velocity becomes the opposite of its old velocity. When two equal mass, perfectly elastic balls collide along a straight line, they exchange velocities according to the conservation laws of energy and momentum of Newtonian physics. However, when such a collision occurs at the same time as the balls reach a wall, we make the idealized assumption that each ball moves away from the wall with a velocity opposite to its old velocity.

$$vel(b, do(c, s)) = v \equiv (\exists w, t)bounce(b, w, t) \in c \wedge v = -vel(b, s) \vee$$
$$\neg(\exists w, t)bounce(b, w, t) \in c \wedge (\exists b', t)[v = vel(b', s) \wedge (collide(b, b', t) \in c \vee$$
$$collide(b', b, t) \in c)] \vee$$
$$v = vel(b, s) \wedge \neg(\exists b', t)[collide(b, b', t) \in c \vee collide(b', b, t) \in c] \wedge$$
$$\neg(\exists w, t)bounce(b, w, t) \in c.$$

Initial Situation:

$$B_1 \neq B_2, \quad W_1 \neq W_2, \quad pos(B_1, S_0) = 0, \quad pos(B_2, S_0) = 120, \quad vel(B_1, S_0) = 10,$$
$$vel(B_2, S_0) = -5, \quad wallLocation(W_1) = 0, \quad wallLocation(W_2) = 120.$$

A domain closure axiom for natural actions:

$$natural(a) \equiv (\exists b_1, b_2, t)[b_1 = B_1 \wedge b_2 = B_2 \wedge a = collide(b_1, b_2, t)] \vee$$
$$(\exists b, w, t)[(b = B_1 \vee b = B_2) \wedge (w = W_1 \vee w = W_2) \wedge a = bounce(b, w, t)].$$

The Natural-World Assumption: $(\forall a)natural(a)$.

Assume No Precondition Interaction Problem for Natural Worlds

Recall that, because of the precondition interaction problem, axiom (7.13) is not a biconditional. However, in the case of natural worlds, for which all actions obey deterministic laws, it is reasonable to suppose that this is a biconditional:

$$Poss(c, s) \equiv coherent(c) \land (\forall a)[a \in c \supset Poss(a, s)].$$

This says that a collection of actions is possible iff it is coherent, and each individual action in the collection is possible. This seems to be an assumption about the accuracy with which the physics of the world has been modeled by equations of motion, in the sense that if these equations predict a co-occurrence, then this co-occurrence really happens in the physical world, so that in our situation calculus model of that world, this co-occurrence should be possible. In our bouncing balls scenario, we include this as an axiom.

Golog Procedure for Executable Situations:

Notice that the above axiomatization satisfies the antecedent conditions of Theorem 7.9.5. Hence, $LNTPC$ holds. Moreover, we are making the Natural-World Assumption that the only actions that can occur are natural actions. Hence, Theorem 7.9.4 justifies the following Golog procedure for computing the executable situation of length n. Theorem 7.9.2, assures us that if it exists, this situation is unique.

> **proc** $executable(n)$
> $\quad n = 0? \mid$
> $\quad n > 0? \; ; \; (\pi c)[\{(\forall a).a \in c \equiv Poss(a) \land lntp(time(a))\}? \; ; \; c] \; ;$
> $\quad executable(n - 1)$
> **endProc**

This completes the specification of the bouncing balls problem. The following is a concurrent, temporal Golog implementation for this axiomatization; it makes use of Prolog's setof construct for computing the set of all simple actions that are possible in a situation's least-natural-time point.

Simulation of Two Balls Bouncing between Two Walls

```
% Procedure to compute the executable situation of length N.

proc(executable(N),
     ?(N = 0) #
     pi(t, ?(N > 0 & lntp(t)) :
          pi(a, pi(c, ?(setof(a, natural(a) &
                                 poss(a) & time(a,t),c)) : c))) :
     pi(n, ?(n is N - 1) : executable(n))).

%   Least-natural-time point.

lntp(S,T) :- natural(A), poss(A,S), time(A,T),
```

```
                     not (natural(A1), poss(A1,S), time(A1,T1), T1 < T), !.

%  Action precondition axioms.

poss(bounce(B,W,T),S) :- vel(B,V,S), not V = 0, start(S,TS),
         pos(B,X,S), wallLocation(W,D), T is TS + (D - X)/V, T > TS.

poss(collide(B1,B2,T),S) :- vel(B1,V1,S), vel(B2,V2,S), not V1 = V2,
                            start(S,TS), pos(B1,X1,S), pos(B2,X2,S),
                            T is TS - (X1 - X2)/(V1 - V2), T > TS.


% Assume no precondition interaction problem; a concurrent action is poss-
% ible iff it is coherent, and each of its primitive actions is possible.

poss(C,S) :- coherent(C), allPoss(C,S).
allPoss([ ],S).
allPoss([A | R],S) :- poss(A,S), allPoss(R,S).

%  Successor state axioms.

pos(B,X,do(C,S)) :- pos(B,X0,S), vel(B,V0,S), start(S,TS),
                    time(C,TC), X is X0 + V0 * (TC - TS).

vel(B,V,do(C,S)) :- vel(B,V0,S),
    (  member(bounce(B,W,T),C), V is -V0 ;
       (member(collide(B,B1,T),C) ; member(collide(B1,B,T),C)),
           not member(bounce(B,W,T),C), vel(B1,V1,S), V is V1 ;
       not member(collide(B,B1,T),C),not member(collide(B1,B,T),C),
           not member(bounce(B,W,T),C), V is V0    ).

%  Initial situation.

start(s0,0.0).
vel(b1,10.0,s0).  vel(b2,-5.0,s0).  pos(b1,0.0,s0).  pos(b2,120.0,s0).
wallLocation(w1,0.0).  wallLocation(w2,120.0).

%  Natural action declarations.

natural(A) :- A = bounce(B,W,T),
              ((B = b1 ; B = b2), (W = w1 ; W = w2)) ;
              A = collide(B1,B2,T), B1 = b1, B2 = b2.

%  Restore suppressed situation arguments.
```

```
restoreSitArg(pos(B,X),S,pos(B,X,S)).
restoreSitArg(vel(B,V),S,vel(B,V,S)).
restoreSitArg(lntp(T),S,lntp(S,T)).
restoreSitArg(setof(X,Generator,Set),S,setof(X,holds(Generator,S),Set)).


% Action occurrence times.

time(bounce(B,W,T),T).    time(collide(B1,B2,T),T).

% Utilities.

prettyPrintSituation(S) :- makeActionList(S,Alist), nl, write(Alist), nl.

makeActionList(s0,[]).
makeActionList(do(A,S),L) :- makeActionList(S,L1), append(L1,[A],L).

simulate(T) :- do(executable(T),s0,S),
               prettyPrintSituation(S), askForMore.
askForMore :- write('More? '), read(n).
```

The following is the output received under ECLIPSE Prolog, for a run of this program for simulating the first 10 concurrent actions for this natural world. The program was run using the interpreter for concurrent, temporal Golog of Section 7.8.

```
[eclipse 2]: simulate(10).

[[collide(b1,b2,8.0)], [bounce(b2,w2,12.0)], [bounce(b1,w1,24.0),
  bounce(b2,w1,24.0), collide(b1,b2,24.0)], [bounce(b2,w2,36.0)],
  [collide(b1,b2,40.0)], [bounce(b1,w1,48.0), bounce(b2,w2,48.0)],
  [collide(b1,b2,56.0)], [bounce(b2,w2,60.0)], [bounce(b1,w1,72.0),
  bounce(b2,w1,72.0), collide(b1,b2,72.0)], [bounce(b2,w2,84.0)]]
More?  y.

no (more) solution.
```

As expected, the balls first collide at time 8.0; then B_2, reversing its direction, bounces against wall W_2 at time 12.0; then B_2 reverses its direction and the two balls meet at wall W_1, causing the concurrent occurrence, at time 24.0, of two *bounce* actions with a *collide* action; then the two balls move off to the right together, etc.

7.9.9   Animating Natural Worlds

With a minimum of additional effort, from a simulation like that above, data can be obtained for generating computer animations of natural worlds. We illustrate how to do this using the earlier bouncing balls program. Add to this program a new natural action:

- $plot(x_1, x_2, t)$. Plot the values, at time t, of the x-coordinates of balls B_1 and B_2.

$$Poss(plot(x_1, x_2, t), s) \equiv t = clock(s) \wedge$$
$$x_1 = pos(B_1, s) + vel(B_1, s) \wedge x_2 = pos(B_2, s) + vel(B_2, s).$$

Here, $clock(s)$ is a new functional fluent, denoting the clock time in situation s. The clock is initialized to 0, and is advanced, by one time unit, only by a $plot$ action.

$$clock(do(c, s)) = t \equiv (\exists x_1, x_2, t')[plot(x_1, x_2, t') \in c \wedge t = t' + 1] \vee$$
$$clock(s) = t \wedge \neg(\exists x_1, x_2, t)plot(x_1, x_2, t) \in c.$$

Finally, the initial situation must be augmented by $clock(S_0) = 0$, $plot$ must be included among the natural actions, and we must augment the domain closure axiom for natural actions of the previous example by a disjunct $(\exists x_1, x_2, t)a = plot(x_1, x_2, t)$.

It is straightforward to verify that the antecedent conditions of Theorem 7.9.5 hold, and therefore, the $LNTPC$ is true, so by Theorem 7.9.4, we can continue using the earlier Golog program for computing the executable situations. To incorporate the $plot$ action into the Golog program for simulating the bouncing balls, we need only add to the above program the following clauses:

```
poss(plot(X1,X2,T),S)  :- clock(T,S), pos(b1,P1,S), vel(b1,V1,S),
                start(S,TS), X1 is P1 + V1*(T - TS), pos(b2,P2,S),
                vel(b2,V2,S), X2 is P2 + V2*(T - TS).

clock(T,do(C,S)) :- member(plot(X1,X2,T1),C), T is T1 + 1 ;
                clock(T,S), not member(plot(X1,X2,T1),C).

clock(0.0,s0).
natural(plot(X1,X2,T)).
restoreSitArg(clock(T),S,clock(T,S)).
time(plot(X1,X2,T),T).
```

The following is the result of executing this plot program for 40 steps. As before, it was run using the interpreter for concurrent, temporal Golog of Section 7.8.

```
[eclipse 2]: simulate(40).

[[plot(0.0,120.0,0.0)], [plot(10.0,115.0,1.0)], [plot(20.0,110.0,2.0)],
 [plot(30.0,105.0,3.0)], [plot(40.0,100.0,4.0)], [plot(50.0,95.0,5.0)],
 [plot(60.0,90.0,6.0)], [plot(70.0,85.0,7.0)], [collide(b1,b2,8.0),
 plot(80.0,80.0,8.0)], [plot(75.0,90.0,9.0)], [plot(70.0,100.0,10.0)],
 [plot(65.0,110.0,11.0)], [bounce(b2,w2,12.0), plot(60.0,120.0,12.0)],
```

```
[plot(55.0,110.0,13.0)], [plot(50.0,100.0,14.0)], [plot(45.0,90.0,15.0)],
[plot(40.0,80.0,16.0)], [plot(35.0,70.0,17.0)], [plot(30.0,60.0,18.0)],
[plot(25.0,50.0,19.0)], [plot(20.0,40.0,20.0)], [plot(15.0,30.0,21.0)],
[plot(10.0,20.0,22.0)], [plot(5.0,10.0,23.0)], [bounce(b1,w1,24.0),
 bounce(b2,w1,24.0), collide(b1,b2,24.0), plot(0.0,0.0,24.0)],
[plot(5.0,10.0,25.0)], [plot(10.0,20.0,9.0)], [plot(30.0,60.0,30.0)],
[plot(35.0,70.0,31.0)], [plot(40.0,80.0,32.0)], [plot(45.0,90.0,33.0)],
[plot(50.0,100.0,34.0)], [plot(55.0,110.0,35.0)], [bounce(b2,w2,36.0),
 plot(60.0,120.0,36.0)], [plot(65.0,110.0,37.0)],[plot(70.0,100.0,38.0)],
[plot(75.0, 90.0, 39.0)]]
More?  y.

no (more) solution.
```

It is easy to imagine how this kind of output could be passed to a graphics routine to generate a computer animation of the bouncing balls scenario.

7.10   Exercises

1. (a) Show that the foundational axioms for the concurrent situation calculus (both temporal and non-temporal versions) entail that

   $(\forall s)\neg Poss(\{\,\}, s).$

   In other words, the empty concurrent action is never possible.

   (b) Show that the foundational axioms for the concurrent temporal situation calculus entail that

   $(\forall c, s).Poss(c, s) \supset (\forall a, a').a \in c \wedge a' \in c \supset time(a) = time(a').$

2. Using the concurrent, non-temporal situation calculus, axiomatize the following table lifting problem. A table on which there is a cup of coffee is resting on the floor with its top horizontal. There are two agents; one can lift the left side of the table, the other the right side. The coffee will not spill iff no lift action occurs, or both agents start to lift their ends of the table together, and subsequently terminate their lifting actions together. Use the actions $startLiftL$, $startLiftR$, $endLiftL$, $endLiftR$ and the fluents $liftingL$, $liftingR$, $spilled$, and give action precondition axioms for the actions and successor state axioms for the fluents. Using these, and assuming initially the coffee is not spilled, prove that after executing the action sequence

   $[\{startLiftL, startLiftR\}, \{endLiftL, endLiftR\}]$

   the coffee will not be spilled, but after the sequence

$[\{startLiftL, \; startLiftR\}, \{endLiftL\}],$

it will be spilled. Why would an interleaving account of concurrency not be appropriate here?

3. For the concurrent, temporal situation calculus, prove:

$$executable(do(c, s)) \equiv executable(s) \land Poss(c, s') \land start(s') \le time(c).$$

4. Give an interleaving axiomatization for the two duelists example by introducing a process fluent $bulletDirectedAt(p)$, initiated by action $shoot(p', p)$ and terminated by $strikes(p)$.

5. Consider the sequential situation calculus in which actions have situation-dependent durations, possibly zero, as well as initiation times.

   (a) Propose suitable foundational axioms for this setting, as well as an appropriate notion of executable situation.

   (b) Using these, implement a Golog interpreter for this setting.

   (c) Modify the coffee delivery program of Section 7.4.1 for this version of Golog and run it. Assume that the $pickupCoffee$ and $giveCoffee$ actions continue to have zero duration.

6. When the time line consists of the integers, prove that the $LNTPC$ is always true.

7. Consider the setting of two balls falling vertically onto a horizontal floor under the influence of gravity. The balls lie in different vertical planes, so they cannot collide. On hitting the floor, a ball bounces, with a rebound coefficient $r > 0$, meaning that it's upward velocity becomes r times its previous downward velocity. Each ball has its own value of r.

   (a) Implement a simulation for this setting.

   (b) With the help of this simulation, illustrate Zeno's paradox, by choosing suitable initial heights, velocities and rebound coefficients for the two balls.

   (c) Finally, modify your simulation to provide a graphical plot of the falling balls.

7.11   Bibliographic Remarks

An early, and very influential account of time and actions was due to James Allen [2]. The door latch problem of Section 7.2.1 is taken from one of his papers [3]; the other papers in the collection containing the latter give an excellent overview of the recent status of Allen's theory. Another early, and quite sophisticated, fully axiomatic account of time and actions was due to McDermott [142]. Here, McDermott addresses the frame problem, continuous time and change, and branching futures quite similar to those of the situation calculus. Chapter 5 of Davis's book [36] describes many of the details of this approach.

Perhaps the earliest treatment, in the situation calculus, of concurrency and actions with durations was by Gelfond, Lifschitz, and Rabinov [61]. By basing it on the language $\mathcal{A}$ of Gelfond and Lifschitz [59], Baral and Gelfond [13] provide a semantic account of concurrency that, although not formulated in the situation calculus, has many similarities with ours. The principal difference is that Baral and Gelfond focus exclusively on concurrency, so their ontology does not include time or natural actions. More recent treatments for concurrency in the situation calculus, again, ignoring time, are by Schubert [192] and Lin and Shoham [127]. See also Pinto [161]. Pelavin [156] addresses the formalization of concurrent actions by extending the ontology of Allen's linear time logic [3] to include histories to represent branching futures, and suitable modal operators semantically characterized with respect to these histories. This gives a rich representation for time and concurrency, somewhat like that of the situation calculus, but at the expense of a rather complicated logic.

The idea of decomposing actions with durations into two instantaneous start and end actions, together with a fluent representing a process, was proposed for the situation calculus by Pinto [159] and Ternovskaia [210]. The precondition interaction problem for concurrent actions is discussed by Pelavin [156] and by Pinto [159]. For an extensive discussion of Zeno's paradox, see Davis [37].

The material on sequential, temporal Golog and the coffee delivery program is taken from Reiter [177], and that on concurrency and natural actions from Reiter [176], which in turn relies heavily on earlier work by Pinto [159]. See also Pinto [162]. For the use of time in the situation calculus for the simulation of physical and mechanical systems, see Kelley [95]. There are several other approaches to modeling natural actions, mostly based upon linear temporal logics. Examples are the work by Miller and Shanahan [194, 144, 145], and Van Belleghem, Denecker, and De Schreye [17], both using extended versions of the event calculus of Kowalski and Sergot [98]. Closely related ideas about representing physical processes were proposed earlier by Sandewall [186]. See also Herrmann and Thielscher [84]. Section 7.9.9 indicated how Golog might be used for computer graphics applications. For a much more interesting exploration of this idea in computer animation that involves sharks, a merman, Velociraptors and a Tyrannosaurus rex, see Funge [55, 56, 57, 54].

A general framework for execution monitor for an agent executing a Golog program on-line is described in (De Giacomo, Reiter, and Soutchanski [68]). This monitor is used by Soutchanski [205], who presents an implementation for the coffee-delivery program of Section 7.4.1 in which the robot monitors its execution of its delivery schedule by sensing and recording the current time in ECLIPSE's temporal constraint store, along the lines discussed in Section 7.4.3.

8 Exogenous Actions, Interrupts, and Reactive Golog

Very few interesting dynamical systems exist in isolation from an external world. This world is itself a dynamical system, and both systems interact. Moreover, these are two-way interactions; through its actions, a system changes its external world, and through its actions, the world affects the behaviour of the system. When we focus on a particular dynamical system inhabiting a particular world, we refer to the primitive system actions—the ones the system is capable of performing—as *control* actions, and those that the world can perform as *exogenous* actions. For the elevator example of Chapter 6, the control actions were $up(n)$, $open$, etc. Its external world, which we did not model in the Golog elevator control program, would have exogenous actions like someone pushing an elevator call button, a fire starting in the building, etc.

Once exogenous actions are allowed, it becomes very useful to write programs that monitor certain conditions, and take appropriate actions when they become true. For example, in the middle of serving a floor, smoke might be detected by the elevator, in which case, it should suspend operations, and sound an alarm until someone (exogenously) puts out the fire and resets the alarm. The natural way to model such *reactive* behaviour is with interrupts, and interleaving concurrency, so that we now think of two programs operating together. The first program describes the system controller—how the system should behave in the absence of exogenous action occurrences. The second program describes the interrupts, in the form of rules. A typical such rule might look something like

$$fire \land \neg alarmOn \rightarrow ringAlarm \ ; \textbf{while } alarmOn \textbf{ do } wait \textbf{ endWhile}.$$

We view such a rule as a condition-action pair; whenever the condition becomes true, the action is performed.

This chapter extends Golog to accommodate the above two features—exogenous actions, and reactivity. It does this by providing Golog with the ability to concurrently interleave two programs.

8.1 Interrupts

The first task is to specify how interrupts are to be represented as Golog programs. We illustrate with an example elevator control problem, for which we enforce the following *condition-action* rules.

1. If there is a fire, and the fire alarm is not on, ring the alarm, then wait until it is off.

    $$fire \land \neg alarmOn \rightarrow ringAlarm \ ; \textbf{while } alarmOn \textbf{ do } wait \textbf{ endWhile}.$$

2. If it is too hot in the elevator, and the fan is off, turn the fan on by toggling it.

$$tooHot \wedge \neg fan \rightarrow toggleFan.$$

3. If it is too cold in the elevator, and the fan is on, turn the fan off by toggling it.

$$tooCold \wedge fan \rightarrow toggleFan.$$

Therefore, for us, a rule will consist of a *condition* part, the left-hand side of the rule, and an *action* part, the right-hand side.

We shall represent these rules by suitable Golog complex actions. For example, the first two interrupts will be:

$$fire \wedge \neg alarmOn? \, ; \, ringAlarm \, ; \, \textbf{while } alarmOn \textbf{ do } wait \textbf{ endWhile}$$

$$tooHot \wedge \neg fan? \, ; \, toggleFan$$

This rule representation has the desired intuitive effect that the action part executes whenever the condition part evaluates true.

We have in mind the following picture for the behaviour of these interrupts in conjunction with exogenous action occurrences: Whenever the elevator performs a primitive action (like going up one floor, or toggling the fan), zero or more exogenous actions (like a fire starting) can occur. At this point, namely after the elevator's primitive action followed by the exogenous actions have occurred, the conditions of the interrupts are tested to determine if any is true in the resulting situation. The rules are selected nondeterministically, and their conditions tested until one such condition tests positively, in which case the action part of the rule is executed. If none of the rules has a condition that tests true, no action is taken; the rules succeed by "falling through". The following Golog procedure captures these requirements:

> **proc** *interrupts* ( )
> $\quad fire \wedge \neg alarmOn? \, ; \, ringAlarm \, ; \, \textbf{while } alarmOn \textbf{ do } wait \textbf{ endWhile } |$
> $\quad tooHot \wedge \neg fan? \, ; \, toggleFan \, |$
> $\quad tooCold \wedge fan? \, ; \, toggleFan \, |$
> $\quad \neg [fire \wedge \neg alarmOn \vee tooHot \wedge \neg fan \vee tooCold \wedge fan]?$
> **endProc**

The "falling through" behaviour of these interrupts is captured by the final test condition

$$\neg [fire \wedge \neg alarmOn \vee tooHot \wedge \neg fan \vee tooCold \wedge fan]?.$$

More generally, rules will often have free variables. For example, in a multi-elevator setting, there might be a rule:

If it is too hot in elevator e, and its fan is off, turn it on.

$$tooHot(e) \wedge \neg fan(e) \rightarrow toggleFan(e).$$

We represent this rule by the Golog complex action:

$$(\pi\, e)[tooHot(e) \wedge \neg fan(e)? \,;\, toggleFan(e)].$$

This has the effect of triggering the $toggleFan(e)$ action whenever, for some elevator e, the test condition $tooHot(e) \wedge \neg fan(e)$ is true.

In general, suppose we wish to represent the following n interrupts as a Golog procedure:

$$\phi_1(\vec{x}_1) \rightarrow \alpha_1(\vec{x}_1),$$

$$\vdots$$

$$\phi_n(\vec{x}_n) \rightarrow \alpha_n(\vec{x}_n).$$

Here, the notation $\phi_i(\vec{x}_i) \rightarrow \alpha_i(\vec{x}_i)$ means that formula ϕ_i has free variables $\vec{x}_i$, and all the free variables (if any) mentioned by the Golog action expression α_i are included in $\vec{x}_i$. Then we represent these n rules by the following Golog procedure:

proc $interrupts$ ( )
   $(\pi\, \vec{x}_1)[\phi_1(\vec{x}_1)? \,;\, \alpha_1(\vec{x}_1)] \mid$
        $\vdots$
   $(\pi\, \vec{x}_n)[\phi_n(\vec{x}_n)? \,;\, \alpha_n(\vec{x}_1)] \mid$
   $\neg[(\exists \vec{x}_1)\phi_1(\vec{x}_1) \vee \cdots \vee (\exists \vec{x}_n)\phi_n(\vec{x}_n)]?$
endProc

This is the general pattern by which interrupts are represented in Golog. So the rule notation $\phi \rightarrow \alpha$ is not an extension of the Golog language; it is a convenient external notation used to compile into a Golog procedure $interrupts$. While it would be simple to implement such a compiler, doing so here would distract us from the main points of this chapter. So we put the burden on the programmer to translate his rules into a suitable Golog procedure like that above.

8.2   The Semantics of RGolog

8.2.1   Intuitive Semantics of RGolog

We have in mind running two Golog programs concurrently, suitably interleaving the two execution traces. Typically, the first will be a control program, like an elevator controller that moves the elevator up or down, serving floors whose call buttons are on. The second program represents the interrupts—what actions the elevator should take the moment some condition becomes true in consequence of an occurrence of an elevator action followed by zero or more exogenous actions. When describing simulations, we shall include a mechanism for generating exogenous actions, for example a call button being pushed. Our picture of exogenous action generation is that these occur after every primitive control action occurrence. Immediately after that, the interrupts are triggered. This means that the execution of the action part of an interrupt may itself induce exogenous action occurrences, followed by further interrupt firing, etc. With luck, these cascaded action occurrences will terminate, in which case, control finally returns to the main control program.

This leads to the following informal evaluation mechanism: In running two Golog programs $prog$ and $rules$ concurrently, begin by first running $prog$. The moment a primitive action of $prog$ is executed, suspend $prog$, allow for the occurrence of zero or more exogenous actions, then execute $rules$ concurrently with $rules$. If this terminates, resume the execution of $prog$ until the next primitive action of $prog$ is executed, at which point exogenous actions are again allowed to occur, then the $rules$ procedure is triggered again, etc. Of course, the execution of the $rules$ procedure, because it is running concurrently with itself, will also allow further exogenous action occurrences after each of its primitive actions, followed by further rule triggering.

8.2.2   Formal Semantics of RGolog

Here we precisely specify the RGolog evaluation mechanism described above. As was the case in defining the semantics of Golog, we appeal to a macro, standing for a suitable situation calculus formula whose meaning will provide a formal statement of this evaluation mechanism. First, it will be convenient to define an auxiliary macro $Do1(\mathcal{A}, Q, s, s')$. Here, $\mathcal{A}$ is any Golog complex action or program, and Q is any binary predicate over situations. $Do1$ is defined inductively over the structure of its first argument:

1. When a is a primitive action,

$$Do1(a, Q, s, s') \stackrel{def}{=}$$
$$Poss(a[s], s) \wedge (\exists s'').exoTransition(do(a[s], s), s'') \wedge Q(s'', s').$$

2. $Do1(\phi?, Q, s, s') \stackrel{def}{=} \phi[s] \wedge s' = s.$

3. $Do1(\alpha \; ; \; \beta, Q, s, s') \stackrel{def}{=} (\exists s'').Do1(\alpha, Q, s, s'') \wedge Do1(\beta, Q, s'', s').$

4. $Do1(\alpha \mid \beta, Q, s, s') \stackrel{def}{=} Do1(\alpha, Q, s, s') \vee Do1(\beta, Q, s, s').$

5. $Do1((\pi \; x)\alpha, Q, s, s') \stackrel{def}{=} (\exists x)Do1(\alpha, Q, s, s').$

6. $Do1(\alpha^*, Q, s, s') \stackrel{def}{=}$
$$(\forall R).(\forall s_1)R(s_1, s_1) \wedge (\forall s_1, s_2, s_3)[Do1(\alpha, Q, s_1, s_2) \wedge R(s_2, s_3) \supset R(s_1, s_3)]$$
$$\supset R(s, s').$$

7. Procedure calls and programs.[1]

Procedure calls:

For any predicate symbol P of arity $n + 2$, taking a pair of situation arguments:

$$Do1(P(t_1, \ldots, t_n), Q, s, s') \overset{def}{=} P(t_1[s], \ldots, t_n[s], s, s').$$

Programs:

$$Do1(\{\textbf{proc } P_1\,(\vec{v}_1)\,\delta_1\,\textbf{endProc}\,;\, \cdots\,;\, \textbf{proc } P_n\,(\vec{v}_n)\,\delta_n\,\textbf{endProc}\,;\; \delta_0\}, Q, s, s')$$

$$\overset{def}{=} (\forall P_1, \ldots, P_n).[\bigwedge_{i=1}^{n}(\forall s_1, s_2, \vec{v}_i).Do1(\delta_i, Q, s_1, s_2) \supset P_i(\vec{v}_i, s_1, s_2)]$$

$$\supset Do1(\delta_0, Q, s, s').$$

$Do1$ is exactly like Golog's Do (Section 6.1) with one exception: For primitive actions a, Do sanctions a transition from s to $s' = do(a, s)$, while $Do1$ sanctions the transition from s to $do(a, s)$, then a transition caused by zero or more exogenous action occurrences from $do(a, s)$ to s'', and finally a transition from s'' to s' whenever $Q(s'', s')$ is true. In fact, if *exoTransition* and Q have no effect, i.e., if both *exoTransition*(s, s') and $Q(s, s')$ are taken to be the relation $s' = s$, then $Do(\mathcal{A}, s, s')$ and $Do1(\mathcal{A}, Q, s, s')$ stand for exactly the same situation calculus formula.

Intuitively, $Do1(\mathcal{A}, Q, s, s')$ abbreviates a situation calculus formula whose meaning is that s' is one of the situations reached from s after executing $\mathcal{A}$, when, after each primitive action of $\mathcal{A}$, we perform this action's transition, then we perform a transition caused by exogenous action occurrences, and finally a transition according to Q. $Do1$ inserts an exogenous action transition, followed by a Q-transition, after each primitive action transition of $\mathcal{A}$.

Finally, suppose that *Rules* is a Golog complex action or program. Define the macro $DoR(\mathcal{A}, Rules, s, s')$ as follows:

$$DoR(\mathcal{A}, Rules, s, s') \overset{def}{=} (\forall Q).(\forall s_1, s_2)[Do1(Rules, Q, s_1, s_2) \supset Q(s_1, s_2)]$$
$$\supset Do1(\mathcal{A}, Q, s, s').$$

$DoR(\mathcal{A}, Rules, s, s')$ is our candidate for the semantics of RGolog's concurrent interleaving of $\mathcal{A}$ with *Rules*. Its situation calculus macro expansion says the following: When Q is the smallest binary relation on situations that is closed under the evaluation of *Rules* with inserted exogenous action and Q-transitions, then any transition (s, s') obtained by evaluating $\mathcal{A}$ with inserted exogenous action and Q-transitions is an RGolog transition for the evaluation of $\mathcal{A}$ concurrently with *Rules*. This smallest relation Q is precisely the set of transitions obtained by an interleaving evaluation of *Rules* with itself, so the inserted

---

1 Refer to Section 6.1, where the semantics of Golog procedures is defined. We use the same notation here for procedure calls, procedures, and programs.

exogenous action and Q-transitions of the evaluation of $\mathcal{A}$ are precisely those caused by evaluating *Rules* after those exogenous actions that follow each primitive action of $\mathcal{A}$.

8.3   An RGolog Interpreter

Here, we present a Prolog interpreter for RGolog. As was the case for the Golog interpreter of Section 6.3.1, it relies on the standard Prolog closed world assumption about the initial database (Section 5.2.3). For many applications, this is a reasonable assumption to make, but it would be unrealistic, for example, in most robotics settings in which many features of the environment would be unknown to the robot. This completeness assumption is a limitation of the implementation, arising from the ease with which an interpreter can be implemented in Prolog. But this is not a feature of RGolog's semantics, and one can imagine a more general interpreter that appeals to a first-order theorem-prover for establishing truths in an incomplete initial situation. The justification for the interpreter relies, in part, on the following equivalences (Exercise 4 below):[2]

1. When a is a primitive action:

$$(\forall s, s').DoR(a, Rules, s, s') \equiv Poss(a, s) \wedge (\exists s'').exoTransition(do(a, s), s'') \wedge$$
$$DoR(Rules, Rules, s'', s').$$

2. $(\forall s, s').DoR(\phi?, Rules, s, s') \equiv \phi[s] \wedge s = s'.$

3. $(\forall s, s').DoR(\alpha \ ; \ \beta, Rules, s, s') \equiv (\exists s'').DoR(\alpha, Rules, s, s'') \wedge$
$$DoR(\beta, Rules, s'', s').$$

4. $(\forall s, s').DoR(\alpha \mid \beta, Rules, s, s') \equiv DoR(\alpha, Rules, s, s') \vee DoR(\beta, Rules, s, s').$

5. $(\forall s, s').DoR((\pi \ x)\alpha, Rules, s, s') \equiv (\exists x)DoR(\alpha, Rules, s, s').$

6. $(\forall s, s').DoR(\alpha^*, Rules, s, s') \equiv s = s' \vee DoR(\alpha \ ; \alpha^*, Rules, s, s').$

An RGolog Interpreter in Prolog

```
doR(A,Rules,S,S1) :- primitive_action(A), poss(A,S),
                        exoTransition(do(A,S),S2), doR(Rules,Rules,S2,S1).
doR(E1 : E2,Rules,S,S1) :- doR(E1,Rules,S,S2), doR(E2,Rules,S2,S1).
doR(?(P),Rules,S,S) :- holds(P,S).
doR(E1 # E2,Rules,S,S1) :- doR(E1,Rules,S,S1) ; doR(E2,Rules,S,S1).
doR(if(P,E1,E2),Rules,S,S1) :- doR(?(P) : E1 # ?(-P) : E2, Rules,S,S1).
doR(star(E),Rules,S,S1) :- S1 = S ; doR(E : star(E),Rules,S,S1).
doR(while(P,E),Rules,S,S1):- doR(star(?(P) : E) : ?(-P),Rules,S,S1).
doR(pi(V,E),Rules,S,S1) :- sub(V,_,E,E1), doR(E1,Rules,S,S1).
doR(P,Rules,S,S1) :- proc(P,B), doR(B,Rules,S,S1).
```

---

2 See Exercise 11 of Chapter 6 to understand why equivalences like these lead naturally to an interpreter.

```
/*  The operator declarations, and clauses for holds and sub are
    the same as for the earlier Golog interpreter.  */
```

8.4   Example: A Reactive Elevator Controller

We begin this section with a complete specification for an elevator controller with exogenous actions and interrupts. First we describe what are the primitive actions and fluents for the example. After that, we specify the domain with action precondition and successor state axioms, and with axioms for the initial situation. Finally, we give the Golog procedures for the elevator controller and the interrupts.

Control Actions

- *goUp*. Move the elevator up one floor.
- *goDown*. Move the elevator down one floor.
- *resetButton(n)*. Turn off the call button of floor n.
- *toggleFan*. Turn the elevator fan on or off.
- *ringAlarm*. The elevator turns on its fire alarm when it detects smoke.
- *wait*. A no-op; has no effect on any fluent.

Exogenous Actions

- *startFire*. Start a fire in the elevator.
- *endFire*. Put out a fire in the elevator.
- *callElevator(n)*. Turn on the call button of floor n.
- *resetAlarm*. Reset the fire alarm.
- *changeTemp*. Cause a unit change in the temperature of the elevator.

Relational Fluents

- *buttonOn(n, s)*. The call button for floor n is on.
- *fire(s)*. There is a fire in the elevator.
- *fan(s)*. The fan is on.
- *alarmOn(s)*. The fire alarm is ringing.

Functional Fluents

- *floor(s)*. The floor the elevator is at.
- *temp(s)*. The temperature in the elevator.

Action Precondition Axioms

$Poss(goUp, s) \equiv floor(s) < TopFloor,$

$Poss(goDown, s) \equiv floor(s) > FirstFloor,$

$Poss(resetButton(n), s) \equiv floor(s) = n \wedge buttonOn(n, s),$

$Poss(toggleFan, s) \equiv true,$

$Poss(ringAlarm, s) \equiv fire(s),$

$Poss(startFire, s) \equiv \neg fire(s),$

$Poss(endFire, s) \equiv fire(s),$

$Poss(callElevator(n), s) \equiv \neg buttonOn(n, s),$

$Poss(changeTemp, s) \equiv true,$

$Poss(resetAlarm, s) \equiv alarmOn(s),$

$Poss(wait, s) \equiv true.$

Successor State Axioms

$buttonOn(n, do(a, s)) \equiv a = callElevator(n) \vee$
$$buttonOn(n, s) \wedge a \neq resetButton(n),$$

$fire(do(a, s)) \equiv a = startFire \vee fire(s) \wedge a \neq endFire,$

$fan(do(a, s)) \equiv \neg fan(s) \wedge a = toggleFan \vee fan(s) \wedge a \neq toggleFan,$

$floor(do(a, s)) = f \equiv a = goDown \wedge floor(s) = f + 1 \vee$
$$a = goUp \wedge floor(s) = f - 1 \vee$$
$$floor(s) = f \wedge a \neq goDown \wedge a \neq goUp,$$

$alarmOn(do(a, s)) \equiv a = ringAlarm \vee alarmOn(s) \wedge a \neq resetAlarm,$

$temp(do(a, s)) = t \equiv temp(s) = t - 1 \wedge \neg fan(s) \wedge a = changeTemp \vee$
$$temp(s) = t + 1 \wedge fan(s) \wedge a = changeTemp \vee$$
$$temp(s) = t \wedge a \neq changeTemp.$$

Abbreviations

$tooHot(s) \stackrel{def}{=} temp(s) > 3,$

$tooCold(s) \stackrel{def}{=} temp(s) < -3,$

$aboveFloor(n, s) \stackrel{def}{=} n < floor(s).$

Initial Situation

$floor(S_0) = 1$, $\neg fan(S_0)$, $temp(S_0) = 0$, $(\forall n)\neg buttonOn(n, S_0)$,
$\neg alarmOn(S_0)$, $\neg fire(S_0)$, $TopFloor = 6$, $FirstFloor = 1$.

Procedures

    proc *control* ( )   % The main elevator control loop. The initial wait action
                             % provides an opportunity for exogenous actions to occur.
      wait ;
      while $(\exists n)buttonOn(n)$ **do**
        $(\pi \; n)[buttonOn(n)? \, ; \, serveFloor(n)]$
      endWhile
    endProc

    proc *serveFloor* (n)
      while $floor \neq n$ **do**
        if $aboveFloor(n)$ **then** *goDown* **else** *goUp*
      endWhile ;
      resetButton(n)
    endProc

    proc *rules* ( )
      $fire \wedge \neg alarmOn?$; *ringAlarm* ; **while** $alarmOn$ **do** *wait* **endWhile** $|$
      $tooHot \wedge \neg fan?$; *toggleFan* $|$
      $tooCold \wedge fan?$; *toggleFan* $|$
      $\neg[fire \wedge \neg alarmOn \vee tooHot \wedge \neg fan \vee tooCold \wedge fan]?$
    endProc

Notice that we do not (and cannot) provide a specification for $exoTransition(s, s')$. Since exogenous action occurrences are, by definition, not predictable by the programmer, she cannot provide this relation. A simulation, however, can issue exogenous action occurrences, and this is what we do here. The next section implements $exoTransition$ by invoking a Prolog clause that interactively requests the user to input an exogenous action. As an alternative mechanism for producing exogenous action occurrences, we also describe an implementation of $exoTransition$ that randomly generates exogenous actions.

8.4.1   A Reactive Elevator with Interactively Generated Exogenous Actions

Here we describe an implementation of the above reactive elevator specification. It provides for exogenous action occurrences via a Prolog clause for the predicate exoTransition by interactively asking the user to input such an action. Notice that the implementation provides for at most one exogenous action occurrence at any time.

A Reactive Elevator Controller with Interactively Generated Exogenous Actions

```
% Primitive action declarations.

primitive_action(goUp).                 primitive_action(goDown).
primitive_action(resetButton(N)).       primitive_action(toggleFan).
primitive_action(ringAlarm).            primitive_action(wait).
primitive_action(startFire).            primitive_action(endFire).
primitive_action(callElevator(N)).      primitive_action(resetAlarm).
primitive_action(changeTemp).


% Golog Procedures

proc(control, wait : while(some(n,buttonOn(n)),
                           pi(n, ?(buttonOn(n)) : serveFloor(n))))).

proc(serveFloor(N), while(-atFloor(N), if(aboveFloor(N), goDown, goUp)) :
                    resetButton(N)).

proc(rules, ?(fire & -alarmOn) : ringAlarm : while(alarmOn,wait) #
            ?(tooHot & -fan) : toggleFan #
            ?(tooCold & fan) : toggleFan #
            ?(-(fire & -alarmOn v tooHot & -fan v tooCold & fan)))).

% exoTransition under the assumption that at most one exogenous action
% can occur after each control action.

exoTransition(S1,S2) :- requestExogenousAction(E,S1),
                        (E = nil, S2 = S1 ;
                         not E = nil, S2 = do(E,S1)).

requestExogenousAction(E,S) :-
        write("Enter an exogenous action, or nil."), read(E1),
  %  IF exogenous action is nil, or is possible THEN no problem
        ((E1 = nil ; poss(E1,S)) -> E = E1 ;
  %  ELSE print error message, and try again.
        write(">> Action not possible. Try again."), nl,
        requestExogenousAction(E,S)).

% Preconditions for Primitive Actions
```

```
poss(goUp,S) :- atFloor(N,S), topFloor(T), N < T.
poss(goDown,S) :- atFloor(N,S), firstFloor(F), F < N.
poss(resetButton(N),S) :- atFloor(N,S), buttonOn(N,S).
poss(toggleFan,S).
poss(ringAlarm,S) :- fire(S).
poss(startFire,S) :- not fire(S).
poss(endFire,S) :- fire(S).
poss(callElevator(N),S) :- not buttonOn(N,S).
poss(changeTemp,S).
poss(resetAlarm,S) :- alarmOn(S).
poss(wait,S).

% Successor State Axioms for Primitive Fluents.

buttonOn(N,do(A,S)) :- A = callElevator(N) ;
                       buttonOn(N,S), not A = resetButton(N).
fire(do(A,S)) :- A = startFire ; not A = endFire, fire(S).
fan(do(A,S)) :- A = toggleFan, not fan(S) ; not A = toggleFan, fan(S).
atFloor(N,do(A,S)) :- A = goDown, atFloor(M,S), N is M - 1 ;
                      A = goUp, atFloor(M,S), N is M + 1 ;
                      not A = goDown, not A = goUp, atFloor(N,S).
alarmOn(do(A,S)) :- A = ringAlarm ; not A = resetAlarm, alarmOn(S).
temp(T,do(A,S)) :- A = changeTemp, temp(T1,S), (not fan(S), T is T1 + 1 ;
                                                fan(S), T is T1 - 1) ;
                   not A = changeTemp, temp(T,S).
% Abbreviations

tooHot(S) :- temp(T,S), T > 3.
tooCold(S) :- temp(T,S), T < -3.
aboveFloor(N,S) :- atFloor(M,S), N < M.


% Initial Situation.

atFloor(1,s0).  temp(0,s0).  topFloor(6).  firstFloor(1).


% Restore suppressed situation arguments.

restoreSitArg(tooCold,S,tooCold(S)). restoreSitArg(fire,S,fire(S)).
restoreSitArg(buttonOn(N),S,buttonOn(N,S)). restoreSitArg(fan,S,fan(S)).
restoreSitArg(tooHot,S,tooHot(S)).
restoreSitArg(atFloor(N),S,atFloor(N,S)).
restoreSitArg(alarmOn,S,alarmOn(S)). restoreSitArg(temp(T),S,temp(T,S)).
restoreSitArg(aboveFloor(N),S,aboveFloor(N,S)).
```

```
restoreSitArg(requestExogenousAction(E),S,requestExogenousAction(E,S)).

elevator :- doR(control,rules,s0,S), prettyPrintSituation(S).
```

The following is a run of this program:

Running the Reactive Elevator with Interactive Exogenous Actions

```
[eclipse 2]: elevator.
Enter an exogenous action, or nil.      callElevator(3).
Enter an exogenous action, or nil.      callElevator(3).
>> Action not possible. Try again.
Enter an exogenous action, or nil.      nil.
Enter an exogenous action, or nil.      changeTemp.
Enter an exogenous action, or nil.      startFire.
Enter an exogenous action, or nil.      changeTemp.
Enter an exogenous action, or nil.      nil.
Enter an exogenous action, or nil.      endFire.
Enter an exogenous action, or nil.      nil.
Enter an exogenous action, or nil.      nil.
Enter an exogenous action, or nil.      callElevator(1).
Enter an exogenous action, or nil.      changeTemp.
Enter an exogenous action, or nil.      resetAlarm.
Enter an exogenous action, or nil.      changeTemp.
Enter an exogenous action, or nil.      nil.
Enter an exogenous action, or nil.      nil.
Enter an exogenous action, or nil.      nil.

[wait, callElevator(3), goUp, goUp, changeTemp, resetButton(3), startFire,
 ringAlarm, changeTemp, wait, wait, endFire, wait, wait, wait,
 callElevator(1), wait, changeTemp, wait, resetAlarm, goDown, changeTemp,
 toggleFan, goDown, resetButton(1)]

yes
```

The execution trace reveals that the occurrence of the exogenous *startfire* action triggers the first interrupt, causing the *ringAlarm* action, and causing the elevator to enter its *wait* loop. It exits this loop upon execution of the exogenous *resetAlarm*. The fourth exogenous *changeTemp* action causes the elevator to become *tooHot*, triggering the *toggleFan* control action. Interleaved with these actions are the various elevator moving actions responding to the exogenous *callElevator* actions.

8.4.2   A Reactive Elevator with Randomly Generated Exogenous Actions

Next, we give a version of the above elevator controller for which exogenous actions are generated randomly. With each exogenous action we specify an interval [i1,i2] over the reals by a declaration: exoAction(action,i1,i2). This interval must be disjoint from the intervals of all the other exogenous actions. Now, the procedure requestExogenousAction generates a random number r; if r lies in the interval [i1,i2] for some exogenous action, and if that action is possible, requestExogenousAction returns that action. Otherwise, it returns nil.

The following is the Prolog code for this version of requestExogenousAction, together with suitable declarations for the exogenous actions:

Modifications of the Reactive Elevator Controller for Randomly Generated Exogenous Actions

```
requestExogenousAction(E,S)  :- randomNumber(R), exoAction(E,I1,I2),
                                I1 =< R, R =< I2, poss(E,S),!, nl,
                                write("Generating exogenous action: "),
                                write(E).
requestExogenousAction(nil,S)  :- nl, write("No exogenous action.").

/* Generate a random number in the interval [0,R], where R has been
   declared to be the range for random numbers. */

randomNumber(Y)  :- frandom(X), % System predicate for random real in [0,1].
                    randomRange(R), Y is X * R.
randomRange(200).

exoAction(changeTemp,0,10).           exoAction(startFire,16,20).
exoAction(endFire,23,27).             exoAction(resetAlarm,42,48).
exoAction(callElevator(1),116,120).   exoAction(callElevator(2),123,127).
exoAction(callElevator(3),130,134).   exoAction(callElevator(4),137,141).
exoAction(callElevator(5),144,148).   exoAction(callElevator(6),151,154).
```

With these clauses replacing that for requestExogenousAction of the previous elevator program, we have an alternative reactive elevator with randomly generated exogenous actions. The following is one of the more interesting executions of this program:[3]

Running the Reactive Elevator with Random Exogenous Actions

```
[eclipse 2]: elevator.
```

---

3 Because exogenous events are randomly generated, most sample runs are rather boring.

```
Generating exogenous action: callElevator(6)
3 output lines: No exogenous action.
Generating exogenous action: callElevator(1)
Generating exogenous action: startFire
No exogenous action.
Generating exogenous action: changeTemp
Generating exogenous action: changeTemp
21 output lines: No exogenous action.
Generating exogenous action: changeTemp
Generating exogenous action: endFire
4 output lines: No exogenous action.
Generating exogenous action: callElevator(4)
10 output lines: No exogenous action.
Generating exogenous action: changeTemp
21 output lines: No exogenous action.
Generating exogenous action: resetAlarm
8 output lines: No exogenous action.

[wait, callElevator(6), goUp, goUp, goUp, goUp, callElevator(1), goUp,
 startFire, ringAlarm, wait, changeTemp, wait, changeTemp, wait, wait,
 wait, wait, wait, wait, wait, wait, wait, wait, wait, wait, wait, wait,
 wait, wait, wait, wait, wait, wait, wait, wait, changeTemp, wait,
 endFire, wait, wait, wait, wait, wait, callElevator(4), wait, wait, wait,
 wait, wait, wait, wait, wait, wait, wait, changeTemp, toggleFan,
 wait, wait, wait, wait, wait, wait, wait, wait, wait, wait, wait, wait,
 wait, wait, wait, wait, wait, wait, wait, wait, wait, resetAlarm,
 resetButton(6), goDown, goDown, resetButton(4), goDown, goDown, goDown,
 resetButton(1)]
yes
```

8.5 Interrupts with Priorities

The elevator example, and the Golog representation for interrupts of Section 8.1 treat all
interrupts as having equal weight. This means that if two or more of the rules can fire, then
one of them is nondeterministically chosen to be activated. No preference is given to some
rules over others in deciding which to fire. Frequently, however, there is a natural ordering
that one would like to impose on a set of rules. For the elevator example, we might prefer
the two temperature-changing rules to have equal priority with each other, but to jointly
take priority over the fire alarm rule. In other words, only when all the conditions of the
temperature-changing rules are false do we test, and possibly trigger, the alarm rule. If the
condition of a temperature-changing rule is true, we do not even test the conditions of the
lower priority alarm rule. Therefore, we want to treat the following two rules at the highest

priority:

$$tooHot \land \neg fan \to toggleFan,$$

$$tooCold \land fan \to toggleFan.$$

At the next priority is the rule:

$$fire \land \neg alarmOn \to ringAlarm \; ; \textbf{while } alarmOn \textbf{ do } wait \textbf{ endWhile}.$$

It is a simple matter to generalize Golog's representation of interrupts to accommodate rules with priorities. For the above example, the result is:

proc *interrupts* ( )
    $\{tooHot \land \neg fan? \; ; \; toggleFan\} \mid$
    $\{tooCold \land fan? \; ; \; toggleFan\} \mid$
    $\{\neg[tooHot \land \neg fan \lor tooCold \land fan]? \; ;$
    $(fire \land \neg alarmOn? \; ; \; ringAlarm \; ; \textbf{ while } alarmOn \textbf{ do } wait \textbf{ endWhile} \mid$
    $\neg(fire \land \neg alarmOn)?)\}$
endProc

In general, suppose $\mathcal{R}$ is the Golog complex action for a set of rules with priorities, and suppose that the following rules all have equal priority with one another, and higher priority than the rules of $\mathcal{R}$:

$$\phi_1(\vec{x}_1) \to \alpha_1(\vec{x}_1),$$

$$\vdots$$

$$\phi_n(\vec{x}_n) \to \alpha_n(\vec{x}_n).$$

Then the following complex action is the Golog representation for all of the above rules with priorities:

$$(\pi \, \vec{x}_1)[\phi_1(\vec{x}_1)? \; ; \; \alpha_1(\vec{x}_1)] \mid$$

$$\vdots$$

$$(\pi \, \vec{x}_n)[\phi_n(\vec{x}_n)? \; ; \; \alpha_n(\vec{x}_1)] \mid$$
$$\neg[(\exists \vec{x}_1)\phi_1(\vec{x}_1) \lor \cdots \lor (\exists \vec{x}_n)\phi_n(\vec{x}_n)]? \; ; \; \mathcal{R}$$

8.6 Discussion

Once exogenous action occurrences are taken seriously, two issues move to the forefront: the question of how a control system comes to know which, if any, exogenous actions have actually occurred, and the distinction between on-line and off-line program execution. The next sections briefly discuss these.

8.6.1   Sensing and Exogenous Actions

A basic issue that was not addressed in the above specification and implementation of
a reactive elevator is how this system becomes aware of exogenous event occurrences.
This was not a problem for us, because we designed the elevator to run only in simulation mode. Therefore, as its designers, we simply arranged for exogenous actions to be
inserted appropriately into the program's execution trace. This was the job of RGolog's
$exoTransition(s, s')$ relation. In a real (non-simulated) environment, the program designers do not get to choose the exogenous action occurrences; nature does. How should a
reactive program, embedded in its physical environment, come to know which exogenous
actions have occurred, and when? The obvious answer is, with sensors that monitor for
exogenous action occurrences. Typically, these sensor readings would be sampled after
each primitive control action occurrence, and interrupts would be triggered by these sensors' outputs. None of these *real time* sensing considerations were modeled in the above
reactive elevator. They were abstracted away in the *exoTransition* relation. We do not
treat these important issues in any great depth in this book, but neither do we ignore them
completely. In Chapter 11 we introduce explicit sensing actions, and provide an account of
how sensing affects an agent's *knowledge* of the world, and in Chapter 12, we revisit exogenous actions in a probabilistic framework, and sensing in the context of Markov Decision
Processes.

8.6.2   On-Line vs. Off-Line Program Execution

Golog programs are designed for off-line execution. After such a program returns an execution trace, this action sequence is passed to a system controller to physically execute
these actions in turn. One can think of this off-line computation as an agent's *deliberative* phase. Having thought things through by computing an execution trace for her program, the agent next physically executes the resulting action sequence. During this off-line
deliberation, backtracking may occur on failed partial executions. Indeed, Golog's nondeterministic operators encourage programming that relies on search, and therefore, on
backtracking. None of this makes much sense for exogenously driven reactive programs.
Such programs rely on *run time* inputs, namely, naturally occurring exogenous actions.
These occurrences cannot be known in advance of running the program, and therefore, it
is impossible to predict exactly what the program's execution history will be. Therefore,
exogenously driven reactive programs are inherently on-line; no amount of off-line deliberation can yield a single action sequence guaranteed to work for all possible exogenous
action occurrences. This means that one must think of such program executions along the
following lines:

1. Begin by actually performing the control program's first primitive action. If, because

of nondeterminism, there is more than one such first action, pick one at random, then actually do it.

2. Next, sense for the actual occurrence of zero or more exogenous actions, and record these in the current execution history.

3. Next, execute the interrupts. These will also sense for exogenous action occurrences after actually performing the primitive actions in the interrupts, and will record these in the current execution history.

4. When (and if) execution terminates on the interrupts, repeat with the next primitive action of the control program.

But what is meant here by "actually" performing an action? Surely, not something so concrete as performing this action in the physical world, if only because nothing like that happens in the above reactive elevator simulations. Instead, we have in mind a more abstract notion; in "actually" performing an action, one *commits* to that action, in the sense that the RGolog interpreter will never consider an alternative execution history to the current one. The interpreter acts as though the action has really been physically performed, and cannot be withdrawn. In other words, *the on-line interpreter will never backtrack past an action it has committed to.* Insofar as the ultimate form of commitment to an action is to physically perform it, this seems intuitively right. Once an agent does something in the world, she can't undo it. Once an exogenous action physically occurs, it can't be undone.

Prolog makes it amazingly simple to realize this notion of commitment; simply replace the first clause of the RGolog interpreter by:

```
doR(A,Rules,S,S1) :- primitive_action(A), poss(A,S), !,
                     exoTransition(do(A,S),S2), !,
                     doR(Rules,Rules,S2,S1).
```

Here, the Prolog cut prevents any execution history from backtracking over the exogenous actions and the control action A. Although it does involve some nondeterminism, the reactive elevator works correctly under the previous non-committing interpreter because none of its execution histories can lead to failure. But to be on the safe side, whenever RGolog is to be used for exogenously driven reactive programs, on-line behaviour of the interpreter should be enforced with the above clause.

On-line execution carries with it the risk that nondeterministic programs may make bad commitments. Because it can't deliberate about the future, the interpreter may may end up following a path through the program that eventually fails. Since backtracking is not permitted, the on-line execution fails, even if there may exist an alternative successful path through the program. However, it is possible to be much more sophisticated than this, by combining on-line program execution with off-line deliberation about the program. Imagine a smarter interpreter that decides which action to do now, but only after performing a certain amount of off-line lookahead into the future, perhaps by ignoring future exogenous actions, or by taking into account only the most likely exogenous occurrences. The action that it commits to now will be one that cannot lead to failure in the future horizon considered during its off-line deliberation. Smart interpreters like this, that combine on-line and off-line behaviours, have been specified and implemented, but pursuing this issue here will take us too far afield. See Section 8.8 below for suitable pointers.

8.7 Exercises

1. **Active databases.** For many database applications, a simple transaction can act as a trigger that causes a complex sequence of other transactions. These are called *active databases*, and in this exercise, we shall explore how to represent this setting with RGolog.

   We continue with the airline reservation database of Exercise 5, Chapter 3. There, the primitive transaction $cancelReservation(person, flight\#, date)$ had a lot of work to do: It affected all three relational fluents, first by increasing by one the number of $seatsAvailable$ on $flight\#$ for $date$, secondly by making $hasReservation$ false for $person$ on $flight\#$ for $date$, thirdly by withdrawing $seatReserved$ for $person$ on $flight\#$ for $date$. Arguably, this is an unnatural and not very modular way to model this database application. A conceptually more natural representation would make $cancelReservation$ affect just the $hasReservation$ fluent. Moreover, any occurrence of a $cancelReservation$ event should trigger an interrupt whose effect is to:

   - Execute a $changeSeatsAvailable(flight\#, date, 1)$ transaction. Here,

     $$changeSeatsAvailable(flight\#, date, m)$$

     is a new primitive transaction whose only effect is to increase n by m in the $seatsAvailable(flight\#, date, n, s)$ fluent, where m can be any integer, positive or negative.

   - Then execute a new primitive transaction

     $$cancelSeatReservation(person, flight\#, date),$$

     whose only effect is the obvious one on the $seatReserved$ relation.

   Similar remarks apply to the $assignSeat(person, seat\#, flight\#, date)$ primitive transaction; it should just affect the $seatReserved$ fluent, and should trigger an interrupt that suitably affects the $seatsAvailable$ relation.

   (a) Specify the interrupts described above.

(b) Design an interrupt, to be triggered by a $reserve(person, flight\#, date)$ primitive transaction, that interactively asks the user to assign $person$ a seat; then, after the user replies, it issues an $assignSeat$ primitive transaction.

(c) Introduce a new primitive transaction $cancelFlight(flight\#, date)$ whose affect is to make the new fluent $flightAvailable(flight\#, date, s)$ false. Change the preconditions of $reserve$ to make sure that $flightAvailable$ is true.

(d) Specify a suitable interrupt for an occurrence of the $cancelFlight$ event.

(e) Implement this active database, and try it out on some database transaction sequences. Notice that exogenous actions play no role in this example.

2. Implement an RGolog program that plays tic-tac-toe (Exercises 3.5, question 3) against an exogenous player. The program's interrupts consist of a single rule that is triggered whenever the program makes a move. The action part of this rule requests a move from the exogenous player. Don't worry about creating a championship player; even one that moves randomly will do.

3. Prove, by induction on the syntactic form of $\mathcal{A}$, that

$$[(\forall s, s').exoTransition(s, s') \equiv s = s'] \supset$$
$$(\forall s, s').Do(\mathcal{A}, s, s') \equiv DoR(\mathcal{A}, true?, s, s').$$

Thus, Golog is a special case of RGolog in which $Rules$ always succeeds without causing any actions, and in which no exogenous actions can occur.

4. Prove the six equivalences listed at the beginning of Section 8.2.2.

8.8   Bibliographic Remarks

There are many conceivable alternatives to RGolog's concurrency control mechanism. One would be to interleave two programs $prog_1$ and $prog_2$ such that $prog_2$ is triggered by every "execution" of a primitive action of $prog_1$, but unlike RGolog, the evaluation of $prog_2$ does not trigger itself. Another possible evaluation mechanism might cause $prog_2$ to be triggered by test actions as well as primitive actions of $prog_1$. Which of the many possible interleaving versions of Golog is most appropriate appears to be application dependent. ConGolog is a very sophisticated concurrent version of Golog that adopts a different interleaving control structure than RGolog and, moreover, allows for nonterminating control programs. It has been defined and implemented at the University of Toronto (De Giacomo, Lespérance, and Levesque [64]), and used in a number of applications: multi-agent systems (Shapiro, Lespérance, and Levesque [197]; Lespérance, Levesque, and Reiter [109]), robotics (Lespérance, Tam, and Jenkin [111]; Tam [208]), and business process modeling

(Lespérance, Kelley, Mylopoulos, and Yu [105]). The reactive elevator of this chapter is an adaptation of the example used in De Giacomo, Lespérance and Levesque [64]. The RGolog formal semantics of Section 8.2.2 was proposed, but never published, by Hector Levesque.

As discussed in Section 8.6.2, it is possible to design interpreters for Golog-like languages that are smart enough to combine on-line program execution with off-line deliberation about possible program futures. One such interpreter for ConGolog is described by De Giacomo and Levesque in [65].

9 Progression

A Golog program of any complexity at all will contain test actions. During the evaluation of such a program, performing a test action requires determining the truth value of a formula in the current situation—that situation built up by evaluating the program to the point where this test action is being performed. This means that performing the test action ϕ? in the current situation $do([A_1, \ldots, A_n], S_0)$ requires proving $\phi[do([A_1, \ldots, A_n], S_0)]$ using the background action precondition, successor state and unique names axioms, together with the initial database. This is the projection problem, whose computational properties we studied extensively in Section 4.6.2. The mechanism proposed there for answering the projection problem was regression. The idea was that regressing the query $\phi[do([A_1, \ldots, A_n], S_0)]$ yields a formula that can be evaluated, using first-order theorem-proving, with reference only to the initial database (Theorem 4.5.5). Indeed, this is the mechanism used by the Golog interpreter to evaluate test expressions. Now, an obvious computational problem arises: For complex Golog programs, whose execution traces can become very long, regressing back to the initial database becomes expensive—at least linear in the number of actions in the trace, and sometimes much worse (problem 13 of Exercises 4.9). Moreover, this is being done again and again, each time a test action is evaluated by the program. At some point during the evaluation of a complex Golog program, the computation may grind to a halt.

The same problem arises in the database setting. Recall that our approach to databases was to represent them as basic action theories in the situation calculus, and to maintain a log of all of the transactions issued thus far to the database; queries were evaluated with respect to this log. Our proposal for query evaluation was to regress the query over the log back to the initial database (Section 4.5). As with the evaluation of complex Golog programs, this approach to query evaluation is expensive when the transaction log becomes very long (as it will in transaction intensive applications).

As an alternative to solving the projection problem using regression, which reasons backward from a query $Q(do([A_1, \ldots, A_n], S_0)$ to the initial database, one can imagine reasoning forward, from the initial database to the query, in the following sense: Suppose we ask the question "What would the world be like if I were to perform action A_1?" given that the initial database describes the world now. With an answer to this question, we can treat this new "snapshot" of the world as the new initial database for the purposes of answering questions about world situations in the future of A_1. We shall call this new database a *progression* of the initial database in response to the action A_1. Moreover, this process can be repeated by progressing this new initial database in response to the action A_2, and so on. After progressing n times in response to the actions $A_1, \ldots, A_n$, we reach a database in which the original query Q can be evaluated directly. So progression would give us an alternative mechanism to regression for the purposes of addressing the projection problem. But, of course, repeated progression is not obviously a better alternative to regression for this purpose; in the first case, one must progress a number of times equal to the length of the log, and in the second case one must regress the same number of times. Since the original motivation in seeking an alternative to regression was the long logs that arise in certain applications, we seem to be no further ahead. But in fact, there are many settings in which progression can be usefully employed:

1. **Robotics.** Consider the coffee delivery robot of Section 7.4.1. Presumably, it will be capable of performing other tasks in its office environment, for example, delivering mail. Imagine it has been given a coffee delivery task, and at the completion of this task, it will be asked to deliver some mail: $do(deliverCoffee(1), S_0, s)$ followed by $do(deliverMail, S_0, s)$. The two instances of S_0 here are not really the same. S_0 in the second request refers to the database in effect at the time the robot has completed its coffee delivery in the physical world. So we must progress the initial database as it was prior to coffee delivery in response to the action sequence computed by the Golog call $do(deliverCoffee(1), S_0, s)$. This progressed database acts as the new initial database for the Golog call $do(deliverMail, S_0, s)$. On this view of how to manage different tasks for the robot, there will be ample time to perform the progression; the robot can use its "mental idle time" to compute the progression, while it is physically delivering coffee.

2. **Databases.** We have seen how to model transaction-centred databases in the situation calculus. Normally, these transactions will be exogenous actions. In the education database example (Section 3.4.2), all of the transactions $register(student, course)$, $drop(student, course)$ and $change(student, course, grade)$ are of this exogenous kind; they would be issued to the database by an external user, in response to real action occurrences in the world, like Sue registering in CS100. Other examples like this are airline reservation systems and automatic bank teller machines. Up to this point, we have imagined that such transactions are maintained in a log, and queries are answered using regression against this log. Instead, because these transactions are exogenous, we can use the database's idle time between transaction requests to progress the current initial database, and answer queries against the resulting shorter log. In the limiting case, we can progress the database in response to each transaction as it is received, in which case query evaluation is always performed with respect to the current database. In fact, this is how transaction-centred database systems are often implemented. Such implementations are feasible precisely because the intervals between transaction occurrences are long relative to CPU cycles, and this is so because the transactions are

exogenous. Notice that unless we continue to record the original initial database, together with the entire transaction log, we can no longer answer historical queries about the database (Section 4.8).

3. **Simulation.** Progression can be viewed as simulation, in the sense that it provides a sequence of world descriptions that are the effects of the performance of a sequence of ground actions $A_1, \ldots, A_n$. Suppose we want the sequence of "world snapshots" that would be obtained as a result of performing these actions in turn, beginning with the initial "world snapshot". We obtain this simulation by first progressing the initial database in response to A_1, then progressing the resulting database in response to A_2, etc. The sequence of progressed databases so obtained is the output of the simulation.

Regression and progression are duals of each other. Whereas regression works backward from a situation to its previous situation, progression works forward from a situation to a successor situation. In view of this, one might expect that progression and regression have analogous logical foundations. Surprisingly, this is not the case. As we shall see in this chapter, progression is a much more subtle and complex operation than regression. In fact, progression is so much more complex that in most cases, it is not computationally feasible. Fortunately, there are a few important cases in which progression is computationally tractable, and these will lead to some interesting connections between progression and planning mechanisms in artificial intelligence.

9.1 Logical Foundations of Progression

Our analysis will be for basic theories of actions, as first defined in Section 4.4. Moreover, to simplify the presentation, we shall deal only with relational fluents, not functional fluents. Recall that a basic action theory has the form:

$$\mathcal{D} = \Sigma \cup \mathcal{D}_{ss} \cup \mathcal{D}_{ap} \cup \mathcal{D}_{una} \cup \mathcal{D}_{S_0}$$

where,

- Σ are the foundational axioms for situations.
- $\mathcal{D}_{ss}$ is a set of successor state axioms. For the purposes of this chapter, these will be successor state axioms for relational fluents only, not for functional fluents.
- $\mathcal{D}_{ap}$ is a set of action precondition axioms.
- $\mathcal{D}_{una}$ is the set of unique names axioms for actions.
- $\mathcal{D}_{S_0}$, the initial database, is a set of first-order sentences uniform in S_0.[1]

---

1 See Definition 4.4.1 for the concept of a uniform formula. Intuitively, the formulas uniform in a situation term σ are those that do not mention the predicates $Poss$ or $\sqsubset$, which do not quantify over variables of sort *situation*, whose equality atoms do not mention terms of sort *situation*, and whose fluents all have σ as their situation

Let α be a ground simple action, e.g. $move(A, B)$, and let S_α denote the situation term $do(\alpha, S_0)$. The motivation behind the concept of progression is that we imagine that α has been performed, and we are looking for a set of sentences $\mathcal{D}_{S_\alpha}$ (the progressed database) that can serve as a new initial database for the basic action theory $\mathcal{D}$ we began with. In other words, we want to throw away $\mathcal{D}_{S_0}$ from $\mathcal{D}$, and replace it with a suitable set of sentences $\mathcal{D}_{S_\alpha}$, obtaining the new theory $\Sigma \cup \mathcal{D}_{ss} \cup \mathcal{D}_{ap} \cup \mathcal{D}_{una} \cup \mathcal{D}_{S_\alpha}$. What properties should $\mathcal{D}_{S_\alpha}$ have?

1. Just as $\mathcal{D}_{S_0}$ is a set of sentences about S_0 only, the sentences of the new initial database $\mathcal{D}_{S_\alpha}$ should be about S_α only.

2. The old theory $\mathcal{D}$ and the new theory $\Sigma \cup \mathcal{D}_{ss} \cup \mathcal{D}_{ap} \cup \mathcal{D}_{una} \cup \mathcal{D}_{S_\alpha}$ should be equivalent with respect to how they describe the possible futures of S_α.

The following attempts to formally capture these two requirements on $\mathcal{D}_{S_\alpha}$:

Definition 9.1.1: Progression
A set of sentences $\mathcal{D}_{S_\alpha}$ is a *progression* of the initial database $\mathcal{D}_{S_0}$ to S_α (with respect to $\mathcal{D}$) iff

1. The sentences of $\mathcal{D}_{S_\alpha}$ are uniform in S_α.

2. The information content of $\Sigma \cup \mathcal{D}_{ss} \cup \mathcal{D}_{ap} \cup \mathcal{D}_{una} \cup \mathcal{D}_{S_\alpha}$ is already present in $\mathcal{D}$:

   $$\mathcal{D} \models \Sigma \cup \mathcal{D}_{ss} \cup \mathcal{D}_{ap} \cup \mathcal{D}_{una} \cup \mathcal{D}_{S_\alpha}.$$

3. For every model M_α of $\Sigma \cup \mathcal{D}_{ss} \cup \mathcal{D}_{ap} \cup \mathcal{D}_{una} \cup \mathcal{D}_{S_\alpha}$ there is a model M of $\mathcal{D}$ such that:

   (a) M and M_α have the same domains.

   (b) M and M_α interpret all predicate and function symbols that do not take any arguments of sort *situation* identically.

   (c) M and M_α interpret all fluents about the future of S_α identically: For every relational fluent F, and every variable assignment v,[2]

   $$\models_M S_\alpha \sqsubseteq s \wedge F(\vec{x}, s)[v] \text{ iff } \models_{M_\alpha} S_\alpha \sqsubseteq s \wedge F(\vec{x}, s)[v].$$

   (d) M and M_α interpret $Poss$ identically for all future situations of S_α: For every variable assignment v,

   $$\models_M S_\alpha \sqsubseteq s \wedge Poss(a, s)[v] \text{ iff } \models_{M_\alpha} S_\alpha \sqsubseteq s \wedge Poss(a, s)[v].$$

---

argument.

2 Refer to Section 2.1.2 for the definition of a variable assignment, and for the associated notation.

Condition 3 says that an observer, standing at S_α in a model M_α of $\Sigma \cup \mathcal{D}_{ss} \cup \mathcal{D}_{ap} \cup$ $\mathcal{D}_{una} \cup \mathcal{D}_{S_\alpha}$ and looking into the future, sees exactly the same domain of individuals and exactly the same truth values as if she were standing at S_α in some model M of $\mathcal{D}$. As far as she is concerned, M_α and M are *indistinguishable* with respect to the individuals populating their domains, and how they describe the possible futures of S_α. But they may well differ on how they interpret the past (namely S_0) and about how they interpret what is true of the perhaps infinitely other situations in the the future of S_0 but not in the future of S_α. In other words, anyone inhabiting a model of $\Sigma \cup \mathcal{D}_{ss} \cup \mathcal{D}_{ap} \cup \mathcal{D}_{una} \cup \mathcal{D}_{S_\alpha}$ and observing the possible futures of S_α might just as well be standing at S_α in a suitable model of $\mathcal{D}$; she can't tell the difference. Condition 2 says the same thing from the vantage point of $\mathcal{D}$: an observer, inhabiting a model M of $\mathcal{D}$ and observing the possible futures of S_α might just as well be standing at S_α in a suitable model (namely M itself) of $\Sigma \cup \mathcal{D}_{ss} \cup$ $\mathcal{D}_{ap} \cup \mathcal{D}_{una} \cup \mathcal{D}_{S_\alpha}$. So taken together, Conditions 2 and 3 formalize the idea that the two theories $\mathcal{D}$ and $\Sigma \cup \mathcal{D}_{ss} \cup \mathcal{D}_{ap} \cup \mathcal{D}_{una} \cup \mathcal{D}_{S_\alpha}$ are equivalent about the futures of S_α; any model of one is indistinguishable from some model of the other with respect to how they interpret the possible futures of S_α.

The first thing to establish is that this definition uniquely characterizes a progression.

Theorem 9.1.2:   *The progression of an initial database is unique, up to logical equivalence. If $\mathcal{D}_{S_\alpha}$ and $\mathcal{E}_{S_\alpha}$ are two progressions of $\mathcal{D}_{S_0}$ to S_α, then $\mathcal{D}_{S_\alpha}$ and $\mathcal{E}_{S_\alpha}$ are logically equivalent.*

There remains something suspicious about our definition of progression. While careful not to say so explicitly, we have been tacitly assuming that $\mathcal{D}_{S_\alpha}$ is a set of first-order sentences. Why should we suppose this? There are plenty of examples of concepts that cannot be captured by sets of first-order sentences. (See Exercise 4 of Chapter 2 for an example. This tells us that no set of first-order sentences, finite or infinite, can capture the collection of all structures with finite domains.) Even worse, how do we know that *any* set of sentences $\mathcal{D}_{S_\alpha}$, in any logical language, can capture the concept of progression we have in mind?

9.1.1   Finite Progression Is Second-Order Definable

While we do not do it here, it is possible to show that, when $\mathcal{D}_{S_0}$ is finite, progression is always second-order definable. In fact, one can do more than this; one can give a procedure that, when given a finite, first-order initial database $\mathcal{D}_{S_0}$ and a ground action term α, constructs a finite set $\mathcal{D}_{S_\alpha}$ of second-order sentences that is a progression of $\mathcal{D}_{S_0}$ to S_α. Moreover, this progression is very easily computed from the given basic action theory.

So we can set our minds to rest about one thing; a progressed database $\mathcal{D}_{S_\alpha}$ always exists, at least for finite initial databases.

9.1.2   Progression Is Not Always First-Order Definable

While for finite initial databases, $\mathcal{D}_{S_\alpha}$ always exists as a set of second-order sentences, one can prove that it is not always definable by a set of first-order sentences. The proof is non-trivial, and we do not consider it here. Needless to say, this is bad news for a general, computational treatment of progression. However, there are some special cases for which progression is first-order, and we shall return to this question later.

9.1.3   But Why Not Do the Obvious?

The above logical foundations for progression are subtle, and at first glance, seem unnecessarily complicated. On encountering the definitions for the first time, most people ask: Why not simply let the progression be, *by definition*, the set $\mathcal{F}_{S_\alpha}$ of first-order sentences uniform in S_α entailed by $\mathcal{D}$? This is conceptually quite clear and, by fiat, eliminates all the problems about non-first-order definability that our semantical definition caused.

To see why this approach is problematic, consider that the fundamental property required of this new definition of progression is the following: For every first-order sentence ψ about the future of S_α,

$$\mathcal{F}_{S_\alpha} \cup \Sigma \cup \mathcal{D}_{ss} \cup \mathcal{D}_{ap} \cup \mathcal{D}_{una} \models \psi \ \text{ iff } \ \mathcal{D} \models \psi. \tag{9.1}$$

Here, we have introduced the concept of a first-order sentence about the future of S_α. Without going into details, this is a condition on the syntactic form of a sentence that constrains it to refer only to situations $\sqsupseteq S_\alpha$, for example $onTable(A, do(move(B, C), S_\alpha))$, $(\forall s).S_\alpha \sqsubseteq s \supset onTable(A, s)$, $(\exists s).S_\alpha \sqsubseteq s \wedge onTable(A, s)$. We know of no proof (or counterexample) for the property (9.1), and currently, the problem remains open.

So, at least for the moment, Definition 9.1.1 of progression is the only game in town, and we commit to it here.

9.2   Two First-Order Progressable Cases

Given the negative results of previous section, it is natural to seek special cases for which progression is first-order, and for which this progression may be easily computed. This section describes two important such cases.

9.2.1   Progressing Relatively Complete Databases

Definition 9.2.1: Relatively Complete Initial Database

$\mathcal{D}_{S_0}$ is *relatively complete* iff it is a set of situation-independent sentences combined with a set of sentences, one for each fluent F, of the form:

$$(\forall \vec{x}).F(\vec{x}, S_0) \equiv \Pi_F(\vec{x}),$$

where $\Pi_F(\vec{x})$ is a situation-independent formula whose free variables are among $\vec{x}$.

When $\mathcal{D}_{S_0}$ is relatively complete, the truth value of each fluent F in the initial situation is completely determined by the truth value of the situation-independent formula $\Pi_F(\vec{x})$. It does not follow that the initial database must be logically complete. It will be only when the initial situation uniquely determines the truth values of the situation-independent predicates. Hence the terminology "relative completeness." For example, in the blocks world, one may want to specify that initially all and only green blocks or yellow blocks are on the table, without saying which blocks are green and which are yellow:

$$onTable(x, S_0) \equiv green(x) \vee yellow(x).$$

Now, consider a basic action theory $\mathcal{D}$ with a relatively complete initial database, $\mathcal{D}_{S_0}$, and a successor state axiom for fluent F:

$$F(\vec{x}, do(a, s)) \equiv \Phi_F(\vec{x}, a, s).$$

Here, $\Phi_F(\vec{x}, a, s)$ is a first-order formula, with free variables among $\vec{x}, a, s$ in which s is the only situation term mentioned by Φ_F, and moreover, any occurrence of s in Φ_F is as an argument to a fluent. Suppose α is a ground action term, and suppose that we are interested in progressing $\mathcal{D}_{S_0}$ to S_α, so we have

$$F(\vec{x}, S_\alpha) \equiv \Phi_F(\vec{x}, \alpha, S_0).$$

Now, we are interested in those sentences that are about S_α only, and while this sentence is about S_α, it is also about S_0, since $\Phi_F(\vec{x}, \alpha, S_0)$ is about S_0 only. Suppose that, in $\Phi_F(\vec{x}, \alpha, S_0)$, S_0 is mentioned by the fluent atom $G(\vec{t}, S_0)$. Then we can eliminate this fluent atom in $\Phi_F(\vec{x}, \alpha, S_0)$, and therefore remove this instance of S_0, by replacing it by $\Pi_G(\vec{t})$, where, because $\mathcal{D}_{S_0}$ is relatively complete, it contains a sentence $(\forall \vec{y}).G(\vec{y}, S_0) \equiv \Pi_G(\vec{y})$. After performing this elimination for all fluent atoms of $\Phi_F(\vec{x}, \alpha, S_0)$, we end up with a formula that does not mention S_0 at all. In other words, using $\mathcal{D}_{S_0}$, we obtain from

$$F(\vec{x}, S_\alpha) \equiv \Phi_F(\vec{x}, \alpha, S_0)$$

a logically equivalent sentence of the form

$$F(\vec{x}, S_\alpha) \equiv \Psi_F(\vec{x}, \alpha).$$

Moreover, $\Psi_F(\vec{x}, \alpha)$ is situation-independent, so this sentence is about S_α only.

Now, form the union of the following sets of sentences:

1. $\mathcal{D}_{una}$.

2. The set of all situation-independent sentences of $\mathcal{D}_{S_0}$. (Remember that $\mathcal{D}_{S_0}$ may contain sentences mentioning no situation term at all, for example $John \neq Mary$, or

$yellow(B_1)$.)

3. The set of sentences $F(\vec{x}, S_\alpha) \equiv \Psi_F(\vec{x}, \alpha)$, as obtained above, one for each fluent F. Then, one can prove:

Theorem 9.2.2: *The set of sentences obtained by steps 1 - 3 above is a progression of $\mathcal{D}_{S_0}$ to S_α.*

Moreover, this progressed set of sentences is also relatively complete. Thus, the above procedure can be applied repeatedly to progress an initial, relatively complete database in response to a sequence of actions. Finally, notice that the progressed database is very easily and efficiently computed.

Example 9.2.3: The following blocks world will provide a running example for the rest of this chapter:

Actions

- $move(x, y, z)$: Move the block x from block y onto block z, provided both x and z are clear, are different blocks, and block x is on top of block y.
- $moveFromTable(x, y)$: Move the block x from the table onto block y, provided x and y are different blocks, x is clear and on the table, and block y is clear.
- $moveToTable(x, y)$: Move block x from block y onto the table, provided x is clear and x is on y.

Fluents

- $clear(x, s)$: Block x has no other blocks on top of it, in situation s.
- $on(x, y, s)$: Block x is on (touching) block y, in situation s.
- $onTable(x, s)$: Block x is on the table, in situation s.

This setting can be axiomatized as follows:

Action Precondition Axioms

$$Poss(move(x, y, z), s) \equiv clear(x, s) \wedge clear(z, s) \wedge on(x, y, s) \wedge x \neq z,$$

$$Poss(moveFromTable(x, y), s) \equiv$$
$$clear(x, s) \wedge clear(y, s) \wedge onTable(x, s) \wedge x \neq y,$$

$$Poss(moveToTable(x, y), s) \equiv clear(x, s) \wedge on(x, y, s).$$

Successor State Axioms

$$clear(x, do(a, s)) \equiv (\exists y, z)a = move(y, x, z) \vee (\exists y)a = moveToTable(y, x) \vee$$
$$clear(x, s) \wedge \neg(\exists y, z)a = move(y, z, x) \wedge \neg(\exists y)a = moveFromTable(y, x),$$

$$on(x, y, do(a, s)) \equiv (\exists z)a = move(x, z, y) \lor a = moveFromTable(x, y) \lor$$
$$on(x, y, s) \land a \neq moveToTable(x, y) \land \neg(\exists z)a = move(x, y, z),$$

$$onTable(x, do(a, s)) \equiv (\exists y)a = moveToTable(x, y) \lor$$
$$onTable(x, s) \land \neg(\exists y)a = moveFromTable(x, y).$$

Example 9.2.4: Here we give an example, using the above blocks world axiomatization, of the progression of the following, relatively complete initial database:

$$yellow(B), \quad green(D), \quad red(C), \quad A \neq C, \quad A \neq B, \quad B \neq C,$$

$$clear(x, S_0) \equiv x = A \lor red(x),$$

$$on(x, y, S_0) \equiv x = A \land y = B \lor x = C \land y = D,$$

$$onTable(x, S_0) \equiv green(x) \lor yellow(x).$$

We progress this in response to the action $move(A, B, C)$, obtaining the following progressed database, in addition to the unique names axioms for actions that we have used to simplify some of the expressions in the progression:

$$yellow(B), \quad green(D), \quad red(C), \quad A \neq C, \quad A \neq B, \quad B \neq C,$$

$$clear(x, do(move(A, B, C), S_0)) \equiv x = A \lor x = B \lor red(x) \land x \neq C,$$

$$on(x, y, do(move(A, B, C), S_0)) \equiv x = A \land y = C \lor x = C \land y = D,$$

$$onTable(x, do(move(A, B, C), S_0)) \equiv green(x) \lor yellow(x).$$

9.2.2 Context-Free Successor State Axioms and the Progression of Isolated Fluents

Recall, from Definition 4.8.1, that a context-free successor state axiom has the form:

$$F(\vec{x}, do(a, s)) \equiv \gamma_F^+(\vec{x}, a) \lor F(\vec{x}, s) \land \neg\gamma_F^-(\vec{x}, a), \tag{9.2}$$

where $\gamma_F^+(\vec{x}, a)$ and $\gamma_F^-(\vec{x}, a)$ are situation-independent formulas whose free variables are among those in $\vec{x}, a$. Intuitively, a successor state axiom for fluent F is context-free iff F's truth value in the next situation $do(a, s)$ depends on F's truth value in the current situation s, but is independent of the truth values of any other fluents in s.

Now, consider a basic action theory satisfying the following conditions:

1. $\mathcal{D}_{S_0}$ is a set of situation-independent sentences, and sentences of the form

$$E \supset (\neg)F(x_1, \ldots, x_n, S_0), \tag{9.3}$$

where F is a fluent, E is a situation-independent formula, and $(\neg)F$ means that the negation sign may, or may not, be present. For example,

$$x = A \land y = B \supset \neg on(x, y, S_0),$$

$onTable(x, S_0),$

$x \neq A \supset \neg onTable(x, S_0),$

$fragile(x) \supset broken(x, S_0),$

are all of this form. The following are not of this form:

$onTable(x, S_0) \lor onfloor(x, S_0),$

$(\exists x)onTable(x, S_0).$

We say that a database of this syntactic form has *isolated its fluents*. Notice that an initial database that isolates its fluents need not be logically complete; there may be sentences about S_0 such that neither they, nor their negations are entailed by the initial database.

2. $\mathcal{D}_{S_0}$ is *coherent* in the sense that for every fluent F, whenever $(\forall \vec{x}).E_1 \supset F(\vec{x}, S_0)$ and $(\forall \vec{x}).E_2 \supset \neg F(\vec{x}, S_0)$ are in $\mathcal{D}_{S_0}$, then

$$\{\phi \mid \phi \in \mathcal{D}_{S_0} \text{ is situation-independent}\} \models (\forall \vec{x}).\neg(E_1 \land E_2).$$

This means that $\mathcal{D}_{S_0}$ cannot use axioms of the form (9.3) to encode situation-independent sentences: For any situation-independent sentence ψ,

$$\mathcal{D}_{S_0} \models \psi \text{ iff } \{\phi \mid \phi \in \mathcal{D}_{S_0} \text{ is situation-independent}\} \models \psi.$$

3. $\mathcal{D}_{ss}$ is a set of context-free successor state axioms.

4. For each fluent F, the following consistency condition is satisfied:

$$\mathcal{D}_{S_0} \cup \mathcal{D}_{una} \models \neg(\exists \vec{x}, a).\gamma_F^+(\vec{x}, a) \land \gamma_F^-(\vec{x}, a), \tag{9.4}$$

where F's successor state axiom has the form (9.2). The consistency condition (9.4) is already familiar to us from Section 3.2.5. It prevented the possible occurrence of an inconsistency deriving from the effect axioms that led, through our solution to the frame problem, to the successor state axiom (9.2).

In the case of basic action theories of the above kind, a first-order progression of $\mathcal{D}_{S_0}$ to S_α can be constructed as follows: Construct a set $\mathcal{S}$, initially empty, of sentences as follows:

1. If $\phi \in \mathcal{D}_{S_0}$ is situation-independent, then $\phi \in \mathcal{S}$.

2. For any fluent F, add to $\mathcal{S}$ the sentences

$\gamma_F^+(\vec{x}, \alpha) \supset F(\vec{x}, do(\alpha, S_0)),$

$\gamma_F^-(\vec{x}, \alpha) \supset \neg F(\vec{x}, do(\alpha, S_0)).$

3. For any fluent F, if $E \supset F(\vec{x}, S_0)$ is in $\mathcal{D}_{S_0}$, then add to $\mathcal{S}$ the sentence

$E \land \neg\gamma_F^-(\vec{x}, \alpha) \supset F(\vec{x}, do(\alpha, S_0)).$

4. For any fluent F, if $E \supset \neg F(\vec{x}, S_0)$ is in $\mathcal{D}_{S_0}$, then add to $\mathcal{S}$ the sentence

$$E \wedge \neg\gamma_F^+(\vec{x}, \alpha) \supset \neg F(\vec{x}, do(\alpha, S_0)).$$

While we do not do it here, it is possible to prove:

Theorem 9.2.5: *For basic action theories of the above kind, $\mathcal{S} \cup \mathcal{D}_{una}$ is a progression of $\mathcal{D}_{S_0}$ to S_α.*

Notice that the new database $\mathcal{S}$ has the same syntactic form as $\mathcal{D}_{S_0}$; it is also coherent (Exercise 1 below). Therefore, this process can be iterated to progress an initial database in response to a sequence of actions. Moreover, the computation of the progressed database can be done very efficiently, and the number of sentences of the resulting database is that of the initial database plus twice the number of fluents, so the progressed databases grow linearly in the number of fluents.

Example 9.2.6: We continue with our running blocks world example. It is easy to verify that all the successor state axioms are context-free, and satisfy the consistency condition (9.4). Consider the following initial database:

$yellow(A), \quad yellow(C), \quad A \neq C, \quad A \neq B, \quad B \neq C, \quad C \neq D,$

$yellow(x) \supset clear(x, S_0),$

$x = A \wedge y = B \vee x = C \wedge y = D \supset on(x, y, S_0),$

$x = y \supset \neg on(x, y, S_0),$

$green(x) \wedge x \neq E \supset \neg onTable(x, S_0).$

According to the above definitions, this database is coherent, and has isolated its fluents. Suppose we wish to progress this in response to the action $move(A, B, C)$. We obtain the following progressed database, in addition to the unique names axioms for actions, which we have used to simplify some of the sentences in the progression. The numbering of the sentences corresponds to that of the above procedure for the construction of $\mathcal{S}$.

1. $yellow(A), \quad yellow(C), \quad A \neq C, \quad A \neq B, \quad B \neq C, \quad C \neq D,$

2. $x = B \supset clear(x, do(move(A, B, C), S_0)),$

    $x = A \wedge y = C \supset on(x, y, do(move(A, B, C), S_0)),$

    $x = C \supset \neg clear(x, do(move(A, B, C), S_0)),$

    $x = A \wedge y = B \supset \neg on(x, y, do(move(A, B, C), S_0)),$

3. $yellow(x) \wedge x \neq C \supset clear(x, do(move(A, B, C), S_0)),$

$$x = C \wedge y = D \supset on(x, y, do(move(A, B, C), S_0)),$$

4. $x = y \supset \neg on(x, y, do(move(A, B, C), S_0)),$

$$green(x) \wedge x \neq E \supset \neg onTable(x, do(move(A, B, C), S_0)).$$

9.3   STRIPS Planning Systems

Section 3.3 provided an introduction to planning in the situation calculus, and we remarked there that this was *not* how planning was normally conceptualized, or done, in the artificial intelligence planning community. Instead, the vast majority of AI planning is done using one variant, or another, of STRIPS, a formalism dating back to the early 1970's. There are many different varieties of STRIPS, but they all provide a set of *operators* and their associated *operator descriptions*, and a data structure called a (STRIPS) *database* that acts as a snapshot of the world. Operators serve as representations of actions, and they map databases into databases. For a given STRIPS operator, this mapping is intended to capture the effects of the action represented by the operator; when applied to a given database (snapshot), the operator produces a new database that is intended to represent the way the world would be after the action corresponding to the operator is performed. Now if all of this sounds like database progression, it should. Our primary intuition about STRIPS operators is that they provide mechanisms for progressing a database, and our purpose in this and succeeding sections is to make this correspondence precise. The advantage of doing so is that we can then provide a logical, situation-calculus-based semantics for STRIPS systems, with the resulting ability to prove the correctness of such systems relative to their associated situation calculus domain axiomatizations. En route, we shall also discover a novel STRIPS system, and using its associated progression semantics, prove its correctness.

9.3.1   STRIPS Databases

A STRIPS database is always a set of sentences in some restricted syntactic form, usually (but not necessarily) a set of atomic sentences, for example:

$\{onTable(C), on(B, C), on(A, B), onTable(E), on(D, E), clear(A), clear(D)\}.$

This might be taken to describe the blocks world scene of Figure 9.1.

Notice that by taking the above STRIPS database to represent the blocks world scene depicted in Figure 9.1, we are adopting certain assumptions about this representation. Specifically, we are assuming that any atoms *not* explicitly mentioned in the database, for example $onTable(A)$, is false, so that the database *implicitly* represents the atom $\neg onTable(A)$. Moreover, the constants A and B are assumed to denote different individuals, so the database also implicitly represents the negative atom $A \neq B$. These two

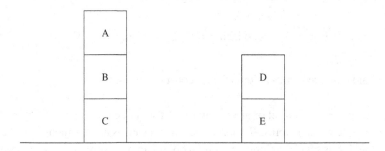

Database = {onTable(C), on(B,C), on(A,B), onTable(E), on(D,E), clear(A), clear(D)}

Figure 9.1: A Blocks World Scene and its STRIPS Database

conventions of the above STRIPS database—that it is a set of ground, atomic facts about predicates other than the equality predicate, and the implicit representation of negative atomic facts, including equality atomic facts—is the distinguishing characteristic of one version of STRIPS, and we shall concentrate on this version here, which we shall henceforth call *relational* STRIPS. Later, we shall investigate a different notion of STRIPS. We call this STRIPS relational because it treats its database exactly as does relational database theory. Specifically, a *relational database* is a finite set of ground atoms of predicates distinct from the equality predicate, where the ground terms are all constants. Any nonequality atom not mentioned in the database is taken to be false. Moreover, whenever A and B are different constants, then they are treated as unequal—$A \neq B$. Instead of representing a relational database as a set of ground atoms, with the above *closed world assumption* about negative information, one can give it an explicit, purely logical axiomatization instead. For the example blocks world, these axioms are:

$$on(x, y) \equiv x = A \wedge y = B \vee x = B \wedge y = C \vee x = D \wedge y = E,$$

$$clear(x) \equiv x = A \vee x = D,$$

$$onTable(x) \equiv x = C \vee x = E,$$

$$A \neq B, \quad A \neq C, \quad B \neq C, \quad etc.$$

This is the *official* meaning of the relational database for the blocks world example. The database itself is merely a compact notation standing for these axioms.

Definition 9.3.1: Official Axiomatization of a Relational Database

Let **D** be a relational database. **D**'s *official axiomatization* Ω is constructed as follows:

1. Suppose $P(\vec{C}^{(1)}), \ldots, P(\vec{C}^{(n)})$ are *all* of the ground atoms of predicate P occurring in **D**, where the $\vec{C}^{(i)}$ are tuples of constant symbols. Then include in Ω, the sentence:

$$P(\vec{x}) \equiv \vec{x} = \vec{C}^{(1)} \vee \cdots \vee \vec{x} = \vec{C}^{(n)}.^3 \qquad (9.5)$$

   If the predicate P has no ground instances in **D**, then include in Ω, the sentence:

$$P(\vec{x}) \equiv false.$$

2. Include in Ω unique names axioms for all constant symbols.

So a relational database, as a set of ground atoms, must *not* be viewed as the logical theory consisting of these ground atoms. Rather, it must be viewed as a convenient, shorthand notation standing for its official axiomatization involving unique names axioms for constants, and logical equivalences of the form (9.5).

Definition 9.3.2: Entailments of a Relational Database
A relational database *entails* a sentence ϕ iff its official axiomatization entails (in the strict logical sense) ϕ.

   Relational databases are logically complete for quantifier-free sentences (Exercises 9.8, question 6 below). This means that the database always entails ϕ or $\neg\phi$ for any quantifier-free sentence ϕ. One consequence of this is that relational databases provide very little scope for representing incomplete information about a domain, for example, that it is unknown whether block A is on the table. For many applications, where one has complete initial information about the state of the world, relational databases are appropriate, but it is easy to imagine settings where such an assumption would be unwarranted.

9.3.2 STRIPS Operator Descriptions

Recall that a STRIPS system provides a database, and a collection of operator descriptions mapping databases into databases. The previous section discussed STRIPS databases, focusing on relational databases as one of many possible kinds of STRIPS databases. This section treats STRIPS operator descriptions and how they affect a database.

   For the blocks world, the following are three such descriptions, corresponding to the operators $move(X, Y, Z)$, $moveFromTable(X, Y)$ and $moveToTable(X, Y)$ respectively:

$move(X, Y, Z)$

   P: $clear(X) \wedge clear(Z) \wedge on(X, Y) \wedge X \neq Z.$

---

3 In general, whenever $\vec{t} = t_1, \ldots, t_n$ and $\vec{\tau} = \tau_1, \ldots, \tau_n$ are two equal length sequences of terms, then $\vec{t} = \vec{\tau}$ denotes $t_1 = \tau_1 \wedge \cdots \wedge t_n = \tau_n$, and $\vec{t} \neq \vec{\tau}$ denotes $\neg(\vec{t} = \vec{\tau})$.

D: $clear(Z), on(X, Y)$.
A: $clear(Y), on(X, Z)$.

$moveFromTable(X, Y)$

P: $clear(X) \land clear(Y) \land onTable(X) \land X \neq Y$.
D: $clear(Y), onTable(X)$.
A: $on(X, Y)$.

$moveToTable(X, Y)$

P: $clear(X) \land on(X, Y)$.
D: $on(X, Y)$.
A: $clear(Y), onTable(X)$.

In STRIPS, an operator description normally consists of four components: The operator's *name*, the description's *precondition*, labeled above by P, its *delete list*, labeled D, and its *add list*, A. When an operator is *applicable* to a given database (in a sense yet to be defined) the database can be modified, first by deleting from it all of the expressions in the operator's delete list, next by adding to the result all of the expressions in the add list. The intended reading of the database that results from these operations is that it is a description of what the world would be like after the performance of the action modeled by the operator, assuming the database we started with describes how the world is now. The operator's precondition describes the conditions under which this action is applicable, and are analogous to the action precondition axioms of the situation calculus. The "variables" $X, Y, \ldots$ occurring in these operator descriptions are not logical variables; they are *schema* variables, and in fact, an operator description is really a schema, standing for all its possible instances formed by instantiating its schema variables by constants denoting individuals in the real world domain being modeled.

We now specify what counts as a STRIPS operator description.

Definition 9.3.3: STRIPS Operator

A STRIPS *operator* has four components:

1. An operator *name*, with a finite number of schema variables.

2. A *precondition*, which is a formula whose only "free variables" (if any) are among the schema variables associated with the operator name. Recall that STRIPS operator definitions are schemas, representing all possible instances formed by replacing its schema variables by ground terms. Therefore, when a precondition formula is so instantiated, it becomes a sentence.

3. An *add* list, which is a a set of formulas, each satisfying the same conditions as the

precondition.

4. A *delete* list, which is a a set of formulas, each satisfying the same conditions as the precondition.

The above three blocks world operator descriptions are examples.

Next, we define when an operator is *applicable* to a given database. This notion also depends on which STRIPS system one is considering; the definition here is for the case of relational STRIPS. Later, when we treat a different version of STRIPS, we shall give a different definition for it.

Definition 9.3.4: Applicable Operator Instance

An instance $A(C_1, C_2, C_3, \ldots)$ of the operator $A(X, Y, Z, \ldots)$ is *applicable* to a relational database iff the database entails (according to Definition 9.3.2) the corresponding instance of the operator's precondition. Here, $C_1, C_2, C_3, \ldots$ are all constants.

When an operator instance is applicable to a database, one can form a successor database as follows:

Definition 9.3.5: Successor Database

Suppose the operator instance $A(C_1, C_2, C_3, \ldots)$ is applicable to a relational database $\mathcal{R}$. Then the *successor* database of $\mathcal{R}$ with respect to $A(C_1, C_2, C_3, \ldots)$ is obtained by first deleting from $\mathcal{R}$ all the instantiated sentences in A's delete list, then adding to this all the instantiated sentences in A's add list.

Notice that these add and delete operations are performed on the relational database, not on its official axiomatization! Notice also that when the operator's add and delete lists consist of non-equality atoms, as is the case for the above blocks world operators, then the successor database will also be relational, so that operators can be applied repeatedly to an initial relational database.

Example 9.3.6: The operator instance $move(A, B, D)$ is applicable to the database of Figure 9.1, and results in the successor database

$$\{onTable(C), on(B, C), on(A, D), onTable(E), on(D, E), clear(A), clear(B)\}.$$

Although we have tried here to be precise about what counts as a STRIPS system, particularly a relational STRIPS system, we have been sloppy on one count. STRIPS' notation for databases and operators obviously appeals to a logical language of some kind, but we have not spelled out the details of this language, nor will we. Its features ought to be clear enough from the examples. However, it is important to notice that this language is *not* the situation calculus; there are no terms of sort *situation* or *action*, and nothing resembling a fluent. Of course, STRIPS does provide an account of varying truth values for atoms like $on(A, B)$ according to the actions that have been "performed", but these truth values are captured by the presence, or absence, of such atoms in the database representing the current world snapshot.

9.3.3   Planning with STRIPS

Within the STRIPS framework, there is a natural way to define the planning problem.

Definition 9.3.7: STRIPS Plan
Suppose D_0 is an initial STRIPS database, and G is a sentence. A sequence of operator instances $\omega_1, \ldots, \omega_n$ is a *plan* for the goal sentence G iff there is a sequence $D_0, D_1, \ldots, D_n$ of STRIPS databases such that, for $i = 1, \ldots, n$:

1. ω_i is applicable to D_{i-1},
2. D_i is a successor database of D_{i-1} with respect to ω_i, and
3. D_n entails G.

Notice that this is a very general definition, suitable for any version of STRIPS for which a notion of entailment from a database is defined. In particular, it applies to relational STRIPS, provided the operator descriptions all map relational databases into relational databases, and the entailment notion is that of Definition 9.3.2.

Example 9.3.8:   For the initial database of Figure 9.1, and the operators given in Section 9.3.2, which together define a relational STRIPS system, the following are plans for the goal $(\exists x).onTable(x) \wedge on(A, x) \wedge \neg clear(E)$:

$move(A, B, D), moveToTable(B, C), move(A, D, B),$

$moveToTable(D, E), move(A, B, D), move(B, C, E),$

$moveToTable(D, E), moveFromTable(D, E), moveToTable(D, E),$
$\quad move(A, B, D), move(B, C, E).$

It is easy to imagine a (not very efficient) planning procedure for such STRIPS systems, at least when there are finitely many ground instances of the operators. Simply generate, in a breadth-first fashion, all possible level 1 successor databases of the initial database, using all possible ground instances of the operators. For each such successor database, check whether it entails the goal. If so, stop with success; else, using these level 1 databases, generate all possible level 2 databases, checking whether any of these entails the goal; etc. If ever success is achieved, return the plan consisting of the sequence of operator instances that led to the successful database. To improve on this brute force approach, many different planning procedures have been developed for STRIPS systems, but our purpose here is not to study more efficient planning mechanisms and heuristics. Rather, it is to provide some insight into the nature of STRIPS systems themselves, with a view towards giving them a purely logical characterization. In this connection, notice that while STRIPS systems do appeal to various concepts from logic (entailment, databases of sentences, goal formulas), they certainly are not axiomatizations in any logic.

1. They do not axiomatize actions and their effects.

2. Operator descriptions are not logical sentences.

3. There is no explicit solution to the frame problem; indeed, it appears that STRIPS systems completely avoid the frame problem by their add and delete list mechanisms.

4. The things that interest us (plans) are not defined in terms of logical entailment from axioms.

Instead, the STRIPS formalism appeals to various extralogical ideas, most notably, operator descriptions with their add and delete lists, and their effects on a database.

Our concern here is with providing a logical foundation for STRIPS systems, specifically, with answering the following questions:

1. What kind of thing is a STRIPS system? Exactly what is the background domain knowledge assumed by the system, including knowledge about actions and their effects, and exactly what does it compute with respect to this domain knowledge.

2. What, if anything, does the STRIPS notion of planning have to do with the classical, situation calculus notion of planning described in Section 3.3?

3. Is there an independent notion of the correctness of a given STRIPS system, and how might such correctness claims be proved?

Our intuition is that these questions can be answered by viewing a STRIPS operator as a *mechanism* for progressing a situation calculus initial database. Different STRIPS systems arise from varying the syntactic form of the sentences in the initial database, and from varying the syntactic form of the successor state axioms. The next sections explore this intuition for two varieties of STRIPS. Specifically, we appeal to our earlier results on progression to obtain a provably correct relational STRIPS system from a suitable situation calculus basic action theory, and we do the same for a new version of STRIPS, called open-world STRIPS.

9.4 Strongly Context-Free Successor State Axioms

The STRIPS systems we shall obtain will be translations of situation calculus action theories whose successor state axioms have a particular syntactic form, which we now define. A successor state axiom is *strongly context-free* iff it has the form:

$$F(\vec{x}, do(a, s)) \equiv$$
$$(\exists \vec{v}^{(1)})a = A_1(\vec{\xi}^{(1)}) \vee \cdots \vee (\exists \vec{v}^{(m)})a = A_m(\vec{\xi}^{(m)}) \vee \qquad (9.6)$$
$$F(\vec{x}, s) \wedge \neg(\exists \vec{w}^{(1)})a = B_1(\vec{\eta}^{(1)}) \wedge \cdots \wedge \neg(\exists \vec{w}^{(n)})a = B_n(\vec{\eta}^{(n)}).$$

Here the A's and B's are function symbols of sort *action, not necessarily distinct from one another.* The $\vec{\xi}$ and $\vec{\eta}$ are sequences of distinct variables that *include all of the variables of* $\vec{x}$; the remaining variables of the $\vec{\xi}$ and $\vec{\eta}$ are those being existentially quantified by the $\vec{v}$ and $\vec{w}$, respectively. $\vec{x}$ could be the empty sequence. Strongly context-free successor state axioms are special cases of the context-free successor state axioms defined in Section 9.2.2. The successor state axioms of the running blocks world example are strongly context-free. The following successor state axiom is context-free but not strongly context- free:

$$onTable(x, do(a, s)) \equiv a = putOnTable(x) \vee$$
$$onTable(x, s) \wedge a \neq tipTable \wedge a \neq pickup(x).$$

This is because the action $tipTable$ does not have x as an argument.

Consider a ground action term α, and the strongly context-free successor state axiom (9.6) for fluent F, relativized to the initial situation S_0. How does α affect the truth value of fluent F in the successor situation $do(\alpha, S_0)$? By the unique names axioms for actions, together with the assumption that the successor state axioms are strongly context-free, this relativized axiom will be logically equivalent to a sentence of the form:

$$F(\vec{x}, do(\alpha, S_0)) \equiv \vec{x} = \vec{X}^{(1)} \vee \cdots \vee \vec{x} = \vec{X}^{(m)} \vee$$
$$F(\vec{x}, S_0) \wedge \vec{x} \neq \vec{Y}^{(1)} \wedge \cdots \wedge \vec{x} \neq \vec{Y}^{(n)}. \qquad (9.7)$$

Here the $\vec{X}$ and $\vec{Y}$ are tuples of ground terms obtained from those mentioned by the ground action term α. This equivalence is at the heart of our proposal for translating from certain basic action theories of the situation calculus into STRIPS systems, a topic we pursue in the next two sections.

Example 9.4.1: Consider the running blocks world axiomatization, and the "generic" ground action $move(X, Y, Z)$. The corresponding instances of (9.7) for the fluents $clear$, on and $onTable$ are logically equivalent to:

$$clear(x, do(move(X, Y, Z), S_0)) \equiv x = Y \vee clear(x, S_0) \wedge x \neq Z,$$

$$on(x, y, do(move(X, Y, Z), S_0)) \equiv$$
$$x = X \wedge y = Z \vee on(x, y, S_0) \wedge \neg[x = X \wedge y = Y],$$

$onTable(x, do(move(X, Y, Z), S_0)) \equiv onTable(x, S_0).$

For the generic ground actions $moveFromTable(X, Y)$ and $moveToTable(X, Y)$ we obtain:

$clear(x, do(moveFromTable(X, Y), S_0)) \equiv clear(x, S_0) \wedge x \neq Y,$

$on(x, y, do(moveFromTable(X, Y), S_0)) \equiv x = X \wedge y = Y \vee on(x, y, S_0),$

$onTable(x, do(moveFromTable(X, Y), S_0)) \equiv onTable(x, S_0) \wedge x \neq X,$

$clear(x, do(moveToTable(X, Y), S_0)) \equiv x = Y \vee clear(x, S_0),$

$on(x, y, do(moveToTable(X, Y), S_0)) \equiv on(x, y, S_0) \wedge \neg[x = X \wedge y = Y],$

$onTable(x, do(moveToTable(X, Y), S_0)) \equiv x = X \vee onTable(x, S_0).$

9.5   Progression and Relational STRIPS

This section gives a precise correspondence between progression and relational STRIPS, showing that its operators are simply mechanisms for progressing relational databases.

The characterization of relational STRIPS starts with situation calculus basic action theories $\mathcal{D}$ of the form $\mathcal{D} = \Sigma \cup \mathcal{D}_{ss} \cup \mathcal{D}_{ap} \cup \mathcal{D}_{una} \cup \mathcal{D}_{S_0}$, with the following properties:

1. The basic action theory $\mathcal{D}$ is expressed in a situation calculus language with sorts *situation, action* and *object*. The sort *object* ranges over all the objects other than situations and actions that arise in an application domain. We assume that the only function symbols of sort *object* are constants.

2. $\mathcal{D}_{S_0}$ contains one sentence of the following form, for each fluent F:

$$F(\vec{x}, S_0) \equiv \vec{x} = \vec{C}^{(1)} \vee \cdots \vee \vec{x} = \vec{C}^{(n)}, \tag{9.8}$$

where the $\vec{C}^{(i)}$ are tuples of constant symbols of sort *object*. These are the only situation dependent sentences of $\mathcal{D}_{S_0}$. Notice that initial databases of this form are special cases of the relatively complete databases defined in Section 9.2.1. The case $n = 0$ is permitted, in which case this axiom is $F(\vec{x}, S_0) \equiv false$. For example, if an agent's hand is initially empty:

$holding(x, S_0) \equiv false.$

If initially, block A is on B, D is on A, C is on E, and no other block is on a block:

$on(x, y, S_0) \equiv x = A \wedge y = B \vee x = D \wedge y = A \vee x = C \wedge y = E.$

3. $\mathcal{D}_{S_0}$ contains *unique names axioms* for all constants of sort *object*: For each pair of distinct constant names C and C' of sort *object*, the axiom $C \neq C'$.

4. Each successor state axiom of $\mathcal{D}_{ss}$ is strongly context-free.

Now we characterize the result of progressing $\mathcal{D}_{S_0}$ under the effects of a ground action α in the case of action theories of the above kind. To do so, we appeal to the results on progressing relatively complete databases of Section 9.2.1. Consider the strongly context-free successor state axiom (9.7) for fluent F relativized to the initial situation S_0. By assumption (9.8) on the syntactic form of $\mathcal{D}_{S_0}$, (9.7) is equivalent to:

$$F(\vec{x}, do(\alpha, S_0)) \equiv \vec{x} = \vec{X}^{(1)} \vee \cdots \vee \vec{x} = \vec{X}^{(m)} \vee$$
$$[\vec{x} = \vec{C}^{(1)} \vee \cdots \vee \vec{x} = \vec{C}^{(n)}] \wedge \vec{x} \neq \vec{Y}^{(1)} \wedge \cdots \wedge \vec{x} \neq \vec{Y}^{(n)}.$$

Let $\vec{C}^{(1)}, \ldots, \vec{C}^{(r)}$ be *all* the $\vec{C}^{(k)}$ that are different tuples than *all* of the $\vec{Y}^{(i)}$. Then, by unique names axioms for constant symbols of sort *object*, the above sentence will be logically equivalent to

$$F(\vec{x}, do(\alpha, S_0)) \equiv \vec{x} = \vec{X}^{(1)} \vee \cdots \vee \vec{x} = \vec{X}^{(m)} \vee \vec{x} = \vec{C}^{(1)} \vee \cdots \vee \vec{x} = \vec{C}^{(r)}. \quad (9.9)$$

Let S be the following set of sentences:

1. Initialize S to $\{\phi \in \mathcal{D}_{S_0} \mid \phi \text{ is situation-independent}\}$.

2. For each fluent F, add the sentence (9.9) to S.

The resulting set S enjoys the property that $S \cup \mathcal{D}_{una}$ is a progression of $\mathcal{D}_{S_0}$ under action α (Theorem 9.2.2). Moreover, S has the same syntactic form as $\mathcal{D}_{S_0}$, and so can serve as a new initial database for the purposes of iterating the above progression mechanism.

The next step is to interpret the above construction of the set S as a relational STRIPS operator. Imagine representing the situation dependent sentences

$$F(\vec{x}, S_0) \equiv \vec{x} = \vec{C}^{(1)} \vee \cdots \vee \vec{x} = \vec{C}^{(n)} \quad (9.10)$$

by the relational database of ground instances $F(\vec{C}^{(1)}, S_0), \ldots, F(\vec{C}^{(n)}, S_0)$. We emphasize that this representation is merely a shorthand for the sentence (9.10). Next, imagine suppressing the situation argument S_0 of all the ground literals of this relational database, producing the STRIPS relational database $\mathcal{D}_0$. Finally, ask what sequence of deletions and additions of ground literals must be performed on $\mathcal{D}_0$, the situation-suppressed relational database version of $\mathcal{D}_{S_0}$, in order to obtain the situation-suppressed relational version of S (i.e. the relational database standing for S, with the situation argument $do(\alpha, S_0)$ suppressed in its sentences). The deletions and additions necessary to achieve this transformation of $\mathcal{D}_0$ to the corresponding relational database representation of S will define the delete and add lists for the STRIPS operator α.

It is easy to see that the following deletions and additions, when applied to $\mathcal{D}_0$, yield the situation-suppressed, relational database representation of S:

For each fluent F do (with reference to (9.7)):

1. Delete from $\mathcal{D}_0$ the sentences $F(\vec{Y}^{(i)})$, $i = 1, \ldots, n$.

2. Add to $\mathcal{D}_0$ the sentences $F(\vec{X}^{(i)})$, $i = 1, \ldots, m$.

Example 9.5.1: The three STRIPS operator descriptions

$$move(X, Y, Z), moveFromTable(X, Y) \text{ and } moveToTable(X, Y)$$

presented in Section 9.3.2 were obtained with this procedure, by "reading off" their add and delete lists from the "generic" sentences of Example 9.4.1.

9.6   An Open-World STRIPS

This section characterizes a different version of STRIPS, whose database is any set of ground, non-equality *literals* over a set of constants (not *atoms* as in relational STRIPS). Moreover, unlike relational STRIPS whose database is merely a compact notation standing for its official axiomatization, this STRIPS database will be taken literally. It *is* a logical theory, and its entailments are its logical entailments. Such databases of ground literals differ qualitatively from relational databases because they allow for open-worlds—open world in the sense that these databases need not be logically complete. For example, by omitting both $onTable(A)$ and $\neg onTable(A)$ from such an open-world database, we are representing that it is unknown whether A is on the table. In other words, such databases permit a certain degree of ignorance about the state of the world, and hence are more realistic for certain kinds of applications, like robotics.

   Our point of departure is an action theory $\mathcal{D} = \Sigma \cup \mathcal{D}_{ss} \cup \mathcal{D}_{ap} \cup \mathcal{D}_{una} \cup \mathcal{D}_{S_0}$, with the following properties:

1. The basic action theory $\mathcal{D}$ is expressed in a situation calculus language with sorts *situation*, *action* and *object*. The sort *object* ranges over all the objects other than situations and actions that arise in an application domain. The only function symbols of sort *object* are constants.

2. Each situation dependent sentence of $\mathcal{D}_{S_0}$ is a ground fluent literal, i.e. of the form $F(\vec{C}, S_0)$ or $\neg F(\vec{C}, S_0)$ for fluent F and constants $\vec{C}$ of sort *object*.

3. $\mathcal{D}_{S_0}$ contains *unique names axioms* for all constants of sort *object*.

4. $\mathcal{D}_{S_0}$ contains no pair of complementary literals (and hence is consistent).

5. Each successor state axiom of $\mathcal{D}_{ss}$ is strongly context-free.

6. For each fluent F, the consistency condition (9.4) is satisfied. It is easy (but tedious) to verify that each fluent of the blocks world Example 9.2.3 satisfies this condition.

In keeping with the intuition that STRIPS systems are mechanisms for progressing situation calculus databases, we want now to characterize the result of progressing $\mathcal{D}_{S_0}$ under the effects of the ground action α in the case of action theories of the above kind. The basis for this will be Theorem 9.2.5 that characterized progression for databases with isolated fluents.

Let S be the following set of sentences:

1. Initialize S to $\{\phi \in \mathcal{D}_{S_0} \mid \phi \text{ is situation-independent}\}$.

2. For each fluent F do (with reference to the instance (9.7) of F's successor state axiom):

   (a) Add to S the sentence $F(\vec{X}^{(i)}, do(\alpha, S_0))$, $i = 1, \ldots, m$.

   (b) For each ground instance $F(\vec{C}, S_0) \in \mathcal{D}_{S_0}$ add the sentence $F(\vec{C}, do(\alpha, S_0))$ to S, whenever $\vec{C}$ is a tuple of constants different from each $\vec{Y}^{(i)}$, $i = 1, \ldots, n$. (Here, we invoke the unique names axioms for constants of sort *object*).

   (c) Add to S the sentence $\neg F(\vec{Y}^{(i)}, do(\alpha, S_0))$, $i = 1, \ldots, n$.

   (d) For each ground instance $\neg F(\vec{C}, S_0) \in \mathcal{D}_{S_0}$ add the sentence $\neg F(\vec{C}, do(\alpha, S_0))$ to S, whenever $\vec{C}$ is a tuple of constants different from each $\vec{X}^{(i)}$, $i = 1, \ldots, m$. (We again invoke the unique names axioms for constants of sort *object*).

By Theorem 9.2.5, the resulting set S enjoys the property that $S \cup \mathcal{D}_{una}$ is a progression of $\mathcal{D}_{S_0}$ under action α. Moreover, the situation dependent sentences of S are all ground literals, and S contains no pair of complementary literals. It follows that S can serve as a new initial database for the purposes of iterating the above progression mechanism.

Now we interpret the above construction of the set S as a STRIPS operator. Imagine suppressing the situation argument S_0 of all the ground literals of $\mathcal{D}_{S_0}$. Next, ask what sequence of deletions and additions of ground literals must be performed on the situation-suppressed version of $\mathcal{D}_{S_0}$ in order to obtain the situation-suppressed version of S (i.e. S with the situation argument $do(\alpha, S_0)$ suppressed in its sentences). The deletions and additions necessary to achieve this situation-suppressed transformation of $\mathcal{D}_{S_0}$ to S will define the delete and add lists for the open-world STRIPS operator α.

It is easy to see that the following deletions and additions, when applied to $\mathcal{D}_0$, the situation-suppressed version of $\mathcal{D}_{S_0}$, yields the situation-suppressed version of S:

For each fluent F do (with reference to the instance (9.7) of F's successor state axiom):

1. Delete from $\mathcal{D}_0$ the sentences $\neg F(\vec{X}^{(i)})$, $i = 1, \ldots, m$.
2. Delete from $\mathcal{D}_0$ the sentences $F(\vec{Y}^{(i)})$, $i = 1, \ldots, n$.
3. Add to $\mathcal{D}_0$ the sentences $F(\vec{X}^{(i)})$, $i = 1, \ldots, m$.
4. Add to $\mathcal{D}_0$ the sentences $\neg F(\vec{Y}^{(i)})$, $i = 1, \ldots, n$.

It is now clear how to define the operator description for α:

1. For each fluent F, include in α's add and delete lists those literals specified above for obtaining the situation suppressed version of S.

2. α's precondition is the situation-suppressed version of the right-hand side of the equivalence in α's situation calculus action precondition axiom.

3. A ground instance of the operator α is applicable in a given open-world database of ground literals iff this database entails the corresponding instance of α's precondition.

Example 9.6.1: Continuing with the blocks world example, we can "read off" the STRIPS operator schema for *move* from the instances of the successor state axioms given in Example 9.4.1:

$move(X, Y, Z)^4$

> P: $clear(X) \wedge clear(Z) \wedge on(X, Y) \wedge X \neq Z$.
> D: $\neg clear(Y), clear(Z), \neg on(X, Z), on(X, Y)$.
> A: $clear(Y), \neg clear(Z), on(X, Z), \neg on(X, Y)$.

The operator description schemas for *moveFromTable* and *moveToTable* are obtained in the same way:

$moveFromTable(X, Y)$

> P: $clear(X) \wedge clear(Y) \wedge onTable(X) \wedge X \neq Y$.
> D: $\neg on(X, Y), onTable(X), clear(Y)$.
> A: $on(X, Y), \neg onTable(X), \neg clear(Y)$.

$moveToTable(X, Y)$

> P: $clear(X) \wedge on(X, Y)$.
> D: $\neg clear(Y), on(X, Y), \neg onTable(X)$.
> A: $clear(Y), \neg on(X, Y), onTable(X)$.

9.7 Correctness of Relational and Open-World STRIPS

The previous sections showed how to obtain two different versions of STRIPS—relational and open-world—from suitable basic action theories in the situation calculus. Now we establish the correctness of these translations of the situation calculus into STRIPS operators, in the sense that for the purposes of planning, the situation calculus axioms and their translations into relational and open-world STRIPS are equivalent.

In Section 9.3.3, we gave the definition of a STRIPS plan. We first discussed planning in the situation calculus in Section 3.3. There, we proposed the following idea. Suppose $G(s)$ is a situation calculus formula with a single free variable s. A sequence of ground action terms $[\alpha_1, \ldots, \alpha_n]$ is a *plan for achieving G* relative to background axioms *Axioms* iff

---

4 Recall that these are *schemas*, standing for the family of operator descriptions obtained by instantiating the "variables" X, Y, and Z of the schema by constants of our situation calculus language.

$Axioms \models executable(do([\alpha_1, \ldots, \alpha_n], S_0)) \wedge G(do([\alpha_1, \ldots, \alpha_n], S_0)).$

It is relatively straightforward to prove:

Theorem 9.7.1: Correctness of Relational STRIPS.

Suppose

1. $\mathcal{D}$ *is a basic action theory satisfying properties 1 - 4 of Section 9.5.*

2. $\mathcal{R}$ *is the relational STRIPS system obtained from $\mathcal{D}$ by the procedure described in Section 9.5.*

3. $[\alpha_1, \ldots, \alpha_n]$ *is a sequence of ground action terms.*

4. $G(s)$ *is a situation calculus formula, with one free variable s, that is uniform in s, and mentions no terms of sort* action.

Then $[\alpha_1, \ldots, \alpha_n]$ is a plan for achieving G in the situation calculus relative to the basic action theory $\mathcal{D}$ iff it is a plan for G in the relational STRIPS system $\mathcal{R}$, where G is $G(s)$ with all its situation arguments suppressed.

In short, the plans for the situation calculus basic action theory of the theorem, according to the classical, deductive definition of planning are precisely the plans for its translation into a relational STRIPS system, according to the STRIPS definition of planning. In other words, this theorem establishes the correctness of our translation, into relational STRIPS, of suitable basic action theories of the situation calculus.

In exactly the same way, one can prove the correctness of the above translation into open-world STRIPS systems.

Theorem 9.7.2: Correctness of Open-World STRIPS.

Suppose

1. $\mathcal{D}$ *is a basic action theory satisfying properties 1 - 6 of Section 9.6.*

2. $\mathcal{O}$ *is the open-world STRIPS system obtained from $\mathcal{D}$ by the procedure described in Section 9.6.*

3. $[\alpha_1, \ldots, \alpha_n]$ *is a sequence of ground action terms.*

4. $G(s)$ *is a situation calculus formula, with one free variable s, that is uniform in s, and mentions no terms of sort* action.

Then $[\alpha_1, \ldots, \alpha_n]$ is a plan for achieving G in the situation calculus relative to the basic action theory $\mathcal{D}$ iff it is a plan for G in the open-world STRIPS system $\mathcal{O}$, where G is $G(s)$ with all its situation arguments suppressed.

To our knowledge, this open-world version of STRIPS is the only variant of STRIPS that provides for an incomplete database of ground literals, and that is provably correct with respect to a logical specification.

9.8 Exercises

1. Prove that the progressed database S, obtained in Section 9.2.2, is coherent. (Hint: Use the facts that the initial database is coherent, and that the consistency condition (9.4) is satisfied.)

2. Compare the blocks world axiomatization of this chapter with the one of Example 6.5.2. What was achieved by modifying the earlier one?

3. Axiomatize the game of tic-tac-toe on a 3×3 board, using strongly context-free successor state axioms and relational database axioms for the initial situation. (See Exercise 3.5, question 3.)

    (a) Progress this initial database in response to the sequence of moves: mark 1 with X, mark 3 with O, mark 6 with X.

    (b) Determine the relational STRIPS operators for the actions of this axiomatization.

4. Consider the axiomatization of the education database of Section 3.4.2. The successor state axiom for $grade(st, c, g, s)$ is *not* strongly context-free. (Why?) To make it so, we can replace the transaction $change(st, c, g)$ by $change(st, c, g, g')$, meaning change the grade of st in course c from g to g'. Axiomatize this revised database using strongly context-free successor state axioms, and determine the open-world STRIPS operators for the actions

$$register(st, c), change(st, c, g, g') \text{ and } drop(st, c).$$

5. The correctness of the translation from suitable basic action theories to the two versions of STRIPS relies on the assumption that all successor state axioms are strongly context-free. A close inspection of these proofs reveals that the only way this strongly context-free property is used is to guarantee that the equivalence (9.7) can be derived from them. From this equivalence, we "read off" the add and delete lists for the two versions of STRIPS. In other words, *any* context-free successor state axioms that yield equivalences of this form will give rise to a correct translation to relational and open-world STRIPS systems, using exactly the same mechanism for "reading off", from (9.7), the operators' add and delete lists. Strongly context-free successor state axioms are simply one class guaranteed to yield such equivalences. Invent some other such classes, but remember, they must be context-free. (Why?)

6. This question explores the extent to which relational databases are logically complete.

(a) Prove that a relational database is complete for ground atoms, i.e. for any such atom γ, a relational database entails γ or it entails $\neg\gamma$.

(b) Hence, prove that a relational database is complete for quantifier-free sentences.

(c) Prove, by example, that a relational database need not be complete for quantified sentences.

(d) Prove that a relational database is complete for quantified sentences of the form $(\forall \vec{x}).A_1 \wedge \cdots \wedge A_n \supset \phi$ where $n \geq 1$, each A_i is a relational atom, every variable of $\vec{x}$ is mentioned by $A_1 \wedge \cdots \wedge A_n$, and ϕ is a quantifier-free formula all of whose free variables are among $\vec{x}$.

(e) A *domain closure axiom* has the form: $(\forall x).x = C_1 \vee \cdots \vee x = C_n$ for constants $C_1, \ldots, C_n$. Prove that if a relational database also includes a domain closure axiom, then it is complete for all first-order sentences.

9.9   Bibliographic Remarks

Most of the material in this chapter is drawn from Lin and Reiter [126], which contains a proof that basic action theories do not always have a first-order progression. Their definition of progression differs from ours, but the two can be proved equivalent. The paper also proves that, for finite initial databases, there is always a second-order progression, and it gives a procedure for computing it. Lakemeyer and Levesque [102] consider progression for a language amalgamating the situation calculus with Levesque's logic of only-knowing [116]. The earliest negative result on progression is due to Pednault [153], who showed that the progression of a finite first-order database need not be finite. The definition of progression is closely related to the more general notion of an arbitrary first-order theory "forgetting" about some of its information content. In our case, progression corresponds to $\mathcal{D}$ forgetting about what is true of those situations not in the future of S_α. This idea is defined and explored by Lin and Reiter [124].

Ever since STRIPS was first introduced (Fikes and Nilsson [49]), its logical semantics has been problematic. There have been many proposals in the literature (e.g. Lifschitz [121]; Erol, Nau, and Subrahmanian [44]; Bacchus and Yang [12]). These all have in common a reliance on meta-theoretic operations on logical theories to capture the add and delete lists of STRIPS operators, but it has never been clear exactly what these operations correspond to declaratively, especially when they are applied to logically incomplete theories. Perhaps the first attempt to provide a logical semantics for STRIPS was by Lifschitz [121]. Pednault [154, 153] was the first to relate a STRIPS database to the initial situation of a situation calculus axiomatization. Our interpretation of such a database, namely as a situation-suppressed situation calculus *theory*, distinguishes our approach from Pednault's, in which these databases are first-order *structures*. So for Pednault, a STRIPS operator is a mapping from first-order structures to first-order structures, where this mapping is defined by the addition and deletion of tuples applied to the relations of the structure. ADL, Pednault's generalization of STRIPS, is defined by just such a mapping between structures. For us, as for Lifschitz [121], a STRIPS operator is a mapping from first-order theories to (possibly second order) theories, where this mapping is effected by add and delete lists of *sentences* applied to the theory.

10 Planning

The situation calculus has occasionally served as a theoretical device for the study of planning in AI, but except for a brief period in the early 1970's in connection with the SRI Shakey robot, it has never been taken seriously in the implementation of planning systems. Instead, variants of STRIPS have been the preferred representations for the planning community. In keeping with one of the main themes of this book—that the situation calculus provides a very general, and practical formalism for modeling dynamical systems—we devote this chapter to the design and implementation of some situation calculus planning systems.

10.1 A Simple Breadth-First Planner

We begin with a seemingly hopeless idea—a breadth-first, iterative deepening planner. The planner first checks whether the goal sentence is true in the initial situation. If so, it succeeds, else it generates all length one sequences of actions satisfying their preconditions, succeeding if any such sequence makes the goal true. Otherwise, it generates all length two sequences of actions satisfying their preconditions, succeeding if any of these satisfies the goal, etc. The process terminates with failure if it ever exceeds some bound on the action sequence lengths. The planner uses *iterative deepening*: Having tried all action sequences of length n, it *recomputes* all sequences of length $\leq n$ in the process of generating potential plans of length $n + 1$. In contrast, one could instead save all the appropriate action sequences of length n, using these to generate the length $n + 1$ sequences, but iterative deepening does not do this, preferring to trade off time against space. Iterative deepening seems to add to the hopelessness of the breadth-first search mechanism, but in fact, its negative effects are not so pronounced as one might initially expect. One can prove (Exercise 4 below) that iterative deepening expands of the order of $b/(b-1)$ times as many nodes of the tree of action sequences as would the alternative space consuming mechanism. Here, b is the branching factor of the tree. In other words, most of the nodes in the tree are found on its fringe. One obvious advantage of a breadth-first planner is that it is guaranteed to find a shortest plan, if it finds one at all.

The following is a Golog program for such a planner. The user supplies a predicate $goal(s)$, which is the goal for which a plan is sought. He must also supply two domain dependent predicates: $primitive\_action(a)$, which is true iff a is one of the primitive action terms of the domain, and $badSituation(s)$, which is true iff, based on domain specific knowledge, and depending on the goal, s is considered to be a bad situation for the planner to consider. It is in $badSituation$ where all the planner's intelligence resides. The rest of *wspbf's* behaviour is simply blind, uncomprehending search.[1]

> **proc** $wspbf(n)$
> $plans(0, n)$
> **endProc**
>
> **proc** $plans(m, n)$
> $m \leq n?\,;\, [actionSequence(m)\,;\, goal?\,|\, plans(m + 1, n)]$
> **endProc**
>
> **proc** $actionSequence(n)$
> $n = 0?\,|$
> $n > 0?\,;\, (\pi a)[primitive\_action(a)?\,;\, a]\,;\, \neg badSituation?\,;$
> $actionSequence(n - 1)$
> **endProc**

The following is a Prolog implementation of this Golog program, suitably embellished with statistics gathering mechanisms.

Implementation of World's Simplest Breadth-First Planner

```
proc(wspbf(N), ?(initializeSitCount) : ?(initializeCPU) : plans(0,N)).

proc(plans(M,N),
        ?(M =< N) :
        (actionSequence(M) : ?(goal) :
         ?(reportSuccess) : ?(prettyPrintSituation) #
         pi(m1, ?(m1 is M + 1) :
         ?(reportLevel(m1)) : plans(m1,N)))).

proc(actionSequence(N),
        ?(N = 0) #
        ?(N > 0) : pi(a,?(primitive_action(a)) : a) :
        ?(-badSituation) : ?(incrementSitCount) :
        pi(n1, ?(n1 is N - 1) : actionSequence(n1))).

planbf(N) :- do(wspbf(N),s0,S), askForMore.

reportLevel(N) :- write('Starting level '), write(N),
                reportCPUtime, write('  Good situations: '),
                getval(sitCount,C), write(C), nl.
```

---

[1] *wspbf* stands for the World's Simplest Breadth-First Planner.

```
initializeSitCount :- setval(sitCount,0). /* Eclipse Prolog provides
                                             global variables.  */

initializeCPU :- cputime(T), setval(cpu,T).

incrementSitCount :- incval(sitCount).  % Increment global variable.

reportCPUtime :- cputime(T),  write('  CPU time (sec): '),
               getval(cpu,T2), T1 is T - T2, write(T1).

reportSuccess :- nl, write('Success.'), reportCPUtime,
    write('  Good situations: '), getval(sitCount,C), write(C), nl.

prettyPrintSituation(S) :- makeActionList(S,Alist), nl, write(Alist), nl.

makeActionList(s0,[]).
makeActionList(do(A,S),L) :- makeActionList(S,L1), append(L1,[A],L).

restoreSitArg(prettyPrintSituation,S,prettyPrintSituation(S)).
restoreSitArg(badSituation,S,badSituation(S)).
restoreSitArg(goal,S,goal(S)).

askForMore :- write('More? '), read(n).
```

10.2   Example: Planning in the Blocks World

In this section, we shall exercise our breadth-first planner on the blocks world of Example 6.5.2 in the Golog chapter.   For convenience, we here repeat the axioms given in that example:

Action Precondition Axioms

$Poss(move(x, y), s) \equiv clear(x, s) \wedge clear(y, s) \wedge x \neq y,$

$Poss(moveToTable(x), s) \equiv clear(x, s) \wedge \neg ontable(x, s).$

Successor State Axioms

$clear(x, do(a, s)) \equiv$
$\quad\quad (\exists y)\{[(\exists z)a = move(y, z) \vee a = moveToTable(y)] \wedge on(y, x, s)\} \vee$
$\quad\quad clear(x, s) \wedge \neg(\exists y)a = move(y, x),$

$on(x, y, do(a, s)) \equiv a = move(x, y) \vee$

$$on(x, y, s) \land a \neq moveToTable(x) \land \neg(\exists z)a = move(x, z),$$

$$ontable(x, do(a, s)) \equiv a = moveToTable(x) \lor$$
$$ontable(x, s) \land \neg(\exists y)a = move(x, y).$$

The following is the straightforward Prolog formulation of these axioms.

Prolog Clauses for a Simple Blocks World

```
%  Action Precondition Axioms.

poss(move(X,Y),S) :- clear(X,S), clear(Y,S), not X = Y.
poss(moveToTable(X),S) :- clear(X,S), not ontable(X,S).

%  Successor State Axioms.

clear(X,do(A,S)) :- (A = move(Y,Z) ; A = moveToTable(Y)), on(Y,X,S) ;
                    clear(X,S), not A = move(Y,X).
on(X,Y,do(A,S)) :- A = move(X,Y) ;
                    on(X,Y,S), not A = moveToTable(X), not A = move(X,Z).
ontable(X,do(A,S)) :- A = moveToTable(X) ;
                    ontable(X,S), not A = move(X,Y).

%  Primitive Action Declarations.

primitive_action(move(X,Y)).    primitive_action(moveToTable(X)).
```

The next task is to characterize the bad situations for the blocks world. As we are about to see, very powerful planning advice can be given that takes the goal into account. Let $goodTower(x, s)$ be true whenever, in situation s, x is a good tower, meaning that x is the top block of a tower of blocks that is a sub-tower of one of the goal towers. For example, if the planning goal calls for the construction of a tower consisting of block A on top of B on top of C, with A the top block and C the bottom, then $goodTower(A, s)$ will be true whenever, in s, A is a three block tower consisting of A on top of B on top of C, with C on the table. $goodTower(B, s)$ will be true whenever, in s, B is a two block tower consisting of B on top of C, with C on the table. Finally, $goodTower(C, s)$ will be true whenever, in s, C is a one block tower, with C on the table. Suppose the planner has available to it a description of all the good towers corresponding to its planning goal. Then the following are all characteristic rules about what to do, and not do, in blocks world planning:

1. Never create a bad (= not good) tower by moving a block onto a tower. This makes sense because a bad tower might contain blocks that will need to be moved later in

the construction of good towers, so there is no point in stacking more blocks on top of them, since the table is always available for the temporary storage of a block.

2. Never move anything from a good tower. This rule makes sense because, in the blocks world, towers are built from the bottom up; having built a good base, one need never disassemble this to achieve the goal. Notice whenever one moves a block from a good tower onto another tower, one is necessarily creating a bad tower, so this case is covered by the previous rule. Hence, the current rule says that one should never move a block from a good tower to the table.

3. *Opportunistic rule:* Don't do an action that creates a bad tower whenever there is an action that creates a good tower. Whenever there is a choice between creating a bad tower and creating a good tower, choose the good tower. Because of the first rule, the only action permitted that can create a bad tower is a *moveToTable* action. So the present rule really says: Never move a block to the table if that block by itself is a bad tower, whenever there is some other action that can be performed that creates a good tower.

Taken together, these rules enforce the following search strategy that is repeated until the goal is satisfied, or some depth bound is exceeded: If it is at all possible to create a good tower, do so; else, move a block to the table, but be sure it doesn't come from a good tower.

Even with the above rules in force, redundancy remains in the search space. For example, suppose that these rules permit two consecutive *move* actions. Then both must be good-tower producing actions. Suppose further that these can be performed in either order. Then doing so gives rise to two plans that will differ only in the order in which these *move* actions were done. The same remark can be made if one of the actions is a *move* and the other is a *moveToTable*, provided the latter creates a good tower. (The rules guarantee that the first creates a good tower.) Similarly, if they are both good-tower producing *moveToTable* actions. These observations yield the following principle for canonically ordering plans with respect to good-tower producing actions:

If there are two good-tower producing actions that can be done in either order, then they can safely be done in the order that moves the lexicographically least block. The only plans eliminated from the search space by doing so are those obtained by performing the two actions in the other order.

All of the above *search control rules* can be encoded in the predicate *badSituation* used by *wspbf*. Only situations that respect these rules will survive during *wspbf's* generation of its search tree; all *badSituation*s, and their successors, will be pruned from the tree. As we shall see, this has a profound effect on the size of the search tree of situations generated by *wspbf*. The following Prolog clauses encode these rules using *badSituation*:

Bad Situations for a Simple Blocks World

```
%  Don't create a bad tower by a move action.

badSituation(do(move(X,Y),S)) :- not goodTower(X,do(move(X,Y),S)).

%  Don't move anything from a good tower to the table.

badSituation(do(moveToTable(X),S)) :- goodTower(X,S).

/*  Opportunistic rule: If an action can create a good tower, don't
    do a bad-tower-creating moveToTable action.  */

badSituation(do(moveToTable(X),S)) :-
                        not goodTower(X,do(moveToTable(X),S)),
                        existsActionThatCreatesGoodTower(S).

existsActionThatCreatesGoodTower(S) :-
                   (A = move(Y,X) ; A = moveToTable(Y)),
                   poss(A,S), goodTower(Y,do(A,S)).

%  Canonical ordering of good-tower producing actions.

badSituation(do(move(X1,Y1),do(move(X2,Y2),S))) :- X1 @< X2,
                   poss(move(X1,Y1),S),
                   poss(move(X2,Y2),do(move(X1,Y1),S)).
badSituation(do(move(X1,Y1),do(moveToTable(X2),S))) :- X1 @< X2,
                   poss(move(X1,Y1),S),
                   poss(moveToTable(X2),do(move(X1,Y1),S)),
                   goodTower(X2,do(moveToTable(X2),S)).
badSituation(do(moveToTable(X1),do(move(X2,Y2),S))) :- X1 @< X2,
                   poss(moveToTable(X1),S),
                   poss(move(X2,Y2),do(moveToTable(X1),S)),
                   goodTower(X1,do(moveToTable(X1),S)).
badSituation(do(moveToTable(X1),do(moveToTable(X2),S))) :- X1 @< X2,
                   poss(moveToTable(X1),S),
                   poss(moveToTable(X2),do(moveToTable(X1),S)),
                   goodTower(X1,do(moveToTable(X1),S)),
                   goodTower(X2,do(moveToTable(X2),S)).
```

10.2.1   A Planning Problem Example

Now, we introduce a blocks world planning problem that will serve as a running example
for the next few sections of this chapter. It has 10 blocks, stacked initially into the three
towers shown. The problem is to find a sequence of actions that will yield the two goal
towers shown. The good towers, used in the specification of the *badSituations*, are all the
possible subtowers of the two goal towers.

A Blocks World Problem

```
/* Initial Situation   u
                       a
                       b   v
                       c   e   w
                       d   f   g                          */

ontable(d,s0).  ontable(f,s0).  ontable(g,s0).  on(u,a,s0).
on(a,b,s0).  on(b,c,s0).  on(c,d,s0).  on(v,e,s0).  on(e,f,s0).
on(w,g,s0).  clear(u,s0).  clear(v,s0).  clear(w,s0).

/* Goal                 u
                        v
                        w
                        d
                        c   g
                        b   f
                        a   e                            */

goal(S) :- ontable(a,S), ontable(e,S), on(u,v,S), on(v,w,S),
           on(w,d,S), on(d,c,S), on(c,b,S), on(b,a,S),
           on(g,f,S), on(f,e,S), clear(u,S), clear(g,S).

% Good towers.

goodTower(a,S)  :- ontable(a,S).
goodTower(b,S)  :- on(b,a,S), goodTower(a,S).
goodTower(c,S)  :- on(c,b,S), goodTower(b,S).
goodTower(d,S)  :- on(d,c,S), goodTower(c,S).
goodTower(w,S)  :- on(w,d,S), goodTower(d,S).
goodTower(v,S)  :- on(v,w,S), goodTower(w,S).
goodTower(u,S)  :- on(u,v,S), goodTower(v,S).

goodTower(e,S)  :- ontable(e,S).
goodTower(f,S)  :- on(f,e,S), goodTower(e,S).
```

```
goodTower(g,S) :- on(g,f,S), goodTower(f,S).
```

With this specification in hand of a planning problem, together with the Golog interpreter, the blocks world axioms and the clauses for *badSituation*, we are ready to try out the planner. But first, just to get some idea of the size of the search space for this problem, we run the planner *without* filtering out the undesirable situations with *badSituations*.[2]

A Breadth-First Run for the Example Planning Problem without badSituations

```
[eclipse 2]: planbf(15).
Starting level 1  CPU time (sec): 0.0  Good situations: 0
Starting level 2  CPU time (sec): 0.01  Good situations: 9
Starting level 3  CPU time (sec): 0.04  Good situations: 114
Starting level 4  CPU time (sec): 0.43  Good situations: 1381
Starting level 5  CPU time (sec): 5.99  Good situations: 18651
Starting level 6  CPU time (sec): 96.17  Good situations: 284278
Starting level 7  CPU time (sec): 1713.18  Good situations: 4849881
^C
Aborting execution ...
```

Without a mechanism for filtering out bad situations, the breadth-first planner has no future. Next, we run the planner *with* the *badSituations*.

A Breadth-First Run for the Example Planning Problem with badSituations

```
[eclipse 2]: planbf(15).
Starting level 1  CPU time (sec): 0.0  Good situations: 0
Starting level 2  CPU time (sec): 0.0  Good situations: 3
Starting level 3  CPU time (sec): 0.01  Good situations: 10
Starting level 4  CPU time (sec): 0.03  Good situations: 21
Starting level 5  CPU time (sec): 0.06  Good situations: 37
Starting level 6  CPU time (sec): 0.1  Good situations: 58
Starting level 7  CPU time (sec): 0.17  Good situations: 84
Starting level 8  CPU time (sec): 0.26  Good situations: 115
Starting level 9  CPU time (sec): 0.37  Good situations: 152
Starting level 10  CPU time (sec): 0.51  Good situations: 196
Starting level 11  CPU time (sec): 0.68  Good situations: 248

Success.  CPU time (sec): 0.7  Good situations: 260

[moveToTable(u), moveToTable(a), move(b, a), move(c, b),
```

2 All CPU times here, and for the rest of this chapter, are for a SUN Enterprise 450, with four 400MHz UltraSPARC-II processors and 4GB of RAM.

```
move(d, c), move(w, d), move(v, w), moveToTable(e), move(f, e),
move(g, f), move(u, v)]
More?  y.
Starting level 12  CPU time (sec): 0.9  Good situations: 307

Success.  CPU time (sec): 0.96  Good situations: 333

[moveToTable(v), moveToTable(e), move(f, e), moveToTable(u),
 moveToTable(a), move(b, a), move(c, b), move(d, c), move(w, d),
 move(g, f), move(v, w), move(u, v)]
More?  y.

Success.  CPU time (sec): 1.06  Good situations: 357

[moveToTable(w), moveToTable(u), moveToTable(a), move(b, a),
 move(c, b), move(d, c), move(w, d), move(v, w), moveToTable(e),
 move(f, e), move(g, f), move(u, v)]
More?  y.
Starting level 13  CPU time (sec): 1.14  Good situations: 370

Success.  CPU time (sec): 1.26  Good situations: 408

[moveToTable(v), moveToTable(e), move(f, e), moveToTable(w),
 move(g, f), moveToTable(u), moveToTable(a), move(b, a), move(c, b),
 move(d, c), move(w, d), move(v, w), move(u, v)]
More?  y.

Success.  CPU time (sec): 1.36  Good situations: 435

[moveToTable(w), moveToTable(v), moveToTable(e), move(f, e),
 move(g, f), moveToTable(u), moveToTable(a), move(b, a), move(c, b),
 move(d, c), move(w, d), move(v, w), move(u, v)]
More?  y.
Starting level 14  CPU time (sec): 1.39  Good situations: 435
Starting level 15  CPU time (sec): 1.65  Good situations: 500
Starting level 16  CPU time (sec): 1.91  Good situations: 565

no (more) solution.
```

The *badSituations* made an enormous difference. The planner quickly found a unique shortest plan, of length 11, two of length 12, and two of length 13. No plans exist of length 14, 15, or 16.

10.3 Planning with Concurrent Actions

With a little extra effort, the breadth-first planner of the previous section can be used for planning with concurrent actions, and this section shows how to do this. The point of departure is the concurrent, non-temporal situation calculus of Section 7.5. So the picture we have in mind is that of a collection of primitive actions, all with equal but unspecified durations, and the co-occurrence of two or more such actions means that they all begin and end together.

First, we need to suitably axiomatize the blocks world. The action precondition axioms for the primitive actions remain the same as for the sequential blocks world. Following the approach to axiomatizing concurrent worlds of Section 7.6, we obtain the following:

Successor State Axioms

$$clear(x, do(c, s)) \equiv$$
$$(\exists y)\{[(\exists z)move(y, z) \in c \lor moveToTable(y) \in c] \land on(y, x, s)\} \lor$$
$$clear(x, s) \land \neg(\exists y)move(y, x) \in c,$$

$$on(x, y, do(c, s)) \equiv move(x, y) \in c \lor$$
$$on(x, y, s) \land moveToTable(x) \notin c \land \neg(\exists z)move(x, z) \in c,$$

$$ontable(x, do(c, s)) \equiv moveToTable(x) \in c \lor$$
$$ontable(x, s) \land \neg(\exists y)move(x, y) \in c.$$

To continue using $wspbf$ for the purposes of concurrent planning requires a tiny modification to the procedure $actionSequence$ called by $wspbf$:

proc $actionSequence(n)$
$n = 0? \mid$
$n > 0?\,; (\pi c)[concurrentAction(c)?\,; c]\,; \neg badSituation?\,;$
$actionSequence(n - 1)$
endProc

Now $actionSequence$ nondeterministically generates a concurrent action to be tested by the predicate $badSituation$ instead of a primitive action.

Next, because $wspbf$ is executed by Golog, the Golog interpreter must be modified slightly to work for concurrent actions instead of simple actions. The clause by which Golog interprets primitive actions is:

```
do(E,S,do(E,S)) :- primitive_action(E), poss(E,S).
```

To have Golog instead interpret concurrent actions, replace this clause by the following two clauses:

```
do(C,S,do(C,S)) :- concurrentAction(C), poss(C,S).
concurrentAction([A | C]).
```

Next, we must specify the *badSituation*'s for concurrent actions. These are natural generalizations of those of Section 10.2 for the sequential blocks world. $do(c, s)$ is a *badsituation* iff:

1. c contains $move(x, y)$ and x is not a good tower in $do(c, s)$, or

2. c contains $moveToTable(x)$ and x is a good tower in s, or

3. c does not contain *all* good-tower-producing actions. This is a generalization of the opportunistic rule of the sequential blocks world. That rule required that if a good-tower-producing action is possible, then the next action to be done must be one of these. In the concurrent setting, we extend this to the *maximally opportunistic rule*: c must contain *all* actions that create a good tower.

In the sequential case, there was also a fourth class of *badSituation*s that imposed a canonical ordering on the good-tower-producing actions, but this is irrelevant in the concurrent setting, because the maximally opportunistic rule collects all of these together into one set.

Finally, we must specify the clauses for $Poss(c, s)$ for concurrent actions c, after which we can try out our concurrent planner. One approach to $Poss(c, s)$ is to write clauses that nondeterministically generate a nonempty set c of primitive actions such that:

1. Each primitive action $a \in c$ is possible.

2. All actions in c are *compatible*. Not any set c of primitive actions can be considered possible. For example, $move(A, B)$ and $moveToTable(A)$ conflict with each other, so c must not contain both of them together. In other words, in the construction of c, the precondition interaction problem of Section 7.6.2 must be taken into account.

With clauses for $Poss(c, s)$ that nondeterministically generate such a set c of compatible primitive actions, we would be done. The Golog interpreter would call $Poss(c, s)$ to generate a concurrent action c, and $wspbf(n)$ would ask *badSituation* whether or not c is acceptable. In principle, this would work, but in practice it is computationally unfeasible. The sizes and the numbers of such sets c become too large. A method is needed to quickly reduce the space of all such sets c. A moment's thought reveals where the problem lies. The above procedure *first* generates one of many possible sets c, and only after doing so does it filter out the bad ones with *badSituation*.

A smarter method would appeal to some of the *badSituation*s earlier, during the generation of the sets c. For example, no action that destroys a good tower should be admitted into c during its generation phase. More generally, certain individual actions

might be known, in advance, to be bad actions, and in generating a potential concurrent
action c, such bad actions should not be permitted. This is what the implementation does.
The following is the Prolog code for the concurrent blocks world; it is commented with a
description of exactly how the clause for poss(C,S) generates concurrent actions C, filtering
out those actions that are specified to be badActions.

Prolog Clauses for a Blocks World with Concurrent Actions

```
/* Poss for concurrent actions. These clauses are independent of
   the blocks world.  */

poss(C,S) :- concurrentAction(C),

    /* First determine all good primitive actions that are
       possible in situation S. */

            setof(A,
                    (primitive_action(A), poss(A,S), not badAction(A,S)),
                    GoodActions),

   /* Next, determine a maximal subset of these whose actions do not
      conflict with one another.   */

            maxCompatibleSubset(GoodActions,Max,S),

% Finally, any subset of these is a possible concurrent action.

            subset(C,Max).

maxCompatibleSubset(C,Max,S) :- getTwoMembers(C,A,B),
                conflict(A,B,S), (delete(A,C,D) ; delete(B,C,D)),
                maxCompatibleSubset(D,Max,S), !.
maxCompatibleSubset(C,C,S).

getTwoMembers([A | L],A,B) :- member(B,L).
getTwoMembers([X | L],A,B) :- getTwoMembers(L,A,B).

/*************************************************************/

        %    Blocks World Specific Clauses.

%   Successor State Axioms.
```

```
clear(X,do(C,S)) :- (member(move(Y,Z),C) ; member(moveToTable(Y),C)),
                        on(Y,X,S) ;
                        clear(X,S), not member(move(Y,X),C).
on(X,Y,do(C,S)) :- member(move(X,Y),C) ;
                        on(X,Y,S), not member(moveToTable(X),C),
                                   not member(move(X,Z),C).
ontable(X,do(C,S)) :- member(moveToTable(X),C) ;
                        ontable(X,S), not member(move(X,Y),C).

%   Action Precondition Axioms

poss(move(X,Y),S) :- clear(X,S), clear(Y,S), not X = Y.
poss(moveToTable(X),S) :- clear(X,S), not ontable(X,S).

conflict(move(X,Y),move(Y,Z),S).  conflict(move(Y,Z),move(X,Y),S).
conflict(move(X,Y),moveToTable(X),S). conflict(moveToTable(X),move(X,Y),S).
conflict(move(X,Y),moveToTable(Y),S). conflict(moveToTable(Y),move(X,Y),S).
conflict(move(X,Y),move(X,Z),S) :- not Y = Z.
conflict(move(X,Y),move(Z,Y),S) :- not X = Z.

%   Bad actions.

badAction(move(X,Y),S) :- not goodTower(X,do([move(X,Y)],S)).
badAction(moveToTable(X),S) :- goodTower(X,S).

%   Bad situation. C doesn't include all good-tower-producing actions.

badSituation(do(C,S)) :- omitsGoodTowerProducingAction(C,S).

omitsGoodTowerProducingAction(C,S) :-
            goodTowerProducingAction(A,S), not member(A,C).

goodTowerProducingAction(A,S):- blockMoved(A,X),
                                goodTower(X,do([A],S)), poss(A,S).

blockMoved(move(X,Y),X).  blockMoved(moveToTable(X),X).

%   Primitive Action Declarations.

primitive_action(move(X,Y)).    primitive_action(moveToTable(X)).
```

We can now run the planner for the example blocks world problem of Section 10.2.1. In doing so, we use the clauses just given, the Golog procedure $wspbf(n)$ and the Golog interpreter, both suitably modified for concurrent actions.

A Breadth-First Run for the Example Blocks World with Concurrent Actions

```
[eclipse 2]: planbf(10).
Starting level 1  CPU time (sec): 0.0   Good situations: 0
Starting level 2  CPU time (sec): 0.0   Good situations: 7
Starting level 3  CPU time (sec): 0.03  Good situations: 32
Starting level 4  CPU time (sec): 0.15  Good situations: 90
Starting level 5  CPU time (sec): 0.49  Good situations: 199
Starting level 6  CPU time (sec): 1.24  Good situations: 376
Starting level 7  CPU time (sec): 2.66  Good situations: 631
Starting level 8  CPU time (sec): 4.97  Good situations: 967


Success.  CPU time (sec): 5.02  Good situations: 975

[[moveToTable(u), moveToTable(v), moveToTable(w)],
 [moveToTable(a), moveToTable(e)], [move(b, a), move(f, e)],
 [move(c, b), move(g, f)], [move(d, c)], [move(w, d)],
 [move(v, w)], [move(u, v)]]
More?  y.


Success.  CPU time (sec): 5.08  Good situations: 983

[[moveToTable(u), moveToTable(v)],
 [moveToTable(a), moveToTable(e), moveToTable(w)],
 [move(b, a), move(f, e)], [move(c, b), move(g, f)],
 [move(d, c)], [move(w, d)], [move(v, w)], [move(u, v)]]
More?  y.


**** 3 plans deleted. ***

Success.  CPU time (sec): 5.27  Good situations: 1005

[[moveToTable(u), moveToTable(v)],
 [moveToTable(a), moveToTable(e)], [move(b, a), move(f, e)],
 [move(c, b)], [move(d, c)], [move(w, d)],
 [move(g, f), move(v, w)], [move(u, v)]]
More?  n.
```

The planner quickly found a number of shortest length plans, too many to show here. However, the plans shown reveal that not all shortest length plans are equally desirable; some require more effort to execute than others. For example, the first plan produced requires a total of 13 block-moving actions, while the last one shown requires 12. So it seems that the natural notion of an optimal concurrent plan involves two minimizations: First find the shortest length plans, then, among these, find one whose execution requires minimal effort. Other notions are also possible, but pursuing these issues here will take us too far afield.

10.4   OCTOPUS: A Multi-Handed Blocks World Agent

Encouraged by the success of the breadth-first planner on the previous examples, we now seek to enrich the blocks world with a multi-handed agent who can concurrently move around several blocks. Of course, the concurrent planner of the previous section concerns just such an agent, but it assumes that all actions are of equal duration, and that the agent has arbitrarily many hands. Here, we seek to relax these assumptions to allow for actions with arbitrary durations, for concurrency with complex action overlapping, and for a bound on how many hands the agent has. To achieve this, we adopt an interleaving account of concurrency, and use the mechanism of instantaneous actions for initiating and terminating processes (Section 7.2). Because we want to allow these processes to have different durations, depending on the action type, the instantaneous process initiation and termination actions will all have temporal arguments. The following are the actions and fluents for the OCTOPUS domain.

Instantaneous Actions:

- $startMove(h, x, y, t, t')$: At time t, hand h initiates the process of moving block x to y, and t' is the termination time of this process.

- $endMove(h, x, y, t, t')$: At time t', hand h terminates the process of moving block x to y, and t is the initiation time of this process.

- $startMoveToTable(h, x, t, t')$: At time t, hand h initiates the process of moving block x to the table, and t' is the termination time of this process.

- $endMoveToTable(h, x, t, t')$: At time t', hand h terminates the process of moving block x to the table, and t is the initiation time of this process.

Primitive Fluents

- $clear(x, s)$: Block x has no other blocks on top of it, in situation s.

- $on(x, y, s)$: Block x is on (touching) block y, in situation s.

- $ontable(x, s)$: Block x is on the table, in situation s.

- $moving(h, x, y, t, t', s)$: In situation s, hand h is in the process of moving block x to y, having initiated this process at time t, with the intention of terminating this process at time t'.

- $movingToTable(h, x, t, t', s)$: In situation s, hand h is in the process of moving block x to the table, having initiated this process at time t, with the intention of terminating this process at time t'.

Abbreviations

- $reserved(x, s)$: In situation s, block x is reserved, in the sense that some block-moving process is active in s and that process is moving a block onto x.

- $handInUse(h, s)$: In situation s, hand h is being used, which is to say, in s there is an active process in which hand h is moving some block.

- $precedesActiveProcessTerminationTimes(t, s)$: Time t precedes the termination times of all processes active in situation s.

The axiomatization for OCTOPUS is relatively straightforward, although the action precondition axioms are somewhat delicate. Consider, for example, the preconditions for $startMove(h, x, y, t, t')$. They require that:

- Blocks x and y must be clear, and different from each other.

- Block x must not be reserved, meaning that no currently active process is moving a block onto x. Block y must also not be reserved, otherwise the $startMove$ action will result in two processes moving blocks onto y.

- Hand h must not be in use by a currently active process.

- t must be the start time of the current situation—no delayed process initiations—and t' must be t plus the duration of the process of h moving x to y.

Next, consider the action preconditions for $endMove(h, x, y, t, t')$. They require that:

- The process of hand h moving x to y, starting at t and ending at t' must be active in situation s, i.e. $moving(h, x, y, t, t', s)$ must be true.

- All currently active processes must be permitted to complete. This means that t', the ending time of the process $moving(h, x, y, t, t')$ that $endMove(h, x, y, t, t')$ is about to terminate, must precede the termination times of all currently active processes. Otherwise, there will be some currently active process whose termination time is $< t'$, and if $endMove(h, x, y, t, t')$ is allowed to occur, this other process cannot terminate (without violating the property that the occurrence times of the actions in a situation must be nondecreasing).

We now present the full axiomatization for OCTOPUS:

Action Precondition Axioms

$$Poss(startMove(h, x, y, t, t'), s) \equiv clear(x, s) \land \neg reserved(x, s) \land$$
$$clear(y, s) \land \neg reserved(y, s) \land x \neq y \land hand(h) \land \neg handInUse(h, s) \land$$
$$t = start(s) \land t' = t + moveDuration(h, x, y, s),$$

$$Poss(startMoveToTable(h, x, t, t'), s) \equiv$$
$$clear(x, s) \land \neg reserved(x, s) \land hand(h) \land \neg handInUse(h, s) \land$$
$$t = start(s) \land t' = t + moveToTableDuration(h, x, s),$$

$$Poss(endMove(h, x, y, t, t'), s) \equiv moving(h, x, y, t, t', s) \land$$
$$precedesActiveProcessTerminationTimes(t', s),$$

$$Poss(endMoveToTable(h, x, t, t'), s) \equiv movingToTable(h, x, t, t', s) \land$$
$$precedesActiveProcessTerminationTimes(t', s).$$

Successor State Axioms

$$clear(x, do(a, s)) \equiv (\exists y)\{[(\exists h, z, t, t')a = startMove(h, y, z, t, t') \lor$$
$$(\exists h, t, t')a = startMoveToTable(h, y, t, t')] \land on(y, x, s)\} \lor$$
$$(\exists h, z, t, t')a = endMove(h, x, z, t, t') \lor$$
$$(\exists h, t, t')a = endMoveToTable(h, x, t, t') \lor$$
$$clear(x, s) \land \neg(\exists h, y, t, t')a = endMove(h, y, x, t, t') \land$$
$$\neg(\exists h, z, t, t')a = startMove(h, x, z, t, t') \land$$
$$\neg(\exists h, t, t')a = startMoveToTable(h, x, t, t'),$$

$$on(x, y, do(a, s)) \equiv (\exists h, t, t')a = endMove(h, x, y, t, t') \lor$$
$$on(x, y, s) \land \neg(\exists h, t, t')a = startMoveToTable(h, x, t, t') \land$$
$$\neg(\exists h, z, t, t')a = startMove(h, x, z, t, t'),$$

$$ontable(x, do(a, s)) \equiv (\exists h, t, t')a = endMoveToTable(h, x, t, t') \lor$$
$$ontable(x, s) \land \neg(\exists h, y, t, t')a = startMove(h, x, y, t, t'),$$

$$moving(h, x, y, t, t', do(a, s)) \equiv a = startMove(h, x, y, t, t') \lor$$
$$moving(h, x, y, t, t', s) \land a \neq endMove(h, x, y, t, t'),$$

$$movingToTable(h, x, t, t', do(a, s)) \equiv a = startMoveToTable(h, x, t, t') \lor$$
$$movingToTable(h, x, t, t', s) \land a \neq endMoveToTable(h, x, t, t'),$$

$$start(do(a, s)) = time(a).$$

Abbreviations

$$handInUse(h, s) \stackrel{def}{=} (\exists x, y, t, t')moving(h, x, y, t, t', s) \lor$$
$$(\exists x, t, t')movingToTable(h, x, t, t', s),$$

$$precedesActiveProcessTerminationTimes(t, s) \stackrel{def}{=}$$
$$(\forall h, x, y, t', t'').[moving(h, x, y, t', t'', s) \lor$$
$$movingToTable(h, x, t', t'', s)] \supset t \leq t'',$$

$$reserved(x, s) \stackrel{def}{=} (\exists h, y, t, t')moving(h, y, x, t, t', s).$$

Action Occurrence Times

$$time(startMove(h, x, y, t, t')) = t,$$

$$time(endMove(h, x, y, t, t')) = t',$$

$$etc.$$

The following is the straightforward translation of these axioms and abbreviations into Prolog:

OCTOPUS Axioms in Prolog

```
% Action Precondition Axioms.

poss(startMove(H,X,Y,T,T1),S) :- start(S,T), clear(X,S), clear(Y,S),
      not reserved(X,S), not reserved(Y,S), hand(H), not handInUse(H,S),
      moveDuration(H,X,Y,S,D), T1 is T + D.

poss(startMoveToTable(H,X,T,T1),S) :- start(S,T), clear(X,S),
      not ontable(X,S), not reserved(X,S), hand(H), not handInUse(H,S),
      moveToTableDuration(H,X,S,D), T1 is T + D.

poss(endMove(H,X,Y,T,T1),S) :- moving(H,X,Y,T,T1,S),
                      precedesActiveProcessTerminationTimes(T1,S).

poss(endMoveToTable(H,X,T,T1),S) :- movingToTable(H,X,T,T1,S),
                      precedesActiveProcessTerminationTimes(T1,S).

% Successor State Axioms.

clear(X,do(A,S)) :- (A = startMove(H,Y,Z,T,T1) ;
                      A = startMoveToTable(H,Y,T,T1)), on(Y,X,S) ;
                  A = endMove(H,X,Z,T,T1) ;
                  A = endMoveToTable(H,X,T,T1) ;
                  clear(X,S), not A = endMove(H,Y,X,T,T1),
                  not A = startMove(H,X,Y,T,T1),
                  not A = startMoveToTable(H,X,T,T1).

on(X,Y,do(A,S)) :- A = endMove(H,X,Y,T,T1) ;
                  on(X,Y,S), not A = startMoveToTable(H,X,T,T1),
                  not A = startMove(H,X,Z,T,T1).

ontable(X,do(A,S)) :- A = endMoveToTable(H,X,T,T1) ;
```

```
                        ontable(X,S), not A = startMove(H,X,Y,T,T1).

moving(H,X,Y,T,T1,do(A,S))  :- A = startMove(H,X,Y,T,T1) ;
              moving(H,X,Y,T,T1,S), not A = endMove(H,X,Y,T,T1).

movingToTable(H,X,T,T1,do(A,S))  :- A = startMoveToTable(H,X,T,T1) ;
        movingToTable(H,X,T,T1,S), not A = endMoveToTable(H,X,T,T1).

% Abbreviations.

handInUse(H,S)  :- moving(H,X,Y,T,T1,S) ; movingToTable(H,X,T,T1,S).

reserved(Y,S)  :- moving(H,X,Y,T,T1,S).

precedesActiveProcessTerminationTimes(T,S)  :-
     not ((moving(H,X,Y,T1,T2,S) ; movingToTable(H,X,T1,T2,S)), T > T2).

% Primitive Action Declarations.

primitive_action(startMove(H,X,Y,T,T1)).
primitive_action(endMove(H,X,Y,T,T1)).
primitive_action(startMoveToTable(H,X,T,T1)).
primitive_action(endMoveToTable(H,X,T,T1)).

% Action Start Times.

time(startMove(H,X,Y,T,T1),T).         time(endMove(H,X,Y,T,T1),T1).
time(startMoveToTable(H,X,T,T1),T).    time(endMoveToTable(H,X,T,T1),T1).

% Situation Start Time.

start(do(A,S),T)  :- time(A,T).
```

The final task is to specify the *badSituations* for the OCTOPUS world. For the most part, these are natural modifications of those given in Section 10.2 for the one-handed blocks world agent. However, the canonical ordering of plans with respect to good-tower producing actions that we exploited for the sequential blocks world does not translate easily into the concurrent setting. Nevertheless, the possibility of concurrency introduces new combinatorial problems, and hence new opportunities for pruning a planner's search tree. We describe these new search control rules now.

1. Impose a canonical ordering on robot hand use: When a free hand is needed, choose the least. This prevents plans that are permutations of one another with respect to hands

being used. This assumes that all hands have identical properties.

2. Different actions are permitted to initiate at the same time. This means that often there will be two plans that differ only in the occurrence order of two such actions. To eliminate such inessential differences, define an ordering on action types, and use this to impose a canonical ordering of such action sequences in plans.

Bad Situations for the OCTOPUS Blocks World

```
/*  Canonical ordering on robot hand use: When a free hand is
    needed, choose the least. This prevents plans that are
    permutations of one another wrt hands being used.   */

badSituation(do(startMove(H,X,Y,T,T1),S)) :- not leastAvailableHand(H,S).
badSituation(do(startMoveToTable(H,X,T,T1),S)) :-
                               not leastAvailableHand(H,S).

leastAvailableHand(H,S) :- not handInUse(H,S),
                           not (hand(H1), H1 < H, not handInUse(H1,S)).

/*  Eliminate permutations of actions whose start times are the same.
    When two identical action types occur at the same times, choose
    the action that moves the lexicographically least block.   */

badSituation(do(A,do(B,S))) :- precedes(A,B),
                               sameOccurrenceTimes(A,B),
                               poss(A,S), poss(B,do(A,S)).

precedes(endMove(H1,X1,Y1,T1,T2),
         startMove(H2,X2,Y2,T3,T4)).
precedes(endMove(H1,X1,Y,T1,T2),
         startMoveToTable(H2,X2,T3,T4)).
precedes(endMoveToTable(H1,X1,T1,T2),
         startMove(H2,X2,Y,T3,T4)).
precedes(endMoveToTable(H1,X1,T1,T2),
         startMoveToTable(H2,X2,T3,T4)).
precedes(startMove(H1,X1,Y,T1,T2),
         startMoveToTable(H2,X2,T3,T4)).
precedes(endMoveToTable(H2,X2,T3,T4),
         endMove(H1,X1,Y,T1,T2)).
precedes(endMoveToTable(H1,X1,T1,T2),
         endMoveToTable(H2,X2,T3,T4)) :- X1 @< X2.
precedes(startMove(H1,X1,Y1,T1,T2),
         startMove(H2,X2,Y2,T3,T4)) :- X1 @< X2.
```

```
precedes(endMove(H1,X1,Y1,T1,T2),
         endMove(H2,X2,Y2,T3,T4)) :- X1 @< X2.

sameOccurrenceTimes(A,B) :- time(A,T), time(B,T).

% Don't create a bad tower by a move action.

badSituation(do(startMove(H,X,Y,T,T1),S)) :-
                not goodTower(X,do(endMove(H,X,Y,T,T1),
                                   do(startMove(H,X,Y,T,T1),S))).

% Don't move anything from a good tower to the table.

badSituation(do(startMoveToTable(H,X,T,T1),S)) :- goodTower(X,S).

/* Opportunistic rule: If an action can create a good tower, don't
   do a bad-tower-creating moveToTable action.  */

badSituation(do(startMoveToTable(H,X,T,T1),S)) :-
        not goodTower(X, do(endMoveToTable(H,X,T,T1),
                            do(startMoveToTable(H,X,T,T1),S))),
        existsActionThatCreatesGoodTower(S).

existsActionThatCreatesGoodTower(S) :-
  (A = startMove(H,Y,Z,T,T1), B = endMove(H,Y,Z,T,T1) ;
   A = startMoveToTable(H,Y,T,T1), B = endMoveToTable(H,Y,T,T1)),
  poss(A,S), poss(B,do(A,S)), goodTower(Y,do(B,do(A,S)))).
```

We are now almost ready to test the planner on OCTOPUS, using the example blocks world of the previous section. The only remaining detail is to augment the clauses of that example with declarations about the start time of the initial situation, the number of hands and their names, and the durations of the blocks-moving processes. We shall assume a two-handed agent. Moreover, although we have the flexibility of allowing process durations to depend on which hand is in use, what blocks are being moved, and what is the current situation, for the purposes of the example, we shall make limited use of this freedom, and simply take the process of moving a block from one block to another to have duration 3, and all other processes (moving a block to/from the table) to have duration 1. Accordingly, the test problem consists of the clauses of the earlier test problem of Section 10.2.1, together with the following clauses:

```
    start(s0,0).
    moveDuration(H,X,Y,S,3) :- not ontable(X,S).
    moveDuration(H,X,Y,S,1) :- ontable(X,S).
```

```
moveToTableDuration(H,X,Y,S,1).
hand(1).  hand(2).
```

The following is a run of the breadth-first planner on this problem:

A Breadth-First OCTOPUS Run for the Example Planning Problem

```
[eclipse 2]: planbf(26).
Starting level 1  CPU time (sec): 0.0  Good situations: 0
Starting level 2  CPU time (sec): 0.0  Good situations: 3
Starting level 3  CPU time (sec): 0.02  Good situations: 13
Starting level 4  CPU time (sec): 0.07  Good situations: 35
Starting level 5  CPU time (sec): 0.22  Good situations: 92
Starting level 6  CPU time (sec): 0.53  Good situations: 171
Starting level 7  CPU time (sec): 1.19  Good situations: 315
Starting level 8  CPU time (sec): 2.39  Good situations: 504
Starting level 9  CPU time (sec): 4.43  Good situations: 803
Starting level 10  CPU time (sec): 7.8  Good situations: 1197
Starting level 11  CPU time (sec): 13.56  Good situations: 1812
Starting level 12  CPU time (sec): 23.15  Good situations: 2680
Starting level 13  CPU time (sec): 40.39  Good situations: 4110
Starting level 14  CPU time (sec): 69.29  Good situations: 6101
Starting level 15  CPU time (sec): 117.11  Good situations: 9197
Starting level 16  CPU time (sec): 193.49  Good situations: 13570
Starting level 17  CPU time (sec): 312.26  Good situations: 20259
Starting level 18  CPU time (sec): 497.45  Good situations: 29820
Starting level 19  CPU time (sec): 765.33  Good situations: 43656
Starting level 20  CPU time (sec): 1165.69  Good situations: 63212
Starting level 21  CPU time (sec): 1700.72  Good situations: 90530
Starting level 22  CPU time (sec): 2446.49  Good situations: 128365

Success.  CPU time (sec): 2446.64  Good situations: 128391

[startMoveToTable(1,u,0,1), startMoveToTable(2,a,0,1),
 endMoveToTable(2,a,0,1), endMoveToTable(1,u,0,1),
 startMove(1,b,a,1,4), endMove(1,b,a,1,4), startMove(1,c,b,4,7),
 endMove(1,c,b,4,7), startMove(1,d,c,7,8), endMove(1,d,c,7,8),
 startMove(1,w,d,8,11), endMove(1,w,d,8,11), startMove(1,v,w,11,14),
 endMove(1,v,w,11,14), startMove(1,u,v,14,15), endMove(1,u,v,14,15),
 startMoveToTable(1,e,15,16), endMoveToTable(1,e,15,16),
 startMove(1,f,e,16,17), endMove(1,f,e,16,17),
 startMove(1,g,f,17,18), endMove(1,g,f,17,18)]
More?  y.
```

```
**** The run produced many more length 22 plans, before it
     was terminated. ****
```

The run succeeded, but just barely. The minimal length (*not* minimal duration) plan for this problem is, of course, twice the minimal length plan found for the sequential blocks world agent of Section 10.2, namely, 22. Unfortunately, the minimal length plans for OCTOPUS tend also to exhibit minimal concurrency. To find highly concurrent plans— ones that make good use of OCTOPUS's two hands—requires searching to a greater depth than 22, but at 2,447 CPU seconds, and growing fast, the program is close to the limits of feasibility. A different strategy is needed.

10.5   A Simple Depth-First Planner

There are several factors working against the breadth-first planner for OCTOPUS:

1. Finding a shortest plan (as the breadth-first planner does) is known to be NP-hard for the blocks world.

2. The planner for OCTOPUS must search twice as deep as for the sequential blocks world agent of Section 10.2, because each action for that agent is encoded in OCTO- PUS using two instantaneous actions.

3. For OCTOPUS, optimal plans need not be the shortest; rather, they are the plans with least duration, because these maximize concurrency.

In view of these observations, it is perhaps wiser to seek feasible, but not necessarily opti- mal plans for the blocks world. In this connection, notice that there is always a sequential plan for an n-block world of length $2n - (k_0 + k_g)$, where k_0 is the number of blocks on the table in the initial situation, and k_g is the number of such blocks in the goal situation. Such a plan simply first places all the blocks onto the table, then builds the goal towers by suitably moving blocks from the table. So there is always an easily computed feasible plan. The problem is to find something better than this, but not necessarily optimal.

One way to compute feasible, but not necessarily optimal, plans is through bounded depth-first search, where the bound is the maximal length plan that one is willing to accept. Here is a Golog program for such a planner, which is even simpler than *wspbf*.

proc $wspdf(n)$
    $goal?\,|\,[n > 0?\,;\,(\pi a)(primitive\_action(a)?\,;\,a)\,;\,\neg badSituation?\,;$
        $wspdf(n-1)]$
endProc

Next, we give an implementation of this planner, with appropriate statistics gathering
features.

Implementation of World's Simplest Depth-First Planner

```
proc(wspdf(N),
    ?(initializeSitCount) : ?(initializeCPU) : plans(N)).

proc(plans(N),
    ?(goal) : ?(reportStats) : ?(prettyPrintSituation) #
    ?(N > 0) : pi(a,?(primitive_action(a)) : a) : ?(-badSituation) :
    ?(incrementSitCount) : pi(n1, ?(n1 is N - 1) :
    plans(n1))).

plandf(N) :- do(wspdf(N),s0,S), askForMore.

reportStats :- nl, cputime(T), write(' CPU time (sec): '),
    getval(cpu,T1), T2 is T - T1, write(T2), getval(sitCount,C),
    write(' Good situations: '), write(C), nl.

% The remaining bookkeeping clauses are the same as for wspbf(n).
```

Next, run this depth-first planner on OCTOPUS.

A Depth-First OCTOPUS Run for the Example Planning Problem

```
[eclipse 2]: plandf(26).

  CPU time (sec): 0.16  Good situations: 26

[startMoveToTable(1,u,0,1), startMoveToTable(2,a,0,1),
 endMoveToTable(2,a,0,1), endMoveToTable(1,u,0,1),
 startMove(1,b,a,1,4), endMove(1,b,a,1,4), startMove(1,c,b,4,7),
 endMove(1,c,b,4,7), startMove(1,d,c,7,8), endMove(1,d,c,7,8),
 startMove(1,w,d,8,11), endMove(1,w,d,8,11), startMove(1,v,w,11,14),
 endMove(1,v,w,11,14), startMove(1,u,v,14,15), endMove(1,u,v,14,15),
 startMoveToTable(1,e,15,16), endMoveToTable(1,e,15,16),
 startMove(1,f,e,16,17), endMove(1,f,e,16,17),
 startMove(1,g,f,17,18), endMove(1, g,f,17,18)]
More?  y.

**** 40 plans edited out ****

  CPU time (sec): 3.61  Good situations: 291
```

```
[startMoveToTable(1,u,0,1), startMoveToTable(2,a,0,1),
 endMoveToTable(2,a,0,1), endMoveToTable(1,u,0,1),
 startMove(1,b,a,1,4), endMove(1,b,a,1,4), startMove(1,c,b,4,7),
 endMove(1,c,b,4,7), startMove(1,d,c,7,8), endMove(1,d,c,7,8),
 startMove(1,w,d,8,11), startMoveToTable(2,v,8,9),
 endMoveToTable(2,v,8,9), startMoveToTable(2,e,9,10),
 endMoveToTable(2,e,9,10), startMove(2,f,e,10,11),
 endMove(2,f,e,10,11), endMove(1,w,d,8,11), startMove(1,v,w,11,12),
 endMove(1,v,w,11,12), startMove(1,g,f,12,13),
 startMove(2,u,v,12,13), endMove(1,g,f,12,13), endMove(2,u,v,12,13)]
More?  n.
```

The planner quickly found a first plan of duration 18, but without much concurrency. After further trials, plans of various durations were generated, until finally one of duration 13 was found, and the session terminated. At this point, it was known that a plan of duration ≤ 13 existed, and an attempt was made to find one of duration < 13. This was done by appealing to *badSituation* to filter out all situations whose start times are ≥ 13, using the following declaration, added to the *badSituation*s:

```
badSituation(S) :- start(S,T), T >= 13.
```

The following run resulted:

A Duration < 13 Time Bounded Depth-First OCTOPUS Run for the Example Blocks World

```
[eclipse 2]: plandf(26).

  CPU time (sec): 2.54  Good situations: 180

[startMoveToTable(1,u,0,1), startMoveToTable(2,a,0,1),
 endMoveToTable(2,a,0,1), endMoveToTable(1,u,0,1),
 startMove(1,b,a,1,4), endMove(1,b,a,1,4), startMove(1,c,b,4,7),
 endMove(1,c,b,4,7), startMove(1,d,c,7,8), startMoveToTable(2,v,7,8),
 endMoveToTable(2,v,7,8), endMove(1,d,c,7,8),
 startMoveToTable(1,e,8,9), startMoveToTable(2,w,8,9),
 endMoveToTable(1,e,8,9), endMoveToTable(2,w,8,9),
 startMove(1,w,d,9,10), endMove(1,w,d,9,10), startMove(1,f,e,10,11),
 startMove(2,v,w,10,11), endMove(1,f,e,10,11), endMove(2,v,w,10,11),
 startMove(1,g,f,11,12), startMove(2,u,v,11,12),
 endMove(1,g,f,11,12), endMove(2,u,v,11,12)]
More?  y.

**** 11 duration 12 plans edited out ****
```

```
  CPU time (sec): 16.51  Good situations: 1006
```

```
[startMoveToTable(1,u,0,1), startMoveToTable(2,a,0,1),
 endMoveToTable(2,a,0,1), endMoveToTable(1,u,0,1),
 startMove(1,b,a,1,4), endMove(1,b,a,1,4), startMove(1,c,b,4,7),
 startMoveToTable(2,v,4,5), endMoveToTable(2,v,4,5),
 startMoveToTable(2,e,5,6), endMoveToTable(2,e,5,6),
 startMove(2,f,e,6,7), endMove(1,c,b,4,7), endMove(2,f,e,6,7),
 startMove(1,d,c,7,8), startMoveToTable(2,w,7,8),
 endMoveToTable(2,w,7,8), endMove(1,d,c,7,8),
 startMove(1,w,d,8,9), endMove(1,w,d,8,9), startMove(1,g,f,9,10),
 startMove(2,v,w,9,10), endMove(1,g,f,9,10), endMove(2,v,w,9,10),
 startMove(1,u,v,10,11), endMove(1,u,v,10,11)]
More?  n.
```

Next, an attempt to find a plan of length 26, with duration < 11 failed, taking 1,152 CPU seconds, after which a run was attempted for a length 28 plan with duration < 11. We do not show it here, but the 18th plan returned by this run was of duration 9. At this point, a search for a length 28 plan with duration < 9 was tried; this failed, using 496 CPU seconds in the attempt. Next, an attempt to find a length 30 plan for this duration yielded the following plans:

A Duration < 9 Time Bounded Depth-First OCTOPUS Run for the Example Blocks World

```
[eclipse 4]: plandf(30).
```

```
  CPU time (sec): 115.37  Good situations: 4758
```

```
[startMoveToTable(1,u,0,1), endMoveToTable(1,u,0,1),
 startMoveToTable(1,a,1,2), startMoveToTable(2,b,1,2),
 endMoveToTable(1,a,1,2), endMoveToTable(2,b,1,2),
 startMove(1,b,a,2,3), startMoveToTable(2,c,2,3),
 endMoveToTable(2,c,2,3), endMove(1,b,a,2,3),
 startMove(1,c,b,3,4), startMoveToTable(2,w,3,4),
 endMoveToTable(2,w,3,4), endMove(1,c,b,3,4),
 startMove(1,d,c,4,5), startMoveToTable(2,v,4,5),
 endMoveToTable(2,v,4,5), endMove(1,d,c,4,5),
 startMove(1,w,d,5,6), startMoveToTable(2,e,5,6),
 endMoveToTable(2,e,5,6), endMove(1,w,d,5,6),
 startMove(1,f,e,6,7), startMove(2,v,w,6,7),
 endMove(1,f,e,6,7), endMove(2,v,w,6,7),
 startMove(1,g,f,7,8), startMove(2,u,v,7,8),
```

```
endMove(1,g,f,7,8), endMove(2,u,v,7,8)]
More?  y.

**** 5 duration 8 plans edited out ****
```

This run produced six length 30, duration 8 plans, terminating after 496 CPU seconds. Finally, an attempt was made to find a length 32 plan of duration < 8; this failed after 271 CPU seconds.

10.6   Open-World Planning

The planners of the previous sections all had in common a reliance on Prolog to reason about the initial situation. This means that Prolog's standard closed-world assumption was being made about the initial situation in those implementations (Definition 5.3.2). If, for example, we only knew that block a is on block b or on block c, or that block a is not on the table (without knowing where it was) we would be unable to represent this information as a Prolog initial database, and the planners developed earlier could not be used in such settings. This section generalizes these closed-world planners to work for incomplete initial situations.

In the interest of preserving as much of the earlier work as possible for the purposes of open-world planning, we continue using the Golog planners $wspbf$ and $wspdf$ of the previous sections, and we also leave the code for the Golog interpreter unchanged. However, we can no longer rely on Prolog to do theorem-proving for us. For example, to evaluate the test expression $on(A, B, do(move(C, D), do(moveToTable(D), S_0)))$, we cannot, as we did with closed worlds, simply pass this expression to Prolog and expect the right answer. Instead, we need to evaluate such expressions with a theorem-prover, using as premises the action precondition and successor state axioms, together with the incomplete initial database axioms. So the principal objective in the next few sections will be the design and implementation of such a theorem-prover for the purposes of open-world planning.

10.6.1   Prime Implicates and Compiling an Initial Database

In the case of open-world planning, the first task is to think about how to implement the theorem-prover. The overriding concern must be to make the theorem-proving task as efficient as possible because the prover will be called each time a test expression must be evaluated, and in the process of searching for a plan, such test expressions are generated and tested a huge number of times.

We begin by thinking about the initial database. Because the concern is with open-world initial databases, these can be any sentences about S_0. Because we are focusing on planning, we can reasonably assume that the only function symbols of sort *object* are constants, and that all quantifiers in sentences of the initial database are *typed*. Formally, a type $\tau(x)$ is an abbreviation for a description of a finite domain of constants:

$$\tau(x) \stackrel{def}{=} x = T_1 \vee \cdots \vee x = T_k,$$

where $T_1, \ldots, T_k$ are all constants. Now, introduce *typed quantifiers* $(\forall x : \tau)$ and $(\exists x : \tau)$ according to:

$$(\forall x : \tau)\phi(x) \stackrel{def}{=} (\forall x).\tau(x) \supset \phi(x),$$

$$(\exists x : \tau)\phi(x) \stackrel{def}{=} (\exists x).\tau(x) \wedge \phi(x).$$

Then typed quantification of formulas can be reduced to conjunctions and disjunctions according to the following equivalences

$$(\forall x : \tau).\phi(x) \equiv \phi(T_1) \wedge \cdots \wedge \phi(T_k),$$

$$(\exists x : \tau).\phi(x) \equiv \phi(T_1) \vee \cdots \vee \phi(T_k).$$

So, we shall assume that all quantifiers in sentences of the initial database are typed, as in, for example

$$(\forall x : train)(\exists y : station)location(x, y, S_0).$$

Moreover, we suppose that the typed quantifiers have been eliminated in favour of conjunctions and disjunctions according to the above equivalences. We are left with quantifier free sentences that we can (and will) convert to a logically equivalent set of *clauses*.[3] In what follows, we adopt the usual convention and represent a clause by the set of its literals.

Next, we replace this set of clauses by a logically equivalent, but in a certain sense simpler set of clauses called *prime implicates*. Prime implicates have the wonderful property that a clause is entailed by the original set of clauses iff it is subsumed[4] by one of the prime implicates of the original set. So, with the prime implicates in hand, proving that a clause about S_0 is entailed by the initial database reduces to testing whether that clause is subsumed by a prime implicate, and this test can be performed very efficiently.

Definition 10.6.1: Prime Implicate

Let $\mathcal{K}$ be a set of clauses. A clause C is a *prime implicate* of $\mathcal{K}$ iff C is not a tautology,[5] $\mathcal{K} \models C$, and there is no clause $C' \neq C$ such that C' subsumes C and $\mathcal{K} \models C'$. In other

---

3 A *clause* is a disjunction of literals, no two of which are identical. We assume here that the reader knows how to convert a set of formulas to clausal form, or at the very least, knows where to find out, and will.

4 Clause C *subsumes* clause C' iff each literal of C occurs in C'. When clauses are represented by sets of literals, then C subsumes C' iff C is a subset of C'.

5 A clause is a *tautology* iff it contains A and $\neg A$ for some atom A.

words, C is a prime implicate of $\mathcal{K}$ iff C is a shortest clause entailed by $\mathcal{K}$.

Theorem 10.6.2: *Suppose $\mathcal{K}$ is a set of clauses, and $pi(\mathcal{K})$ is the set of all of $\mathcal{K}$'s prime implicates. Then*

1. *$\mathcal{K}$ and $pi(\mathcal{K})$ are logically equivalent; each clause in one set is entailed by the other set.*
2. *For any clause C, $\mathcal{K} \models C$ iff there is a clause $\Pi \in pi(\mathcal{K})$ such that Π subsumes C.*

Proof: Exercise 10 below. ∎

This theorem tells us, first, that we can safely replace $\mathcal{K}$ by the set of all its prime implicates, and secondly, with this equivalent set of clauses in hand, we can very quickly determine whether a given clause is entailed by $\mathcal{K}$. So it seems that we need only to compute $\mathcal{K}$'s prime implicates, and thereafter we have efficient theorem-proving, efficient in the sense that it can be performed in time linear in the number of prime implicates. These prime implicates act like a compiled form of $\mathcal{K}$: All the "hard" reasoning is done at compile time, in computing the prime implicates; after that, reasoning becomes easy. Of course, there is no free lunch, so we have to expect that the compilation phase will have high complexity, and indeed, this is so. In the worst case, the number of prime implicates of a set of clauses is exponential in the number of distinct atoms in those clauses. So we must simply hope that this does not occur for the planning problems we want to solve.

The next task is to find an algorithm for computing the prime implicates. There are many approaches, almost all based on resolution.

Definition 10.6.3: Resolvent

Let C and C' be two clauses such that $A \in C$ and $\neg A \in C'$ for some atom A. A *resolvent* of C and C' is the clause $(C - \{A\}) \cup (C' - \{\neg A\})$. In other words, delete A from C and $\neg A$ from C', and combine the results into a new clause.

It is possible to prove that the following procedure will generate all prime implicates of a finite set $\mathcal{K}$ of non-tautological clauses:

1. Choose two clauses of $\mathcal{K}$ that have a resolvent R that is not a tautology, and that is not subsumed by a clause of $\mathcal{K}$.
2. Delete from $\mathcal{K}$ all clauses subsumed by R, then add R to the resulting set of clauses.
3. Repeat the above steps with the clauses resulting from the previous step until no new clauses are produced.

On termination of the above procedure, we are left with the set of prime implicates of

$\mathcal{K}$. This is what the implementation does, with the exception that it gives preference to resolvents of clauses C and C' where one of C, C' is a *unit clause*, namely, a clause of length one. The nice property of such a resolvent is that it subsumes one of its parent clauses, so that this parent can be discarded. The resulting resolvent is also more likely to subsume other clauses in the set of clauses computed thus far, and therefore these too can be discarded. The algorithm is the following, assuming we begin with a database $\mathcal{K}$ of non-tautologous clauses:

1. Index each clause of $\mathcal{K}$ by 0, its starting level. Initialize the variable *level* to 0: *level* $\leftarrow$ 0.

2. For each pair of clauses of the database such that one of them is indexed by *level* and also one of them is a unit clause, determine whether the pair has a resolvent R, and if so, compute it. If R is subsumed by a clause in the database, or if R is a tautology, forget it. Otherwise, delete from the database all clauses at any level that are subsumed by R. Finally, index R by *level* $+ 1$ and add it to the database.

3. For each pair of clauses of the database such that one of them is indexed by *level* and also neither of them is a unit clause, determine whether the pair has a resolvent R, and if so, compute it. If R is subsumed by a clause in the database, or if R is a tautology, forget it. Otherwise, delete from the database all clauses at any level that are subsumed by R. Finally, index R by *level* $+ 1$ and add it to the database.

4. If a new clause was computed at step 2 or step 3, *level* $\leftarrow$ *level* $+ 1$; go to 2.

5. Exit; the database is the set of prime implicates of $\mathcal{K}$.

The implementation assumes that the initial database—the sentences about S_0—are Prolog assertions of the form axiom(W), where W is a sentence about the initial situation. Examples for the blocks world are:

```
axiom(on(b,c,s0)).
axiom(on(a,b,s0) v on(a,e,s0)).
axiom(all([x,block],all([y,block], on(x,y,s0) => -on(y,x,s0)))).
```

Here, we have introduced a type block; notice the syntax for typed quantifiers. The first stage of the implementation uses the Prolog procedure clausifyAxioms to convert these assertions about the initial situation to clausal form. In doing so, it first invokes the procedure processQuantifiers to eliminate quantifiers in these assertions by appealing to user-supplied declarations of the form domain(Type,D), where D is a list of the finitely many individuals in the domain of Type. It also makes use of various logical simplifications, for example, replacing X = X by true, -true by false, P & true by P, etc. The resulting clauses are then asserted into Prolog's global database, indexed by level 0. Next, the implementation calls the Prolog procedure resolveAll(0) to compute the prime implicates of these clauses, using the resolution algorithm given above. The following is the entire program:

A Program for Generating Prime Implicates

```
:- op(900,xfy,==>).   % Simplification Rules.
:- dynamic(clause/2).

compile :- initializeCompileCPU, clausifyAxioms,
           reportClausifyStats, resolveAll(0), reportPrimeImpStats.

clausifyAxioms :- axiom(W), processQuantifiers(W,W1),
                  simplify(W1,Simp), clausalForm(Simp,Clauses),
                  assertClauses(Clauses,0), fail.
clausifyAxioms.

processQuantifiers(W1 & W2,I1 & I2) :- processQuantifiers(W1,I1),
                                       processQuantifiers(W2,I2).
processQuantifiers(W1 v W2,I1 v I2) :- processQuantifiers(W1,I1),
                                       processQuantifiers(W2,I2).
processQuantifiers(W1 => W2,I) :- processQuantifiers(-W1 v W2,I).
processQuantifiers(W1 <=> W2,I) :-
                processQuantifiers((W1 => W2) & (W2 => W1),I).
processQuantifiers(-W,-I) :- processQuantifiers(W,I).
processQuantifiers(some([X,T],W),I) :-
                          processQuantifiers(-all([X,T],-W),I).
processQuantifiers(all([X,T],W),I) :- sub(X,var(X),W,WR),
        /* The substitution predicate of the GOLOG interpreter. Here, we
           rename each quantified variable X by var(X). This prevents any
           possible clash between variable and domain element names.  */
        processQuantifiers(WR,I1),
        domain(T,D), eliminateUniversal(I1,var(X),D,I).
processQuantifiers(A,A) :- isAtom(A).

eliminateUniversal(W,X,[E],I) :- sub(X,E,W,I).
eliminateUniversal(W,X,[E1,E2 | R],I1 & I2) :- sub(X,E1,W,I1),
                                eliminateUniversal(W,X,[E2 | R],I2).

clausalForm(L,[[L]]) :- isLiteral(L).
clausalForm(W1 & W2,Clauses) :- clausalForm(W1,C1),
                        clausalForm(W2,C2), union(C1,C2,Clauses).
clausalForm(-(-W),Clauses) :- clausalForm(W,Clauses).
clausalForm(W1 v W2,Clauses) :-
                clausalForm(W1,Clauses1), clausalForm(W2,Clauses2),
                findall(U, C1^C2^(member(C1,Clauses1),
```

```
                                        member(C2,Clauses2),
                                        union(C1,C2,U)),
                             Clauses).
clausalForm(-(W1 & W2),Clauses) :- clausalForm(-W1 v -W2,Clauses).
clausalForm(-(W1 v W2),Clauses) :- clausalForm(-W1 & -W2,Clauses).

isLiteral(A) :- isAtom(A).
isLiteral(-A) :- isAtom(A).

assertClauses([],N).
assertClauses([C | R],N) :- assertClause(C,N), assertClauses(R,N).

assertClause(C,N) :- tautology(C), !.
assertClause(C,N) :- subsumed(C), !.
assertClause(C,N) :- retractSubsumedClauses(C), assert(clause(C,N)).

retractSubsumedClauses(C) :- clause(K,N), subsumes(C,K),
                             retract(clause(K,N)), fail.
retractSubsumedClauses(C).

subsumes([],C).
subsumes([L | R],C) :- member(L,C), subsumes(R,C).

% Subsumption is expensive, so optimize a little.

subsumed([L]) :- clause([L],N).
subsumed([L1,L2 | C]) :- clause(K,N), subsumes(K,[L1,L2 | C]).

tautology([true]).
tautology([L1,L2 | C]) :- member(A,[L1,L2 | C]), isAtom(A),
                          member(-A,[L1,L2 | C]).

resolveAll(N) :- unitResolve(N), nonUnitResolve(N).
resolveAll(N) :- N1 is N + 1,
        % Was a new resolvent produced at the previous level?
                clause(C,N1), resolveAll(N1).
resolveAll(N).

unitResolve(N) :- N1 is N + 1,
        (clause([L],N), clause(C,J) ; clause([L],J),  J < N, clause(C,N)),
        unitResolvent([L],C,R), retractSubsumedClauses(R),
        assert(clause(R,N1)), fail.
unitResolve(N).
```

```
unitResolvent([L],C,R) :- complement(L,N), member(N,C), delete(N,C,R).

nonUnitResolve(N) :- N1 is N + 1,
                     clause([L1,L2 | R],N), clause([F1,F2 | T],J),
                     resolvent([L1,L2 | R],[F1,F2 | T],C),
                     assertClause(C,N1), fail.

resolvent(C1,C2,C) :- member(L1,C1), complement(L1,L2), member(L2,C2),
                         delete(L1,C1,K1), delete(L2,C2,K2), union(K1,K2,C).

complement(A,-A) :- not A = -W.
complement(-A,A).

initializeCompileCPU :- cputime(T), setval(compileCPUtime,T).

reportClausifyStats :- nl,
        write('Clausal form completed.   CPU time (sec): '),
        getval(compileCPUtime,T1), cputime(T), T2 is T - T1,
        setval(clausifyTime,T2), write(T2), countClauses(N),
        write('  Clauses: '), write(N), nl.

reportPrimeImpStats :- nl,
     write('Database compiled.   CPU time (sec): '), cputime(T),
     getval(clausifyTime,T1), T2 is T - T1, write(T2),
     countClauses(N), write('  Prime implicates: '), write(N), nl.

countClauses(N) :- setval(clauseCount,0), clause(C,J),
                    incval(clauseCount), fail.
countClauses(N) :- getval(clauseCount,N).

simplify(W1 & W2,S) :- simplify(W1,S1), simplify(W2,S2),
                         simplify1(S1 & S2,S), !.
simplify(W1 v W2,S) :- simplify(W1,S1), simplify(W2,S2),
                         simplify1(S1 v S2,S), !.
simplify(-W,S) :- simplify(W,S1), simplify1(-S1,S), !.
simplify(A,S) :- simplify1(A,S).

simplify1(W,Simp) :- W ==> Simp, !.
simplify1(W,W).

% Simplification Rules

true & P ==> P.         P & true ==> P.        false & P ==> false.
P & false ==> false.    true v P ==> true.     P v true ==> true.
```

```
false v P ==> P.        P v false ==> P.        -true ==> false.
-false ==> true.        X = X ==> true.
X = Y ==> false :- not X = Y.
```

10.6.2   A Regression-Based Theorem-Prover

We now have in hand an implementation for converting an initial database to prime implicate form. The final task is to describe and implement the theorem-prover prove. For the
purposes of planning, what kinds of sentences do we want to prove? The planners $wspbf$
and $wspdf$ work by generating potential plans of the form $do([\alpha_1, \ldots, \alpha_n], S_0)$, where the
α_i are action terms; then they test these potential plans against $goal$ and $badSituation$.
So the test expressions that must be evaluated are of the form $W(do([\alpha_1, \ldots, \alpha_n], S_0))$, for
formulas $W(s)$ with a single free situation variable s. Now, these are exactly the kinds of
sentences for which regression was designed (Section 4.5). Essentially, regression replaces
a regressable sentence of the form $W(do([\alpha_1, \ldots, \alpha_n], S_0))$ by a logically equivalent sentence *about the initial situation only*, and the original sentence is provable iff the regressed
sentence is provable *using only the initial database together with the unique names axioms
for actions*. So our strategy will be this, assuming we already have an initial database in
prime implicate form:

1. Eliminate the quantifiers of the sentence $W(do([\alpha_1, \ldots, \alpha_n], S_0))$. We assume here,
   as we did for the sentences in the initial database, that all quantifiers of W are typed.

2. Regress the resulting sentence to a sentence about the initial situation only.

3. Convert the regressed sentence to clausal form.

4. For each clause of this clausal form determine whether it is subsumed by a prime
   implicate. If so, report QED; else report failure.

This is what the implementation does, with one important difference: Rather than regress
the entire sentence to the initial situation, it does a depth first regression of the components
of the sentence, hoping that the regressed component will simplify in such a way that the
remaining components need not be regressed. For example, suppose we want to regress
$P \wedge Q$, and we first regress P to get R. If R simplifies to $false$, then it is clearly a waste
of time to next regress Q, since in any event, the regressed form of $P \wedge Q$ will be $false$
and cannot be entailed by the initial database. There is a similar principle for regressing
formulas of the form $P \vee Q$.

Regression requires successor state axioms, and we allow for these by user-provided
Prolog assertions of the form Atom <=> Expression. For example, in the blocks world, one

such assertion is:[6]

```
clear(X,do(A,S)) <=> (A = move(Y,Z) v A = moveToTable(Y)) & on(Y,X,S) v
                      clear(X,S) & -(A = move(Y,X)).
```

Now we can describe the final details of the regression theorem-prover. In regressing an atom A, there are two possibilities:

1. A has a definition of the form A <=> W. This means that A has a successor state axiom or is a defined atom, and to regress A, we need to regress W.

2. A does not have a definition of the form A <=> W. This means that either A is not a fluent, or it is, but its situation argument is s0, so the regression is finished. In this case, because depth-first regression is being done, we do a quick test to see whether the database entails this atom, returning true if it does, and false if it entails the negation of A. As observed earlier in connection with depth-first regression, such truth values can improve the efficiency of the regression algorithm by sometimes eliminating the need for regressing the rest of the formula of which A is a component.

The following is the Prolog implementation for prove, as just described:

A Regression Theorem-Prover for an Initial Situation of Prime Implicates

```
prove(W):- processQuantifiers(W,I), simplify(I,Simp), regress(Simp,R),
           clausalForm(R,Clauses), databaseEntails(Clauses).

databaseEntails([]).
databaseEntails( [C | R]) :- (tautology(C), ! ; subsumed(C)),
                             databaseEntails(R).

regress(P & Q, R) :- regress(P,R1),
                     (R1 = false, R = false, ! ;
                      regress(Q,R2), simplify(R1 & R2,R)).
regress(P v Q, R) :- regress(P,R1),
                     (R1 = true, R = true, ! ;
                      regress(Q,R2), simplify(R1 v R2,R)).
regress(-P,R) :- regress(P,R1), simplify(-R1,R).
regress(A,R) :- isAtom(A), A <=> W,      /* A is a defined atom. Retrieve
                                            and regress its definition. */
                processQuantifiers(W,I), simplify(I,S), regress(S,R).
regress(A,R) :- isAtom(A),
```

---

6 Actually, to simplify the implementation, our planner does not use general successor state axioms of this form, but instead instantiates the action variable A by each action term of the domain. See the next section for the details.

```
not A <=> W,    /* A is an atom, but it has no definition,
                    so the regression is finished. */
(A = false, R = false, ! ;
 databaseEntails([[A]]), R = true, ! ;
 databaseEntails([[-A]]), R = false, ! ;
 R = A).
```

10.6.3 Bad Situations for Open-World Planning

The concept of a *bad Situation* continues to make sense for open-world planning, but
some minor modifications are required to ensure that the appropriate test conditions are
evaluated by the theorem-prover prove instead of Prolog. For the blocks world, we continue using the same program for badSituation as in Section 10.2, but with all tests for a
goodTower evaluated by prove. For example, the first rule of that program becomes:

```
badSituation(do(move(X,Y),S)) :- prove(-goodTower(X,do(move(X,Y),S))).
```

The opportunistic rule becomes:

```
badSituation(do(moveToTable(X),S)) :-
                prove(-goodTower(X,do(moveToTable(X),S))),
                existsActionThatCreatesGoodTower(S).

existsActionThatCreatesGoodTower(S) :-
                (A = move(Y,X) ; A = moveToTable(Y)),
                poss(A,S), prove(goodTower(Y,do(A,S))).
```

The remaining rules are similarly modified, and we do not show them here. Notice that
poss remains a Prolog predicate; in the blocks world implementation below, it will be
poss's responsibility to invoke prove appropriately on the action preconditions.

10.6.4 Axiomatizing Incomplete Initial Situations

To specify a planning problem, the initial database must be axiomatized. For closed-world
planning, this was not problematic: The initial theory was a relational database (Definition
9.3.1), and therefore a special kind of closed initial database (Section 5.3.2). Open worlds
are more complicated. The following are general facts about blocks that must be true of
the initial situation:

$on(x, y, S_0) \supset \neg on(y, x, S_0),$

$on(y, x, S_0) \land on(z, x, S_0) \supset y = z,$

$on(x, y, S_0) \land on(x, z, S_0) \supset y = z.$

So these must be included in any axiomatization of an initial blocks world database.[7] Two questions immediately come to mind:

1. If these sentences are true of every initial situation, why were they not included in the closed-world initial databases of the previous planning problems?

2. These sentences are true not just of the initial situation, but of *all situations*:

$$on(x, y, s) \supset \neg on(y, x, s),$$
$$on(y, x, s) \wedge on(z, x, s) \supset y = z, \qquad\qquad (10.1)$$
$$on(x, y, s) \wedge on(x, z, s) \supset y = z.$$

This being so, why were these sentences not included in the earlier blocks world axiomatizations? Perhaps some essential information about blocks has not been captured by the successor state and action precondition axioms. How do we know that some perfectly good plans have not been precluded by omitting these axioms?

The answer to the first question is relatively easy. The previous planners worked on an initial relational database formulated in a situation calculus language whose only function symbols not of sort *situation* are constants—the names of the blocks—and these constants are pairwise unequal (Definition 9.3.1). Now, it is easy to prove (Exercise 11b below) that for each of the above three sentences about S_0, the relational database that axiomatizes the fluents of such an initial situation either entails the sentence, or it entails the negation of the sentence. This means that the relational database *plus* these three sentences is either logically equivalent to the relational database itself, or is inconsistent. So, either these sentences are redundant, or they tell us that something is wrong with the description of the initial situation. Notice that it is extremely easy to give a questionable initial database, for example, $\{on(A, B, S_0), on(B, A, S_0)\}$, and without sentences of the above kind, there would be no way to tell that a mistake has been made. So the role of such sentences is to detect logical inconsistencies in an initial relational database. Whenever such a database is consistent with these sentences, it must entail them, so they can safely be discarded. We did exactly this with the planners for the ongoing blocks world example of Section 10.2, while remaining silent until now about the underlying consistency assumption for the initial database. Now the secret is out, and one can easily verify that the relational database for the initial situation of that example does entail the above three sentences (Exercise 11a below), and therefore is consistent with them.

These observations have an important consequence: For open-world initial databases, which certainly are not relational, none of these properties are true and the above three sentences about S_0 must be included in any axiomatization of the initial situation.

---

7 Incidentally, this is why the open-world STRIPS of Section 9.6 is not suitable for this blocks world problem. The initial STRIPS database treated there must consist of *literals*; here more general clauses must be included.

The second question is much more subtle and interesting. The sentences (10.1) are examples of so-called *state constraints*, which we first encountered in Section 4.3.2. There are many kinds; we consider here only the simplest—sentences of the form $(\forall s)C(s)$, where $C(s)$ is a formula with one free variable s that is uniform in s (Definition 4.4.1). For example, $C(s)$ for the first state constraint of (10.1) is $(\forall x, y).on(x, y, s) \supset \neg on(y, x, s)$. State constraints specify properties that are true of all situations. Using induction for the situation calculus and the action precondition and successor state axioms for the blocks world, one can prove that whenever $\mathcal{D}_{S_0}$ contains $C(S_0)$ for each of the sentences (10.1) (together with $C(S_0)$ for one other state constraint—see Exercise 12 below for the details):

$$(\forall s).executable(s) \supset C(s).$$

This says something very interesting: Provided the constraints hold in the initial situation, they are guaranteed to hold at all future executable situations. It doesn't guarantee the same for non-executable future situations, but we never care about these, because they correspond to "ghost" situations—action sequences where one or more actions violates its preconditions. So we conclude that the essential information content of these state constraints is already included in the basic action theory itself; *the constraints contribute no new information to what is already present in these axioms*. This justifies omitting these constraints from the blocks world axiomatization.

There still remains something mysterious in these considerations. How did the action precondition and successor state axioms come to embody the information content of the state constraints to begin with? Is this an accidental property of the blocks world, or are there some general principles at work? We shall return to this question in Appendix B, in connection with the qualification problem, that we have already discussed briefly in Section 3.1.3, and in connection with the so-called *ramification* problem, that is closely related to the frame problem. There, some of the mystery will be explained.

10.6.5   A Blocks World with Incomplete Initial Situation

At last, we can present an example open-world blocks problem. It has 12 blocks, arranged as indicated in the figure. Block m is known to be clear, and not on the table, but its location is otherwise unknown. f is known not to be on the table; otherwise, it may or may not be clear, and its location is unknown. a is known to be on b or on e, and exactly one of b and e is known to be clear. And so forth; the axioms say it all.

A Blocks World Problem with Incomplete Initial Situation

```
/* Initial situation: Only the blocks so indicated have been
   specified to be clear.
```

```
                              d
        clear --> p           a              m <--- clear; not on table
   not on table --> n         .
                          ? . . ?                  f <--- not on table
                            .  .
                    g     b    .
                    h     c    e    k
                    ---------------------------

Goal situation       d    k
                     h    g
                     b    m
                     e    f
                     a    c
                     -----------                              */
```

```prolog
goal(S) :- prove( on(d,h,S) & on(h,b,S) & on(b,e,S) & on(e,a,S) &
           ontable(a,S) & on(k,g,S) & on(g,m,S) & on(m,f,S) &
           on(f,c,S) & ontable(c,S) ).

goodTower(X,S) <=> X = a & ontable(a,S) v
    X = e & on(e,a,S) & ontable(a,S) v
    X = b & on(b,e,S) & on(e,a,S) & ontable(a,S) v
    X = h & on(h,b,S) & on(b,e,S) & on(e,a,S) & ontable(a,S) v
    X = d & on(d,h,S) & on(h,b,S) & on(b,e,S) & on(e,a,S) & ontable(a,S) v
    X = c & ontable(c,S) v
    X = f & on(f,c,S) & ontable(c,S) v
    X = m & on(m,f,S) & on(f,c,S) & ontable(c,S) v
    X = g & on(g,m,S) & on(m,f,S) & on(f,c,S) & ontable(c,S) v
    X = k & on(k,g,S) & on(g,m,S) & on(m,f,S) & on(f,c,S) & ontable(c,S).
```

/* Initial database. Notice that all references to clear and ontable
    have been eliminated, via their definitions, in favour of on. This
    considerably improves the efficiency of prime implicate generation. */

```prolog
axiom(all([y,block],-on(y,m,s0))).            % m is clear.
axiom(all([y,block],-on(y,p,s0))).            % p is clear.
axiom(all([x,block],-on(k,x,s0))).            % k is on the table.
axiom(all([x,block],-on(c,x,s0))).            % c is on the table.
axiom(all([x,block],-on(e,x,s0))).            % e is on the table.
axiom(all([x,block],-on(h,x,s0))).            % h is on the table.
axiom(on(b,c,s0)).    axiom(on(d,a,s0)).
axiom(on(g,h,s0)).    axiom(on(p,n,s0)).
axiom(on(a,b,s0) v on(a,e,s0)).               % a is on b or on e,
```

```
axiom(all([x,block],on(x,b,s0) => x = a)).        % and no other block
axiom(all([x,block],on(x,e,s0) => x = a)).        % is on b or on e.
axiom(some([x,block],on(f,x,s0))).                % f is not on the table.
axiom(some([x,block],on(m,x,s0))).                % m is not on the table.
axiom(some([x,block],on(n,x,s0))).                % n is not on the table.
axiom(all([x,block],all([y,block], on(x,y,s0) => -on(y,x,s0))))).
axiom(all([x,block],all([y,block], all([z,block],
              on(y,x,s0) & on(z,x,s0) => y = z)))).
axiom(all([x,block],all([y,block], all([z,block],
              on(x,y,s0) & on(x,z,s0) => y = z)))).


/*  clear and ontable defined in the initial situation. This is
    needed by the regression theorem-prover to eliminate clear
    and ontable in favour of on in regressed formulas.  */

clear(X,s0) <=> all([y,block],-on(y,X,s0)).
ontable(X,s0) <=> all([y,block],-on(X,y,s0)).


%  Domain of individuals.

domain(block, [a,b,c,d,e,f,g,h,k,m,n,p]).


%  Action preconditions.

poss(move(X,Y),S) :- domain(block,D),
                     findall(Z,(member(Z,D), prove(clear(Z,S))),L),
                     member(X,L), member(Y,L), not X = Y.
poss(moveToTable(X),S) :- domain(block,D), member(X,D),
                          prove(clear(X,S) & -ontable(X,S)).


/* Successor state axioms instantiated by action terms to
   simplify implementation of the regression theorem-prover. */

clear(X,do(move(U,V),S)) <=> on(U,X,S) v -(X = V) & clear(X,S).
clear(X,do(moveToTable(U),S)) <=> on(U,X,S) v clear(X,S).

on(X,Y,do(move(U,V),S)) <=> X = U & Y = V v -(X = U) & on(X,Y,S).
on(X,Y,do(moveToTable(U),S)) <=> -(X = U) & on(X,Y,S).

ontable(X,do(move(U,V),S)) <=> -(X = U) & ontable(X,S).
ontable(X,do(moveToTable(U),S)) <=> X = U v ontable(X,S).

primitive_action(move(X,Y)).   primitive_action(moveToTable(X)).
```

There are three things to note about this axiomatization:

1. The initial database is defined only using the fluent *on*, and not *clear* and *ontable*. In the blocks world, the fluent *on* is primitive, and fluents *clear* and *ontable* can be defined in terms of it:

$$clear(x, s) \equiv (\forall y)\neg on(y, x, s),$$

$$ontable(x, s) \equiv (\forall y)\neg on(x, y, s).$$

Thus, instead of representing the initial fact that h is on the table by $ontable(h, S_0)$, we elected instead to use $\neg(\exists x)on(h, x, S_0)$, and similarly for *clear*. So *on* will be the only fluent mentioned in the initial database. Why adopt this indirect representation? The main reason is computational efficiency. With this choice, the initial database does not include facts about *clear* and *ontable*. This means that there will be far fewer prime implicates for the initial database, and since the prime implicate calculation is expensive, there is a considerable gain in efficiency. However, one pays a small price for this. We continue to have successor state axioms for *clear* and *ontable*; therefore, when the regression theorem-prover regresses a formula back to the initial situation, that regressed formula may mention *clear* or *ontable*. But the prime implicates are exclusively in terms of *on*. So the theorem-prover must replace any atom in *clear* or *ontable* of the regressed formula by its definition in terms of *on*, after which it can determine whether the prime implicates entail the regressed formula. For this reason, we have included the initial situation definitions of *clear* and *ontable* among the blocks world clauses.

2. The clauses for poss assume responsibility for calling prove on appropriate formulas. Similarly, the clause for goal explicitly invokes prove.

3. The successor state axioms are not the same as those of the earlier examples. For example, in the blocks world of Section 10.2, the Prolog successor state axiom for clear was:

```
clear(X,do(A,S))  :-  (A = move(Y,Z) ; A = moveToTable(Y)), on(Y,X,S) ;
                       clear(X,S), not A = move(Y,X).
```

This universally quantifies over all actions A. In contrast, the open-world blocks world axiomatization uses two clauses for clear, one for action move(U,V), the other for action moveToTable(U). There is no deep reason for this choice. It was made only to simplify the implementation of the simplification routine simplify used by the regression theorem-prover. To see why, consider the equivalence of the successor state axiom that this Prolog clause represents:

$$clear(x, do(a, s)) \equiv$$

$$(\exists y)\{[(\exists z)a = move(y, z) \lor a = moveToTable(y)] \land on(y, x, s)\} \lor$$
$$clear(x, s) \land \neg(\exists y)a = move(y, x).$$

Now, consider an instance $move(u, v)$ of a in this sentence that would be suitable for regressing an atom of the form $clear(x, do(move(u, v), s))$:

$$clear(x, do(move(u, v), s)) \equiv (\exists y)\{[(\exists z)move(u, v) = move(y, z) \lor$$
$$move(u, v) = moveToTable(y)] \land on(y, x, s)\} \lor$$
$$clear(x, s) \land \neg(\exists y)move(u, v) = move(y, x).$$

This can be simplified using the unique names axioms for actions, and some elementary logic:

$$clear(x, do(move(u, v), S)) \equiv on(u, x, s) \lor x \neq v \land clear(x, s).$$

This is the logical form of the first clause for clear in the open-world blocks world axiomatization. Obtaining this logical form from the general successor state axiom was straightforward, but required a lot of simplification based on reasoning about quantifiers, equality and unique names axioms for actions. To avoid having to implement such simplification routines we have opted instead for the user of the system to do this himself, in advance, and to represent the results of these simplifications directly by successor state axioms, particularized to each action, as done in the above Prolog axiomatization.

Now we try the implementation on the above example, using the same Golog interpreter and program $wspdf$ as for the closed world planners. An initial run with maximal depth 16, that we do not show here, yielded several plans, among which was one of length 14. Next, we ran the planner searching for plans of length ≤ 14, with the following result.

A Depth-First Run for the Example

```
[eclipse 2]: compile.

Clausal form completed.   CPU time (sec): 7.31  Clauses: 495

Database compiled.   CPU time (sec): 10.63   Prime implicates: 248

yes.
[eclipse 3]: plandf(14).

  CPU time (sec): 3.57  Good situations: 14

[moveToTable(m), moveToTable(p), moveToTable(n), moveToTable(f),
 moveToTable(d), moveToTable(a), move(e, a), move(b, e), move(f, c),
```

```
move(m, f), move(g, m), move(h, b), move(d, h), move(k, g)]
More?   y.

  CPU time (sec): 20.51  Good situations: 54

[moveToTable(p), moveToTable(m), moveToTable(n), moveToTable(f),
 moveToTable(d), moveToTable(a), move(e, a), move(b, e), move(f, c),
 move(m, f), move(g, m), move(h, b), move(d, h), move(k, g)]
More?   y.

  CPU time (sec): 37.22  Good situations: 93

[moveToTable(p), moveToTable(n), moveToTable(m), moveToTable(f),
 moveToTable(d), moveToTable(a), move(e, a), move(b, e), move(f, c),
 move(m, f), move(g, m), move(h, b), move(d, h), move(k, g)]
More?   y.

no (more) solution.
```

The initial database was transformed to clausal form in 7.31 CPU seconds, and it took a further 10.63 seconds to compile these clauses to prime implicates. The planner ran to completion, taking 68.75 CPU seconds to search the entire space of plans of length ≤ 14. Since the run produced only plans of length 14, we conclude that 14 is the minimum length of a plan for this problem.

10.7   Planning vs. Nondeterministic Programming

This chapter has presented two planners: $wspbf$, which searches breadth first, and $wspdf$, which executes depth first. Both are general purpose, domain independent planners. To run them on a specific problem, one must provide suitable domain axioms, together with domain specific search control heuristics via the $badSituation$ predicate. But the planners themselves are fixed in their structure. The procedures $wspbf$ and $wspdf$ are designed to work for all planning problems.

Another point of view is possible and often useful. Suppose someone seeking to solve planning problems in some application domain knows a lot about that domain, in particular, about good ways to search through the space of possible plans. For example, in the blocks world, she might know that a good strategy for finding a plan is always to create a good tower by moving a lexicographically least block onto an existing good tower, and failing that, to move any block onto the table, provided it's not the top of a good tower. This is a nondeterministic procedure; it still requires search to find a plan, but it is easy to describe as a Golog program that does this search in a depth first manner:

> **proc** $blocksPlanDF(n)$
> $\quad goal? \mid [n > 0? \,;\, moveOneBlock \,;\, blocksPlanDF(n-1)]$
> **endProc**

> **proc** $moveOneBlock$
> $\quad (\pi\, a)[actionCreatesGoodTower(a) \wedge actionMovesLeastBlock(a)? \,;\, a] \mid$
> $\quad \neg(\exists a)actionCreatesGoodTower(a)? \,;$
> $\quad (\pi\, x)[clear(x) \wedge \neg goodTower(x)? \,;\, moveToTable(x)]$
> **endProc**

The procedure *moveOneBlock* appeals to the following abbreviations:

$$actionCreatesGoodTower(a, s) \overset{def}{=}$$
$$Poss(a, s) \wedge (\exists x).blockMoved(a, x) \wedge goodTower(x, do(a, s)),$$

$$blockMoved(a, x) \overset{def}{=} a = moveToTable(x) \vee (\exists y)a = move(x, y),$$

$$actionMovesLeastBlock(a, s) \overset{def}{=} blockMoved(a, x) \wedge$$
$$(\forall a', y).actionCreatesGoodTower(a', s) \wedge blockMoved(a', y) \supset \neg y < x.$$

We omit the straightforward translation of this program into Prolog. For the example of Section 10.2.1, it produced all five plans in .42 CPU seconds, using a depth bound of 15.

Here is an amazingly simple variant of the previous procedure that computes all plans, in no particular order, and with no fixed length bound:

> **proc** $blocksPlan$
> $\quad$ **while** $\neg goal$ **do** $moveOneBlock$ **endWhile**
> **endProc**

For the example of Section 10.2.1, it produced all five plans in .41 CPU seconds.

The above are special purpose planning procedures; they work only for the blocks world. To plan in another domain, you would need to write special procedures for that domain. These examples demonstrate that there can be a very thin line between general purpose planning and nondeterministic programming. But there can also be important differences. While the planners are much more general, the procedures can be much more transparent and efficient. Suppose the goal is to get all the blocks onto the table. *wspdf* and *wspbf* will both solve this problem, but you will need to specify a lot of domain specific information about good towers and bad situations. On the other hand, the following procedure is much more direct, transparently encodes what every child knows about how to solve this particular problem, and will certainly be faster:

> **proc** $allToTable$

$$\textbf{while } (\exists x)\neg ontable(x) \textbf{ do } (\pi\, x)moveToTable(x) \textbf{ endWhile}$$
$$\textbf{endProc}$$

This is a simple example of what might be called *procedural knowledge*—small pieces of highly domain specific, prestored code representing what we humans know about various ways to best change the world. On this view, representing knowledge about a domain goes beyond "simply" writing static axioms; one must also include procedural knowledge. Just as logic gives an account of how to use axioms (entailment, theorem-proving, etc.), we also need a story about how to use procedural knowledge: which pieces are relevant to a given task, how are pieces combined, how do we reason about the effects of procedures, etc. Many of these issues are the province of classical computer science, involving, as they do, programming language semantics, and automatic program synthesis and verification. From this perspective, the planning problem becomes how to combine appropriate chunks of procedural knowledge in the right way to achieve a prespecified goal or class of goals. This is often referred to as *hierarchical planning*.

It is a subtext of much of this book that, at least for complex system control tasks, general purpose planning to synthesize the system's behaviour might not be computationally feasible. It will often be preferable for a programmer to encode his domain specific knowledge about this task as a collection of (possibly nondeterministic) Golog procedures, and we have often done just that in this book. For example, we solved the coffee delivery problem of Section 7.4.1 by writing a temporal Golog program. We could instead have posed this as a planning problem, whose goal is that everyone who wants coffee at her preferred times has coffee, but it is extremely unlikely that any current general purpose planners could solve this problem in a reasonable amount of time. Of course, relying on the system designer to program the solution side-steps many of the artificial intelligence issues concerned with how a robot might come up with these programs by itself. Perhaps hierarchical planning relative to a (large) database of procedural knowledge will some day resolve this issue, but at the moment, we are a long way from that dream. Until that day arrives, the Golog family of languages provides a computationally attractive alternative to general purpose planning for complex control tasks, while at the same time, its nondeterminism gives its users the ability to program search, when that is required to solve a problem.

10.8   Exercises

1. **The missionaries and missionaries problem.** This is a thinly disguised rephrasing of a classical AI problem. *m* Catholic missionaries and an equal number of Protestant missionaries are traveling together and arrive at the left side a river at which an empty

rowboat, whose capacity is b people, is moored. The Catholic missionaries are so persuasive that if ever their numbers on any bank of the river, or in the boat, exceed the Protestants, the Catholics will convert them all (or vice versa—take your pick). Find a plan for getting all the missionaries across the river while preserving their ecumenical spirit. First try the case $m = 3$, $b = 2$, which is the standard textbook formulation of the problem. Next, experiment with various other combinations, and when you are confident of your solution, try out your program, in depth-first mode, for large m (of the order of 100), and $b = 4$. It is known that there is no solution for $m = 4$, $b = 2$. In formulating your *badSituations*, be sure to filter out repeated states, i.e., when, in the current situation, the missionary numbers on the left bank and the boat location are the same as in some prior situation. Also, encode in your *badSituations* the sensible requirement to maximize the number of missionaries transported from left to right, and to minimize the number returning from right to left.

2. Implement a bounded blocks world planner, for which empty space on the table is limited to at most three blocks. You will have to revise the blocks world axioms suitably, as well as modify the search control principles for *badSituation*. Invent some planning problems, and try out your program.

3. Consider a blocks world where every block is coloured blue, green or red. Suppose the plans of interest are those that satisfy the goal, but also have the property that the sequence of blocks moved by the plan must consist of zero or more blue blocks, followed by one or more green blocks, followed by two or more red ones. Build a planner for this problem, and try it out. Notice that now there may be goals for which no plan exists.

4. Suppose a search tree has a constant branching factor b. For large n, prove that an iterative deepening search through the tree to depth n expands of the order of $b/(b-1)$ times as many nodes as does a simple, breadth-first search.

5. This exercise is a follow-up of question 5 of Exercises 7.10. With the version of Golog developed there, *wspbf* and *wspdf* are planners for sequential actions with durations. Modify the blocks world axioms for this case, and try out these planners on some problems of your invention. Consider finding minimal duration plans, as well as minimal length plans.

6. Revisit question 12 of Exercises 4.9. Formulate search control rules for this setting, and derive a plan for exchanging the values of two program variables. Formulate various other "program synthesis" problems involving multiple program variables, for example, sorting the values of several variables, and experiment with deriving plans for these. Of course, the only programs you can synthesize this way are straight line programs—no loops, no conditionals—but it's a start.

7. Axiomatize a blocks world in which, whether or not a block x has other blocks above it, it is always possible to move x; moreover, all blocks stacked above x move with it. Formulate suitable notions of *badSituations* for complete and incomplete initial situations, and experiment with the resulting planning systems.

8. Implement breadth-first and depth-first planners for concurrent actions with incomplete initial situation, and try them out.

9. As we have seen, regression is not always a good idea because the regressed formula might be exponentially long in the number of actions (Exercise 13 of Section 4.9). Show that for the blocks world axioms in the program of Section 10.6.5 the regression of a ground atom grows at most linearly in the number of actions. Formulate some general conditions on the syntactic form of successor state axioms that will guarantee this desirable property.

10. Prove Theorem 10.6.2.

11. Refer to the discussion about open blocks world initial databases of Section 10.6.4.

    (a) Show that the initial relational database underlying the ongoing blocks world example of Section 10.2 entails each of the three sentences of Section 10.6.4 about the initial situation.

    (b) Suppose an initial blocks world database is relational. Show that for each of the three sentences of Section 10.6.4 about the initial situation, the relational database entails the sentence or its negation. (Hint: See question 6 of Exercises 9.8.)

12. Refer to the discussion about open blocks world initial databases of Section 10.6.4. As observed there, each of the three state constraints (10.1) has the general form $(\forall s)C(s)$. In addition to these, consider the constraint:

$$clear(x, s) \supset \neg(\exists y)on(y, x, s).$$

For each of these four state constraints, prove, using induction for the situation calculus, that the following is entailed by the basic action theory whose action precondition and successor state axioms are those we have been using for the blocks world, and $\mathcal{D}_{S_0}$ contains these four constraints relativized to S_0:

$$(\forall s).executable(s) \supset C(s).$$

Hint: You will probably find that proving these one at a time won't work. Instead, consider doing simultaneous induction on $\bigwedge C(s)$, where the conjunction is over all four of the constraints.

13. Consider a blocks world in which at most two blocks can fit on the table.

    (a) Formulate a state constraint that expresses this.

    (b) Write a suitable action precondition axiom for $moveToTable(x)$, and using this, prove that the state constraint holds in all executable situations, provided it holds initially.

14. Refer to the theorem-proving problem of question 9 of the exercises in Appendix A. We recast this here as a planning problem. There are three blocks, A, B and C, all initially on the table. A is green, C is not green, and the colour of B is unknown. Using the open-world planning system of this chapter, find all plans of length three or less to achieve the goal that there is a green block on top of a non-green block. Since the problem does not specify a final goal configuration as an explicit set of towers, you cannot use the $badSituations$ of this chapter to filter out useless action sequences, but this problem is so simple, these are unnecessary.

15. **The bomb and the toilets problem.** It is known that exactly one of a number of packages contains a bomb, and that one way to disarm a bomb is by immersing it in a toilet, of which there is at least one available. A toilet can contain just one package, but by flushing it, room becomes available for another package. Formalize this problem with the following predicates, fluents and actions, propose a suitable $badSituation$ predicate, and find some plans to achieve the goal $\neg dangerous(s)$ for various numbers of packages and toilets.

    • $in(pkg)$: The bomb is in package pkg.

    • $dangerous(s)$: Situation s is dangerous, meaning that there is a package containing a bomb that has not yet been disarmed.

    • $clogged(t, s)$: Toilet t is clogged, meaning it contains a package.

    • $disarmed(pkg, s)$: Package pkg has been disarmed by placing it into a toilet.

    • $flush(t)$: The action of flushing toilet t, which is always possible. Its effect is to remove any package that might have been in the toilet.

    • $dunk(pkg, t)$: The action of placing package pkg into toilet t. This is possible only when the toilet doesn't currently contain a package.

10.9 Bibliographic Remarks

All of the planners of this chapter are based on a very simple idea: Systematically generate potential plans of increasing length, filter out those that are clearly bad according to suitable domain specific knowledge, and test those that pass the filter against the goal. This is not a new idea. In 1981, Kibler and Morris [96] noticed how useful this procedure can be for the blocks world, and implemented a successful planning system based on it. For mysterious reasons, their paper had no impact, and remained lost in time. In the early 1990's,

Bacchus and Kabanza [10, 9, 11] independently rediscovered this idea, and recognized its wider applicability than just the blocks world. Unlike ours, their implementation uses a linear temporal logic coupled with a STRIPS representation for actions and a STRIPS database. The temporal logic is used for representing goals, as well as assertions about which STRIPS databases should be considered bad; progression is invoked to explicitly create these databases. Initial, systematic experiments by Bacchus and Kabanza on various planning problems in a number of different domains have been very encouraging. So this approach seems to be a viable—in many cases preferable—alternative to more "classical" approaches, that have been based on working backwards, via regression, from the goal statement to the initial situation (e.g., PRODIGY [30], McAllester and Rosenblitt's SNLP [134, 204]). Srivastava and Kambhampati [206] have also explored the advantages of domain specific control information for planners, and have confirmed the observations of Bacchus and Kabanza that such planners can significantly outperform more traditional systems. Many members of the planning research community object to exploiting user-supplied domain specific information in planning systems; they argue that somehow, this is cheating. In response to this criticism, research is being done on methods for automatically extracting control information from domain descriptions; see, for example, Bacchus [7], and Gerevini and Schubert [62].

The concurrent planner of Section 10.3 produces what are normally called *partial order plans* (Russell and Norvig [184], Chapter 11). Such a plan consists of a set of action terms, together with a partial order on these terms, with the property that any linearization of this partial order produces a sequential plan for the problem. In the case of the concurrent situation calculus, the situation $do([C_1, \ldots, C_n], S_0)$ defines a partial order plan with respect to the partial order: $A_i \prec A_j$ for all $A_i \in C_i$, $A_j \in C_j$, $i < j$. However, not every partial order plan can be represented in the concurrent situation calculus; Russell and Norvig [184] Figure 11.5 provides an example. Most partial order planners in the literature are based on STRIPS-like representations for actions, and use regression in their search for plans (e.g., Chapman's TWEAK [31], Soderland and Weld's SNLP [204] based on McAllester and Rosenblitt [134], and Blum and Furst's Graphplan [21]).

There has been very little work on open-world planning. Exceptions are Conformant Graphplan of Smith and Weld [203], and planners by Cimatti and Roveri [34] and by Rintanen [181]. The open-world planner of this chapter was reported in Finzi, Pirri, and Reiter [52].

Most work on open-world planning focuses on a very interesting, but different approach than ours, namely on how to devise plans that, during their execution, use sensing to obtain information unavailable during the planning phase. Typically, such plans involve *conditionals* coupled with sensing actions, for example:

senseTrafficLight; **if** *red* **then** *stop* **else** *go*.

Etzioni et al [46] give a procedural approach to planning with sensing actions for a STRIPS-like representation. Levesque [117] provides an elegant logical specification for such conditional plans based on the situation calculus. In Chapter 11 we shall deal with the approach to sensing actions that underlies Levesque's account of planning. A quite different logical specification for planning with sense actions is (De Giacomo, Iocchi, Nardi, and Rosati [63]).

The first uses for prime implicates in computer science were in the synthesis of digital circuits, and there is an early literature on how to compute them (e.g. Tison [215]). The importance of prime implicates for artificial intelligence was first pointed out by Reiter and de Kleer [179] in connection with so-called assumption-based truth maintenance systems, and since that time, there has been considerable work done on better computational methods than simple-minded resolution (e.g., de Kleer [38]; Jackson and Pais [92]; Palopoli, Pirri, and Pizzuti [151]). In particular, the program given in this chapter for computing prime implicates is particularly naive compared with more recent implementations that are based on very restrictive forms of resolution. Cadoli and Donini [29] give a survey of knowledge base compilation techniques.

Another class of problems for which little work exists is planning in the presence of natural actions (Section 7.9). Here, there are natural actions, under nature's control and whose occurrences are governed by known laws, and a repertoire of free-will actions under an agent's control. For a planning system for such problems based on the ideas of this chapter and Section 7.9, see Pirri and Reiter [166].

The most important foundational paper on planning is by Green [71]; it provides the theoretical underpinning for all of the results of this chapter. The NP-hardness of optimal blocks world planning was established by Gupta and Nau [74]. For a systematic study of the complexity of blocks world planning, including algorithms for finding near-optimal plans and mechanisms for generating random problem instances, see Slaney and Thiébaux [201]. An excellent, general book on planning is by Yang [219]; consult also the relevant chapters in Russell and Norvig [184]. On the relationships between planning and automatic program synthesis see Manna and Waldinger [132]. Hierarchical planning is an idea that has been around for a long time (Sacerdoti [185]); see Erol [43] for a modern treatment. For a discussion of why nondeterministic programming might be preferable to planning for complex control tasks, see Levesque and Reiter [112].

11 Sensing and Knowledge

To this point in the book, we have been (implicitly) assuming that agent-performed actions only affect the state of that agent's external world. We have overlooked a basic ability possessed by many dynamical systems, especially robotic and other agents, which is that they can actively *sense* various features of the world they inhabit, and by doing so, can acquire new information about their environment. Unlike "ordinary" actions like picking up a block, such sensing actions have no effect on the agent's external world. Instead, they affect the perceiver's *mental* state; by performing the action of sensing its distance from a wall, a robot comes to *know* how far it is from the wall. For this reason, these are often called *knowledge-producing* actions.

We have also been assuming (again, implicitly) that action precondition axioms can always be formulated in terms of what is true of an agent's external world. But this is not always the case. Consider the preconditions for calling someone on the telephone. You must be next to a telephone, and you must *know* the telephone number of the person you are calling:

$$Poss(call(x), s) \equiv (\exists t).telephone(t) \wedge nexto(t, s) \wedge \mathbf{KRef}(telNumber(x), s).$$

Here, *knowing the referent of telNumber(x)* in situation s is not a truth about the physical world, but about the mental state of knowledge of the agent doing the calling.

For these and other reasons, we need to expand our picture of the situation calculus to accommodate knowledge-producing actions and their effects on an agent's mental state, and that is the purpose of this chapter. First, we shall need a mechanism for representing knowledge in the situation calculus. To do so, we shall use situations as surrogates for the possible worlds with which modal logics normally formalize knowledge. This will require modifying the foundational axioms for situations. Just as was the case for ordinary actions, we shall need to solve a frame problem associated with knowledge. Having done so, we shall revisit regression as a reasoning mechanism, and extend it appropriately to this more general setting. Finally, we shall introduce the concept of knowledge-based programming, and develop an implementation for an important special case.

11.1 Knowledge in the Situation Calculus

The first problem to solve is how to represent an agent's knowledge within the situation calculus, and to keep the story simple, we shall consider just one agent. The classical approach would be to pass from first-order logic to an appropriate *modal* logic, using the possible-worlds semantics first anticipated by Leibniz in the 17th century and formalized by Kripke, Hintikka, and others around 1960. An alternative proposal, due to Robert Moore, starts with the observation that situations can serve as the possible worlds of modal logic. Moreover, because situations (unlike possible worlds in modal languages) are terms *in the language of the situation calculus*, one can directly represent knowledge in the language by introducing a suitable new fluent standing for an accessibility relation. This is the approach we take here.

11.1.1 Accessibility Relations and Knowledge

Just as we are accustomed to saying that a formula ϕ is true in situation s, we want also to be able to say that it is true of a situation s that an agent *knows* ϕ. So our first technical problem is to formulate what might be meant by this. To ground the discussion, consider the familiar blocks world, and ask what might be meant by the claim that in S_0 an agent knows that block A is clear. One intuition about this claim, which we pursue here, is that because typically he will lack some knowledge about the world he inhabits, the agent is uncertain about which world he is really in, and therefore, can imagine that there are other possible worlds he could be inhabiting. Nevertheless, because he knows that A is clear, there can be no uncertainty about this fact, so $clear(A)$ must be true in every one of these possible worlds. In all the ways the agent thinks the actual world S_0 could have been, $clear(A)$ must be true. We can picture this in terms of an agent inhabiting S_0, and imagining all possible alternative situations to the one he is in. Figure 11.1 illustrates such an agent who is uncertain about whether A is on the table or on B, but he's quite sure that there are four blocks A, B, C and D, and that B, C and D are on the table. So he can imag-

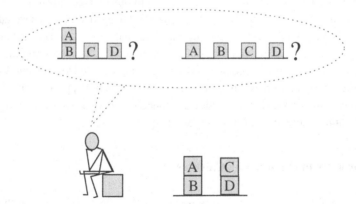

Figure 11.1: Two alternative worlds to an actual world.

ine two alternative worlds to the one he is in. Notice that the actual world is not among those he considers possible, although there is nothing in the theory we are developing that prevents it from being included. With respect to this scenario, we shall say that, in S_0, the following are among the things the agent knows:

$clear(A),\ clear(C),\ clear(D),\ onTable(C),\ \neg on(A,C),\ \neg on(A,D),$
$on(A,B) \vee onTable(A),\ (\forall x).\neg on(x,B) \supset onTable(x).^{1}$

The following are among the things the agent doesn't know:

$clear(B),\ \neg clear(B),\ onTable(A),\ \neg onTable(A).$

Notice that in this example, much of his knowledge is actually mistaken. Thus, he knows that $clear(D)$, but in the actual world, namely S_0, D is not clear. If the agent had also considered the actual world among his alternatives, his knowledge would no longer be mistaken. But this would increase his uncertainty; he would know less than before. For example, in S_0 he would no longer know $clear(D)$ or $onTable(C)$, although he would continue to know $onTable(B), onTable(D), clear(A)$, etc. On the other hand, if the agent had considered the first alternative in his cloud to be the only alternative world, then in S_0 he would know everything about this blocks world, namely $on(A,B), onTable(B), clear(C)$, etc. These examples illustrate a general property of the above approach to knowledge: The more worlds an agent considers possible, the more uncertainty there is in his mind about which world he actually inhabits, and therefore, the less he knows.

The example also illustrates that, without further constraints on what kinds of worlds an agent can consider possible, our use of the word "knowledge" to describe his state of mind might be an overstatement. Perhaps "belief" would be a better term; or "desire" or "intention" or any of a range of so-called *propositional attitudes*. In fact, possible worlds have been traditionally used to characterize all these concepts; the differences among them result from placing different constraints on the worlds an agent considers possible. So the above approach to defining knowledge is perfectly consistent with this tradition, and we shall continue to use the term "knowledge", while keeping in mind that only under suitable conditions (that we will consider later) will "knowledge" resemble knowledge.

To summarize, we have the following general picture: An agent inhabiting S_0 imagines a set of worlds that, as far as he is concerned, represents all the worlds he might be in. If ϕ is true in each world of this set, then we say that *relative to this set*, the agent knows ϕ in S_0. If, no matter what set of worlds he imagines, he knows ϕ in S_0 relative to that set, then we will say that he (absolutely) knows ϕ in S_0. The intuition behind this concept of

---

1 Notice that these are situation-suppressed expressions. and therefore, are not strictly speaking sentences of the situation calculus. They are expressions like those occurring in Golog test actions. In general, when we speak of an agent knowing ϕ in some situation, ϕ will be such a situation-suppressed expression. As in Golog, when we wish to restore a missing situation argument s in such an expression to obtain a legitimate situation calculus formula, we shall write $\phi[s]$.

knowledge is that, no matter how hard he tries, the agent can't imagine a set of worlds he might be inhabiting without ϕ being true everywhere in this set. Therefore, there can be no uncertainty in his mind about the truth of ϕ; therefore, he must know ϕ.

What kinds of things are these possible worlds, and how can they be represented in the situation calculus? We propose to represent worlds by situations, so when, in S_0, an agent is imagining a set of possible worlds, we intend that he is imagining a set of situations. To represent the fact that s is one of the situations that an agent in S_0 considers possible, we shall write $K(s, S_0)$, where K is a new binary predicate symbol that we add to the language of the situation calculus. Following common practice in modal logic, we call K an *accessibility relation*. We now have the following proposal for representing, in the situation calculus, that an agent knows ϕ in situation S_0:

$$(\forall s).K(s, S_0) \supset \phi[s].^2$$

For example, to assert that initially, an agent knows that all the blocks on the table are clear, one writes:

$$(\forall s).K(s, S_0) \supset (\forall x).onTable(x, s) \supset clear(x, s).$$

Of course, we shall need to provide axioms characterizing the K relation, but for now, we defer this decision.

11.1.2   Alternatives to the Initial Situation

The question now arises: Where do the alternative situations to S_0 come from? In the situation calculus as we know it, there are plenty to choose from. In the blocks world, apart from S_0, there are

$$do(move(A, B), S_0), \quad do(moveToTable(B), S_0),$$
$$do(move(A, B), do(moveToTable(B), S_0)), \quad \text{etc.,}$$

an infinite supply of situations. The problem is that, with the exception of S_0, none of these can serve as a possible alternative world to S_0. To see why, consider, for example, $do(move(A, B), S_0)$. We have an agent who actually inhabits S_0, but she is considering $do(move(A, B), S_0)$ as a possible world that she could be inhabiting. But initially, there should be no uncertainty in the agent's mind about what actions she has performed; after all, she hasn't done anything yet. However, if she imagines $do(move(A, B), S_0)$ as a possible alternative world to S_0, then she imagines she might be be in a world that she reached by doing the action $move(A, B)$, and this conflicts with her certainty that she has done nothing yet. So the only situation that can serve as an alternative to S_0 is S_0 itself,

---

2 Recall that ϕ is a situation-suppressed expression, and that $\phi[s]$ denotes the result of restoring situation argument s back into ϕ.

and that doesn't leave us with very many possible worlds. The way out of this difficulty will be to enrich the situation calculus with more initial situations that can therefore serve as alternatives to S_0, and this we shall do in Section 11.5.1 below. For the moment, we shall simply assume the availability of an unlimited supply of other initial situations.

11.1.3 Knowing a Referent

We can now give an account of what it means for an agent to know the referent of a term, as in knowing Mary's telephone number. For an agent in situation S_0 to know the referent of $telNumber(Mary)$, she must find it impossible to imagine two different alternative situations to S_0 in which the values of $telNumber(Mary)$ are different. In other words, in all situations s K-related to S_0, the denotations of the term $telNumber(Mary)$ are identical. We can express this by:

$$(\exists x)(\forall s).K(s, S_0) \supset x = telNumber(Mary, s).$$

This says that a single x serves as the value of $telNumber(Mary, s)$ in all situations s accessible from S_0.

11.1.4 Knowledge and Action

The above example blocks world was static, and the only account of knowledge that has been given so far is of knowledge in the initial situation. Next, we consider how to adapt the possible worlds view of knowledge to accommodate an agent acting on the world. Figure 11.2 illustrates what we have in mind. There, we have the same initial situations as in Figure 11.1, but now we consider how these initial situations should evolve in response to agent-performed actions. The agent is in the actual situation S_0, but as far as she is concerned, she could be in any of the two initial situations K-related to S_0. Now she performs the action $move(C, A)$, causing the actual situation to evolve to a successor actual situation $do(move(C, A), S_0)$, with the resulting indicated configuration of blocks. But the agent imagines she could have started in any one of the two initial alternatives to S_0 and therefore, she imagines that the action $move(C, A)$ caused these situations to evolve to the two configurations shown. Therefore, she is actually in situation $do(move(C, A), S_0)$, but as far as she is concerned, she could be in any one of these two other configurations. This means that these two configurations should be treated as alternatives to the actual situation $do(move(C, A), S_0)$, and therefore, we show them as K-related to it in the figure. Now it makes sense to talk about the agent's knowledge in situation $do(move(C, A), S_0)$. For example, in this situation she knows that $on(C, A)$, $onTable(B)$, $on(A, B) \vee onTable(A)$. She does not know $onTable(A)$ or $\neg onTable(A)$.

Suppose the agent next performs $move(D, C)$. This causes the second level situations of Figure 11.2 to evolve to those at the third level. Reasoning as before, we obtain two

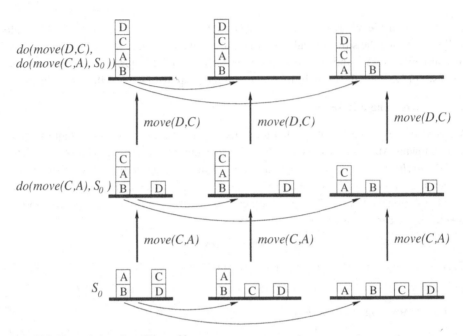

Figure 11.2: The evolution of possible worlds.

configurations K-related to the actual situation $do(move(D, C), do(move(C, A), S_0))$. Therefore, as before, we can meaningfully talk about the agent's knowledge in situation $do(move(D, C), do(move(C, A), S_0))$, some examples of which are

$$on(D, C), \quad on(A, B) \vee onTable(A), \quad (\forall x).onTable(x) \supset x = A \vee x = B.$$

11.1.5 Knowledge Defined

The above example illustrates the need to extend the concept of the accessibility relation K to include situations accessible from any actual situation $do([\alpha_1, \ldots, \alpha_n], S_0)$. But if we are prepared to go this far, we might as well go all the way and generalize this relation to allow situations accessible from any situation, not just actual ones. Now the predicate K will be defined over all pairs of situations, and we will take $K(s', s)$ to mean that s' is accessible from s. This leads to the following proposal for expressing that, in situation s, an agent knows ϕ:

$$(\forall s').K(s', s) \supset \phi[s'].$$

Now we can express thoughts about what an agent would know in non-actual situations, for example:

$$(\exists s).K(s, S_0) \land s \neq S_0 \land (\forall s').K(s', s) \supset \phi[s'].$$

This says that there is an alternative situation to the actual initial situation in which the agent knows ϕ. Granted, we don't often need to express thoughts like this, but consider the following:

$$(\forall s')[K(s', S_0) \supset \phi[s']] \supset (\forall s').K(s', S_0) \supset (\forall s^*).K(s^*, s') \supset \phi[s^*].$$

This expresses a genuinely useful thought, namely, that if in S_0 an agent knows ϕ, then in S_0 she knows that she knows ϕ.

Continuing in the same spirit, we generalize the account of Section 11.1.3 of what it means for an agent to know the referent of a situation calculus functional fluent, for example, in situation s to know the referent of $telNumber(Mary)$:

$$(\exists x)(\forall s').K(s', s) \supset x = telNumber(Mary, s').$$

11.1.6   Some Consequences of This Approach

Independently of any special properties we might in future attach to the K relation, we can draw a number of important conclusions:

1. If ϕ is a situation independent sentence of the situation calculus that is part of the agent's background axioms, then no matter what situation she is in, the agent knows ϕ. This is so because ϕ entails $(\forall s, s').K(s', s) \supset \phi$ when ϕ mentions no situation term. This means, for example, that an agent always knows her unique names axioms for actions.

2. When t is a situation-independent term of the situation calculus, then an agent always knows the referent of t. This is so because always knowing the referent of t is formally represented by $(\forall s)(\exists x)(\forall s').K(s', s) \supset x = t[s']$, and when $t[s']$ does not mention s', this sentence is valid.

3. When a sentence of the form $(\forall s)\phi(s)$ is part of the agent's background axioms, then the agent knows ϕ. This is so because $(\forall s)\phi(s)$ entails $(\forall s, s').K(s', s) \supset \phi[s']$. This means, for example, that an agent knows his successor state and action precondition axioms. It does not follow that he knows his initial state axioms.

4. **Logical omniscience:** An agent knows all the logical consequences of her knowledge; if she knows ϕ and if ψ is a logical consequence of ϕ, then she knows ψ. More precisely, if $(\forall s).\phi(s) \supset \psi(s)$ is a valid sentence, then whenever the agent knows ϕ, i.e. $(\forall s, s').K(s', s) \supset \phi[s']$ holds, then she also knows ψ, i.e. $(\forall s, s').K(s', s) \supset \psi[s']$ holds. Logical omniscience is an unrealistic property of an agent's knowledge: Can anyone know all the logical consequences of Peano arithmetic? Despite this, virtually all formalizations of knowledge and belief have this property, and we'll just have to live with it. In Section 11.2.1 below, we return to this question to clarify exactly

in what sense logics of knowledge ascribe logical omniscience to an agent.

11.1.7   A Useful Notation

We now introduce the convenient and suggestive notation $\mathbf{Knows}(\phi, \sigma)$, meaning that, in situation σ, the agent *knows* ϕ. Of course, we take this to mean that ϕ is true in all situations s' accessible from σ:

$$\mathbf{Knows}(\phi, \sigma) \stackrel{def}{=} (\forall s').K(s', \sigma) \supset \phi[s']. \tag{11.1}$$

Therefore, $\mathbf{Knows}(\phi, \sigma)$ is an abbreviation (a macro in the way that Do was in the definition of Golog); it is *not* a formula in the language of the situation calculus. ϕ as it occurs in $\mathbf{Knows}(\phi, \sigma)$ is an expression like those occurring in Golog test actions. So it also is not a formula in the language of the situation calculus; rather, it is obtained from a situation calculus formula by suppressing its situation arguments. Therefore, as we did with Golog, $\phi[s]$ denotes that situation calculus formula obtained from ϕ by restoring the situation argument s to its rightful place.

Example 11.1.1:

1. $\mathbf{Knows}(raining, \sigma)$ expands to

   $(\forall s').K(s', \sigma) \supset raining(s')$.

2. $\mathbf{Knows}(broken(x), do(drop(x), \sigma))$ expands to

   $(\forall s').K(s', do(drop(x), \sigma)) \supset broken(x, s')$.

3. $\mathbf{Knows}(\phi, s) \supset \mathbf{Knows}(\mathbf{Knows}(\phi), s)$ expands to

   $(\forall s')[K(s', s) \supset \phi[s']] \supset (\forall s').K(s', s) \supset (\forall s^*).K(s^*, s') \supset \phi[s^*]$.

4. $\mathbf{Knows}(telNumber(Bill) = telNumber(Mary), \sigma)$ expands to

   $(\forall s').K(s', \sigma) \supset telNumber(Bill, s') = telNumber(Mary, s')$.

5. As remarked in Section 11.1.6, an agent always knows her action precondition axioms:

   $(\forall s)\mathbf{Knows}((\forall x).Poss(drop(x)) \equiv holding(x), s)$.

   This expands to

   $(\forall s)(\forall s').K(s', s) \supset (\forall x).Poss(drop(x), s') \equiv holding(x, s')$.

As convenient as it is, the notation $\mathbf{Knows}(\phi, \sigma)$ suffers from one limitation: ϕ must be a situation-suppressed expression, and therefore, its situation restored version $\phi[\sigma]$ must be uniform in σ. Therefore, the $\mathbf{Knows}$ notation can only express knowledge about uniform formulas. Normally, these are the kinds of formulas we shall deal with, but occasionally we shall need to express knowledge about other kind of formulas. Accordingly, we expand the class of expressions ϕ by introducing a special symbol *now*, and we allow $\phi(now)$ to be any situation-suppressed expression that may also mention the special term *now*. In such cases, the abbreviation (11.1) becomes:

$$\mathbf{Knows}(\phi(now), \sigma) \stackrel{def}{=} (\forall s').K(s', \sigma) \supset \phi(s').$$

Example 11.1.2:

1. $\mathbf{Knows}((\exists s^*)now = do(a, s^*), do(a, s))$ expands to

   $$(\forall s').K(s', do(a, s)) \supset (\exists s^*)s' = do(a, s^*).$$

2. As observed in Section 11.1.6 an agent always knows her successor state axioms:

   $$(\forall s)\mathbf{Knows}((\forall x, a).holding(x, do(a, now)) \equiv a = pickup(x) \vee$$
   $$holding(x, now) \wedge a \neq drop(x), s).$$

   This expands to

   $$(\forall s)(\forall s').K(s', s) \supset (\forall x, a).holding(x, do(a, s')) \equiv a = pickup(x) \vee$$
   $$holding(x, s') \wedge a \neq drop(x),$$

   and it is easy to see that this is entailed by the successor state axiom for *holding*.

We introduce two further notational conventions:

1. In situation σ, an agent *knows whether* ϕ iff he knows ϕ or he knows $\neg\phi$:

   $$\mathbf{KWhether}(\phi, \sigma) \stackrel{def}{=} \mathbf{Knows}(\phi, \sigma) \vee \mathbf{Knows}(\neg\phi, \sigma).$$

2. In situation σ, an agent *knows the referent* of the term t iff there is an individual x such that x and t are the same in all situations accessible from σ:

   $$\mathbf{KRef}(t, \sigma) \stackrel{def}{=} (\exists x)(\forall s').K(s', \sigma) \supset x = t[s'].$$

   Here, t does not mention x, and $t[s']$ denotes that term in the language of the situation calculus obtained from t by restoring the situation argument s' to its correct place in t. Notice that this definition is equivalent to:

   $$\mathbf{KRef}(t, \sigma) \stackrel{def}{=} (\exists x)\mathbf{Knows}(x = t, \sigma).$$

11.1.8 Quantifiers and Knowledge

Consider the claim that initially, an agent knows the American president is a philanderer. Let the functional fluent $presidentUSA(s)$ denote who the president is in situation s. There are at least two possible readings of the claim that the president is a philanderer:

$$\mathbf{Knows}((\exists x).x = presidentUSA \wedge philanderer(x), S_0),$$

$(\exists x)\mathbf{Knows}(x = presidentUSA \wedge philanderer(x), S_0).$

The first is called the *de dicto* reading; it expresses that the agent knows that the president, *whoever that might be*, is a philanderer. So in one alternative situation to S_0, say S_1, the denotation of $presidentUSA(S_1)$ might be Bill, in another, say S_2, $presidentUSA(S_2)$ might be Hillary. Nevertheless, no matter what the denotation is in a situation accessible to S_0, *philanderer* is true of that denotation. So the agent does not know who the president is, but does know he/she is a philanderer.

The second sentence, which is often called the *de re* reading, is quite different. It claims that, in addition to knowing that the president is a philanderer, the agent knows who the president is. De re knowledge is often called WH-knowledge—knowing who, what, where, when—and is expressed by the pattern $(\exists x)\mathbf{Knows}(-, -)$. This is an example of what is called *quantifying into a modal context*.

The important point about this example is that subtle differences in meaning can be captured by explicitly representing an agent's knowledge, and that these differences depend on the quantifier structure of the sentence.

11.2   Knowledge and the Designer's Perspective

The moment one chooses to take knowledge seriously in axiomatizing a domain, it becomes very important to understand the role of the designer—the person who writes the axioms—and her relationship to the agent whose state of knowledge she is axiomatizing. The designer is normally best thought of as an external observer, looking down on the world. Whatever she sees to be true, she expresses axiomatically. Not only can she see "objective" truths—that block A is on the table, or that all dogs are mammals—she can also see "subjective" truths—that John knows that block B is red, or that John does not know whether block A is on the table. Whatever truths she sees from her eye-in-the-sky perspective, she expresses axiomatically. In the standard *external design stance*, the designer is entirely external to the world she is formalizing. In particular, she is not the same as the agent inhabiting that world. $\mathbf{Knows}(\phi, S_0)$ does not mean "I, the designer, know ϕ." It means that I, the designer, am looking down on some world inhabited by an agent, and I can see that, in the initial situation, this agent knows ϕ. Similarly, $onTable(A, S_0)$ means that I can see that initially, A is on the table. If a designer writes $onTable(A, S_0) \wedge \neg\mathbf{Knows}(onTable(A), S_0)$, she is asserting that initially, A is on the table, but the agent doesn't know this.

Having said all this, we emphasize that nothing about logics of knowledge precludes a *self-reflective design stance*, in which the designer is identical to the agent she is axiomatizing. In this case, her eye-in-the-sky is looking inside her own head, and expressing what *she* knows. Under these circumstances, the designer is not entirely free about the axioms she can write. For example, $onTable(A, S_0) \land \neg\textbf{Knows}(onTable(A), S_0)$ wouldn't make much sense. More generally, we would expect that whatever she can see to be true must be known to her: $P[S_0] \supset \textbf{Knows}(P, S_0)$ for every sentence $P[S_0]$. If, moreover, the designer is committed to the truth of what she knows, so that she includes $\textbf{Knows}(P, S_0) \supset P[S_0]$ for every sentence $P[S_0]$, then knowledge and truth would collapse into one; $\textbf{Knows}(P, S_0) \equiv P[S_0]$, in which case knowledge would be doing no real work in the axiomatization. For these, and other reasons, the self-reflective design stance is seldom used, and we shall restrict ourselves to the external stance in what follows.

11.2.1 Logical Omniscience Revisited

The design perspective clarifies what the logical omniscience problem is for knowledge, and what the designer claims when she ascribes logical omniscience to an agent. Picture yourself as the designer, and suppose you have just written some sentences about a world. Certainly, you will be committed to any logical consequences of these sentences, but nothing about this story implies that you are *aware* of all these logical consequences, only that, whenever one is pointed out to you (presumably accompanied by a proof), you will assent to it. Therefore, on this view, *you are not taken to be aware of all the logical consequences of your axioms*, and this is as it should be. On the other hand, it is easy to see that whenever $V[S_0]$ is a valid first-order sentence, $\textbf{Knows}(V, S_0)$ is valid. In other words, you have proved the following metatheorem: "For every valid sentence $V[S_0]$, $\textbf{Knows}(V, S_0)$ is valid." Therefore, *you are aware that the agent you are axiomatizing must know all valid sentences, and hence, you are ascribing logical omniscience to that agent.* Notice that in the unusual case that you are axiomatizing your own knowledge (the self-reflective design stance), you will be ascribing logical omniscience to yourself, in the sense that you will be aware that you know all valid sentences! Perhaps this is another reason why a self-reflective design stance is best avoided.

11.3 Knowledge-Producing Actions

Now that we have a formal concept of knowledge within the situation calculus, we need to provide for actions that can affect an agent's state of knowledge. This we do by supposing that for each of finitely many relational fluents there is a *sense* action whose purpose is to determine the truth value of its fluent, for example, a sense action $sense_{on}(x, y)$, whose purpose is to determine whether the fluent $on(x, y, s)$ is true in s. If $F(\vec{x}, s)$ is such a fluent, we denote its sense action by $sense_F(\vec{x})$, and we want it to be the case that after an agent performs a $sense_F$ action, the agent will know whether F, i.e. that

$(\forall s, \vec{x})\mathbf{KWhether}(F(\vec{x}), do(sense_F(\vec{x}), s)).$

We shall assume that the agent has a fixed, finite repertoire of sense actions $sense_{F_1}, \ldots,$ $sense_{F_m}$.

Similarly, we suppose that for each of finitely many functional fluents there is a *read* action whose purpose is to determine the referent of its fluent, for example, a read action $read_{colour}(x)$, whose purpose is to determine the value of the functional fluent $colour(x, s)$ in s. If $f(\vec{x}, s)$ is such a fluent, we denote its read action by $read_f(\vec{x})$, and we want it to be the case that by performing a $read_f$ action, an agent will come to know the referent of f, i.e. that

$(\forall s, \vec{x})\mathbf{KRef}(f(\vec{x}), do(read_f(\vec{x}), s)).$

We assume that the agent has a fixed, finite repertoire of read actions $read_{f_1}, \ldots, read_{f_n}$.

These knowledge-producing actions participate in the unique names axioms for actions in the usual way.

11.4   The Frame Problem for Knowledge-Producing Actions

To represent knowledge, we have introduced a new predicate symbol K that acts as an accessibility relation on situations, where $K(s', s)$ means that s' is accessible from s. Because K takes a situation argument—in fact, it takes two—it behaves like a relational fluent; its truth value varies from one situation to another. But ordinary fluents take just one situation argument, while K takes two. To resolve this ambiguity, we shall view $K(s', s)$ as a relational fluent whose official situation argument is s, and we shall treat s' like any other argument to a fluent.

Now, having introduced knowledge-producing actions and a new fluent K as an accessibility relation on situations, we need to solve the frame problem for K. In other words, we want to obtain a successor state axiom for K, something of the form $K(s', do(a, s)) \equiv \phi(a, s', s)$. Before doing so, we need first to consider how the successor state axioms for ordinary fluents are affected by the introduction of knowledge-producing actions.

11.4.1   The No-Side-Effects Assumption for Knowledge-Producing Actions

For fluents other than K, we suppose that they are provided with successor state axioms in the same way as has been done throughout this book. But in the presence of knowledge-producing actions, there is always the possibility that such actions can affect these fluents, as in, for example:

$$eyesOpen(do(a, s)) \equiv a = senseForObstacle \vee$$
$$eyesOpen(s) \wedge a \neq closeEyes.$$

For reasons that will soon become apparent, we do not want to allow knowledge-producing actions to have such side-effects on ordinary fluents; in the formal story we develop here, such actions are only permitted to affect the K fluent. In other words, for each sense action $sense_F$, and read action $read_f$, and each relational fluent G, we require that G's successor state axiom, together with the other background axioms that we shall specify in Section 11.5.3 below, entails:

$$(\forall \vec{x}, \vec{y}, s).G(\vec{x}, s) \equiv G(\vec{x}, do(sense_F(\vec{y}), s)),$$

$$(\forall \vec{x}, \vec{z}, s).G(\vec{x}, s) \equiv G(\vec{x}, do(read_f(\vec{z}), s)),$$

and for each functional fluent g, that g's successor state axiom and other background axioms entail:

$$(\forall \vec{x}, \vec{y}, s)g(\vec{x}, s) = g(\vec{x}, do(sense_F(\vec{y}), s)),$$

$$(\forall \vec{x}, \vec{z}, s)g(\vec{x}, s) = g(\vec{x}, do(read_f(\vec{z}), s)).$$

These conditions will be needed to obtain a successor state axiom for K in the next section. They will also guarantee the intuitively necessary property that by virtue of performing a knowledge-producing action, an agent will come to know the outcome of that action (Section 11.4.4 below).

One might argue that the no-side-effect assumption is unreasonable, that sense actions often produce a change in the state of ordinary fluents, as in the above $senseForObstacle$ example. The counter argument is that, indeed, certain preconditions (e.g. $eyesOpen$) may be necessary for sense actions to occur, but then separate actions—not sense actions— should be provided by the axioms to achieve these preconditions (e.g. $openEyes$). Then to perform a sense action, one must first perform the appropriate state changing actions to establish that sense action's preconditions. This is the perspective we adopt here.

11.4.2   A Successor State Axiom for K

Here, we obtain a successor state axiom for K. So we are concerned with filling in the details of Figure 11.3, where we imagine that an agent is in some situation s, but with respect to what he can be said to know, he could just as easily be in any of the situations K-related to s. Then he performs action a, which takes him from s to $do(a, s)$, and we want to characterize the alternative situations to $do(a, s)$ that he could be in.

To begin, consider how we would expect a non knowledge-producing action a to affect the K fluent. What situations should be considered possible for an agent after he performs such an action? In situation s, the agent could just as well be in any situation s^* K-related to s. After performing action a, the agent enters situation $do(a, s)$. But he could just

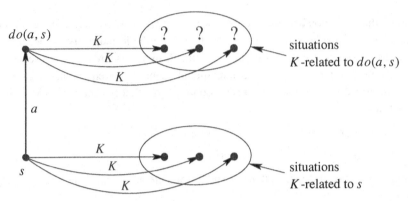

Figure 11.3: What situations are K-related to $do(a, s)$?

as well have been in s^*, in which case performing a would have taken him to situation $do(a, s^*)$. Therefore, we want $do(a, s^*)$ to be K-related to $do(a, s)$. This provides us with the following characterization of K when a is not a knowledge-producing action:

$$K(s', do(a, s)) \equiv (\exists s^*).s' = do(a, s^*) \wedge K(s^*, s).$$

In other words, when a is not a knowledge-producing action, the situations K-related to $do(a, s)$ should be the images, under the performance of action a, of those situations K-related to s. Figure 11.4 illustrates this requirement. (See also Figure 11.2 and its accompanying discussion in Section 11.1.4.)

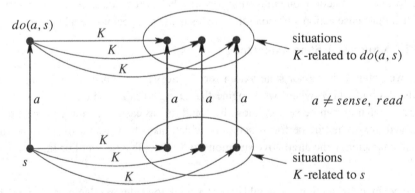

Figure 11.4: K-related situations for non knowledge-producing actions.

We summarize this condition on K by the following:

$$a \neq sense_{F_1}(\vec{x}_1) \wedge \cdots \wedge a \neq sense_{F_m}(\vec{x}_m) \wedge$$
$$a \neq read_{f_1}(\vec{y}_1) \wedge \cdots \wedge a \neq read_{f_n}(\vec{y}_n) \tag{11.2}$$
$$\supset [K(s', do(a, s)) \equiv (\exists s^*).s' = do(a, s^*) \wedge K(s^*, s)].$$

Next, consider how we expect a knowledge-producing action $sense_F$ to affect the K fluent. As before, we consider the situations K-related to s, and the images of these situations under the performance of action $sense_F$ (Figure 11.5).

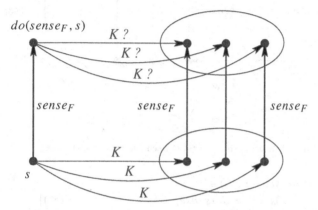

Figure 11.5: What situations are K-related to $do(sense_F, s)$?

If $sense_F$ were an ordinary action, these images would be precisely the situations K-related to $do(sense_F, s)$, so that the arrows labeled K? in Figure 11.5 would be labeled K. But unlike ordinary actions, $sense_F$ is understood to inform the agent about the truth value of F. Therefore, after the agent performs this action, certain situations in the set of images must not be considered possible, namely, those assigning a different truth value to F than it has in $do(sense_F, s)$. Thus, with reference to Figure 11.6, suppose that F is true in $do(sense_F, s)$. Then we want that, in situation $do(sense_F, s)$, the agent knows that F is true. Hence, F must be true in all the situations K-related to $do(sense_F, s)$. Therefore, to obtain the situations K-related to $do(sense_F, s)$, we must select out, from the image set, those situations in which F is true (Figure 11.6). This gives the following condition on K:

$$F(do(sense_F, s)) \supset [K(s', do(sense_F, s)) \equiv$$
$$(\exists s^*).s' = do(sense_F, s^*) \wedge K(s^*, s) \wedge F(do(sense_F, s^*))].$$

The no-side-effects assumption (Section 11.4.1) yields

$$(\forall s).F(do(sense_F, s)) \equiv F(s),$$

so the above condition on K becomes:

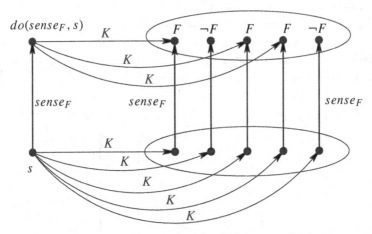

Figure 11.6: The situations K-related to $do(sense_F, s)$ when $F(do(sense_F, s))$ is true.

$$F(s) \supset [K(s', do(sense_F, s)) \equiv$$
$$(\exists s^*).s' = do(sense_F, s^*) \wedge K(s^*, s) \wedge F(s^*)].$$

A similar argument yields the following condition on K:

$$\neg F(s) \supset [K(s', do(sense_F, s)) \equiv$$
$$(\exists s^*).s' = do(sense_F, s^*) \wedge K(s^*, s) \wedge \neg F(s^*)].$$

It is straightforward, but tedious, to show that these two sentences are logically equivalent to:

$$K(s', do(sense_F, s)) \equiv \tag{11.3}$$
$$(\exists s^*).s' = do(sense_F, s^*) \wedge K(s^*, s) \wedge F(s^*) \equiv F(s).$$

In other words, the situations K-related to $do(sense_F, s)$ are precisely the images, under the action $sense_F$, of those situations K-related to s that assign the same truth value to F as does s.

Generalizing (11.3) to allow for fluents with arbitrary argument structure, and introducing an action variable, we obtain the following, for each of the knowledge-producing actions $sense_{F_1}, \ldots, sense_{F_m}$:

$$a = sense_{F_i}(\vec{x}_i) \supset$$
$$[K(s', do(a, s)) \equiv \tag{11.4}$$
$$(\exists s^*).s' = do(a, s^*) \wedge K(s^*, s) \wedge F_i(\vec{x}_i, s^*) \equiv F_i(\vec{x}_i, s)].$$

By a similar argument, we establish that for each of the knowledge-producing actions $read_{f_1}, \ldots, read_{f_n}$:

$$a = read_{f_j}(\vec{x}_j) \supset$$
$$[K(s', do(a, s)) \equiv \tag{11.5}$$
$$(\exists s^*).s' = do(a, s^*) \wedge K(s^*, s) \wedge f_j(\vec{x}_j, s^*) = f_j(\vec{x}_j, s)].$$

Finally, we can put it all together by observing that (11.2), (11.4) and (11.5) are logically equivalent to:

$$K(s', do(a, s)) \equiv$$
$$(\exists s^*).s' = do(a, s^*) \wedge K(s^*, s) \wedge$$
$$(\forall \vec{x}_1)[a = sense_{F_1}(\vec{x}_1) \supset F_1(\vec{x}_1, s^*) \equiv F_1(\vec{x}_1, s)] \wedge \cdots \wedge$$
$$(\forall \vec{x}_m)[a = sense_{F_m}(\vec{x}_m) \supset F_m(\vec{x}_m, s^*) \equiv F_m(\vec{x}_m, s)] \wedge \tag{11.6}$$
$$(\forall \vec{y}_1)[a = read_{f_1}(\vec{y}_1) \supset f_1(\vec{y}_1, s^*) = f_1(\vec{y}_1, s)] \wedge \cdots \wedge$$
$$(\forall \vec{y}_n)[a = read_{f_n}(\vec{y}_n) \supset f_n(\vec{y}_n, s^*) = f_n(\vec{y}_n, s)]].$$

11.4.3 More General Knowledge-Producing Actions

Often, we want to be able to sense truth values for arbitrary conditions, not simply relational fluents, for example, a sense action $sense_{between}(x, y)$, whose purpose is to determine whether $(\exists z).object(z) \wedge leftOf(z, y, s) \wedge leftOf(x, z, s)$ is true in s. It is straightforward to adapt the above argument that led to (11.6) to obtain the following more general successor state axiom, where here, each sense action $sense_{\psi_i}(\vec{x}_i)$, $i = 1, \ldots, m$, is associated with a condition $\psi_i(\vec{x}_i, s)$ whose truth value in situation s the action is designed to determine:

$$K(s', do(a, s)) \equiv$$
$$(\exists s^*).s' = do(a, s^*) \wedge K(s^*, s) \wedge$$
$$(\forall \vec{x}_1)[a = sense_{\psi_1}(\vec{x}_1) \supset \psi_1(\vec{x}_1, s^*) \equiv \psi_1(\vec{x}_1, s)] \wedge \cdots \wedge$$
$$(\forall \vec{x}_m)[a = sense_{\psi_m}(\vec{x}_m) \supset \psi_m(\vec{x}_m, s^*) \equiv \psi_m(\vec{x}_m, s)] \wedge \tag{11.7}$$
$$(\forall \vec{y}_1)[a = read_{f_1}(\vec{y}_1) \supset f_1(\vec{y}_1, s^*) = f_1(\vec{y}_1, s)] \wedge \cdots \wedge$$
$$(\forall \vec{y}_n)[a = read_{f_n}(\vec{y}_n) \supset f_n(\vec{y}_n, s^*) = f_n(\vec{y}_n, s)]].$$

This is our final proposal for a successor state axiom for K.

Having introduced more general sense actions $sense_\psi$, we shall need to generalize the no-side-effects assumption of Section 11.4.1, to require that no such general sense action can affect the values of any fluents.

11.4.4 Some Consequences of this Solution

The successor state axiom (11.7) leads to a number of intuitively correct conclusions (Exercise 2 below).

1. Using the no-side-effects assumption, one can prove that after sensing whether ψ in a world where ψ is true, an agent knows ψ.

   $(\forall \vec{x}, s).\psi(\vec{x}, s) \supset \mathbf{Knows}(\psi(\vec{x}), do(sense_\psi(\vec{x}), s)).$

   Similarly, after sensing whether ψ in a world where ψ is false, an agent knows $\neg\psi$.

   $(\forall \vec{x}, s).\neg\psi(\vec{x}, s) \supset \mathbf{Knows}(\neg\psi(\vec{x}), do(sense_\psi(\vec{x}), s)).$

   From these it follows that after performing a $sense_\psi$ action, an agent will know whether ψ:

   $(\forall s, \vec{x})\mathbf{KWhether}(\psi(\vec{x}), do(sense_\psi(\vec{x}), s)).$

2. Using the no-side-effects assumption, one can prove that by performing a $read_f$ action, an agent comes to know the referent of f:

   $(\forall s, \vec{x})\mathbf{KRef}(f(\vec{x}), do(read_f(\vec{x}), s)).$

3. After performing a non knowledge-producing action, an agent knows the effects of that action. For example, if an action A causes F to become true, so that $(\forall s)F(do(A, s))$, then this and K's successor state axiom imply that $(\forall s)\mathbf{Knows}(F, do(A, s))$.

4. If an agent knows F before doing the action A, and if A has no effect on F, i.e. $(\forall s)F(s) \equiv F(do(A, s))$, then the agent knows F after doing the action:

   $(\forall s).\mathbf{Knows}(F, s) \supset \mathbf{Knows}(F, do(A, s)).$

   Similarly, if the agent doesn't know F initially, and if its action A has no effect on F, then the agent doesn't know F after doing the action:

   $(\forall s).\neg\mathbf{Knows}(F, s) \supset \neg\mathbf{Knows}(F, do(A, s)).$

   In other words, an agent remembers what she knew and didn't know in earlier situations, provided the intervening actions have no effect on this earlier knowledge.

5. In situation $do(a, s)$, an agent knows that she has just performed the action a. We take this to mean that in situation $do(a, s)$ she knows that whatever situation she really is in, it is the result of performing action a in some previous situation. We express this by

   $(\forall a, s)\mathbf{Knows}((\exists s^*)now = do(a, s^*), do(a, s)).$

Example 11.4.1: How to Open a Safe

Consider an agent who wants to open a safe whose combination is written on a piece of paper. Initially, the agent knows that the paper contains the combination needed to open the safe. We want to prove that after the agent reads what is written on the paper she can dial the combination of the safe, and thereafter, the safe will be open.

We include the following actions:

- $dialCombo(x)$. Dial the combination of the safe x and also pull the handle.
- $read(x)$. A knowledge-producing action meaning read the contents of x.

We also include the following fluents:

- $open(x, s)$. Safe x is open.
- $combo(x, s)$. A functional fluent denoting the combination of safe x.
- $info(x, s)$. A functional fluent denoting what is written on paper x.

We use the following preconditions for $dialCombo(x)$ and $read(x)$:

$$Poss(dialCombo(x), s) \equiv \textbf{KRef}(combo(x), s),$$

$$Poss(read(x), s) \equiv true.$$

Successor state axioms for "ordinary" fluents:

$$open(x, do(a, s)) \equiv a = dialCombo(x) \vee open(x, s) \wedge a \neq lock(x),$$

$$info(x, do(a, s)) = y \equiv a = write(y, x) \vee$$
$$info(x, s) = y \wedge \neg(\exists z)a = write(z, x), \tag{11.8}$$

$$combo(x, do(a, s)) = y \equiv a = changeCombo(x, y) \vee$$
$$combo(x, s) = y \wedge \neg(\exists z)a = changeCombo(x, z). \tag{11.9}$$

It is easy to see that these satisfy the no-side-effects assumption for knowledge-producing actions.

Successor state axiom for K:

$$K(s', do(a, s)) \equiv (\exists s^*).K(s^*, s) \wedge s' = do(a, s^*) \wedge$$
$$[a = read(x) \supset info(x, s) = info(x, s^*)]. \tag{11.10}$$

So $read(x)$ is the only knowledge-producing action, and its effect is to make $info(x)$ known.

We take $\mathcal{D}_{S_0}$ to include:

$$\textbf{Knows}(info(Ppr) = combo(Sf), S_0).$$

Note that these axioms do not entail $Poss(dialCombo(Sf), S_0)$. Sentences (11.10) and (11.8) ensure that the axioms entail:

$$\textbf{KRef}(info(Ppr), do(read(Ppr), S_0)). \tag{11.11}$$

Since $\mathcal{D}_{S_0}$ includes $\textbf{Knows}(info(Ppr) = combo(Sf), S_0)$, sentences (11.8), (11.9) and (11.10) ensure that

$$\textbf{Knows}(info(Ppr) = combo(Sf), do(read(Ppr), S_0)). \tag{11.12}$$

Therefore, by (11.11), (11.12), and properties of equality (Exercise 1e below), the axioms entail

$$\textbf{KRef}(combo(Sf), do(read(Ppr), S_0)).$$

Since the successor state axioms ensure that a *read* action does not change *combo* and *info*, it is the case that

$$Poss(dialCombo(Sf), do(read(Ppr), S_0)).$$

In other words, after reading what is on the paper, the agent can dial the combination of the safe. Finally, the axioms entail

$$open(Sf, do(dialCombo(Sf), do(read(Ppr), S_0))),$$

and therefore, the safe will be open as a result.

11.5   Accessibility in the Initial Situation

Thus far, we have proposed a solution to the frame problem for the K fluent, and this places strong constraints on the accessibility relation. Nevertheless, this solution says nothing about properties of K in the initial situation; it simply characterizes $K(s', do(a, s))$, namely K in the next situation $do(a, s)$, in terms of the current situation s. To fully characterize K, we need to specify its properties in the initial situation. Before doing so, we need to think about how to provide alternative initial situations to S_0, and for this we need to reconsider the foundational axioms for the situation calculus.

11.5.1   New Foundational Axioms for Situations

Recall the original foundational axioms for situations, before the K fluent was introduced:

$$do(a_1, s_1) = do(a_2, s_2) \supset a_1 = a_2 \wedge s_1 = s_2, \tag{11.13}$$

$$(\forall P).P(S_0) \wedge (\forall a, s)[P(s) \supset P(do(a, s))] \supset (\forall s)P(s), \tag{11.14}$$

$$\neg s \sqsubset S_0, \tag{11.15}$$

$$s \sqsubset do(a, s') \equiv s \sqsubseteq s'. \tag{11.16}$$

These have the property that any of their models consists of a tree of situations, rooted at the interpretation of S_0 in that model (Figure 4.1). For the purposes of axiomatizing the K fluent, this will not do; we need additional initial situations to serve as alternatives to S_0. So we still need S_0, which serves as the *actual* initial situation, but we must allow for other initial situations that can be K-related to S_0 and to one another.

What modifications must be made to the above foundational axioms to allow for multiple initial situations? Consider the induction axiom (11.14). It says that the set of all situations in any model consists of S_0, together with those situations obtained by applying *do* a finite number of times to S_0. None of these situations different than S_0 can serve as an initial situation, because they all have predecessors. To allow for other initial situations, this axiom needs weakening, which is what we now do. First, introduce an abbreviation:

$$Init(s) \stackrel{def}{=} \neg(\exists a, s')s = do(a, s').$$

Next, formulate a weaker version of the old induction axiom (11.14):

$$(\forall P).(\forall s)[Init(s) \supset P(s)] \wedge (\forall a, s)[P(s) \supset P(do(a, s))]$$
$$\supset (\forall s)P(s). \tag{11.17}$$

Consider the foundation axioms given above, but with the induction axiom (11.17) instead of (11.14). A model of these axioms will consist of a forest of isomorphic trees, one rooted at S_0, the others rooted at the other initial situations in the model (Figure 11.7). All these roots can serve in specifying a K relation over initial situations.

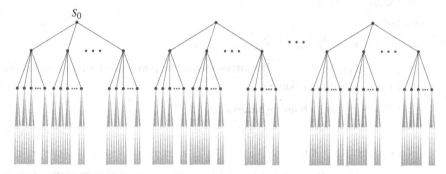

Figure 11.7: A forest of isomorphic situation trees rooted at initial situations.

Finally, insist that only initial situations can be K-related to an initial situation:

$$K(s, s') \supset [Init(s) \equiv Init(s')]. \tag{11.18}$$

The new foundational axioms for the situation calculus with the K fluent consist of (11.13), (11.15), (11.16), (11.17) and (11.18).

One question remains: How do we now provide inductive proofs of properties that are not about the K fluent? In other words, with these new foundational axioms, how can we inductively prove the kinds of properties we were accustomed to proving in the earlier chapters of this book? These were properties of the form $(\forall s)\phi(s)$, and we had to show that $\phi(s)$ was true of all situations s according to the old foundational axioms. Relative to the new axioms, $\phi(s)$ must be shown to be true of all situations on the tree rooted at S_0. In other words, instead of proving $(\forall s)\phi(s)$, prove its *relativized* form $(\forall s).S_0 \sqsubseteq s \supset \phi(s)$.

To do this, we can use the following induction principle for such relativized sentences, which is provable from the new foundational axioms (Exercise 3 below).

$$(\forall P).P(S_0) \wedge (\forall a, s)[P(s) \wedge S_0 \sqsubseteq s \supset P(do(a, s))]$$
$$\supset (\forall s).S_0 \sqsubseteq s \supset P(s). \tag{11.19}$$

11.5.2   Some Possible Accessibility Relations

In modal logics, various conditions on accessibility relations are imposed in order to achieve suitable intuitive properties for knowledge and belief. The following are some common examples:

1. Reflexivity:

   $$(\forall s)K(s, s).$$

   From this condition it follows that whatever is known must be true:

   $$(\forall s)\mathbf{Knows}(\phi, s) \supset \phi[s].$$

2. Transitivity:

   $$(\forall s, s', s'').K(s, s') \wedge K(s', s'') \supset K(s, s'').$$

   From this is obtained the **positive introspection** property: If in s an agent knows ϕ, then in s he knows that he knows ϕ.

   $$(\forall s).\mathbf{Knows}(\phi, s) \supset \mathbf{Knows}(\mathbf{Knows}(\phi), s).$$

3. Symmetry:

   $$(\forall s, s').K(s, s') \supset K(s', s).$$

   Using this and transitivity, we obtain the **negative introspection** property: If in s an agent does not know ϕ, then in s she knows that she does not know ϕ.

   $$(\forall s).\neg\mathbf{Knows}(\phi, s) \supset \mathbf{Knows}(\neg\mathbf{Knows}(\phi), s).$$

4. Euclidean:

   $$(\forall s, s', s'').K(s', s) \wedge K(s'', s) \supset K(s', s'').$$

The Euclidean property is a logical consequence of symmetry and transitivity, and it alone is sufficient to guarantee negative introspection.

It is a remarkable fact about the solution (11.7) to the frame problem for K that, provided any one of the above reflexive, transitive, symmetry and Euclidean properties on accessibility relations is true in all initial situations, then it will be true in all situations.

Theorem 11.5.1: *Suppose that any one of the following properties holds:*

1. Reflexive in initial situations:

$(\forall s).Init(s) \supset K(s, s)$.

2. *Symmetric in initial situations:*

$(\forall s, s').Init(s) \wedge Init(s') \supset [K(s, s') \supset K(s', s)]$.

3. *Transitive in initial situations:*

$(\forall s, s', s'').Init(s) \wedge Init(s') \wedge Init(s'') \supset [K(s, s') \wedge K(s', s'') \supset K(s', s'')]$.

4. *Euclidean in initial situations:*

$(\forall s, s', s'').Init(s) \wedge Init(s') \wedge Init(s'') \supset [K(s', s) \wedge K(s'', s) \supset K(s', s'')]$.

Then the property holds for all situations. For example, with reference to the symmetry property, the following is a consequence of the new foundational axioms and the solution (11.7) to the frame problem for K:

$$(\forall s, s')[Init(s) \wedge Init(s') \supset [K(s, s') \supset K(s', s)]]$$
$$\supset (\forall s, s').K(s, s') \supset K(s', s).$$

Proof: Exercise 8 below. ∎

This theorem guarantees that whatever subset of the properties of reflexivity, symmetry, transitivity, and Euclidean we choose in modeling knowledge, it will be sufficient merely to include their initial situation axioms; the successor state axiom for K guarantees that they hold in all situations.

11.5.3   Basic Action Theories for Knowledge

We can now generalize our earlier basic action theories of Section 4.4 to accommodate knowledge. Such a theory has the form:

$$\mathcal{D} = \Sigma \cup \mathcal{D}_{ss} \cup \mathcal{D}_{ap} \cup \mathcal{D}_{una} \cup \mathcal{D}_{S_0} \cup \mathcal{K}_{Init}$$

where,

- Σ are the new foundational axioms.
- $\mathcal{D}_{ss}$ is a set of successor state axioms for functional and relational fluents, including an axiom (11.7) for K. These must satisfy the no-side-effect conditions of Section 11.4.1.
- $\mathcal{D}_{ap}$ is a set of action precondition axioms. These may mention expressions of the form **Knows**(ϕ, s) and **KRef**(t, s).
- $\mathcal{D}_{una}$ is the set of unique names axioms for actions. These will include unique names axioms for knowledge-producing actions.
- $\mathcal{K}_{Init}$ consists of any subset of the initial accessibility axioms 1 - 4 of Theorem 11.5.1. (In fact, other initial accessibility axioms can also be included, so long as they also

have the property that, by virtue of the successor state axiom for K, they will be true in all situations.)

- $\mathcal{D}_{S_0}$ is a set of first-order sentences uniform in S_0. Without going into details, by this we mean that such sentences are constructed from fluent terms and atoms whose only situation terms are S_0, together with expressions of the form **Knows**(ϕ, S_0) and **KRef**(t, S_0).

11.6 Regression for Knowledge-Producing Actions

As was the case for ordinary actions, we want a systematic, regression-based mechanism for formulas involving sense actions and knowledge, in order to answer queries about hypothetical futures by regressing them to equivalent queries about the initial situation only. As before, this has the advantage of reducing query evaluation to a theorem-proving task only with respect to the initial database.

Begin by assuming a background basic theory of actions with knowledge. First, we need some notation for describing the regression of situation-suppressed expressions. Recall that when W is such an expression, and σ a situation term, then $W[\sigma]$ is that situation calculus formula resulting from adding an extra situation argument σ to every situation-suppressed fluent mentioned by W. We henceforth assume that W does not use the special symbol *now* introduced in Section 11.1.7, so that W mentions no situation terms at all. Introduce a "one-step" regression operator, $\rho^1(W, \alpha)$, whose role is to regress a situation-suppressed expression W through the action term α, as follows: Let s^* be a new situation variable distinct from any mentioned in α. (Therefore, we allow α to mention functional fluents, and therefore, situation terms.) $\rho^1(W, \alpha)$ is that situation-suppressed expression obtained from W by first replacing all fluents in $W[do(\alpha, s^*)]$ with situation argument $do(\alpha, s^*)$ by the corresponding right-hand sides of their successor state axioms, and next, suppressing the situation arguments in the resulting formula. Clearly, $\rho^1(W, \alpha)[s^*]$ is logically equivalent to $W[do(\alpha, s^*)]$ relative to the successor state axioms.

We now extend the notion of regression to accommodate knowledge-producing actions and expressions of the form **Knows**(W, σ). So the regression operator will satisfy all of the conditions of Definition 4.7.4 of Section 4.7, and some additional conditions that we now describe.

1. $\mathcal{R}[\mathbf{Knows}(W, S_0)] = \mathbf{Knows}(W, S_0)$.

2.   Whenever α is not a knowledge-producing action,

$$\mathcal{R}[\mathbf{Knows}(W, do(\alpha, \sigma))] = \mathcal{R}[\mathbf{Knows}(\rho^1(W, \alpha), \sigma)].$$

The following justifies this regression operation.

Proposition 11.6.1: *Suppose $W(\vec{x})$ is a situation-suppressed expression with free variables $\vec{x}$, and $A(\vec{y})$ is not a sense action. Then,*

$$\mathcal{D} \models (\forall \vec{x}, \vec{y}, s).\mathbf{Knows}(W(\vec{x}), do(A(\vec{y}), s)) \equiv \mathbf{Knows}(\rho^1(W(\vec{x}), A(\vec{y})), s).$$

Proof: Exercise 10 below. ∎

3. Whenever α is a sense action determining the agent's state of knowledge about the condition ψ, i.e. $\alpha = sense_\psi(\vec{t})$ for terms $\vec{t}$,

$$\mathcal{R}[\mathbf{Knows}(W, do(\alpha, \sigma))] =$$
$$\mathcal{R}[\{\psi(\vec{t}, \sigma) \supset \mathbf{Knows}(\psi(\vec{t}) \supset \rho^1(W, \alpha), \sigma)\} \wedge$$
$$\{\neg\psi(\vec{t}, \sigma) \supset \mathbf{Knows}(\neg\psi(\vec{t}) \supset \rho^1(W, \alpha), \sigma)\}].$$

The following justifies this regression operation.

Proposition 11.6.2: *Suppose $W(\vec{x})$ is a situation-suppressed expression with free variables $\vec{x}$, and $sense_\psi(\vec{y})$ is a sense action. Then,*

$$\mathcal{D} \models (\forall \vec{x}, \vec{y}, s).\mathbf{Knows}(W(\vec{x}), do(sense_\psi(\vec{y}), s)) \equiv$$
$$\{\psi(\vec{y}, s) \supset \mathbf{Knows}(\psi(\vec{y}) \supset \rho^1(W(\vec{x}), sense_\psi(\vec{y})), s)\} \wedge$$
$$\{\neg\psi(\vec{y}, s) \supset \mathbf{Knows}(\neg\psi(\vec{y}) \supset \rho^1(W(\vec{x}), sense_\psi(\vec{y})), s)\}.$$

Proof: Exercise 10 below. ∎

4. Whenever α is a read action determining the agent's state of knowledge about the functional fluent term t,

$$\mathcal{R}[\mathbf{Knows}(W, do(\alpha, \sigma))] = \mathcal{R}[(\exists y)\mathbf{Knows}(t = y \supset \rho^1(W, \alpha), \sigma)]. \qquad (11.20)$$

Exercise 11 below asks you to justify this regression operator.

In the regression rules above, nothing prevents W in $\mathbf{Knows}(W, do(\alpha, \sigma))$ from also mentioning $\mathbf{Knows}$, but of course, since W is a situation-suppressed expression, so also must be any of W's subexpressions in $\mathbf{Knows}$, i.e. they must have the form $\mathbf{Knows}(\psi)$.

Recall that the Regression Theorem 4.5.5 of Section 4.5 reduced query evaluation for regressable sentences to a theorem-proving task relative to the initial database and unique names axioms for actions. This result generalizes to our present circumstances. Without going into details, we first need to generalize the notion of a regressable formula to include expressions like $\mathbf{Knows}(\psi, do([\alpha_1, \ldots, \alpha_n], S_0))$. Moreover, in such an expression, we require that each of the α_i be of the form $A(\vec{t})$ where A is the name of some action function; this way, one can tell whether α_i is an ordinary action, or a knowledge-producing action, something that the regression operator defined above needs to be able to determine.

Finally, we require that $\psi[do([\alpha_1, \ldots, \alpha_n], S_0)]$ must be regressable. Expressions of the form $\textbf{Knows}(\psi, do([\alpha_1, \ldots, \alpha_n], S_0))$ are the only knowledge specific expressions that a regressable formula is allowed to mention. Therefore, expressions of the form $\textbf{KRef}(t, \sigma)$ are assumed to have been replaced by $(\exists x)\textbf{Knows}(x = t, \sigma)$. It is then possible to prove:

Theorem 11.6.3: (The Regression Theorem with Knowledge) *Suppose that $\mathcal{D}$ is a basic action theory for knowledge, and that Q is a regressable sentence. Then*

1. *$\mathcal{D} \models Q$ iff $\mathcal{D}_{una} \cup \mathcal{D}_{S_0} \cup \mathcal{K}_{Init} \cup \{(11.18)\} \models \mathcal{R}[Q]$*

2. *Moreover, whenever $\mathcal{K}_{Init}$ consists of any subset of the accessibility relations Reflexive, Symmetric, Transitive, Euclidean,*

$$\mathcal{D} \models Q \quad \textit{iff} \quad \mathcal{D}_{una} \cup \mathcal{D}_{S_0} \cup \mathcal{K}_{Init} \models \mathcal{R}[Q]$$

Similar to the case for the situation calculus without sensing actions and knowledge, query evaluation reduces to first-order theorem-proving in the initial database $\mathcal{D}_{S_0} \cup K_{Init}$ together with unique names axioms for actions, possibly together also with axiom (11.18).

Example 11.6.4: How to Test for Acidity.

Show that after an agent performs a litmus paper test on an acidic solution, the agent will know that the solution is acidic. The litmus paper turns red if the solution is acidic. The actions include $test$ (insert litmus paper into solution) and $sense_{red}$ (sense whether the paper turns red). $\mathcal{D}_{S_0}$ includes $acid(S_0)$, and $\textbf{Knows}(\neg red, S_0)$. Assume that the action preconditions are all $true$, and that we have the following successor state axioms:

$$red(do(a, s)) \equiv acid(s) \wedge a = test \vee red(s), \tag{11.21}$$

$$acid(do(a, s)) \equiv acid(s) \wedge a \neq dilute. \tag{11.22}$$

We want to prove that after performing the litmus test and sensing the colour of the litmus paper, the agent will know that the solution is acidic:

$$\textbf{Knows}(acid, do(sense_{red}, do(test, S_0))). \tag{11.23}$$

This we do by regressing (11.23), and appealing to Theorem 11.6.3. After performing the "one-step" regression we obtain:

$$\begin{aligned} &\mathcal{R}[[red(do(test, S_0)) \supset \textbf{Knows}(red \supset acid, do(test, S_0))]] \wedge \\ &\mathcal{R}[[\neg red(do(test, S_0)) \supset \textbf{Knows}(\neg red \supset acid, do(test, S_0))]]. \end{aligned} \tag{11.24}$$

By (11.21), $red(do(test, S_0))$ regresses to $acid(S_0) \vee red(S_0)$. By (11.21) and (11.22),

$$\textbf{Knows}(red \supset acid, do(test, S_0)) \text{ and } \textbf{Knows}(\neg red \supset acid, do(test, S_0))$$

regress to

$$\textbf{Knows}(acid \vee red \supset acid, S_0) \text{ and } \textbf{Knows}(\neg acid \wedge \neg red \supset acid, S_0)$$

respectively. Therefore, regressing (11.24) produces:

$$[acid(S_0) \vee red(S_0) \supset \mathbf{Knows}(acid \vee red \supset acid, S_0)] \wedge$$
$$[\neg acid(S_0) \wedge \neg red(S_0) \supset \mathbf{Knows}(\neg acid \wedge \neg red \supset acid, S_0)].$$

This is entailed by $acid(S_0)$ and $\mathbf{Knows}(\neg red, S_0)$, so (11.23) is entailed by the original theory.

11.7   Knowledge-Based Programming

We are now positioned to write *knowledge-based programs*—Golog programs that appeal to knowledge and actions, including sense actions. As an example, consider the blocks world, and a program that explicitly refers to an agent's knowledge, and to the sense actions she can perform to gain information about the world. Imagine that initially, the agent is positioned in front of a table of blocks, with no prior knowledge about which blocks are where. The only information she is given in advance is an enumeration of all the blocks. Of course, the agent must know this is a blocks world, so we include the standard blocks world axioms of Example 6.5.2. Because the action precondition and successor state axioms universally quantify over situations, the agent also knows these. And she knows the unique names axioms for actions, because these are situation independent. But she definitely does not know anything about the initial configuration of blocks. For that matter, neither do we, the designers. The program we write will allow her to gain the information she needs, and to carry out the actions required to place all the blocks onto the table:

> **proc** $allToTable(b)$
> $\mathbf{Knows}((\forall x)ontable(x))?$ |
> $(\pi\ x).x \notin b?$;
>   **if** $\neg\mathbf{KWhether}(clear(x))$ **then** $sense_{clear}(x)$ **endIf** ;
>   **if** $\mathbf{Knows}(\neg clear(x))$ **then** $allToTable(\{x\} \cup b)$
>   **else if** $\neg\mathbf{KWhether}(ontable(x))$ **then** $sense_{ontable}(x)$ **endIf** ;
>   **if** $\mathbf{Knows}(ontable(x))$ **then** $allToTable(\{x\} \cup b)$
>   **else** $moveToTable(x)$; $allToTable(\{\ \})$ **endIf**
>   **endIf**
> **endProc**

The parameter b in $allToTable(b)$ stands for the set of those blocks that the agent has considered, and rejected, as candidates for moving to the table since her last $moveToTable$ action. The test action $x \notin b?$ prevents her from ever reconsidering such a block. Thus, the initial call to this procedure is with $allToTable(\{\ \})$. The procedure assumes two knowledge-producing actions, $sense_{ontable}(x)$ and $sense_{clear}(x)$, whose action preconditions are always *true*. Notice that this program attempts to minimize the number of *sense* actions the agent performs by first checking that she doesn't currently know the truth value of the sensed fluent. For example, the program fragment

if ¬**KWhether**(*clear*(*x*)) **then** *sense_clear*(*x*) **endIf**

instructs the agent to sense whether *x* is clear only when she doesn't already know whether *x* is clear.

While on the face of it, this program seems perfectly intuitive, there are a number of technical problems lurking behind the scenes, particularly what it would take to implement it:

1. **Knowledge and lack of knowledge.** The background axiomatization must character-ize the agent's knowledge about the initial situation, and also her *lack of knowledge*. So, for example, her ignorance about which blocks are where can be represented by

    $(\forall x, y)\neg$**KWhether**($on(x, y), S_0$).

    This can be a bit tricky when the agent does know something about the positions of some blocks, but not about others, for example, if she knows that *A* is on *B* and *B* is on *C*, but nothing else:

    Knows($on(A, B), S_0$), **Knows**($on(B, C), S_0$),
    $(\forall x, y)$.**KWhether**($on(x, y), S_0$) $\supset x = A \land y = B \lor x = B \land y = C$.

    Representing lack of knowledge becomes particularly problematic when an agent has complex knowledge about the initial situation:

    Knows(($\forall x$).$red(x) \supset ontable(x), S_0$),
    Knows($red(B) \lor red(C), S_0$),
    Knows($on(A, B) \lor on(A, C), S_0$),
    Knows(($\exists x$)$on(x, C), S_0$),
    Knows(($\forall x, y, z$).$on(y, x) \land on(z, x) \supset y = z, S_0$).

    Assuming that the above characterizes all that the agent knows, what does the agent *not* know in this example? Whatever that might be, it must somehow be axiomatized because it does represent a truth about the agent's knowledge. This is a very commonly occurring problem. Beginning with a collection $\mathcal{K}$ of axioms about what an agent *does* know, we want to make a *closed-world assumption about knowledge* to the effect that $\mathcal{K}$ captures everything that the agent knows; any knowledge sentences not following logically from $\mathcal{K}$ are taken to be false. The problem here, of course, is to somehow capture this closed-world assumption in a way that relieves the designer from having to figure out the relevant lack of knowledge axioms when given what the agent does know.[3]

2. **On-line execution.** Because the program appeals to sense actions, it is designed for on-line execution. This means that it must never backtrack over a sense action; once such an action is performed, it cannot be undone. (Recall the discussion in Section 8.6.2.) Knowledge-based programs that invoke information gathering actions must be carefully designed to prevent execution traces that include sense actions but that eventually lead to dead-ends. The above program has this property.

3. **Implementing sense actions.** What should be done when such a program encounters a sense action? The program is executing on-line, so that each action in an execution trace is meant to be performed as it is generated during a program run. Performing an ordinary action, like $moveToTable(A)$, is unproblematic; in a setting where the program is controlling a robot, the robot would simply perform the action, and the action term would be added to the situation history being constructed by the program interpreter. Performing a sense action is a different matter. Consider the robot receiving the on-line program request $sense_{clear}(A)$ when the current situation is S. It will respond with one of "yes" or "no", depending on its sense action's outcome. If "yes", then the robot now knows that A is clear: **Knows**$(clear(A), do(sense_{clear}(A), S))$. If "no", then **Knows**$(\neg clear(A), do(sense_{clear}(A), S))$. Normally, neither of these facts will be logical consequences of the underlying axioms; they provide new information about the robot's world. Therefore, one way to provide an on-line implementation of the sense action $sense_{clear}(A)$ is to dynamically *add* one of

$$\textbf{Knows}(clear(A), do(sense_{clear}(A), S)),$$
$$\textbf{Knows}(\neg clear(A), do(sense_{clear}(A), S))$$

to the background axioms, depending on the actual outcome of the sense action.

4. **A knowledge-based Golog interpreter.** For knowledge-based programs like *allTo-Table* above, we can no longer depend on the earlier Golog interpreters of this book, all of which relied on closed initial databases. To see why, first recall that an initial database is closed provided all its fluents are definitional: $F(\vec{x}, S_0) \equiv \psi_F(\vec{x}, S_0)$. Next, recall from item 1 above that we want to make the closed-world assumption about knowledge. So, for example, suppose there are two fluents $P(s)$ and $Q(s)$, and only P is known initially: **Knows**(P, S_0). Then under this closed-world assumption, $\neg$**Knows**(Q, S_0) and $\neg$**Knows**$(\neg Q, S_0)$ must be included in the initial database. This last sentence is an abbreviation for $(\exists s).K(s, S_0) \wedge Q(s)$, and this is an existential

---

3 The closed-world assumption for knowledge is much like related phenomena encountered elsewhere in this book. The frame problem amounts to axiomatically specifying what does not change on the assumption that all the ways that things do change have been specified. The Clark Completion of a database amounts to axiomatically characterizing what is false on the assumption that the database completely axiomatizes what is true.

sentence. As we saw in Section 5.3.2, existential facts are essentially open-world; they cannot be recast in definitional form. So there appears to be no way to represent initial databases about knowledge in the form necessary for the Prolog-based Golog interpreter. A different approach is needed.

For the above reasons, it is problematic to directly execute knowledge-based programs like *allToTable* using a closed-world Golog interpreter. The stance we shall take here is to view such programs as *specifications* for agent behaviours, and seek an alternative representation for them that can be executed under standard closed-world Golog.

11.7.1 Two Simplifying Assumptions

In the interest of simplifying this presentation on knowledge-based programming, we shall make two notationally undesirable but otherwise inessential assumptions about the underlying language of the situation calculus:

1. The language has no functional fluents. Non-fluent function symbols are permitted. To represent a functional fluent, e.g. $numberOfBlocksOnTable(s)$, the axiomatizer should use a relational fluent, e.g. $numberOfBlocksOnTable(n, s)$, and should enforce, via its truth value in the initial database and via its successor state axiom, that n must always exist and be unique.

    Because *read* knowledge-producing actions sense functional fluent values, this assumption allows us to ignore *read* actions in treating knowledge-based programs with sensing.

2. Except for the equality predicate, $\sqsubset$ and *Poss*, the language has no non-fluent predicate symbols. To represent such an "eternal" relation like $isPrimeNumber(n)$, the axiomatizer is required to use a relational fluent, e.g. $isPrimeNumber(n, s)$, and to assign it the successor state axiom

    $$isPrimeNumber(n, do(a, s)) \equiv isPrimeNumber(n, s).$$

    Moreover, any assertion about $isPrimeNumber(n)$ in the initial database must be made in terms of $isPrimeNumber(n, S_0)$.

    This assumption is introduced for purely technical reasons. It simplifies a condition (Definition 11.7.11 below) on basic action theories that seems to be needed to justify the interpreter that we shall design in this section for knowledge-based programs.

11.7.2 Sense Actions

Since we assume there are no functional fluents in the language, we do not need to worry about *read* actions; all sensing actions have the form $sense_\psi(\vec{x})$, where $\psi(\vec{x})$ is a situation-suppressed expression. To prove the main theorem of this section, it is necessary to be a bit careful about the syntactic form of ψ. Hence, the following definition:

Definition 11.7.1: Objective Situation-Suppressed Expressions

These are inductively defined as follows:

1. If $F(\vec{t}, \sigma)$ is a relational fluent atom, then $F(\vec{t})$ is an objective situation-suppressed expression.

2. If t_1 and t_2 are terms not of sort *situation*, then $t_1 = t_2$ is an objective situation-suppressed expression.

3. If ϕ and ψ are objective situation-suppressed expressions, so are $\neg\phi$, $\phi \vee \psi$, and $(\exists v)\psi$, where v is not a *situation* variable.

Therefore, objective expressions are situation-suppressed statements only about the world, not the agent's mental state; they do not involve expressions of the form **Knows**(ϕ). An *objective situation-suppressed sentence* is an objective situation-suppressed expression without any free variables. In what follows, we shall simply say "ϕ is objective " in place of the long-winded "ϕ is an objective situation-suppressed sentence".

In the remainder of this chapter, we shall assume that all sense actions have the form $sense_\psi(\vec{x})$, where $\psi(\vec{x})$ is an objective situation-suppressed expression.

11.7.3 Reducing Knowledge to Provability for the Initial Situation

The starting point for an implementation of knowledge-based programs is the observation that in a certain important special case, knowledge is reducible to provability. Here, we describe what we mean by this, and give suitable conditions under which it will be true.

First, we need a simple consequence of the Regression Theorem:

Lemma 11.7.2: *Whenever $\mathcal{D}$ is a basic action theory with knowledge, $\mathcal{K}_{init}$ consists of any subset of the accessibility relations Reflexive, Symmetric, Transitive, Euclidean, and ϕ is objective,*

$$\mathcal{D} \models \textbf{Knows}(\phi, S_0) \text{ iff } \mathcal{K}_{init} \cup \mathcal{D}_{una} \cup \mathcal{D}_{S_0} \models \textbf{Knows}(\phi, S_0).$$

Proof: By the Regression Theorem 11.6.3, and the fact that **Knows**(ϕ, S_0) regresses to itself. ∎

Next, we introduce a special class of initial databases. Suppose the sentences of $\mathcal{D}_{S_0}$ are all of the form **Knows**$(\kappa_i, S_0), i = 1, \ldots, n$, where each κ_i is objective. In other words, the initial database consists exclusively of sentences declaring what the agent knows about the world he inhabits, but there are no sentences declaring what is actually true of the world, or what he knows about what he knows. So $\mathcal{D}_{S_0} = \{\mathbf{Knows}(\kappa_1, S_0), \ldots, \mathbf{Knows}(\kappa_n, S_0)\}$, and since this is logically equivalent to $\mathbf{Knows}(\kappa_1 \wedge \cdots \wedge \kappa_n, S_0)$, we can simply suppose that $\mathcal{D}_{S_0}$ consists of a single sentence of the form $\mathbf{Knows}(\kappa, S_0)$, where κ is objective, and that is what we shall do from here on.

Lemma 11.7.3: *Suppose that ϕ is objective, that $\mathcal{D}_{S_0} = \mathbf{Knows}(\kappa, S_0)$ where κ is objective, and that $\mathcal{K}_{init}$ consists of any subset of the accessibility relations Reflexive, Symmetric, Transitive, Euclidean. Then,*

$$\mathcal{D} \models \mathbf{Knows}(\phi, S_0) \text{ iff } \mathcal{D}_{una} \cup \{\kappa[S_0]\} \models \phi[S_0].$$

Proof: Exercise 15 below. ∎

Therefore, for the initial situation, the entailment problem for knowledge sentences has been reduced to that of knowledge-free sentences. Keep in mind that this result relies on the stated assumptions that:

1. $\mathcal{D}_{S_0}$ consists of a sentence of the form $\mathbf{Knows}(\kappa, S_0)$, where κ is objective. Therefore, $\mathbf{Knows}((\forall x).clear(x) \vee ontable(x), S_0)$ qualifies, but $(\exists x)\mathbf{Knows}(\kappa(x), S_0)$ would not. Neither would $\mathbf{Knows}(\mathbf{Knows}(\kappa), S_0)$, or $\mathbf{Knows}(\kappa_1, S_0) \vee \mathbf{Knows}(\kappa_2, S_0)$, or $\neg\mathbf{Knows}(\kappa, S_0)$, or $\mathbf{Knows}(now = S_0, S_0)$.

2. The sentence to be proved has the form $\mathbf{Knows}(\phi, S_0)$, where ϕ is objective.

   Lemma 11.7.3 provides a provability story for entailments from $\mathcal{D}$ having the form $\mathbf{Knows}(\phi, S_0)$. What about entailments of the form $\neg\mathbf{Knows}(\phi, S_0)$? We defer treating negative knowledge until Section 11.7.6 below, where we shall introduce the *closed-world assumption on knowledge*, whose effect will be that entailments of negative knowledge will reduce to non-provability of knowledge-free sentences.

11.7.4   On-Line Execution of Knowledge-Based Programs

As discussed earlier, we have in mind executing knowledge-based programs like that for *allToTable* on-line. This means that each time a program interpreter adds a new program action to its action history, the robot also physically performs this action. Some of these actions will be sense actions; since these normally increase the robot's knowledge of its world, this means that its axioms must be augmented by knowledge about the outcomes of its on-line sense actions. To capture this idea formally, some notation is needed to describe this incrementally growing set of axioms. Initially, before it has performed any actions on-line, the robot's background consists of a basic action theory $\mathcal{D}$, as defined in Section 11.5.3. Suppose that σ is the current situation recording all the actions performed on-line by the robot. We can suppose that σ mentions no variables, since it makes no sense to perform a non-ground action on-line. We want to define the result of augmenting $\mathcal{D}$ with knowledge about the outcomes of all the sense actions occurring in σ. To do this, we introduce the concept of the *sense outcomes* of a given on-line action sequence σ.

Definition 11.7.4: Sense Outcome Function

A *sense outcome function* is any mapping Ω from ground situation terms to knowledge sentences, such that:

1. $\Omega(S_0) = \{\,\}$,

2. If α is not a sense action,

   $\Omega(do(\alpha, \sigma)) = \Omega(\sigma)$.

3. If α is a sense action $sense_\psi(\vec{g})$,

   $\Omega(do(\alpha, \sigma)) = \Omega(\sigma) \cup \{\mathbf{Knows}(\psi(\vec{g}), do(sense_\psi(\vec{g}), \sigma))\}$ or

   $\Omega(do(\alpha, \sigma)) = \Omega(\sigma) \cup \{\mathbf{Knows}(\neg\psi(\vec{g}), do(sense_\psi(\vec{g}), \sigma))\}$.

In general, our interest will be in $\mathcal{D} \cup \Omega(\sigma)$, namely, the original basic action theory $\mathcal{D}$, augmented by knowledge of the outcomes of all sense actions in the action history σ, according to the sense outcome function Ω. Recall that one of the simplifying assumptions of Section 11.7.1 is that there are no functional fluents, and that is why $read$ actions were not treated in the above definition of Ω.

11.7.5 Reduction of Knowledge to Provability for On-Line Programs

Here, we focus on conditions under which the theory $\mathcal{D} \cup \Omega(\sigma)$, consisting of the original theory $\mathcal{D}$ augmented by the outcomes of all sense actions in σ, entails sentences of the form $\mathbf{Knows}(\phi, \sigma)$.

Lemma 11.7.5:

$\mathcal{D} \models (\forall \vec{y}, s).\mathbf{Knows}(\psi(\vec{y}), do(sense_\psi(\vec{y}), s)) \equiv \psi(\vec{y}, s) \vee \mathbf{Knows}(\psi(\vec{y}), s),$

$\mathcal{D} \models (\forall \vec{y}, s).\mathbf{Knows}(\neg\psi(\vec{y}), do(sense_\psi(\vec{y}), s)) \equiv \neg\psi(\vec{y}, s) \vee \mathbf{Knows}(\psi(\vec{y}), s).$

Proof: Take W to be ψ, then $\neg\psi$, in Proposition 11.6.2, and use the no-side-effects assumption for sense actions. ∎

Corollary 11.7.6: *When $\mathcal{K}_{Init}$ includes the reflexivity axiom,*

$\mathcal{D} \models (\forall \vec{y}, s).\mathbf{Knows}(\psi(\vec{y}), do(sense_\psi(\vec{y}), s)) \equiv \psi(\vec{y}, s),$

$\mathcal{D} \models (\forall \vec{y}, s).\mathbf{Knows}(\neg\psi(\vec{y}), do(sense_\psi(\vec{y}), s)) \equiv \neg\psi(\vec{y}, s).$

Proof: Use Lemma 11.7.5, and the fact that when reflexivity holds in the initial situation, it holds in all situations, so that what is known in s is true in s. ∎

Lemma 11.7.7:   *When $\mathcal{K}_{Init}$ includes the reflexivity axiom,*

$$\mathcal{D} \models (\forall \vec{x}, \vec{y}, s).\mathbf{Knows}(\psi(\vec{y}), do(sense_\psi(\vec{y}), s)) \supset$$
$$\mathbf{Knows}(\phi(\vec{x}), do(sense_\psi(\vec{y}), s)) \equiv \mathbf{Knows}(\psi(\vec{y}) \supset \phi(\vec{x}), s),$$

$$\mathcal{D} \models (\forall \vec{x}, \vec{y}, s).\mathbf{Knows}(\neg\psi(\vec{y}), do(sense_\psi(\vec{y}), s)) \supset$$
$$\mathbf{Knows}(\phi(\vec{x}), do(sense_\psi(\vec{y}), s)) \equiv \mathbf{Knows}(\neg\psi(\vec{y}) \supset \phi(\vec{x}), s).$$

Proof: By Proposition 11.6.2 and Corollary 11.7.6. ∎

The following bits of notation will be useful:

Definition 11.7.8: $\rho(\phi, \sigma)$, $\Omega^\rho(\sigma)$

1. Here, we define the "multi-step" regression operator on situation-suppressed expressions. Let σ be a ground situation term. $\rho(\phi, \sigma)$ is the regression of the situation-suppressed expression ϕ through the actions of σ, defined by

$$\rho(\phi, S_0) = \phi,$$

$$\rho(\phi, do(\alpha, \sigma)) = \rho(\rho^1(\phi, \alpha), \sigma),$$

where $\rho^1(\phi, \alpha)$ is the one-step regression of ϕ through action α defined in Section 11.6. Clearly, $\rho(\phi, \sigma)[S_0]$ and $\mathcal{R}[\phi[\sigma]]$ are logically equivalent, relative to the background basic action theory.

2. Suppose Ω is a sense outcome function, and σ is a ground situation term.

$$\Omega^\rho(\sigma) = \bigwedge\{\rho(\psi(\vec{g}), \sigma') \mid \mathbf{Knows}(\psi(\vec{g}), do(sense_\psi(\vec{g}), \sigma')) \in \Omega(\sigma)\} \wedge$$
$$\bigwedge\{\rho(\neg\psi(\vec{g}), \sigma') \mid \mathbf{Knows}(\neg\psi(\vec{g}), do(sense_\psi(\vec{g}), \sigma')) \in \Omega(\sigma)\}.$$

So, for example, if

$$\Omega(\sigma) = \{\mathbf{Knows}(\psi_1, do(sense_{\psi_1}, \sigma_1)), \mathbf{Knows}(\neg\psi_2, do(sense_{\psi_2}, \sigma_2)),$$
$$\mathbf{Knows}(\neg\psi_3, do(sense_{\psi_3}, \sigma_3))\},$$

then

$$\Omega^\rho(\sigma) = \rho(\psi_1, \sigma_1) \wedge \rho(\neg\psi_2, \sigma_2) \wedge \rho(\neg\psi_3, \sigma_3).$$

Notice that $\Omega^\rho(\sigma)$ is a situation-suppressed sentence. By convention, $\Omega^\rho(\sigma) = true$ when $\Omega(\sigma) = \{\ \}$.

Lemma 11.7.9:   *When $\mathcal{K}_{Init}$ includes the reflexivity axiom, then $\Omega(\sigma)$ and $\Omega^\rho(\sigma)[S_0]$*

are logically equivalent,[4] *relative to* $\mathcal{D}$. *Recall that the notation* $\Omega^\rho(\sigma)[S_0]$ *stands for the result of restoring situation argument* S_0 *back into the situation-suppressed sentence* $\Omega^\rho(\sigma)$.

Proof: Corollary 11.7.6. ∎

Lemma 11.7.10: *Suppose* ϕ *is objective,* σ *is a ground situation term, and* $\mathcal{K}_{Init}$ *includes the reflexivity axiom. Then*

$$\mathcal{D} \cup \Omega(\sigma) \models \mathbf{Knows}(\phi, \sigma) \equiv \mathbf{Knows}(\Omega^\rho(\sigma) \supset \rho(\phi, \sigma), S_0).$$

Proof: Exercise 16 below. ∎

Definition 11.7.11: Deciding Equality Sentences

Suppose T is any situation calculus theory. We say that T *decides all equality sentences* iff for any sentence β over the language of T whose only predicate symbol is equality, $T \models \beta$ or $T \models \neg\beta$.

The following is a purely technical lemma that turns out to be very useful in establishing our principal results.

Lemma 11.7.12:   *Suppose that* $\mathcal{D}_{S_0} = \mathbf{Knows}(\kappa, S_0)$ *where* κ *is objective, that* $\mathcal{D}_{una} \cup \{\kappa[S_0]\}$ *decides all equality sentences, and* $\mathcal{K}_{init}$ *consists of any subset of the accessibility relations Reflexive, Symmetric, Transitive, Euclidean. Suppose further that* $\psi_0, \dots, \psi_n$ *are objective, and that*

$$\mathcal{D} \models \psi_0[S_0] \vee \mathbf{Knows}(\psi_1, S_0) \vee \cdots \vee \mathbf{Knows}(\psi_n, S_0).$$

Then for some $0 \leq i \leq n$, $\mathcal{D} \models \mathbf{Knows}(\psi_i, S_0)$.

Proof: Exercise 17 below. ∎

Something like the assumption that $\mathcal{D}_{una} \cup \{\kappa[S_0]\}$ decides all equality sentences in the above lemma seems necessary. To see why, consider:

Example 11.7.13:   Let F and G be unary fluents, and let κ be the conjunction of the following three sentences:

$$a = b \vee c = d, \quad a = b \supset F, \quad c = d \supset G.$$

---

4 We are slightly abusing terminology here; strictly speaking, we should say that the conjunction of the sentences in $\Omega(\sigma)$ is logically equivalent to $\Omega^\rho(\sigma)[S_0]$.

Then it is easy to see that

$$\mathbf{Knows}(\kappa, S_0) \models a = b \vee \mathbf{Knows}(F, S_0) \vee \mathbf{Knows}(G, S_0),$$

but

$$\mathbf{Knows}(\kappa, S_0) \not\models \mathbf{Knows}(a = b, S_0), \ \mathbf{Knows}(\kappa, S_0) \not\models \mathbf{Knows}(F, S_0) \text{ and}$$
$$\mathbf{Knows}(\kappa, S_0) \not\models \mathbf{Knows}(G, S_0).$$

Theorem 11.7.14: *Suppose that ϕ is objective, $\mathcal{D}_{S_0} = \mathbf{Knows}(\kappa, S_0)$ where κ is objective, $\mathcal{D}_{una} \cup \{\kappa[S_0]\}$ decides all equality sentences, σ is a ground situation term, and $\mathcal{K}_{Init}$ includes the reflexivity axiom. Then*

$$\mathcal{D} \cup \Omega(\sigma) \models \mathbf{Knows}(\phi, \sigma) \ \textit{iff} \ \mathcal{D}_{una} \cup \{\kappa[S_0], \Omega^{\rho}(\sigma)[S_0]\} \models \mathcal{R}[\phi[\sigma]].$$

Proof: Exercise 18 below. ∎

This is the central result of this section; it completely characterizes entailments of the form $\mathbf{Knows}(\phi, \sigma)$ relative to $\mathcal{D} \cup \Omega(\sigma)$ in terms of provability, in the initial situation, for knowledge-free sentences. What about entailments of the form $\neg\mathbf{Knows}(\phi, \sigma)$? That is the topic of the next section.

11.7.6   The Dynamic Closed-World Assumption

We now consider the problem, discussed in item 1 of Section 11.7, of characterizing an agent's lack of knowledge, and we begin first by considering knowledge in the initial situation $\mathcal{D}_{S_0} = \mathbf{Knows}(\kappa, S_0)$. Here, we shall make the *closed-world assumption on knowledge*, namely, that $\mathbf{Knows}(\kappa, S_0)$ characterizes *everything* that the agent knows initially, and whatever knowledge does not follow from this will be taken to be lack of knowledge. How can this closed-world assumption be characterized in a way that relieves the axiomatizer from having to figure out the relevant lack of knowledge axioms when given what the agent does know? We propose the following:

$$closure(\mathcal{D}) = \mathcal{D} \cup \{\neg\mathbf{Knows}(\theta, S_0) \mid \theta \text{ is objective and } \mathcal{D} \not\models \mathbf{Knows}(\theta, S_0)\}.$$

Under the closed-world assumption on knowledge, the *official* basic action theory is taken to be $closure(\mathcal{D})$. To make his life easier in specifying the initial database, the axiomatizer is asked only to provide a specification of the positive initial knowledge $\mathcal{D}_{S_0}$ that the robot has of its domain, but this is understood to be a convenient shorthand for what holds initially, and $closure(\mathcal{D})$, as defined above, specifies the actual basic action theory.

Example 11.7.15:   Here, we specify the positive initial knowledge available to the agent inhabiting the blocks world. While she knows nothing about which blocks are where, this does not mean she knows nothing at all. There are state constraints associated with this world, and we must suppose the agent knows these. Specifically, she must know that these constraints hold initially, and therefore, her initial database consists of the following:

$\textbf{Knows}((\forall x, y).on(x, y) \supset \neg on(y, x), S_0),$

$\textbf{Knows}((\forall x, y, z).on(y, x) \land on(z, x) \supset y = z, S_0),$

$\textbf{Knows}((\forall x, y, z).on(x, y) \land on(x, z) \supset y = z, S_0).$

By making the closed-world assumption about this initial database, the axiomatizer need not concern himself with writing additional lack of knowledge axioms like

$\neg\textbf{Knows}((\exists x, y)on(x, y), S_0),$ or $\neg\textbf{Knows}((\exists x).clear(x) \land ontable(x), S_0).$

Neither does he have to worry about whether he has succeeded in expressing *all* the relevant lack of knowledge axioms. The closed world-assumption takes care of these problems for him.

However, as noted above, the axioms of $\mathcal{D}$ are being continuously augmented by sentences asserting knowledge about the outcomes of the sense actions performed during the on-line execution of a program, and $\mathcal{D} \cup \Omega(\sigma)$ specifies what these axioms are, when the program is currently in situation σ. Therefore, under the closed-world assumption in situation σ, we are supposing that $\mathcal{D} \cup \Omega(\sigma)$ characterizes all of the agent's positive knowledge about the initial situation, so we are really interested in the closure of $\mathcal{D}_{S_0}$ relative to $\mathcal{D} \cup \Omega(\sigma)$. Therefore, here we are actually making a *dynamic closed-world assumption*.

Definition 11.7.16: Dynamic Closed-World Assumption on Knowledge

$closure(\mathcal{D} \cup \Omega(\sigma)) =$
$\mathcal{D} \cup \Omega(\sigma) \cup \{\neg Knows(\theta, S_0) \mid \theta$ is objective and $\mathcal{D} \cup \Omega(\sigma) \not\models Knows(\theta, S_0)\}.$

Under the dynamic closed-world assumption on knowledge, the *official* basic action theory, when the on-line execution of a program is in situation σ, is taken to be $closure(\mathcal{D} \cup \Omega(\sigma))$.

Next, we need to study the properties of $closure(\mathcal{D} \cup \Omega(\sigma))$, with the ultimate objective of reducing negative knowledge to non-provability.

Lemma 11.7.17: *Suppose that $\mathcal{D}_{S_0} = \textbf{Knows}(\kappa, S_0)$ where κ is objective, $\mathcal{D}_{una} \cup \kappa[S_0]$ decides all equality sentences, and $\mathcal{K}_{Init}$ includes the reflexivity axiom, together with any subset of the accessibility relations Symmetric, Transitive, Euclidean. Then*

$closure(\mathcal{D} \cup \Omega(\sigma))$ *is satisfiable iff* $\mathcal{D}_{una} \cup \{\kappa[S_0], \Omega^p(\sigma)[S_0]\}$ *is satisfiable.*

Proof: Exercise 19 below. ∎

Lemma 11.7.18: *Suppose $\mathcal{D}_{S_0} = \mathbf{Knows}(\kappa, S_0)$ where κ is objective, $\mathcal{D}_{una} \cup \kappa[S_0]$ decides all equality sentences, σ is a ground situation term, and $\mathcal{K}_{Init}$ includes the reflexivity axiom. Suppose further that ϕ is objective and $closure(\mathcal{D} \cup \Omega(\sigma))$ is satisfiable. Then*

$$closure(\mathcal{D} \cup \Omega(\sigma)) \models \mathbf{Knows}(\phi, \sigma) \text{ iff } \mathcal{D}_{una} \cup \{\kappa[S_0], \Omega^\rho(\sigma)[S_0]\} \models \mathcal{R}[\phi[\sigma]].$$

Proof: Exercise 20 below. ∎

Definition 11.7.19: Subjective Sentences
A sentence is a *subjective sentence about* a ground situation term σ iff it has the form $\mathbf{Knows}(\beta, \sigma)$, where β is objective, or the form $\neg W$, where W is a subjective sentence about σ, or the form $W_1 \vee W_2$, where W_1 and W_2 are subjective sentences about σ.

Lemma 11.7.20:   *Suppose $\mathcal{K}_{Init}$ includes the reflexivity axiom. Then for any subjective sentence W about a ground situation term σ,*

$$closure(\mathcal{D} \cup \Omega(\sigma)) \models W \text{ or } closure(\mathcal{D} \cup \Omega(\sigma)) \models \neg W.$$

Proof: Exercise 21 below. ∎

Finally, combine Lemmas 11.7.17, 11.7.18 and 11.7.20 to obtain the main result:

Theorem 11.7.21: *Let Ω be a sense outcome function. Suppose that*

1. *$\mathcal{D}_{S_0} = \mathbf{Knows}(\kappa, S_0)$, where κ is objective.*
2. *$\mathcal{D}_{una} \cup \{\kappa[S_0]\}$ decides all equality sentences.*
3. *σ is a ground situation term.*
4. *$\mathcal{D}_{una} \cup \{\kappa[S_0], \Omega^\rho(\sigma)[S_0]\}$ is satisfiable.*
5. *$\mathcal{K}_{Init}$ consists of the reflexivity axiom, together with any subset of the accessibility axioms Symmetric, Transitive, Euclidean.*

Then,

1. *When ϕ is objective,*

    $$closure(\mathcal{D} \cup \Omega(\sigma)) \models \mathbf{Knows}(\phi, \sigma) \text{ iff}$$
    $$\mathcal{D}_{una} \cup \{\kappa[S_0], \Omega^\rho(\sigma)[S_0]\} \models \mathcal{R}[\phi[\sigma]].$$

2. *When W is a subjective sentence about σ,*

    $$closure(\mathcal{D} \cup \Omega(\sigma)) \models \neg W \text{ iff } closure(\mathcal{D} \cup \Omega(\sigma)) \not\models W.$$

3. *When W_1 and W_2 are subjective sentences about σ,*

    $$closure(\mathcal{D} \cup \Omega(\sigma)) \models W_1 \vee W_2 \text{ iff}$$

$closure(\mathcal{D} \cup \Omega(\sigma)) \models W_1$ or $closure(\mathcal{D} \cup \Omega(\sigma)) \models W_2$.

11.7.7   Interpreter for Knowledge-Based Programs with Sensing

Under the stated conditions, Theorem 11.7.21 justifies the following decisions in implementing an interpreter for an on-line knowledge-based program:

- **Initial Database.** If $\mathcal{D}_{S_0} = \mathbf{Knows}(\kappa, S_0)$, the implementation uses $\kappa[S_0]$ as its initial database.

- **Regression after Sense Actions.** Whenever a $sense_\psi(\vec{g})$ action is performed by the program in a situation σ, the implementation adds the regression of $\psi(\vec{g}, \sigma)$ or $\neg\psi(\vec{g}, \sigma)$ to the current initial database, depending on the sense action's outcome.

- **Evaluating Program Test Conditions.** Suppose a test condition W is evaluated by the program in a situation σ. Using items 2 and 3, the implementation recursively breaks down $W[\sigma]$ into appropriate subgoals of proving, or failing to prove, sentences of the form $\mathbf{Knows}(\phi, \sigma)$. By item 1, these reduce to proving, or failing to prove, the regression of $\phi[\sigma]$ relative to the current initial database. So for these base cases, the implementation performs this regression step, then invokes a theorem prover on the regressed sentence, using the current initial database (plus unique names for actions) as premises. Notice the assumption here, required by the theorem, that every test condition W of the program be such that $W[\sigma]$ is a subjective sentence about σ.

- **Guarded Sense Actions.** Condition 4 of Theorem 11.7.21 requires the satisfiability of $\mathcal{D}_{una} \cup \{\kappa[S_0], \Omega^\rho(\sigma)[S_0]\}$. Therefore, an implementation must perform this satisfiability test. However, there is one natural condition on a knowledge-based program that would eliminate the need for such a test, and that is that every sensing action in the program be *guarded*. By this, we mean that a sense action is performed only when its outcome is not already known to the robot. In the *allToTable* program, the statement **if** $\neg\mathbf{KWhether}(clear(x))$ **then** $sense_{clear}(x)$ **endIf** provides such a guard for the action $sense_{clear}(x)$. Whenever the program guards all its sense actions, as *allToTable* does, then condition 4 of Theorem 11.7.21 reduces to requiring the satisfiability of $\mathcal{D}_{una} \cup \{\kappa[S_0]\}$, and this can be performed once only, when the initial database is first specified. This is the content of the following:

Proposition 11.7.22:   *Under the conditions of Theorem 11.7.21, let $sense_\psi(\vec{g})$ be a ground sense action, and suppose that $closure(\mathcal{D} \cup \Omega(\sigma)) \models \neg\mathbf{KWhether}(\psi(\vec{g}), \sigma)$. Then $\mathcal{D}_{una} \cup \{\kappa[S_0], \Omega^\rho(do(sense_\psi(\vec{g}), \sigma))[S_0]\}$ is satisfiable.*

Proof: Exercise 22 below. ∎

11.7.8 Computing Closed-World Knowledge

The reduction of knowledge to provability under the closed-world assumption on knowledge makes little computational sense for full first-order logic, because its provability relation is not computable. Therefore, in what follows, we shall restrict ourselves to the quantifier-free case. Specifically, we shall assume:

1. The only function symbols not of sort *action* or *situation* are constants.

2. $\mathcal{D}_{S_0}$ includes knowledge of unique names for these constants:

   Knows$(C \neq C', S_0)$, for distinct constant symbols C and C'.

3. All quantifiers mentioned in $\mathcal{D}_{S_0}$, and all quantifiers mentioned in test expressions of a knowledge-based program are typed, and these types are abbreviations for descriptions of finite domains of constants, as described in Section 10.6.1:

$$\tau(x) \overset{def}{=} x = T_1 \vee \cdots \vee x = T_k,$$

   where there will be one such abbreviation for each type τ.

Therefore, typed quantifiers can be eliminated in formulas in favour of conjunctions and disjunctions, as described in Section 10.6.1, so we end up with sentences of propositional logic, for which the provability relation is computable. Because the agent has knowledge of unique names, $\mathcal{D}_{una} \cup \mathcal{D}_{S_0}$ will decide all typed equality sentences. Therefore, the conditions of Theorem 11.7.21 will hold.

11.7.9 Putting It All Together

Theorem 11.7.21 provides the theoretical foundations for implementing programs like *allToTable*(b). The following is a generic Golog interpreter for knowledge-based programs with sense actions using provability in propositional logic to implement knowledge. It assumes that all sense actions in the program are guarded, and it therefore does not perform the consistency check required by condition 4 of Theorem 11.7.21. It is generic in the sense that the theorem-prover prove is left unspecified, as are clauses for updateInit-Database, whose purpose is to add the regression of the outcome of a sense action to the initial database, thereby incorporating the new information obtained from the sense action into the old axioms. The interpreter is designed for implementing simulations, hence its interactive component querying the user about sense action outcomes.

A Generic Golog Interpreter for Knowledge-Based Programs with Sense Actions Using Provability to Implement Knowledge

```
/* The clauses for do remain as for standard Golog, except that
   do(pi(V,E),S,S1) is modified to associate, with variable V, a type T
```

with finite domain, and an extra clause is added to treat sense actions
by interactively asking the user for the outcome of the action, and
updating the initial database with the regression of this outcome. This
clause for sense actions appeals to a user-provided declaration
senseAction(A,SensedOutcome), meaning that A is a sense action, and
SensedOutcome is the formula whose truth value the action A is designed
to determine. */

```
do(pi([V,T],E),S,S1) :- domain(T,D), member(M,D), sub(V,M,E,E1),
                        do(E1,S,S1).
```

/* In the following, regress is exactly as in the prime implicate-based
   open-world planning program in Chapter 10. */

```
do(A,S,do(A,S)) :- senseAction(A,SensedOutcome), poss(A,S),
                   queryUser(SensedOutcome,YN),
                   restoreSitArgThroughout(SensedOutcome,S,Outcome),
                   regress(Outcome,R),
                   (YN = y, updateInitDatabase(R) ;
                    YN = n, updateInitDatabase(-R)).

queryUser(SensedOutcome,YN) :- nl, write("Is "),
      write(SensedOutcome), write(" true now? y or n."), read(YN).
```

/* The following clauses are added to those for holds in the
   standard Golog interpreter. */

```
holds(kWhether(W),S) :- holds(knows(W),S), ! ; holds(knows(-W),S)).
holds(knows(W),S) :- restoreSitArgThroughout(W,S,F), prove(F).
```

/* Finally, replace the last holds clause in the standard
   Golog interpreter by the following: */

```
holds(A,S) :- restoreSitArg(A,S,F), F ;
              not restoreSitArg(A,S,F), isAtom(A),
              not (A = knows(W) ; A = kWhether(W)), A.
```

/* restoreSitArgThroughout(W,S,F) means F is the result of restoring
   the situation argument S into every fluent mentioned by the formula W. Its clauses are straightforward, and we omit them. */

Next, we describe a particular implementation of this generic Golog interpreter. This means we must provide the update procedure updateInitDatabase and the theorem-prover prove used in the program. Any sound and complete theorem-prover for propositional logic will do, but since we already have such a program based on prime implicates, used in Section 10.6 for open-world planning, we shall exploit this. Recall that in this planning setting, the initial database was first compiled into prime implicate form (using the clauses for compile of Section 10.6). The theorem-prover, prove, took a regressable sentence, regressed it, converted the result to clausal form, and finally tested each of these clauses for subsumption by one of the initial database's prime implicates. We shall use this same program for prove to implement the above generic Golog interpreter, and we shall maintain the initial database in prime implicate form. The only remaining task is to implement updateInitDatabase(R), whose purpose is to add the regression R of the information obtained from a sense action, to the current initial database. This we do by adding the clausal form of R to the initial database, and computing the prime implicates of this new initial database, exploiting the fact that the old database was already in prime implicate form.

Clauses for Updating an Initial Database of Prime Implicates

```
/* updateInitDatabase receives a regressed sentence R, converts it
   to clausal form, then uses assertClauses and resolveAll to
   compute the prime implicates of R's clauses together with the
   current initial database (which is in prime implicate form). It
   uses the Prolog predicates clausalForm, assertClauses, clause,
   and resolveAll, which are exactly as in the prime implicate-
   based open-world planning program in Chapter 10.   */

updateInitDatabase(R) :- clausalForm(R,Clauses),
                getMaxClauseIndex(Max), NextIndex is Max + 1,
                assertClauses(Clauses,NextIndex),
                resolveAll(NextIndex).

getMaxClauseIndex(N) :- clause(C,N), not (clause(K,M), M > N).
```

Finally, we can return to the blocks world program $allToTable(b)$. Because $\mathcal{D}_{S_0}$ includes knowledge of domain closure and unique names for all the domain constants, $\mathcal{D}_{una} \cup \mathcal{D}_{S_0}$ decides all equality sentences, so the conditions for the correctness of the Golog interpreter for knowledge-based programs hold for this domain. Next, we provide the implementation of $allToTable(b)$, together with the relevant blocks world clauses. Notice that, in keeping with the assumption that the agent has no prior knowledge about the specific initial configuration of blocks, the initial situation consists only of state constraints, relativized to S_0.

How to Move All the Blocks to the Table: Prolog Implementation

```
%  The Golog Program.

proc(allToTable(B),
    ?(knows(all([x,block],ontable(x)))) #
    pi([x,block],
        ?(-member(x,B)) :
        if(-kWhether(clear(x)), senseClear(x)) :
        if(knows(-clear(x)), allToTable([x | B]),
  /* ELSE */ if(-kWhether(ontable(x)), senseOnTable(x)) :
            if(knows(ontable(x)), allToTable([x | B]),
        /* ELSE */ moveToTable(x) :
                    ?(report(moveToTable(x))) :
                    allToTable([]))))).

report(A) :- nl, write('Performing '), write(A), write('.'), nl.

run :- do(allToTable([]),s0,S), nl, write('Final situation: '),
       prettyPrintSituation(S).

          %  The Blocks World Clauses.

%  Initial Situation. Nothing else is known to the agent.

axiom(all([x,block], all([y,block], on(x,y,s0) => -on(y,x,s0)))).
axiom(all([x,block], all([y,block], all([z,block],
        on(y,x,s0) & on(z,x,s0) => y = z)))).
axiom(all([x,block], all([y,block], all([z,block],
        on(x,y,s0) & on(x,z,s0) => y = z)))).

%  clear and ontable defined in the initial situation.

clear(X,s0) <=> all([y,block],-on(y,X,s0)).
ontable(X,s0) <=> all([y,block],-on(X,y,s0)).

%  Preconditions for sense actions.

poss(senseClear(X),S).  poss(senseOnTable(X),S).

%  Misc declarations.

senseAction(senseClear(X),clear(X)).
```

```
senseAction(senseOnTable(X),ontable(X)).

domain(block,[a,b,c,d]).   % A four block domain.
```

```
/* The remaining clauses consist of the action precondition and
   successor state axioms, and the primitive_action declarations
   and restoreSitArg declarations for the open blocks world
   planning problem of the planning chapter 10.   */
```

This is all the code needed to run the example program:

Running the Program for Four Blocks

```
[eclipse 2]: compile.

Clausal form completed.   CPU time (sec): 0.06  Clauses: 34

Database compiled.   CPU time (sec): 0.04   Prime implicates: 34

yes.
[eclipse 3]: run.

Is clear(a) true now? y or n.   y.

Is ontable(a) true now? y or n. y.

Is clear(b) true now? y or n.   n.

Is clear(c) true now? y or n.   y.

Is ontable(c) true now? y or n. n.

Performing moveToTable(c).

Is clear(b) true now? y or n.   n.

Performing moveToTable(d).

Final situation:
[senseClear(a), senseOnTable(a), senseClear(b), senseClear(c),
 senseOnTable(c), moveToTable(c), senseClear(b), moveToTable(d)]

yes.
```

Notice how smart the program is: After learning that a is clear and needn't be moved, and after moving c to the table and learning that b is still not clear, it figures that d must therefore be on b and that b must be on the table, so it simply moves d.

11.8 Discussion

In the context of computational vision and robotics, there is much that is naive about our treatment of sensing actions. We have totally ignored the incredibly complex problems associated with extracting useful information from noisy images (e.g. regions, edges, texture, depth), and with the recognition phase of image processing: What things are out there, and how are they spatially related to one another? In effect, for example in the program for moving all the blocks to the table of Section 11.7, we are treating a robot's visual system as a black box whose inputs are requests for information about the scene—Is there a cat on the sofa?—and whose outputs provide answers to these requests. The truth is that contemporary vision research is nowhere near delivering such black boxes. Moreover, it is not even clear what should count as a primitive sense action. Surely, $sense_{catOnSofa}$ is not. Presumably, this should be something more like $(\pi\ x).sense_{sofa}(x); (\pi\ y)sense_{catOn}(x, y)$. Or maybe it should be $(\pi\ y).sense_{cat}(y); (\pi\ x).sense_{on}(y, x); sense_{sofa}(y)$. Even something like $(\pi\ x)sense_{sofa}(x)$ is problematic, quite independently of the difficulties contemporary vision systems might have with actually recognizing sofas in a typical living room. Where should the camera be pointed initially? How should the camera systematically scan the room? Are the camera actions under the control of the black box vision system, or the robot? For reasons like these, we are a long way from integrating theories of high level robot sensing and control with existing vision systems. Nevertheless, it is a very interesting idea that robot control programs can explicitly call sense actions, in a top-down way, to look for particular properties of a scene, for example, whether there is a cat on the sofa. This promises to add an important top-down component to existing image processing systems, which tend to be highly bottom-up.

Despite these real obstacles to our view of sensing for computer vision, it is important to remember that not all sensing is visual, and that there are other domains for which a top-down, black box approach to sensing is quite realistic. The simplest examples include industrial control systems where a system's state is continuously monitored by sensors that return information about temperature, pressure, flow rates, etc. More interesting applications concern so-called *softbots*—software autonomous robots. A simple example might be a Unix-based softbot, implemented in Golog with sensing, whose job is to help you manage your files, for example, by periodically roaming through your directories to compress all your old files. To do that, the softbot would need the ability to sense the contents of a directory (using the Unix *ls* command), and perhaps also to sense file contents. There are many more examples of softbot sense actions that fit our black box perspective; these include sensing the date and time using a computer's internal clock, whether your electronic mailbox contains any messages, whether the Nasdaq has dropped by more than 50% in the last hour, etc. So while the current outlook is bleak for visual sense actions, there still remain many interesting, unproblematic forms of sensing, and many uses for such sense actions, especially in applications involving internet agents and softbots.

11.9   Exercises

1. Using only the abbreviation for **Knows**(ψ, σ), prove the following results, which are therefore independent of any special properties of the K fluent (including our solution to the frame problem):

    (a)   **Knows**$(\phi_1 \wedge \phi_2, s) \equiv$ **Knows**$(\phi_1, s) \wedge$ **Knows**(ϕ_2, s).

    (b)   **Knows**$(\phi, s) \wedge$ **Knows**$(\phi \supset \psi, s) \supset$ **Knows**(ψ, s).

    (c)   **Knows**$(\phi, s) \wedge$ **Knows**$(\phi \equiv \psi, s) \supset$ **Knows**(ψ, s).

    (d)   **Knows**$(\phi(x), s) \wedge$ **Knows**$(x = y, s) \supset$ **Knows**$(\phi(y), s)$.

    (e)   **Knows**$(x = y, s) \wedge$ **KRef**$(x, s) \supset$ **KRef**(y, s).

    (f)   **Knows**$((\forall x)\phi(x), s) \equiv (\forall x)$**Knows**$(\phi(x), s)$.[5]

2. Prove the claims of Section 11.4.4.

3. Prove that the relativized induction principle (11.19) follows from the new foundational axioms for situations needed for knowledge of Section 11.5.1. Hint: Take $P(s)$ to be $S_0 \sqsubseteq s \supset Q(s)$ in (11.17), where Q is a unary predicate variable.

4. Prove that in the presence of the successor state axiom for K, the new foundational axiom (11.18) can be weakened to:

    $K(s, s') \supset [Init(s) \supset Init(s')]$.

5. (a) Prove that in any initial situation, an agent knows he is in an initial situation:

    $Init(s) \supset$ **Knows**$(Init(now), s)$.

    (b) Prove that if there is just one situation accessible to S_0, then in S_0 an agent knows where he is:

    $(\exists! s)K(s, S_0) \supset$ **KRef**(now, S_0).

    (c) Prove that if there are at least two situations accessible from S_0, then in S_0 an

---

5 The right-to-left implication of this sentence is known as the *Barcan formula*. It is valid in first-order modal logics of knowledge and belief that make the *common domain assumption* that all the possible worlds in a Kripke structure have the same domain. When these worlds have different domains of individuals, it is not valid.

agent doesn't know where he is:

$$(\exists s, s')[K(s, S_0) \wedge K(s', S_0) \wedge s \neq s'] \supset \neg\textbf{KRef}(now, S_0).$$

6. Prove that a consequence of the new foundational axioms is that the trees rooted at different initial situations are disjoint:

$$\neg(\exists s, s', s'').Init(s') \wedge Init(s'') \wedge s' \neq s'' \wedge s' \sqsubseteq s \wedge s'' \sqsubseteq s.$$

7. With reference to Section 11.5.2, prove the claims made there about the relationships between reflexive, transitive, symmetric and Euclidean accessibility relations and knowledge as truth, and positive and negative introspection.

8. Prove Theorem 11.5.1.

9. An accessibility relation K is said to be *serial* iff every situation has an accessible situation: $(\forall s)(\exists s')K(s', s)$.

   (a) Prove that for such an accessibility relation, an agent cannot know both ϕ and $\neg\phi$:

   $$\neg(\exists s).\textbf{Knows}(\phi, s) \wedge \textbf{Knows}(\neg\phi, s).$$

   (b) Suppose K is serial in initial situations. Does it follow from the new foundational axioms for situations and the successor state axiom for K that it will be serial in all situations?

10. Prove Propositions 11.6.1 and 11.6.2.

11. Justify the regression operator (11.20) for $read$ actions.

12. With reference to the acidity testing Example 11.6.4, suppose that the initial database consists only of the sentence $\textbf{Knows}(\neg red, S_0)$. Derive that

   $$\textbf{KWhether}(acid, do(sense_R, do(test, S_0))).$$

13. Imagine a robot that lives in a 1-dimensional world, and that can move towards or away from a fixed wall. The robot also has a sonar sensor that tells it when it is close to the wall, that is, less than 10 units away. So we might imagine three actions, *forward* and *backward* that move the robot one unit towards and away from the wall, and a *sonar* sensing action. There are two fluents, $wallDistance(s)$, which gives the actual distance from the robot to the wall in situation s, and the K fluent.

   (a) Write successor state axioms for $wallDistance$ and K.

   (b) Assume the robot is located initially 6 units away from the wall in S_0. Show that after reading the sonar and then moving towards the wall, the robot would know that it was close. In other words, derive

   $$\textbf{Knows}(close, do(forward, do(sonar, S_0))),$$

   where $close(s)$ is an abbreviation for $wallDistance(s) < 10$.

(c) The robot would still be close to the wall if it read the sonar in S_0 and then moved one unit away from the wall. Explain why the robot might not *know* it was close in this situation.

(d) State a reasonable condition on the K fluent in S_0 such that

$$\neg\mathbf{Knows}(close, do(backward, do(sonar, S_0)))$$

follows logically, and show the derivation.

14. The successor state axiom (11.7) for the K fluent does not say anything about the predicate $Poss$. However, it might be reasonable to insist that after performing an action, an agent always comes to know, among other things, that the action was possible. (Perhaps this should not hold if the action is *impossible* in the actual situation, but this need not concern us, since the situation that results from performing an impossible action is not executable anyway.)

(a) Modify K's successor state axiom to incorporate this requirement using the $Poss$ predicate.

(b) Imagine we have the following precondition axiom for the action of picking up an object:

$$Poss(pickup(obj), s) \equiv \neg tooHeavy(obj, s).$$

Moreover, nothing affects whether or not an object is too heavy:

$$tooHeavy(obj, do(a, s)) \equiv tooHeavy(obj, s).$$

Show that your new successor state axiom works properly by deriving a formal version of the following: *If an agent picks up an object, then in the resulting situation, she knows that the object is not too heavy.*

15. Prove Lemma 11.7.3. Hint: First, use Lemma 11.7.2. For the $\Leftarrow$ direction, use the fact that the sentences of $\mathcal{D}_{una}$ are known, and that all logical consequences of what is known are also known. For the $\Rightarrow$ direction, suppose that $\mathcal{K}_{init} \cup \mathcal{D}_{una} \cup \{\mathbf{Knows}(\alpha, S_0), \neg\mathbf{Knows}(\phi, S_0)\}$ is unsatisfiable. Then it must continue to be so with $K(s, s')$ taken to be $s = s'$. Show that this implies the unsatisfiability of $\mathcal{D}_{una} \cup \{\alpha[S_0], \neg\phi[S_0]\}$.

16. Prove Lemma 11.7.10. Hint: Use induction on the number of actions in σ. For the inductive case $do(\alpha, \sigma)$, consider two cases: (1) α is not a sense action, and (2) α is a sense action.

17. Prove Lemma 11.7.12. This takes a bit of proof theory, specifically, the Craig Interpolation Theorem. First, use Theorem 11.6.3 to establish that

$$\mathcal{K}_{init} \cup \mathcal{D}_{una} \cup \{\mathbf{Knows}(\kappa, S_0), \neg\psi_0[S_0], \neg\mathbf{Knows}(\psi_1, S_0), \ldots, \neg\mathbf{Knows}(\psi_n, S_0)\}$$

is unsatisfiable. Therefore, after expanding the **Knows** notation, we have that

$$\mathcal{K}_{init} \cup \mathcal{D}_{una} \cup \{(\forall s).K(s, S_0) \supset \kappa[s], \neg\psi_0[S_0], (\exists s).K(s, S_0) \wedge \neg\psi_1(s), \ldots,$$
$$(\exists s).K(s, S_0) \wedge \neg\psi_n(s)\}$$

is unsatisfiable. Therefore, after skolemizing the existentials, we get that

$$\mathcal{K}_{init} \cup \mathcal{D}_{una} \cup$$
$$\{(\forall s).K(s, S_0) \supset \kappa[s], \neg\psi_0[S_0], K(\sigma_1, S_0), \neg\psi_1(\sigma_1), \ldots, K(\sigma_n, S_0), \neg\psi_n(\sigma_n)\}$$

is unsatisfiable. It remains unsatisfiable if we take

$$K(s, s') = (s = S_0 \vee s = \sigma_1 \vee \cdots \vee s = \sigma_n) \wedge (s' = S_0 \vee s' = \sigma_1 \vee \cdots \vee s' = \sigma_n).$$

With this choice for K, all sentences of $\mathcal{K}_{init}$ become tautologies, and therefore

$$\mathcal{D}_{una} \cup \{\kappa[S_0], \neg\psi_0[S_0]\} \cup \{\kappa[\sigma_1], \neg\psi_1[\sigma_1]\} \cup \cdots \cup \{\kappa[\sigma_n], \neg\psi_n[\sigma_n]\}$$

must be unsatisfiable. Let

$$\{\{\kappa[\sigma_1], \neg\psi_1[\sigma_1]\}, \ldots, \{\kappa[\sigma_m], \neg\psi_m[\sigma_m]\}\}$$

be a minimal subset of

$$\{\{\kappa[\sigma_1], \neg\psi_1[\sigma_1]\}, \ldots, \{\kappa[\sigma_n], \neg\psi_n[\sigma_n]\}\}$$

such that

$$\mathcal{D}_{una} \cup \{\kappa[S_0], \neg\psi_0[S_0]\} \cup \{\kappa[\sigma_1], \neg\psi_1[\sigma_1]\} \cup \cdots \cup \{\kappa[\sigma_m], \neg\psi_m[\sigma_m]\}$$

is unsatisfiable. If $m = 0$, then $\mathcal{D}_{una} \cup \{\kappa[S_0], \neg\psi_0[S_0]\}$ is unsatisfiable, so by Lemma 11.7.3, the result is immediate. Therefore, we can suppose that $m \geq 1$. Next, appropriately use the Craig Interpolation Theorem, noticing that the resulting intersection language consists of equality sentences only.

18. Prove Theorem 11.7.14.

19. Prove Lemma 11.7.17. Hint: Use compactness, and Lemma 11.7.12.

20. Prove Lemma 11.7.18.

21. Prove Lemma 11.7.20. Hint: Use induction on the syntactic form of W, using Lemma 11.7.10 to help prove the base case.

22. Prove Proposition 11.7.22. Hint: Use Lemmas 11.7.10 and 11.7.3.

23. Specify a knowledge-based program for creating a single tower of all the blocks. Give its implementation using provability, and run it on an example blocks world that initially *does* include prior knowledge about the locations of some blocks, for example, that A is on the table, and that B is on A, but that the locations of the remaining blocks is not known.

11.10   Bibliographic Remarks

The possible worlds semantics for modal logics were independently proposed by a number of people, including Kripke [99] and Hintikka [85]. Hintikka's [86] was the first book to treat logics of knowledge. Two excellent sources for modal logics and their applications in artificial intelligence and computer science are Halpern and Moses [79] and Fagin, Halpern, Moses, and Vardi [48]. Two classical textbooks on modal logic are by Hughes and Cresswell [90] and Chellas [33].

The K fluent approach to knowledge in the situation calculus is originally due to Moore [148, 149], and the safe-opening and litmus testing examples are adapted from the latter paper. However, Moore did not propose a solution to the frame problem; that advance was due to Scherl and Levesque [190]. Much of this chapter, including the material on regression, is based on their paper.

There are many important consequences, for dynamical systems modeling, of having a formal account of knowledge in the situation calculus. Within this framework, Bacchus, Halpern, and Levesque [8] have given a probabilistic account of noisy sensors and effectors, and of the problem of interpreting noisy signals from multiple sensors (the sensor fusion problem). Levesque [117] uses knowledge to specify what counts as a plan when the planning agent can sense its environment. Recent work on logical agent specification languages introduces additional modalities corresponding to desires, intentions, etc. Wooldridge [217] provides a comprehensive treatment of this approach to agents within the framework of a temporal logic.

In many respects, our account of **KRef**(t, s) is inadequate for modeling agent knowledge. For example, the referent in situation s of $location(A)$, the physical location of object A, is some objective quantity, say the co-ordinates $(10, 20)$. But we would want to say that an agent knows where A is provided she can locate A *relative* to her own location (three steps forward, then four to the left) *even if she doesn't know her own objective location*. Similarly, we would want to say of an agent that she knows when the bus will arrive if she knows that will be 10 minutes from now, even if she doesn't know what time (in objective terms) it is now. These are examples of *indexical* knowledge, i.e. agent-centred knowledge relative to the agent's current frame of reference. Lespérance and Levesque [106] provide a formal account of indexicals within the framework of traditional modal logic, and Scherl, Levesque, and Lespérance [191] adapt this earlier approach to the situation calculus. For a different treatment of indexical time in the setting of dynamical systems, see Ismail and Shapiro [91].

The logical omniscience problem has troubled many researchers, especially in artificial intelligence, and there have been attempts to overcome it. See, for example, Levesque [113] and Fagin and Halpern [47], both of which formalize a distinction between an agent's implicit and explicit (conscious) knowledge. This latter kind of knowledge does not suffer from full logical omniscience. Chapter 9 of Fagin, Halpern, Moses, and Vardi [48] treats this topic in some detail, and provides a survey of other approaches.

Levesque has given a formal account of the closed-world assumption on knowledge in his logic of *only knowing* [116]. His results have been considerably extended (to include an account within the situation calculus of knowledge) by Lakemeyer and Levesque [118, 103].

The concept of knowledge-based programming was first introduced by Halpern and Fagin [78]. Chapter 7 of Fagin, Halpern, Moses, and Vardi [48] contains an extensive discussion. The material of Section 11.7 on knowledge-based programs with sensing is taken from Reiter [178]. Programs that appeal to knowledge play a prominent role in the literature on agent programming; see, for example, Shoham [200].

Treatments for the effects of sensing actions for Golog programs have been provided by De Giacomo and Levesque [65, 67] and Lakemeyer [101]. An account of on-line sensing that has much in common with ours is given by Pirri and Finzi [164].

With a story for knowledge in hand for the situation calculus, it now becomes possible to give an account of what it means for an agent to be *able* to execute a Golog program (Lespérance, Levesque , Lin, and Scherl [108]). This is important, for example, in modeling multiple agents who are co-operating to achieve some task. In such settings, it only makes sense for one agent to ask another to perform some subtask if the second agent is able to do it, i.e. has enough knowledge to be able to execute the appropriate program for that subtask.

How to integrate reasoning and perception, especially vision, is one of the most important open problems in artificial intelligence. There are very few papers that even attempt an account of how an agent's background knowledge about a world conditions what he sees. See Chella et al [32], Reiter and Mackworth [180] and Grüninger [73] for representative examples. See also Pirri and Finzi [164] for preliminary work on integrating theories of actions with sometimes erroneous sensing, and Bacchus, Halpern, and Levesque [8] for a treatment of noisy sensors, knowledge, and dynamical system modeling.

Agent programming and softbots have become very active research and application areas. Etzioni [45] gives a very readable account of the interesting kinds of problems that can arise in this setting, and the role of active sensing in designing and implementing such systems.

As might be expected, sensing plays an important role in cognitive robotics. Shanahan [193] describes the theory and implementation of a logic-based physical robot (a Rug Warrior) that includes sensing. Cassie is a logic-based robot architecture that takes sensing seriously; it has been under development for many years at the University of Buffalo. For an overview, see Shapiro [198]. Soutchanski [205] describes a robot implementation for the coffee-delivery program of Section 7.4.1 in which the robot monitors its execution of its delivery schedule by sensing and recording the current time in ECLIPSE's temporal constraint store, recomputing a new schedule after each such sense action, then continuing its deliveries under the resulting schedule. Subsumption (Brooks [27]) is a layered architecture for designing reactive agents with sensing—the foundation for what is now called *behaviour-based robotics*. Amir and Maynard-Reid II have axiomatized (in the situation calculus) and implemented (for a Nomad 200 autonomous robot) a real-time subsumption-based controller using first-order theorem-proving to compute the control actions [4].

12 Probability and Decision Theory

Two kinds of uncertainty can arise in modeling dynamical systems (or any other aspect of the world, for that matter). *Logical* uncertainty is typically expressible with disjunction, existential quantification and negation. Flipping a coin has outcome heads *or* tails, but we are uncertain about which will actually occur. After dropping a coin, *there is some* place on the floor where it will end up, but we don't know where that will be. Perhaps we know that John is *not* married to Sue, but we may remain uncertain about who his wife is. *Probabilistic* uncertainty goes beyond such course grained logical representations by quantifying—no pun intended—one's degree of uncertainty. The probability of flipping a head is 0.5; the probability that a dropped coin will end up within distance r of its contact point with the floor is $r * e^{-r^2/2}$.

To this point in the book, we have been concerned only with representing logical uncertainty, and because we allow full first-order logic, all aspects of logical uncertainty are expressible in the situation calculus. For example, an initial database for a basic action theory can be any set of first-order sentences, and therefore, may involve any of the logical connectives. The situation calculus semantics of the nondeterministic choice operators in Golog are expressed with disjunction and existential quantification.

It is often believed that logic and probability theory simply don't mix. Logic is cold and authoritarian, uncompromisingly committed to an all-or-nothing view of the world; propositions are either true or false, with nothing in between. In contrast, probability theory is warm and fuzzy, admitting vague judgements, and a continuum of truth values. Maybe so, but a harmonious marriage of the two is possible, and this chapter shows one way to do it for the purpose of modeling dynamical systems.

12.1 Stochastic Actions and Probability

Stochastic actions are actions with uncertain outcomes that an agent can perform: Flipping a coin, picking up a slippery object, sensing colours at dusk. Moreover, the outcomes of such actions have associated with them suitable probability distributions. How are we to represent such actions and their probability distributions in the situation calculus? The first obstacle is that, throughout this book, the foundations for representing actions and their effects rest on successor state axioms, and these presuppose that all primitive actions are deterministic—they cannot have uncertain outcomes. If the current state of the world is known (as the values of all the fluents) then after performing a primitive action, the successor state axioms predict exactly what will be the resulting state of the world. So if we are to preserve all the hard-earned gains of this book, we cannot treat stochastic actions as primitive actions. The approach we shall take, which is actually pretty standard in probability and decision theory, is to decompose stochastic actions into deterministic primitives.

As an example of this approach, consider a robot whose purpose is to deliver coffee and mail to the inhabitants of an office. We introduce a *stochastic* action $giveCoffee(p)$, meaning that the robot gives a cup of coffee to person p, and we have in mind that this action may succeed or fail (e.g., by the robot spilling the coffee) with certain known probabilities. We decompose the stochastic action $giveCoffee(p)$ into two *deterministic* actions $giveCoffeeS(p)$, meaning the action succeeds, and $giveCoffeeF(p)$, meaning it fails. We view the stochastic action $giveCoffee(p)$ to be under the robot's control; it can choose to perform, or withhold this action. If it elects to perform it, nature steps in and performs exactly one of the deterministic actions $giveCoffeeS(p)$, or $giveCoffeeF(p)$, and there will be probabilities associated with which of these she actually does. Notationally, we characterize this setting by:

$$choice(giveCoffee(p), a) \stackrel{def}{=} a = giveCoffeeS(p) \lor a = giveCoffeeF(p).$$

Introduce one other stochastic action $go(l)$, meaning that the robot goes to location l. It too can succeed or fail:

$$choice(go(l), a) \stackrel{def}{=} a = endUpAt(l) \lor a = getLost(l).$$

Here, $endUpAt(l)$ corresponds to the successful performance of the $go(l)$ action, with the effect that the robot ends up at location l; $getLost(l)$ means that in the process of going to location l, the robot gets lost. We emphasize that neither of these actions are under the robot's control. It gets to decide whether or not to perform a $go(l)$ action; if it chooses to do this action, nature decides which of $endUpAt(l)$ and $getLost(l)$ actually occurs.

In addition, we include a deterministic agent action, $puMail$, meaning that the robot picks up all the mail present in the mail room. We also view such actions as stochastic, but in this case, nature has just one choice as the outcome of the action:

$$choice(puMail, a) \stackrel{def}{=} a = puMail.$$

There is one other deterministic action, $giveMail(p)$, meaning that the robot gives to person p all the mail it is carrying that is addressed to p.

$$choice(giveMail(p), a) \stackrel{def}{=} a = giveMail(p).$$

Introduce the following fluents:

- $mailPresent(p, s)$: There is mail for person p present in the mail room.
- $carryingMail(p, s)$: The robot is carrying mail for person p.
- $loc(s)$: A functional fluent denoting the robot's location.

- $coffeeRequested(p, s)$: Person p has requested a coffee delivery.

Because nature's actions $endUpAt(l)$, $getLost(l)$, $giveCoffeeS(p)$, $giveCoffeeF(p)$, $puMail$ and $giveMail(p)$ are deterministic, it is predictable how they change the state of the world.

$$mailPresent(p, do(a, s)) \equiv mailPresent(p, s) \wedge a \neq puMail,$$

$$carryingMail(p, do(a, s)) \equiv a = puMail \wedge mailPresent(p) \vee$$
$$carryingMail(p, s) \wedge a \neq giveMail(p),$$

$$coffeeRequested(p, do(a, s)) \equiv coffeeRequested(p, s) \wedge$$
$$a \neq giveCoffeeS(p),$$

$$loc(do(a, s)) = l \equiv a = endUpAt(l) \vee (\exists l')a = getLost(l') \wedge l = BlackHole \vee$$
$$loc(s) = BlackHole \wedge l = BlackHole \vee$$
$$loc(s) \neq BlackHole \wedge \neg(\exists l')[a = endUpAt(l') \wedge loc(s) \neq l'] \wedge$$
$$\neg(\exists l')a = getLost(l') \wedge l = loc(s).$$

The last axiom introduces a special location, $BlackHole$, from which there is no escape. The effect of a $getLost(l)$ action is to locate the robot in the $BlackHole$, and once it gets lost, it stays lost.

Nature's actions have preconditions:

$$Poss(endUpAt(l), s) \equiv l \neq BlackHole \wedge loc(s) \neq BlackHole \wedge loc(s) \neq l,$$

$$Poss(getLost(l), s) \equiv l \neq BlackHole \wedge loc(s) \neq BlackHole \wedge loc(s) \neq l,$$

$$Poss(puMail, s) \equiv loc(s) = MR \wedge (\exists p)mailPresent(p, s),$$

$$Poss(giveMail(p), s) \equiv carryingMail(p, s) \wedge loc(s) = office(p),$$

$$Poss(giveCoffeeS(p), s) \equiv coffeeRequested(p, s) \wedge loc(s) = office(p),$$

$$Poss(giveCoffeeF(p), s) \equiv coffeeRequested(p, s) \wedge loc(s) = office(p).$$

So the robot can attempt to give coffee to person p iff it is in p's office, and p has asked for coffee. Therefore, we are supposing that the robot always has coffee to give. So the scenario we have in mind here is one in which, for example, the robot is equipped with an urn of coffee which it is always carrying, and it dispenses coffee from it as needed. Notice that the action preconditions for nature's choices for the $go(l)$ stochastic action are identical. Similarly for the $giveCoffee(p)$ stochastic action. This will often be the case, but not always. In Section 12.5.1 below, we shall encounter an example, in connection with stochastic sensing actions, where they must be different.

It is not known which of nature's choices actually gets done, but their probabilities are known, and we now consider how to represent this information. This is a little bit delicate, mainly because it is necessary to align the information in an action's precondition axioms with its probabilistic information. Specifically, we must require that whenever one of nature's action's precondition is false, that action will have zero probability, and conversely. Notationally, let $prob(a, \beta, s)$ denote the probability that nature selects deterministic action a as the outcome of stochastic action β in situation s. The above requirements on the relationship between action preconditions and probabilities lead to the following proposal for defining $prob$:

$$prob(a, \beta, s) = p \stackrel{def}{=} choice(\beta, a) \wedge Poss(a, s) \wedge p = prob_0(a, \beta, s) \vee$$
$$[\neg choice(\beta, a) \vee \neg Poss(a, s)] \wedge p = 0. \qquad (12.1)$$

Here, $prob_0(a, \beta, s)$ will be a specification of the probability that a is selected in situation s as the outcome of stochastic action β, given that a is one of nature's choices for β and, moreover, *that a is possible in s*. Specifying probabilities in this way modularizes the axiomatizer's job, and this notation will be adopted in what follows. For the delivery robot, we declare the following probabilities:

$$prob_0(giveCoffeeS(p), giveCoffee(p), s) \stackrel{def}{=} 0.95,$$

$$prob_0(giveCoffeeF(p), giveCoffee(p), s) \stackrel{def}{=} 0.05,$$

$$prob_0(puMail, puMail, s) \stackrel{def}{=} 1,$$

$$prob_0(giveMail(p), giveMail(p), s) \stackrel{def}{=} 1,$$

$$prob_0(endUpAt(l), go(l), s) \stackrel{def}{=} \frac{1000}{1000 + dist(loc(s), l)},$$

$$prob_0(getLost(l), go(l), s) \stackrel{def}{=} \frac{dist(loc(s), l)}{1000 + dist(loc(s), l)}.$$

We have made the probabilities for $endUpAt(l)$ and $getLost(l)$ depend on the distance the robot must travel; the greater this distance, the greater the probability it gets lost.

Notice that according to this definition of $prob$,

$$prob(puMail, giveCoffee(p), s) = 0,$$

$$prob(giveCoffeeS(p), giveMail(p'), s) = 0,$$

and these are intuitively necessary properties for the example.

There is a small anomaly in this story that must be kept in mind. Suppose, in situation s, that the robot is not in person p's office, so that both $\neg Poss(giveCoffeeS(p), s)$ and $\neg Poss(giveCoffeeF(p), s)$. Then according to the definition (12.1) of $prob$,

$$prob(giveCoffeeS(p), giveCoffee(p), s) +$$
$$prob(giveCoffeeF(p), giveCoffee(p), s) = 0.$$

But if $giveCoffeeS(p)$ and $giveCoffeeF(p)$ are the only possible outcomes of the stochastic action $giveCoffee(p)$, their probabilities should sum to 1. This is a general property of definition (12.1): Whenever none of nature's choices are possible for stochastic action β, then their probabilities are all zero, and this runs counter to the principles of probability theory. One technical way to overcome this anomaly in the definition of $prob$ is to introduce a null action for β, in addition to β's choices, and require that the null action occur with probability 1 whenever none of β's choices is possible. Doing so would introduce a lot of notational clutter into our story. Instead, in what follows, we shall be careful to make probability calculations using the above definition of $prob$ only when it is known in advance that at least one of β's choices is possible.

The last remaining task is to specify the initial database. In this, our preliminary excursion into probability theory for the situation calculus, we shall assume that there is no uncertainty about this initial state; we have a complete description of the initial situation:

$$\neg mailPresent(p, S_0), \quad loc(S_0) = MR,$$

$$coffeeRequested(p, S_0) \equiv p = Sue \vee p = Alf,$$

$$carryingMail(p, S_0) \equiv p = Pat \vee p = Sue \vee p = Alf.$$

Of course, this assumption of a complete initial database is unrealistic in general. More likely, probability distributions over the initial fluent values would be given, for example, that the probability of mail being present for Sue is .78, of the robot being in the mail room is .23, etc. Later we shall treat this more general setting, but the moment, we assume a complete initial situation.

There is one important observation to make about the above specification of a delivery robot. *Nowhere have we extended the ontology of the situation calculus.* All probabilistic concepts have been introduced with abbreviations. So, for example, $prob$ and $prob_0$ are not new function symbols of the situation calculus; $choice$ is not a new predicate symbol. Even the stochastic actions $go(l)$ and $puMail$ are not primitive actions in the language. The only action symbols in the language are nature's choices, and these are the deterministic actions required to define a basic action theory. *Taken together, the above axioms are a standard situation calculus basic action theory.* The abbreviations allow one to compute probabilities with the help of this basic action theory, but formally, they are not part of the theory.

12.1.1   How to Specify a Probabilistic Domain: A Guide for the Perplexed

Here, we summarize all the steps needed to formalize a probabilistic domain in the situation calculus.

  1. **Decide on the actions.** There are two kinds:

(a) *Stochastic actions.* Conceptually, these are under the control of the agent, and normally, like $go(l)$, have uncertain outcomes. Syntactically, these are not first class citizens of the situation calculus; they provide an external notation whose meaning is obtained in terms of primitive actions like $getLost(l)$ via suitable abbreviations. In this respect, they are like Golog programs, which also are not terms in the language of the situation calculus, but whose meaning arises from the abbreviation Do.

(b) *Nature's choices.* These are deterministic actions, from which nature can select in response to an agent-performed stochastic action. Syntactically, these are primitive actions of the situation calculus axiomatization for a probabilistic domain; they are first class citizens.

2. **Specify nature's choices.** For each stochastic action $A(\vec{x})$, with finitely many nature's choices $N_1(\vec{x}), \ldots, N_k(\vec{x})$, provide an abbreviation:

$$choice(A(\vec{x}), a) \stackrel{def}{=} a = N_1(\vec{x}) \vee \cdots \vee a = N_k(\vec{x}).$$

The case $k = 1$ is permitted, in which case $A(\vec{x})$ is deterministic, and the convention will be that this *choice* abbreviation is:

$$choice(A(\vec{x}), a) \stackrel{def}{=} a = A(\vec{x}).$$

Notice the assumption here—one we make throughout this chapter—that for each stochastic action nature has just finitely many choices.

3. **Specify the probabilities.** To compute probabilities according to the definition (12.1) for $prob$, it is sufficient to specify $prob_0(\alpha, \beta, s)$ for each of nature's choices α for β. This is the probability that α will be the outcome of stochastic action β, given that α is possible in s.

4. **Verify that a proper probability distribution has been defined.** The axiomatizer must verify that the probabilities specified in item 3 have the right properties. Specifically, the axiomatizer is responsible for verifying that the following two properties follow from her specification:

(a) $prob_0(a, \beta, s)$ is the probability that primitive action a is the outcome of stochastic action β given that it is one of β's choices and that it is possible in s. Therefore, because a is possible in s, this probability must be positive. Therefore, with reference to item 2, the axiomatizer must prove that

$$Poss(N_i(\vec{x}), s) \supset prob_0(N_i(\vec{x}), A(\vec{x}), s) > 0, \qquad i = 1, \ldots, k. \qquad (12.2)$$

(b) If any of nature's choices is possible, then the probabilities of these choices must sum to 1. Therefore, the axiomatizer must prove that

$$Poss(N_1(\vec{x}), s) \vee \cdots \vee Poss(N_k(\vec{x}), s) \supset$$

$$\sum_{i=1}^{k} prob(N_i(\vec{x}), A(\vec{x}), s) = 1. \tag{12.3}$$

It is routine to verify that the earlier specification for the delivery robot has these properties.

5. **Provide a complete initial database.** This means that initially, there is no uncertainty about the initial state of the world. Later, we shall relax this unrealistic assumption.

6. **Provide the rest of the basic action theory.** In other words, give action precondition axioms for each of nature's actions, successor state axioms for each fluent in terms of nature's actions, and unique names axioms for all the primitive actions. We emphasize again that the only primitive actions of this situation calculus theory are those that nature can choose, and these are all deterministic. Stochastic actions, like $go(l)$ are not mentioned anywhere in these axioms.

12.1.2   Some Properties of the Specification

Provided the actions are chosen and specified in accordance with the previous section, a number of essential properties are guaranteed.

Lemma 12.1.1:   *Let $A(\vec{x})$ be a stochastic action with nature's choices determined by*

$$choice(A(\vec{x}), a) \overset{def}{=} a = N_1(\vec{x}) \vee \cdots \vee a = N_k(\vec{x}).$$

Suppose that properties (12.2) and (12.3) have been verified. Then the following sentences follow from these properties, and the definition (12.1) of $prob$:

1. All probabilities are bounded by 0 and 1:

$$(\forall a, \vec{x}, s).0 \le prob(a, A(\vec{x}), s) \le 1.$$

2. All non-outcomes of $A(\vec{x})$ have probability 0.

$$(\forall a, \vec{x}, s).\neg choice(A(\vec{x}), a) \supset prob(a, A(\vec{x}), s) = 0.$$

3. Nature's choices are possible iff they have non-zero probability.

$$(\forall \vec{x}, s).Poss(N_i(\vec{x}), s) \equiv prob(N_i(\vec{x}), A(\vec{x}), s) > 0.$$

Proof: Exercise 1 below. ∎

12.2   Derived Probabilities

With a specification for a probabilistic domain in hand, like that for the delivery robot above, we now inquire what it is good for. One important use is in determining how probable some state of affairs will be after an agent performs a sequence of stochastic actions. For example, consider the sequence

$$go(office(Sue)) \, ; \; giveMail(Sue) \, ; \; giveCoffee(Sue) \, ; \; giveCoffee(Sue).^1$$

We might wish to know the probability that *Sue* has coffee after this program is performed. Figure 12.1 indicates how we propose to answer such questions. There has been drawn the tree of all possible outcomes of this program, together with fluent truth values for the robot's locations and for properties of *Sue* in all the situations in this tree, together with the probabilities of nature's choices at each situation. The leaves of this tree are of particular interest; they are the terminating situations of the above action sequence. The two topmost leaves are self-explanatory. Consider next the leftmost leaf, $do([endUpAt(office(Sue)), giveMail(Sue), giveCoffeeS(Sue)], S_0)$, which embodies a convention that we now discuss. Because $\neg coffeeRequested(Sue)$ is true in this situation, none of nature's choices for the second $giveCoffee(Sue)$ in the program are possible, so the remainder of the program, namely $giveCoffee(Sue)$ cannot be executed. Similarly, at the rightmost leaf $do(getLost(office(Sue)), S_0)$, the remainder of the program, namely $giveMail(Sue) \, ; \; giveCoffee(Sue) \, ; \; giveCoffee(Sue)$ cannot be executed because the preconditions for $giveMail(Sue)$ are false. These are examples of a general convention that we shall adopt: *When nature cannot choose an executable outcome for a sequential program's stochastic action, treat this situation as a premature program termination point, and make it a leaf for the program's tree of situations.* In effect, this convention says that whenever an impossible stochastic action is encountered while executing a program, stop the program execution.

One could imagine other conventions, for example, continuing with the next program action instead of creating a premature program termination point. But some such convention is needed because of the peculiar character of straight-line programs. In practice, no one would want to write unnatural programs like that of Figure 12.1. Instead, programs would take into account the contingent outcomes of their stochastic actions by explicitly testing for these outcomes, along the following lines:

$go(office(Sue))$;
if $loc = BlackHole$ **then** *stop*
else if $carryingMail(Sue)$ **then** $giveMail(Sue)$;
    if $coffeeRequested(Sue)$ **then** $giveCoffee(Sue)$;
                            if $hasCoffee(Sue)$ **then** *stop*
                            else $giveCoffee(Sue)$

---

1 Our choice of Golog's ; notation for sequence is no accident here. Later we shall generalize these sequential programs to include a larger class of Golog programs.

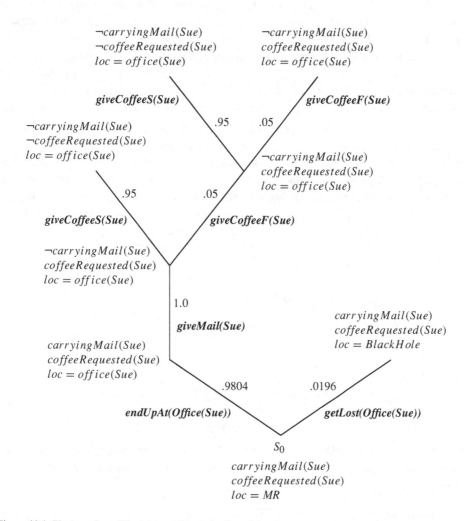

Figure 12.1: The tree of possible outcomes for stochastic action sequence
go(office(Sue)); *giveMail(Sue)*; *giveCoffee(Sue)*; *giveCoffee(Sue)*.

For programs like this, premature termination cannot occur, so the above convention is irrelevant. In the next section, we shall provide for such programs, but for the moment, we consider only straight-line programs like that of Figure 12.1, unrealistic as they might be.

Figure 12.1 provides all the information needed to compute probabilities for various states of affairs after the execution of the above action sequence. For example, the probability that *Sue* will not be requesting coffee is just the sum of the probabilities of those leaf situations in which $\neg coffeeRequested(Sue)$ is true, namely, $.9804 \times 1.0 \times .95 + .9804 \times 1.0 \times .05 \times .95$.[2] The probability that the robot will be carrying mail for *Sue* is .0196. The probability that *Sue* will not be requesting coffee or the robot will be carrying mail for *Sue* is $.0196 + .9804 \times 1.0 \times .05 \times .95 + .9804 \times 1.0 \times .95$. The probability that the robot will not be in the mail room is 1. In general, *the probability of any situation-suppressed sentence ψ is simply the sum of the probabilities of those leaf situations in which ψ is true.*

We can now specify an interpreter for stochastic action sequences that terminates in a situation iff it is a leaf of the tree of situations for that sequence; in addition, the interpreter returns the probability that this leaf is the result of the stochastic action sequence. The interpreter, $stDo$, expects a sequence $\alpha_1 ; \alpha_2 ; \cdots ; \alpha_n ; nil$, where the α_i are stochastic actions, and nil is a dummy symbol indicating the end of the sequence. nil is needed because, in processing the current action in the sequence, $stDo$ must "look ahead" to the next action, and therefore, there must always be a next action, in particular, when the current action is α_n.

$$stDo(nil, p, s, s') \stackrel{def}{=} s = s' \wedge p = 1.$$

Associate the sequence operator to the right:

$$stDo((\alpha ; \beta) ; \gamma, p, s, s') \stackrel{def}{=} stDo(\alpha ; (\beta ; \gamma), p, s, s').$$

Whenever α is a stochastic action,

$$\begin{aligned} stDo(\alpha ; \beta, p, s, s') &\stackrel{def}{=} \\ &\neg(\exists a)[choice(\alpha, a) \wedge Poss(a, s)] \wedge s = s' \wedge p = 1 \vee \\ &(\exists a).choice(\alpha, a) \wedge Poss(a, s) \wedge \\ &\quad (\exists p').stDo(\beta, p', do(a, s), s') \wedge p = prob(a, \alpha, s) * p'. \end{aligned} \qquad (12.4)$$

With the help of $stDo$, we can define what is meant by the probability that some situation-suppressed sentence ψ will be true after executing a sequence of stochastic actions γ:

$$probF(\psi, \gamma) \stackrel{def}{=} \sum_{\{(p,\sigma) | \mathcal{D} \models stDo(\gamma ; nil, p, S_0, \sigma) \wedge \psi[\sigma]\}} p. \qquad (12.5)$$

Here, $\mathcal{D}$ stands for the background basic action theory, for example, the one for the delivery robot. In other words, the probability of ψ after executing the sequence of stochastic actions γ is simply the sum of the probabilities of those leaves in the tree of possible outcomes for γ in which ψ is true.

---

2 We here suppose $dist(MR, office(Sue)) = 20$; hence the numbers .9804 and .0196.

12.2.1 stGolog: Stochastic Golog

Having developed the above story for sequences of stochastic actions, it is only natural
to generalize this to a larger class of Golog-like programs, and that is what we now do.
Specifically, we consider *stGolog programs* that can be constructed from stochastic actions
together with the Golog program constructors sequence, tests, while loops, conditionals
and procedures. Notice that these differ from "traditional" Golog programs because they
are based on stochastic actions, not, as in Golog, on primitive actions.[3] Notice especially
that stGolog programs do *not* involve any form of nondeterminism; neither the nondeter-
ministic choice, |, of two actions, nor the π operator are allowed. In this sense, stGolog
programs are entirely deterministic.

   We can now generalize the *stDo* interpreter of the previous section to cover all stGolog
programs. Rather than give its formal specification in full—a straightforward exercise—we
simply give its Prolog code.

An stGolog Interpreter

```
stDo(nil,1,S,S).
stDo(A : B,P,S1,S2) :- stochastic(A),
   (not (choice(A,C), poss(C,S1)), !,   % Program can't continue.
   S2 = S1, P = 1 ;                      % Create a leaf.
  % once is an Eclipse Prolog built-in. once(G) succeeds the first time
  % G succeeds, and never tries again under backtracking. We use it here
  % to prevent stDo from generating the same leaf situation more than
  % once, when poss has multiple solutions.
   choice(A,C), once(poss(C,S1)), prob(C,A,S1,P1),
   stDo(B,P2,do(C,S1),S2), P is P1 * P2 ).
stDo((A : B) : C,P,S1,S2) :- stDo(A : (B : C),P,S1,S2).
stDo(?(T) : A,P,S1,S2) :- holds(T,S1), !, stDo(A,P,S1,S2) ;
                          S2 = S1, P = 1. % Program can't continue.
                                          % Create a leaf.
stDo(if(T,A,B) : C,P,S1,S2) :- holds(T,S1), !, stDo(A : C,P,S1,S2) ;
                          stDo(B : C,P,S1,S2).
stDo(A : B,P,S1,S2) :- proc(A,C), stDo(C : B,P,S1,S2).
stDo(while(T,A) : B,P,S1,S2) :- holds(T,S1), !,
                          stDo(A : while(T,A) : B,P,S1,S2) ;
                          stDo(B,P,S1,S2).

prob(C,A,S,P) :- choice(A,C), poss(C,S), !, prob0(C,A,S,P) ; P = 0.0 .
```

---

3 Recall that stochastic actions are not primitive; only nature's choices are. Indeed, stochastic actions are not
even terms in the language of the situation calculus.

```
stochastic(A) :- choice(A,N), !.

% The clauses for holds are those of the standard Golog interpreter.
```

The stGolog interpreter generates the leaves of the tree of possible outcomes of an stGolog program, together with their probabilities. In this more general setting, (12.5) continues to define the probability that a situation-suppressed sentence ψ will be true after executing an stGolog program γ. Implementing this is straightforward.

Probabilities for stGolog Programs

```
probF(F,Prog,Prob) :- findall(P,
                              S^(stDo(Prog : nil,P,s0,S), once(holds(F,S))),
                              PS),
                      addNumbers(PS,Prob).
addNumbers([],0.0).
addNumbers([N | Ns],Sum) :- addNumbers(Ns,Sum1), Sum is Sum1 + N.
```

We are now positioned to compute some probabilities. First, translate into Prolog the specification for the delivery robot.

Delivery Robot in Prolog

```
% Declare nature's choices.

choice(giveCoffee(P),C) :- C = giveCoffeeS(P) ; C = giveCoffeeF(P).
choice(go(L),C) :- C = endUpAt(L) ; C = getLost(L).
choice(puMail,C) :- C = puMail.
choice(giveMail(P),C) :- C = giveMail(P).

% Action precondition and successor state axioms.

poss(puMail,S) :- loc(mr,S), mailPresent(P,S).
poss(giveMail(P),S) :- carryingMail(P,S), loc(office(P),S).
poss(giveCoffeeS(P),S) :- coffeeRequested(P,S), loc(office(P),S).
poss(giveCoffeeF(P),S) :- coffeeRequested(P,S), loc(office(P),S).
poss(endUpAt(L),S) :- not L = blackHole, loc(L1,S), not L1 = blackHole,
                      not L1 = L.
poss(getLost(L),S) :- not L = blackHole, loc(L1,S), not L1 = blackHole,
                      not L1 = L.

mailPresent(P,do(A,S)) :- not A = puMail, mailPresent(P,S).
coffeeRequested(P,do(A,S)) :- coffeeRequested(P,S), not A = giveCoffeeS(P).
carryingMail(P,do(A,S)) :- A = puMail, mailPresent(P,S) ;
```

```
                                carryingMail(P,S), not A = giveMail(P).
loc(L,do(A,S)) :- A = endUpAt(L) ; A = getLost(L1), L = blackHole ;
                  loc(blackHole,S), L = blackHole ;
                  loc(L,S), not L = blackHole, not A = getLost(L1),
                  not (A = endUpAt(L1), not L = L1).
```

% Probabilities.

```
prob0(giveCoffeeS(P),giveCoffee(P),S,Pr) :- Pr = 0.95 .
prob0(giveCoffeeF(P),giveCoffee(P),S,Pr) :- Pr = 0.05 .
prob0(giveMail(P),giveMail(P),S,Pr) :- Pr = 1.0 .
prob0(puMail,puMail,S,Pr) :- Pr = 1.0 .
prob0(endUpAt(L),go(L),S,Pr) :- loc(L0,S), dist(L0,L,D),
                                Pr is 1000 / (1000 + D).
prob0(getLost(L),go(L),S,Pr) :- loc(L0,S), dist(L0,L,D),
                                Pr is D / (1000 + D).
```
% Initial database.

```
loc(mr,s0).
carryingMail(p,s0) :- P = pat ; P = sue ; P = alf.
coffeeRequested(P,s0) :- P = sue ; P = alf.
```

% The offices are strung out along a single line. mr is on the left.
% office(pat) is to its immediate right at a distance of 10. office(sue)
% is to the immediate right of office(pat) at a distance of 10. Etc.

```
distances([mr,10,office(pat),10,office(sue),10,office(ann),10,
           office(bob),10,office(sam),10,office(alf)]).
```

```
dist(X,Y,D) :- distances(A), (dist0(X,Y,A,D), ! ; dist0(Y,X,A,D)).
```

```
dist0(X,X,A,0).
dist0(X,Y,A,D) :- tail([X,DX | [Z | L]],A),
                  dist0(Z,Y,[Z | L],DR), D is DX + DR.
```

```
tail(L,L).
tail(L,[X | Xs]) :- tail(L,Xs).
```

```
restoreSitArg(coffeeRequested(P),S,coffeeRequested(P,S)).
restoreSitArg(mailPresent(P),S,mailPresent(P,S)).
restoreSitArg(loc(L),S,loc(L,S)).
restoreSitArg(carryingMail(P),S,carryingMail(P,S)).
```

Next, load the stGolog interpreter and Prolog code for probF given above, and the robot program, and compute some probabilities.

Computing Probabilities for Various Sentences and stGolog Programs

```
% First, verify the leaves of Figure 12.1.

[eclipse 2]: stDo(go(office(sue)) : giveMail(sue) : giveCoffee(sue) :
                giveCoffee(sue) : nil,P,s0,S).
P = 0.931372523
S = do(giveCoffeeS(sue), do(giveMail(sue),
      do(endUpAt(office(sue)), s0))))      More? (;)


P = 0.0465686284
S = do(giveCoffeeS(sue), do(giveCoffeeF(sue), do(giveMail(sue),
      do(endUpAt(office(sue)), s0))))      More? (;)


P = 0.00245098048
S = do(giveCoffeeF(sue), do(giveCoffeeF(sue), do(giveMail(sue),
      do(endUpAt(office(sue)), s0))))      More? (;)


P = 0.0196078438
S = do(getLost(office(sue)), s0)      More? (;)
no (more) solution.

% Next, verify that the probabilities sum to 1.

[eclipse 3]: probF(true,
                go(office(sue)) : giveCoffee(sue) : go(office(pat)),P).
P = 1.0

% Finally, compute some other probabilities for the robot.

[eclipse 4]: probF(coffeeRequested(sue),
                go(office(sue)) : giveCoffee(sue) :
                if(-coffeeRequested(sue), giveMail(sue),
                                        giveCoffee(sue)), P).
P = 0.0220588241

[eclipse 5]: probF(coffeeRequested(sue) <=> carryingMail(sue),
                go(office(sue)) : giveCoffee(sue) : giveMail(sue), P).
P = 0.950980365

[eclipse 6]: probF(-carryingMail(sue),
                go(office(sue)) : giveCoffee(sue) :
                ?(-coffeeRequested(sue)) : giveMail(sue), P).
```

```
P = 0.931372523

[eclipse 7]: probF(some(x,some(y,coffeeRequested(x) &
                        loc(office(y)) & -(x = y))),
               go(office(sue)) : giveCoffee(sue) : go(office(pat)), P).

P = 0.970685303
```

12.3 Exogenous Events

In addition to selecting the outcomes of agent initiated stochastic actions, nature can initiate her own *exogenous* actions. One desirable property of the delivery robot is that it respond appropriately to a request from *Pat* for some coffee, and also to the arrival of mail to be delivered to *Sue*. Conceptually, neither of these actions—*Pat* requesting coffee, mail arriving for *Sue*—is under the robot's control, and therefore, relative to designing control programs for this agent, they must be viewed as exogenous.

We now generalize the stGolog interpreter to accommodate exogenous action occurrences. This we do by generalizing the transition relation (12.4) for a stochastic agent action:

$$stDo(\alpha\,;\,\beta, p, s, s') \stackrel{def}{=} \neg(\exists a)[choice(\alpha, a) \wedge Poss(a, s)] \wedge s = s' \wedge p = 1 \vee$$
$$(\exists a).choice(\alpha, a) \wedge Poss(a, s) \wedge$$
$$(\exists p', s'').exoTransition(\alpha, a, p', s, s'') \wedge (\exists p'').stDo(\beta, p'', s'', s') \wedge$$
$$p = p' * p''.$$

Here, we are taking a very general approach in specifying the effects of exogenous events; $exoTransition(\alpha, a, p, s, s')$ is left completely open. Its intended meaning is that s' is one of the situations resulting from performing the outcome a of stochastic action α *in conjunction with any exogenous actions that also occur*, and p is the probability of the resulting transition. Notice the similarity in the treatment here of exogenous actions and that of Section 8.2.2 for reactive Golog. If exogenous actions are not being taken into account, simply declare

$$exoTransition(\alpha, a, p, s, s') \stackrel{def}{=} s' = do(a, s) \wedge p = prob(a, \alpha, s),$$

thereby recovering the earlier stGolog interpreter of Section 12.2.1.

This is much too general to implement; a commitment is needed to a specific exogenous event model describing, via $exoTransition(\alpha, a, p, s, s')$, exactly how exogenous events relate to the action a, and how to compute the probability p of the transition from s to s'. There are many possibilities for this. Often, the literature provides an interleaving event model, under which some number of exogenous events may occur between every pair of stochastic action outcomes in an execution history. That is what we shall do here, by way of an illustrative example. To maintain a high level of generality, we shall allow the interleaved exogenous events to be described by an arbitrary Golog program called *exoProgram*. Notice how the Golog interpreter *Do* is invoked on this exogenous event program in the following specification:

$$exoTransition(\alpha, a, p, s, s') \stackrel{def}{=} Do(exoProgram, do(a, s), s') \wedge$$
$$p = prob(a, \alpha, s) * exoTransitionProb(do(a, s), s').$$

Here, $exoTransitionProb(s, s')$ denotes the probability of the transition from s to s' via a sequence of exogenous events, defined by:

$$exoTransitionProb(s, s) \stackrel{def}{=} 1,$$

$$exoTransitionProb(s, do([e_1, \ldots, e_k], s)) \stackrel{def}{=}$$
$$exoProb(e_k, do([e_1, \ldots, e_{k-1}], s)) *$$
$$exoTransitionProb(s, do([e_1, \ldots, e_{k-1}], s)).$$

The above description of $exoTransition(\alpha, a, p, s, s')$ specifies that first the action a occurs, followed by the exogenous action sequence resulting from evaluating the Golog program *exoProgram*. We could as easily have decided that the exogenous actions occur first, followed by a, or that a gets inserted into the middle of the exogenous actions.

The above specifications translate into Prolog in the usual way:

Clauses for Exogenous Transitions

```
stDo(A : B,P,S1,S2) :- stochastic(A),
 (not (choice(A,C), poss(C,S1)), !, S2 = S1, P = 1 ; % Program can't
                                                 % continue. Create a leaf.
  choice(A,C), once(poss(C,S1)),
  exoTransition(A,C,P1,S1,S3), stDo(B,P2,S3,S2), P is P1 * P2).

exoTransition(A,C,P,S1,S2) :- setof(S,do(exoProgram,do(C,S1),S),Ss),
             member(S2,Ss), exoTransitionProb(do(C,S1),S2,P2),
             prob(C,A,S1,P1), P is P1 * P2.

exoTransitionProb(S,S,1).
exoTransitionProb(S1,do(E,S2),P) :- exoTransitionProb(S1,S2,P1),
                              exoProb(E,S2,P2), !, P is P1 * P2.
% Notice the cut! exoProb(E,S2,P2) might have multiple solutions (all the
% same if the probabilities have been correctly axiomatized). The cut
% prevents stDo from generating multiple identical branches in its tree.
```

We continue now with the ongoing delivery robot, and include some exogenous actions, of which there are three kinds, for the purposes of this example:

1. Someone requests delivery of a cup of coffee.
2. Mail arrives for someone in the mail room.
3. All the mail that the robot is carrying gets stolen.

One way to represent these exogenous actions is to introduce them explicitly:

$$requestCoffee(p), \ mailArrives(p), \ \text{and} \ stealMail.$$

We could then give them suitable action precondition axioms, and appropriately modify the successor state axioms of Section 12.1 to take them into account. A conceptually and computationally simpler representation, which we shall adopt, is to introduce a single, monolithic exogenous action $exo(m, c, sm)$. Here, m and c are subsets of the set of all people in the delivery domain, and sm is one of $StealMail$ or $NoStealMail$. $exo(m, c, sm)$ is that action whose effects are that mail arrives for all and only the members of m, coffee is requested by all and only the members of c, and mail is, or is not, stolen according to the value of sm. Here is its action precondition axiom:

$$Poss(exo(m, c, sm), s) \equiv (\forall p)[p \in m \supset person(p)] \wedge$$
$$(\forall p)[p \in c \supset person(p) \wedge \neg coffeeRequested(p, s)] \wedge$$
$$[sm = StealMail \wedge (\exists p)carryingMail(p, s) \vee sm = NoStealMail].$$

$exo(m, c, sm)$ affects many of the fluents in the delivery domain, and therefore, these need to be redefined:

$$mailPresent(p, do(a, s)) \equiv (\exists m, c, sm)[a = exo(m, c, sm) \wedge p \in m] \vee$$
$$mailPresent(p, s) \wedge a \neq puMail.$$

$$coffeeRequested(p, do(a, s)) \equiv (\exists m, c, sm)[a = exo(m, c, sm) \wedge p \in c] \vee$$
$$coffeeRequested(p, s) \wedge a \neq giveCoffeeS(p).$$

$$carryingMail(p, do(a, s)) \equiv mailPresent(p, s) \wedge a = puMail \vee$$
$$carryingMail(p, s) \wedge a \neq giveMail(p) \wedge \neg(\exists m, c)a = exo(m, c, StealMail).$$

Next, we consider appropriate conditions under which $exo(m, c, sm)$ occurs, interleaved with the robot's control actions. To best model this in a realistic fashion, we should conceptualize the delivery domain in terms of processes,[4] and imagine that exogenous actions can occur only while these processes are in progress. For the delivery domain, a natural process is $going(l, s)$, meaning that the robot is in the process of going to location l. We could also introduce other processes—giving coffee, picking up mail, giving mail—but we shall view these actions as taking an insignificant amount of time compared to that of traveling from one location to another, and we shall treat these as instantaneous

---

4 See Section 7.3, and also the coffee delivery robot of Section 7.4.1.

actions, with no associated processes. Therefore, $going(l, s)$ will be the only process, and only while $going(l, s)$ is true will exogenous events be allowed to occur. Conceptually, we are now viewing the robot's $go(l)$ action as initiating the process $going(l, s)$. Since $go(l)$ is now a deterministic process initiating action, it will no longer have $endUpAt(l)$ and $getLost(l)$ as nature's choices. Instead, we shall use these to terminate any $going(l)$ process initiated by $go(l)$. One way to do this is to provide a stochastic agent action $endGo(l)$, with nature's choices $endUpAt(l)$ and $getLost(l)$. The downside to this is that the robot (or more accurately, the robot's programmer) now must issue an $endGo(l)$ action after every $go(l)$ action, much as for the coffee delivery robot in Section 7.4.1. But if $endGo(l)$ is obligatory after a $go(l)$, there is something artificial about forcing the programmer to explicitly include it in his programs. In Section 7.4.1, we had no mechanism for avoiding this annoying problem, but now we do. Simply make $endUpAt(l)$ and $getLost(l)$ exogenous, forcing one of them to occur during each $going(l, s)$ process.

So the current picture is this: $go(l)$ is now a deterministic agent action that initiates a $going(l, s)$ process, $exo(m, c, sm)$ occurs only during this process, and $endUpAt(l)$ and $getLost(l)$ are exogenous actions that terminate this process. To axiomatize these properties, we must make the following changes to the delivery specification of Section 12.1:

$$choice(go(l), a) \stackrel{def}{=} a = go(l).$$

$$prob_0(go(l), go(l), s) \stackrel{def}{=} 1.0,$$

$$Poss(go(l), s)) \equiv l \neq loc(s) \wedge loc(s) \neq BlackHole \wedge l \neq BlackHole \wedge$$
$$\neg(\exists l')going(l', s).$$

$$Poss(endUpAt(l), s) \equiv going(l, s),$$

$$Poss(getLost(l), s) \equiv going(l, s),$$

$$going(l, do(a, s)) \equiv a = go(l) \vee going(l, s) \wedge a \neq endUpAt(l) \wedge a \neq getLost(l).$$

Finally, probability distributions must be specified for the exogenous actions. We use the same distributions for $endUpAt$ and $getLost$ as in Section 12.1:

$$exoProb(endUpAt(l), s) \stackrel{def}{=} \frac{1000}{1000 + dist(loc(s), l)},$$

$$exoProb(getLost(l), s) \stackrel{def}{=} \frac{dist(loc(s), l)}{1000 + dist(loc(s), l)}.$$

Assume independence of the component exogenous actions in $exo(m, c, sm)$:

$$exoProb(exo(m, c, sm), s) \stackrel{def}{=} exoProbMailArrives(m, s) *$$
$$exoProbRequestCoffee(c, s) *$$
$$exoProbMailStolen(sm, s).$$

The probability that mail gets stolen depends on how far the robot is traveling:

$$exoProbMailStolen(sm, s) = pr \stackrel{def}{=} (\exists p)carryingMail(p, s) \wedge$$
$$(\exists l)[going(l, s) \wedge (sm = StealMail \wedge pr = \frac{dist(loc(s),l)}{5000+dist(loc(s),l)} \vee$$
$$sm = NoStealMail \wedge pr = \frac{5000}{5000+dist(loc(s),l)})] \vee$$
$$\neg[(\exists p)carryingMail(p, s) \wedge (\exists l)going(l, s)] \wedge$$
$$(sm = StealMail \wedge pr = 0.0 \vee sm = NoStealMail \wedge pr = 1.0).$$

$exoProbMailArrives(m, s)$ is the probability that mail arrives exogenously for all and only those people in m. Therefore, it is the product of the probabilities that mail arrives for each $p \in m$ times the product of the probabilities that mail doesn't arrive for each $p \notin m$:

$$exoProbMailArrives(m, s) \stackrel{def}{=} \prod_{p \in m} probMailArrives(p, s) *$$
$$\prod_{\{p \mid p \notin m, \ \mathcal{D} \models person(p)\}} (1 - probMailArrives(p, s)).$$

In treating stolen mail, we made the probability depend on the distance the robot is traveling. We resist being this fancy again, and simply take the probability of mail arriving for a single person p to be 0.005, even though intuitively, this probability also depends on how long the robot's $going$ process takes, and also on who p is—maybe Sue gets more mail than Pat.

$$probMailArrives(p, s) \stackrel{def}{=} 0.005.$$

The probability for exogenous coffee requests is much the same:

$$exoProbRequestCoffee(c, s) \stackrel{def}{=} \prod_{p \in c} probRequestsCoffee(p, s) *$$
$$\prod_{\{p \mid p \notin c, \ \mathcal{D} \models person(p)\}} (1 - probRequestsCoffee(p, s)).$$

Again, we won't be too fancy:

$$probRequestsCoffee(p, s) = pr \stackrel{def}{=} coffeeRequested(p, s) \wedge pr = 0.0 \vee$$
$$\neg coffeeRequested(p, s) \wedge pr = 0.01.$$

Finally, to implement the above interleaving event model, we need to fix on a program $exoProgram$. As discussed above, we shall monitor for exogenous events only while the robot is $going$ from one location to another, and all such $going$ processes are terminated, not by the robot, but by the exogenous occurrence of one of $endUpAt$ or $getLost$. Therefore, take the exogenous program to be:

proc $exoProgram$
$\neg(\exists l)going(l)? \mid$
$(\pi \ l, m, c, sm).going(l)? ; exo(m, c, sm) ; (endUpAt(l) \mid getLost(l))$

endProc

We now present the Prolog code for the above specification of a delivery robot with exogenous actions. The code departs from the specification in only one respect, which we now discuss. Recall that the parameters m and c of $exo(m, c, sm)$ stand for subsets of all the people—say there are n of them—inhabiting the office. This means that, including the two values that sm can take on, there can be as many as 2^{2n+1} possible exogenous actions occurring during a *going* process; even for small n ($n = 6$ in the example below) this can make the tree of situations produced by stGolog impossibly large. Accordingly, some way is needed to improve the combinatorics of the problem, and this we do in the program by ignoring instances of $exo(m, c, sm)$ with very small probabilities. See the clause for poss(exo(M,C,Sm),S) for the details.

Clauses for the Delivery Robot with Exogenous Events

```
% We give only the clauses that differ from those of the previous
% section for the delivery robot in the absence of exogenous events.

% Declare nature's choices.

choice(go(L),C) :- C = go(L).

% Action precondition and successor state axioms.

poss(go(L),S) :- not going(L1,S), not L = blackHole,
                 loc(L1,S), not L1 = blackHole, not L1 = L.
poss(endUpAt(L),S) :- going(L,S).
poss(getLost(L),S) :- going(L,S).

poss(exo(M,C,Sm),S) :- findall(P,person(P),Ps),
     findall(P,(member(P,Ps), not coffeeRequested(P,S)),Cs),
     findall([M,C,Sm],
             P^Prm^Prc^Prob^
             (subset(M,Ps),
             % Filter out those sets of mail arrivals with very
             % small probabilies.
              exoProbMailArrives(M,S,Prm), Prm > 0.0001,
              subset(C,Cs),
             % Filter out those sets of mail arrivals and coffee
             % requests with very small combined probabilities.
              exoProbRequestCoffee(C,S,Prc), Prob is Prm * Prc,
              Prob > 0.0001,
              (Sm = stealMail, once(carryingMail(P,S)) ;
               Sm = noStealMail)),
```

```
                  Args),
        member([M,C,Sm],Args).

going(L,do(A,S)) :- A = go(L) ; going(L,S), not A = endUpAt(L),
                                 not A = getLost(L).
mailPresent(P,do(A,S)) :- A = exo(M,_,_), member(P,M) ;
                          not A = puMail, mailPresent(P,S).
coffeeRequested(P,do(A,S)) :- A = exo(_,C,_), member(P,C) ;
                              coffeeRequested(P,S), not A = giveCoffeeS(P).
carryingMail(P,do(A,S)) :- A = puMail, mailPresent(P,S) ;
                           carryingMail(P,S), not A = giveMail(P),
                           not A = exo(_,_,stealMail).


% Probabilities.

prob0(go(L),go(L),S,Pr) :- Pr = 1.0 .

exoProb(endUpAt(L),S,Pr) :- loc(L0,S), dist(L0,L,D),
                            Pr is 1000 / (1000 + D).
exoProb(getLost(L),S,Pr) :- loc(L0,S), dist(L0,L,D), Pr is D / (1000 + D).
exoProb(exo(M,C,SM),S,Pr) :- exoProbMailArrives(M,S,PM),
                             exoProbRequestCoffee(C,S,PC),
                             exoProbMailStolen(SM,S,PS),
                             Pr is PM * PC * PS.
exoProbMailStolen(SM,S,Pr) :- carryingMail(P,S), going(L,S),
                              loc(L0,S), dist(L0,L,D),
                              (SM = stealMail, Pr is D / (5000 + D) ;
                               SM = noStealMail, Pr is 5000 / (5000 + D)) ;
                              not (carryingMail(P,S), going(L,S)),
                              (SM = stealMail, Pr is 0.0 ;
                               SM = noStealMail, Pr is 1.0).
exoProbMailArrives(M,S,Pr) :-
            % First compute the probability, Pr1, that mail arrives for
            % all people in M.
               findall(Prob,
                    P^(member(P,M), probMailArrives(P,S,Prob)),
                    ProbList1),
               multiplyNumbers(ProbList1,Pr1),
            % Next, compute the probability, Pr2, that mail doesn't
            % arrive for those people not in M.
               findall(P,person(P),Ps),
               findall(Prob,
                    P^ProbM^(member(P,Ps), not member(P,M),
                             probMailArrives(P,S,ProbM),
```

```
                                    Prob is 1 - ProbM),
                          ProbList2),
                  multiplyNumbers(ProbList2,Pr2),
                  Pr is Pr1 * Pr2.

probMailArrives(P,S,Pr) :- Pr = 0.005 .

exoProbRequestCoffee(C,S,Pr) :-
            % First compute the probability, Pr1, that all people
            % in C issue a request for coffee.
              findall(Prob,
                      P^(member(P,C), probRequestsCoffee(P,S,Prob)),
                      ProbList1),
              multiplyNumbers(ProbList1,Pr1),
            % Next, compute the probability, Pr2, that those people
            % not in C do not request coffee.
              findall(P,person(P),Ps),
              findall(Prob,
                      P^ProbC^(member(P,Ps), not member(P,C),
                               probRequestsCoffee(P,S,ProbC),
                               Prob is 1 - ProbC),
                      ProbList2),
              multiplyNumbers(ProbList2,Pr2),
              Pr is Pr1 * Pr2.

probRequestsCoffee(P,S,Pr) :- coffeeRequested(P,S), Pr = 0.0 ;
                              not coffeeRequested(P,S), Pr = 0.01 .
multiplyNumbers([],1.0).
multiplyNumbers([P | Ps],Prod) :- multiplyNumbers(Ps,Pr), Prod is P * Pr.

% Initial situation. This is the same as before, but we need to enumerate
% the people.

person(P) :- P = pat ; P = sue ; P = alf ; P = sam ; P = ann ; P = bob.

% Misc declarations.

restoreSitArg(going(L),S,going(L,S)).
primitive_action(endUpAt(_)).  primitive_action(getLost(_)).
primitive_action(exo(_,_,_)).

% Golog procedure describing exogenous event occurrences.

proc(exoProgram,
```

```
?(-some(l,going(l))) #
pi(l,?(going(l))) :
     pi(m, pi(c, pi(sm, exo(m,c,sm)))) :
     (endUpAt(l) # getLost(l)))).
```

All the code needed to test our ideas has now been developed. This consists of the exogenous transition version of the stGolog interpreter, the above code for the delivery robot and the Golog procedure *exoProgram*, the clauses for *Do* of the Golog interpreter, and the clauses for probF of Section 12.2.1. After loading these programs, we compute some probabilities.

Computing with stGolog Programs and Exogenous Events

```
% First, generate some leaves for the tree of outcomes for a program.

[eclipse 2]: stDo(go(office(sue)) : giveCoffee(sue) : giveMail(sue) :
                go(mr) : nil,P,s0,S).
P = 0.779201269
S = do(endUpAt(mr), do(exo([], [], noStealMail), do(go(mr),
     do(giveMail(sue), do(giveCoffeeS(sue), do(endUpAt(office(sue)),
        do(exo([], [], noStealMail), do(go(office(sue)), s0)))))))))    More?(;)
P = 0.0.00311680487
S = do(endUpAt(mr), do(exo([], [], stealMail), do(go(mr),
     do(giveMail(sue), do(giveCoffeeS(sue), do(endUpAt(office(sue)),
        do(exo([], [], noStealMail), do(go(office(sue)), s0)))))))))    More?(;)
P = 0.00787071884
S = do(endUpAt(mr), do(exo([], [ann], noStealMail), do(go(mr),
     do(giveMail(sue), do(giveCoffeeS(sue), do(endUpAt(office(sue)),
        do(exo([], [], noStealMail), do(go(office(sue)), s0)))))))))    More?(;)
P = 3.14828758e-05
S = do(endUpAt(mr), do(exo([], [ann], stealMail), do(go(mr),
     do(giveMail(sue), do(giveCoffeeS(sue), do(endUpAt(office(sue)),
        do(exo([], [], noStealMail), do(go(office(sue)), s0)))))))))    More?(;)

*** Several output lines deleted. The next line corresponds to a
    premature program termination. Why? ***

P = 0.00345882843
S = do(giveCoffeeS(sue), do(endUpAt(office(sue)),
     do(exo([], [], stealMail), do(go(office(sue)), s0))))       More? (;)

*** More output lines deleted. ***

P = 3.21221108e-07
```

```
S = do(endUpAt(mr), do(exo([], [bob], stealMail), do(go(mr),
      do(giveMail(sue), do(giveCoffeeS(sue), do(endUpAt(office(sue))),
        do(exo([], [ann], noStealMail), do(go(office(sue)), s0))))))))    (;)
```

*** Lots more. ***

`% Next compute some probabilities.`

```
[eclipse 3]: probF(true,go(office(sue)) : giveCoffee(sue) :
                          go(office(pat)), P).
P = 0.995263457
```

```
[eclipse 4]: probF(some(x,mailPresent(x) & some(y,loc(office(y)) &
                                                -(x = y))),
                    go(office(pat)) : ?(loc(office(pat))) :
                    go(office(sue)), P).
P = 0.0452927761
```

```
[eclipse 5]: probF(all(x,person(x) => -coffeeRequested(x)),
                    go(office(alf)) : giveCoffee(alf) : go(office(sue)) :
                    giveCoffee(sue),P).
P = 0.747314274
```

`% Finally, test the limits of what can be feasibly computed.`

```
[eclipse 6]: cputime(T1),
              probF(true,go(office(sue)) : go(office(pat)) : go(mr) :
                          go(office(alf)),P), cputime(T2), T is T2 - T1.
P = 0.991928697
T = 1080.04
```

Notice the errors introduced by the approximation to exogenous event probabilities. The final computation, involving four *going* processes, took 1080 seconds.[5] This is about the limit of what can be done with this example; adding a fifth process would lead to an intolerable computation. Such cases are not unusual in probabilistic reasoning, where the search spaces tend to grow exponentially with problem size. To solve large problems, approximation techniques become necessary, normally involving Monte Carlo sampling methods, but such considerations are far beyond the scope of this chapter.

The above approach to exogenous events relies on explicitly providing exogenous actions and their probabilities, together with some mechanism for combining these event occurrences with the outcomes of the stochastic actions. This is often called an *explicit ex-*

---

5 On a SUN Enterprise 450, with four 400MHz UltraSPARC-II processors and 4GB of RAM.

ogenous event model. An explicit approach can be computationally very expensive, especially when there are many exogenous actions, because they considerably enlarge the tree of possible outcomes for an stGolog program. An alternative to this, which we do not pursue here, is to provide an *implicit exogenous event model*. Here, the probabilities of exogenous events are *folded* into the probabilities for the stochastic action outcomes, and there are no explicit exogenous actions in the model. So, for example, instead of providing the $exo(m, c, sm)$, $endUpAt(l)$ and $getLost(l)$ exogenous actions, we would instead return to the original style of (exogenous-free) axiomatization of Section 12.1. Within that framework, we would create four nature's choices for $go(l)$, corresponding to whether or not mail got stolen en route: $endUpAtWithMail(l)$, $endUpAtWithoutMail(l)$, $getLost-WithMail(l)$, $getLostWithoutMail(l)$, and we would assign probabilities to these actions that reflect their intended effects. This can quickly get out of hand. Consider that to incorporate all the exogenous events of the delivery robot requires expanding $go(l)$ into

$$coffeeRequestedAndMailArrivesAndEndUpAtWithMail(p_1, p_2, p_3, l),$$

and so forth. Not a pretty picture.

12.4 Uncertainty in the Initial Situation

Up to this point, we have assumed a complete initial database; there has been no provision for uncertainty in the initial situation. This section remedies this limiting assumption.

As an example of what we have in mind, suppose that initially, there is uncertainty only about whether there is mail present for Pat, and about where the robot is located. Specifically, assume it is known that the probability is 0.9 that mail is present for Pat, and the probability is 0.4 that the robot is located in the mail room, and 0.6 that it is located in Sue's office. For all other fluent values, there is no uncertainty, and for the purposes of this example, we shall assume that everyone has requested coffee, there is mail present for Sue, but not for anyone else other than Pat, the robot is not carrying any mail, neither is it in the process of *going* anywhere.[6]

This gives rise to four possible complete states of affairs for the initial database, where, in assigning probabilities to each of the following initial databases, we assume that the robot's location is independent of the *mailPresent* relation.

1. $loc(S_0) = MR$, $mailPresent(p, S_0) \equiv p = Pat \lor p = Sue$,
   with probability 0.4×0.9.
2. $loc(S_0) = MR$, $mailPresent(p, S_0) \equiv p = Sue$,

---

6 So we assume the exogenous event model of the previous section, in which a $go(l)$ action initiates a process $going(l, s)$.

with probability 0.4×0.1.
3. $loc(S_0) = office(Sue)$, $mailPresent(p, S_0) \equiv p = Pat \vee p = Sue$, with probability 0.6×0.9.
4. $loc(S_0) = office(Sue)$, $mailPresent(p, S_0) \equiv p = Sue$, with probability 0.6×0.1.

Moreover, in each of the above possible initial databases

$$\neg carryingMail(p, S_0),   coffeeRequested(p, S_0),   \neg going(l, S_0).$$

In other words, each of these four possible initial databases *is a complete theory about the initial situation*. Also, a probability is associated with each of these complete theories.

Now, imagine starting out with an arbitrary, but fixed, initial database. Any one will do; its properties will turn out to be irrelevant. Next, imagine a stochastic action $bigBang$ with four outcomes, $bang_1, \ldots, bang_4$. Imagine also that the successor state axioms for the delivery robot augmented with the primitive actions $bang_1, \ldots, bang_4$ have been so cunningly crafted that, regardless of what is true in S_0, the effect of $bang_i$ is to deterministically cause all the fluents to take on values that satisfy, in $do(bang_i, S_0)$, all the sentences in complete theory i above. For example, the successor state axioms will entail

$$loc(do(bang_2, S_0)) = MR,   mailPresent(p, do(bang_2, S_0)) \equiv p = Sue,$$

and also

$$\neg carryingMail(p, do(bang_2, S_0)),   coffeeRequested(p, do(bang_2, S_0)),$$
$$\neg going(l, do(bang_2, S_0)).$$

With such a magic stochastic action $bigBang$, we could reduce probabilistic reasoning with uncertainty in the initial situation to the problem, which we have already solved, of probabilistic reasoning with a complete initial database. First, take the probability of $bang_i$ to be that of database i. For example, $prob_0(bang_2, bigBang, s) \stackrel{def}{=} 0.4 \times 0.10$. Secondly, take $Poss(bang_i, s) \equiv s = S_0$. Then, provided that the stGolog program γ does not mention the $bigBang$ stochastic action, we can simply compute $probF(\psi, bigBang ; \gamma)$ whenever we wish to know the probability of ψ after executing γ when there is uncertainty in the initial situation.

It remains only to describe how to design successor state axioms to give $bigBang$ the above properties. Suppose, in the absence of the $bigBang$ stochastic action, F's successor state axiom is

$$F(\vec{x}, do(a, s)) \equiv \phi_F(\vec{x}, a, s),$$

so that $\phi_F(\vec{x}, a, s)$ mentions none of the $bang_i$. Suppose there are n initial complete databases, so that $bigBang$ has outcomes $bang_1, \ldots, bang_n$, and that in the i-th such database, F is completely described by the sentence

$$F(\vec{x}, S_0) \equiv \psi_F^i(\vec{x}),$$

where $\psi_F^i(\vec{x})$ is a situation-independent formula. Then take as F's new successor state axiom,

$$F(\vec{x}, do(a, s)) \equiv \bigvee_{i=1}^{n} [a = bang_i \wedge \psi_F^i(\vec{x})] \vee$$
$$a \neq bang_1 \wedge \cdots \wedge a \neq bang_n \wedge \phi_F(\vec{x}, a, s).$$

Now it should be clear that there really is no need to introduce the $bigBang$ action at all. Its sole purpose is to initially create for us four complete theories, one in each of $do(bang_i, S_0), i = 1, \ldots 4$. Instead of adopting this cumbersome approach to the creation of these four theories, we can introduce four "initial situations", $S_0^1, \ldots, S_0^4$, and associate the required four initial theories with these. Declare these as initial:

$$init(s) \stackrel{def}{=} s = S_0^1 \vee s = S_0^2 \vee s = S_0^3 \vee s = S_0^4.$$

Assign them appropriate probabilities:

$$initProb(S_0^1) \stackrel{def}{=} 0.4 \times 0.9,$$
$$\vdots$$
$$initProb(S_0^4) \stackrel{def}{=} 0.6 \times 0.1.$$

Finally, associate four complete theories with these initial situations:

$$loc(S_0^1) = MR, \quad mailPresent(p, S_0^1) \equiv p = Pat \vee p = Sue,$$
$$\neg carryingmail(p, S_0^1), \quad coffeeRequested(p, S_0^1), \quad \neg going(l, S_0^1).$$

$$\vdots$$

$$loc(S_0^4) = office(Sue), \quad mailPresent(p, S_0^4) \equiv p = Sue,$$
$$\neg carryingmail(p, S_0^4), \quad coffeeRequested(p, S_0^4), \quad \neg going(l, S_0^4).$$

There is one serious problem with above approach to representing uncertainty about the initial situation: The number of initial databases can easily grow exponentially with the number of individuals. If there are n people in the office, and probability distributions associated with each person for the relation $carryingMail$, then potentially there will be 2^n initial databases just to represent the uncertainty of $carryingMail$. This problem is most commonly addressed by using a Bayesian network to compactly represent the initial probability distributions over the fluents, but pursuing this approach here would take us too far afield.

By introducing multiple initial situations, we have dramatically departed from the earlier approach to representing probabilities using basic action theories of the situation calculus. What has now been introduced has the flavour of the possible worlds account of knowledge in Chapter 11. There, an agent's uncertainty about how the actual world might be was captured by introducing alternative situations to S_0. Here, we are doing exactly the same thing, but in addition, we attach probabilities to these alternative initial situations. In fact, a theoretical account of probability theory can be given in exactly this way within the possible worlds framework for knowledge in the situation calculus. Uncertainty in the initial situation is captured by postulating a probability distribution over the situations accessible from S_0. Stochastic actions are represented exactly as we have done in terms of their deterministic outcomes. The Scherl-Levesque solution to the frame problem for the accessibility relation given in Chapter 11 determines how these initial situations and their probabilities evolve. Finally, sensing actions affect an agent's knowledge about the probability distributions over the possible situations that he might inhabit.[7] While this chapter could have taken a possible worlds approach to probability theory, we have instead opted for what seems to us to be a more intuitive account within the conventional situation calculus. This has taken us a long way, but at this point, we are forced to deviate from the standard story by introducing these multiple initial situations, each with its own associated initial database. For the purists, perhaps it is best to view this move as a trick for implementing the big bang approach; each S_0^i stands for $do(bang_i, S_0)$, $initProb(S_0^i)$ is just $prob_0(bang_i, bigBang, S_0)$, and the initial database associated with S_0^i simply represents the global effects of $bang_i$.

It is straightforward to suitably generalize the definition (12.5) of $probF$ to take initial uncertainty into account:

$$probF(\psi, \gamma) \stackrel{def}{=} \sum_{\{s | \mathcal{D} \models init(s)\}} initProb(s) * \left[\sum_{\{(p,\sigma) | \mathcal{D} \models stDo(\gamma\,;\,nil,p,s,\sigma) \wedge \psi[\sigma]\}} p \right].$$

So the probability of ψ after executing the stGolog program γ is simply the sum, over all the trees in the forest of trees rooted at initial situations, of the probabilities of ψ in each tree, weighted by the probabilities of the roots of these trees. As expected, this reduces to (12.5) when S_0 is the only initial situation, with probability 1.

Here is the code for this generalization for $probF$, together with the necessary modifications to the delivery program to handle the above example of uncertainty in the initial situation.

Modifications to probF to Accommodate Uncertainty in the Initial Situation, and the Delivery Robot Example

```
probF(F,Prog,Prob) :- findall(P,
                        S0^S^P0^Pr^(init(S0), initProb(S0,P0),
```

---

7 Section 12.5.1 below treats sensing actions.

```
                                      stDo(Prog : nil,Pr,S0,S),
                                      once(holds(F,S)), P is Pr * P0),
                       PS),
               addNumbers(PS,Prob).
```

```
      % Delivery robot with uncertain initial database.

init(S) :- S = s01 ; S = s02 ; S = s03 ; S = s04.

% Initial Database #1

loc(mr,s01).  mailPresent(P,s01) :- P = pat ; P = sue.
initProb(s01,P) :- P is 0.4 * 0.9 .  coffeeRequested(P,s01).

% Initial Database #2

loc(mr,s02).  mailPresent(P,s02) :- P = sue.
initProb(s02,P) :- P is 0.4 * 0.1 .  coffeeRequested(P,s02).

% Initial Database #3

loc(office(sue),s03).  mailPresent(P,s03) :- P = pat ; P = sue.
initProb(s03,P) :- P is 0.6 * 0.9 .  coffeeRequested(P,s03).

% Initial Database #4

loc(office(sue),s04).  mailPresent(P,s04) :- P = sue.
initProb(s04,P) :- P is 0.6 * 0.1 .  coffeeRequested(P,s04).
```

12.5 Markov Decision Processes

We continue with the delivery robot of Section 12.1, ignoring exogenous actions to simplify the presentation. Suppose that different states of affairs have different values for the robot. For example, a situation reached by giving mail to someone is worth more than one reached by giving coffee; mail delivery is more important than coffee delivery. Similarly, successfully giving someone coffee is worth more than failure. In decision theory, assigning such normally subjective values to states of affairs is done using a real valued *reward function*, $reward(a, s)$, denoting the reward accrued to an agent for doing action a when in situation s. For the delivery robot, we propose the following simple-minded reward function:

$$reward(puMail, s) \stackrel{def}{=} 20,$$

$$reward(giveMail(p), s) = r \overset{def}{=} p = Ann \wedge r = 80 \vee p = Alf \wedge r = 100 \vee$$
$$person(p) \wedge p \neq Ann \wedge p \neq Alf \wedge r = 50,$$

$$reward(giveCoffeeS(p), s) = r \overset{def}{=} p = Ann \wedge r = 60 \vee p = Alf \wedge r = 90 \vee$$
$$person(p) \wedge p \neq Ann \wedge p \neq Alf \wedge r = 50,$$

$$reward(giveCoffeeF(p), s) = r \overset{def}{=} p = Ann \wedge r = -40 \vee p = Alf \wedge r = -60 \vee$$
$$person(p) \wedge p \neq Ann \wedge p \neq Alf \wedge r = -30,$$

$$reward(endUpAt(l), s) \overset{def}{=} 25,$$

$$reward(getLost(l), s) \overset{def}{=} -100.$$

Moving around is costly because it consumes some of the robot battery's charge:

$$cost(endUpAt(l), s) \overset{def}{=} 0.25 * dist(loc(s), l),$$

$$cost(getLost(l), s) \overset{def}{=} 0.50 * dist(loc(s), l).$$

All other actions are cheap:

$$cost(puMail, s) \overset{def}{=} 0, \quad cost(giveMail(p), s) \overset{def}{=} 0,$$

$$cost(giveCoffeeS(p), s) \overset{def}{=} 0, \quad cost(giveCoffeeF(p), s) \overset{def}{=} 0.$$

It is possible to tell a slightly different story that eliminates the cost function by folding it into the reward function, but conceptually, it is often more natural to keep them separate. Many dynamic domains include the concept of resources that are consumed by performing certain actions—driving uses up gas, eating consumes food, etc.—and in such cases, the cost function provides a natural mechanism for measuring this consumption. A resource for a delivery robot is its battery's charge; actions like moving from one location to another consume this resource, and it is convenient to represent this in a cost function, separately from the reward function.

The above specification is an example of a *Markov decision process* (MDP), as expressed in the situation calculus. In general, an MDP consists of a specification of a dynamic probabilistic domain, as described in Section 12.1.1, together with two real valued functions: A *cost function*, $cost(\alpha, s)$, defined for each of the deterministic outcomes α of a stochastic action, together with a *reward function*, $reward(\alpha, s)$. MDPs quantify different states of affairs by means of these two functions. There are various ways of doing this, but most commonly, such values are defined using a linear combination of the accumulated costs and rewards in a history. Whenever σ is a ground situation term,

$$value(do(a, \sigma)) \overset{def}{=} value(\sigma) + reward(a, \sigma) - cost(a, \sigma). \tag{12.6}$$

We shall take this expression to define a measure of the subjective value an agent assigns to a situation; the bigger the value of the situation he finds himself in, the happier the agent.[8] Capable, as he is, of free will behaviour, an agent can elect to perform some action sequence that will stochastically take him through a sequence of situations. If he is smart about the actions he chooses, he will end up in a happy situation; if he is particularly smart, he will end up in the happiest of all possible situations—one whose value is maximal over all situations. Strictly speaking, this is too much to hope for; the agent can only perform stochastic actions, and therefore, is incapable of predicting the actual outcomes of his actions, whereas (12.6) defines values in terms of actual outcomes. The best he can do is choose a sequence of stochastic actions to perform that maximizes the *expected value* of his value function. For any sequence $\alpha_1 ; \cdots ; \alpha_n$ of stochastic actions, define

$$eValue(\alpha_1 ; \cdots ; \alpha_n) \overset{def}{=} \sum_{\{(p,\sigma)|\mathcal{D}\models stDo(\alpha_1 ; \cdots ; \alpha_n ; nil, p, S_0, \sigma)\}} value(\sigma) * p.$$

Smart agents choose to perform stochastic action sequences with maximal *eValue*s.

Notice that the above definition of *eValue* assumes a single initial database, and therefore does not accommodate uncertainty in the initial situation. This is easily remedied, as was done for *probF* in Section 12.4, and while we are at it, we might as well generalize *eValue* to arbitrary stGolog programs γ in the natural way:

$$eValue(\gamma) \overset{def}{=} \sum_{\{s|\mathcal{D}\models init(s)\}} initProb(s) * \left[\sum_{\{(p,\sigma)|\mathcal{D}\models stDo(\gamma ; nil, p, s, \sigma)\}} value(\sigma) * p \right].$$

This is implemented in the usual way.

Expected Value for StGolog Programs and Uncertainty in the Initial Situation

```
eValue(Prog,Val) :- findall(VV,
                    S0^S^P0^P^V^(init(S0), initProb(S0,P0),
                                 stDo(Prog : nil,P,S0,S),
                                 value(S,V), VV is P0 * P * V),
                    Vals),
               addNumbers(Vals,Val).

value(S0,V) :- init(S0), initValue(S0,V).
value(do(A,S),V) :- value(S,VS), cost(A,S,C), reward(A,S,R),
                    V is VS + R - C.
```

The ability to generalize the concept of expected value to arbitrary stGolog programs

---

8 Other notions of value are treated in decision theory, the most common of which provides a *discounted* measure of value; the farther one is from the initial situation, the less reward one accumulates. Our primary purpose here is to show how decision theoretic concepts can be axiomatized in the situation calculus, by focusing on the above definition of value. Alternative notions can be easily expressed along the same lines.

is fortunate, because restricting agent behaviours to just sequences of stochastic action is extremely limiting. To see why, we must now think seriously about an agent's sensing abilities.

12.5.1 Sensing and stGolog Programs

Let us return to Section 12.2.1, and think a little harder about what exactly we had in mind when we spoke there about executing an stGolog program. Many such programs, that of Figure 12.1 for example, are more than a little bit odd, if we think of them as robot control programs. After executing $go(office(Sue))$, the robot has no idea where it is, so it seems strange to ask it next to $giveCoffee(Sue)$, independently of whether or not the go action took it to Sue's office. What's missing here is any capacity, on the robot's part, of coming to know where it is. More generally, it lacks the ability to sense its environment to determine what are the outcomes of the stochastic actions it performs. A much more reasonable variant of the program of Figure 12.1, one that would be suitable for a robot to actually execute, is something like the following:

$go(office(Sue))$; $sense_{go}(office(Sue))$;
if $\neg outcomeIs(observe_{loc}(office(Sue)))$ **then** $soundAlarm$; $stop$
else $giveCoffee(Sue)$; $sense_{giveCoffee}(Sue)$;
    if $outcomeIs(observe_{giveCoffeeS}(Sue))$ **then** $stop$ (12.7)
    else $giveCoffee(Sue)$; $sense_{giveCoffee}(Sue)$;
        if $outcomeIs(observe_{giveCoffeeF}(Sue))$ **then** $soundAlarm$; $stop$
        else $stop$

The above is a conditional stGolog program, all of whose stochastic action occurrences spawn sense actions that are followed, in turn, by conditionals instructing the robot what to do next, depending on what it actually observed as a result of these sense actions. We call such stGolog programs *policies*.[9]

To begin, having now introduced a new kind of action into the MDP framework, namely sense actions, we inquire about how to represent these in the situation calculus. The above policy supposes that the robot has a sensor, denoted by $sense_{go}(l)$—the action of sensing the world immediately after performing a stochastic $go(l)$ action. Markov decision theory takes sensing seriously in two ways: 1) By considering the possibility that an agent might obtain only partial information about its world through its sensors, and 2) By modeling the possibility that an agent's sensors can be mistaken. This leads to what are called *partially observable* MDPs. The limiting case—where the agent's sensors are

---

9 Strictly speaking, this is an example of what the MDP literature calls a *non-stationary policy tree* (because a conditional stGolog program has the structure of a tree), but since these are the only kinds we shall consider, we shall continue referring to them simply as policies.

perfect, and where those sensors are sufficient to keep the agent always informed about the entire state of its environment—is called a *fully observable* MDP. Continuing with the $sense_{go}$ action, imagine that this sensor can be subject to error, so that there are multiple possible observations that can result from performing a $sense_{go}$ action, with suitable probabilities. For example, one such observation for the stochastic action $go(office(Sue))$ might be the action $observe_{loc}(MR)$, meaning that one possible outcome of performing the $sense_{go}(office(Sue))$ action is observing that it is in MR; another might be $observe_{loc}(office(Sue))$, meaning that the robot thinks it is in $office(Sue)$ as a result of performing the action $go(office(Sue))$. Notice especially that $observe_{loc}(MR)$—the action of observing that it is in MR—need not mean that the robot actually is in the mail room. Its sensor tells it that it's there, but the sensor could be reporting false information. These observational actions have probabilities, and these will typically depend on where the robot actually is when it performs its $sense_{go}$ action. For example, if the sensor is fairly reliable, we might expect the observation $observe_{loc}(MR)$ to occur with high probability, say 0.99, whenever the robot is actually in the mail room, but with probability 0.01, say, when the robot is in someone's office.

It should now be clear where we are heading: We shall treat $sense_{go}(l)$ as a stochastic action, exactly as we treated "ordinary" stochastic actions in Section 12.1, and treat the observations associated with $sense_{go}$ as nature's choices, that are selected as the outcomes of the $sense_{go}$ stochastic action according to a specified probability distribution. So in the above stGolog program, $observe_{loc}(office(Sue))$ will be one of nature's choices for the stochastic action $sense_{go}(office(Sue))$. As before, nature's choices $observe_{loc}(l)$ are deterministic, and therefore will have action precondition axioms, and associated probabilities. Just what forms stochastic sense action choices have, and what their axioms will look like depends on whether one is modeling a fully observable or a partially observable MDP, and we shall consider this issue below. For the moment, we suppose simply that each stochastic action has associated with it a sense action, denoted by the symbol *sense*, with suitable parameters and a suitable subscript, and is formalized as a stochastic action with finitely many nature's choices, denoted by the symbol *observe*, with suitable parameters and subscripts, as suggested by the above policy.

Because there are now two kinds of stochastic actions, some terminology will be needed to distinguish them. By an *ordinary stochastic action* we shall mean one that does not involve sensing, like $go(l)$, $giveCoffee(p)$, etc.; those for sensing we shall call *stochastic sense actions*, or sometimes, simply *sense actions*.

The above policy appeals to a situation-suppressed expression $outcomeIs(o)$, whose intended meaning is that o is the outcome chosen by nature for the immediately preceding stochastic sense action in the policy. This is simply an abbreviation:

$outcomeIs(o,s) \overset{def}{=} (\exists s')s = do(o,s').$

The next task is to define exactly what counts as a policy. To do so requires two prior concepts:

Definition 12.5.1: Associated Sense Action
We assume that for each ordinary stochastic action α there is a unique stochastic sense action, and we call this *the sense action associated with* α.

Definition 12.5.2: Sense Outcome Condition
A *sense outcome condition for* a stochastic sense action *sense* is any situation-suppressed sentence constructed from atoms of the form $outcomeIs(o)$, where o can be any term denoting one of nature's choices for *sense*.

We can now define exactly what counts as a policy:

Definition 12.5.3: Policy
A policy is an stGolog program inductively defined by:

1. An ordinary stochastic action is a policy.
2. If α is an ordinary stochastic action, $sense_\alpha$ is the sense action associated with α, $\omega_1, \ldots, \omega_k$ are sense outcome conditions for $sense_\alpha$, and $\rho_1, \ldots, \rho_k, \rho_{k+1}$ are policies, then the following is a policy:

α ; $sense_\alpha$; **if** ω_1 **then** ρ_1
　　　　　　　　else if ω_2 **then** ρ_2
　　　　　　　　　　　$\vdots$
　　　　　　　　else if ω_k **then** ρ_k
　　　　　　　　else ρ_{k+1}

So a policy is an stGolog program constructed from ordinary and sensing stochastic actions in which every ordinary stochastic action is immediately followed by its associated sense action, which in turn is immediately followed by a conditional that branches on test conditions formulated in terms of the observations that can result from performing the sense action. Policies are meant to capture the following kind of on-line execution behaviour for an agent: Perform an ordinary action; then sense for some properties of the world as specified by the sense action; then, depending on what was observed, do some other things.

Notice that there are no restrictions on what the sense action associated with the ordinary action α actually senses *for*. Its purpose is to allow an agent to sense her environment immediately after performing α, but what properties of the environment she seeks to discover are left completely open to the axiomatizer. Normally, because α is stochastic and therefore has multiple possible outcomes, an axiomatizer will give its associated sense action the capacity to observe which of these outcomes actually occurred. For example, the sense action $sense_{flipCoin}$, associated with stochastic action $flipCoin$, would typically have $observe_{head}$ and $observe_{tail}$ as nature's choices, in order to allow the agent to determine what was the actual result of flipping the coin. But the axiomatizer is perfectly free instead to take $observe_{tigerInRoom}$, $observe_{raining}$ and $observe_{trainIsLate}$ as nature's choices for $sense_{flipCoin}$ provided, of course, the probabilities of these observational actions sum to one.

POLICIES AND DELIBERATION

As defined above, policies are constructed from stochastic actions and conditionals whose branching conditions (sense outcome conditions) are specified *entirely in terms of the outcomes of an agent's sensors. In executing a policy, the agent has no need of the underlying domain axioms.* Its resulting behaviour depends only on the outputs of its sensors. In other words, a policy is a procedure requiring no deliberation on the part of the agent, and is designed for on-line execution.

None of this is meant to suggest that the underlying axioms and probability distributions are useless. On the contrary, they are essential, but only to the *designer* of policies to be executed by a robot. Policy execution itself is a mindless affair.

12.5.2 Fully Observable MDPs

As observed above, there are various kinds of MDPs, depending on what one assumes about the range and reliability of an agent's sensors. The limiting case, which we consider first, is when these sensors are perfect, and when they can sense enough features of the environment to keep the agent fully informed, at all times, about which state he is in. These assumptions characterize what is called a *fully observable* MDP (FOMDP). This setting can be formally characterized as follows:

Definition 12.5.4: The Full-Observability Assumption

1. **Range of possible observations.** Sense actions are stochastic, and therefore their possible outcomes must be specified. In the fully observable case, these take the following form: If $sense_A(\vec{x})$ is the sense action associated with stochastic action $A(\vec{x})$, and if nature's choices for A have the form

$$choice(A(\vec{x}), c) \stackrel{def}{=} c = N_1(\vec{x}) \lor \cdots \lor c = N_k(\vec{x}),$$

then nature's choices for $sense_A$ are specified by

$$choice(sense_A(\vec{x}), c) \overset{def}{=} c = observe_{N_1}(\vec{x}) \vee \cdots \vee c = observe_{N_k}(\vec{x}).$$

In other words, in the fully observable case, the sense action associated with an ordinary stochastic action is intended to observe the actual outcome of that action.

2. **Accurate sensing.** Under the full observability assumption, sense action outcomes are characterized as follows, for $i = 1, \ldots, k$:

$$Poss(observe_{N_i}(\vec{x}), s) \equiv (\exists s')s = do(N_i(\vec{x}), s'), \,^{10}$$

$$prob_0(observe_{N_i}(\vec{x}), sense_A(\vec{x}), s) \overset{def}{=} 1.$$

To see why these capture the intuitive concept of accurate sensing, notice that by the definition (12.1) of $prob$, we can derive

$$prob(observe_{N_i}(\vec{x}), sense_A(\vec{x}), s) = 1 \equiv (\exists s')s = do(N_i(\vec{x}), s').$$

In other words, no matter what situation an agent is in, if she senses for the outcome of an ordinary stochastic action immediately after performing that action, she will observe, with probability 1, what that outcome really was.

3. **No uncertainty about the initial situation.** The initial situation is taken to be a single, complete theory about S_0, unlike the treatment of uncertainty in Section 12.4. The idea here is that, because her sensors are infallible and comprehensive, the agent will come to know the complete state of her world after performing a stochastic action, *provided she knew the state of the world before doing this action.* Therefore, if initially, before executing a policy, an agent knows the exact state of the world, she will continue to know what state she is in throughout the execution of this policy. So to guarantee this property of complete knowledge about an agent's world state, we assume a complete initial database.

Continuing with the delivery example, we represent the full observability assumption for the two sense actions $sense_{go}(l)$ and $sense_{giveCoffee}(p)$, designed to sense which action nature chose when the robot performed a $go(l)$ action, and which one she chose for a $giveCoffee(p)$ action. First we focus on the $sense_{go}$ action. By the above specifications for fully observable MDPs:

$$choice(sense_{go}(l), c) \overset{def}{=} c = observe_{endUpAt}(l) \vee c = observe_{getLost}(l),$$

---

10 We are here bending the rules a bit for basic action theories by allowing the right-hand side of an action precondition axiom to refer to an earlier situation than the current one. It's clear enough that no damage is done by this move, either representationally or computationally, and we won't worry about this simple extension to the theory. In effect, we are no longer enforcing the Markov property here for basic action theories.

$$Poss(observe_{endUpAt}(l), s) \equiv (\exists s')s = do(endUpAt(l), s'),$$

$$Poss(observe_{getLost}(l), s) \equiv (\exists s')s = do(getLost(l), s').$$

Assign probability 1 to these observations:

$$prob_0(observe_{endUpAt}(l), sense_{go}(l), s) \stackrel{def}{=} 1,$$

$$prob_0(observe_{getLost}(l), sense_{go}(l), s) \stackrel{def}{=} 1.$$

Next, specify the full observability assumption for $sense_{giveCoffee}(p)$:

$$choice(sense_{giveCoffee}(p), c) \stackrel{def}{=} c = observe_{giveCoffeeS}(p) \lor$$
$$c = observe_{giveCoffeeF}(p).$$

Observing that the coffee delivery succeeded (failed) is possible iff that delivery actually succeeded (failed).

$$Poss(observe_{giveCoffeeS}(p), s) \equiv (\exists s')s' = do(giveCoffeeS(p), s),$$

$$Poss(observe_{giveCoffeeF}(p), s) \equiv (\exists s')s' = do(giveCoffeeF(p), s).$$

Finally, guarantee that the appropriate observations occur with probability 1:

$$prob_0(observe_{giveCoffeeS}(p), sense_{giveCoffee}(p), s) \stackrel{def}{=} 1,$$

$$prob_0(observe_{giveCoffeeF}(p), sense_{giveCoffee}(p), s) \stackrel{def}{=} 1.$$

Strictly speaking, we must also assign sensors to $giveMail(p)$ and $puMail$, even though these are actually deterministic actions. But since they are deterministic, there is not much point in doing so in the fully observable case; such sensor readings can provide no new information. Therefore, we require only that truly stochastic actions have associated sense actions, and we relax the definition 12.5.3 of a policy to require that only such stochastic actions must be immediately followed by a sense action. Therefore, we do not give sense axioms corresponding to $giveMail(p)$ and $puMail$. We emphasize here that this simplification applies only in the fully observable case, and not for the more general partially observable MDPs treated below.

Because observations have been introduced as first class citizens into the situation calculus, we are obliged to specify cost and reward functions for them. This is perhaps less of an obligation than an opportunity, because now one can represent the potential value to an agent of *information gathering* activities. This raises lots of interesting possibilities, but we resist pursuing them here. Instead, we shall remain neutral, and simply take the costs and rewards for observational actions to be 0.

Finally, notice that observational actions are deterministic and therefore can, in principle, participate in successor state axioms; they could conceivably affect fluents. However, just as Chapter 11 assumed that sense actions do not change the state of the world (the no-side-effects assumption of Section 11.4.1), FOMDPs (and also partially observable MDPs, which we consider next) make the same assumption for observations, and we shall do that here.

12.5.3   Partially Observable MDPs

When the full observability assumption is relaxed, things become much more complicated. First, uncertainty must be allowed in the initial situation. Secondly, the agent may be capable of observing only part of his environment; for example, he may be incapable of observing whether mail has exogenously arrived, unless he is present in the mail room. Or he may be entirely incapable of sensing the values of one or more fluents; perhaps he simply doesn't have a sensor for observing mail arrivals. Finally, insofar as he has sensors, they may be noisy, allowing him, for example, to sometimes sense that he is in Sue's office when in fact, he is in Sam's. Partially observable MDPs (POMDPs) provide mechanisms for representing these aspects of uncertainty.

  We already know how to represent uncertainty in the initial situation. That is what Section 12.4 was about, and we shall continue to use that approach in the POMDP setting. Therefore, we focus now on representing partial observability. Continuing with the delivery robot, without exogenous actions, we suppose that the robot's location sensor, $sense_{go}(l)$, whose purpose is to sense the robot's current location after performing a $go(l)$ action, is subject to error. The following specifies a probability distribution for this location sensor:[11]

1. If, after performing a $go(l)$ action, the robot is lost (its current location is $BlackHole$), then with probability 1 its sensor will tell it so.

2. If, after a $go(l)$ action, the robot is not lost, then with probability 0.95, its sensor will correctly tell it where it is.

3. If the robot is not lost (so it is in some room), then its sensor will (incorrectly) tell it that it is in one of the other rooms with probability $0.05/(numberOfRooms - 1)$.

First, specify nature's choices for $sense_{go}(l)$:

$$ choice(sense_{go}(l), c) \stackrel{def}{=} (\exists l').location(l') \wedge c = observe_{loc}(l'). $$

So we are supposing that the robot's location sensor can report that it ended up at any location in the office, including the $BlackHole$. We need to specify action preconditions and probabilities for $observe_{loc}(l')$. The above specifies all the conditions under which this sensor model assigns a non-zero probability to $observe_{loc}(l')$. Therefore, the associated

---

11 This is an example of what is often called a *sensor model*.

action precondition axiom is[12]

$$Poss(observe_{loc}(l), s) \equiv loc(s) = BlackHole \wedge l = BlackHole \vee$$
$$loc(s) = l \wedge l \neq BlackHole \vee$$
$$loc(s) \neq BlackHole \wedge l \neq BlackHole \wedge l \neq loc(s).$$

The above description of a sensor model leads to the following expression for $prob_0$:

$$prob_0(observe_{loc}(l), sense_{go}(l'), s) = pr \overset{def}{=}$$
$$loc(s) = BlackHole \wedge l = BlackHole \wedge pr = 1.0 \vee$$
$$loc(s) = l \wedge l \neq BlackHole \wedge pr = 0.95 \vee$$
$$loc(s) \neq BlackHole \wedge l \neq BlackHole \wedge l \neq loc(s) \wedge$$
$$pr = 0.05/(numberOfRooms - 1).$$

Next, consider $sense_{giveCoffee}(p)$, the sense action associated with the ordinary action $giveCoffee(p)$, and whose purpose is to inform the robot about the results of its coffee deliveries. In contrast to the fully observable case, we introduce a third outcome:

$$choice(sense_{giveCoffee}(p), c) \overset{def}{=} c = observe_{giveCoffeeS}(p) \vee$$
$$c = observe_{giveCoffeeF}(p) \vee c = observe_{zipAboutCoffee}(p).$$

Here, $observe_{zipAboutCoffee}(p)$ allows for the possibility that $sense_{giveCoffee}(p)$ provides no information about whether $giveCoffee(p)$ succeeds or fails, namely, when it's too dark to tell.

$$Poss(observe_{giveCoffeeS}(p), s) \equiv (\exists s')s = do(giveCoffeeS(p), s) \wedge$$
$$\neg dark(loc(s)),$$

$$Poss(observe_{giveCoffeeF}(p), s) \equiv (\exists s')s = do(giveCoffeeF(p), s) \wedge$$
$$\neg dark(loc(s)),$$

$$Poss(observe_{zipAboutCoffee}(p), s) \equiv dark(loc(s)).$$

Unlike the $sense_{go}$ action, we assume that the robot's coffee delivery sensors are perfect, provided the sensing conditions are right. If it successfully gave coffee to p, its sensor tells it so, but only if there is enough light, and conversely. Similarly, if it failed in giving coffee. But if the room is dark, its sensor returns no information. We assign probabilities that reflect this perfect sensor assumption:

$$prob_0(observe_{giveCoffeeS}(p), sense_{giveCoffee}(p), s) \overset{def}{=} 1.0,$$

$$prob_0(observe_{giveCoffeeF}(p), sense_{giveCoffee}(p), s) \overset{def}{=} 1.0,$$

---

12 Recall that the action precondition axioms for a stochastic action's outcomes must characterize all conditions under which these outcomes have non-zero probability (Section 12.1.1).

$$prob_0(observe_{zipAboutCoffee}(p), sense_{giveCoffee}(p), s) \overset{def}{=} 1.0.$$

Compare this account for $sense_{giveCoffee}(p)$ with the representation in the fully observable case. Despite the fact that under the right conditions the sensors are perfect, we do not have full observability here because there are situations—when the office is dark—when $observe_{giveCoffeeS}(p)$ and $observe_{giveCoffeeF}(p)$ both have probability 0.

Unlike FOMDPs, a POMDP need not give a sensor model to each stochastic action.[13] Moreover, again unlike FOMDPs, a POMDP can assign a nontrivial sensor model to a *deterministic* action, like $giveMail(p)$. This may seem a bit odd, but maybe the robot uses mail deliveries to remind itself to check the charge in its batteries. In the treatment of the delivery POMDP, we choose not to assign a sensor model to the deterministic $giveMail(p)$ and $puMail$ actions. In such cases, there is no need for policies to sense and branch after such actions, and we relax the definition 12.5.3 of a policy to allow this.

This completes the specification of a POMDP for the delivery robot. The following Prolog clauses implement this:

Additional Clauses for the Delivery Robot POMDP

```
choice(senseGo(L),C) :- location(L1), C = observeLoc(L1).
choice(senseGiveCoffee(P),C) :- C = observeGiveCoffeeS(P) ;
            C = observeGiveCoffeeF(P) ; C = observeZipAboutCoffee(P).

poss(observeLoc(L),S) :- loc(Loc,S),
                        (L = blackHole, Loc = blackHole ;
                         Loc = L, not L = blackHole ;
                         not (Loc = blackHole ; L = Loc ; L = blackHole)).
poss(observeGiveCoffeeS(P),S) :- S = do(giveCoffeeS(P),S1),
                                loc(L,S), not dark(L).
poss(observeGiveCoffeeF(P),S) :- S = do(giveCoffeeF(P),S1),
                                loc(L,S), not dark(L).
poss(observeZipAboutCoffee(P),S) :- loc(L,S), dark(L).

prob0(observeLoc(L),senseGo(L1),S,Pr) :- loc(Loc,S),
                        (L = blackHole, Loc = blackHole, Pr = 1.0 ;
                         Loc = L, not L = blackHole, Pr = 0.95 ;
                         not Loc = blackHole, not L = Loc, not L = blackHole,
                         numberOfRooms(N), Pr is 0.05/(N-1) ).
prob0(observeGiveCoffeeS(P),senseGiveCoffee(P),S,Pr) :- Pr = 1.0 .
prob0(observeGiveCoffeeF(P),senseGiveCoffee(P),S,Pr) :- Pr = 1.0 .
prob0(observeZipAboutCoffee(P),senseGiveCoffee(P),S,Pr) :- Pr = 1.0 .
```

---

13 Strictly speaking, it must assign a sensor model to each ordinary action, but unlike FOMDPs, this can be the trivial no-information sense action.

```
dark(L) :- L = office(sue) ; L = office(sam).
numberOfRooms(N) :- findall(P,person(P),Ps), length(Ps,M), N is M + 1.
location(L) :- L = mr ; L = blackHole ; person(P), L = office(P).

outcomeIs(O,S) :- S = do(O,S1).
restoreSitArg(outcomeIs(O),S,outcomeIs(O,S)).

% Rewards and costs for observations.

cost(observeGiveCoffeeS(P),S,C) :- C = 0.
cost(observeGiveCoffeeF(P),S,C) :- C = 0.
cost(observeZipAboutCoffee(P),S,C) :- C = 0.
cost(observeLoc(L),S,C) :- C = 0.
reward(observeGiveCoffeeS(P),S,R) :- R = 0.
reward(observeGiveCoffeeF(P),S,R) :- R = 0.
reward(observeZipAboutCoffee(P),S,R) :- R = 0.
reward(observeLoc(L),S,R) :- R = 0.

% Value is 0 for all initial databases.

initValue(S,0.0) :- init(S).

% Rewards and costs for ordinary stochastic actions.

reward(puMail,S,R) :- R = 20.
reward(giveMail(P),S,R) :- P = ann, R = 80 ; P = alf, R = 100 ;
                           person(P), not P = ann, not P = alf, R = 50.
reward(giveCoffeeS(P),S,R) :- P = ann, R = 60 ; P = alf, R = 90 ;
                           person(P), not P = ann, not P = alf, R = 50.
reward(giveCoffeeF(P),S,R) :- P = ann, R = -40 ; P = alf, R = -60 ;
                           person(P), not P = ann, not P = alf, R = -30.
reward(endUpAt(L),S,R) :- R = 25.
reward(getLost(L),S,R) :- R = -100.
cost(puMail,S,C) :- C = 0.0 .
cost(giveMail(P),S,C) :- C = 0.0 .
cost(giveCoffeeS(P),S,C) :- C = 0.0 .
cost(giveCoffeeF(P),S,C) :- C = 0.0 .
cost(endUpAt(L),S,C) :- loc(L0,S), dist(L0,L,D), C is 0.25 * D.
cost(getLost(L),S,C) :- loc(L0,S), dist(L0,L,D), C is 0.50 * D.

person(P) :- P = pat ; P = sue ; P = alf ; P = sam ; P = ann ; P = bob.
```

Now we can compute expected values of policies for the delivery robot POMDP. To do that, load the above clauses, the stGolog interpreter, the delivery program of Section 12.2.1 but with the four initial databases of Section 12.4 to accommodate uncertainty in the initial situation, and the code for expected values of stGolog programs of Section 12.5.

Computing Expected Values of Policies for the Delivery Robot POMDP

```
[eclipse 2]: eValue(go(office(sue)) :
                   senseGo(office(sue)) :
                   if(-outcomeIs(observeLoc(office(sue))) &
                      -outcomeIs(observeLoc(blackHole)),
                            go(office(sue)),
                   /*else*/ if(outcomeIs(observeLoc(blackHole)),
                                     ?(true),
                               /*else*/ puMail : go(office(sue)))),
                   V).
V = 6.98039246
```

% Notice the use above of ?(true) as a no-op "action".

```
[eclipse 3]: eValue(go(office(sue)) :
                   senseGo(office(sue)) :
                   if(outcomeIs(observeLoc(office(sue))),
                            giveCoffee(sue) :
                            senseGiveCoffee(sue) :
                            if(outcomeIs(observeGiveCoffeeS(sue)),
                                   giveMail(sue),
                            /*else*/ giveCoffee(sue)),
                   /*else*/ if(outcomeIs(observeLoc(mr)),
                                puMail :
                                go(office(pat)) :
                                senseGo(office(pat)) :
                                if(outcomeIs(observeLoc(
                                                  office(pat))),
                                        givemail(pat),
                                /*else*/ ?(true)),
                            /*else*/ ?(true))),
                   V).
V = 24.9745083
```

12.5.4 Implementing Policies: Run-Time Sense Actions

While the formal definition 12.5.3 of a policy is suitable for the theoretical foundations of MDPs, the concept of an associated sense action and its outcomes remains too abstract for a policy to actually specify an agent's run-time behaviour. We did not require that policies describe *what concrete properties of his environment an agent should sense for* immediately after performing an ordinary stochastic action. Instead, we simply assumed that each of his sense actions, for example, $sense_{giveCoffee}(Sue)$, has a range of possible outcomes, and that nature miraculously reveals this outcome to him—$outcomeIs(observe_{zipAboutCoffee}(Sue))$—after which he takes the appropriate branch in executing his policy. But in reality, an agent's sensors work by determining the values of concrete properties of his environment—sense the value of my location, sense whether *Sue* has her coffee. So a "real" location sense action is better denoted by $sense(loc, l)$, whose intended reading is something like: Sense for the value of the functional fluent $loc(s)$, and bind variable l to what the sensor returns. Similarly, there might be a "real" sense action $sense(hasCoffee(p), t)$, with intended reading: Sense the truth value of relational fluent $hasCoffee(p, s)$, and bind variable t to that truth value. This perspective brings us closer to the concept of a sense action of Section 11.3.

Somewhat more formally, define a *run-time sense action* to be an expression of the form $sense(p, v)$ where p is a situation-suppressed expression or term called a *sense condition*, and v is a *run-time variable* that gets bound by an agent's sensors to the value that p has when $sense(p, v)$ is executed. With this notation we can now formulate programs using these run-time sense actions, with branching conditions determined by the values of their run-time variables, as in the following run-time variant of policy (12.7):

> $go(office(Sue))$; $(\pi\ l).sense(loc, l)$;
> **if** $l \neq office(Sue)$ **then** $soundAlarm$; $stop$
> **else** $giveCoffee(Sue)$; $(\pi\ t).sense(hasCoffee(Sue), t)$;
>   **if** $t = true$ **then** $stop$
>   **else** $giveCoffee(Sue)$; $(\pi\ t).sense(hasCoffee(Sue), t)$;
>   **if** $t = false \vee t = unknown$ **then** $soundAlarm$; $stop$
>   **else** $stop$

This is a program an agent can actually execute, provided it has the required sensing abilities. Notice that in formulating this run-time program, we had in mind the delivery POMDP of Section 12.5.3. There, the sense action associated with the $giveCoffee(p)$ action had three possible outcomes: $observe_{giveCoffeeS}(p)$, $observe_{giveCoffeeF}(p)$ and $observe_{zipAboutCoffee}(p)$. Corresponding to these, we are viewing the run-time variable t of $sense(hasCoffee(Sue), t)$ as ranging over $\{true, false, unknown\}$.

We emphasize that the above specification of run-time sense actions, and the resulting run-time programs, are not ingredients of the much more abstract theory of policies and their expected values given in the previous sections. Rather, such programs serve as *implementations* for these abstract policies, and they do so by making explicit the sense and branching conditions that enable direct execution by an agent with the capacity to observe the values of these sense conditions in his environment.

Finally, notice that in the fully observable case, the sense condition $\phi(\vec{x})$ for a run-time sense action $sense(\phi(\vec{x}), v)$ must uniquely determine the outcome of the ordinary stochastic action $A(\vec{x})$ with which it is associated. Specifically, with reference to definition 12.5.4, the distinct values that can be taken by the run-time variable v, say $\{V_1, \ldots, V_k\}$, must correspond 1-1 with the outcomes of A, and the following must be entailments of the background action theory:

$$(\forall \vec{x}, s)\phi(\vec{x}, do(N_i(\vec{x}), s)) = V_i \quad i = 1, \ldots, k.$$

It is an interesting, but largely unexplored problem, to automatically generate suitable sense conditions for FOMDPs from the underlying basic action theory.

12.5.5 Exogenous Actions

The above treatment of policies for MDPs ignored exogenous actions. To take these into account, one must introduce an explicit sense action for each exogenous action, and modify the Definition 12.5.3 of a policy to provide occurrences of these sense actions. Normally, MDPs model exogenous action occurrences by requiring them to occur between stochastic agent-performed actions, as in Section 12.3. Therefore, a policy that explicitly senses for exogenous events will require such sense actions to immediately precede these agent actions, to be immediately followed by conditionals that branch according to the results of these sense actions. Exercise 9 below asks you to give an account of policies in the presence of exogenous actions.

12.5.6 Solving MDP Planning Problems

This section has focused exclusively on how to specify MDPs, observability conditions, and policies. With respect to the latter, the implicit assumption has been that the system designer will write suitable control policies, and apart from perhaps wanting to know the expected values of the policies she writes, this is the end of the story. But in fact, decision theory is far more ambitious than that. Much of its literature is concerned with automatically synthesizing *optimal* (or near-optimal) policies, namely policies with maximal expected values. This notion depends on the class of policies over which one is optimizing. One such class consists of *finite horizon* policies, in which some positive integer h—the *horizon*—is supposed given, and one seeks an optimal policy over all policy trees of height h. Another class concerns *infinite horizon problems with discounting*, in which the policy trees are potentially unbounded, but where discounting causes policy values to converge at some finite h. Most solution techniques appeal to dynamic programming; value and policy iteration are the most common examples. Regardless of how these algorithms work, we shall not treat them here, for one simple reason: No one has yet formulated these, or any other techniques for solving MDPs in the situation calculus. The main reason is that these classical algorithms rely on having an explicit enumeration of a system's states, while the situation calculus is based on situations, and these are not the same as states. The following section discusses this issue in greater detail.

12.6 Discussion

Most people who work with MDPs—queuing theorists, decision analysts, economists, control theorists—will find our situation calculus formulation of decision theory somewhat peculiar. It is not the standard story on MDPs—although for computer scientists, it is perhaps a more natural story because policies are stGolog *programs*, with explicit sensing actions that act just like input statements of conventional programming languages, and that conditionally branch on the outcomes of these inputs. In contrast, the standard account of MDPs is *state based*. One imagines being given a (usually finite, but not always) set of possible system states together with probability distributions, over these states, for stochastic action outcomes, including sense action outcomes. Similarly, reward and cost functions are defined over these states, and value functions are defined accordingly. With this apparatus in place, one can define the notion of a policy and its expected value, and therefore formulate the concept of a solution to an MDP as a policy with maximal expected value. The big advantage of our approach—indeed any approach formulated in a sufficiently expressive logic—is that one can freely specify MDPs using *logical sentences* to capture the regularities of the problem domain. Almost all the axioms for this chapter's delivery robot express such regularities, primarily by exploiting quantifiers. For highly structured application domains, like the delivery robot, such sentential representations tend to be extremely concise, and have an intuitive clarity lacking in state based formalisms where the states and their stochastic transitions are explicitly enumerated. But this is a purely *representational* advantage. Does it pay off computationally? On this, the jury is still out, and the reason is due precisely to the differences between states and situations. The classical, state based foundation for decision theory has led to many dynamic programming algorithms (e.g. value/policy iteration) for solving MDPs. We, however, don't have states, only situations, and as has been emphasized so often in this book, situations are not states; they are finite sequences of actions. Of course, with each ground situation term there is an associated state, namely the set of fluent values in that situation, *but this state is not part of the ontology of the situation calculus*; the language cannot talk about states. This makes it awkward to directly translate state based algorithms, like dynamic programming, into the situation calculus. But fortunately, this does appear to be possible, and moreover, in an elegant way. It turns out that the classical dynamic programming algorithms for solving MDPs are intimately related to regression, and from this perspective, the situation calculus appears to be well suited computationally to exploit these algorithms. However, these ideas are still preliminary and are the subject of ongoing research. Section 12.8 below gives a pointer to this work.

Policies are for MDPs what classical plans (Chapter 10) are for artificial intelligence. But there is a fundamental difference between the two, apart from the simple observation that policies involve sensing. Classical plans, involving, as they do, the concept of a goal, are all or nothing affairs; either there is a plan for a given goal, or there isn't. It may be that no plan exists to deliver coffee to everyone within some prespecified time frame. If we restrict ourselves to classical planning here, no one gets coffee; everyone is unhappy. But an optimal policy will always exist. Some people won't get their coffee under such a policy, but at least some will, and in a way that maximizes "the greatest good for the greatest number". In this sense, MDPs provide a much more flexible framework for describing behaviours than does classical planning.

Throughout this chapter, we have assumed that stochastic actions have just finitely many outcomes. For example, in modeling the $go(l)$ stochastic action, we assumed that l ranges over finitely many offices, and that $go(l)$ has just two possible outcomes—the robot ends up at location l, or it gets lost, ending up at the special location $BlackHole$. A more realistic representation would allow l to range over all (x, y) coordinates, and the outcomes of $go(l)$ to be something like $endUpAt(x', y')$ with x' and y' ranging over the reals. While we do not do so here, it is possible to give situation calculus representations for stochastic actions (including sense actions) having a continuum of outcomes, and their associated continuous probability distributions. Section 12.8 below contains pointers to some proposed approaches.

Perhaps the most important lesson of this chapter is that the purely logical approach to modeling dynamical systems can be seamlessly integrated with the numerical and state based paradigms of probability and decision theory. Which is not to say that this has been demonstrated in its full generality. The most significant omission has been of algorithms for solving MDPs, i.e., for computing optimal policies. So it is still an article of faith that the situation calculus can gracefully accommodate all aspects of probability and decision theory, especially their computational features. Many of these issues are currently active research topics (Section 12.8 below), but all the evidence suggests that it is only a matter of time and careful thinking.

12.7   Exercises

1. Prove Lemma 12.1.1.

2. In defining what counts as an stGolog program, we emphasized that these must be deterministic. Why?

3. By drawing the situation tree of possible outcomes for the stochastic programs for the delivery robot on which we tested the stGolog implementation (Section 12.2.1), verify that the probabilities computed are correct.

4. Prove that the probabilities of the leaves of the tree of possible outcomes for an stGolog program sum to 1.

5. Consider the urn beloved throughout the world by teachers of probability. Initially, it contains some numbers of red, white and blue balls. Balls are randomly drawn from this, and we are asked to answer questions about the probabilities of various final states of the urn.

   (a) Axiomatize this problem with the following fluents and actions:

   Fluents:

   - $urn(r, w, b, s)$. In situation s, the urn contains r, w and b red, white and blue balls respectively.

   Actions:

   - $add(c)$. A deterministic agent action meaning put a ball with colour c into the urn.
   - $remove$. A stochastic agent action meaning remove a ball from the urn. This has deterministic choices

     $removeRed, removeWhite, removeBlue,$

     meaning remove a ball of the indicated colour from the urn.

   (b) Translate your specification to Prolog, and compute probabilities for various stGolog programs and conditions on their terminating situations. Assume a complete initial situation in which

     $$urn(r, w, b, S_0) \equiv r = 1 \wedge w = 2 \wedge b = 3.$$

   (c) Now introduce an exogenous event $sneak(c)$, meaning that someone surreptitiously adds a ball with colour c to the urn. Assign some probability to this, suitably modify your axioms to accommodate this new action, and test out the resulting program.

   (d) Finally, suppose we do not have a complete initial situation, but only a probability distribution over the initial configuration of balls in the urn. For example, suppose we know that $urn(1, 2, 3, S_0)$ with probability .5, that $urn(1, 0, 1, S_0)$ with probability .1, and $urn(3, 2, 0, S_0)$ with probability .4. Suitably modify the above specification, and again compute probabilities for various stGolog programs and conditions on their terminating situations.

6. Consider a variant of Russian roulette consisting of an executioner and several players. The gun initially has a single bullet in one of its six chambers. There is a stochastic action $shootAt(x)$, meaning that the executioner points the gun at person x and pulls the trigger. We have in mind a particularly lethal form of this game in which a $shootAt$ action advances the gun's chamber; the executioner does not spin the chamber after a $shootAt$ action. Decompose $shootAt(x)$ into two deterministic actions $shootYes(x)$, meaning a bullet is fired and x is no longer alive, and $shootNo(x)$, meaning no bullet is fired (but the chamber is advanced), and x continues to live. In addition, include a deterministic agent action, $reload$, meaning that the executioner reloads the gun. Axiomatize this setting, and experiment with an implementation. Be sure to consider the possibility of exogenous actions, for example the gun jamming, and of an uncertain initial situation.

7. (a) Axiomatize a blocks world in which the move actions may succeed or fail with certain probabilities, so that the actions $move(x, y)$ and $moveToTable(x)$ are stochastic. Decompose these stochastic actions into deterministic outcomes as follows:

   - $moveS(x, y)$, meaning that the $move$ action succeeds in achieving its intended effect that x will be on y.
   - $moveNull(x, y)$, meaning that the $move$ action fails by leaving x where it was before the action attempt.
   - $moveFall(x, y)$, meaning that the $move$ action causes x to fall to the table.
   - $moveToTableS(x)$, meaning that the action succeeds in achieving its intended effect that x will be on the table.
   - $moveToTableNull(x)$, meaning that the $move$ action fails by leaving x where it was before the action attempt.

   (b) Play around with an implementation of this blocks world, along the lines suggested in the previous exercise.

   (c) Expand your stochastic blocks world to include sense actions $sense_{onTable}(x)$ and $sense_{on}(x, y)$. First, specify these for the fully observable case. Next, propose a suitable noisy sensor model for $sense_{on}(x, y)$, for example, that it will sense, with some non-zero probability, that x is on y when it is actually on $z \neq y$. In addition, specify a sensor model for $sense_{onTable}(x)$ that correctly senses whether or not x is on the table whenever x is clear, but returns no information otherwise.

   (d) Finally, write some policies for your POMDP, and compute their expected values using the code provided here.

8. Design and implement a policy-evaluating stGolog interpreter that issues appropriate sense actions after each ordinary stochastic action, thereby eliminating the nuisance of the policy designer having to explicitly write these sense actions as part of a policy.

9. **Policies for exogenous events**

   (a) Augment our account of policies for MDPs to include exogenous actions. This means there must be a sense action associated with each exogenous action. Moreover, the definition 12.5.3 of a policy must be modified to require occurrences of sense actions for exogenous events. Normally, MDPs model exogenous action occurrences by requiring them to occur between stochastic agent-performed actions, as in Section 12.3. Therefore, a policy that explicitly senses for exogenous events will require such sense actions to immediately precede these agent actions, to be immediately followed by conditionals that branch according to the results of these sense actions.

   (b) Corresponding to the exogenous action $exo(c, m, sm)$ of Section 12.3, introduce an appropriate sense action to monitor this exogenous event occurrence, and specify it for the fully observable case. Then make some reasonable assumptions to turn it into an interesting partially observable sense action, and specify it axiomatically. Finally, write some policies that monitor for exogenous event occurrences, and compute their expected values using the code provided here, for the partially observable case.

12.8   Bibliographic Remarks

By far, the most influential source for probability theory in artificial intelligence is the book by Pearl [152]. For an account combining logic with probability theory, see Bacchus [6] and also Halpern [77].

There have been a few proposals for embedding probability theory into the situation calculus. Bacchus, Halpern, and Levesque [8] is a foundational study that gives an account of an agent's probabilistic beliefs based on the Scherl-Levesque theory [190] of knowledge and sensing actions in the situation calculus. Our decomposition of stochastic actions into deterministic nature's choices with associated probabilities derives from their paper. In addition, our treatment of uncertainty in the initial situation parallels their use of an accessibility relation on initial situations for representing an agent's degree of belief about which situation he is initially in. Poole [167] embeds probability theory into the situation calculus, and also decision theory, but his ontology for the language is substantially different than ours, and a comparison is difficult. A closer approach to ours for embedding probability theory into the situation calculus is by Pinto, Sernadas, Sernadas, and Mateus

[163]. In subsequent work, these authors, together with Pacheco, have provided a very sophisticated extension of the previous paper to include continuous probability distributions, and a Mathematica implementation [133]. A probabilistic extension to Golog is by Grosskreutz and Lakemeyer [72]. As we have seen elsewhere in this book, the STRIPS planning formalism is closely related to the situation calculus. Therefore, it should not be surprising that there is a probabilistic version of STRIPS (Hanks and McDermott [81]; Kushmerick, Hanks, and Weld [100]), with many similarities to our situation calculus account of probability theory.

The standard text on FOMDPs is by Puterman [168]. For an excellent survey of decision theoretic planning, see Boutilier, Dean, and Hanks [23]. For a survey of solution techniques for POMDPs, see Lovejoy [130], and for recent results on POMDP algorithms, Kaelbling, Littman, and Cassandra [94]. The concept of run-time sense actions and their run-time variables of Section 12.5.4 is adapted from Pirri and Finzi [164].

Preliminary work by Boutilier, Reiter, Soutchanski, and Thrun [26] describes decision theoretic Golog (dtGolog), which is Golog augmented with stochastic elementary actions, probabilities and decision theory. The idea is that, as with Golog, one writes nondeterministic control programs, but unlike Golog, decision-theoretic principles are invoked to resolve this nondeterminism. To do so, the off-line interpreter uses programmer-specified probabilities and reward functions to select a program execution trace with maximum expected value. A dtGolog version of the coffee delivery program of Section 7.4.1 has been successfully tested on an RWI B21 autonomous robot at the University of Toronto.

As remarked in Section 12.6, there remains the problem of finding techniques to compute optimal policies for MDPs in the situation calculus. As it happens, classical dynamic programming algorithms for solving MDPs are intimately related to regression, and from this perspective, the situation calculus does appear to have a natural mechanism for approaching this problem. Moreover, the resulting *symbolic dynamic programming* algorithm applies to problem descriptions in first-order logic, and therefore can exploit regularities in these descriptions. Preliminary results along these lines are described by Boutilier, Reiter, and Price [25]. A related, but less general, non-logical regression-based algorithm for MDPs is found in Boutilier, Dearden, and Goldszmidt [24].

13 Concluding Remarks

It's time to step back and assess what has, and what has not, been achieved in this book. In many respects, ours is something like the physicists' grand quest for a Theory of Everything. If we had such a thing, our TOE would be a sufficiently expressive language to represent all the phenomena associated with dynamical systems, while at the same time lending itself to efficient implementation. It is arguable who faces the harder problem.

It is remarkable how far we have managed to come with the simple ontology provided by the situation calculus. The only ingredients needed were actions, fluents, and the ability to construct finite action sequences. (We also needed less glamorous primitives like the reals for time, locations, probability, etc., and naive set theory, but these will be essential for any proposed representation of the commonsense world.) With only this minimal ontology, we have developed situation calculus accounts for time, processes, concurrency, procedures, exogenous events, reactivity, sensing and knowledge, probabilistic uncertainty, and decision theory. It remains an open question how easily this ontology can be expanded to accommodate other features of an agent's representation for the commonsense world: space, shape, fluids, qualitative physics, etc. This ontology must also be enlarged to include properties of agents themselves: goals, commitment, obligation, abilities, communication, etc. As anyone who has worked on these problem knows, none of these are trivial, suggesting that the ultimate goal of a dynamical systems TOE is a very long way off.

It is also of interest to step back and inspect the computational properties of the situation calculus developed in this book. Many years ago, Hector Levesque argued that feasible implementations for large, complex AI systems will require what he called *vivid representations* [114, 115]. These require, at their foundation, a base theory in what Levesque calls *database form*, the key property of which is that there are available efficient methods for storing and querying very large amounts of information contained in it. The canonical example of such a base theory is a relational database, for which very sophisticated commercial implementations exist, but nothing in Levesque's account requires that this role be played by a relational database, or even that the base theory be logically complete, as it would be for a relational database. The only condition is that it support efficient information storage and retrieval. The second crucial component of a vivid representation is a tower of definitions, supported by the base theory. This means that the predicates and functions of the base theory are treated as primitive, and new concepts are introduced into the theory by defining them in terms of the primitives and previously defined concepts. To evaluate a query against such a vivid axiomatization, one need only unwind the query, via the definitions, to obtain an equivalent query involving only the database primitives, then evaluate this against the base theory. This, of course, is exactly the idea behind regression.

This book is an illustration of the computational power of the idea of a vivid representation. In our case, the base theory consists of the foundational axioms for situations, together with an application-dependent initial database. In its full generality, this base theory need not be in database form for two reasons: 1) Including, as they do, an induction axiom, the foundational axioms for situations hardly support efficient reasoning. 2) The initial database can be any first order theory about S_0. The Regression Theorem 4.5.5 allowed us to sidestep the first problem, because it guaranteed that for a large class of queries—the regressable sentences—the foundational axioms can be ignored. To get around the second problem, at least for most of the implementations of this book, we assumed a very special kind of initial database, namely, the closed databases of Section 5.3, an assumption that justified using Prolog to handle all processing for the base theory. This gave us an efficiently implementable base theory. Next, we made this base into a support for a tower of definitions, consisting of action precondition and successor state axioms, definitions for the executable situations, for the least-natural-time point, for probabilities and value functions, etc., and perhaps most importantly, for the control structures for the various dialects of Golog that we used in the book.[1] In all cases, the implementation unwinds these definitions, either by regression alone or, in the case of Golog, by macro-expansion of a program followed by regression. On completion of this unwinding, the resulting expression is evaluated against the base theory. At heart, every Prolog programmer knows this principle of structuring a knowledge base. As Clark's semantics for Prolog tells us, clauses really are definitions, and the base theory is a collection of atoms that acts like a relational database. These are precisely the properties that make logic programming computationally feasible. We can summarize these intuitions by the following slogan:

> Efficient implementation = Base theory in database form + Tower of definitions

But what if the base theory is not in database form? We did treat examples of this possibility, first in the case of open-world planning (Section 10.6), and secondly for knowledge-based programming with sensing (Section 11.7). In both cases, we had to appeal to general theorem-proving techniques because we were not justified in assuming a closed initial database. Sometimes such forms of intensive deliberation may be acceptable, especially if they are performed off-line, but for real-time agent behaviours, the computational overhead will normally be unacceptable. What can be done in such cases? The problem is certainly real, at least for applications in cognitive robotics; it is unrealistic to assume that a robot will have complete information about its environment, and this alone precludes starting it out with a closed initial theory of the world. One possible approach, which is an active

---

1 We are here conflating the distinction between a definition, which is a biconditional sentence, and an abbreviation, which is a macro. But computationally, they are treated in the same way.

research theme in the complexity literature, is to determine classes of base theories with provably good theorem-proving computational complexity. Such is the case, for example, with propositional Horn theories. But it is likely that a more general approach will be needed. A very interesting, and intuitively plausible, possibility is to rely on a robot's sensors to fill in the gaps in its open database. But we don't want our robot to randomly wander around sensing its environment; it should act according to suitable sense-only-as-needed criteria. One such criterion is provided by De Giacomo and Levesque [66] who describe how regression can be guaranteed to determine a sentence's truth value, even with open initial databases, provided the current situation and the robot's sensor readings satisfy the property of being *just-in-time*. Roughly speaking, this means that at the time the sentence needs to be evaluated, there will be enough information available to do this, from the sensor readings and from the open initial database. This idea has been further extended by De Giacomo, Levesque, and Sardiña [67], who combine this just-in-time regression algorithm with an on-line version of ConGolog—a concurrent version of Golog. The resulting language, called IndiGolog, allows writing on-line robot control programs with sensing and open initial databases. IndiGolog's just-in-time criterion encourages a different style of programming, one in which the programmer must ensure that her program explicitly calls for sensing information, and at just the right time, to guarantee that just-in-time regression will apply to any sentence that the program needs to evaluate at the next step.

Open worlds pose other problems that have not been dealt with in this book. One concerns belief, in contrast to knowledge, where an agent's representation of the world might be mistaken, or too course-grained. The only way an agent can determine such discrepancies between her mental state and external reality is through sensing. Having sensed that there is a conflict, how should she revise her beliefs? Closely related to this is the problem of execution monitoring: An agent has formulated a mental plan of actions, and then proceeds to execute it, using her sensors to check whether everything is going according to plan. This requires a subtle combination of off- and on-line behaviours, that integrates sensing, belief revision, and replanning.

Apart from open worlds and their related problems, there are many other issues that have not been addressed in this book. A partial list would include multiple co-operating agents and their associated modalities (promising, requesting, etc.), hybrid systems requiring combined discrete and continous control programs, non-terminating processes like a controller governing a robot's lifetime behaviour, and qualitative probability and decision theory for expressing an agent's preferences in the absence of numerical information about rewards and probabilities.

Finally, it should be noted that the entire framework of this book relies on the concept of a primitive action. Plans, Golog programs, stochastic actions, are all defined in terms of them. Therefore, perhaps we should ask ourselves what counts as a primitive action? This raises more questions than anyone currently knows how to answer. Consider a robot's blocks world "primitive" action $moveToTable(x)$. This abstracts away many features of the world; moving a block involves first positioning the robot's hand (which surely involves sensing), then grasping, then lifting, etc. So $moveToTable(x)$ is far from primitive; it's more like a Golog procedure. By focusing on one of the "primitives" of this Golog program, say $grasp(x)$, we discover that even at this finer level of granularity, it is not primitive either. Instead, its structure is that of a while loop, with pressure sensing actions: While the pressure is less than p, close the gripper by ϵ, then sense the pressure. Moreover, the value of p depends on how heavy the block is, whether it is slippery, made of wood or paper, etc., so the $grasp(x)$ action is sensitive to what the robot knows about these properties. $moveToTable(x)$ should not take responsibility for transmitting to $grasp(x)$ the value of this knowledge-sensitive parameter p; such concerns are inappropriate to $moveToTable$'s level of abstraction, which deals only with planning course-grained action sequences. Thus, the $grasp$ procedure must have access to the robot's beliefs about the world. We can plausibly take this to be a sufficient condition for $grasp$ not to be primitive. A good case can be made that this is also necessary. Therefore, action primitives must be "cognitively impenetrable" behaviours (Pylyshyn [169]); their executions are independent of the agent's belief state. As such, they can be designed as "informationally encapsulated" modules requiring no access to the logical sentences making up the agent's beliefs about the world. But what behaviours have this property? Perhaps some day principles of good design will provide the answers; perhaps, instead, we shall have to wait for psychologists and neurophysiologists to come up with the right empirically determined behavioural primitives. Whatever these primitives turn out to be, we can expect a hierarchy of action types, where primitives at one level have the fine structure of procedures involving lower level "primitives". Within this framework, how should an agent's beliefs be stratified and transmitted from one level to another? In execution monitoring, how do failures at one level propagate to other levels, and who does what to recover from failures? For preliminary results on such hierarchically structured, logic-based action theories, see Amir and Maynard-Reid II [4] and Finzi, Pirri, Romano, and Vaccaro [53]. These issues are instances of the more general problem of representing and reasoning with knowledge at different levels of *granularity*. Hobbs [88] was perhaps the first to address this problem from a logical perspective. More recent results on granularity can be found in [19].

I can't remember its title or author, but many years ago I recall reading a science fiction story about a future world that has run out of Ph.D. thesis topics, and a desperate student sells his soul to the devil for a subject. Perhaps someday physics students will find themselves in this sorry state, but I suspect that, even as the physicists bargain away their souls, cognitive robotics Ph.D. candidates will still be struggling with the mysteries of modeling human-level behaviours.

A Appendix:
Some Useful First-Order Inference Rules

For finding proofs by hand of complex logical theorems, the following rules are very useful (and natural). They are not complete, but seem to work well surprisingly often. Of course, they are sound.

In the following, A is always a set of formulas; λ, with or without subscripts, denotes a literal; ϕ and ψ denote formulas. In a theorem-proving context, the notation $A \Rightarrow \phi$ is read as: The current goal is to prove that the *premise* A entails the *consequent* ϕ. The following inference rules always replace a current goal by one or more *subgoals*.

A.1 Decomposition Rules

These reduce goals to simpler subgoals.

D1 **Splitting a conjunctive consequent.** Goal: $A \Rightarrow \phi \land \psi$, where ϕ and ψ have no free variables in common.
   Subgoals: $A \Rightarrow \phi$ and $A \Rightarrow \psi$.
   In other words, to establish the original goal, it is sufficient to establish both of the subgoals.

D2 **Equivalence elimination in the consequent.** Goal: $A \Rightarrow \phi \equiv \psi$.
   Subgoals: $A, \phi \Rightarrow \psi$ and $A, \psi \Rightarrow \phi$.

D3 **Implication elimination in the consequent.** Goal: $A \Rightarrow \phi \supset \psi$.
   Subgoal: $A, \phi \Rightarrow \psi$.

D4 **Or-elimination in the consequent.** Goal: $A \Rightarrow \phi \lor \psi$.
   Subgoal: $A, \neg\phi \Rightarrow \psi$ or $A, \neg\psi \Rightarrow \phi$.
   In other words, to establish the original goal, it is sufficient to establish one of the two subgoals.

D5 **Skolemize universals in the consequent.** Goal: $A \Rightarrow (\forall x)\phi$.
   Subgoal: $A \Rightarrow \phi|^{x}_{sk(\vec{y})}$ where $\vec{y}$ are all the free variables of $(\forall x)\phi$, distinct from x, and sk is a new function symbol, distinct from any occurring in the proof thus far.[1]

D6 **Remove existentials in the consequent.** Goal: $A \Rightarrow (\exists x)\phi$.
   Subgoal: $A \Rightarrow \phi$.
   Hence, free variables in consequents are implicitly existentially quantified. (Before removing such an existential, make sure—by renaming if necessary—that the variable x is different than any of the other variables, quantified or not, of $(\exists x)\phi$.)

---

1 In general, when ϕ is a formula, x a variable, and t a term, $\phi|^{x}_{t}$ denotes that formula obtained from ϕ by substituting t for all free occurrences of x in ϕ.

D7 **Guess values for free variables in the consequent.** Goal: $A \Rightarrow \phi$, where variable x occurs free in ϕ.

In this case, the freedom of x in ϕ arose from dropping an existential quantifier as in the previous rule, and heuristically we are seeking an instance of x for which the consequent is provable. Accordingly, this leads to:

Subgoal: $A \Rightarrow \phi|_t^x$, where t is a ground term[2] that you must cleverly guess. This is the most "creative" of all the rules.

D8 **Backchaining.** Goal: $A \Rightarrow \lambda$, where A contains a formula of the form $\phi \supset \lambda'$ and where λ and λ' unify with unifier μ.

Subgoal: $A \Rightarrow \phi\mu$.

Notice that ϕ here can be an arbitrary formula, but λ and λ' must be literals. Here, by a *unifier* μ of two literals λ and λ', we mean a substitution of terms for the free variables of λ and λ' that makes the resulting two literals identical, and by $\phi\mu$ we mean the formula obtained by making this substitution for the free variables of ϕ. When two literals have a unifier, we say that they *unify*. In obtaining the unifier μ, make sure, by renaming variables if necessary, that the two formulas $\phi \supset \lambda'$ and λ have no free variable in common.

D9 **Try for proof by contradiction.** Goal: $A \Rightarrow \phi$.

Subgoal: $A, \neg\phi \Rightarrow false$. Usually most successful when ϕ is a negated formula.

D10 **Proof by cases.** Goal: $A \Rightarrow \phi$ and A contains a formula of the form $\psi_1 \vee \psi_2$, where ψ_1 and ψ_2 have no free variables in common.

Subgoals: $A, \psi_1 \Rightarrow \phi$ and $A, \psi_2 \Rightarrow \phi$.

D11 **Equality substitution into the consequent.** Goal: $A \Rightarrow \phi$ and A contains $t_1 = t_2$ for terms t_1 and t_2. Suppose that ϕ mentions a term t_1', and that μ is a substitution for the free variables (if any) of t_1 such that $t_1\mu$ is identical to t_1'.

Subgoal: $A \Rightarrow \phi'$, where ϕ' is obtained from ϕ by replacing the occurrence of t_1' in ϕ by $t_2\mu$.

In other words, if t_1 has an instance that is identical to t_1', you can replace t_1' in ϕ by the corresponding instance of t_2. There is a symmetric rule interchanging t_1 and t_2. A good heuristic is to substitute syntactically simpler terms for complex ones.

D12 **Equivalence substitution into the consequent.** Goal: $A \Rightarrow \phi$ and A contains the formula $P(\vec{t}) \equiv \psi$, where P is a predicate symbol, $\vec{t}$ are terms, and ψ is a formula. Often, this will be a a formula of the form $P(\vec{x}) \equiv \psi$, where the $\vec{x}$ are different variables, in which case it is a definition of P. Suppose that ϕ mentions an atom of the form $P(\vec{t'})$ for terms $\vec{t'}$, and μ is a substitution for the free variables (if any) of t such

---

2 A *ground* term is one that mentions no variables.

that $\vec{t}\mu$ is identical to $\vec{t}'$.

Subgoal: $A \Rightarrow \phi'$, where ϕ' is obtained from ϕ by replacing the occurrence of $P(\vec{t}')$ in ϕ by $\psi\mu$.

In other words, if $P(\vec{t})$ has an instance that is identical to $P(\vec{t}')$, you can replace $P(\vec{t}')$ in ϕ by the corresponding instance of ψ. Notice the parallel with the previous rule for equality substitution into the consequent.

A.2   Generation Rules

These sanction the derivation of new premises using those of A.

G1 **Remove universals in the premise.** Whenever A contains a formula $(\forall x)\phi$, replace it by ϕ. Thus, free variables in formulas of A are implicitly universally quantified. (Before doing this, make sure, by renaming if necessary, that the variable x is different than any of the other variables, quantified or free, of $(\forall x)\phi$.)

G2 **Skolemize existentials in the premise.** Whenever A contains a formula $(\exists x)\phi$, replace it by $\phi|_{sk(\vec{y})}^{x}$ where $\vec{y}$ are all the free variables of $(\exists x)\phi$, and sk is a new function symbol, distinct from any occurring in the proof thus far. (Before doing this, make sure, by renaming if necessary, that the variable x is different than any of the other variables, quantified or free, of $(\exists x)\phi$.)

G3 **And-elimination in the premise.** Whenever A contains a conjunction $\phi \wedge \psi$ of two formulas, replace this conjunction by the two formulas ϕ and ψ.

G4 **Generalized modus ponens (forward chaining).**
Suppose A contains a formula of the form $\lambda_1 \wedge \cdots \wedge \lambda_n \supset \phi$, together with n literals $\lambda_1', \ldots, \lambda_n'$, and suppose that μ is a unifier such that, for $i = 1, \ldots, n$, $\lambda_i\mu = \lambda_i'\mu$. Then add to A the formula $\phi\mu$. In obtaining the unifier μ, make sure, by renaming variables if necessary, that the formulas $\lambda_1 \wedge \cdots \wedge \lambda_n \supset \phi$ and $\lambda_1', \ldots, \lambda_n'$ have no free variable in common. Notice that ϕ here need not be a literal.

G5 **Unit resolution.** If A contains a formula $\lambda \vee \phi$ and it also contains the literal $\neg\lambda'$, and if λ and λ' unify with unifier μ, then add to A the formula $\phi\mu$. In obtaining the unifier μ, make sure, by renaming variables if necessary, that the formulas $\lambda \vee \phi$ and λ have no free variable in common. Notice that ϕ need not be a clause.

G6 **Equality substitution into the premise.** Suppose A contains $t_1 = t_2$ for terms t_1 and t_2. Suppose also that A contains a formula ϕ that mentions a term t_1', and that μ is a substitution for the free variables (if any) of t_1 such that $t_1\mu$ is identical to t_1'.

Then add to A the formula ϕ' where ϕ' is obtained from ϕ by replacing the occurrence of t_1' in ϕ by $t_2\mu$.

In other words, if t_1 has an instance that is identical to t_1', you can replace t_1' in ϕ by the corresponding instance of t_2. There is a symmetric rule interchanging t_1 and t_2. A good heuristic is to substitute syntactically simpler terms for complex ones.

G7 **Equivalence substitution into the premise.** Suppose that A contains a biconditional formula $P(\vec{t}) \equiv \psi$, where P is a predicate symbol, $\vec{t}$ are terms, and ψ is a formula. Often, this will be a a a formula of the form $P(\vec{x}) \equiv \psi$, where the $\vec{x}$ are different variables, in which case it is a definition of P. Suppose further that A contains a formula ϕ that mentions an atom of the form $P(\vec{t'})$ for terms $\vec{t'}$, and μ is a substitution for the free variables (if any) of t such that $\vec{t}\mu$ is identical to $\vec{t'}$.

Then "expand" this biconditional in ϕ, namely, add to A the formula ϕ' where ϕ' is obtained from ϕ by replacing the occurrence of $P(\vec{t'})$ in ϕ by $\psi\mu$.

Notice the parallel with the previous rule for equality substitution into the premise. Notice also that the corresponding rules for equality and equivalence for consequents (decomposition rules 11 and 12) are basically the same as those for premises; they talk about equality and equivalence substitution into the right hand side of the $\Rightarrow$, whereas here we are considering substitution into the left side. We could have combined these four rules into one that simply says "Substitute for equality and equivalence throughout the goal $A \Rightarrow \phi$".

A.3   Success Rules

S1 Goal: $A \Rightarrow \lambda$.

QED, if λ unifies with a literal of A. In performing this unification test, make sure that the two literals have no variables in common.

S2 Goal: $A \Rightarrow t_1 = t_2$.

QED, if there is a substitution of terms for the free variables of t_1 and t_2 that makes them identical.

S3 **Proof by contradiction.** Goal: $A \Rightarrow \phi$.

QED, if A contains two complementary literals whose atoms unify, i.e. A contains an atom α and a literal $\neg\beta$ such that α unifies with β. In performing this unification test, make sure that these two literals have no variables in common.

S4 **Proof by contradiction: equality.** Goal: $A \Rightarrow \phi$.

QED, if A contains the inequality literal $\neg t_1 = t_2$, and there is a substitution of terms for the free variables of t_1 and t_2 that makes them identical.

A.4   Proof Rules for Unique Names Axioms

Often, in artificial intelligence applications, a domain theory will include so-called *unique names axioms*. These specify that certain designated function symbols of the domain theory satisfy two properties:

1. Whenever f and g are two such designated function symbols, then

$$f(\vec{x}) \neq g(\vec{y})$$

   is part of the domain theory.

2. Whenever f is such a designated n-ary function symbol, then

$$f(x_1, \ldots, x_n) = f(y_1, \ldots, y_n) \supset x_1 = y_1 \wedge \cdots \wedge x_n = y_n$$

   is part of the domain theory.

When the function symbol f is a constant symbol, so $n = 0$, the second unique names axiom is vacuously true, and is omitted.

We often encounter such unique names axioms in this book. For example, the foundational axioms for situations of Chapter 4 provide unique names axioms for the designated function symbols do and S_0. Such axioms lead to the following natural proof rules:

Suppose f and g are designated unique names function symbols.

1. Replace the atom $f(\vec{t}) = g(\vec{\tau})$ by *false* wherever it occurs in a proof. Here, $\vec{t}$ and $\vec{\tau}$ are any tuples of terms of arity suitable as arguments to f and g. Notice that $f(\vec{t}) \neq g(\vec{\tau})$ is a notational convention standing for $\neg(f(\vec{t}) = g(\vec{\tau}))$, and so by this rule it gets replaced by $\neg false$.

2. If f is an n-ary function symbol, $n \geq 1$, replace the atom $f(t_1, \ldots, t_n) = f(t'_1, \ldots, t'_n)$ by $t_1 = t'_1 \wedge \cdots \wedge t_n = t'_n$ wherever it occurs in a proof. Here, the t_i and t'_i are any terms.

A.5   Simplification Rules

Since we have introduced the special atom *false*, we need simplification rules for this. And while we are at it, we shall include additional simplification rules that are often very useful. In the following rules, $\phi \rightarrow \psi$ means replace ϕ by ψ wherever ϕ occurs in a proof.

$\neg false \rightarrow true$	$\neg true \rightarrow false$	$false \wedge \phi \rightarrow false$
$true \wedge \phi \rightarrow \phi$	$false \vee \phi \rightarrow \phi$	$true \vee \phi \rightarrow true$
$t = t \rightarrow true$	$\neg(\phi \wedge \psi) \rightarrow \neg\phi \vee \neg\psi$	$\neg(\phi \vee \psi) \rightarrow \neg\phi \wedge \neg\psi$
$\neg\neg\phi \rightarrow \phi$	$(\exists x).x = t \wedge \phi(x) \rightarrow \phi(t)$	$(\forall x).x = t \supset \phi(x) \rightarrow \phi(t)$

In the last two rules, the term t must not mention x. They are particularly useful when reasoning about equality, and rely on the fact that, on the stated assumption about t, the left and right hand sides of the arrow are logically equivalent in first-order logic with equality (Exercise 10 below).

A.6 Additional Success Rules

Having introduced the atoms *true* and *false*, we need to augment the success rules so that the following goals succeed:

$$A \Rightarrow true \qquad A, false \Rightarrow \phi$$

A.7 Examples of Proofs

Example A.7.1: The top level goal is:

$(\forall x, y).E(x, y) \equiv S(x, y) \wedge S(y, x),$
$(\forall x, y, z).I(z, f(x, y)) \equiv I(z, x) \vee I(z, y),$
$(\forall x, y).S(x, y) \equiv (\forall z).I(z, x) \supset I(z, y)$
$\Rightarrow$
$(\forall x, y).E(f(x, y), y) \equiv S(x, y)$

In other words, we want to show that the premise preceding the $\Rightarrow$ symbol entails the sentence following it.

Skolemize the consequent (rule D5) with the constants X, Y and drop redundant universal quantifiers in the premise (rule G1), to get the new goal:

$E(x, y) \equiv S(x, y) \wedge S(y, x), \quad I(z, f(x, y)) \equiv I(z, x) \vee I(z, y),$
$S(x, y) \equiv (\forall z).I(z, x) \supset I(z, y)$
$\Rightarrow$
$E(f(X, Y), Y) \equiv S(X, Y)$

D2 gives two subgoals:

1. $\quad E(x, y) \equiv S(x, y) \wedge S(y, x), \quad I(z, f(x, y)) \equiv I(z, x) \vee I(z, y),$
$S(x, y) \equiv (\forall z).I(z, x) \supset I(z, y), \quad E(f(X, Y), Y)$
$\Rightarrow$
$S(X, Y)$

2. $\quad E(x, y) \equiv S(x, y) \wedge S(y, x), \quad I(z, f(x, y)) \equiv I(z, x) \vee I(z, y),$
$S(x, y) \equiv (\forall z).I(z, x) \supset I(z, y), \quad S(X, Y)$
$\Rightarrow$
$E(f(X, Y), Y)$

First pursue subgoal 1. By D12 (equivalence substitution into the consequent):

$E(x, y) \equiv S(x, y) \wedge S(y, x), \quad I(z, f(x, y)) \equiv I(z, x) \vee I(z, y),$
$S(x, y) \equiv (\forall z).I(z, x) \supset I(z, y), \quad E(f(X, Y), Y)$
$\Rightarrow$
$(\forall z).I(z, X) \supset I(z, Y)$

By D5 (Skolemize the variable z of the consequent) followed by D3:

$$E(x, y) \equiv S(x, y) \wedge S(y, x), \quad I(z, f(x, y)) \equiv I(z, x) \vee I(z, y),$$
$$S(x, y) \equiv (\forall z).I(z, x) \supset I(z, y), \quad E(f(X, Y), Y), \quad I(Z, X)$$
$$\Rightarrow$$
$$I(Z, Y)$$

By G7 (equivalence substitution) followed by G3 (and-elimination):

$$E(x, y) \equiv S(x, y) \wedge S(y, x), \quad I(z, f(x, y)) \equiv I(z, x) \vee I(z, y),$$
$$S(x, y) \equiv (\forall z).I(z, x) \supset I(z, y), \quad E(f(X, Y), Y), \quad I(Z, X),$$
$$S(f(X, Y), Y), \quad S(Y, f(X, Y))$$
$$\Rightarrow$$
$$I(Z, Y)$$

By G7 (equivalence substitution) followed by G1 (remove the quantifier $\forall z$):

$$E(x, y) \equiv S(x, y) \wedge S(y, x), \quad I(z, f(x, y)) \equiv I(z, x) \vee I(z, y),$$
$$S(x, y) \equiv (\forall z).I(z, x) \supset I(z, y), \quad E(f(X, Y), Y), \quad I(Z, X),$$
$$S(f(X, Y), Y), \quad S(Y, f(X, Y)), \quad I(z, f(X, Y)) \supset I(z, Y)$$
$$\Rightarrow$$
$$I(Z, Y)$$

By D8 (backchaining):

$$E(x, y) \equiv S(x, y) \wedge S(y, x), \quad I(z, f(x, y)) \equiv I(z, x) \vee I(z, y),$$
$$S(x, y) \equiv (\forall z).I(z, x) \supset I(z, y), \quad E(f(X, Y), Y), \quad I(Z, X),$$
$$S(f(X, Y), Y), \quad S(Y, f(X, Y)), \quad I(z, F(X, Y)) \supset I(z, Y)$$
$$\Rightarrow$$
$$I(Z, f(X, Y))$$

By D12 (equivalence substitution into the consequent):

$$E(x, y) \equiv S(x, y) \wedge S(y, x), \quad I(z, f(x, y)) \equiv I(z, x) \vee I(z, y),$$
$$S(x, y) \equiv (\forall z).I(z, x) \supset I(z, y), \quad E(f(X, Y), Y), \quad I(Z, X),$$
$$S(f(X, Y), Y), \quad S(Y, f(X, Y)), \quad I(z, F(X, Y)) \supset I(z, Y)$$
$$\Rightarrow$$
$$I(Z, X) \vee I(Z, Y)$$

By D4 (or-elimination):

$$E(x, y) \equiv S(x, y) \wedge S(y, x), \quad I(z, f(x, y)) \equiv I(z, x) \vee I(z, y),$$
$$S(x, y) \equiv (\forall z).I(z, x) \supset I(z, y), \quad E(f(X, Y), Y), \quad I(Z, X),$$
$$S(f(X, Y), Y), \quad S(Y, f(X, Y)), \quad I(z, F(X, Y)) \supset I(z, Y), \quad \neg I(Z, Y)$$
$$\Rightarrow$$
$$I(Z, X)$$

QED by S1.

Next we prove subgoal 2, which we do with a minimum of editorial comment.

$E(x, y) \equiv S(x, y) \wedge S(y, x), \quad I(z, f(x, y)) \equiv I(z, x) \vee I(z, y),$
$S(x, y) \equiv (\forall z).I(z, x) \supset I(z, y), \quad S(X, Y)$
$\Rightarrow$
$S(f(X, Y), Y) \wedge S(Y, f(X, Y))$

2.1 $E(x, y) \equiv S(x, y) \wedge S(y, x), \quad I(z, f(x, y)) \equiv I(z, x) \vee I(z, y),$
           $S(x, y) \equiv (\forall z).I(z, x) \supset I(z, y), \quad S(X, Y)$
           $\Rightarrow$
           $S(f(X, Y), Y)$

2.2 $E(x, y) \equiv S(x, y) \wedge S(y, x), \quad I(z, f(x, y)) \equiv I(z, x) \vee I(z, y),$
           $S(x, y) \equiv (\forall z).I(z, x) \supset I(z, y), \quad S(X, Y)$
           $\Rightarrow$
           $S(Y, f(X, Y))$

First, pursue 2.1.

$E(x, y) \equiv S(x, y) \wedge S(y, x), \quad I(z, f(x, y)) \equiv I(z, x) \vee I(z, y),$
$S(x, y) \equiv (\forall z).I(z, x) \supset I(z, y), \quad S(X, Y)$
$\Rightarrow$
$(\forall z).I(z, f(X, Y)) \supset I(z, Y)$

$E(x, y) \equiv S(x, y) \wedge S(y, x), \quad I(z, f(x, y)) \equiv I(z, x) \vee I(z, y),$
$S(x, y) \equiv (\forall z).I(z, x) \supset I(z, y), \quad S(X, Y)$
$\Rightarrow$
$I(Z, f(X, Y)) \supset I(Z, Y)$

$E(x, y) \equiv S(x, y) \wedge S(y, x), \quad I(z, f(x, y)) \equiv I(z, x) \vee I(z, y),$
$S(x, y) \equiv (\forall z).I(z, x) \supset I(z, y), \quad S(X, Y), \quad I(Z, f(X, Y))$
$\Rightarrow$
$I(Z, Y)$

$E(x, y) \equiv S(x, y) \wedge S(y, x), \quad I(z, f(x, y)) \equiv I(z, x) \vee I(z, y),$
$S(x, y) \equiv (\forall z).I(z, x) \supset I(z, y), \quad S(X, Y), \quad I(Z, f(X, Y)),$
$I(Z, X) \vee I(Z, Y)$
$\Rightarrow$
$I(Z, Y)$

By D10 (proof by cases):

2.1.1 $E(x, y) \equiv S(x, y) \wedge S(y, x), \quad I(z, f(x, y)) \equiv I(z, x) \vee I(z, y),$
$S(x, y) \equiv (\forall z).I(z, x) \supset I(z, y), \quad S(X, Y), \quad I(Z, f(X, Y)),$
$I(Z, X)$
$\Rightarrow$
$I(Z, Y)$

2.1.2 $E(x, y) \equiv S(x, y) \wedge S(y, x), \quad I(z, f(x, y)) \equiv I(z, x) \vee I(z, y),$
$S(x, y) \equiv (\forall z).I(z, x) \supset I(z, y), \quad S(X, Y), \quad I(Z, f(X, Y)), I(Z, Y)$
$\Rightarrow$
$I(Z, Y)$

For 2.1.2 we immediately have QED by S1. So, pursue 2.1.1.

$E(x, y) \equiv S(x, y) \wedge S(y, x), \quad I(z, f(x, y)) \equiv I(z, x) \vee I(z, y),$
$S(x, y) \equiv (\forall z).I(z, x) \supset I(z, y), \quad S(X, Y), \quad I(Z, f(X, Y)),$
$I(Z, X), \quad I(z, X) \supset I(z, Y)$
$\Rightarrow$
$I(Z, Y)$

By G4 (modus ponens):

$E(x, y) \equiv S(x, y) \wedge S(y, x), \quad I(z, f(x, y)) \equiv I(z, x) \vee I(z, y),$
$S(x, y) \equiv (\forall z).I(z, x) \supset I(z, y), \quad S(X, Y), \quad I(Z, f(X, Y)),$
$I(Z, X), \quad I(z, X) \supset I(z, Y), \quad I(Z, Y)$
$\Rightarrow$
$I(Z, Y)$

QED by S1.

We leave it to the reader to establish subgoal 2.2.

Example A.7.2: The proof for the previous example was excessively wordy, and not very easy to follow. Figure A.1 presents a more compact and transparent tree-structured proof format for the following goal:

$$\Rightarrow (\exists x)T(x) \wedge (\forall x, y)[T(x) \wedge T(y) \supset x = y] \equiv (\exists x)(\forall y).T(y) \equiv y = x$$

Notice especially that when a proof is organized in this way as a tree, there is no need to continually copy all the premises of a goal from one proof step to the next. Premises inherit downward in the tree; the available premises at a tree node consist of those explicitly indicated, together with all premises explicitly indicated at all its ancestor nodes in the tree.

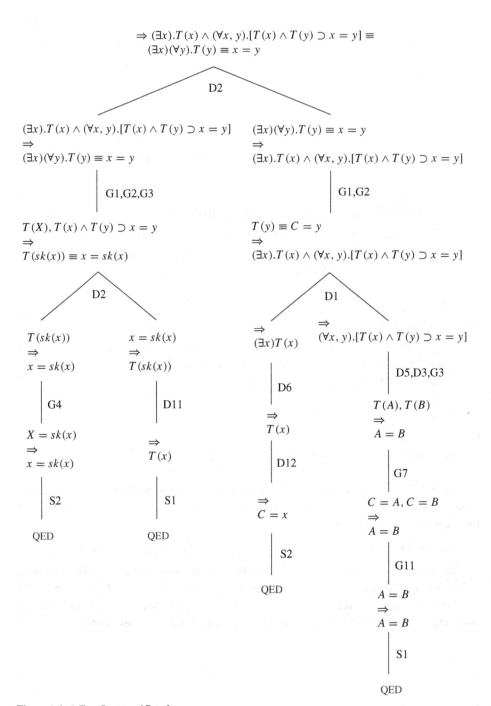

398   Appendix A

Figure A.1: A Tree-Structured Proof.

A.8 Exercises

Prove the following goals:

1. $(\exists x)P(x) \equiv (\exists y)Q(y),$
    $(\forall x, y).P(x) \wedge Q(y) \supset [R(x) \equiv S(y)]$
    $\Rightarrow$
    $(\forall x)[P(x) \supset R(x)] \equiv (\forall y)[Q(y) \supset S(y)].$

2. $(\exists x)F(x), (\exists x)G(x)$
    $\Rightarrow$
    $(\forall x)[\{F(x) \supset H(x)\} \wedge (\forall y)\{G(y) \supset J(y)\}] \equiv$
    $\qquad\qquad (\forall x, y)[F(x) \wedge G(y) \supset H(x) \wedge J(y)].$

3. Russell's paradox: there is no set containing exactly those sets that are not members of themselves.
    $\Rightarrow \neg(\exists x)(\forall y).F(y, x) \equiv \neg F(y, y).$

4. $(\forall x, y).Q(x, y) \equiv (\forall z).F(z, x) \equiv F(z, y)$
    $\Rightarrow$
    $(\forall x, y).Q(x, y) \equiv Q(y, x).$

5. $(\forall x).F(x) \wedge (\forall y)[F(y) \supset G(y)] \supset G(x),$
    $(\exists x)[F(x) \wedge \neg G(x)] \supset (\exists y)[F(y) \wedge \neg G(y) \wedge$
    $\qquad\qquad (\forall z)\{F(z) \wedge \neg G(z) \supset J(y, z)\}],$
    $(\forall x, y).F(x) \wedge F(y) \supset \neg J(y, x)$
    $\Rightarrow$
    $(\forall x).F(x) \supset G(x).$

6. $A = B \vee C = D, A = C \vee B = D \Rightarrow A = D \vee B = C.$

7. $(\exists z, w)(\forall x, y).F(x, y) \equiv x = z \wedge y = w$
    $\Rightarrow$
    $(\exists w)(\forall y)[(\exists z)(\forall x)\{F(x, y) \equiv x = z\} \equiv y = w].$

8. $\Rightarrow (\forall x).F(x, f(x)) \equiv (\exists y).(\forall z)[F(z, y) \supset F(z, f(x))] \wedge F(x, y).$

9. There are three blocks, A, B and C. A is on B and B is on C. A is green and C is not green. Then there is a green block on top of a non-green block.

$$\Rightarrow green(A) \wedge \neg green(C) \wedge on(A, B) \wedge on(B, C) \supset$$
$$(\exists x, y).green(x) \wedge \neg green(y) \wedge on(x, y)$$

10. Prove that when the term t does not mention x, and when $\phi(x)$ is a first-order formula with one free variable x, the following equivalences are valid. (These are the bases for the last two simplification rules of this appendix.)

$$(\exists x)[x = t \wedge \phi(x)] \equiv \phi(t),$$

$$(\forall x)[x = t \supset \phi(x)] \equiv \phi(t),$$

11. Present the proof of Example A.7.1 in the form of a tree.

12. Suppose the following facts are true for a collection of blocks placed along a straight line on a table:

   (a) Every block on the table is either a cube or a tetrahedron.

   (b) Whenever a cube x lies to the left of another cube, x must be red.

   (c) Every red tetrahedron lies to the left of at least one blue cube.

   (d) Nothing can be both red and blue.

   (e) Whenever x is to the left of y, and y is to the left of z, then x is to the left of z.

   Axiomatize the information in (a)-(e), and prove that no blue cube can lie to the left of a red block.

B Appendix: The Qualification and Ramification Problems

On several occasions in this book, notably in Section 4.3, we have encountered so-called *state constraints*, or as they are called in database theory, *integrity constraints*. These describe global properties that must hold in all situations. In Section 4.3.2, we observed that such constraints are intimately connected with the frame and qualification problems, and that they pose particularly difficult questions for theories of actions. While treating these in depth would overly lengthen this book, the subject is sufficiently important that we here describe what the problems are, and indicate how they might be approached.

We begin by noting that there are often natural sentences that one might write in describing dynamical domains. We encountered many examples in the book. For the blocks world, two such constraints are:

$$on(x, y, s) \supset \neg on(y, x, s),$$

$$on(y, x, s) \land on(z, x, s) \supset y = z.$$

Other examples arose naturally in the database setting. One of those, stating that no one's salary may decrease, is of interest because it illustrates that constraints may depend on situations s' other than the global one s:

$$(\forall s, s', p, \$, \$').s' \sqsubseteq s \land sal(p, \$', s') \land sal(p, \$, s) \supset \$' \leq \$.$$

The first question that naturally arises about constraints is this: Why do basic action theories make no provision for these to be included among their axioms? They are, after all, truths about the world, so what justifies us ignoring them? The answer is, as described in Section 4.3, because such constraints must be inductive entailments of the basic action theory. As such, their information content is already present in the theory, and so they can be ignored. But this raises another question. How is it that constraints will always be logical consequences of the basic action theory? How can we be so lucky, and what guarantees are there that this will always be the case? It almost seems that in formulating a particular basic action theory, we are subconsciously taking the domain's state constraints into account. If so, exactly how do we take them into account?

B.1 Constraints and the Ramification Problem

An example of what is called a *ramification* constraint is the fact that if an object is painted, then its component parts are also painted:

$$painted(x, s) \land partOf(y, x) \supset painted(y, s).$$

Intuitively, this axiom implicitly conveys causal information about the action of painting something, namely, that painting x causes each of x's component parts y to also become painted. Let's see how such a causal law can be extracted from this state constraint plus the causal law for painting. This latter is expressed by the effect axiom:

$painted(x, do(paint(x), s))$.

This, together with the state constraint, entails

$partOf(y, x) \supset painted(y, do(paint(x), s))$.

So from the old effect axiom and the state constraint, a new effect axiom is obtained. Now recall that our solution to the frame problem was based on the causal completeness assumption that an explicit enumeration of *all* the causal laws of the domain is given in the form of effect axioms. The presence of state constraints means that those effect axioms "hidden" in the constraints must be made explicit before one can solve the frame problem by transforming effect axioms to successor state axioms. This illustrates the intimate connection between state constraints and the frame problem.

Using the above two effect axioms to determine a successor state axiom for *painted*, we get

$$painted(x, do(a, s)) \equiv a = paint(x) \vee (\exists y)[partOf(x, y) \wedge a = paint(y)] \vee painted(x, s).$$

Next, we show that this successor state axiom, together with the constraint relativized to S_0, contains all the information of the original constraint. Specifically, it is easy to prove, by induction on situations, that this successor state axiom, together with the sentence

$painted(x, S_0) \wedge partOf(y, x) \supset painted(y, S_0)$,

entails the original constraint. This means that the original constraint can be ignored by any basic action theory that includes the above successor state axiom, and whose initial database includes the constraint relativized to S_0. Its information content has been compiled into the basic action theory. This example indicates why basic action theories do not include axioms for state constraints. But one does pay a price for this luxury: One must be conscious of how state constraints might contain implicit causal laws, and take these laws into account in formulating successor state axioms.

Solving the frame problem when given a set of effect axioms and state constraints as initial data is called the *ramification problem*. It was first observed by Finger [51].

B.2   Constraints and the Qualification Problem

We first encountered the qualification problem in Section 3.1.3, which observed that action preconditions can have an indefinite number of minor qualifications, in addition to the major ones:

$$Poss(pickup(r, x), s) \supset [(\forall z)\neg holding(r, z, s)] \wedge \neg heavy(x) \wedge nextTo(r, x, s) \wedge$$
$$\neg gluedToFloor(x, s) \wedge \neg armsTied(r, s) \wedge \neg hitByTenTonTruck(r, s) \wedge \cdots$$

We decided there to simply ignore the minor qualifications, in favour of action precondition axioms, defined in terms of necessary and sufficient conditions on the major qualifications. In effect, our proposal was the following: For each action type $A(\vec{x})$, list as many necessary conditions on $Poss$ as you think are important, say $\pi_1(\vec{x}, s), \ldots, \pi_n(\vec{x}, s)$, where the $\pi_i(\vec{x}, s)$ are A's major qualifications. Next, make a closure assumption to the effect that these are all and only the qualifications you wish to consider, and get A's action precondition axiom:

$$Poss(A(\vec{x}), s) \equiv \pi_1(\vec{x}, s) \wedge \cdots \wedge \pi_n(\vec{x}, s).$$

But constraints can add a new dimension to this problem. They may contain implicit major qualifications, just as, in the case of the ramification problem, they may contain hidden effect axioms. To see this, consider that whenever $(\forall s)C(s)$ is a constraint, we certainly want to restrict the ability to perform an action so that C will be true after its performance. Therefore, we want to enforce the sentence

$$Poss(a, s) \supset C(do(a, s)). \tag{B.1}$$

By performing a single regression step on $C(do(a, s))$, we get a logically equivalent formula $R(a, s)$, and therefore, a possibly new qualification for A:

$$Poss(A(\vec{x}), s) \supset R(A(\vec{x}), s). \tag{B.2}$$

If indeed this is a new qualification for A, distinct from the π_i above, then in forming the above action precondition axiom, we would have prematurely closed off the qualifications.

As an example, consider the blocks world constraint $(\forall x, s)\neg on(x, x, s)$. To enforce it, impose the following necessary condition on $Poss$:

$$Poss(a, s) \supset (\forall x)\neg on(x, x, do(a, s)).$$

Therefore,

$$Poss(move(u, v), s) \supset (\forall x)\neg on(x, x, do(move(u, v), s)).$$

Next, use unique names axioms for actions together with the successor state axiom for on of Section 10.2, do some logical manipulation, and get the logically equivalent sentence

$$Poss(move(u, v), s) \supset u \neq v.$$

This is one of the standard qualifications for the *move* action, and we *derived* it from a state constraint.

As in the case of ramification constraints, we can begin to see how qualification constraints might be already entailed by a basic action theory $\mathcal{D}$, and, therefore, how we are

justified in excluding them from the theory's axioms. For suppose that, having obtained
(B.2) above, we took it into account in forming A's action precondition axiom of $\mathcal{D}$. In
other words, this axiom has the form

$$Poss(A(\vec{x}), s) \equiv R(A(\vec{x}), s) \wedge \cdots$$

Because $R(A(\vec{x}), s)$ and $C(do(A(\vec{x}), s))$ are logically equivalent relative to $\mathcal{D}$'s successor
state axioms, $\mathcal{D}$ entails

$$Poss(A(\vec{x}), s) \supset C(do(A(\vec{x}), s)).$$

Suppose further that we have done this for all action types $A(\vec{x}), \ldots, T(\vec{z})$, so $\mathcal{D}$ entails

$$Poss(A(\vec{x}), s) \supset C(do(A(\vec{x}), s)),$$

$$\vdots$$

$$Poss(T(\vec{z}), s) \supset C(do(T(\vec{z}), s)).$$

Finally, suppose $\mathcal{D}$ includes a domain closure assumption on the action types:

$$(\forall a).(\exists \vec{x})a = A(\vec{x}) \vee \cdots \vee (\exists \vec{z})a = T(\vec{z}).$$

Then $\mathcal{D}$ entails (B.1). From this, using induction on executable situations, and assuming
that $\mathcal{D}_{S_0} \models C(S_0)$, we get

$$\mathcal{D} \models (\forall s).executable(s) \supset C(s),$$

i.e, the constraint holds in all executable situations. Since these are the only situations that
ever interest us, we are justified in omitting the state constraint from $\mathcal{D}$'s axioms.

Determining action preconditions when given a set of qualifications for an action together with a set of state constraints is called the *qualification problem*. McCarthy [137]
first pointed out the qualification problem without state constraints. He, however, had in
mind a more subtle concept than that discussed above. McCarthy sought to formalize minor qualifications in such a way that when they are not known to be false—we don't know
that the robot's arms are not tied—the action is seen as possible, but when given that they
are true—its arms are tied—the action is taken to be impossible. Ginsberg and Smith [69]
appear to have been the first to recognize how constraints further complicate the problem.

B.3   Solving the Qualification and Ramification Problems

There is a substantial literature on these topics, and we do not have space here to describe
all the approaches. The situation is further complicated by the fact that different researchers
use different action ontologies and axiomatizations in formulating their proposals. Nevertheless, there are commonalities, and we describe these here. Basically, there are two steps

that are followed in addressing the problem:

Step 1: Adapt classical logic to include *nonmonotonicity*, and use such logics to axiomatize dynamical systems. (Very) roughly speaking, nonmonotonicity allows you to say, for example in the case of the ramification problem, that the effect axioms derivable from the initially specified effect axioms and state constraints are all and only the effect axioms in force—the standard closure assumption for the frame problem. In approaching the problem this way, researchers have preferred McCarthy's circumscription formalism [138, 139], but occasionally Reiter's default logic [171] is used. For in-depth studies of how this is done, see Sandewall [187] and Shanahan [195]. A number of authors have adopted this very general methodology; these include Thielscher [211], Lin [122]. McCain and Turner [135], Sandewall [188], and Gustafsson and Doherty [75]. An interesting feature of all these approaches is that they require an explicit causality relation on fluents. The end result of this step is a nonmonotonic specification of what counts as a solution to the ramification and qualification problems. This still leaves open the computational problem: How is the entailment relation for the nonmonotonic logic computed?

Step 2: Address the implementation problems raised in step 1. Here, there are two basic approaches. The first provides a theorem prover for the nonmonotonic logic, usually by giving a translation of the logic into a suitable nonmonotonic executable logic programming language, e.g. Gelfond and Lifschitz [60], Baral and Lobo [14]. The second approach compiles the nonmonotonic specification into classical (monotonic) axioms. In the case of the situation calculus, this means compiling the state constraints into the action precondition and successor state axioms. This amounts to using deduction to extract the effect axioms and action qualifications hidden in the state constraints. Once these are made explicit, the successor state and action precondition axioms can be obtained in the usual way, and the state constraints discarded, as indicated above. Lin and Reiter [125] were the first to propose this. Their approach was further refined and extended by McIlraith [143], Pinto [158, 160], and Ternovskaia [209].

Some researchers (e.g., Schubert [192]) argue that the ramification problem need not be taken seriously, that it is not a significant burden on an axiomatizer to take ramifications into account when writing effect axioms for a domain. In effect, we have implicitly taken Schubert's stance throughout this book, where we have seldom worried about state constraints, and simply assumed that action precondition and successor state axioms will be easy to write, as they have been for the examples considered. Nevertheless, this will not always be the case. In domains with complex chains of causal influences. as often arise in engineering systems—see McIlraith [143] for an example of a power plant feedwater system—it is much more natural, and modular, to represent these causal influences with ramification constraints. In fact, for McIlraith's example, it is far from easy to directly write the successor state axioms without first considering these constraints.

All of this is further complicated by the fact that there are no purely syntactic grounds for distinguishing between ramification and qualification constraints (Lin and Reiter [125]). In fact, there are examples where the same sentence acts as both a ramification and a qualification constraint. The axiomatizer must be aware of the causal consequences of her domain constraints, and also the impact they might have on action preconditions, and take these into account when using the given constraints to address the ramification and qualification problems.

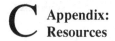

C Appendix: Resources

The Knowledge-in-Action Web Site

   http://www.cs.toronto.edu/cogrobo/kia/

This is where all the code used in this book resides. It is freely available for downloading, with the usual disclaimers. If you have developed any interesting situation calculus-based programs, or additional useful exercises relevant to this book that you would like to make generally available through this site, please let me know (reiter@cs.toronto.edu).

Legolog

   http://www.cs.toronto.edu/cogrobo/Legolog/

Legolog [119] is a Prolog-based, inexpensive system, designed and implemented by Hector Levesque and Maurice Pagnucco to encourage teaching and experimenting in Cognitive Robotics. What makes it inexpensive, and especially easy to work with, is its "robot" platform, which is constructed using the LEGO® MINDSTORMS™ Robotics Invention System™. The robot is a small vehicle equipped with a light sensor, and in its current incarnation, it runs on a track, performing pick-up and delivery tasks relative to different stations on the track. It is controlled by IndiGolog, an on-line variant of Golog with sensing, but provisions have been made for other user-defined control languages, not necessarily based on the situation calculus. This means that for an initial investment of about $US 200, one can experiment with a wide variety of possible robot designs, and high level control programs. The system is particularly nice for teaching basic concepts in Cognitive Robotics.

Research Groups for Reasoning about Actions

   http://www.ucl.ac.uk/ uczcrsm/ReasoningAboutActions.html

There are many research groups throughout the world devoted to logical approaches to modeling dynamical systems; the above web site maintains an up-to-date list of these.

Electronic Transactions on Artificial Intelligence

   http://www.ida.liu.se/ext/etai/

Established by Erik Sandewall, ETAI provides an electronic forum for publications in AI. It also supports a wide variety of special interest groups, the most relevant of which are, for readers of this book, the Reasoning about Actions and Change and the Planning and Scheduling groups. Here, submitted papers are publicly discussed before being peer reviewed. There are also often public discussions on particular themes, research problems, technical matters, etc., and a calendar of relevant workshops and conferences is posted. Well worth subscribing to if you have any interest at all in AI, and especially in the subject matter of this book.

Planning Resources and Benchmark Problems

   http://www.cs.toronto.edu/aips2000

In recent years, the International Conference on Artificial Intelligence Planning and Scheduling Systems (AIPS) has sponsored planning competitions in conjunction with its conference. Various implemented planners from around the world compete on suites of benchmark problems. If you have implemented a planning system, and are looking for interesting examples on which to exercise it, you can find descriptions of the problems used in the AIPS2000 competition at the above web site. These files also include solutions and timing information obtained by the competitors.

   http://www.csc.ncsu.edu/faculty/stamant/planning-resources.html

Created and maintained by Rob St. Amant, this is an excellent general site that includes pointers to benchmark problems and planning research groups.

Eclipse Prolog

   http://www.icparc.ic.ac.uk/eclipse

This is the Prolog dialect used throughout this book. It is available, without charge, to universities and non-profit research groups.

Guide to Axiomatizing Domains in First-Order Logic

   http://cs.nyu.edu/faculty/davise/guide.html

Written by Ernie Davis, this is a short, but very useful set of guidelines to follow, and pitfalls to avoid, when logically specifying application domains.

The Common Sense Web Page

   http://www.cs.nyu.edu/cs/davise/commonsense01

The Common Sense Symposia are periodic meetings of researchers devoted to logical formalizations of the knowledge agents need to function in the same real world as we do. Representative topics include axioms for, and reasoning about, space, time, shape, causality, actions, qualitative physics, granularity, belief change, social interactions between agents, nonmonotonicity, and context. Associated with the symposium web page is the Common Sense Problem Page that provides benchmark problems and proposed axiomatizations.

References

[1] S. Abiteboul. Updates, a new frontier. In *Second International Conference on Database Theory*, pages 1–18. Springer, 1988.

[2] J.F. Allen. Towards a general theory of action and time. *Artificial Intelligence*, 23(2):123–154, 1984.

[3] J.F. Allen. Temporal reasoning and planning. In J.F. Allen, H.A. Kautz, R.N. Pelavin, and J.D. Tenenberg, editors, *Reasoning about Plans*, pages 1–68. Morgan Kaufmann Publishers, San Francisco, CA, San Mateo, CA, 1991.

[4] E. Amir and P. Maynard-Reid II. LiSA: A robot driven by logical subsumption. In *Proc. 5th Symposium on Logical Formalizations of Commonsense Reasoning (Common Sense 2001)*, New York, May 20–22, 2001. www.cs.nyu.edu/faculty/davise/commonsense01.

[5] K. Apt and E-R. Olderog. *Verification of Sequential and Concurrent Programs*. Springer Verlag, 1997. Second edition.

[6] F. Bacchus. *Representing and Reasoning with Probabilistic Knowledge*. MIT Press, 1990.

[7] F. Bacchus. Computing domain specific information. In H.J. Levesque and F. Pirri, editors, *Logical Foundations for Cognitive Agents: Contributions in Honor of Ray Reiter*, pages 29–40. Springer, 1999.

[8] F. Bacchus, J.Y. Halpern, and H.J. Levesque. Reasoning about noisy sensors in the situation calculus. *Artificial Intelligence*, 111:171–208, 1999.

[9] F. Bacchus and F. Kabanza. Planning for temporally extended goals. In *Proceedings of the National Conference on Artificial Intelligence (AAAI'96)*, pages 1215–1222, 1996.

[10] F. Bacchus and F. Kabanza. Using temporal logic to control search in a forward chaining planner. In M. Ghallab and A. Milani, editors, *New Directions in Planning*, pages 141–153. IOS Press, 1996.

[11] F. Bacchus and F. Kabanza. Using temporal logics to express search control knowledge for planning. *Artificial Intelligence*, 116(1-2):123–191, 2000.

[12] F. Bacchus and Q. Yang. Downward refinement and the efficiency of hierarchical problem solving. *Artificial Intelligence*, 71(1):41–100, 1994.

[13] C. Baral and M. Gelfond. Reasoning about effects of concurrent actions. *Journal of Logic Programming*, 31:85–118, 1997.

[14] C. Baral and J. Lobo. Defeasible specification in action theories. In *Proceedings of the Fifteenth International Joint Conference on Artificial Intelligence (IJCAI'97)*, pages 1441–1446, 1997.

[15] J. Barwise and J. Etchemendy. *Language, Proof and Logic*. Seven Bridges Press, Center for the Study of Language and Information, Stanford, California, 1999.

[16] K. Van Belleghem, M. Denecker, and D. De Schreye. On the relation between situation calculus and event calculus. *Journal of Logic Programming*, 31(1-3):3–37, 1994.

[17] K. Van Belleghem, M. Denecker, and D. De Schreye. Representing continuous change in the abductive event calculus. In P. Van Hentenrijck, editor, *Proc. 1994 Int. Conf. on Logic Programming*, pages 225–240, 1994.

[18] L. Bertossi, M. Arenas, and C. Ferretti. SCDBR: An automated reasoner for specifications of database updates. *Journal of Intelligent Information Systems*, 10(3):253–280, 1998.

[19] C. Bettini and A. Montanari, editors. *Spatial and Temporal Ganularity: Papers from the AAAI Workshop*. The AAAI Press, Menlo Park, California, 2000.

[20] W.W. Bledsoe and P. Bruell. A man-machine theorem-proving system. *Artificial Intelligence*, 5(1):51–72, 1974.

[21] A. Blum and M. Furst. Fast planning through planning graph analysis. *Artificial Intelligence*, 90(1-2):281–300, 1997.

[22] A.J. Bonner and M. Kifer. A logic for programming database transactions. In J. Chomicki and G. Saake, editors, *Logics for Databases and Information Systems*, chapter 5, pages 117–166. Kluwer Academic Publishers, March 1998.

[23] C. Boutilier, T. Dean, and S. Hanks. Decision-theoretic planning: Structural assumptions and computational leverage. *Journal of Artificial Intelligence Research*, 11:1–94, 1999.

[24] C. Boutilier, R. Dearden, and M. Goldszmidt. Stochastic dynamic programming with factored

representations. *Artificial Intelligence*, 121:49–107, 2000.

[25] C. Boutilier, R. Reiter, and R. Price. Symbolic dynamic programming for solving first-order Markov decision processes. In *Proceedings of the Sixteenth International Joint Conference on Artificial Intelligence (IJCAI'01)*, Seattle, Washington, 2001.

[26] C. Boutilier, R. Reiter, M. Soutchanski, and S. Thrun. Decision-theoretic, high-level agent programming in the situation calculus. In *Proceedings of the National Conference on Artificial Intelligence (AAAI'00)*, pages 355–362. AAAI Press/MIT Press, 2000.

[27] R.A. Brooks. A robust layered control system for a mobile robot. *IEEE Journal of Robotics and Animation*, RA-2(1):14–23, 1986.

[28] F.M. Brown, editor. *The frame problem in artificial intelligence. Proceedings of the 1987 workshop.* Morgan Kaufmann Publishers, San Francisco, CA, Los Altos, California, 1987.

[29] M. Cadoli and F.M. Donini. A survey on knowledge compilation. Technical report, Dipartimento di Informatica e Sistemistica, Università di Roma "La Sapienza", 1997.

[30] J.G. Carbonell, J. Blythe, O. Etzioni, Y. Gill, R. Joseph, D. Khan, C. Knoblock, S. Minton, A. Pérez, S. Reilly, M. Veloso, and X. Wang. Prodigy 4.0: The manual and tutorial. Technical report, School of Computer Science, Carnegie Mellon University, 1992.

[31] D. Chapman. Planning for conjunctive goals. *Artificial Intelligence*, 32(3):333–377, 1987.

[32] A. Chella, M. Frixione, and S. Gaglio. A cognitive architecture for artificial vision. *Artificial Intelligence*, 89(1,2):73–111, 1997.

[33] B.F. Chellas. *Modal Logic.* Cambridge University Press, Cambridge, U.K., 1980.

[34] A. Cimatti and M. Roveri. Conformant planning via symbolic model checking. *Journal of Artificial Intelligence Research*, 13:305–338, 2000.

[35] K.L. Clark. Negation as failure. In H. Gallaire and J. Minker, editors, *Logic and Data Bases*, pages 292–322. Plenum Press, New York, 1978.

[36] E. Davis. *Representations of Commonsense Knowledge.* Morgan Kaufmann Publishers, San Francisco, CA, 1990.

[37] E. Davis. Infinite loops in finite time: some observations. In *Proceedings of the Third International Conference on Principles of Knowledge Representation and Reasoning (KR'92)*, pages 47–58. Morgan Kaufmann Publishers, San Francisco, CA, 1992.

[38] J. de Kleer. An improved incremental algorithm for generating prime implicates. In H.J. Levesque and F. Pirri, editors, *Logical Foundations for Cognitive Agents: Contributions in Honor of Ray Reiter*, pages 103–112. Springer, 1999.

[39] M. Dixon. *Embedded Computation and the Semantics of Programs.* PhD thesis, Department of Computer Science, Stanford University, Stanford, CA, 1991. Also appeared as Xerox PARC Technical Report SSL-91-1.

[40] P. Doherty, J. Gustafsson, L. Karlsson, and J. Kvarnström. TAL: Temporal action logics language specification and tutorial. *Linköping Electronic Articles in Computer and Information Science*, 3(15), 1998. http//www.ep.liu.se/ea/cis/1998/01fl/.

[41] C. Elkan. Reasoning about action in first-order logic. In *Proc. of the Ninth Biennial Conf. of the Canadian Society for Computational Studies of Intelligence (CSCSI'92)*, pages 221–227. Morgan Kaufmann Publishers, San Francisco, CA, 1992.

[42] H.B. Enderton. *A Mathematical Introduction to Logic.* Academic Press, 1972.

[43] K. Erol. *Hierarchical Task Network Planning: Formalization, Analysis, and Implementation.* PhD thesis, University of Maryland, 1995. Available at http:www.cs.umd.edu/users/kutluhan/Papers/thesis.ps.gz.

[44] K. Erol, D.S. Nau, and V.S. Subrahmanian. On the complexity of domain-independent planning. In *Proceedings of the National Conference on Artificial Intelligence (AAAI'92)*, pages 381–386, San Jose, CA, 1992. American Association for Artificial Intelligence.

[45] O. Etzioni. Intelligence without robots (a reply to Brooks). *AI Magazine*, December 1993.

[46] O. Etzioni, S. Hanks, D. Weld, D. Draper, N. Lesh, and M. Williamson. An approach to planning with incomplete information. In B. Nebel, C. Rich, and W. Swartout, editors, *Proceedings of the Third International Conference on Principles of Knowledge Representation and Reasoning (KR'92)*, pages 115–125, Cambridge, Mass, 1992.

[47] R. Fagin and J.Y. Halpern. Belief, awareness, and limited reasoning. *Artificial Intelligence*, 34:39–76, 1988.

[48] R. Fagin, J.Y. Halpern, Y.O. Moses, and M.Y. Vardi. *Reasoning about Knowledge*. MIT Press, Cambridge, Mass, 1995.

[49] R.E. Fikes and N.J. Nilsson. STRIPS: a new approach to the application of theorem proving to problem solving. *Artificial Intelligence*, 2(3/4):189–208, 1971.

[50] R.E. Fikes and N.J. Nilsson. STRIPS, a retrospective. *Artificial Intelligence*, 59(1/2):227–232, 1993.

[51] J. Finger. *Exploiting Constraints in Design Synthesis*. PhD thesis, Stanford University, Stanford, CA, 1986.

[52] A. Finzi, F. Pirri, and R. Reiter. Open world planning in the situation calculus. In *Proceedings of the National Conference on Artificial Intelligence (AAAI'00)*, pages 754–760. AAAI Press/MIT Press, 2000.

[53] A. Finzi, F. Pirri, M. Romano, and M. Vaccaro. Autonomous mobile manipulators managing perception and failure. In *Proc. 5th Int. Conf. on Autonomous Agents*, Montreal, Canada, May 28–June 1, 2001.

[54] J. D. Funge, X. Tu, and D. Terzopoulos. Cognitive modeling: Knowledge, reasoning and planning for intelligent characters. In *SIGGRAPH 99*, Los Angeles, CA, August 11-13, 1999.

[55] J.D. Funge. *Making Them Behave: Cognitive Models for Computer Animation*. PhD thesis, Department of Computer Science, University of Toronto, 1998.

[56] J.D. Funge. *AI for Games and Animation: A Cognitive Modelling Approach*. A.K. Peters, Natick, Massachusetts, 1999.

[57] J.D. Funge. Cognitive modeling for games and animation. *Communications of the ACM*, 43(7):40–48, 2000.

[58] A. Gabaldon. Non-Markovian control in the situation calculus. In *Proceedings of the Second International Cognitive Robotics Workshop*, Berlin, Germany, August 2000.

[59] M. Gelfond and V. Lifschitz. Representing actions in extended logic programs. In *Proc. Joint Int. Conf. and Symp. on Logic Programming*, pages 559–573, 1992.

[60] M. Gelfond and V. Lifschitz. Representing action and change by logic programs. *Journal of Logic Programming*, 17:301–321, 1993.

[61] M. Gelfond, V. Lifschitz, and A. Rabinov. What are the limitations of the situation calculus? In *Working Notes, AAAI Spring Symposium Series on the Logical Formalization of Commonsense Reasoning*, pages 59–69, 1991.

[62] A. Gerevini and L. K. Schubert. Inferring state constraints for domain-independent planning. In *Proceedings of the National Conference on Artificial Intelligence (AAAI'98)*, pages 905–912, 1998.

[63] G. De Giacomo, L. Iocchi, D. Nardi, and R. Rosati. Planning with sensing for a mobile robot. In *Preprints of the Fourth European Conf. on Planning*, pages 158–170, Toulouse, France, 1997.

[64] G. De Giacomo, Y. Lespérance, and H.J. Levesque. ConGolog, a concurrent programming language based on the situation calculus. *Artificial Intelligence*, 121(1-2):109–169, 2000.

[65] G. De Giacomo and H.J. Levesque. An incremental interpreter for high-level programs with sensing. In G. De Giacomo, editor, *Proceedings of the AAAI Fall Symposium on Cognitive Robotics*, pages 28–34. AAAI Technical Report FS-98-02, 1998.

[66] G. De Giacomo and H.J. Levesque. Projection using regression and sensors. In *Proceedings of the Sixteenth International Joint Conference on Artificial Intelligence (IJCAI'99)*, pages 160–165, 1999.

[67] G. De Giacomo, H.J. Levesque, and S. Sardiña. Executing programs over guarded theories. *ACM Transactions on Computational Logic*, 2001. To appear.

[68] G. De Giacomo, R. Reiter, and M. Soutchanski. Execution monitoring of high-level robot programs. In A.G. Cohn and L.K. Schubert, editors, *Principles of Knowledge Representation and Reasoning:*

Proceedings of the Sixth International Conference (KR'98), pages 453–464. Morgan Kaufmann
Publishers, San Francisco, CA, 1998.

[69] M.L. Ginsberg and D.E. Smith. Reasoning about actions II: The qualification problem. *Artificial
Intelligence*, 35:311–342, 1988.

[70] R. Goldblatt. *Logics of Time and Computation.* CSLI Lecture Notes No. 7. Center for the Study of
Language and Information, Stanford University, Stanford, CA, 2nd edition, 1987.

[71] C.C. Green. Theorem proving by resolution as a basis for question-answering systems. In B. Meltzer
and D. Michie, editors, *Machine Intelligence 4*, pages 183–205. American Elsevier, New York, 1969.

[72] H. Grosskreutz and G. Lakemeyer. Turning high-level plans into robot programs in uncertain domains.
In W. Horn, editor, *ECAI2000, Proc. 14th European Conf. on Artificial Intelligence*, Berlin, 2000. IOS
Press, Amsterdam.

[73] M.J. Grüninger. *Foundations of Shape-Based Object Recognition.* PhD thesis, Department of Computer
Science, University of Toronto, 2000.

[74] N. Gupta and D.S. Nau. On the complexity of blocks-world planning. *Artificial Intelligence*,
56:223–254, 1992.

[75] J. Gustafsson and P. Doherty. Embracing occlusion in specifying the indirect effects of actions. In
*Proceedings of the Fifth International Conference on Principles of Knowledge Representation and
Reasoning (KR'96)*, pages 87–98, 1996.

[76] A. R. Haas. The case for domain-specific frame axioms. In F. M. Brown, editor, *The frame problem in
artificial intelligence. Proceedings of the 1987 workshop*, pages 343–348, Los Altos, California, 1987.
Morgan Kaufmann Publishers, San Francisco, CA.

[77] J.Y. Halpern. An analysis of first-order logics of probability. *Artificial Intelligence*, 46:311–350, 1990.

[78] J.Y. Halpern and R. Fagin. Modelling knowledge and action in distributed systems. *Distributed
Computing*, 3(4):159–179, 1989.

[79] J.Y. Halpern and Y.O. Moses. A guide to completeness and complexity for modal logics of knowledge
and belief. *Artificial Intelligence*, 54:319–379, 1992.

[80] S. Hanks and D. McDermott. Default reasoning, nonmonotonic logics, and the frame problem. In
Proceedings of the National Conference on Artificial Intelligence (AAAI'86), pages 328–333, 1986.

[81] S. Hanks and D. McDermott. Modeling a dynamic and uncertain world I: Symbolic and probabilistic
reasoning about change. *Artificial Intelligence*, 66(1):1–55, 1994.

[82] D. Harel, D. Kozen, and J. Tiurin. *Dynamic Logic.* MIT Press, Cambridge, Mass., 2000.

[83] E.C.R. Hehner. *A Practical Theory of Programming.* Springer, New York, 1993.

[84] C.S. Herrmann and M. Thielscher. Reasoning about continuous processes. In *Proceedings of the
National Conference on Artificial Intelligence (AAAI'96)*, pages 639–644. AAAI Press/MIT Press, Menlo
Park, 1996.

[85] J. Hintikka. Modalities and quantification. *Theoria*, 27:119–128, 1961.

[86] J. Hintikka. *Knowledge and Belief.* Cornell University Press, Ithaca, N.Y., 1992.

[87] C.A.R. Hoare. An axiomatic basis for computer programming. *C. ACM*, 12(10):576–583, 1969.

[88] J.R. Hobbs. Granularity. In *Proceedings of the Ninth International Joint Conference on Artificial
Intelligence (IJCAI'85)*, pages 432–435, Los Angeles, California, 1985.

[89] S. Hölldobler and J. Schneeberger. A new deductive approach to planning. *New Generation Computing*,
8:225–244, 1990.

[90] G.E. Hughes and M.J. Cresswell. *An Introduction to Modal Logic.* Methuen, London, 1968.

[91] H.O. Ismail and S.C. Shapiro. Two problems with reasoning and acting in time. In A.G. Cohn,
F. Giunchiglia, and B. Selman, editors, *Proceedings of the Seventh International Conference on
Principles of Knowledge Representation and Reasoning (KR'00)*, pages 355–365. Morgan Kaufmann
Publishers, San Francisco, CA, 2000.

[92] P. Jackson and J. Pais. Computing prime implicants. In *Proc. of CADE-90*, pages 543–557, 1990.

[93] M. Jenkin, Y. Lespérance, H.J. Levesque, F. Lin, J. Lloyd, D. Marcu, R. Reiter, R.B. Scherl, and K. Tam.

A logical approach to portable high-level robot programming. In *Proceedings of the Tenth Australian Joint Conference on Artificial Intelligence (AI'97)*, Perth, Australia, 1997. Invited paper.

[94] L.P. Kaelbling, M.L. Littman, and A.R. Cassandra. Planning and acting in partially observable stochastic domains. *Artificial Intelligence*, 101(1-2):99–134, 1998.

[95] T.G. Kelley. Modeling complex systems in the situation calculus: A case study using the Dagstuhl steam boiler problem. In L.C. Aiello, J. Doyle, and S.C. Shapiro, editors, *Principles of Knowledge Representation and Reasoning: Proceedings of the Fifth International Conference (KR'96)*, pages 26–37. Morgan Kaufmann Publishers, San Francisco, CA, 1996.

[96] D. Kibler and P. Morris. Don't be stupid. In *Proceedings of the Seventh International Joint Conference on Artificial Intelligence (IJCAI'81)*, pages 345–347, 1981.

[97] R. Kowalski and F. Sadri. The situation calculus and event calculus compared. In M. Bruynooghe, editor, *Proc. of the International Logic Programming Symposium*, pages 539–553. MIT Press, 1994.

[98] R.A. Kowalski and M.J. Sergot. A logic-based calculus of events. *New Generation Computing*, 4:267, 1986.

[99] S. Kripke. A semantical analysis of modal logic I: normal modal propositional calculi. *Zeitschrift für Mathematische Logik und Grundlagen der Mathematik*, 9:67–97, 1963.

[100] N. Kushmerick, S. Hanks, and D. Weld. An algorithm for probabilistic planning. *Artificial Intelligence*, 76:239–286, 1995.

[101] G. Lakemeyer. On sensing and off-line interpreting in GOLOG. In H.J. Levesque and F. Pirri, editors, *Logical Foundations for Cognitive Agents: Contributions in Honor of Ray Reiter*, pages 173–189. Springer, 1999.

[102] G. Lakemeyer and H.J. Levesque. Query evaluation and progression in AOL knowledge bases. In *Proceedings of the Sixteenth International Joint Conference on Artificial Intelligence (IJCAI'99)*, pages 124–131, 1999.

[103] G. Lakemeyer and H.J. Levesque. AOL: a logic of acting, sensing, knowing, and only knowing. In *Proc. of KR-98, Sixth International Conference on Principles of Knowledge Representation and Reasoning*, pages 316–327, June 1998.

[104] D. Leivant. Higher order logic. In D.M. Gabbay, C.J. Hogger, and J.A. Robinson, editors, *Handbook of Logic in Artificial Intelligence and Logic Programming*, pages 229–321. Clarendon Press, Oxford, 1994.

[105] Y. Lespérance, T.G. Kelley, J. Mylopoulos, and E.S.K. Yu. Modeling dynamic domains with ConGolog. In *Proc. Advanced Information Systems Engineering, 11th International Conference, CAiSE-99*, pages 365–380. LNCS vol. 1626, Springer-Verlag, Berlin, 1999.

[106] Y. Lespérance and H.J. Levesque. Indexical knowledge and robot action – a logical account. *Artificial Intelligence*, 73:69–115, 1995.

[107] Y. Lespérance, H.J. Levesque, F. Lin, D. Marcu, R. Reiter, and R. Scherl. A logical approach to high-level robot programming – a progress report. In *Control of the Physical World by Intelligent Systems, Working Notes of the 1994 AAAI Fall Symp.*, pages 79–85, 1994.

[108] Y. Lespérance, H.J. Levesque, F. Lin, and R.B. Scherl. Ability and knowing how in the situation calculus. *Studia Logica*, 66(1):165–186, October 2000.

[109] Y. Lespérance, H.J. Levesque, and R. Reiter. A situation calculus approach to modeling and programming agents. In M. Wooldridge and A. Rao, editors, *Foundations and Theories of Rational Agency*, pages 275–299, 1999.

[110] Y. Lespérance, H.J. Levesque, and S.J. Ruman. An experiment using Golog to build a personal banking assistant. In L. Cavedon, A. Rao, and W. Wobke, editors, *Intelligent Agent Systems: Theoretical and Practical Issues. Lecture Notes in Computer Science, Volume 1209.*, pages 27–43. Springer-Verlag, 1997.

[111] Y. Lespérance, K. Tam, and M. Jenkin. Reactivity in a logic-based robot programming framework (extended version). In H.J. Levesque and F. Pirri, editors, *Logical Foundations for Cognitive Agents: Contributions in Honor of Ray Reiter*, pages 190–207. Springer, 1999.

[112] H. J. Levesque and R. Reiter. High-level robotic control: beyond planning. Position paper. AAAI 1998 Spring Symposium: Integrating Robotics Research: Taking the Next Big Leap. Stanford University,

March 23-25, 1998. http://www.cs.toronto.edu/˜cogrobo/.

[113] H.J. Levesque. A logic of implicit and explicit belief. In *Proceedings of the National Conference on Artificial Intelligence (AAAI'84)*, pages 198–202, 1984.

[114] H.J. Levesque. Making believers out of computers. *Artificial Intelligence*, 30:81–108, 1986.

[115] H.J. Levesque. Logic and the complexity of reasoning. *Journal of Philosophical Logic, Special Issue on AI and Logic*, 17:355–389, 1988.

[116] H.J. Levesque. All I know: A study in autoepistemic logic. *Artificial Intelligence*, 42:263–309, 1990.

[117] H.J. Levesque. What is planning in the presence of sensing? In *Proceedings of the National Conference on Artificial Intelligence (AAAI'96)*, pages 1139–1146, 1996.

[118] H.J. Levesque and G. Lakemeyer. *The Logic of Knowledge Bases*. MIT Press, 2001.

[119] H.J. Levesque and M. Pagnucco. Legolog: Inexpensive experiments in cognitive robotics. In *Proc. 2nd Int. Cognitive Robotics Workshop*, 2000. Aug 21-22, Berlin, Germany. http://www-i5.informatik.rwth-aachen.de/LuFG/cogrob2000/.

[120] H.J. Levesque, R. Reiter, Y. Lespérance, F. Lin, and R. Scherl. GOLOG: a logic programming language for dynamic domains. *J. of Logic Programming, Special Issue on Actions*, 31(1-3):59–83, 1997.

[121] V. Lifschitz. On the semantics of STRIPS. In *Reasoning about Actions and Plans: Proceedings of the 1986 Workshop*, pages 1–9. Morgan Kaufmann Publishers, San Francisco, CA, 1986. June 30–July 2, Timberline, Oregon.

[122] F. Lin. Embracing causality in specifying the indirect effects of actions. In *Proceedings of the Fourteenth International Joint Conference on Artificial Intelligence (IJCAI'95)*, pages 1985–1991, 1995.

[123] F. Lin and H.J. Levesque. What robots can do: Robot programs and effective achievability. *Artificial Intelligence*, 101(1-2):201–226, 1998.

[124] F. Lin and R. Reiter. Forget it! In R. Greiner and D. Subramanian, editors, *Working Notes of the AAAI Fall Symposium on Relevance*, pages 154–159. The American Association for Artificial Intelligence, Menlo Park, CA, 1994.

[125] F. Lin and R. Reiter. State constraints revisited. *J. of Logic and Computation, special issue on actions and processes*, 4:655–678, 1994.

[126] F. Lin and R. Reiter. How to progress a database. *Artificial Intelligence*, 92:131–167, 1997.

[127] F. Lin and Y. Shoham. Concurrent actions in the situation calculus. In *Proceedings of the National Conference on Artificial Intelligence (AAAI'92)*, pages 590–595, 1992.

[128] Y. Liu. Hoare logic for GOLOG programs. Master's thesis, Department of Computer Science, University of Toronto, 2000.

[129] J.W. Lloyd. *Foundations of Logic Programming*. Springer Verlag, second edition, 1987.

[130] W. S. Lovejoy. A survey of algorithmic methods for partially observed Markov decision processes. *Annals of Operations Research*, 28:47–66, 1991.

[131] D. Maier. *The Theory of Relational Databases*. Computer Science Press, Rockville, Maryland, 1983.

[132] Z. Manna and R. Waldinger. How to clear a block: A theory of plans. *Journal of Automated Reasoning*, 3:343–377, 1987.

[133] P. Mateus, A. Pacheco, J. Pinto, A. Sernadas, and C. Sernadas. Probabilistic situation calculus. Technical report, Section of Computer Science, Department of Mathematics, Instituto Superior Ticnico, 1049-001 Lisboa, Portugal, March, 2000.

[134] D. McAllester and D. Rosenblitt. Systematic nonlinear planning. In *Proceedings of the National Conference on Artificial Intelligence (AAAI'91)*, pages 634–639, 1991.

[135] N. McCain and H. Turner. A causal theory of ramifications and qualifications. In *Proceedings of the Fourteenth International Joint Conference on Artificial Intelligence (IJCAI'95)*, pages 1978–1984, 1995.

[136] J. McCarthy. Situations, actions and causal laws. Technical report, Stanford University, 1963. Reprinted in Semantic Information Processing (M. Minsky ed.), MIT Press, Cambridge, Mass., 1968, pages 410-417.

[137] J. McCarthy. Epistemological problems of artificial intelligence. In *Proceedings of the Fifth*

International Joint Conference on Artificial Intelligence (IJCAI' 77), pages 1038–1044, Cambridge, MA, 1977.

[138] J. McCarthy. Circumscription - a form of non-monotonic reasoning. *Artificial Intelligence*, 13:27–39, 1980.

[139] J. McCarthy. Applications of circumscription to formalizing commonsense knowledge. *Artificial Intelligence*, 28:89–116, 1986.

[140] J. McCarthy and T. Costello. Combining narratives. In A.G. Cohn and L.K. Schubert, editors, *Principles of Knowledge Representation and Reasoning: Proceedings of the Sixth International Conference (KR' 98)*, pages 48–59. Morgan Kaufmann Publishers, San Francisco, CA, 1998.

[141] J. McCarthy and P. Hayes. Some philosophical problems from the standpoint of artificial intelligence. In B. Meltzer and D. Michie, editors, *Machine Intelligence 4*, pages 463–502. Edinburgh University Press, Edinburgh, Scotland, 1969.

[142] D. McDermott. A temporal logic for reasoning about processes and plans. *Cognitive Science*, 6:101–155, 1982.

[143] S.A. McIlraith. Integrating actions and state constraints: A closed-form solution to the ramification problem (sometimes). *Artificial Intelligence*, 116(1-2):87–121, 2000.

[144] R. Miller. A case study in reasoning about actions and continuous change. In *Proc. 12th European Conf. on Artificial Itelligence (ECAI' 96)*, pages 624–628. John Wiley and Sons, 1996.

[145] R. Miller and M. Shanahan. Reasoning about discontinuities in the event calculus. In L.C. Aiello, J. Doyle, and S.C. Shapiro, editors, *Principles of Knowledge Representation and Reasoning: Proceedings of the Fifth International Conference (KR' 96)*, pages 63–74. Morgan Kaufmann Publishers, San Francisco, CA, 1996.

[146] R. Miller and M. Shanahan. The event calculus in classical logic - Alternative axiomatizations. *Linköping Electronic Articles in Computer and Information Science*, 4(16), 1999. http://www.ep.liu.se/cis/1999/016/.

[147] J. Minker, editor. *Foundations of Deductive Databases and Logic Programming*. Morgan Kaufmann Publishers, San Francisco, CA, Los Altos, CA, 1988.

[148] R.C. Moore. Reasoning about knowledge and action. Technical report, SRI International, 1980. Technical Note 191.

[149] R.C. Moore. A formal theory of knowledge and action. In Jerry B. Hobbs and Robert C. Moore, editors, *Formal Theories of the Commonsense World*, chapter 9, pages 319–358. Ablex Publishing Corp., Norwood, New Jersey, 1985.

[150] Y.N. Moschovakis. *Elementary induction on abstract structures*. North-Holland Publishing Company, Amsterdam, 1974.

[151] L. Palopoli, F. Pirri, and C. Pizzuti. Algorithms for selective enumeration of prime implicants. *Artificial Intelligence*, 111:41–72, 1999.

[152] J. Pearl. *Probabilistic Reasoning in Intelligent Systems: Networks of Plausible Inference*. Morgan Kaufmann Publishers, San Francisco, CA, 1988.

[153] E.P.D. Pednault. *Toward a Mathematical Theory of Plan Synthesis*. PhD thesis, Department of Electrical Engineering, Stanford University, 1986.

[154] E.P.D. Pednault. ADL: Exploring the middle ground between STRIPS and the situation calculus. In R.J. Brachman, H.J. Levesque, and R. Reiter, editors, *Proceedings of the First International Conference on Principles of Knowledge Representation and Reasoning (KR' 89)*, pages 324–332. Morgan Kaufmann Publishers, San Francisco, CA, 1989.

[155] E.P.D. Pednault. ADL and the state-transition model of action. *J. Logic and Computation*, 4(5):467–512, 1994.

[156] R.N. Pelavin. Planning with simultaneous actions and external events. In J.F. Allen, H.A. Kautz, R.N. Pelavin, and J.D. Tenenberg, editors, *Reasoning about Plans*, pages 127–211. Morgan Kaufmann Publishers, San Francisco, CA, San Mateo, CA, 1991.

[157] F. J. Pelletier. Seventy-five problems for testing automatic theorem provers. *J. of Automated Reasoning*,

2(2):191–216, 1986.

[158] J. Pinto. Compiling ramification constraints into effect axioms. *Computational Intelligence*, 15(3):280–307, 1999.

[159] J.A. Pinto. *Temporal Reasoning in the Situation Calculus*. PhD thesis, University of Toronto, Department of Computer Science, 1994.

[160] J.A. Pinto. Causality in theories of action. In R. Miller and M. Shanahan, editors, *Proc. Fourth Symposium on Logical Formalizations of Commonsense Reasoning (Queen Mary and Westfield College, London, U.K)*, 1998. http://www.ida.liu.se/ext/etai/nj/fcs-98/listing.html.

[161] J.A. Pinto. Concurrent actions and interacting effects. In *Proceedings of the Sixth International Conference on Principles of Knowledge Representation and Reasoning (KR'98)*, pages 292–303, 1998.

[162] J.A. Pinto. Integrating discrete and continuous change in a logical framework. *Computational Intelligence*, 14(1):39–88, 1998.

[163] J.A. Pinto, A. Sernadas, C. Sernadas, and P. Mateus. Non-determinism and uncertainty in the situation calculus. *Int. Journal of Uncertainty, Fuzziness and Knowledge-Based Systems*, 8(2):127–149, 2000.

[164] F. Pirri and A. Finzi. An approach to perception in theory of actions: Part 1. *Linköping Electronic Articles in Computer and Information Science*, 4, 1999. http://www.ep.liu.se/ea/cis/1999/041/.

[165] F. Pirri and R. Reiter. Some contributions to the metatheory of the situation calculus. *Journal of the ACM*, 46(3):261–325, 1999.

[166] F. Pirri and R. Reiter. Planning with natural actions in the situation calculus. In J. Minker, editor, *Logic-Based Artificial Intelligence*, pages 213–231. Kluwer Academic Press, 2000.

[167] D. Poole. Decision theory, the situation calculus, and conditional plans. *LinKöping Electronic Articles in Computer and Information Science*, 3(8), 1998. http//www.ep.liu.se/ea/cis/1998/008/.

[168] M.L. Puterman. *Markov decision Processes: Discrete Stochastic Dynamic Programming*. John Wiley and Sons, 1994.

[169] Z.W. Pylyshyn. *Computation and Cognition: Toward a Foundation for Cognitive Science*. MIT Press, Cambridge, Mass., 1984.

[170] Z.W. Pylyshyn, editor. *The robot's dilemma: The frame problem in artificial intelligence*. Ablex Publishing Corporation, Norwood, New Jersey, 1987.

[171] R. Reiter. A logic for default reasoning. *Artificial Intelligence*, 13:81–132, 1980.

[172] R. Reiter. Nonmonotonic reasoning. *Annual Reviews in Computer Science*, 2:147–186, 1987.

[173] R. Reiter. The frame problem in the situation calculus: a simple solution (sometimes) and a completeness result for goal regression. In Vladimir Lifschitz, editor, *Artificial Intelligence and Mathematical Theory of Computation: Papers in Honor of John McCarthy*, pages 359–380. Academic Press, San Diego, CA, 1991.

[174] R. Reiter. Proving properties of states in the situation calculus. *Artificial Intelligence*, 64:337–351, 1993.

[175] R. Reiter. On specifying database updates. *Journal of Logic Programming*, 25:25–91, 1995.

[176] R. Reiter. Natural actions, concurrency and continuous time in the situation calculus. In L.C. Aiello, J. Doyle, and S.C. Shapiro, editors, *Principles of Knowledge Representation and Reasoning: Proceedings of the Fifth International Conference (KR'96)*, pages 2–13. Morgan Kaufmann Publishers, San Francisco, CA, 1996.

[177] R. Reiter. Sequential, temporal GOLOG. In A.G. Cohn and L.K. Schubert, editors, *Principles of Knowledge Representation and Reasoning: Proceedings of the Sixth International Conference (KR'98)*, pages 547–556. Morgan Kaufmann Publishers, San Francisco, CA, 1998.

[178] R. Reiter. On knowledge-based programming with sensing in the situation calculus. *ACM Trans. on Computational Logic*, 2001. To appear.

[179] R. Reiter and J. de Kleer. Foundations for assumption-based truth maintenance systems: Preliminary report. In *Proceedings of the National Conference on Artificial Intelligence (AAAI'87)*, pages 183–188, 1987.

[180] R. Reiter and A.K. Mackworth. A logical framework for depiction and image interpretation. *Artificial Intelligence*, 41:125–155, 1990.

[181] J. Rintanen. Constructing conditional plans by a theorem-prover. *Journal of Artificial Intelligence Research*, 10:323–352, 1999.

[182] S.J. Rosenschein and L.P. Kaelbling. The synthesis of digital machines with provable epistemic properties. In Joseph Y. Halpern, editor, *Proceedings of the 1986 Conference on Theoretical Aspects of Reasoning about Knowledge*, pages 83–98. Morgan Kaufmann Publishers, San Francisco, CA, Monterey, CA, 1986.

[183] S.J. Ruman. Golog as an agent-programming language: Experiments in developing banking applications. Master's thesis, Department of Computer Science, University of Toronto, Toronto, ON, 1996.

[184] S.J. Russell and P. Norvig. *Artificial Intelligence: A Modern Approach*. Prentice Hall, 1995.

[185] E.D. Sacerdoti. Planning in a hierarchy of abstraction spaces. *Artificial Intelligence*, 5:115–135, 1974.

[186] E. Sandewall. Combining logic and differential equations for describing real-world systems. In R.J. Brachman, H.J. Levesque, and R. Reiter, editors, *Proceedings of the First International Conference on Principles of Knowledge Representation and Reasoning (KR'89)*, pages 412–420. Morgan Kaufmann Publishers, San Francisco, CA, 1989.

[187] E. Sandewall. *Features and Fluents: The Representation of Knowledge about Dynamical Systems*. Oxford University Press, 1994.

[188] E. Sandewall. Assessment of ramification methods that use static domain constraints. In *Proceedings of the Fifth International Conference on Principles of Knowledge Representation and Reasoning (KR'96)*, pages 99–110, 1996.

[189] E. Sandewall. Cognitive robotics logic and its metatheory: Features and fluents revisited. *Linköping Electronic Articles in Computer and Information Science*, 3(17), 1998. http//www.ep.liu.se/ea/cis/1998/017/.

[190] R. Scherl and H.J. Levesque. The frame problem and knowledge producing actions. In *Proc. AAAI-93*, pages 689–695, Washington, DC, 1993.

[191] R. Scherl, H.J. Levesque, and Y. Lespérance. The situation calculus with sensing and indexical knowledge. In M. Koppel and E. Shamir, editors, *Proc. BISFAI'95: The Fourth Bar-Ilan Symposium on Foundations of Artificial Intelligence*, pages 86–95, Ramat Gan and Jerusalem, Israel, 1995.

[192] L.K. Schubert. Monotonic solution of the frame problem in the situation calculus: an efficient method for worlds with fully specified actions. In H.E. Kyberg, R.P. Loui, and G.N. Carlson, editors, *Knowledge Representation and Defeasible Reasoning*, pages 23–67. Kluwer Academic Press, 1990.

[193] M. Shanahan. A logical account of the common sense informatic situation for a mobile robot. *Linköping Electronic Articles in Computer and Information Science*, 4, 1999. http://www.ep.liu.se/ea/cis/1999/010/.

[194] M.P. Shanahan. Representing continuous change in the event calculus. In *Proceedings ECAI 90*, pages 598–603, 1990.

[195] M.P. Shanahan. *Solving the Frame Problem: A Mathematical Investigation of the Common Sense Law of Inertia*. MIT Press, 1997.

[196] S. Shapiro. *Specifying and Verifying Multiagent Systems Using the Cognitive Agents Specification Language (CASL)*. PhD thesis, Department of Computer Science, University of Toronto, 2001.

[197] S. Shapiro, Y. Lespérance, and H.J. Levesque. Specifying communicative multi-agent systems. In Wayne Wobcke, Maurice Pagnucco, and Chengqi Zhang, editors, *Agents and Multi-Agent Systems — Formalisms, Methodologies, and Applications*, volume 1441 of *LNAI*, pages 1–14, Berlin, 1998. Springer-Verlag.

[198] S.C. Shapiro. Embodied Cassie. In *Proc. AAAI Fall Symposium on Cognitive Robotics*, pages 136–143. AAAI Press, Menlo Park, CA, 1998.

[199] Y. Shoham. *Reasoning about Change: Time and Causation from the Standpoint of Artificial Intelligence*. MIT Press, 1988.

[200] Y. Shoham. Agent oriented programming. *Artificial Intelligence*, 60(1):51–92, 1993.

[201] J. Slaney and S. Thiébaux. Blocks world revisited. *Artificial Intelligence*, 125(1–2):119–153, 2001.

[202] B.C. Smith. *Reflection and semantics in a procedural language*. PhD thesis, MIT, Cambridge, Mass., 1982.

[203] D.E. Smith and D.S. Weld. Conformant graphplan. In *Proceedings of the National Conference on Artificial Intelligence (AAAI'98)*, pages 889–896. AAAI Press/MIT Press, 1998.

[204] S. Soderland, T. Barrett, and D. Weld. The SNLP planner implementation. Technical report, Department of Computer Science, University of Washington, 1990. Contact bug-snlp@cs.washington.edu.

[205] M. Soutchanski. Execution monitoring of high–level temporal programs. In *Robot Action Planning, Proceedings of the IJCAI-99 Workshop*, Stockholm, 1999. Available at: http://www.cs.toronto.edu/˜mes/papers.

[206] B. Srivastava and S. Kambhampati. Synthesizing customized plans from specifications. *J. of Artificial Intelligence Research*, 8:93–128, 1998.

[207] J.E. Stoy. *Denotational Semantics*. MIT Press, 1977.

[208] K. Tam. Experiments in high-level robot control using ConGolog — reactivity, failure handling, and knowledge-based search. Master's thesis, Dept. of Computer Science, York University, 1998.

[209] E. Ternovskaia. Inductive definability and the situation calculus. In B. Freitag, H. Decker, M. Kifer, and A. Voronkov, editors, *Transactions and Change in Logic Databases, Lecture Notes in Computer Science, Vol. 1472*, pages 227–248. Springer, Berlin, 1998.

[210] E. Ternovskaia. Interval situation calculus. In *Proc. of ECAI'94 Workshop W5 on Logic and Change*, pages 153–164, Amsterdam, August 8-12, 1994.

[211] M. Thielscher. Ramification and causality. *Artificial Intelligence*, 89(1–2):317–364, 1997.

[212] M. Thielscher. Introduction to the fluent calculus. *Linköping Electronic Articles in Computer and Information Science*, 3(14), 1998. http//www.ep.liu.se/ea/cis/1998/'1'/.

[213] M. Thielscher. From situation calculus to fluent calculus: State update axioms as a solution to the inferential frame problem. *Artificial Intelligence*, 111:277–299, 1999.

[214] M. Thielscher. The fluent calculus: A specification language for robots with sensors in nondeterministic, concurrent, and ramifying environments. Technical Report CL-2000-01, Computational Logic Group, Department of Computer Science, Dresden University of Technology, October 2000.

[215] P. Tison. Generalized consensus theory and applications to the minimization of boolean functions. *IEEE Transactions on Electronic Computers*, 4:446–456, 1967.

[216] R. Waldinger. Achieving several goals simultaneously. In E. Elcock and D. Michie, editors, *Machine Intelligence 8*, pages 94–136. Ellis Horwood, Edinburgh, Scotland, 1977.

[217] M.J. Wooldridge. *Reasoning about Rational Agents*. MIT Press, Cambridge, Mass., 2000.

[218] M.J. Wooldridge and N.R. Jennings. Intelligent agents: Theory and practice. *Knowledge Engineering Review*, 10(2), 1995.

[219] Q. Yang. *Intelligent Planning*. Springer Verlag, 1997.

Index

Printed in the United States
By Bookmasters